TABLE OF CONTENTS

SECTION ONE

Manners

SECTION TWO
Ceremonies and Events

SECTION THREE

Weddings

SECTION FOUR
Household Customs

SECTION FIVE
Furnishing a House

SECTION SIX

Entertaining

SECTION SEVEN
Correspondence

SECTION EIGHT
Clothes

1

Introduction: More Than Manners

ETIQUETTE is an important subject because it is concerned with human beings and their relations to one another. It is a system for the complex business of living in a community. Like life and people, it is full of paradoxes. Etiquette is based on tradition, and yet it can change. Its ramifications are trivialities, but its roots are in great principles. It is part of the web of customs, beliefs, laws, and morals which sustains and restrains every society of men.

When we apply this definition to our daily life, we can understand the changes etiquette has undergone. The origin of the word "etiquette" was supposedly the "ticket" of entrance to court ceremonies in France, on which rules of court behavior were written; and for us, the primary point of etiquette is still human relations. But now almost every degree of relationship is included in its scope. Reaching out beyond this field, it is now concerned with inanimate objects and ways of handling them—silver, glass, writing paper, and many more. It prescribes the procedure of family events such as weddings and christenings; and in minute detail it covers the smallest technicalities, such as how to address a letter or eat an artichoke.

Etiquette is a big subject, but it's no secret. And this is significant of the revolutionary change in its character. In the last twenty years, particularly in America, etiquette has become less arbitrary and more democratic, because it has discarded the old source of its authority and taken up a new one. The old sanction for its rules was, "The inner circle (or the 'best' people) behave this way." Its new standards of behavior are based on what millions of people have accepted as right or wrong. There is no longer any question of admission "by ticket only." It's a forum for citizens, open to anyone who cares about the amenities of living. Good behavior is everybody's business, and good taste can be everyone's goal.

The simplest proofs of this change are its casualty list. Pretentiousness, which was once considered quite understandable, is now laughable if not pathetic. Condescension has disappeared. And "noblesse oblige," which might have been translated, "Aristocrats acknowledge the responsibilities of privilege," now reads, "Citizens admit the responsibilities of freedom." These are the general outlines of the change.

A more specific example is the matter of entertaining. Earlier etiquette treated entertaining as a solemn business, an opportunity to show off the family position. "You have to have footmen," it hinted. "Otherwise you'll look like nobodies. And if you haven't footmen, don't entertain." Later, it stressed the "smartly-dressed maid," complete with cap and buckled shoes, implying that this figure was one no hostess could do without. The present attitude, as far as help of any kind is concerned, is "the more the merrier, as a matter of convenience; but better no service, than service for show." In other words, if the part-time cook is anxious and strained about waiting on table, she should stay happily in the kitchen rather than be urged into the uncomfortable and unaccustomed role of waitress just because there is company for dinner. As a matter of common sense, if there is any service, it is better to have it done well than badly; but any service which smacks of pretentiousness is far worse than none. The contemporary spirit, of which this is just one example, is liberated from much of the burden of what used to be called "keeping up." It is much more honest and simple than it was.

This new spirit has suddenly become apparent, but it has been forming for many years. All changes in behavior come slowly, through great shifts in economic conditions, through education and a change of heart. What we do stems directly from what we believe. It is interesting to find the roots of etiquette and behavior in ethics and religion. In this country, a man cannot beat a dog unmercifully without public disapproval, and this small fact can be traced back through the present laws against cruelty to animals, and all the important laws for the protection of the helpless, to its origin in religion. From religion comes the principle that kindness and good will are more admirable than strength and courage, or even justice. The strong are admired when they protect the weak, and our society has developed very definite rules of etiquette in support of this view. The simplest examples are the conventions which convey the attitude of protection, respect, and deference which a man is expected to show toward a woman. These conventions are so deeply ingrained in our customs and point of view that we think it quite natural for men to take off their hats to women, or walk on the outer, less protected, side of the pavement. In other societies, where customs rest on different principles, such actions and attitudes would be considered eccentric. A great deal is summed up in the fact that, in some countries, public opinion does not censure a man who rides comfortably down the road, while his wife trudges along, heavily laden, in the dust behind him.

Any change in customs as basic as these takes generations to accomplish, and must come about by general consent. Even a superficial study of sociology shows the futility of past efforts to make a lasting change in manners by an act of will or authority. The French revolutionists tried it. But it is significant that, although they were able to destroy the stability of the monarchical system, they were unable for more than a short time to make the French people call each other "Citizen" instead of "Monsieur" or "Madame." Professor William Sumner, the great Yale sociologist, once wrote, "This is the last and greatest lesson of the revolution: it is impossible to abolish mores and replace them by new ones rationally invented. To change a monarchy into a republic is trifling."

Indeed, from the vantage point of sociology, etiquette has considerable scientific importance: as a part of what sociologists call our "mores," or "ways," etiquette ranks with law and government as a subject for study. We take our manners for granted, but it is amusing to think how seriously they may be discussed in the future. In a treatise about our times, some professor may write, "These people always greeted each other with an inquiry about the other's health, perhaps because of the extraordinary value their ethic placed on human life." Or, "Their eating habits were stiff with taboos as to which animal organs could be eaten and which could not. They ate at set times and in set places, owing to their dependence on schedules and fresh foods." Or, "Their wedding traditions were a fairly accurate reflection of the diversity of their cultural origins, and included the customs of many religions other than their own."

It may be, of course, that some of our customs will survive intact and will, therefore, seem less curious to the professor. But two things will be sure, just as they are now: The first is that there will have to be a code of behavior of some kind, and the second is that that code will be an expression of contemporary taste.

A code of behavior is an inevitable part of life in any community, and if we hadn't inherited ours, we should have had to invent one. A system, or a set of rules, is vital for anything in which human beings are involved. Think of bridge, or golf, without rules. Think of traffic without laws or lights, and ball games without a conventional seating system. Whenever egos touch, and conflicts of interest arise, common sense demands a system. The practical beauty of etiquette is that it is precise, detailed, and widely accepted. Many hands, both literally and metaphorically, would be left hanging in mid-air if etiquette did not exist. It is essential to the amenities of a civilized life.

But because life changes, and tastes change, every generation discards certain minor rules which no longer seem relevant, and develops others which seem good. Our generation is no exception. The deciding factor is always the current definition of good taste, a complicated formula which can be applied to situations far beyond the scope of etiquette. The rules of etiquette are made for our daily lives, and for stock situations which come up all the time; they can be set down, and they can be learned. But good taste is a matter of feeling, as well as knowledge. It must be understood. The essence of good taste is a sense of values, and a sense of values is the pivotal point of good living. One of the keys to our present definition of good taste is that it is better to be kind than to be "correct." There is no situation in which it is smart to be nasty. This maxim may seem a little obvious—a little like Calvin Coolidge's preacher who was "against sin." But it is actually a great advance, and a new one.

Another development in our sense of values is a greater collective conscience. Concern for mass welfare is a basic part of the formula of good taste, as proved by the remark of Mayor O'Dwyer of New York, who questioned the plans for a city jubilee: "Is it good taste, in view of world conditions?" This is a long step from the fiddle that played while Rome burned, and from the big dances which were given in time of breadlines and depressions.

On the debit side, it must be admitted that with this great gain in concern for the many, we have lost some of our concern for the individual. We have a greater sense of the rights of others, and less interest in the feelings or convenience of an individual. That is why there is more rudeness in shops, more jostling and fewer apologies on busses. That's why hostesses wait longer for answers to their invitations, and guests are more often late. This comparative indifference toward the individual is a great loss, and unless we recognize it as such, it will not be recouped. But, on the whole, the gains have been many, and in the right direction. Certainly, as proved by the changes in our customs, simplicity and common decency are now much greater factors in our conception of good taste than they ever used to be.

All this being so, readers may wonder why so much conventional detail can be found in this book. If honesty and decency are the basic elements of good taste, why need the details be written down? Specifically, if the contemporary spirit is one of simplicity, why are such elaborate weddings and such elaborate ways of entertaining described in detail? There are two answers and they need a little explaining.

The first answer is that much of the detail is included for practical reasons. Although big households are few in comparison to the many small ones, there are still many, particularly official ones, which are run in the most traditional pattern. There are still those who wish to give big weddings, and wish to, or must for official reasons, entertain in an elaborate way. And in every country, but particularly in America, there are still many who are new to this, and want information about it. Running a big household is no simple job. That's the first reason for including the detailed outlines of household departments and all the other details of the same kind.

A bigger reason, because it applies so much more widely, is that it is impossible to make decisions intelligently about housekeeping, or about anything else, without a grasp of the whole subject. Just as the rules of etiquette cannot particularize about every conceivable situation, so an outline of entertaining, or of wedding procedure, cannot describe every subtle shading in the degrees of formality. But the theory and the standards can be explained, and no book of etiquette is worth printing which does not do this so fully that every reader can work out his own good decisions for special situations. The reason for including the details of the elaborate forms is not that the extreme of formality is nearest the ideal. The biggest dinner party is not necessarily more nearly perfect than a smaller one. But the most formal dinner, or the biggest wedding, includes the maximum of elaboration and procedure. And it is always easier to cut something down to fit than to build it up piecemeal. The ideal wedding or entertainment is always the one that best fits the particular circumstances, and a wealth of information always makes this much easier to achieve. With an understanding of all possibilities, it is easier to decide what to discard and what to keep, how best to compromise between the perfect and the practicable.

Now comes the question, is etiquette necessary, since a good heart is the true source of good taste? Some exponents of etiquette have said, mistakenly, I think, that in a world of perfect characters, it would be superfluous. It would be truer to say that, in such a world, etiquette would be inevitable. One of the elements of a perfect character is surely good sense, and why waste time deciding every day where to put the forks? Business and government and law have their forms, and it is obvious that human relationships and daily living should also. In fact, it is quite likely that in a perfect world we should be taught etiquette as we are now taught arithmetic, art, and civics: because it is a practical and attractive system which contributes to the general welfare.

Broken down into its three parts, the value of etiquette can be analyzed as follows: It has a practical value, because it has made time-and-thought-saving decisions on technicalities, such as the wording and forms of invitations, which are notably within the province of etiquette. It has an attractive side, an aesthetic value, in that many of its rules and customs (flowers on the table, for example) are designed purely for the sake of beauty or gracefulness. Finally, it has great civic value, and this is the prime contribution of etiquette. Its civic value lies in the fact that etiquette imposes consideration for others. It demands willingness to discipline oneself for the sake of others, or for a principle. It acknowledges high standards of behavior and is valuable to the community because, by acknowledging these standards, it strengthens them. Etiquette has sometimes been questioned because it can serve as a substitute for kindness or gratitude. But the one who pretends to a virtue he lacks is not as dangerous to society as the one who convinces others that virtue is unnecessary.

7

The greatest value of etiquette, however, is none of these. It is its value to the individual. Good behavior may be useful to society, but it is part of a man. Dozens of philosophers, from Aristotle to Emerson, have pointed out this truth. "Manners make the man." The rules of behavior do not depend upon material things. In the end your behavior is "you." It is part of your character, and you can't escape it or leave it behind.

It may seem surprising to some that in a book of etiquette there is so much about morals and principles. But a study of etiquette must go beyond the technicalities to the spirit which lies behind them. And fortunately, when one studies our contemporary etiquette this is what one finds. There are morals in etiquette because our good taste has put them there. They are part of our taste because they are part of our principles. There is no wishful thinking in this book, and no motive except to write an honest textbook about the manners and customs of our times. Out of respect for the subject and for the reader, nothing is here simply because it is moral, or because it is, or might be, popular. No allowances are made on the grounds that the "uninitiated" would not be interested in the finest points, or in some possibly inconvenient truth.

The assumption is that, although few may have the time or the opportunity to study the developments in etiquette, most Americans are interested in the amenities of living. We understand good living to include good manners and good usage and, in the very fullest sense, good taste. And we believe this book to be an outline of good living, as it is given to our generation to understand the meaning of good. When the definition changes, or when usage widens the field of etiquette still further, we'll take up the subject again.

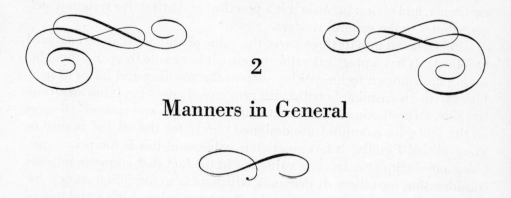

2

Manners in General

THE MANNERS outlined in this chapter are more important than almost any others. Most of them are small points which cannot be listed as rules. But all of them are examples of a code of behavior which must at once override and underlie all other manners. All merely technical rules must be broken, whenever necessary to accord with the attitude on which this code of behavior is based. For it is from this attitude toward one's fellow man that the rest of one's behavior should spring. The core of it is respect for others—for their feelings, their sensibilities, their opinions, and their welfare. It may, at first, seem elaborate and artificial to suggest that a short, inelastic set of rules, such as the rules of table manners, can have any connotation of such importance. But it has. The technique of eating at table is an integral part of the conventions which are symbols of respect for others. The community does not demand, although it would very much enjoy, continuously heartfelt good will. It does, however, demand enough good will to insure lip service, at least, to the code it has devised.

This code of behavior need not, and indeed, cannot, be learned by rote. It must be understood in the heart. One might break many of the rules given in other parts of this book (the rules of club etiquette, for example) and be thought guilty of nothing more than limited experience. One might issue wedding invitations printed in red and gold, and merely be thought somewhat eccentric as well as inexperienced. But if one ignores this code of behavior one gives a regrettable indication of one's character and disposition. Thoughtlessness, selfishness, or even greed and an unkind heart, can be made obvious to others by rudeness. And, although no arbitrary code should ever be used as a substitute for an inner virtue, to flout an accepted pattern is the quickest way to make the absence of that virtue obvious.

"I know what I think when I see what I do." If this is true (and it is, for a great many fuzzy-minded people), how much more true is "I know what to think of you when I see what you do"! A code of behavior is made up, like life itself, of little things. Even the smallest action, if others are involved, has a double significance. First, for oneself, as an expression of discrimination and taste, or of the principles one lives by. And, second, for others, as an expression of one's feelings toward them. The suggestions which follow are important only in these ways. Each one is small, but the sum is significant.

THE ROLE OF THE CUSTOMER OR EMPLOYER

A full understanding of the role of the customer-employer is one of the key points of good manners and that is why it is listed before any other. It has often been said that all the rest of etiquette might be thrown away and, keeping only this one point, the other rules of behavior could easily be reconstructed. This is probably not quite true, but still, it would be difficult to break the pattern laid down for this relationship between employer and employee, or customer and salesman, without making all the rest of one's behavior somewhat suspect.

The axiom is an old one: "In all one's relationships with those who are employed to give personal service, one must be more polite, more considerate, more careful than in any others." This applies not only to one's own employees, to waiters in restaurants and hotels, to stewards in clubs, but also to saleswomen and salesmen, to workers in beauty parlors, to telephone operators, elevator men, doormen, etc. All these people are employed to give service, and politeness toward them is the very essence of good manners. Rudeness always involves a loss of dignity, but rudeness to an employee is vulgar in the extreme. It implies that one is taking advantage of an economically superior position, counting on the fact that the employee may endanger his livelihood if he answers back.

The truth has nothing to do with class distinctions or condescension. Its basis is economic and rests on the power of two old, and, incidentally, very ugly, sayings, "The customer is always right," or, "The one who pays the piper calls the tune." Most Americans have jobs and, from this point of view, they lead dual lives. Half the time, they are "pipers," or employees; and the other half, they are paying the piper—either as customers or employers. It is just conceivable that an employee with good manners, driven beyond bearing, might be a little rude to a customer. But no one with good manners would ever dream of allowing himself to be equally rude to an employee.

For all these reasons, one should be extremely careful about complaining to an employer or manager about an employee; no matter what the provocation, a complaint must always be made with complete composure and in the mildest terms. For example, if a waiter or a saleswoman is unbearably rude or negligent, one can quite properly speak to the headwaiter or the section manager, and ask that another waiter be assigned to one's table or that one be given another saleswoman. The accepted formula is, "I wonder if you could send another waiter to this table, please? This one seems to be very busy," or, "There seems to have been a little misunderstanding." An awkward, loud-voiced scene—like any scene in public—is the absolute low point of manners.

MANNERS IN PUBLIC PLACES

Most of this chapter will be concerned with behavior toward people who are acquaintances, at least—not strangers. In this small section, however, we shall discuss one's relation to the general public. Good manners in public, because of their very anonymity and the fact that they can in no way be prompted by self-interest, are perhaps more than anything else the mark of a civilized man. They are the achievement of a civilized people. Without them, what should be a perfectly normal, if boring, action, such as getting on the bus or waiting in line for a ticket, can be turned into a maddening and tumultuous experience. We have listed some suggestions here, alphabetically and not in order of importance. They are, as a matter of fact, all equally important.

Decorum

Decorum is a pretty old-fashioned word which has, unfortunately, almost disappeared from modern vocabularies. Even more unfortunately, the practice of decorum is not always conspicuous in our streets and public places. The bases of decorum, which are respect for others and an innate sense of modesty, are still as valid as they ever were. But some of the standards have changed, and many people are confused into thinking that the whole idea has been abandoned.

A salient example of the change in standards is in the matter of clothes, women's clothes especially. It used to be said that no "lady" left the house without a hat on her head and gloves on her hands. Decorum demanded these, even for a country outing. Today bare heads and bare hands, and even bare legs, are an accepted part of any summer street scene. But the rule of decorum, as far as clothes are concerned, is still exactly what it was: It is extremely bad taste to wear in public clothes that depart widely from the accepted norm. Any clothes which make an obvious bid for public attention are offensive evidence of indiscrimination and exhibitionism. A bare-headed, bare-legged young girl, for example, may wear a short-sleeved print dress in the street without immodesty or exhibitionism. But one who wears pink pajamas, or long red stockings with a peasant blouse and skirt, is guilty of both, although she may be covered from her chin to her heels.

To a lesser extent, men's clothes, also, can express a lack of the sense of decorum. Brightly colored suits or trousers, open shirts, turtle-neck sweaters—all these would be surprising, and indecorous, on the streets of most big cities. Decorum often demands discipline, even sacrifice of comfort. It always implies a certain personal reticence. It is the opposite of the characteristic which prefers any attention, whether favorable or unfavorable, to none at all.

Like the clothes worn in public, the manners shown to the public should also be characterized by modesty and reticence. It is perfectly all right for a woman to put on powder and lipstick in public, and even to pat a stray hair into place, but she should never put on mascara or rouge, or comb her hair thoroughly, except in a dressing room. An unobtrusive touching up is permitted, but a complete job of making up is unacceptable. Men should never look in the mirror nor comb their hair in public. At most, a man may straighten his necktie and smooth his hair with his hand. It is probably unnecessary to add that it is most unattractive to scratch one's head, to rub one's face or touch one's teeth, or to clean one's fingernails in public. All these things should be done privately. Even a mannerism such as passing one's finger over the cheek or behind the ear can be most unattractive, particularly if it is done in an abstracted, searching way.

A longing for attention from others—even more, perhaps, than lack of respect for them—causes some people to talk and laugh loud in public places; it makes them conspicuous on the street, in busses, or wherever else there may be an audience big enough to impress. Lack of consideration permits such people to sprawl on park benches, to spread over their allotted space in streetcars and busses, to scatter peanut shells and candy wrappers about them. It makes them barge along the street, bumping into others, apparently, and perhaps all but subconsciously, oblivious of them. It allows women to smoke on the street, as though they were at home. It gives an impression of one who feels, "This street and this park were made for my convenience," instead of, "These were made for all to share."

All these dictums obviously have a certain civic worth, a certain value to the community. But in case any reader might feel that decorum is just another boring, if extremely worthy, civic virtue, we must emphasize that our reasons for including it here have nothing to do with being worthy. Apart from any of its civic connotations, decorum is a personal asset which will probably have value for its possessor as long as worldliness exists. All decorum suggests a certain civic consciousness, but there is a great deal of behavior which is quite compatible with

11

altruism and civic-mindedness and is still not decorous. For example, it is not decorous to sing or whistle on the street, and even less so in a crowded elevator. It is not decorous to express even the most patriotic sentiments in an uninhibited and expansive way, in front of other people who cannot help but hear. It is decorous to be quiet, controlled, and dignified in public.

Deportment in Church

An attitude of deference and respect whenever one enters a place of worship, of whatever faith, should be taught children at the earliest possible age. As a matter of fact, it should be unnecessary to outline church manners, because the proper behavior ought to be absorbed by the young from the attitude and behavior of their seniors. But it is the deplorable truth that, in church, behavior which is shocking from the point of view of manners (not to mention other more important connotations) is all too prevalent.

The first point is that a church is not a social meeting place. Heads turned to look for friends in the congregation, merry nods and smiles, gay greetings, and a distracted restlessness are all out of place in church. If one happens to catch a friend's eye, certainly there is no reason to withhold a glance of recognition and a short subdued smile; but respect for the place and concentration on the ceremony should be the basis of all one's behavior.

At funerals this is particularly true, and it applies especially to those who sit in the front pews. It is very bad taste, when one is going to a seat far forward in the church, to cast cheerful and smiling glances at friends and acquaintances all up the aisle.

At joyful religious ceremonies, such as weddings and christenings, a little more leniency is expected; but even here greetings should be subdued, and personal or social relationships subordinated to the ceremony. Guests at a wedding may quite properly turn their heads to smile at friends who are coming in, and of course to watch the bride come up the aisle. But the parents of the bride and groom and members of the wedding procession should not treat the occasion as a triumphal progress; there may be a few smiles and nods, particularly on the return down the aisle, but there should be no unrestrained gaiety and certainly no waving.

Inconsiderateness

The difference between inconsiderateness and lack of decorum is that inconsiderateness is usually based on thoughtlessness, rather than exhibitionism. Thoughtless men and women stand in a doorway blocking the way. A thoughtless driver blocks the road, and ignores a honk behind him; and he never dims his headlights when approaching a car on a road at night. Thoughtless people whisper penetratingly at the theater or a concert; smoke pipes and cigars in closed places, sitting close to strangers.

Littering the Streets

Littering the streets is a mark of an antisocial man. The antisocial man, if he lives in an apartment house, will drop his cigarette stubs and empty packages in the hallways or outside the door, subconsciously bolstered by the knowledge that others may be blamed. He will throw lighted cigarettes in dangerous places, happily sure that he will soon be far away. He will park his car in front of someone else's door in order to leave his own doorway free. The antisocial man is irresponsible and ill-bred.

Standing in Line

Standing in line without pushing and without sneaking up to a higher place is one of the basic decencies of manners in public. If one wants to make private arrangements to avoid the line and go in by another entrance, so much the better and less tiring. But once one has taken one's place in the line, there is no alternative but to keep it patiently and good-humoredly, or leave it. This applies equally to making one's way through crowded doorways: Patient fair play must be the keynote.

Staring and Glaring

Glaring furiously at innocent members of the public who may unwittingly have stepped on one's toe or bumped one's elbow is a very frequent and offensive form of bad manners. Chronic offenders in this are not even mollified by an apology. In crowded places one may often be pushed and jostled, even stepped on, by one's neighbor. The best reaction is to try, pleasantly and quietly, to get out of the way. In any case, one should always accept an apology, however curt or casual, in an agreeable way. It is probably unnecessary to add that one should never stare at conspicuously unfortunate people. Those who are crippled, or in tears, or very shabbily dressed, or otherwise marked by misfortune, should at least be granted the dignity of privacy. The only exception might be the serious attention which is the prelude to an offer to help one who is in distress.

Response to a Beggar

If one is approached on the street by a beggar and does not wish to give him money, any one of three courses may be followed: One may spare the beggar the embarrassment of a refusal by pretending not to notice his appeal; or one may refuse, saying, "No, I'm sorry"; or one may stop and offer help by suggesting a charitable organization to which the unfortunate can apply. A kind heart may extend this list even further, but the essential point is that if one is asked for charity, an apology must accompany a refusal. Quite apart from its other connotations, any sign of anger or impatience is brutally ill-mannered.

SUBTLE POINTS OF BEHAVIOR

In this section are discussed a few fine points of manners which are often overlooked.

Compliments

So much has been said about the danger of making personal remarks that there is no need to go into it here. No one is going to make the obvious mistake of drawing attention to a spot on someone's dress, because disagreeable truths are rarely considered a part of good manners. But a word should be said about compliments, which many people believe to be always acceptable. One of the points of good manners is to give pleasure to others, and certainly a judicious number of

13

compliments always give pleasure to the one who receives them. But there is a further reach which good manners should also be able to cover: Giving a compliment to one person in front of others is very often a negative form of rudeness to the others. Under certain circumstances, even a stock compliment such as, "What a beautiful dress!" may be rude because it may suggest to the other guests that their dresses are not as pretty or, at least, are less conspicuously so. Or else it may suggest that the one who gives the compliment is more interested in pleasing one person than in pleasing the others. A compliment such as this is not, therefore, in the fullest sense, good manners.

The most exquisite manners go further, holding that "What a becoming hat!" is not an entirely felicitous comment, because it suggests that the woman's other hats have been found less becoming. Few, however, are even aware of such subtleties and they are perhaps a little precious. A good common sense rule is to avoid giving pointedly selective compliments in the presence of others.

On the Telephone

Telephone manners are often thought to begin and end with "Hello" and "Good-bye," but the matter is a little more complicated than that. "Hello" is, of course, the standard greeting in answering the telephone and it should always be used except when one is answering the telephone as part of one's work. A nurse in a doctor's office says, "Dr. Wheeler's office"; a butler says, "Mrs. Bradley's residence"; a switchboard operator in a hotel says, "Ritz-Carlton Hotel"; or in a business firm, "Lincoln Engineering Company." But all of these at home would answer the telephone with "Hello."

A second point, which involves a more important question of manners, is the modern custom of calling a person to the telephone before one is ready to speak oneself. This is never polite, but if a man does it to a woman it is extremely rude. No matter how important or busy he may be, a man must never keep a woman waiting on the telephone, unless he is calling a junior member of his staff on business. His secretary may get the number for him, but he should be on the wire when the woman comes to the telephone. Should she answer the telephone herself, all he can do, of course, is to come to the telephone as quickly as possible. But it is rude beyond any acceptable standard for a man to allow his secretary to call the number, to ask for the woman in his name, and to wait until she is on the wire before turning the telephone over to him. If some emergency has unavoidably broken this rule, he must apologize and explain. This rule should be followed by women as well as men; and it applies whether a child, a maid, a private secretary, or a business secretary is the one who does the preliminary work of calling.

"Good-bye" is, of course, the accepted end of a telephone conversation; but again, as in the case of "Hello," there are certain exceptions. As described on page 503, a butler or maid ends the conversation with "Thank you," not "Good-bye," and in many business firms this practice is followed also by switchboard operators, secretaries, and others who answer routine calls.

Rudeness Toward the Uninvited

One of the most egregious forms of rudeness is to give an invitation to one person in front of another, who is not included. There is literally no excuse for this, since it can be avoided easily. Another form of the same rudeness is to refer to an invitation one has received, unless one is sure that the others present have also been invited. Even an indirect reference—asking, "What time is dinner tonight? Eight o'clock?"—is bad manners. Almost equally bad are compliments to one's hostess for a party to which others present were not invited; such as, "We had such fun the other night; and wasn't Mary amusing about Saratoga!"

The reasons why such invitations or remarks are rude are fairly obvious. References to past pleasures make others feel left out; reference to a future engagement may put the hostess in the awkward position of being almost forced to invite also the others in the room; an invitation given to one and not to another is obviously not flattering.

But there is a still more delicate point. In giving an invitation to one person in the presence of a second person who has already refused, the hostess should make clear the fact that the second person has also been invited. For example, if Mrs. A. has just accepted an invitation to lunch, within hearing of Mrs. B., the hostess should say, "I am so pleased you will be able to come. Isn't it a pity that Mrs. B. can't be there?" Otherwise, Mrs. A. and Mrs. B. will both feel awkward: Mrs. A. because she is abashed at such apparent rudeness to Mrs. B., and Mrs. B. because she is well aware that Mrs. A. will think her slighted.

The Previous Engagement

There is a fine point of good manners which is involved whenever one must refuse a friend's invitation to dinner. In America, it is considered stiff and somewhat unfriendly to refuse a friend's invitation by saying only, "I'm so sorry, we've already accepted an invitation to dinner for that evening." Although this system is widely used abroad and is almost standard practice in America in refusing an invitation from an acquaintance, it is often considered inadequate when a friend is concerned, especially in a small community. However, the alternative, "I'm sorry, we're dining with the Clarks that night," is not in some cases the very best manners, either. If "the Clarks" are mutual friends, the one who is giving the invitation may feel a little left out. The difficulty is that one is caught between two conflicting points of good manners: One wants to be friendly and agreeable to the friend whose invitation must be refused, and to give her every assurance that only a previous and valid engagement prevents one from accepting; on the other hand, one does not want to hurt this same friend's feelings by bringing to her attention a party to which she has not been invited, or even to involve "the Clarks" in a difficulty with a mutual friend. The best solution is to avoid the direct statement if possible. For example, one might say, "Oh dear, I *am* sorry, I'm afraid that we've accepted something for that evening. We should have loved to come, and George will be so disappointed."

If one has accepted an invitation from someone who is not a mutual friend there is, of course, no reason not to be as explicit in refusing as one wants to be.

Conversation

It has been generally agreed that conversation is a lost art. And from one point of view there is little to be said here which will help to restore it. The first requisite, as in any art, is that those who would practice it must have something interesting and valuable to express. But it is nevertheless true that most conversations, even the most brilliant, start very simply. The weather, the surroundings, the news—all these are classic opening gambits, and the only possible objection to them is that they have been called clichés. As a matter of fact, too much has been said against clichés and too little in their defense. A cliché is chiefly objectionable when it is pronounced, with great satisfaction and no little pomposity, as though it were an extraordinary and original thought. The cliché is not objectionable, but on the contrary most acceptable and civilized, when it is only the tentative opening of a conversation with a stranger. Certainly remarks such as "What a beautiful house!" or "What a terrible day this has been!" are not strikingly original; but they are the accepted starting points of conversation, even among those who may be consistently brilliant and original from that point on.

The second requisite of the art of conversation is a simple matter of good manners, which are quite easy to describe and even easier to carry out. All general conversation, whether at the level of a great art or a little pleasure, should be conducted within this set of civilized limits:

No monologues. This scarcely needs elaboration. An informative speech, however interesting, cannot be considered conversation.

No languages which everyone present cannot understand. If one of the group speaks only a foreign language which the others cannot understand, a separate conversation should be conducted with him.

No member of a group should be left out. This does not refer to the obvious language barrier which is discussed immediately above, but to another form of rudeness which is much more common. In any conversation, the one who is speaking should always look from one guest to another until each member of the group can feel that the words are directed to him as much as to any other one person. Even though the conversation may for the moment have turned into a discussion between two people, this rule should be observed by the one who is speaking. Newcomers to the conversation should be brought up to date with a brief outline of the subject under discussion, and of the direction the conversation has taken.

No topic too difficult for any member of the group. This may at first seem like an elaboration of the rule against leaving members of the group out of the conversation, but it goes beyond that rather simple situation. Very often, among a group of well-informed people there will be one who, though joining quite happily in the conversation, is obviously beyond his depth. In such circumstances, it is better to steer the conversation to a subject on which his views will be more interesting to the rest of the conversationalists. If he seems interested, though silent, and particularly if he asks intelligent questions from time to time, this maneuver is not necessary.

No blanket attacks on religions, nationalities, political parties, or races. Attacks are out of the question, but the word "attack" does not, of course, mean reasonable discussion.

No strong categorical pronouncements on moral or ethical questions. Again, this does not exclude reasonable discussion.

(See also "General Conversation," pages 461 to 462, and "Conversation," on page 441.)

ENGAGEMENTS—ABUSES AND EXCUSES, VALID AND INVALID

Issuing, accepting, and regretting invitations are essentially a matter of form, and they are discussed from that point of view in a chapter beginning on page 501. But there are two forms of opportunism and bad manners connected with these subjects which must be discussed in this section concerning behavior.

The Delayed Acceptance

The first is an innovation in the technique of receiving verbal invitations: the response, "May I let you know?" Nothing could be more inconvenient or annoying to a hostess, except the other form of opportunism which is discussed immediately below. The delaying tactics of "May I let you know?" are a corruption of a perfectly polite and often quite necessary form: "We'd love to come, but I am afraid George may be going to Boston; we won't know until tomorrow, and I'm sure you want an answer, so I'm afraid we must say no." This longer form suggests that one would like to come, but hesitates to cause the hostess inconvenience. Hostesses usually reply, "Oh, no, do let me know tomorrow; we'd like so much to see you," etc. The short form suggests, "A more amusing (or important) invitation may turn up. Therefore, may I let you know?"

Canceling an Engagement

The second form of opportunism is less simple than this one. It is concerned with invitations already issued or accepted by hostesses and guests who would like to change their minds. As far as guests are concerned (and we shall discuss guests first because their position is more subtle) the traditional social code has an inflexible ruling: no invitation can be used as an excuse to avoid one already accepted, unless the second invitation is official or royal. One cannot refuse an invitation to the White House, for example, or to the house of a member of a reigning royal family, no matter what one's previous engagement may have been. (See page 497 for the accepted way to break engagements in these circumstances.) Official duties can also take precedence over most social engagements. But otherwise there is no polite way of getting out of one invitation in order to accept a later one, no matter how alluring. This rule exists because of the normal reactions of a hostess who finds that some other dinner party is preferred to her own. She would think her guest rude to imply that, of two invitations of a voluntary and unofficial nature, another is more attractive than hers. And she would be quite right. It *is* rude—and selfish—to seek pleasure at the cost of annoyance and inconvenience to others.

In practice, this excellent rule has a few exceptions. If one has planned to dine alone with a very old friend and is suddenly invited to meet the most famous statesman of the moment, one can call up and explain, and no damage will be done. But it will annoy any but the most understanding and tolerant friend if the excuse is only that one wants to dine with another equally old and easily available friend. Just as one cannot put off one social invitation for another purely social invitation, so one cannot put off a simple cozy dinner for another of the same kind.

In view of these patent difficulties, the most usual excuse for getting out of a dinner party is not another invitation. Before discussing the excuses which are considered acceptable, it might be useful to outline the different categories, or priority ratings, of invitations. There are three.

First, cocktail parties, tea parties, dances, late evening parties. In this first category one need only regret by telephone, unless there is some special circumstance. For example, if a tea party is being given in one's honor, the invitation is as binding as a dinner invitation.

Second, women's luncheons, picnics. A family obligation or a minor business engagement will suffice here as an excuse, provided, of course, that one makes suitable expressions of regret.

Last, a dinner or luncheon to which men and women have been invited in equal numbers; invitations to the theater, opera, concert, or anything else for which tickets have been bought; week ends, of course, most of all. The rule in this third category is that one must go wherever one has promised to go unless there is an adequate excuse. And so we come to the question, "What is considered adequate?"

The first point to remember in making any excuse is that one must impress on the hostess how sorry one is not to be able to keep the engagement. No matter what one's reasons or personal feelings may be, this is a required minimum of politeness. The second point is that, whenever one has determined to break an engagement, exaggeration of the importance of one's excuse is a virtue rather than a vice. It is accepted as proper politeness and consideration, not as hypocrisy. And, incidentally, one *good* excuse is enough: two always sound more artificial than one. For these reasons, however truthful the excuse may be, its verisimilitude and importance must increase in direct ratio to the possible inconvenience to one's hostess. Three grounds, enlarged upon, or minimized, to fit the circumstances, are always considered valid.

First, personal or family illness, either critical or contagious. No forms, of course, are necessary for canceling an engagement with an intimate friend on the plea of illness, but there are accepted forms for canceling the usual social engagements. In case of personal illness, unless it is critical, one can send a message such as this: "Mr. and Mrs. Bradley are very sorry that they will not be able to dine with Mr. and Mrs. Humphries this evening, as Mrs. Bradley has an attack of grippe." When a hostess receives a message of this kind, she can telephone and ask if Mr. Bradley would like to come to dinner anyway; and Mr. Bradley may accept, or regret on the plea of keeping Mrs. Bradley company. Or, if the guests are older and more experienced than the hostess, the refusal may include the offer, "If it would be more convenient for Mrs. Humphries, Mr. Bradley would, of course, be delighted to come."

If there is a serious or contagious illness in the family, some not too explicit hint of this is given in the message: "Mr. and Mrs. Bradley are very sorry that they will not be able to dine with Mr. and Mrs. Humphries this evening, as one of their children has been quarantined;" or, ". . . owing to the critical illness of Mrs. Bradley's mother."

There is a further convention which permits women to be excused from an engagement for an illness too slight to serve as an excuse for a man. Mothers and daughters can quite properly plead a parent's or a child's illness which is uncomfortable for the patient, rather than grave. But no illness serious enough to make a man's presence necessary should fail to bind his wife also. Only in special circumstances should a wife allow her husband to go alone to his relative's bedside.

Apart from any question of a serious illness, it is extremely considerate to telephone and offer to stay home if one has a cold. In this case, one must speak directly to the hostess, because one must explain that, if the hostess prefers, one is entirely prepared to come.

Second, business: a trip to another city, an important meeting or conference. The established expressions are, "has a very important business meeting," or "must be away on business." For example, in the case of a married couple, the wife might telephone, or send the following message: "Mr. and Mrs. Bradley are very sorry that they will not be able to dine with Mr. and Mrs. Humphries on Tuesday evening as Mr. Bradley has just been notified of a very important business conference on that evening"; or, ". . . has just learned that he must be in Detroit on business." As in the case of illness, if the guests are older and more experienced than the hostess, they may add to the message, "If it would be more convenient for Mrs. Humphries, Mrs. Bradley will be delighted to come." Or, if the hostess is the more experienced, she may telephone to ask if Mrs. Bradley would like to come alone. This courtesy must, however, be extended with some discretion on the part of the hostess, because it may be that the excuse is not a true one. In other words, if the hostess has any reason to suppose that Mr. Bradley has not been called out of town, it would not be tactful to put Mrs. Bradley in the position of having to make further excuses for herself.

In the case of a single man or woman, the same kind of message is left at the hostess' house; for example, "Miss Bradley is very sorry she will not be able to dine with Mr. and Mrs. Humphries on Tuesday as planned, as she must be away on business." To be quite polite, all men, and any women conspicuously younger than the hostess, should follow this message with a telephone call or letter, expressing regret and giving a little fuller explanation of the circumstances. These forms are not, of course, followed exactly when the guest speaks to the hostess or to a member of her family. But they are always used otherwise, because they are so clear and convenient.

Last, family events: weddings, funerals, or christenings; the arrival or departure of an intimate member of the family at the end or beginning of a long separation.

It is probably unnecessary to say that a family funeral is always a valid excuse. In fact, in this case, one is open to criticism for keeping, not breaking, one's engagement. Naturally, the degree of kinship and the degree of intimacy are factors which must be taken into consideration; it might be a little exaggerated to refuse to dine with four or five friends on the evening of the funeral of a distant, and not at all intimate, relative. But it is better to err on this side than on the other.

If one is using a family wedding or christening as an excuse, one must explain a bit why so little notice was given of such important events. For example, "Mr. and Mrs. Bradley are very sorry that they will not be able to lunch with Mr. and Mrs. Humphries on Wednesday because the date of the wedding of Mrs. Bradley's sister has been advanced, owing to her fiancé's sudden transfer," or, ". . . because the christening of Mrs. Bradley's godchild, of which Mrs. Bradley was notified only this morning, has been set in the country for that date." If the reason is complicated, a simple message should be followed by a fuller explanation on the telephone or in a letter.

Family arrivals and departures must be used with more discretion, because the obligation on the part of the guest is less obvious than in the case of a funeral, wedding, or christening. In time of war, or in the case of a long and well-known family separation, such an excuse is always valid. But, however much one might like to, one cannot give as a reason the arrival of a beloved sister whom one sees quite regularly every few months.

To sum up: Any situation which is understandable and convincing, even in its barest outlines, is a valid excuse, because there is no danger of hurting the feelings of one's hostess. She may be almost a stranger, who cannot be expected to be deeply concerned with one's private life; but if the situation is one involving obvious emotions, she will be able to understand without much explanation. A more complicated and subtle situation, where there are personal reasons for emotions beyond the obvious, can be used as an excuse only when the hostess is an intimate friend, with whom reticence is unnecessary.

Canceling an Invitation

All this is even more binding upon those who have sent the invitations. The law of hospitality ranks higher than that of social obligation. An invitation, once issued, cannot be lightly canceled. One cannot call up and inform guests that a dinner, or even a tea party, has been called off, without giving one of the three valid excuses suggested above. There are no priority ratings for invitations issued, as there are for invitations accepted (see page 17). If the cook becomes ill on the afternoon of the dinner, the hostess should either get another cook for the evening or take her guests to a restaurant. If one of her children, or other member of her family, is ill, it is a valid excuse for canceling a dinner; but, if it is a question of a contagious, rather than a serious, disease, all she can do is telephone each guest and warn him. Hostesses should, however, be sure to do this. Measles may not seem formidable to an experienced mother, but her guests may take another view.

If one cannot give a dinner as planned, it is more polite to postpone than to cancel the invitation. Informal invitations given on the telephone may be changed a day or so later with little or no excuse; pleading a "mistake" is enough. But if the invitation has been one of long standing, or if the engagement is imminent, the reasons for changing it will have to be full and valid. This is even more true of an invitation which is canceled than of one postponed. The hostess must explain fully, with many expressions of regret. In the case of a death in the family, of course, the hostess need neither telephone nor write herself, and no further explanations are necessary. (Canceling and changing formal and official invitations are described in the chapter "Invitations, Acceptances, and Regrets." See page 516.)

Any excuse must be used with a sense of values and proportion. An invitation, whether issued or accepted, entails an obligation and all obligations demand a certain amount of self-discipline. A refusal to accept this self-discipline is one of the marks of an opportunist, willing to sacrifice others to his ambition, self-interest, or greed for amusement. But without a sense of values the other extreme can be worse. The opportunist is, after all, more innocent and more excusable than one who puts social obligations above friendship and family affection. It may be snobbish and a little cheap to put off Mrs. A. for Mrs. B., but it would be appallingly bad taste, and most unnatural, to dine out when a member of the family has just died or is dying.

BORROWING AND LENDING

Borrowing, lending, and asking favors, which seem such simple interchanges among friends, are in fact quite ticklish matters.

As a borrower, or as one who asks favors, one must be quick and sensitive to the reactions of the lender. One must be able to gauge the strain one's request may put upon a friend. One must be prepared to take infinite pains in a long search to replace a borrowed object if one breaks it.

As a lender, or as one who grants a favor, one must be quick-witted enough to evaluate all the possible consequences before answering yes or no. The less intimate a friend, the more this is true.

This, with all its drawbacks, is the pleasanter side of borrowing and lending. There is a seamy side as well for borrowers and lenders alike. It is expressed in the attitude, "I'll take advantage of him." Borrowers take advantage of a generosity which subconsciously they tend to consider weakness. An exaggeration of this eventually causes borrowers to feel positively cheated, if help is not granted, or even not offered. Lenders take advantage of the obligation under which the borrower is bound. A typical victim of this attitude is the poor relation who is almost ordered to run errands and who is never given the best guest room, even when there are no other guests.

Another unfortunate feature of the borrower-lender relation derives from one of the weaknesses of small natures, the inability to carry the weight that an obligation entails. In an equal interchange of favors this is expressed in a tight-lipped adherence to a strict quid pro quo, as though favors were part of an arithmetical formula which could be balanced if only one tried hard enough! In extreme cases, when the obligation is such that an equal return cannot be made, the borrower often turns on the lender, cloaking in enmity his inability to repay.

Fortunately, however, borrowing and lending are usually not such unhappy matters. As in the rest of etiquette, a good heart, sympathy for others, understanding of their problems and their feelings, and true generosity of spirit, dictate the rules and accepted customs. If one had received many favors, with a heart such as this, one would be moved to return them by affection and gratitude, not by a spirit of bookkeeping. If one had given much to another, one would feel recompensed by the pleasure in giving. If one had borrowed and broken something belonging to another, one would make every effort to replace it, through regret, affection, and concern for the feelings of the other person. As one who had loaned an object which had been broken or lost, one's first concern would be to spare the feelings of the borrower. On this attitude, the following common-sense rules are based.

Obligations of the Borrower

Return anything borrowed promptly, as promised.

If one cannot return something borrowed on the day for which it was promised, one should warn the lender as early as possible and try to agree upon a mutually convenient and satisfactory postponement.

If any damage has been done, notify the lender immediately, offering to have it repaired by any workman the owner recommends. This is particularly important if the object is valuable; inexpert repairs can be almost as damaging as the original breakage.

If the object is lost, or damaged beyond repair, the borrower should replace it, or at least make every effort to do so. If it is irreplaceable, all he can do is to find a similar object of the same, or even greater, value. In these circumstances, it is wise to make sure that whatever one buys can be returned for credit or cash, preferably either. The point is that one should not return money for the broken or lost object, but should arrange matters so that the lender can have either cash or credit, as he prefers. Only then has one made the fullest possible reparation. When this has been arranged, one should always make it clear to the lender; for example, "I'm sorry about this; I know that this platter can never take the place of the one that was broken, but do go back to the shop if this proves not to be useful; they'll exchange or credit it for you."

Before borrowing anything, except of course money, one should have a pretty clear idea as to its value. If it seems to be at all valuable, one can ask the lender, "But isn't this pretty valuable? If I were to insure it, what do you think I ought to insure it for?" This may be only a hypothetical question, but the answer will give an indication of what amount of money one should be prepared to pay if the object is lost. One should never borrow valuable things—furs, jewelry, furniture, or paintings—unless they are covered by insurance, or unless one is prepared to make good the loss.

One must consider as a refusal the slightest hint of reluctance or even hesitation on the part of the owner. Like all refusals, it must be most gracefully accepted. At best, it is embarrassing for an owner to refuse to lend something; and it is the duty of the would-be borrower, since he has put the owner into this embarrassing position, to extricate him as easily as possible. This can be done by changing one's request immediately; or better still, perhaps, by working out some quick solution so that no borrowing is necessary.

It is probably unnecessary to add that one should never borrow anything which is obviously needed for a party unless the lender has been invited. There are exceptions to this rule, such as lenders who are older relatives, or great friends whom one entertains constantly. And the rule need not be observed if one is giving a party, such as a committee meeting, in which the lender is not interested. But apart from such exceptions, this is a sound general rule.

The last important point is that one is responsible for something borrowed from the moment it leaves the owner's jurisdiction. If the owner has offered to deliver a bridge table, for example, and it is broken on the way to the borrower's house, the borrower is not responsible. But the borrower is responsible for anything that may happen while the object is in his care, whether it is damaged in transit, by a guest in his house, or by himself.

Obligations of the Lender

Never lend anything so valuable, whether sentimentally or otherwise, that its loss might cause a serious breach or a change of feeling toward the borrower. Lending an uninsured jewel, or an irreplaceable china platter, is not always pure generosity. It can be weakness, or the desire to be thought a good fellow, or even a form of showing off. It is indeed more difficult, but much wiser, to say, "I'm awfully sorry; I'd love to lend it to you, but I'd feel so dreadfully if anything happened to it. Would something else be useful to you?"

If an object has been lost or broken, one must minimize its value and importance. The moment to demur was the moment of lending. After that, one must accept the consequences gracefully. This is a rule as binding as the rule which forces one to minimize any damage done by a guest in one's house.

Whenever a borrower asks the value of the object he wants to borrow, the lender should be quite frank in answering. The borrower is trying to protect himself from borrowing something he cannot afford to replace, or from borrowing something which, apart from its intrinsic worth, may be particularly valuable to the owner. And certainly he deserves every co-operation in this effort. But there is another and more subtle point on which he may need help. Suppose, for example, that twelve quite expensive whiskey-and-soda glasses are in question. If the owner would greatly mind their loss, and if he suspects that the borrower has not a clear understanding of their value, he should try to indicate it. "I'd love to lend them to you, but they *are* a nuisance, because they're English glass and ridiculously expensive." This may seem a little awkward to say, but it is much more fair to the borrower than to allow him to believe he is taking twelve glasses which can quite easily be replaced at the nearest department store counter. If, as sometimes happens, there is no way the borrower can learn the true value of what he has broken and if the owner is generously prepared to accept an inexpensive substitute without rancor, none of this is necessary.

The really awkward moments in the whole transaction of lending come when the borrower fails to return an object as promised. How the owner is to get it back depends somewhat on how intimate a friend the borrower is, but even more on one's guess as to the reason for the delay. If the cause is simple forgetfulness, a polite letter may be written; but the loan should not be mentioned to others, or when others are present. If it is a matter of chronic forgetfulness, any amount of pressure, private or public, immediate or postponed, is permissible because such a borrower will not be seriously embarrassed. When these fail, great tact is necessary. As a general rule, it is better not to keep reminding the delinquent. One might wait to meet the borrower and mention it casually, rather than write again or make a special telephone call. If one plans to go past the borrower's house, one may offer to pick up the object, but this should only be done if it would be a real convenience to the borrower. Otherwise, this offer would suggest an impolite lack of confidence. If the object is valuable and if the owner does not mind losing a friend and making an enemy, he can write stiff notes. But the need for such stringent action is only further proof that the important moment of lending is in the act of lending.

When money is involved, the situation is a little different. We are not discussing here the ethics of business practice or loans made on a business basis. We are concerned only with loans made on the basis of friendship. And the suggestions given here apply particularly, although not exclusively, to women. (In spite of the fact that they are the majority property owners in the United States, women usually borrow and lend money on this basis.) These loans fall into three categories, for two of which there are accepted techniques of retrieval.

In the first group are the very small amounts, between five cents and a dollar, which might be borrowed for a tip or taxi. One cannot gracefully ask to have such small amounts returned, but it is perfectly simple to allow the borrower, without comment, to pay the next tip and taxicab, or even to borrow the money from her in order to do so oneself.

In the second category, the loans involved are small, but not inconsiderable, sums: five or ten dollars. It is perfectly simple to remind the borrower about a debt of this kind, after allowing a reasonable interval, two days to a week, for voluntary repayment. But one must wait to see the borrower, or create an opportunity to see her, in order to remind her. A written reminder is not a suitable way to collect a debt of this size. One of the easiest reminders is, "I'm terribly sorry; I meant to cash a check this morning but forgot. Could you give me the ten dollars?"

The third kind of loan involves any considerable sum of money which may be loaned to help a friend out of a critical financial situation. These are the most unwise and the most difficult of all loans between friends. When one is asked for such a loan there are only three ways in which the matter should be considered. First, the easiest and the most pleasant, if one can afford it, is to acquiesce immediately, mentally writing off the loan as a gift. If this is not practical, the second course is to facilitate in every way, with advice, sympathy, effort, information, the friend's securing a regular commercial loan on the usual business basis. The third course is to refuse, with many expressions of regret and sympathy and with some explanation as to the financial factors which make the refusal necessary. If one wants to be sure of a continuing friendship, no course is open other than these three, unless the circumstances are most exceptional.

HOSPITAL MANNERS

The primary elements of all correct hospital behavior are dictated by common sense. Visitors should walk and talk quietly in elevators and corridors, and never talk about illness within the earshot of others. Patients should keep their radios low and remember that the telephone, unlike a hotel telephone, is a concession on the part of the hospital and not standard equipment. In addition to these general reminders, we offer a few suggestions which may be useful to visitors and patients.

Presents to Patients

Flowers are the standard present to patients in the hospital. But when one sends flowers to patients on floor care, it is best to send them in vases or containers, all arranged, so that the nurse need only fill the vase with water; or, during a long visit, to send a small vase with one or two flowers (a camellia, for example) and to send flowers for the same vase once or twice a week.

Books or magazines, carefully chosen to suit the patient's taste, are ideal presents.

A bedjacket is a very good present, whether it is the plain, open-front model, or a cape which can be worn backwards. The new copies of hospital nightgowns, made in pretty, silky materials, are wonderful presents, but quite expensive.

Attractive packets of matches are a good present for a long-term patient who smokes.

A thermos ice bucket is useful for a patient on floor care, especially for one who is not very ill and will have many visitors.

A pencil box, complete with stamps, pencils, erasers, and perhaps even a fountain pen, is another good present for a long-term patient.

The Patient's Part

The question most often asked by patients about to leave the hospital is, "Whom do I tip, and how much?" One does not tip a trained nurse, but one may tip chambermaids, pantryboys, and others. Wages of hospital employees are not predicated on their receiving tips, so tips are not an essential matter of justice, as they are in a hotel. But nevertheless, it is always attractive and kind to give some sign of gratitude to those who have given service, and the following is the usual scale for patients who have private or semi-private rooms; ward patients are not expected to give tips.

For chambermaids, or attendants who do the rooms and bathrooms, a dollar each for a five-to-ten-day visit; a dollar a week, or three dollars a month for a long stay. Sums smaller than a dollar are not given.

A doorman who has helped to carry a patient's luggage down to the door is given fifty cents, usually by the friend or relative who has come to fetch the patient. If the doorman has called many taxis for the family and visitors during the patient's stay, the tip is a dollar.

Pantryboys who bring the trays, and delivery boys who bring newspapers, cigarettes, etc., are not tipped unless one has stayed a month or so. After a stay of a month, five dollars is the standard tip, to be divided among them all.

Presents to Nurses

As we have said, nurses are never tipped, but there is a very sound and sensible and attractive practice of making a small present (candy or fruit, for example) to the floor nurse. The best present is one which can be enjoyed by all the nurses on floor duty.

After a stay of a week or two, one gives individual presents to the nurse or nurses who have been especially kind. Soap, handkerchiefs, sachet powder, eau de cologne are standard examples of the presents usually given. It is probably unnecessary to add that a present inscribed, "To the night nurse," will never give as much pleasure as one that is sent, "For Miss Morris—with many thanks."

A final suggestion: It is very nice to send extra flowers, books, and magazines to the other patients in the hospital. The head floor nurse will know which ones will most appreciate them.

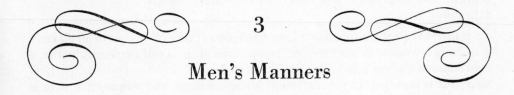

3

Men's Manners

MEN'S MANNERS, like their clothes, should be unobtrusive. A woman's manners may be noticeably good, although the best manners fit so easily that one thinks, "What a friendly woman!" rather than, "What beautiful manners!" But noticeably good manners, according to the Anglo-American standard, are almost unattractive in a man. Lifting his hat should be an automatic reflex action, not a flowing, unctuous, obviously self-conscious exhibition of courtesy. Moving to the outer edge of the sidewalk should be done smoothly, without losing a stride or a syllable. The following suggestions which, for convenience' sake, are separated into different sections, are all based on this theory.

These suggestions are not, however, a full guide. To them should be added many other rules and customs concerning procedure and behavior. Politenesses expected from a man at a dance are discussed not only on page 78 in the chapter, "Dances," but also on page 47 in the chapter, "Concerning the Young," since all these customs should be learned at an early age. Another example is in the section about dining with a woman in a restaurant, on page 30, which should be read together with the suggestions as to men's behavior in restaurants, on page 27, and the section, "Entertaining in Clubs, Restaurants, Night Clubs, etc.," on page 452. Ways of handling unsatisfactory waiters are discussed in the section, "The Role of the Customer or Employer," on page 9. The same applies to all other questions of behavior. Most of the suggestions in this book apply to men and women alike; the suggestions in this chapter are those which apply specifically to men.

ACCEPTED CUSTOMS

A Man's Hat

Outdoors a man takes off his hat

a. when being introduced, or saying good-bye;
b. as a salutation when passing in the street;
c. while conversing, particularly with an older man, an ecclesiastic, or anyone else who is owed special respect;
d. when he is with someone who recognizes a woman passing by, even if the woman is unknown to him.

Indoors a man takes his hat off, except

a. in Orthodox Jewish synagogues and in some Conservative synagogues;
b. in public buildings such as railroad stations and post offices;
c. in entrance halls and corridors of office buildings or hotels;
d. in stores.

It used to be a strict rule that a man must always take off his hat in an elevator if there is a woman in the elevator; now, although it is still extremely polite, a man does not always take off his hat in the elevator of an office building, particularly if it is crowded. In an apartment house, or hotel, and whenever a man is accompanying a woman, he should take his hat off in the elevator.

A Man at the Theater

a. checks his hat and coat only if he wants to; often he folds his coat and puts it with his hat under his seat (see also "Entertaining at the Theater and Movies," page 457);

b. should get up, fold up his seat, and stand while others are passing him on their
way between their seats and the aisle.

A Man in a Restaurant

a. checks his hat and coat;
b. waits at the door of the dining room until the headwaiter comes to him;
c. asks the headwaiter, "Have you a table for two?" and follows him, or the
subordinate whom the headwaiter will assign, to his table;
d. changes tables by asking for the headwaiter, if the table is too near the door
or is otherwise unsatisfactory (if the waiter is unsatisfactory, see page 9,
"The Role of the Customer or Employer");
e. may share the check with other men, unless there is a host. This is fully discussed on page 456, "When There Is No One Host."

When a Man Calls

Unless there is a previous arrangement to the contrary, a man who comes to
call for or fetch a friend goes to the door of the house or apartment, rings, says,
"Would you please tell Miss Blank (or Mr. Blank) that Mr. Doe is here?" He
waits in the hall unless some other suggestion is made to him. (See also page 470,
"Formality with the Staff," and page 362, "At the Door."

Gloves

Gloves are worn out of doors, whenever a hat may be worn, and are taken off
indoors when a man takes off his hat. (See the exceptions in the paragraph below.) The old-fashioned rule was that one should never shake hands with a
woman with one's gloves on; and this is still observed to the extent that, if convenient, one tries to avoid doing so. But it is much better to shake hands with a
glove on, than it is to fumble wildly while a woman stands waiting with her hand
outstretched. In no case, should a man apologize for shaking hands with his
gloves on.

The only time a man wears gloves indoors is when he is acting as an usher at
a wedding or a funeral, or, very rarely nowadays, at a most formal and elaborate
dance.

Bowing

When standing, a man should draw his feet together and bow from the waist.
The deeper the bow, the greater the respect shown. If, while he is sitting, he recognizes a woman acquaintance or an older man at a distance, he should half-rise
while bowing. A man should not sit and bow, as a woman does, except to men
who are his contemporaries or younger than he.

Smoking

Smoking is, technically, a most informal practice and there are certain definite
rules about it. The old-fashioned rule was that a man might smoke a cigarette or
cigar in public in the city, but that a pipe was only for the country, preferably out

of doors, or for the privacy of his library. Another old rule about smoking, which is mentioned later in this section, was that a man should not smoke a pipe or cigar in an automobile with a woman. These rules are no longer observed, but the following are still very much the custom: a man

a. should never smoke while dancing;
b. should never smoke when he is taking part in a formal official procession or when, in formal dress, he is preparing to enter a church or an official residence;
c. should take his cigarette or pipe out of his mouth before lifting his hat, bowing, greeting others, or saying good-bye.

WHEN A MAN IS WITH MEN

A Younger Man

a. calls an older man "Sir";
b. gets up when an older man comes into the room;
c. allows an older man to pass ahead of him through a doorway, but should the older man suggest that he go first, he should do so. It is bad manners for a younger man to persist against an older man's suggestions.
d. waits until an older man speaks to him;
e. lifts his hat to an older man on the street; and, if he is smoking, he must take his cigarette or pipe out of his mouth before lifting his hat.

There are two further customs which are still polite but are no longer strictly observed: A younger man

f. allows an older man to sit at his right when being driven in the back seat of an automobile;
g. walks on the outer side of the pavement.

MEN'S MANNERS TOWARD WOMEN

The whole relation of men to women, as far as etiquette is concerned, is based on the assumption that woman is a delicate, sensitive creature, easily tired, who must be fêted, amused, and protected, to whom the bright and gay side of the picture must always be turned. This is what causes men to hide the check at restaurant dinners, to walk on the outer or seamy side of the sidewalk, to get up and give women their seats in busses and subways. (What causes men *not* to get up and give their seats to women is a question for the modern sociologist.) The fact that men are relaxing somewhat from this agreeable attitude is one of the minor sorrows of modern life. It is perhaps natural, and in accord with the times, for men no longer to feel that every woman who gives a dinner party must be reassured by flowers and a polite word sent the next day that her dinner was a success; or, if they fail to be the first to reach the taxicab door, no longer to worry about the frail creature's wrist or wounded feelings. But they cannot relax entirely. Men still raise their hats when they meet a woman in the street. As host at an informal dinner, a man still accompanies her to the door of her car; or, if she is leaving a big apartment house, at least to the door of the elevator. He does, that is, unless he wants her to feel that such rudeness can only be an obscure technique.

Apart from this basic assumption, there is only one big difference between the customs that apply generally and the customs that apply specifically to men in their relation to women. None of the hesitancy described on page 502 in the section on "Entertaining" need apply to a man who is inviting a woman he has met for the first time. Conduct which might be considered pushing in one woman toward another, and would be unthinkable in a woman toward a man, is entirely acceptable in a man toward a woman, because it can be attributed to admiration. No woman in her right mind would be annoyed to think that a man has been struck with her beauty and charm, although she might be annoyed to think that she was considered a useful social acquisition by another woman.

Invitations from a married man will, of course, have to be made through his wife. But an unmarried man can telephone a woman the day after he meets her for the first time, without any risk of being thought rude or pushing. To some extent, also, the unmarried man is exempt from the rule (see page 434) which makes it mandatory to invite one's hosts the first time one invites a new acquaintance met in their house. If he is planning to invite several people, among them the new acquaintance, certainly his hosts should be invited too. But he can quite properly invite a woman to lunch or dine alone without inviting their hosts or anyone else. This is true in America; but see page 124 concerning foreign customs.

A Man Addressing a Woman

a. always waits to call a woman by her first name until she has taken the initiative. A woman may make a point of the change by saying, "*Please*, don't call me Mrs. Edwards"; or she may simply start calling the man by his first name. But, unless the man is very much older than the woman, he should never fall into the modern rudeness of saying, "Do call me George." (See page 59, "In Private Houses.")

A Man Accompanying a Woman

a. opens the door for her and holds it for her to go through. At a revolving door, he starts it off with a push and waits for her to go through. (See also the point immediately below.)

b. allows a woman to precede him, if single file formation is necessary, unless there is some service he can do for her by going first. In crossing a drawing room, for example, a woman precedes a man. When they reach the door, a very conventional woman, or a foreign woman, may pause so that the man can open it for her. But, in going through a train, when one heavy door after the other will have to be opened, men very often precede women. For the same reason, if a revolving door opens into a dark room where there might be a step or some other difficulty, a man might precede a woman in order to be in a position to help her when she reaches the other side.

In the Street, a Man

a. walks on the outside of the pavement, nearest the traffic. This is the accepted custom, but it must be followed with common sense: If a change is necessary for a short moment only, he does not dart back and forth.

b. carries packages and suitcases. Men in uniform, particularly officers, are not supposed to carry packages, but this military and naval rule is often not observed.

c. lifts his hat in passing salutation. This can vary between raising the hat an inch and taking off the hat completely; but the higher the lift, the greater the respect shown. A man in uniform salutes, but does not take off his hat.

d. lifts his hat when walking with a woman who recognizes a passerby. Again, if he is in uniform, he merely salutes.

e. keeps his hat off when standing and conversing with a woman, unless it is very bad weather or unless he is a very much older man. Men in uniform, however, do not follow this rule. Having saluted, they keep on their hats during the conversation and salute again when saying good-bye.

f. takes his hat off when he greets a woman or when he says good-bye to her. This applies particularly when a man kisses a woman.

g. lifts his hat when he is apologizing to a woman stranger or thanking her; or accepting her apologies or thanks.

h. holds the umbrella over a woman and himself when they are walking together.

i. does not hold a woman's elbow crossing the street or when she is stepping up or down at the curb, unless such an attention is really necessary; for example, if the woman is very old or incapacitated, or if the streets are very icy, and if the traffic is really dangerously congested, he holds her arm, but not otherwise.

A Man at the Theater

a. allows a woman to precede him down the aisle, following the usher; if he must look for the usher, he precedes her until the usher comes to show the way;

b. helps a woman to take off her coat, and puts the shoulders of the coat over the back of the seat;

c. asks a woman if she would like to smoke during the intermissions; and accompanies her to the lobby, even if he does not smoke himself. If she does not smoke and wants to stay in her seat, he may leave her but he must come back well before curtain time.

A Man in a Restaurant

a. allows a woman to precede him to the table;

b. pulls out her chair for her, unless the waiter does it;

c. asks her what she would like before ordering for himself (see also page 452, "Entertaining in Restaurants");

d. suggests it is time to go on to the next entertainment, movie, theater, or other, by saying, "I think we might be moving along, don't you?" (or colloquially, "Let's get out of here") and by asking for the check. He does not, however, suggest that it is time to go home: That is up to the woman.

In and Out of an Automobile

A man should be the first to get out of the car and the last to get in. This is a basic rule on which many customs depend. It is designed so that a man can not only open and shut the door for a woman, but so that he can, if necessary, also help her to get in or out. This rule holds even if there is a doorman or footman whose duty it is to open and shut the door. Therefore:

a. Even if there is a doorman, a man should stand by and pay attention to any woman who is getting in or out of a car. The old-fashioned rule that he should take her elbow, or her hand, is no longer observed except in the case of very old or invalid women, or unless the running board or the streets are very slippery. Modern usage demands no more than vague gestures toward taking her arm, but it does insist that he should not at this moment pay the taxi-driver, turn his back, or gaze off into space.

b. If he is calling for a woman, a man should get out of the car and greet her, unless he is driving and for an obvious reason cannot leave his place at the wheel. He should open and close the door for her, if there is no doorman. No man should sit in a car and allow a woman to climb in by herself, no matter how many doormen or other people may be around to open and shut doors for her.

c. If the man is driving, these rules may need to be altered a little. Technically, a man should go around the car and open the door for a woman who is getting out; but, if there is an obstruction or a great deal of traffic on his side, this may be impossible. In this case, he excuses himself by saying, "I'm sorry but I think I'd better get out on your side," leaning across her and opening the door for her. Or, if a man is leaving a woman in the midst of so much traffic that it would not be feasible to park the car for even a short while, he may again lean across her and open the door, excusing himself by saying, "I'm afraid I'll have to drop you here." In modern usage, women often get out of a car without waiting for a man to open the door. But a man should be prepared for these gestures, and should at least start making them, even if the woman's quickness makes it impossible for him to follow through.

d. A man gives any necessary directions to the chauffeur or to the driver of a taxicab.

e. A man should, theoretically, seat a woman at his right hand. This applies only to the back seat of a car and is only followed strictly when driving to official or very formal entertainments or occasions. In other words, at a state funeral one should observe this custom; on a trip to the movies, the woman usually seats herself furthest from the door, so that the man need not climb over her feet.

f. There is a further old-fashioned rule, now observed only on most formal occasions, which is that a man should never smoke a pipe or cigar in an automobile with a woman.

Lighting a Woman's Cigarette

The small matter of lighting a woman's cigarette offers a clear example of the American standard of good manners for men. The basic rule is that a man should light a woman's cigarette for her. According to the standard of good manners which obtains in all Latin countries, this means that a man must, if necessary, get up from his seat, cross the room, strike and hold the match for her. For an American man, such an action would be considered almost unattractively exaggerated, except in the case of an older woman. The American standard is that a man need not get up to light a woman's cigarette, but that he must do so if he has an easy and obvious opportunity. For example, at a dining-room table, when a lighter has not been brought to the guests; at a restaurant table; when he

31

is sitting on the same sofa or near a woman in the living room; and particularly, of course, when he and she have taken cigarettes at the same moment.

Offering a Woman a Cigarette

A man should always offer a woman a cigarette when he takes one himself. Of course, if he knows that she does not smoke, this politeness is unnecessary. But if she has refused by saying only, "Not just now, thank you," he must repeat the offer every time he decides to have a cigarette himself.

Politenesses Not Mandatory

It is good manners but not essential to send flowers with one's visiting card to one's hostess a day or so after one has dined with her for the first time. In such cases, the "Mr." is struck off the visiting card in ink. Sometimes, but not always or necessarily, a phrase such as, "Thank you so much for a most pleasant evening" or "With many thanks for a most agreeable evening," is written on the face of the card. It is even more polite for a man who is leaving the city to send flowers with a visiting card to all the women in whose houses he has often lunched or dined. If the relationship is a formal one, nothing is written on the card except the letters "P.p.c." in the lower left-hand corner. P.p.c. is the abbreviated form of the French expression "pour prendre congé"—to take leave—the classic formal good-bye for visiting cards. Less formally: "Mr." is struck off the card and one writes a message such as, "With so many thanks for your kind hospitality" or "I hope I may telephone and come to see you as soon as I come back."

POLITENESSES TOWARD STRANGERS

On the street, in subways and busses, and in all public places, a man may and should perform any of the following services for women strangers or for very much older men. He may:

a. offer his seat in any public conveyance;
b. offer to carry a heavy parcel or a suitcase, whenever there is a particularly difficult moment; for example, up or down stairs, or in and out of busses or trains;
c. pick up anything that has been dropped;
d. open heavy doors;
e. help when it seems necessary; as, for example, when someone has fallen.

On any of these occasions, the one who has been helped says, "Thank you," and the man raises his hat. This need not be a full gesture; the hat need only be raised an inch or so and dropped back immediately. But the gesture, such as it is, must be made.

4

Women's Manners

As IN THE case of the preceding chapter, which outlined men's manners, this chapter cannot be considered a full guide to a woman's behavior. It treats only the manners of women as such, without any other qualification. Here a woman is considered neither as a hostess nor as a guest, nor even as a dancing partner (this last is discussed on page 79). All her other roles are discussed elsewhere under different headings and it is wise, of course, to read them all.

The first point about women's manners is made obvious by the difference in the size of this chapter as compared to the chapter on men's manners. Men's manners are fairly definite and prescribed, a matter of rule and action. Women's manners are more subtle, a matter of attitude rather than rule. In other words, a man is clearly told to open the door, and a woman is expected to walk gracefully through it. The few rules—if they can be called rules—which women are expected to observe are listed below, but the question of attitude is basic, and must be discussed first.

THE IDEAL ATTITUDE

The ideal attitude which should underlie all women's manners expresses kindness, gentleness, good will, sensitive understanding, self-respect and, when it is appropriate, deference. A great deal has been said about the deference expected of men; indeed, many rules of men's manners impose deference in forms so long accepted that the spirit has almost been lost. But little has been said about the charm that proper deference can give to women's manners. Deference toward older women is a point of good behavior which women express in the following ways:

Women rise when an older woman enters the room, unless there are more than ten or twelve people present.

Women rise to speak to an older woman and remain standing as long as she stands nearby. (See also "Introductions, Acknowledgments, Greetings and Goodbyes," on p. 56.

Women allow an older woman to go first through doorways, but if the older woman insists, the younger should go first. She should not persist in her own courtesy above that of an older woman.

Women stand when an older woman comes to the table at a restaurant.

Women walking with an older woman offer to carry parcels for her.

Women offer older women their seats in crowded busses and subways.

This deference is shown also toward clergymen and officials. And as suggested on page 57, in "Introductions," it is through the respect due such men that women rise when being introduced to their wives. Women should rise, also, to greet a very much older man; young girls should stand when speaking to the father of a friend, as well as to the mother or aunt. Nothing is more unbecoming to a woman than a harsh attitude of carelessness and self-absorption. And now we come to the more delicate question of politeness toward husbands.

HUSBANDS

It must be admitted that in spite of all the charm which frankness and friendliness give to American women, they are often unwittingly, and most unbecomingly, careless in their attitude toward their husbands. Deference is perhaps too strong a word to describe the perfect attitude, but certainly there should be a noticeable deferring, on the part of the wife, toward the husband as head of the house. It is difficult to explain how this is conveyed, because the shadings of behavior are extremely subtle, but one or two examples will give the idea.

A very common example of bad manners is that of the wife who says "I" or "my" instead of "we" or "our": "I decided it was wiser for the children . . . ," instead of "We thought it wiser . . . ," or best of all perhaps, "Henry thought it wiser . . ." Another is the wife who rises and says good night to her hosts, without even consulting her husband or waiting for his sign or initiative, expecting him to follow her lead with no more to-do. A third is the wife who sharply corrects her husband, or impatiently informs him that he has told the same story before. All these are bad manners because a subordinate position is most unbecoming to a man. A woman can gracefully play second fiddle, but a man who is obviously subordinated to a dominating woman is a pathetic and foolish figure.

So much for a woman's attitude. The rest of the suggestions concerning her behavior are more specific.

ACCEPTED CUSTOMS

Bowing

A word should be said about bowing, because one so often hears such phrases as "a woman bows first to a man" or "a woman bows to friends across the opera house." Actually, of course, a woman need not bow, in the way a man does, except when being presented to a high official of Church or State. (See "Introductions," page 61.) A woman's bow might be described as a slow nod, combined with a slight forward movement from the waist. The action should be a natural one, a seemingly spontaneous inclination toward a friendly acquaintance. Indeed, many women with a gift for graceful manners bow slightly each time they shake hands. As a point of rule, women need bow only when greeting acquaintances at a distance, when a wave would be too informal; or, as we have said, when being introduced to officials. The old dictum that women must greet men first is now almost obsolete, except among the most tradition-and-protocol minded. This rule is reversed abroad and it is a point of protocol there that men should "salute" women first.

Gloves

Traditionally, gloves are a mark of the formally dressed woman. A generation ago, as we said on page 11, no "lady" left her front door without gloves on her hands. Now, modern usage holds that gloves should be worn on occasions such as these: going to a formal luncheon, dinner, reception, or dance; in the streets of large towns and cities; going to and from church; going to official receptions or entertainments.

On the other hand, a woman should always take off her gloves before she starts smoking, playing cards, eating, drinking, or putting on make-up. When one is wearing long, elbow-length gloves (as, for example, at a very big dinner) one should take them off as soon as one is seated at the dining table, before touching food or drink. At dances and receptions, gloves are left on for dancing and one may unbutton them at the wrist, tucking the finger ends of the glove into the wrist opening, whenever one wants to smoke, drink, or powder one's nose. This system can also be followed at supper at a dance, but gloves should never be left on the arm at the dinner table. Bracelets may be worn over long gloves (except, of course, at the dinner table) but rings should *never* be worn outside a glove.

Hats

Women should never wear hats when entertaining at home, except out of doors or after a religious ceremony such as a wedding or a christening at home. At a garden party, for example, the hostess may wear a hat but not at luncheon or tea. This rule applies also to daughters of the house and to any house guests. Other guests who have worn hats for the trip from their own houses may keep them on, although in the country many leave them with their coats. It should be unnecessary to add that in almost all places of worship it is a rule that a woman's head be covered.

The only other point about hats is that a woman must always, when asked, take off her hat in a theater or movie house; and she must do it gracefully and apologetically, not crossly.

Thanks to a Stranger

Women must thank all those, including strangers, who do them little services. For example, if a stranger, man or woman, opens a door for a woman, or picks up something she has dropped, a woman should not allow timidity or shyness to stop her from saying thank you in a pleasant impersonal way. If the stranger seems to be trying to start an unwelcome conversation, one can, still with politeness but with increasing firmness, refuse to converse. But it is more attractive to take for granted that the gesture was motivated by politeness only than it is immediately to suspect another motive. One should never be afraid to be kind, or to put a generous interpretation on the actions of others. It is better to risk a little trouble than to risk a narrow, ungenerous habit of mind.

Time to Go Home

When a woman is lunching or dining with a man, it is she who suggests that it is time to go home. She does not, however, suggest "moving along." The man with whom she is dining may have planned to spend the evening in the restaurant, lingering over dinner; or he may have planned to meet other people at a certain time. It is up to him to take the initiative in making any further arrangements for the evening (frankly, because he will have to pay for them), unless he asks her for suggestions. But it is she who suggests that it is getting late, and time to end the evening.

Smoking

Women (and men, too, of course) should not smoke while dancing. Neither should women smoke while walking on the street or waiting in front of a shop or theater; they may smoke while sitting in an automobile.

Walking Arm in Arm

Women should not walk arm in arm with a man in the street, as a general practice. The old-fashioned rule was that, with certain exceptions, a woman should never take a man's arm except on formal occasions (e.g., going in to a very formal dinner, or going up the aisle at a church wedding) or for reasons of practical necessity or convenience (in a crowd, on very steep steps, etc.). The exceptions were her husband, a close relative, or—to be a little more daring—her fiancé. This rule is no longer observed by less conservative women, but no woman should unhesitatingly take the arm of a casual acquaintance, particularly if he is a foreigner, for no reason other than that it is a pleasant way to walk. A woman may, of course, walk arm in arm with another woman, although this is usually a young girl's habit, rather than a grown woman's.

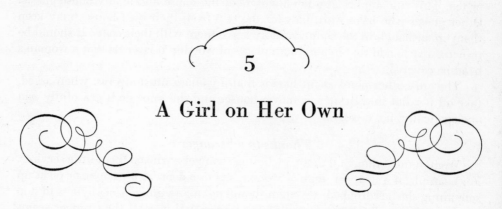

5

A Girl on Her Own

IN EARLIER DAYS, it would have been quite unnecessary to write a chapter about "a girl on her own." There were no girls on their own. If young girls or young unmarried women took jobs, they lived with their parents, or an elderly relative, or at least an older woman, who chaperoned them. The rules were laid down for them, and most of the questions that many young girls meet every day, in our times, never touched them at all.

Now, in almost every American city, there are hundreds and thousands of young girls, working in jobs of their own choosing, living entirely alone in rooms and apartments they have chosen for themselves. Inexperienced, often without any guidance or advice more worldly than that of other girls of their own age, they find it extremely puzzling to work out a pattern of behavior that will be both wise and attractive. They do not want to seem either too dashing or too severe, and, though they may be blessed with plenty of good common sense, they are often wise enough to know that common sense without much knowledge is not always a full and perfect guide.

Some of the old rules were pretentious and tiresome. "Nice (meaning respectable) girls don't live alone" completely ignored the fact that the girl may have no available relatives and may be unable to afford a paid chaperone. "Nice girls don't powder their faces in public" was so impossibly severe that it broke, almost as soon as it was formed, under the weight of woman's legitimate interest in her appearance. These rules, like many others, have been discarded. But many of the other old rules remain, and it is the fact that some old rules are still considered sensible while the rest are only laughed at, which makes it difficult for a young girl to decide on her course. Like signposts, the old rules hemmed in the sides of the road, marking each turn so clearly that, if one followed them, one could never be misunderstood, and one could never be traveling a road which one had not intended to take. Now, many of the old signposts have fallen, and, of those still standing, some are regarded seriously and others are not. It is hard for the inexperienced traveler to know which are still there.

At this point, perhaps, it should be made clear that we are not here discussing questions of morals or of conscience. It is perfectly possible, of course, to live in the most impeccable morality under almost any conditions, no matter how unconventional they might seem. It is equally possible to live in utter depravity within an apparently flawless shell of convention. What we are discussing here is the facade that a young girl presents to the world, the modern concept of her behavior, the present-day signposts. If the modern signposts for behavior are followed, no sensible contemporary can raise any eyebrow, no sensible young man will say to himself, "She's attractive all right, but, as a wife . . . ?"

And by "young girl," for the purposes of this chapter, we mean an unmarried woman, who is, or looks, young enough to need the guidance and protection of parental rules and care.

WHERE TO LIVE AND HOW

If expense were no object, it would be easy to say that every young girl who lives away from her parents, in a strange city, should live in an apartment house which has a doorman and elevator man, with an eminently respectable and elderly woman servant, preferably one chosen by her mother and responsible to her mother. This, certainly, is the most unequivocal pattern for living that such a young girl might follow, short of the old-fashioned, elderly-relative or paid-chaperone standard. It could not be misunderstood, or give an impression that the young girl was unaware, or heedless, of the conventional standards of behavior. Its big and immediately obvious flaw is that it is impossibly unrealistic. Most young girls who live alone do so in order to work, and very few are successful enough to maintain such an establishment.

Two entirely different ways of living are open to the young girl who arrives alone in a strange city. The first is to live under organizational rules in a non-profit club such as the Y.W.C.A.; in a professional club; in a "girls' residence"; or in a woman's hotel. (These last two both have very strict rules concerning visitors.) In very large cities all these are available, and for the very young girl who cannot afford the paid-chaperone arrangement mentioned above, one of these four possibilities is definitely advisable.

In the second way open to her, there are no restrictions on her behavior beyond those the young girl chooses to make for herself. There are five choices for living quarters and we list them in the order of their desirability.

The first is an apartment in a good apartment building with an elderly woman servant chosen by her mother. The second is an apartment shared with one or two other young girls. The third possibility is to board with a family; and this, like the joint apartment, is a very sound arrangement, although sometimes difficult to manage.

The advantage of both these latter suggestions is that they afford perhaps the best solution to a budget problem; the drawback is that such communal living requires the greatest tact and compatibility. It is never wise to rush into such an arrangement, unless the other people involved are old friends; and it is always wise to set a definite time limit at the very beginning so that one can slip out of it gracefully if it is not a success.

The fourth possibility is a room or small apartment in a quiet hotel, the kind that is always called a "family hotel." The fifth advisable solution to the question of where to live is to take an apartment in a building where there are friends or members of the family. In many cities, a walk-up apartment in a made-over house is much less expensive than an apartment in a big building with an elevator and doorman; but, unless a relative or elderly friend is to be a close neighbor, this is the least desirable choice for a young girl.

In the end, when one has considered all the possible choices, it becomes obvious that, from a worldly point of view, the question of where to live is not difficult to solve. The choices are many, the limitations comparatively few. If one cares about appearances, the conventions, and the opinion of the world, one should not flout them all by ignoring the generally accepted concepts of behavior. The effect to be avoided—and this cannot be overstressed—is that of a young girl who lives entirely alone, except for the services of a part-time maid, in an obviously expensive apartment. Because the budget is apparently no problem, such a young girl gives the impression of not knowing, or not caring, what the conventions are; and the world assumes, perhaps unfairly, that the less apparent facts of her behavior will follow the same insouciant pattern. But no one will dare raise an eyebrow at the young girl who, struggling to meet a budget, must sacrifice some of the conventions in the process; her regard for the conventions, though not stressed, is likely to be assumed unless her behavior indicates otherwise. One pattern is evidence of unconventionality, and it will take consistently conventional behavior to disprove it; the other is evidence of nothing more than an attempt to meet an economic reality.

MEN

It has been estimated that young girls, no matter how seriously they may be working, spend at least half their free time thinking about men. And how right they are! A job may not last a lifetime, but it is always to be hoped that a marriage will. What could be more important, or more worthy of the deepest concentration? The most difficult thing about men and marriage, a fact which every young girl discovers after ten minutes of the lightest thought, is that being thoughtful or even clever about marriage is not enough; in fact, a marriage made through cleverness alone is almost doomed from the start. Ten minutes' more thought brings her to the realization that although this is true, it is also true that, through foolishness, many a young girl has lost what might have been a marriage—or, at least, a very cheering and pleasant proposal.

Anita Loos's Lorelei stated the whole case very succinctly: "Gentlemen prefer blondes, but they marry brunettes." They like dash and unconventionality and bright lights, but they marry sweetness and dependability. Blondeness, as Lorelei saw it, is a state of mind, or a pattern of behavior. What we are concerned with here is the pattern of behavior that will not strike any man, or any woman of the world, as "blonde." As in all other matters, here there are infinite shades and variations. One can behave so strictly as to seem almost unattractively suspicious; or so gaily as to be alarming to a prospective bridegroom. The first is boring, the second is embarrassing and foolish; but it is well to remember that most men, when they think of themselves as husbands, would rather be bored by a wife than embarrassed or fooled by her.

Here follow two sets of rules for behavior, as far as men are concerned; the first is traditional and conventional, the second, the most unconventional that is sanctioned by modern usage.

The Strictest Set of Rules

a. Never dine alone with a married man, unless his wife is your great friend.
b. Never accept an invitation through a man to the house of someone else.
c. If you have met a man and his wife together, and the man asks you to a party at his house, do not accept: his wife should invite you. If she is away, of course, there is no discourtesy implied, and if he invites you to a party, you may accept.
d. Never drink anything alcoholic, except sherry, or a glass of wine with dinner.
e. Never encourage stories that are risqué.
f. Never allow a man to come into your apartment if you are alone in it, or to stay on when other guests have left.
g. Never go alone with a man to his apartment, or stay on in his apartment when other guests have gone.
h. Never go alone with a man to his hotel room, even if he has a sitting room.
i. Never accept a valuable present from a beau or possible beau—a very old rule and very sound.

If she follows the above rules, no young girl could conceivably be considered fast or cheap. She could never be misunderstood. If she refuses an invitation, a drink, or a present in a prim and righteous way, she may be considered stuffy. If she refuses all these gracefully, with a smile, she will be thought charming and well brought up by the world at large and, by young men, eminently wifely material.

A More Lenient Set of Rules

a. Never dine repeatedly with the same married man.
b. Never drink enough alcohol to be even slightly affected by it. Even this should be limited. "She can certainly hold her liquor" is not a compliment.
c. Never allow a man to come into your apartment if you are alone in it, except in the daytime or before going out to dinner in the evening.
d. Never go to a man's apartment after the dinner hour if he is alone.
e. Never go alone with a man to his hotel room; if he has a sitting room, never go there after the dinner hour.

. . . and three rules that are unchanged:

f. Never allow a man guest to stay on in your apartment after the other guests have gone.
g. Never stay on in a man's apartment after the other dinner guests have left.
h. Never accept a valuable present from a beau or possible beau.

If she follows the above rules, no young girl will be seriously criticized. The more conservative people may question a little and reserve judgment; but although there is nothing immediately reassuring in such a pattern of behavior, there is also nothing startlingly or uncompromisingly unconventional. Eligible young men may be a little more on their guard, a little slower in recognizing in this pattern a young girl's pre-eminently wifely characteristics, but for all but the most conservative there is nothing alarming.

Some Things Out of the Question

Any young girl who breaks all the above rules is asking for trouble. It is not only a question of what the world in general will think but of the much more important impression that men will form. Because women are so often blamed for all the gossip, it takes a little time and experience to realize how much men gossip. But they do. Not only among themselves, but with their wives, their sisters, and their friends. If they meet an attractive young girl who seems to be living in a very unconventional way, they will not hesitate to convey the fact, every time her name is mentioned, that they found her both attractive *and* very unconventional. It is not a question entirely of what they say—often it is nothing more than, "She's *something*"!—but there is a nuance in their manner that conveys an unmistakable whistle. This is, of course, inexcusable on their part, but it happens. They may be admiring; they may say that she's beautiful; but every other man in the room will prick up his ears, file the name in his memory, and meet the young girl in question with the impression that, with her, his best behavior is not necessary. If young girls could hear men discuss women and their ways, they would cling to convention like a limpet to its rock. Men, like the rest of the world, have been conditioned to recognize certain conventions as symbols of a certain way of life, or as identification tags of a certain kind of character. In young girls, they expect to find behavior governed by certain conventions, the rules of the game. If the rules are not followed, they imagine that the game is not being played; the rules are off; it's free-for-all, and in a free-for-all, all that a loser gets is a laugh.

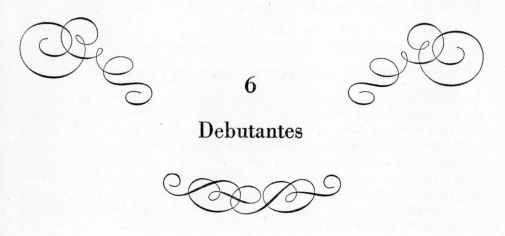

6

Debutantes

THE PATTERN of events which mark the time when a young girl becomes a debutante is a very elastic one. In some cities, she is formally presented to society and a dance is given in her honor. But in most of the United States, a girl is a debutante when she has finished school or when she is about eighteen years old. Some debutantes are seventeen and a few may even be nineteen years old.

These are some other ways of marking a young girl's debut:

Instead of "coming out" at a dance given specially in her honor, the debutante "comes out" at a big dance given for many debutantes, often a subscription dance.

Instead of giving a dance or joining in a subscription dance, the debutante's mother invites women of her own age and friends of her daughter's to come to tea. Invitations to a very formal afternoon reception always used to be engraved according to the standard form, shown on page 511. But such formal receptions are almost unheard of today. Much more usual are informal receptions, for which invitations are sent by letter or by telephone: "Mrs. Bourne and Miss Ann Bourne would like to know if Mrs. and Miss . . ." Debutante luncheons are a thing of the past.

Instead of giving a dance or reception, the debutante's mother gives a dinner party for her daughter before one of the debutante dances.

Apart from these special events which mark a young girl's debut, there is a change in what a debutante, as compared to a younger girl, is allowed to do.

41

BEHAVIOR OF A DEBUTANTE

A debutante

a. is allowed to go to movies, restaurants, and night clubs alone with a boy;
b. is not allowed to visit or stay overnight, even in a group, without a chaperone;
c. should still be invited for a visit by a friend's mother, particularly by a boy's mother;
d. is allowed to smoke but, if her parents are wise, not to drink.

The behavior of girls older than debutantes has been discussed on pages 36 to 40; that of younger girls follows at the end of the next chapter.

DEBUTANTE DANCES AND RECEPTIONS

At informal dances and receptions given for debutantes, there is no change in the usual procedure of entertaining. But at big dances, or receptions, when there is to be a receiving line, the debutante receives with her parents. The mother stands first in line with her daughter next to her; then her husband. This is the standard arrangement; but nowadays the mother and daughter very often stand alone to receive the guests while the father circulates, as he does at a wedding reception. Otherwise, there is no change from the usual procedure of any dance, discussed on page 443 in the section, "Entertaining." See also page 510, where invitations to dances given for debutantes are described.

7

Concerning the Young

THE RUDIMENTS of good manners should be taught to children at a very early age. And the arrival of relatives or guests is usually the first moment. Almost before they can talk, and as soon as they begin to toddle around on their own, they should be presented to strangers. They will soon realize that it is a part of life to be drawn away from an interesting game, to be propelled forward (arm held out by the elbow) to an overhanging and strange face, and will accept all this philosophically and with good grace.

The proper handling of this situation will probably strike the child as mildly boring but not unduly painful. To psychologists, it is a good way to start teaching the child to fit into the family pattern, a valuable factor in later adjustments. But to practicing mothers it is, above all, a preparation for one of the facts of life: that living in company with others imposes limitations on one's conduct, restrictions on one's freedom, and certain sacrifices of purely personal ends. A game may be fun but, if guests have arrived, the child should co-operate with the rest of the family in welcoming them. A great deal could be said (although this is not, perhaps, the place to say it) concerning the value of such early training for a future citizen, a citizen who must not only accept, but impose on himself, similar restrictions in the interest of society. In any case, without considering its psychological or democratic implications, a sense of obligation toward others stands on its own merits as one of the great factors in making life easier for everyone concerned.

So much for the inarticulate and barely ambulatory stage. As soon as children can operate under their own steam, there is a little ritual of elementary procedure that they really should learn. It is an essential ritual, but it is only a collection of tricks unless it is basically a true expression of an attitude toward life and people. It would be impossible, of course, to expect any three-year-old child to have a well-formed attitude toward anything but the vital facts of nourishment, physical comfort, and sleep, so the little ritual he is taught must be an accurate expression of the parents' attitude. "Don't interrupt" is one of the first things a child should learn in his relations with strangers; but how can it be anything but a trick unless the child sees his parents observing this rule in their relations with each other and with other people, including himself? If his father wanders vaguely into the dining room, walking straight in ahead of everybody, how can a child learn to wait at doorways? And if his mother is sharp to the maid, how can a child know that one of the fundamental decencies is to be polite to employees?

Example, then, is one of the best ways of teaching children. They are not always quick to learn, but they are always impressionable. They soak up impressions, as though through their skin. They see everything, hear everything, and say nothing. They are logical and shrewd. They are penetrating in character analysis. And they have a fine sense of justice. The father who hurries to fetch something his wife has asked him for will teach his son courtesy much more quickly than the one who spends twenty minutes in a laborious, pseudo-psychological argument about coming quickly when Daddy calls. The other extreme ("Do as I say, not as I do"), fortified with frequent spankings or unjust severity, will either make the child rebellious or break his spirit utterly.

The instinctive reactions of parents to such everyday situations, rather than what they say to the child, are the basis of his scale of values. Kindness, moderation, consideration, and the vital importance of truth— all these are taught by the parents' easy and often unemphasized acceptance of these as valuable. To the pitiless logic of a child's mind, tact is an incomprehensible compromise with truth: "If I thought the party was horrid, shouldn't I say so, when she asked me?" But the child whose mother really cares about both truth and kindness, will learn very quickly to avoid the unpleasant truth, and search for a pleasant one: "The ice cream was wonderful." It is impossible to teach very young children that the real betrayal in human relations is to give lies in return for truth; but in casual relations with strangers, one is not usually on a plane where absolute truths are involved. If the parents know where tact ends and truth begins, the children will soon learn. If they are clever in keeping awkward situations on a trivial plane, and if, above all, they are firm in their conviction that in a final showdown, everything must be sacrificed to truth, they need never worry about their children.

On this basis, the following list is compiled. Children should start learning it at four years old, and practice it unfailingly by the time they are nine. There is little waste motion in it, because all of it, excepting only the bow and curtsey, should stick with them to the grave. And even these may be useful, if the children turn out to have a bent for diplomacy or international committee work.

WHAT CHILDREN UNDER TEN YEARS OLD SHOULD LEARN

1. To say "How do you do?" and "Good-bye"; and, almost more important, to look at the one they are shaking hands with.
2. To bow (for boys) and to curtsey (for girls), whenever they say, "How do you do?" or, "Good-bye," to adults.
3. To say, "Yes, thank you" and "No, Mummy" and "Yes, Mrs. Smith"; not just "Yes" and "No."
4. To say, "Thank you for a very nice afternoon," or, "Thank you, I had a lovely time," when they say good-bye to their hostess.
5. Not to interrupt older people.
6. To wait at doorways until older people have gone through. Boys should also learn to let girls precede them.
7. To take hats off in the house or when talking to older people; this, of course, for boys.
8. To answer when they are spoken to.
9. To eat neatly, without dawdling, and without argument. (See also "Rules for Children" in the chapter, "Table Manners.")
10. To be scrupulously polite always to nurses, maids, waiters—to anyone who receives wages in return for service. The kind of rudeness which should never be tolerated is that which refers to the fact that these people are employed.

In addition to these rules, there are a few basic responsibilities which a child should learn as soon as he can recognize them. The most important is a sense of responsibility for the belongings of others. As a borrower, guest, or visitor, he must learn to treat the belongings of others far more carefully than he does his own. Quite apart from its charm for others, this is really a vital precept. It is a good step toward honesty in money matters, and it makes a firm foundation for the good citizen's respect for the rights of others.

OTHER RESPONSIBILITIES

Other responsibilities are more purely social. Children must learn as soon as possible to answer invitations themselves and to write thank-you letters for presents and visits. They should go to any party for which they have accepted an invitation, whether or not a more promising second invitation should arrive later. And very early in life they should be confronted with their responsibilities as hosts and guests: "Don't spoil the party," "Don't hurt others' feelings." These are the first steps. As a basis for the later rule, "Always dance with your hostess," boys must learn to be especially polite to the little girl who is giving the party. And finally, all children should know that it is part of a proper family feeling, as well as good manners, to be polite, at least, to the children of their parents' friends. So much for the old and very sound general rules. With these well in hand, we come to more specific questions. (See also "Children at Meals," page 444.)

CHILDREN AND OLDER PEOPLE

The desire to please older people, and to be praised by them, comes naturally to small children, and it is most regrettable that within a few years, usually at about eight or ten years of age, children begin to lose it. Ideally, of course, the indiscriminate desire to please should be replaced by a growing understanding of the responsibilities and dignity of older people; but practically, if children were left to their own untutored devices, many of them (quite logically, it must be admitted) would strive to please only the powerful (their parents or teachers) and exercise their developing personalities in pertness to other adults.

One of the first lessons a child should learn is respect for older people as such, an attitude which is expressed in many conventional forms, such as rising, bowing, answering politely, and in many subtler and more personal ways—an attitude of respectful attention, for example. As always, children will learn this most quickly and easily by the example of their parents. They will learn that special respect is owed to women, to all old people, and to clergymen. And they will see that this is not a lesson for childhood only, but one that they will need to remember until there is no one older or more respectworthy than they. The forms used by grown men and women are outlined on pages 25 to 32 and 33 to 34. Children should begin to learn them at the age of four or five and should have mastered them all by the time they are twelve or fourteen.

CHILDREN AND HOUSE GUESTS

When there are house guests, a whole new set of questions arises. The primary points are these: Children are not allowed in the guest's room unless specifically invited; they are kept very quiet in the morning so that the guest can sleep; they do not walk, talk, sit, or tag along with the guest unless he specifically asks them to. This is the beginning, but now we come to the more complicated, if no less usual, question of errands and odd jobs and presents from the guest.

As a rule, children may accept a present from a friend of their parents, but they should not accept a present, whether money or anything else, given in return for an errand or an odd job. For example, if a child has run upstairs to fetch a paper, or if he has helped to wash a guest's car, he should be taught to refuse any present in return. Ideally, the child should feel that he is a secondary host; anything he can do to help a family guest is done as a member of the family, and he refuses payment politely and firmly, as his parents would refuse payment for their hospitality. Guests must co-operate in this, realizing that it may be hard for the young to strike a note which is both polite and firm. For the same reason if a child has a garden, he can offer to give the visitor radishes but he should never ask him to buy; the infant businessman at work on a guest is no more charming a picture than his father would be. On the other hand, presents given by a guest on arrival, on birthdays, at Christmas, or "because you've grown so much" are quite another thing. These are accepted quite naturally, with great pleasure and many thanks.

Another minor point is that children shouldn't play the radio, or change stations, when guests are in the room. Finally, lest mothers feel appalled at all these rules and strictures, it must be said that many guests find the attentions of children extremely flattering. Children, like dogs, can give subtle compliments quite beyond the scope of adults, and success with children is often accepted as the recognition of a most commendable trait of character. If the children know that these are the rules, and if they and the guests seem happy, keeping in light touch with the situation is quite enough.

CHILDREN'S CHORES

The question of how much work a child can, with taste, be allowed to do around the house is in many ways the most difficult in outlining the child's pattern of behavior. Children have always run errands for their parents, although one marvels at their patience when they are asked with the maddening phrase, "Would you *like* to run up . . . ?" And now, under the conditions of the modern domestic situation, they have very naturally and properly taken an increased share in the actual work of running the house. Almost every child makes his own bed and keeps his own room tidy, and many share with their parents in general work such as sweeping the steps or gardening. These are practical but purely family matters which have little to do with a child's charm or manners. The question of how much work he should do from this point of view is governed by a sound axiom: He may help his parents and do any kind of auxiliary work, but he should not be used as a substitute for a servant. For example, no child should be allowed to take dishes and crumbs off the table while his parents and their guests sit still. This does not mean, of course, that children should not help their parents. As soon as they are able, they should share in whatever work is to be done.

For other, obvious, reasons a child this age should never be allowed to bring the cocktails or to mix drinks. He may go to the pantry to fetch the biscuits or the ice, but his father is the one to go to the cellar for the gin. "Why, he's as good as a bartender" is as dubious a compliment to a child as "She certainly can hold her liquor" to a woman.

THE NOT SO VERY YOUNG—TEN TO SIXTEEN

At some point near the ten- or twelve-year mark the relationship between parents and children changes completely. It is no longer a question of prompting the children in what they should do, but rather one of anxious decision as to what they may be permitted to do. They who, in their relations with strangers, have been rather like obedient actors, repeating more or less well the author's lines, now want to ad lib. on their own. And the parents, who have been the authors, now find themselves acting more as directors, permitting this innovation, explaining that this other new idea simply will not do. The day will come, of course, when the parents will sit among the audience of strangers, proud, anxious, or in despair, no longer directing.

For this "director" period, then, there is no list of little phrases for children to learn, of simple little acts of politeness to be performed. The children will think up their own lines, a vigorous new crop every day, and parents must decide which to encourage and which, if possible, to nip in the bud. What the children think up will be due partly to early conditioning, partly to environment, and partly to their own developing personalities; and what to permit is often a delicate and difficult decision. Since the herd instinct is now operating in full swing, the question of what other children are allowed to do is a very important one. (See page 640 for the early importance of the herd instinct in dress.) If every other twelve-year-old goes to school by himself in the subway, your child probably should be allowed to, also. If every other fifteen-year-old girl wears dark-red nail polish, unattractive as it may seem to you, your daughter might perhaps be allowed to. Every wise parent will know which are the basically unimportant issues and which are the ones that do not admit compromise.

The list that follows cannot, therefore, be ironclad. It is only a record of what most children in America are permitted or forbidden to do at a given age, according to the generally accepted standard, and subject to the herd instinct, to the parents' predilections, and innumerable special circumstances.

Boys Up to Sixteen

The question of what boys may and may not be permitted to do is much simpler than that concerning girls. It is not so much a matter of a code as it is of common sense. If they are old enough to find their way around alone, they should be encouraged to do so. They shouldn't go to the movies without an older person, unless they are old enough to sit quietly and not annoy others, or go to late movies, because they need a lot of sleep. They shouldn't drink or smoke, not only because it looks dreadful, but chiefly because it is bad for their health. Apart from these practical dictums, there are really only four things, as far as manners and appearances go, that can be considered a code for boys:

1. He must be made to answer invitations, and go to all dances and dinner parties to which he has promised to go. This is the time to lay the foundation for an

attitude which should be an integral part of his behavior. (See page 16, "Engagements.")

2. He must always dance with:

    a. the girl with whom he came to the party;

    b. the girl who is giving the dance or in whose honor the dance is being given;

    c. the girl who invited him to dinner before the dance, or the one in whose honor the dinner was given; or both;

    d. the two girls who sat beside him at dinner. This is not absolutely mandatory, as the other categories are, but it is an attractive and polite thing to do, because it shows the girls that he liked them.

There is no escape from these obligations. All men and boys must assume them, from the moment an unwilling eleven-year-old is sent off to his first dancing-class party until he is too old to dance more than a few steps with his granddaughter at her wedding.

3. He should never go to poolrooms, bowling alleys or any other such places, unless the places are well-run, respectable, and eminently un-tough.

4. He shouldn't go to prize fights without an older man.

Beyond this, in the matter of night clubs, restaurants, and chaperones, boys' conduct will be governed by the restrictions imposed on the girls of their own age. As a rule, the girls are the ones who do all the inviting, and their mothers make the rules for the evening. If a boy's mother is giving a party for him, she need only know what the girls are permitted to do. If a boy wants to send a girl flowers, candy, or a book, he should be allowed to; any present more valuable, from such a young boy to such a young girl, will probably, and quite properly, be returned.

Girls of Ten, Eleven, and Twelve

1. are not allowed make-up, but are allowed a permanent wave, even an obvious one.

2. are allowed to go to dances specifically given for children of their age, which end at nine o'clock or thereabouts.

3. are not allowed to go to these dances, even in groups, unless an older man or woman is to take them and bring them home.

4. are not allowed to go to the movies, even in the afternoon, without an older person, unless the town is so small that the theater owner, the ushers, and everyone else knows very well who the girls are.

5. are not allowed to meet boys at the corner drugstore for a soda.

6. are allowed to be alone in the daytime at such places as country clubs, under the assumption that, at this age, they will have learned to be quiet and considerate and not to annoy older members.

7. are not allowed to go about the streets of a big city alone, except to and from school or the school bus-stop.

Girls of Thirteen and Fourteen

1. are allowed a little face powder and (but only if necessary to conform with the group) pink pomade or the smallest amount of lipstick. Needless to say, no make-up should be encouraged for such a young girl. But, if the child longs for it and looks old enough to carry it off, it can be permitted in the above

amounts. Any more may look grotesque. At children's parties a little more leeway is allowed than at other times.

2. are allowed to go to the movies in the afternoon in groups of three or four other girls without a chaperone. They should not be allowed to go out in the evening without a chaperone, unless they can be home before seven, or unless they live in a very small town where the movie theater is fairly near their house. It does not look well to allow such young girls to be without supervision at night, even if two or three are together.
3. are allowed to go to the movies in the afternoon in a group without a chaperone, with boys who are well known to the girls' parents.
4. are allowed to stay at children's dances until about ten-thirty.
5. are not allowed to go to these dances, even in groups, without a chaperone.
6. are not allowed to go to a night club, with or without a chaperone.
7. are not allowed to dine with boys in a restaurant unless chaperoned.
8. are allowed to meet boys, in groups in the afternoon, for a soda at a drugstore or in a tearoom.
9. are allowed to go about, in groups of two or three, in even the biggest city, but only in the daytime.

Girls of Fifteen and Sixteen

1. are allowed moderate make-up; powder, a little lipstick, and pink nail polish; but never rouge or eye make-up.
2. are allowed to go to the movies or dances in groups, with boys or without them, without a chaperone. Strict parents insist that girls without a chaperone must be home no later than ten o'clock; less strict ones set the deadline at midnight.
3. are not allowed to go to any night clubs, except to dine in a very staid one with older people. At this age, they should be chaperoned by a couple, rather than by a woman who is too obviously "the Chaperone."
4. are allowed to dine without a chaperone in groups, but not alone with a boy, in what is called abroad a "family restaurant": a quiet, eminently respectable place.
5. are not allowed to go to prizefights with a boy, or with a group of boys and girls.

THE SUB-DEBUTANTE AGE

Boys over Sixteen

Boys over sixteen follow the girls' lead, as before, in the matter of restaurants, night clubs, chaperones, etc. The rest of their behavior pattern is a question of safety and common sense, rather than etiquette.

Girls of Seventeen

1. are allowed to go to movies, dances, and restaurants with boys in groups without a chaperone.
2. are often allowed to go to night clubs, chosen by the family, in groups without a chaperone.
3. are still not allowed to go to prizefights without an older person.

See also "Debutantes," page 41.

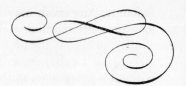

8

Table Manners

LIKE ALL MANNERS, table manners should not be put on and taken off from day to day. They must be an inherent part of the whole man, an expression of his personality, an indication of the kind of man he is. In this, table manners are quite unlike the other customs that surround eating and drinking. It is obvious that one can cook and wait on oneself one day and be waited on by four footmen the following day, without any effect on the character. But it is impossible to eat boorishly in private, and politely in company, without subjecting oneself to all the effects of any hypocrisy.

The primary purpose of almost all our ritual of table manners is dual: to convey nourishment to the body, and to do so gracefully, with the utmost consideration of others. What has come to be accepted as offensive or pleasant to ourselves and our public is a matter which involves our whole conception of aesthetics. (All this is more fully discussed in the chapter on "Manners in General," on page 9, and in the Introduction on page 3.) But it is in the light of this premise that table manners are discussed in this chapter. We're taking for granted such basic precepts as "Chew silently and with your mouth closed," "Don't talk with your mouth full," "Don't put one mouthful in on top of another."

TWENTY-THREE RULES

For the sake of brevity, the standard pattern of table manners is broken down into twenty-three rules.

1. Napkins belong on the lap. They should never be tucked in, or tied around the neck, except in the case of very small children, under seven years of age.
2. The back should be straight without rigidity. The perfect posture is that described as an "easy seat" in riding. And the food should be brought up to the mouth, not the mouth down to the food.
3. The arms should move freely in bringing food to the mouth. The elbows should never be anchored to the table or the ribs, but they should stay down, near the sides, even when cutting the toughest meat.
4. When soup is served in a plate, the spoon should always be filled with a motion away from the table edge. The old-fashioned ironclad rule used to be that one should drink only from the side of the spoon, tilting the soup gently into the mouth. This is no longer strictly observed, and neither is the rule against tilting the soup plate itself. If the plate is tilted, it should be away from, and not toward, the edge of the table.

50

5. When one has finished one's soup, the spoon is left in the soup plate, handle to the right, over the edge of the plate, parallel to the edge of the table; but it should never be left in a soup cup or any other cup. The spoon should lie on the saucer of the cup. Never, even for a moment, should a spoon be left sticking up out of the cup.

6. Anything served in a cup with a handle should be drunk from the cup. For example, one might sip one spoonful of tea or coffee or soup; but after that, one should drink from the cup. If there are vegetables or noodles in the soup, they may, of course, be finished off with the spoon after the soup has been drunk. But, on the whole, when anything is served in a cup with handles, a spoon should be used only for stirring and tasting.

7. The little finger should never be crooked; the corners of the mouth should never be too delicately touched with the point of the napkin. In other words, pretentious refinement here, at table, is as bad as it is anywhere else.

8. Food should be kept within the center part of the plate, away from the flat rim.

9. Food should be cut and handled neatly; it should not be pushed around or messed up, and neither the fork nor the plate should ever be overloaded.

10. Only one piece of meat, or anything else, should be cut at a time. (See also rule 3, on page 52.)

11. Two bites should never be taken from the same forkful, or two sips from the same spoonful.

12. When one pauses in the midst of eating (to drink or to eat bread, for example) the fork should lie across the middle of the plate, the handle to the right and just over the edge of the plate. The knife is put across the upper third of the plate, with the handle to the right, and with the point of the blade, as well as the handle, resting on the rim of the plate, as it is whenever it is not being used. The habit of resting the handles of implements on the table, with the ends on the plates, is a very bad one.

13. As soon as one has finished eating, the fork and knife should be put across the middle of the plate, in line with the edge of the table, handles to the right, with the ends inside the rim of the plate and with the fork nearest to the table edge. The tines of the fork should be turned upward, not downward as in foreign countries, and the edge of the knife blade should be toward the table edge. Oyster forks should stay on the plate between the oyster shells. When one has finished a soup which demands a fork and knife as well as a spoon (Hochepot Normande, for example), all the implements should be put across the middle of the plate as suggested above, the knife farthest from the table edge, the spoon next, and the fork nearest. The reason for all this is not only to make the plate look neat, but, most importantly, to put all the implements across the plate in such a way as to prevent their slipping into the center of the plate or to prevent heavy-handled implements from falling as the plate is being taken away.

14. The mouth should be wiped before drinking, to keep the edge of the glass attractively clean, and the mouth must be empty.

15. Bread, rolls, and muffins should always be broken in half, or in even smaller pieces, before they are buttered or eaten. Small biscuits and bite-size sandwiches should not be broken. Small muffins should be split horizontally, unless, of course, they are treated as a sandwich and stuffed with filling; in this case, they are taken up whole.

16. Sauces should not be sopped up with bread, and neither should any bread, biscuit, or roll be dipped into coffee, tea, soup, or any other liquid. These are old rules, and the last one holds without exception. But the first is often broken by those whose manners could be called informal, although not "bad." Sopping up sauce or gravy with a piece of bread is standard practice in the good, hearty eating ways of middle-class Continental Europe; here, in the modern atmosphere of impatience with anything "refined," it is regarded as a little eccentric, but flattering to the hostess. The right way to do it is to drop a bite-sized piece of bread into the plate, spear it with the fork, and then sop up the gravy. The bread should never be held in the fingers.

17. Salad should not be cut with a knife, but broken with the side of the fork in-

51

stead. If, however, one is presented with a rocklike quarter-head of iceberg lettuce—an unfortunate kind of salad, at best—one can only resort to the knife.

18. Anything that must be taken from the mouth and put back on the plate is dealt with according to a very simple rule: If it went in on a spoon, it comes out on a spoon (peach and cherry stones in a cooked compote, for example); if it goes in by hand, it comes out by hand (grape stones, olive pits, bits of nut shell, etc.). Exceptions to this rule are made in the case of small clean things, such as fish bones and pieces of shot which are often found in game. These, though put in on a fork, are taken from the mouth by hand. At best, of course, these moments are avoided as much as possible. Fat, gristle, and skin are cut away from meat before they are put into the mouth; peach, plum, and prune pits are cut away and left on the plate. And, beyond this, there must be a certain amount of Spartan restraint. One may find a mouthful of food unpleasant-tasting; but a willingness to upset one's neighboring guests, in preference to swallowing it down, is brutally egocentric. The only thing that is worse is an over-genteel effort to hide the removal of something as inoffensive as a fishbone—furtive glance, napkin held as a screen for the operation, etc.

19. An implement which has been used by one person should never be used to take food from any dish which contains food for others. One's butter knife should never go into the jam pot; one's coffee spoon should stay out of the sugar bowl.

20. Condiments, butter, jam, or a stiff sauce such as the hard sauce that goes with plum pudding are put directly from the serving dish onto the plate, not onto another food. Honey goes on the butter plate first, not on the muffin; tomato catsup beside, not on top of, the baked beans. Gravies and liquid or semiliquid sauces are exempt from this rule, and are poured directly over the food.

21. No food is ever put directly into the mouth from the platter without being put down first on a plate. For example, a small cake or a sandwich should be set down on a plate first, and then taken up to be eaten.

22. Soup, oysters, or any food that is served already "portioned" should never be refused. And one should take a little of at least the majority of the other courses—or, better, a little of each one. Wine is refused by a negative gesture toward the glass, just as the wine is about to be poured. The glass should never be turned down, because it breaks the rule that one must not refuse anything ostentatiously, lest it suggest disapproval (drink) or dislike (food).

23. Fingers should never be used to push food onto the fork.

OUTDATED DICTUMS

There are five more old-fashioned rules, once ironclad, now broadened and relaxed and, in some cases, reversed.

1. "Reaching across the table is rude." The fact that this rule is no longer observed typifies one of the best changes in modern etiquette. The old-fashioned rule laid all the emphasis on how one would appear to the rest of the guests ("Don't appear greedy"). Modern etiquette sanctions any reaching that doesn't inconvenience other guests, on the assumption that it is better to risk appearing a little greedy than it is to risk disturbing other people.

2. "No one should begin eating until everyone has been served." This rule, too, was designed to avoid the appearance of being greedy, a preoccupation that no longer seems important. After one or two others have been served, there is no reason not to begin eating.

3. "The fork must be switched from the left hand to the right hand as soon as each piece of meat has been cut"; in other words, the food must never be carried to the mouth by the left hand. This was always an American rule only, never part of the English or Continental code of manners. Today, it is reversed so commonly that the left-

handed method is almost preferred to the other. Both are perfectly good usage, but it is now axiomatic that whenever food is cut with a knife, the left hand can quite naturally carry it up to the mouth.

4. "Leave a little on your plate for Lady Manners." The form, to say nothing of the content, of this rule is so outdated that no further comment is needed.

5. "Food should be eaten as little as possible with the fingers" (see "Cake and Sandwiches," page 54, for a further discussion of this) and "Meat bones must never be taken up by hand at table." This still holds as far as meat bones are concerned, but the genteel and dainty approach the rule suggests is completely out of date. Fruit, sandwiches, candy, cookies, and anything else which is eaten by hand should be taken up naturally, with no effort to emphasize a delicate fingertip grip; forks should be used only for a very sticky cake or a big wedge of cake eaten with, or as, dessert or at tea time.

TABLE MANNERS OF THE HOSTESS

The only way in which a hostess's table manners differ from anyone else's is that she must never eat so quickly as to finish everything on her plate before every guest has finished. She should always leave on her plate a little food which she can peck at from time to time, in order to keep a very slow eater company.

RULES FOR CHILDREN

Ideally, these rules should apply in full to children. In practice, they cannot all apply until the child is at least six or seven years old. Rule 9, for example, cannot obtain before that age. Meat will have to be cut up all at once by an adult, for a child who cannot manage a knife; salad, too, will probably have to be cut. And elbows, when one is beginning to learn how to use a knife, will certainly not always stay down near the ribs. The essential point is to exact as high a standard of performance as one can reasonably expect the child to be able to manage. The first effort should be to train the child to eat neatly and without fuss or coaxing. Most modern doctors agree that the best way to train a child to eat without being urged is never to make him eat what he doesn't want. But if a child persists in refusing food, one should get a doctor's advice. And it should be stressed that the purpose of manners is not to make an impression, but to show consideration of others. In other words, "That's most unattractive," and not, "That's not like a little gentleman."

The only other permissible deviation from general practice is that children need not help themselves from the platters of food as they are passed around. If the child's mother is serving from platters set in front of her, she will probably cut up his food for him as she serves his plate. A waitress or butler can serve the child from the platter, or cut and prepare his food in the pantry. (See "Children at Meals," on page 444, in the chapter on "Entertaining.")

Other differences between children and grownups at table are more a matter of behavior and attitude than manners and technique. But they are vitally important, more important at table than anywhere else. Children should not interrupt, and they should not dominate the conversation. This should be one of the fundamentals of a child's code of manners, which is more fully discussed on page 45, in the chapter, "Concerning the Young."

SPECIAL CUSTOMS AND TECHNIQUES

The twenty-three eating rules given above are accepted everywhere in the United States. As a matter of course, they should be so ingrained as to become automatic reflexes. The suggestions that follow below, however, are not at all in this category. Although they describe the accepted techniques for eating certain foods, these are more a matter of custom than of rule; and knowledge or ignorance of these customs is an indication of the extent of one's experience and nothing more. For example, if one had lived in a community where Japanese persimmons were unknown, one would obviously not have needed to develop a system for eating them. The only important point is that one should never be flustered or upset if one's inexperience has been proved. Furtive efforts to correct a mistake, a worried, apologetic manner, are more to be avoided than the mistake itself. It is much better to do whatever need be done calmly, openly, and without embarrassment.

Artichokes are eaten leaf by leaf, in the fingers, with each leaf dipped first into the sauce. The only part of the leaf that is eaten is the soft base. When the heart has been reached, the fuzz is scraped off with a knife and fork, and the heart is eaten with the fork.

Asparagus is eaten with a fork. One mouthful of the soft part is cut at a time, with the side of the fork and, to follow the informal custom, the stem is then taken up and finished in the fingers. More conventional manners demand that only the fork be used. Asparagus holders or special asparagus servers are unnecessary.

Cake and Sandwiches are always eaten by hand. Only a very sticky cake, or a cake served alone as dessert, should be eaten with a fork; sandwiches, never. Very big double-decker sandwiches may be cut in half or into smaller pieces with a knife, but they should be eaten by hand. The so-called "hot sandwiches" served with gravy are not, of course, sandwiches at all. They are "turkey on toast" or "chicken on toast" or whatever, and they are eaten with a knife and fork.

Candy, whether offered on a plate or in a box, should be taken with its little paper frill. The main points are not to touch other pieces and not to hesitate in choosing, as though some of the candies might not be good. It is probably unnecessary to say that it is barbaric to bite, poke, squeeze, or break candies to investigate the contents, and then put them back in the box.

Caviar is eaten on toast, in the fingers; never with a fork. (See also page 305 for a description of how it is served.)

Custard or Eggs, served in cups, must be eaten with the cup flat on the plate. The cup is steadied with the left hand. The usual implement is a teaspoon.

Finger Bowls are taken off the plate, with the little doily that usually comes underneath, and put to the upper left of the plate, the silver having first been set down at each side. Unfortunately, this is not always all there is to the finger bowl situation. Sometimes, finger bowls are brought with a doily and underplate (usually glass) on top of the dessert plate. In this case it is a question whether to remove finger bowl, doily, and underplate, or whether to remove the finger bowl and doily only, leaving the glass underplate as a protection for the dessert plate. If one is not the guest of honor, it is perfectly simple to wait and see what others, particularly the hostess, will do. If one is the guest of honor and there is no opportunity to observe anyone else before the dessert platter comes, the best thing is to remove everything—the glass plate, the finger bowl, and the doily.

Fish, if served with the head and tail, should be neatly boned as follows: Cut off the head and tail and put them to one side of the plate; cut away a small edging of the fish all along the stomach, to remove the small bones; slit the fish along the backbone, and lift away the top filet. The backbone will then lie exposed and the filet that has been cut away will be entirely free of bones. When this has been eaten, slip the knife between the other filet and the backbone. Lift away the backbone and put it next to the head and tail.

Fruit eaten at the dining-room table may be eaten in either of two ways—the American way or the Continental. In the Continental technique, the hand never touches the fruit except to take it from the platter and put it on the plate. The fruit is skinned, halved, stoned, cut into small pieces, and eaten entirely with the knife and fork. The American technique is less elaborate. The fruit is halved, quartered, and stoned with the fork and knife, but it is rarely skinned (except in the case of peaches), and the quarters are eaten in the fingers. These techniques apply to all the usual table fruits: apples, pears, peaches, nectarines, plums, and apricots. At a formal dinner table such fruit should never be eaten whole, in the fingers; nor should it be dipped into a finger bowl except in a questionably clean restaurant.

Grapes and Cherries are eaten whole, by hand; pits are removed in the fingers. Like other fruit, they should never be dipped in the finger bowl before being eaten, although this rule is sometimes broken by those who like the taste of fresh water on fruit. At formal dinners, a pair of scissors is usually put on the platter with grapes, so that small clusters can be cut from the branch.

Grapefruit served, so to speak, on the half-shell, is eaten with a teaspoon. At all but the most informal meals, extra juice must be scooped out with the spoon. Squeezing the fruit to get the last drop of juice is not an attractive custom.

Honey is often, and quite unnecessarily, the cause of a great deal of untidiness. The technique of handling it is so simple and effective that one wonders why it is not used more often. Thin liquid honey is the most difficult to handle, but even so, all that is necessary is to take a spoonful, and with a twisting motion which catches any drops of honey as they fall, transfer it to the butter plate. The thinner the honey, the more rapid the twisting motion will have to be. And that's all there is to it.

Ice Cream and Other Desserts are eaten with both a fork and spoon. There is no practical basis for this as a spoon would often suffice, and it is certainly not a rule. But for some reason, when one is given the two implements, as one is for dessert, it is more attractive not to use the spoon only. The fork is used for the solid part of ice cream, the spoon for the part which has melted.

Olives should not be put whole into the mouth. They are held in the fingers, and the flesh is bitten away until only the stone remains. The reason for this is that the flesh doesn't come easily away from the stone, as does the flesh of a ripe cherry. Exceptions are stuffed olives and almost free-stone, ripe Greek olives which are very small and are preserved in a special way.

Oysters and Clams should never be cut. No matter how big they are, an oyster fork is the only legitimate implement.

Pâté de Foie Gras is eaten on toast or crackers, in the fingers, except when it is served as a salad course. (See page 306.)

Persimmons—specifically the big Japanese ones—may be eaten in two ways. The first requires a fork and knife only. The persimmon is set upright on the plate, stem end down, and cut in quarters, which are then opened out until they lie flat on the plate. The flesh is cut into convenient pieces and eaten with a fork. The second system requires a fork, knife, and spoon. The persimmon is cut horizontally, like a grapefruit, rather than vertically; and the flesh is eaten with a spoon, as a melon or grapefruit would be. Under either system, the skin is never eaten.

Pickles are eaten in the fingers when they are served with a sandwich. Pickles served with meat, at the dining-room table, are eaten with a fork.

Spaghetti is eaten with a fork only. The system of using a fork and spoon is bad usage both in Italy and here. Ideally, a few strands are speared by the fork, and the fork is then twisted in such a way as to wrap the strands neatly around it, like a cocoon. Practically, the strands are often cut with the side of the fork before winding. But they must never be bitten off.

9

Introductions, Acknowledgments, Greetings, and Good-byes

INTRODUCING one person to another, like the law of gravity, follows the principle of the lesser approaching the greater body. This is the rule of thumb: The younger woman is presented to the older one, the younger man to the older man. This part of the rule applies without exceptions other than those dependent on rank or official position. The other part of the rule, which is that men must be introduced to women, demands a little more discretion in its application. Women, no matter how young or old, are always presented to chiefs of state, to members of a reigning family, and to dignitaries of the church. In addition, a young girl (up to seventeen or eighteen) is presented to everyone except her own contemporaries. When she is old enough to go to her parents' dinner parties, or after she has been officially presented to society, she may still be presented by her parents, but not by others, to men in official positions, or to men of her father's generation. After this, with the exceptions noted above, all men are presented to her.

WHEN TO INTRODUCE

The question of when to introduce has been the subject of a great deal of unnecessary debate. The simplest answer is, "Whenever it seems natural and sensible, or whenever it makes a social situation easier"; but to be useful, this answer must be more specific.

The first point to consider is the nature of the occasion. Strangers may be introduced at *any* social occasion. And this is a rule which we hope will end many earlier and really irrelevant dictums about their so-called "relative social position." A visit to the drugstore or to a filling station is not a social occasion, and a friend need not be introduced to the pharmacist or the attendant unless he, also, happens to be a friend.

Strangers are also introduced to each other in business meetings which are not based on routine service to the public. In other words, if the pharmacist and drug salesman are brought together for business, or social, reasons by a mutual friend, the usual introductions will naturally be made.

The only other factor in deciding whether or not to introduce two strangers is the length of time they will have to spend together. For example, if one is walking on the street with two friends and meets another friend, introductions are in order if there is any conversation longer than "Hello, how are you?" or "How do you do, Mrs. Adams?" Occasionally the two friends will walk slowly on ahead and there is no need to corral them in order to make a forced, and, in the circumstances, somewhat unnecessary introduction. But a group of four is awkward unless introductions are made. This is the key to hundreds of other similar situations.

Quasi-introductions, such as those which are made between the household staff and members of the family, are discussed on page 364.

Mandatory introductions which are referred to elsewhere in the book concern the following situations: when one brings a stranger to a party (page 437); and when one is hostess (page 437). (Letters of introduction are on page 456.)

RISING

A man stands when he is being introduced to a woman, to a clergyman, to a man older than he, to an official, or to one who holds an official position higher than his. The only exceptions to this rule are the obvious ones: illness or extreme age.

Women stand when they are being introduced to any woman older than they, or to any church dignitary or important state official; and they should, as a matter of courtesy, rise to shake hands when an older man is being introduced. Out of respect for official positions and for the clergy, a woman stands, also, when she is being introduced to the wife of a clergyman or an important official. Again, the only exceptions to this are illness and old age.

When a woman comes into the room, all the men should stand, except, of course, in a very big room when a man who is sitting in a group of people might not have noticed her entrance. Younger women should rise when an older woman approaches, and particularly if an older woman speaks to them. And they must remain standing until the older woman sits down or goes away. Men should rise for women, young or old, and for older men, also.

OFFERING ONE'S HAND

The one who is being presented must not be the first to offer his hand. If a younger man is being introduced to an older one, for example, he must not put out his hand unless the older man has first done so. If the older man bows, instead of offering to shake hands, the younger man must follow suit. And this is true of all introductions, whether between two women, a man and woman, or two men. If the one who is being introduced should proffer his hand, out of turn as it were, it is up to the other to reciprocate as quickly and smoothly as possible, so that embarrassment may not be the result of a simple friendly gesture.

In foreign countries, it is the custom to shake hands with anyone who is being presented to you (see page 122), but in America a man or woman who is being presented to a group of people does not usually shake hands. (Opening gambits for conversation after introduction are suggested on page 15.)

BASIC RULE FOR SIMPLE INTRODUCTIONS

In America and England, the form of introduction is as simple as possible. Very often only the names are mentioned, but if so, it is a fundamental point that the name of the one who is being introduced must always be mentioned first. The basis for this rule is that the one who is doing the introducing is addressing himself first to the more important of the two. In introducing Mr. Carpenter to Mrs. Walcott, one may say, "Mr. Carpenter—Mrs. Walcott," but never, "Mrs. Walcott—Mr. Carpenter." On the other hand, if the introduction is a full sentence, addressed to Mrs. Walcott, it is quite correct to say, either, "Mrs. Walcott, may I present Mr. Carpenter?" or, "May I present Mr. Carpenter?—Mrs. Walcott." In presenting someone to the President or to a Cardinal (who is a Prince of the Church), one addresses oneself only to the more important person. (See forms below.) But other introductions are easier and more agreeable if they are broken in two, the first half addressed to the more important person and the second to the one who is being introduced. Each half contains the information necessary to each of the people involved.

A very natural and attractive informal introduction is: "Mary"—to attract her attention—"this is Mr. Carpenter"—and, turning to Mr. Carpenter—"Mrs. Walcott." If one wanted to be a little more formal, one might say only, "This is Mr. Carpenter—Mrs. Walcott." But, in any case, it would be absurd to address an intimate friend as "Mrs. Walcott" in any normal introduction. Therefore, the form, "Mrs. Walcott, may I present (or "this is") Mr. Carpenter?" should be used only if one is on fairly formal terms with Mrs. Walcott. The form given immediately below can be used whether Mrs. Walcott is a most formidable dowager or a most intimate friend.

THE FORMAL ANGLO-AMERICAN INTRODUCTION

"May I present Mr. Carpenter?—Mrs. Walcott."

LESS FORMAL INTRODUCTIONS

"Do you know Mr. Carpenter?—Mrs. Walcott."
"This is Mr. Carpenter—Mrs. Walcott."
"Mr. Carpenter—Mrs. Walcott."

Introducing Relatives.—A child: "This is my daughter Mary—Mr. McCann"; a grown woman: "This is Mr. McCann—my sister, Mrs. Pyne" or "This is my sister-in-law, Mrs. Dulany—Mrs. Elwell" (or daughter-in-law, son-in-law, etc.).

Introducing Couples.—"Mrs. and Mrs. Walker—Mr. and Mrs. Philips."

Introducing a Man to a Group.—"Mr. Davis—Mrs. Walker, Mr. Walker, Mr. Parker, Mrs. Ellis . . ." and so on around the room.

Introducing a Group to a Woman.—"Mrs. Walker, Mr. Walker, Mr. Parker, Mrs. Ellis—Mrs. Francis."

Between the Young, who do not yet address each other as "Mr." and "Miss."— "You know Jack Bradley, don't you?—Mary Anson."

Between the Young, Collectively.—"Jack Bradley, Elaine Mortimer, Bob Payson —Mary Anson."

INCORRECT WORDING OF INTRODUCTIONS

"May, this is John," is wrong because the use of first names only, without surnames, does not constitute a proper introduction. Worse still is, "Josh, this is Mary." Another very frequent mistake is to refer to a business or occupation when making an introduction: "This is Mr. Brown of the Standard Oil Company." It is almost necessary at business meetings, but it has no place in the living room.

SELF-INTRODUCTIONS

In introducing oneself, whether face to face or on the telephone, one should be extremely careful to avoid using "Mr.," "Mrs.," or any other title. The only times when it is correct to use a title is in speaking to an unknown person on the telephone, or in speaking to children, employees, and tradesmen.

Telephone conversations which illustrate the correct forms used in speaking to members of the household staff are given on pages 360 and 503, but the rule must be emphasized here as a point of manners. It is extremely bad form, for example, to say to an acquaintance, "I am Mrs. Whitney," or "My name is Mrs. Whitney," whether the acquaintance is older or younger, male or female. And it is even worse for a man to say, "I am Mr. Whitney," particularly to a woman. With the exceptions given above, one should always introduce oneself with one's full name: "Mary Whitney," for example, or "Henry Whitney"; never "Mrs.," "Mr.," "Miss," or "Dr." (See also "Introducing Members of the Staff," page 364.)

"Do You Remember Me?"

If an acquaintance seems to have forgotten an earlier introduction, it is never wise to say only, "Do you remember me?" Instead, one should say, "Oh, how do you do? I'm Mary Whitney. We met at Mrs. Bradley's." The first leaves the acquaintance floundering between the politeness of saying, falsely, "Of course I remember you perfectly," and the difficulties which such a phrase may entail. The second removes any possibility of awkwardness and, in one short phrase, accomplishes what manners are meant to accomplish: a smooth and easy relationship with others.

In Private Houses

In a private house, introductions are not supposed to be necessary, following the old saying that, "The roof constitutes an introduction." Actually, as suggested further on in "Entertaining at Home," page 437, American hostesses usually introduce a stranger to all the guests at a small party and to a few, at least, at a very big party. Nevertheless, it is still true that in a private house, or at any party, a guest may speak to any other guest without an introduction of any kind.

Sometimes in the course of conversation, it may happen that some informal self-introduction seems indicated. A man says, "My name is Henry Whitney," as suggested above; and a woman answers, "Mine is Jessica Harper." This does not, of course, mean that they will immediately call each other "Henry" and "Jessica." "Mr. Whitney" and "Mrs. Harper" are used until the woman suggests otherwise.

ACKNOWLEDGMENTS

"How do you do?" is used both by the one who is being introduced and by the one to whom he is being introduced.

UNDESIRABLE ACKNOWLEDGMENTS

"I am glad (or happy, or pleased, or delighted, or anything else) to know (or meet, or make the acquaintance of) you" should never be used as an acknowledgment. As a hostess, one may say to the guest a friend has brought, "I am so pleased you were able to come." If one has been introduced to the friend of a friend, one may say, "I am delighted to see you at last. I have heard so much of you from Alice." But these are obviously special circumstances and, if one must look for a rule, "How do you do?" is the only acknowledgment that can be called a rule. Another acknowledgment to be avoided is the questioning repetition of the other's name: "Mr. Carpenter,—?"

GREETINGS

The formal ceremonious greeting is "Good morning," "Good afternoon," or "Good evening," and this is still used as a mark of respect in greeting older people or those to whom special respect is due.

Less formally, "How do you do?" is the standard phrase. "Hello" is most informal and should be used only in greeting a friend or contemporary. (This is not true of the telephone greeting, of course; see page 14.)

SAYING GOOD-BYE

In the Anglo-American tradition, no very great point is made of saying good-bye. At a small dinner or luncheon, one should say good-bye to all the guests; but at a big party one need only say good-bye to one's hosts and to those in the group one was talking to. No special phrases other than "Good-bye" are necessary. A woman leaving a bridge table may say, "Good-bye; it has been such a pleasant game," to the other players. Or, to the one with whom she has been chatting after dinner, she might say, "I'm afraid I must go home now; I've enjoyed our conversation so much." In saying good-bye to one's host and hostess, there are special forms (see "Saying Good-Bye," on page 441), and if one wants to be particularly friendly one can always use a phrase such as, "Good-bye, I hope so much that we'll see you soon again." But except in such rather special circumstances, nothing more than "Good-bye" is actually required.

As a form of leave-taking, the ceremonious old-fashioned "Good morning," "Good afternoon," and "Good evening," are now seldom if ever used except with tradespeople and the domestic staff. For instance, when leaving a dinner party a very formal guest may say "Good evening" to the butler, instead of "Good night."

In saying good-bye, men and women rise as they do when being introduced. (See page 57, above.)

OFFICIAL INTRODUCTIONS

The titles of officials and prelates will be found on pages 558 to 581 in the chapter, "Forms of Address." For most of these, the forms of spoken address and introduction are also given and therefore in this section we shall discuss only those whose rank demands special forms and ceremonies.

To the President

"Mr. Carpenter"—the official presentation, usually made by an aide.

"Mr. President, may I present Señora de Blanco?"—the unofficial presentation.

When one is presenting either a man or a woman to a chief of state, one addresses only the important official. At a White House reception, the aide mentions only the name of the one who is being presented; on less official occasions, the second form is used. But the rule is that, in any case, both men and women are presented to the President and the one who is making the presentation addresses himself only to him.

When presented to the president of any country, men bow deeply. If the president offers his hand, men bow as they shake hands. Women incline their heads. As shown in the chapter "Forms of Address," one addresses the president as "Mr. President" and refers to him as "the President."

To Royalty

"Mr. Carpenter."

When one is presenting someone to a king or queen, or to a member of a reigning family, as in the case of a president, one mentions the name of the person who is being presented only.

Men are expected to bow deeply, as they do when they are presented to the president. Women curtsey to all royal personages. The question of whether or not American women should curtsey to royalty has often been discussed. But this is, after all, only a form of politeness, and since it is the accepted form, there seems no valid reason not to follow it. At court, the curtsey is deep and sweeping. In private houses and in public places, it is usually only a small bob. Kings and queens are addressed as, "Your Majesty," and in the third person: "Would Your Majesty like to come in to dinner?" In the course of a conversation, "Your Majesty" can be varied with "Sir" to the king and "Ma'am" to the queen. The same forms are followed with royal highnesses. They are addressed very formally as "Your Royal Highness"; less formally, "Your Highness," and "Sir," or "Ma'am."

To a Cardinal

"Your Eminence, may I present Mr. Carpenter?"

Again, as in the case of introductions to a president, only the cardinal is

61

addressed. When Roman Catholics are presented to a cardinal, both men and women are expected to kneel as they kiss his ring. Usually, this rule is interpreted as follows: The cardinal holds out his hand, and the one who is being presented drops one knee almost to the ground; at the same time, holding the cardinal's hand lightly in his fingers, he bends so that his lips almost touch the cardinal's ring. Non-Catholics, both men and women, should bow deeply. In conversation, "Your Eminence" is used by Catholics and non-Catholics alike.

To a Patriarch
"Your Holiness, may I present Mr. Carpenter?"

To All Other Church Dignitaries
Men and women are presented as, "May I present Mr. Carpenter?—Bishop Tucker"; or, "Bishop Tucker, may I present Mrs. Walcott?"

To State Officials
Men are presented: "May I present Mr. Carpenter?—the Chief Justice."

State officials are presented to women in the usual form: "May I present Governor Johnson?—Mrs. Parker."

The correct titles of other officials and the forms by which they should be introduced and addressed will be found in the chapter, "Forms of Address."

No ceremony is involved in these introductions, other than the usual courtesy which makes it mandatory that the one who is being presented must wait for the other to offer his hand.

10

Presents

WHAT PRESENT TO GIVE, when, and how to give it, are largely matters of feeling and friendship rather than of etiquette or usage. But there are a few points which are accepted as an integral part of our modern customs.

BASIC CONSIDERATIONS

The three basic considerations in present-giving are these:
1. the nature of the occasion. Most present-giving involves reciprocity, and this

is particularly true on certain occasions. Everyone has a birthday, and Christmas comes to everyone. Acquaintances, therefore, usually maintain a more or less equal return at these times. It would be unwise, for example, and not very good taste, to overwhelm a friendly acquaintance with a valuable birthday present which he might feel obliged to answer with an equally valuable one. Presents given for weddings, christenings, and week ends are not in the same category, because reciprocity is not so immediately involved.

2. the degree of intimacy in the relationship, if friendship or affection is the reason for giving. As in the case of entertaining, the essential consideration in present-giving between friends is not the absolute, but the relative, return. Friends and family may give very valuable presents, for which carefully thought-out, or homemade, presents may be a more than adequate exchange. This rule applies also to presents given through a sense of social obligation— that shadow of friendship. The hostess who has entertained many guests who cannot return her hospitality in kind will probably receive many presents more elaborate than those she sends.

3. the nature of the relationship, if obligation, or any reason other than friendship or affection, is the chief reason for giving. Reciprocity is not as important when one is giving a present of this kind. But a sense of obligation is, nevertheless, involved. It is like an invisible second present, slipped into every package. It is always more tactful, therefore, and more considerate of the feelings of another, to give a valuable present at the end of a relationship, rather than earlier. The reasons for this are very sound. At the end of a relationship, the giver has nothing to gain from whatever gratitude or obligation the receiver may feel. The present is obviously given without any selfish motive. Suppose, for example, that a business man has just concluded a long and difficult negotiation with the very valuable assistance of a junior associate. The moment for present-giving is naturally at the end of the negotiations; but if he or the associate should be going away in a short while, a tactful man will always delay giving the present until the eve of departure. (See also, "Jobs," page 111.)

Wedding presents, christening presents, week-end presents, presents from men to young girls, and from boys to girls are discussed under their separate headings on pages 224, 131, 471, 39 and 48. Presents to patients in the hospital, and presents given instead of tips, are discussed on pages 24 and 476. The only other subjects that need to be mentioned here are: flowers, candy, and current books, which are not considered as presents in the sense in which we have used the word in this chapter; the giving of money as a present; and, for the record, the traditional lists of birthstones and wedding anniversary presents.

FLOWERS, CANDY, BOOKS

Flowers, candy, and current books (as distinct from rare or specially bound books) are not in the same category as other presents. They involve no obligation other than polite thanks, because they can be considered as "attentions," rather than presents. They are almost like a visit, or a letter, and they are the classic presents which a woman may accept from a man without hesitation.

MONEY

In theory, money is not a good present and in practice it is never given as a present except to younger and very intimate members of the family, or to employees. Large amounts have always been given in checks and now that gold pieces are out of circulation, smaller amounts should be also. Bonds and stocks are considered as money, but "gift certificates" are not.

Unlike money, a gift certificate may be given as a present to younger friends, although the letter or card accompanying it often contains a word of apology. The standard phrases are, "I couldn't decide what you would really like so I hope you will choose for yourself. With much love and all best wishes ... ," etc.; or "I am so sorry that I didn't get back in time" (or "get well in time") "to choose a present for you myself. But this brings you all my best wishes for a Merry Christmas and a Happy New Year and much love. ... "

BIRTHSTONES

This is the list of stones traditionally believed to "belong" to each month:

January	Garnet
February	Amethyst
March	Bloodstone or aquamarine
April	Diamond
May	Emerald
June	Pearl or moonstone or agate
July	Ruby
August	Sardonyx or peridot or, sometimes, carnelian
September	Sapphire
October	Opal or tourmaline
November	Topaz
December	Turquoise or lapis lazuli

Alternates are listed in the order of their popularity.

WEDDING ANNIVERSARY PRESENTS

As we said on page 512, no guest at a wedding anniversary party is under an obligation to bring a present. But these are appropriate for the different years:

First	Paper		*Thirteenth*	Lace
Second	Cotton		*Fourteenth*	Ivory
Third	Leather		*Fifteenth*	Crystal
Fourth	Linen or silk		*Twentieth*	China
Fifth	Wood		*Twenty-fifth*	Silver
Sixth	Iron		*Thirtieth*	Pearls
Seventh	Wool or copper		*Thirty-fifth*	Coral or jade
Eighth	Bronze or		*Fortieth*	Rubies
	electrical appliances		*Forty-fifth*	Sapphires
Ninth	Pottery		*Fiftieth*	Gold
Tenth	Tin or aluminum		*Fifty-fifth*	Emeralds
Eleventh	Steel		*Sixtieth*	Diamonds
Twelfth	Silk or linen		*Seventy-fifth*	Diamonds

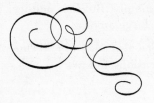

11

Tipping

IN THIS CHAPTER about tipping, there are dozens of specific suggestions and, besides, there is a set of four short rules that apply to tipping in general. But much more important than any of these is the spirit in which the tip is given and the manners with which that spirit is conveyed. If the service has been good, any money that is given as a tip should be given as though it were secondary, supporting evidence of gratitude. The idea that prompts good manners is this: "Thank you very much. Everything has been very pleasant and satisfactory. I am grateful for what you have done for me." The manners are these: a smile, a direct look, and "Thank you" or "Thank you very much."

If the service has been perfunctory, or barely adequate, tipping becomes purely a matter of justice, rather than gratitude, and the "Thank you" will be perfunctory also. But it is unkind and unattractive to reward willing service by pushing money toward the one who has been helpful, carelessly forgetting even to look in his direction. If tipping is done in the right spirit, it is a mutually pleasant interchange of good feelings, of appreciation and understanding and good will.

GENERAL RULES

1. All those who are usually tipped *must* be tipped as a matter of justice, because their wages are predicated on this custom. Only open rudeness or willful neglect on their part justifies a failure to tip them in the customary amounts.
2. Never tip the owner or the manager, even if he is acting in a capacity which would usually entail tipping. For example, if the owner of a beauty parlor has given service, he is not tipped, although one of his employees definitely would be. In a restaurant, however, if the owner has waited on table, a tip can be left on the plate with the check, on the assumption that an employee has collaborated in the service.
3. Never tip employees of private clubs. Members will probably be asked to contribute to a Christmas fund for the employees, but they should never give an employee a tip. (But see also "Four Customary Rules," on page 90.)
4. Extra tips must always be given for extra service, but lavish and unwarranted over-tipping is not desirable. If one has been ill, or if one has asked for any

special service, one must be prepared to tip proportionately. But it is neither good taste, nor fair to others, to tip carelessly in very large amounts.

These rules apply to all tipping, here, and abroad. (See also page 117, " 'One World' Etiquette.") Specific suggestions for specific occasions follow.

AIRPLANES

Stewards and stewardesses in airplanes are never tipped; neither is the chauffeur of the airline bus, who drives passengers from the terminal to the airport. A fee is usually collected for this trip, but no tip is given beyond the fee. If one has given one's baggage to the airline officials of the terminal, one need not tip the airline porters who see that it gets into the airplane. But if one drives to the airport in a taxi or a private car, the porters at the airport should be tipped unless they are employees of the airline. Airline employees are easily recognizable: Ground crews and airport employees usually wear coveralls embroidered with the airline's name. Airport porters, who wear tags like those of railroad station porters, are tipped at the same scale as porters in railroad stations: a little more than fifteen cents a bag if there are many bags, or twenty-five cents for one big bag.

APARTMENT HOUSES

Those who live in apartment houses must tip the elevator men, the doormen, the janitor, and the superintendent at least once a year, usually at Christmas time. The amount of the tips depends largely on the amount of one's rent. Provided one has asked for no special service, the total amount divided among all the employees should be about two per cent or two and one-half per cent of one's annual rent. If there were three elevator men, two doormen, a janitor and a superintendent, and one's rent were $1800 a year, the total tips would amount to $36 or $45 or about $5 to $7 each. If the apartment rent were $5000 a year, or if the apartment were a large one with an extra janitor and service-elevator man, porter, doorman, etc., one might give about $100 in tips.

As a guest, one need tip only the doorman of an apartment house and then only for special service. For example, if the doorman has made an effort in very cold or rainy weather to find one a taxi, he should be given about 25¢.

BARBER SHOPS

In barber shops in big cities the rule of thumb is 25¢ for each separate service —haircut, shampoo, facial, or manicure; and 35¢ to 50¢ for a haircut and shampoo, or for any two services. In very expensive barber shops, a man who has had the same barber for many years may give 35¢ or even 50¢ as a tip to the barber who cuts his hair. In small towns and inexpensive barber shops, 15¢ or 20¢ is a more usual tip than 25¢, or 25¢ for two services. But the sums we have suggested are the basic average.

BARS

In bars where only beer is sold, it is usually customary to tip only if one has been served at a table; and the tip is at least 10¢ for one person, or 25¢ for three.

At other bars, whether one is served at the bar or at the table, the usual tip is 15¢ to 25¢ for one drink each, for one or two people. Above that, the tip should be a generous 15 per cent of the bill. For example, if the bill is $1.50, the tip should be 25¢ or 30¢; if the bill is $2.50, the tip should be 40¢ or 50¢.

BEAUTY PARLORS

There is a very wide variation in the amounts charged for services in different beauty parlors, but the tips vary comparatively little. If a manicure costs 50¢, the tip is either 15¢ or 20¢; but whether a manicure costs 75¢ or $1.50, the tip is still 25¢. The standard tip for a shampoo is also 25¢, unless the shampoo costs 65¢ or less, in which case the tip is 15¢. In very expensive beauty parlors, where men often set one's hair, a man may be given 40¢ or 50¢ for this service (this is particularly true if the coiffure is very elaborate); but, as a rule, 25¢ is the standard tip for setting the hair also. For a permanent wave, the tip is 10 per cent of the cost or $1.00, whichever is greater. (This should not be taken too exactly: if a permanent wave costs $12.00, $1.50 would be the right tip.) For a facial, or for any more complicated service, such as a hair dye, the tip should be about 10 per cent of the bill, with a 50¢ minimum. In very elaborate establishments, where classes are held for reducing exercises, it is not customary to tip those who are teaching the class.

BOOTBLACKS

If a shoeshine costs 10¢, the tip is 5¢; if it costs 15¢, the bootblack is given either a 5¢ or 10¢ tip. It is not necessary to tip for shoe repairing.

DELIVERY BOYS

Delivery boys are not tipped as a matter of custom. For routine deliveries from department stores, no tip is necessary or even expected. Delivery boys from florist shops and Western Union messengers are not always tipped unless it is late, or bad weather, or unless the delivery has been specially made; in these cases they are given anything from 10¢ to 25¢. Western Union messengers who have done some service other than a routine telegram delivery are often tipped in very large amounts: For a singing telegram, they are often given anywhere from 25¢ to $1.00, depending on the feelings of the one who receives it. Their wages are not, however, predicated on their receiving tips and the policy of the Western Union Company officially ignores the practice of tipping. Any tips that are given, therefore, are a matter of politeness and appreciation rather than justice.

Grocery delivery boys are sometimes tipped, especially for an extra service such as taking away a case of empty bottles. Drugstore delivery boys, who may often be working after school hours, are also given 10¢ to 25¢ every now and then.

DEPARTMENT STORES

The only department store employee who is ever tipped is the doorman. In very bad weather, if a doorman has made efforts to find one a taxi, he should be given 25¢. If he has done nothing more difficult than open the door of a waiting taxicab, he need not be tipped at all.

DOMESTIC EMPLOYEES

See pages 474 to 476, "Tipping after a Visit."

FISHING AND HUNTING TRIPS

The employees of a private fishing club, like those of all clubs, are not tipped; and neither are guides who receive a regular fee and are in the position of an "owner-manager" rather than that of an employee.

HIRED CARS

If one has hired a car and chauffeur for the evening, the usual tip is 20 per cent of the bill. For longer periods, 15 per cent would be enough.

HOSPITALS

See page 24, "Hospital Manners."

HOTELS

Meals

If one is lunching or dining in a hotel, the waiters and doorman are tipped exactly as they would be in any restaurant. (See "Restaurants" below.)

Short Stays

An overnight or weekend guest tips according to this scale:

Bellboys: In a fairly expensive hotel, 25¢ to the bellboy who carries the bag up to the room, unlocks the door, turns on the light, etc; 50¢ in an expensive hotel, even if he has carried nothing but one bag and the key; $1.00 divided among three bellboys who have brought many bags to the room; 5¢ for bringing a newspaper; 10¢ for delivering cigarettes or small packages; 25¢ for heavy, large, or very valuable packages.

Chambermaids: About 10 per cent of the cost of the room.

Doorman: 25¢ for any special service.

Porters: $1.00 for a special service on a moderate scale: for example, for securing a section or compartment for an overnight railroad trip; 50¢ for reserving a Pullman chair for a day trip; $2.00 or more for very luxurious train or ship accommodations, or for any difficult special service.

Room waiters: In an inexpensive hotel, 15¢ or 20¢ minimum per person; in an expensive hotel or a moderately expensive hotel, 25¢ minimum; if the bill is between $2.00 and $10.00, 40¢ or 50¢ a person has become the standard tip. Over that, 10 or 15 per cent can be applied, depending on how good the service was and how expensive the hotel (dining-room waiters are tipped as they would be in a restaurant; see "Restaurants" below).

Valets: Hotel valets are often not employed by the hotel, but instead pay the hotel for the concession. In such cases, therefore, they are in the owner-manager position and are not tipped, except for a bonus for exceptional service.

Long Stays

If one is staying a week or longer in a hotel, the following scale should be used:

Bellboys: The scale suggested above can be applied, but those who are spending any length of time in a hotel very often like to give a regular tip every week to the head bellboy, rather than be bothered to tip each bellboy each time a package is delivered. If one has needed very little service (about a dozen deliveries during the week), the head bellboy is given a dollar. If a great many packages have been delivered or if many heavy packages have had to be taken up to one's room, one might give as much as $5.00 a week. Permanent hotel residents often give a monthly tip of a $1.00 each to the porter, the bellboys, the doormen, and the package-room employees. The total amount may be given either to the bell captain or to the head porter who will distribute the dollar to each one.

Chambermaids: For one room for one person in an expensive hotel, $2.00 for four or five nights, or $3.00 for one week. For two people, these sums should be raised to $3.00 and $5.00. For two rooms for one or two people, $5.00 a week, or $8.00 a week for three rooms for two people in an expensive hotel. In a less expensive hotel, $5.00 a week for two rooms; $6.00 a week for three. If one is spending a week or more in a hotel, the night chambermaid should be tipped as well as the day chambermaid. The tips for the night chambermaid are very much less since she does comparatively little work: $2.00 or $3.00 a week for one room; $3.00 for two bedrooms, in an expensive hotel; in an inexpensive hotel, a dollar a week for one room; $2.00 a week for two or three rooms. If one is living permanently in a hotel, one may tip either weekly or monthly and the scale is a little lower. The minimum is 25¢ per day per room, or $2.00 per week minimum; the maximum, for exceptionally good service, is 50¢ a room. The night chambermaid is rarely given more than a steady $2.00 a week. Tips to the chambermaid who often relieves the day maid as a routine matter are included in the $2.00—$3.50

weekly tips. In other words, if one has two rooms and the relief maid works two days a week, the regular day maid would be given $2.50 a week minimum and the relief maid would be given $1.00.

Doormen: For any special service, 25¢. Guests who stay longer than a week often tip regularly, usually $1.00 for two weeks, if one has needed a good deal of service. Permanent residents often give $1.00 a month, if they require little service; and this is often given through the bell captain (see "Bellboys").

Elevator men: No tips are necessary unless the elevator man performs a special service. If one has a baby carriage or a wheel chair, or if one needs any special help, the head elevator man may be tipped $1.00 to $2.00 a week. Permanent residents often give occasional tips, perhaps only three or four times a year and especially at Christmas.

Porters: For bringing three trunks, or two very large trunks, from the dock or railroad station, $1.00. This tip is usually given in advance to the head porter. For railroad or steamship accommodations, see scale suggested above.

Dining-room waiters: Visitors staying for a week or so tip as in a restaurant (see "Restaurants" below.) Permanent guests in an expensive hotel tip $3.00 to $5.00 every two weeks to the headwaiter. Table waiters are tipped as in a restaurant. In inexpensive hotels, $5.00 every three or four weeks to the headwaiter.

Room waiters: Whether one is staying for a weekend or for six months, room waiters are usually tipped according to the "short visit" scale given above on page 68. The only differences are that $10.00 is given head room waiters every four or five months or twice a year, and that permanent residents often prefer to write in the amount of the tip when they sign the check, rather than give money each time.

Valets: See page 68 above.

LUNCH COUNTERS

In some big cities, there is a new custom of tipping for lunch-counter service. The amounts are: 5¢ for a cup of coffee; 10¢ for coffee and a sandwich; 15¢ for coffee, a sandwich, and fruit juice, or for coffee, a sandwich, and pie; 25¢ if the service has been very good or if the check is over a dollar.

MASSEURS

A masseur (or masseuse) who is on his own, and not employed by anyone else, is not tipped, again because he is in the position of "owner-manager." Those who are employed in beauty parlors or health gymnasiums are given 50¢ for an hour's massage.

NIGHT CLUBS

Cigarette girls: 10¢ or 15¢.

Doormen: 25¢ on departure, whenever one is driving away from the night club; 25¢ if one's motor has been parked nearby.

Hat-check girls: In expensive night clubs, 25¢; in inexpensive night clubs, 10¢ or 15¢ for a hat; 15¢ to 25¢ for a hat and coat.

Headwaiters: Tipping the headwaiter is not a matter of justice, but entirely a matter of choice. If one does not go often and if one does not care about a "good" table, no tips are necessary. On the other hand, in a crowded, expensive night club strangers often give the headwaiter $2.00 or $3.00 on arrival, when they ask for a small table—perhaps even $5.00 for a big table—thus managing to get a "good" table right away. Those who go often to the same night club usually tip the head-waiter as they leave, giving him about $5.00 every third or fourth time. But, again, this is a custom observed only by those who want to be sure of getting a table in some particularly comfortable or desirable part of a room.

Ladies'-room attendant: 25¢ in an expensive night club or for any special service; 10¢ or 15¢ as a matter of course in any inexpensive night club; 50¢ or more for more complicated service such as sewing up a hem or removing a spot.

Waiters: 25¢ per person minimum, or a very generous 10 per cent of the bill —whichever is greater.

Wine stewards: $1.00 minimum, or a very generous 10 per cent of the bill.

PORTERS

Pullman

After a day trip in a Pullman car, one usually gives the porter 25¢ if he has given any service, no matter how slight. For one night in an upper berth, the usual tip is 50¢; in a lower berth, 75¢; in a roomette or compartment, $1.00; for two people in a compartment, $1.50; for a drawing room, $2.00. For longer trips of two or three nights, the porter is tipped on a slightly lower scale: $5.00 for a three-night trip in a drawing room; $2.00 or $3.00 for two people for three nights in a compartment; $2.00 for one person for three nights in a roomette or compartment; $1.50 or $2.00 for three nights in a lower berth; $1.00 for three nights in an upper berth.

Railroad Station

In many railroad stations, particularly in very large cities, a fee of 10¢ or 15¢ per suitcase has been established as the official tip to the porter. As a rule, whether or not this official fee is in question, the following scale is used: 15¢ minimum for one small light bag; 25¢ for two small bags or one big bag; 50¢ for three or four. This scale applies whether the porter has carried the bags or put them on a dolly truck.

RESTAURANTS

Headwaiters

(See also "Entertaining in Restaurants," page 452, and "Being Entertained in Restaurants," page 471, for suggestions concerning when and how to tip, how to order, etc.)

If one has discussed the arrangements of a dinner party beforehand with the headwaiter, he should be given a generous 10 per cent of the bill; but always in round dollar sums, and after dinner. For example, if the dinner has cost $9.00 or less, the headwaiter's tip must be a dollar; if the dinner has cost $10.00 in an inexpensive restaurant, the headwaiter should be given at least $1.00, or $2.00 if the service has been particularly good or if the restaurant is an expensive one. If the dinner has cost from $10.00 to $20.00, the tip is $2.00; if the check has been $20.00 or more, the tip should be $3.00, or $5.00 if he has given particularly good service.

If one makes no plans beforehand and if the headwaiter does nothing more than escort one to the table, tipping the headwaiter is not a matter of justice but purely a matter of choice. As in the case of headwaiters in night clubs, a great many people tip the headwaiter only in order to be sure that they will have a good table whenever they come. Strangers tip on arrival when they ask for a table; frequent patrons tip on the way out. One need not search out the head-waiter; he is tipped at the door of the dining room, if he is standing conveniently nearby—as he usually is. The sums vary with each restaurant: The more expensive it is, the higher the tip. In very expensive restaurants, there are five different categories of employees. Some are not tipped; others are. These are the categories, and the amounts usually given in the most expensive restaurants:

The head headwaiter, or manager: This one is never tipped. His only role is to greet the guests and to supervise.

The headwaiter of the room or department: This one is tipped, if one wants to be sure of a good table in an expensive and popular restaurant. A woman who lunches often in the same restaurant gives him $5.00 each four or five times; a man, each three or four times.

The headwaiter of the section: This one brings the menu card and takes the order. Since he does nothing but this, it is not necessary to tip him unless one has had a long discussion with him about the meal, or unless he has suggested special dishes not on the menu. If he is tipped, he usually is given $1.00 for one or two people, or $2.00 if there were four guests or more.

71

The table waiter: This one does all the work of bringing the food and is tipped according to the usual scale. (See below.)

Bus boy: This one has no role other than to bring bread, fill the water glasses, etc. He is more or less an apprentice waiter and is not tipped.

Hat-check girls: As in night clubs; see above.

Waiters and Waitresses

In any restaurant, except perhaps the most expensive, if the check is

Under 50¢	the tip should be 10¢ or 15¢
From 50¢ to $ 1.00	the tip should be 20¢
From $ 1.00 to $ 2.25	the tip should be 25¢
From $ 2.25 to $ 8.00	the tip should be a generous 10 per cent of the check: If the check is $4.00, the tip is 50¢; if it is $6.60, 75¢
From $ 8.00 to $ 9.50	the tip should be $1.00
From $ 9.50 to $11.50	the tip should be $1.50
From $11.50 to $15.50	the tip should be $2.00
From $15.50 to $19.00	the tip should be $2.50

In the most expensive restaurants, waiters have now become accustomed to a minimum tip of about 50¢ a person for any meal; or a dollar, at least, for three people. From $20.00 up, the question of how much to tip should depend on the number of people who have been served. If two people have had a most expensive dinner costing $22.00, the tip would be $2.00, or $3.00 if the service has been particularly good. On the other hand, if ten people have had a $2.25 table d'hôte dinner, the tip should certainly be $4.00, or if the service has been particularly good, $5.00.

Wine Stewards

10 per cent of the bill, or $1.00 minimum, whichever is greater.

SHIPS

The general rule is that one should allot an amount equal to 10 per cent of the cost of one's passage to be used for tipping. The question of how one divides this sum must depend on who has given the most service. Granted a normal passage, with breakfast in one's cabin and two meals a day in the dining room, the following is the scale:

Barroom Steward: About 15 or 20 per cent of the bar bill, which is presented at the end of the trip, unless one has tipped each time. This is over and above the 10 per cent figure set aside for tips.

Bath Steward: 10 per cent of the sum set aside for tipping, or a little more in order to bring it up to a round figure. Tips given to stewards who have performed regular service should always be in round sums. Tips are given in silver only for casual services, such as those given by the barroom steward. If there is no bath steward, the amount planned for him should be given to the cabin steward.

Cabin Steward: 30 per cent of the total amount set aside for tipping. The cabin steward does all the work of making the beds and cleaning the cabin.

Deck Steward: A little less than 20 per cent of the total amount for tipping, if one has a deck chair which one has used regularly.

Dining-room Steward: About 30 per cent of the money allotted for tipping.

Stewardesses: About 10 per cent of the money allotted for tipping. Steward-esses, as a rule, do comparatively little for a passenger. Of course, if one has been ill and has spent a great deal of time in one's cabin with the stewardess in attend-ance, most of the money set aside for the deck steward would be given to her.

On cruises, tips are often given weekly, the full sum being divided by the number of weeks the cruise is to last. But the full sum is still 10 per cent of the total cost of one's trip.

SHOOTING

As a guest for a long week end of shooting, the usual tip is about $15.00; or $25.00 for a married couple. This tip is usually given to the man who is in charge of the shooting (sometimes called the "factor"), although some hosts have a box in the hall of the house, where guests can leave tips. When giving a tip to the fac-tor, one must be careful to make it plain that the tip is for the men who take care of the horses and shooting dogs, and that one is only asking him to distribute it between them; many factors, particularly in the South, would never dream of ac-cepting a tip for themselves. The classic phrase is, "Would you be kind enough to distribute this whichever way you think best? And" (shaking hands) "good-bye and thank you for such fine shooting." In addition to this tip, one must give $5.00 ($10.00 from a married couple) to the man who has cleaned one's guns. The household staff must also be tipped as described on page 474, "Tipping After a Visit."

STABLES

Private Stables

Guests, for a week end or for any longer period, must tip the grooms if they have ridden their host's horses more than once. A single woman, who has only had one short ride, might not give any tips, but a man would usually give the head groom a dollar. For a day's hunting, a single man would tip the head groom $3.00; for two hunts, $5.00. If a husband and wife had both hunted, the husband would give the head groom $5.00, even if they had only been out once. The "strap-per," or second groom, who brings the horses to the meet and who may very well be asked to come and fetch the horses at the end of the day, should be given about $2.00. If one has brought one's own horses, these tips should be increased propor-tionately. In most hunting communities, it is customary to tip the head groom when horses have been brought out for the usual Sunday afternoon inspection. A dollar or so is the usual tip, depending on the number of horses.

Riding Stables

In commercial riding stables when horses are hired by the hour, the groom is given 25¢ or 50¢ depending on the amount of the charge. If one has hired a horse for a hunt, the charge will be much greater, and the usual tip to the groom is a dollar. If the groom has brought the horse from the stable to the meet, the tip is still a dollar, if the distance is short; if the meet is a mile or more from the stable, the tip should be $2.00.

TAXIS

In big cities, this is the scale of tips for three people or fewer:

Up to 50¢	the tip is 10¢;
from 50¢ to 70¢	the tip is 15¢;
from 70¢ to $1.00	the tip is 20¢;
from $1.00 to $1.50	the tip is 25¢;
from $1.50 to $2.00	the tip is 35¢;
from $2.00 to $3.50	the tip is 50¢;
from $3.50 to $5.00	the tip is 75¢;
up to $10.00	the tip is $1.00.

If there are four or five people in the taxi, these tips might be raised a little, particularly in the upper brackets. At night, too, the tip is often a little higher. In some small towns, particularly university towns, no tipping is customary; nor is it in some cities where there is a fixed charge for taxi-rides.

THEATERS

No tipping is necessary in theaters unless one has asked for some special service. If a ladies'-room attendant must be tipped—if she has sewn up a hem, for example—she should be given at least 25¢. If a doorman has fetched a taxi, he is usually given 25¢. Ushers are not tipped in America, and it is not necessary to pay for theater programs as it often is abroad. See page 120 in the chapter " 'One World' Etiquette."

TRAINS

The only employees who are usually tipped on trains are Pullman porters (see "Pullman Porters" above) and dining-car waiters. In "lunch-counter" cars, they are tipped according to the regular lunch-counter scale; in dining cars, according to the regular restaurant scale. On long transcontinental trips, the steward or headwaiter in the dining car is sometimes tipped as a headwaiter in a restaurant would be. If one were traveling with children, for example, one would almost surely tip him.

Conductors are not tipped unless one has asked for some unusual service. The typical example of this is watching out for an unaccompanied child. For a short day trip, a conductor who is keeping his eye on a child traveling alone is given 50¢; for a longer day trip, $1.00. If a child is spending the night on the train, he will presumably be old enough to look out for himself to a greater extent. A dollar, therefore, would still be enough, if the child is traveling in a coach. If the child is traveling in a Pullman car, the conductor is not tipped, but instead, a dollar should be added to the usual tip given to the Pullman porter.

WEEK ENDS

Tips given after a week end are discussed on pages 474 through 476; "Tipping after a Visit," in the section "Entertaining."

YACHTS

As a guest on a big yacht, one tips exactly as one does for a week end. Even on longer trips, tips are given not weekly, but only when the trip is over. If the trip has lasted a month or more, the tips are usually given in round figures: $15.00 or $20.00 to the cabin steward, depending on the amount of service one has asked; $10.00 or $15.00 to the head dining-room steward. On yachts that are specially chartered for the trip, one usually tips less than on yachts where the stewards are regular employees of one's host. The captain of a big yacht is never tipped. On any boat under fifty feet, the guests are usually expected to co-operate in the sailing, and the crew, if any, is small. The captain is very seldom tipped, and one should hesitate before tipping any member of the crew. A good rule of thumb is that a guest tips only for personal service, but not for handling the boat. And an even better rule, if in doubt, is to ask the owner, "I'd like to give Ted something; do you think he'd mind?" On a small yacht if there is a steward to be tipped, he is given about $15.00 or $20.00 after a voyage of a month or so. For short trips on both small and big yachts, tips are given according to the scale suggested on page 474 for week-end visits ashore.

12

Traveling

MANY OF the rules of good manners which should be observed while traveling are mentioned in other parts of this book. Decorum, for example, that vital characteristic of every attractive traveler, is discussed in detail on pages 10 to 12. In its application specifically to traveling, decorum means no loud and jolly parties on trains and planes, where others cannot help but hear and see; no messy box luncheons when one has a near neighbor who is forced to witness the untidiness (a neat sandwich in waxed paper is one thing, a juicy orange quite another); no argument or laughter which others cannot help but hear, especially after bed-time hours.

Other points concerning travel will be found in "Tipping," on pages 65 to 74, in "Women's Clothes," pages 632 to 633, and in "Visiting," page 471. Travel abroad is discussed on pages 117 to 125 in the chapter " 'One World' Etiquette." In this section we need discuss only a few specific points which seem to need clarification or emphasis.

TRAVELING WITH CHILDREN

Consideration for others, the basis of all good manners in traveling, is part-ticularly important when one must travel with children. An ordeal at best for the poor parent in charge of the expedition, traveling with small children can be a nightmare to others. The ideal solution for train travel is to keep the children within the privacy of a compartment, but, of course, this is not always possible. In a bus or airplane, or in a coach or chair car, the only hope is to keep them busy with books and games.

The root of the matter, of course, lies far back of the trip itself, in an early and consistent training in discipline and consideration for the rights of others. But all of us have known quite well-behaved children who seem to choose traveling as the time of all others for "self-expression." In these circumstances, all one can do is to make great efforts to keep the children from annoying the other travelers. Trips up the platform (not through the corridors) when the train has stopped, to see the engine; trips down the platform to see the observation car—all these are sound ideas because a child's traveling problem is usually that he hates sitting still. And, to be quite frank, they are sound ideas also because the thing that really annoys other travelers is not only the noise and the interruption of children. A great deal of their annoyance often springs from the fact that the parents are not even trying to spare their feelings. A mother who struggles to keep her children from bothering the other passengers is usually spoken of as, "That nice woman who was having such a hard time keeping her little boy quiet." Those whose atti-tude toward their children is, "I don't care what you do as long as you stop bother-ing *me*," are often lumped with the children as, "That awful noisy family on the train."

TRAVELING IN A PULLMAN CAR

An overnight journey in a Pullman berth is one of the test moments of the traveler. Some do it gracefully and easily; others bring in a note of strain, for themselves and everyone else. It is very easy to share a section with an experi-enced traveler who has good manners, but a novice with bad manners is a very difficult companion.

Experienced travelers will wait considerately until a reasonable hour before asking the porter to make up the section. They will not feel it necessary to start a conversation about it, but instead will confine themselves to a polite, "Would you mind if I asked the porter to make up my berth now?" or, if they are really provi-dent, ". . . to make up the berths at 9:30?"

They will do all their undressing in their berths, after washing and not before. And should they want to make another trip later, they will wear a tailored dress-ing gown and plain slippers.

In the washrooms, they will keep their belongings neatly to themselves, not spread over the whole dressing table. They usually have a neat "sponge bag" for toothbrushes, etc., or a small fitted case. In the morning they dress again in their berths and slip away almost noiselessly—a joy to late sleepers. They speak to the porter, asking him for the ladder or whatever, in a low voice and seem to need so little extra help from him that he is always free to help others. They are a blessing to everyone who travels with them because they are experienced enough to know what makes traveling agreeable for others, and disciplined enough to be willing to live up to its rules.

TRAVELING ON SHIPS

Everything we have said about consideration for others while traveling applies equally, of course, to travel on a ship. As in the case of other traveling, women's clothes are discussed on pages 632 to 633, and tipping on pages 65 to 74. The only things that need be discussed here are steamer chairs and the question of sitting at the captain's table.

As a rule, most travelers speak to the head dining-room steward about reserving a table almost as soon as they come on board. Some of them, however, particularly officials or important personages, are asked to sit at the captain's table. This is always a compliment, but accepting is entirely a matter of choice. In refusing, the classic phrases are, "Please thank the captain very much, but we are very bad sailors so perhaps we had better not accept," or ". . . but we are traveling with friends and do not like to leave them." Invitations to a single meal are difficult to refuse unless one is really not well. Those who sit at the captain's table are usually introduced to each other, but whether they are or not, they converse anyway, as they would at any dinner table to which they were invited.

A steamer chair, like a dining-room table, should be reserved as soon as one gets on board. If there is a special place which one prefers, this is the moment to ask for it. The purser, or any steward, will know where the deck steward may be found.

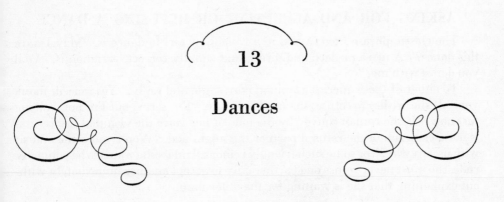

13

Dances

THE PERFECT attitude at a dance is a mixture of gaiety and decorum: gay hosts who are still mindful of their guests' well-being; gay guests who, while enjoying themselves, are still aware of their responsibilities as guests. Granted this attitude as the ideal, the rest of good behavior at a dance is a matter of technique.

SAYING GOOD EVENING

The first rule of manners, as always, is that guests must say good evening to their hosts, and this applies to all dances. At a subscription dance, if members of the committee are receiving, guests must greet them. At a dance in a college fraternity or sorority house, guests must say "How do you do?" to the chaperone or housemother. If the hostess is dancing, men guests who come alone must cut in; women guests greet her at the earliest possible opportunity, perhaps on the floor but certainly before supper. If the host is dancing, he will usually stop for a moment to greet newly arrived guests, particularly a woman. But men guests must find an opportunity to nod or bow, at least, in greeting.

DUTY DANCES

As stated in the chapter concerned with the manners of the young, all men guests should dance with the following at least once:

The hostess, and any daughters of the hostess.
Any woman guest of honor.
The hostess of the dinner given before the dance and any woman guest of honor there.

If a man has been "brought" to the party by a woman guest, or by a subscription party member, he must dance repeatedly with her and invite her to have supper with him. "Will you have supper with me?" is the classic question. It is also very polite, but not mandatory, for a man to dance with the two women between whom he sat at dinner. (See also "Night Clubs," page 455.)

ASKING FOR AND ACCEPTING OR REFUSING A DANCE

The classic phrase used in asking a woman or girl to dance is, "May I have this dance?" A more modern and direct, and equally correct, variation is, "Will you dance with me?"

To either of these queries a woman may smile and reply, "Yes indeed, thank you." If she wishes to refuse, she need only say, "I'm sorry, but I'm not dancing just now." If she cannot convey by the tone of her voice the idea that her refusal is not a criticism of the refused partner she might add, "Won't you come and sit with us, anyway?" or some such friendly remark. Unless she wants to be pointedly rude, she must never refuse one partner only to accept another immediately without explaining that she is waiting for the other man.

CUTTING IN

Cutting in offers an excellent example of the direct connection between manners and sociological facts: It is unheard of in settled and traditional European society, but it is an accepted part of manners in America, where there was probably a chronic shortage of women at every dance from 1650 to 1900. At most American dances today, this is the accepted form for cutting in: When a man wants to cut in on a couple who are contemporaries or friends, he taps the man's shoulder or touches his arm, without comment, or perhaps with a short, "Cut, please." When he is cutting in on an older man, he goes up to the couple, bows to catch the older man's eye and, without touching him, says, "May I cut in, please?"

CUTTING BACK

"Cutting back," which is against all rules, even among the youngest dancers, means cutting in on the same man who has himself just cut in. For example, if Miss A is dancing with Mr. B and Mr. C cuts in, Mr. B cannot cut back. He cannot dance with Miss A until she has a new partner, or until the music stops.

GETTING STUCK

"Getting stuck," or dancing overlong with one partner, is probably one of the nightmares of every young girl who goes to dances in America. The milder foreign equivalent is called "having no partner," but it lacks the sting which "getting stuck" has for the young. And very often it is only thanks to the duty-dance rule that it is not a young hostess' nightmare also. Just as cutting in is an example of the connection between fact and manners, so getting stuck is an example of the time lag which often occurs between a new fact and an established pattern. At a certain moment in this century, there were for the first time as many women as men in America, and although there are always more men than women at a dance, the pattern of the men's behavior is based on a shortage of women more acute than the present one. A new system will certainly have to be devised unless men guests will take more seriously their obligation to dance at a dancing party. Abroad, a man returns his partner to the place where he found her unless another partner comes to claim her. Here, a few hostesses have seen the wisdom of this system and, when the ballroom is big, have arranged tables around it to which couples who have danced enough may retire. But too often there is no system and women, who are responsible under the code, must rely on whatever makeshift arrangements they are clever enough to devise.

The beginning of wisdom is to accept the fact that one has danced long enough with one partner and that he might like to change. A woman who clings for hours, pathetic though she may be, will not soon dance with that partner again. Failing that perfect refuge, a table and a group of friends, she should suggest leaving the floor quite quickly, as soon as getting stuck seems likely. The classic phrase for this is, "It's so hot—would you like a drink?" or, "Let's sit down for a bit." Once away from the floor, she and her partner should join a group of friends—better a group than a couple—unless a man comes up to speak to her, at which point her partner may slip away. At a dance where there are not many extra men, or where few of the extra men are dancing, she will probably find several couples in the same situation; it is quite easy to change the combinations of partners during a general conversation, and the problem of getting stuck with one partner is solved for the time being, at least.

It is not too difficult, perhaps, for an older woman to accept the fact that she is not the universal ideal of a dancing partner, but it is not at all easy for young girls. When the situation seems completely out of hand, when there are no friends sitting in groups and no boys she knows anywhere in sight and everyone else is dancing gaily, the best thing to do is to go home. Young girls who come in a group to a chaperoned dance may ask the chaperone to make arrangements for them to leave; or, better still, her parents should make a previous arrangement with her, so that she can telephone and be fetched if she wants to come home before the dance ends. A girl old enough to go to a party with a man can ask him to take her home, on the plea of being tired or feeling ill.

Finally—although this has nothing to do with manners except in so far as it is part of a proper sense of values—parents should not urge their daughters to go to dances unless the girls want to go; and women should not feel that if there is a dance and they are invited they *must* be there. A dance should be fun and if it isn't, there's no point in it.

SAYING GOOD-BYE

Saying good-bye to one's hosts is as binding as saying good evening. And, as in the case of saying good evening, "hosts" means housemothers, chaperones, and reception committee members, not only the hosts in a private house or at a private dance. (The forms are in "Entertaining at Home," on page 441.)

14

Games and Sports

SPORTSMANSHIP applies to all competitive games, from tennis to checkers. And these are its rules: One must play one's best always; one must be a generous opponent, slow to take advantage of technicalities in one's favor, quick to give others the benefit of the doubt; one must accept defeat gracefully and victory with deprecating modesty. The man who boasts about winning or bewails his bad luck, or stops trying when he is far behind, is a bad sport.

The ideal attitude of any player is expressed in the old saying, "Play for the sake of the game; not only to win." When the game is over, the ideal attitude of winner and loser is expressed in this short conversation, not necessarily to be repeated verbatim after each game, but conveying the ideal attitude perfectly:

Loser: That was a good game.
Winner: You had awfully bad luck.
Loser: No question of luck at all; you played well.

All rules of sportsmanship are based on the following premises:

1. If one breaks a rule, one must accept an opponent's correction immediately and willingly, with some phrase such as, "Oh, of course; I'm so sorry." Infringements that may not have been noticed by one's opponents should be rectified and apologized for at once. (But see "Bridge," below, on this point.)
2. Upbraiding a partner for an error in judgment or for poor playing is the height of bad sportsmanship. As the offending partner one should say, "That was horrible. I let you down badly," to which the answer can only be, "Not at all. I should have done the same," or "Not at all. You had a tough break."
3. Delaying the game, for deep thought, to study conditions, or whatever, is boring to all concerned and should be avoided. The only possible exceptions to this rule are games such as croquet, where delay is part of the battle strategy. But it is a technique best used among friends. Righteous impatience is even more rude and unsporting. Tapping, whistling, moving about, whether to indicate impatience or not, are impossible in any game.
4. In any game, the most attractive player is the one who is the quickest to accept the rules and playing customs of others.

These four are all general rules, but some games and sports have a further set of almost specialized manners. These are listed alphabetically below.

BRIDGE

It is curious, but it is a fact, that the rules of sportsmanship in bridge permit one to be silent about mistakes which would benefit the opponents, although one is expected to rectify immediately any mistakes which carry no penalty. For example, if one has revoked or has led from the wrong hand, one is permitted to keep silent and hope that nobody will notice. This refers, of course, only to unpremeditated revokes or misleads; deliberate ones are out of the question. In bridge, even more than in some other games, it is bad taste to hunt down every technicality in one's favor, and to pounce on every error that an opponent may have made in an ostensibly friendly, sociable game. (See also "Gambling," page 84.)

GOLF

On the first tee there is no order of precedence, but it is polite to suggest to a guest or an older person that he take the first drive. Women, too, usually tee off before men, unless the women's tee is so placed that a lot of fussing and walking about would be necessary.

Technically, two people on a golf course can always go through a foursome, on the assumption that two can cover the course much more quickly than four.

It is very good manners, however, for two people who are playing slowly to allow a foursome to go through. And this should always be done if the people in the foursome are very much older or very much better players than the other two.

As a member of a foursome, one should always ask two people to go through. It is true that the two have the right of way and that they can very well ask, "May we go through?" but it is much more attractive to invite them to do so. Three people playing together have no standing at all on a golf course, and they are expected to ask two people or a foursome to go through.

A further point of manners at golf is that one must be absolutely still and silent when others are addressing the ball, particularly on the putting green. But in return for this, players must also avoid delaying their shots. It is probably unnecessary to warn anyone against such antisocial habits as neglecting to replace divots. (See also "Golf Courses," page 93 in the chapter, "Clubs.")

TENNIS

Quite apart from any of the rules of tennis, there are three accepted forms of good manners. The first is that one must never serve without being sure that one's opponent is ready. It is wise to cling to the form of saying "Ready?" before serving, although this is not necessary if one's opponent is obviously poised and waiting. But it is not enough to say "Ready?" without looking to be sure that one's opponent has heard. The reverse of this is that one must try not to delay the server by picking up unnecessary balls, or by being out of place when the server is ready. Nothing is more unattractive than the opponent who returns with deliberate slowness to the ready position.

The second point of good manners is that one must always offer to play over a doubtful point if the element of doubt is in one's favor. When an opponent fails to return the ball the server should be quick to offer to serve again if there is any chance that the first serve might have been a let ball. Equally, the opponent must be as quick to offer to play the point over if his return was suspiciously near the back line.

The third point of manners is that one must send over to the server whatever balls may be on one's side of the net at the end of each game. As a rule, in order to avoid delay to the server, one should not send back balls after each point unless the server really needs them.

FOX HUNTING

Riding clothes, including those worn for hunting, are discussed separately on pages 633 to 635. Riding manners are purely a matter of common sense and need no special consideration, but fox-hunting manners are somewhat formalized and need a little discussion. These are the general outlines:

1. When one arrives at the meet, unless a big crowd makes it impossible, one should ride up to the Master and say, "Good morning." When one is going home, if the moment is suitable, one should ride up to the Master again, and thank him for a good day's sport.

2. No one should ride between the Master and the hounds; no one except a huntsman or whip should precede the

Master over a fence or across a field.

3. One must stop when the Master says, "Hold hard, gentlemen, please," and one must not use this moment to jockey for a better position nearer the front of the field.

4. If anyone has a fall, men are always expected to stop and see if they can help, even if the rider is a stranger. Women need stop only if the fallen rider is a woman or if no men are nearby.

5. Men are not expected to show women any special courtesy, such as to let women precede them over fences or through gates in the middle of a run; but everyone is expected to ride carefully and with enough consideration not to be a menace to the field.

6. When there is a crowd at a gap or a narrow place, one must be sure to wait one's turn.

7. Guests should be meticulous in paying the "cap" (a fee owed by anyone who has hunted and is not a regular subscriber to the hunt); the usual procedure is to send a check to the hunt secretary a day or two after the hunt.

8. If one is riding a strange horse, or a very difficult one, one should be careful to keep in the background and avoid interfering with or impeding the other members of the hunt.

9. Novices should not wander off by themselves. There is always danger of heading the fox, or riding across planted or posted land.

10. If someone gets off his horse to open a gate, one should wait for him to remount and not gallop off heedlessly.

11. The last member of the field, riding through a gate which has been opened for the hunt, must be sure it is closed before going on.

12. A rider whose horse has refused a fence should pull aside and allow others to jump before facing his horse at the fence again.

13. Riders should keep still and avoid conversation when hounds are drawing or casting nearby.

14. Riders should keep a sharp lookout for the hunted fox. A novice who views the fox takes off his hat and holds it out, with a straight arm, pointing at the animal. A proper "view holloa" is better left to experts. He must be sure, however, that a member of the hunt staff has noticed his signal. He may be the only one to see the fox and so be able greatly to improve the day's sport.

YACHTING AND SAILING

Most of the rules of good manners are based on common-sense principles that apply anywhere. As a guest on a boat of any size, whether a ten-foot frostbite dinghy or a big ocean-going yacht, the first rule is to take one's cue from the owner. Some owners, particularly on very big yachts, observe strict, almost naval etiquette. Others are more easygoing. The question of what to wear is discussed on page 635, "Women's Clothes," and on page 621, "Men's Clothes." Here follows a short list of pointers for novices, both owners and guests, on what to do:

1. It is a point of good manners, as well as common sense, to wear rubber-soled or rope-soled shoes on a boat. High heels and hard-soled shoes are slippery and scar soft wooden decks which are often the pride and joy of the owner and his crew. On long cruises, one can bring high heels and hard-soled shoes for going ashore, but one should always expect to wear soft shoes on board.

2. The mark of a well-run boat is neatness, and owners who are easygoing in everything else may be fanatics on this point. Guests should not leave clothes, glasses, etc. lying about. They should never stamp out a cigarette or drop ashes on the deck. They should never throw a lighted cigarette overboard on the windward side of the boat (the side from which the wind is blowing).

3. The owner is responsible for his boat, for those aboard her, and for any accident in which she may be involved. Therefore, if the owner appears preoccupied, the novice guest should efface himself. "Sit down and keep quiet," is often the owner's silent prayer. It is also a good policy to follow whenever the boat is getting under way, anchoring, entering or leaving port.

4. On all boats, and particularly larger yachts, guests should be extremely conservative in their relations with the crew. The "paid hands," as they are usually called, are extremely proud of their profession and of their knowledge of the sea; and, indeed, many a paid captain commanded a naval ship in the war. Guests should never ask for food, drinks, the use of a small boat, or any other service out of the ordinary routine except through the owner.

5. A paid captain is usually called "Captain"; other members of the crew on big yachts are called by their last names, on smaller boats often by their first names or nicknames. Guests should take their cue from the owner; on a big yacht, if one does not know the crew members' names, the ones who take care of the dining room, bedroom, etc., can be called "Steward."

6. When there is a paid captain, he does not as a rule eat with the owner and guests. He has his own quarters and is served there.

7. The owner should be the last to leave the yacht and get into the launch or dinghy in which the trip is made to the shore; leaving the shore, he is again the last to get into the launch. Transferring from the small boat to the yacht, he is the first to leave the small boat. This is a rigid rule in the Navy, but it is not always observed on yachts, particularly very small ones.

Incidentally, to clear up a few points of terminology: Dinghies, motor launches, tenders, rowboats, and the different kinds of skiffs can be generally described as boats; anything used for sport—racing, cruising, or pleasure sailing—can be called a yacht. Ships are, technically, large vessels over a hundred feet long. Naval vessels and ocean liners should all be referred to as ships. A dinghy is a small boat which usually has oars or an outboard motor; a launch is a small boat with an inboard motor. A final word of caution: The sea has a highly technical language of its own and nautical terms should never be used without a full grasp of their meanings.

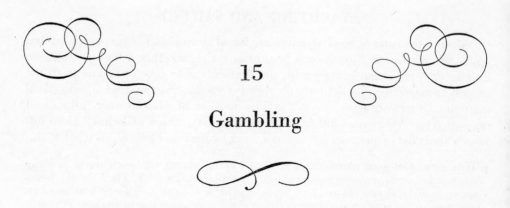

15

Gambling

GAMBLING involves a code of behavior which is, in some ways, very like the old dueling code. In the first place, neither is supported by the law: one can no more sue for money won at gambling than for injuries received in dueling. In the second place, both rest on mutual acceptance of the validity of this extracurricular, extralegal code. Finally, and most of all, both are intimately concerned with what used to be called "a gentleman's honor." Perhaps at this point we should make it clear that we are discussing a code for gambling in particular, and not for games in general. The primary law of decency in regard to games, or anything else, is honesty. No one who cheats is a gentleman, whether or not he pays his debts with meticulous promptness. The gambling code, like the dueling code, is a question of technique rather than fundamental principle.

Happily, in this country, dueling is a dead issue, but happily or unhappily, gambling is not. Gambling debts are still debts of honor, and disciplined good manners in everything connected with gambling should still be part of everyone's code. The essence of good manners in gambling is indifference to the stakes; indifference whether one wins or loses; indifference, if one wins, as to when and how one will be paid. Because there is no legal recourse, an unbreakable part of the code is that gambling debts should be paid at once. These rules are equally important. Fierce disappointment, if it is not carried too far, can be quite amusing in a parchesi game played for love. But any suggestion of disappointment can be disturbing to the winner in a poker game played for money.

The first rule of good sense, therefore, is never to play for any stakes which one cannot conveniently afford. It is not only foolish to become involved in a game where the stakes are too high but, if one's opponents are aware of one's situation, it is also bad taste and to some extent bad sportsmanship. As soon as one sits down to a game, before the cards are dealt, the stakes should be set. If anyone feels that the stakes are uncomfortably high, this is the moment for him to speak. The stakes will then be lowered, or else he will be put "on the table"; i.e., the difference between the stakes and the amount he wants to play for will be divided among his opponents. If this course is decided upon, it must be accepted by the low-stake man. It is extremely unattractive to refuse to be put "on the table" if the others seem to desire it, or to make fussy excuses when the stakes are lowered.

Furthermore, the slightest suggestion that the stakes may be too high for one of the players must be met by the most ready acceptance on the part of the others. It is true that no one should hesitate to speak up, but it is often difficult for a shy stranger to do so. Therefore all suggestions as to stakes should be tentative, particularly in any game with strangers. A useful opening phrase, when there is any uncertainty, is, "What do you like to play for, if anything?" This will make it easier for a conscientious objector to say, "Well, I hope you don't mind, I don't play for any stakes." If, however, one's opening gambit has no response other than a merry laugh, the next question might be, "Well, what stake would you like? I honestly don't mind; anything from —————— to —————— suits me," and the figures one mentions should be one's maximum stake and a ridiculously low minimum. But if one's usual stake is a high one, there is a further delicate point of tact involved. To opponents whose maximum stake may be one-tenth of a cent a point, one obviously should not say, "Anything from one-fortieth to two cents suits me." If one thinks the stranger's stake might be low, it is much better to say, "Anything from one-fortieth to one-fourth suits me," because he will then have less hesitation in saying, "Would a tenth of a cent be all right?" If there is no indication as to what stakes he might like, one can take cover under exaggeration: "What do you like to play for: a fortieth, a quarter of a cent, a penny, or would you like to play for more?"

This detailed discussion about money may seem contrary to the "indifference to the stakes" principle of the gambling code, but, actually, it is like a modern prologue to the eighteenth century play of gambling. Once these preliminaries are over and the stakes are agreed upon, the old code holds in full. One must never, by any hint or expression, show any emotion other than complete indifference as far as the money end of the game is concerned.

SETTLING UP

The second major premise of the gambling code, as we have said, is that gambling debts must be paid immediately. Ideally, therefore, all scores should be settled and all debts paid before any player leaves the table. Furthermore, whatever form of payment a debtor suggests must be agreed to immediately. An older person can say to a younger, "Let it go until next time; we'll be playing soon again." But this is not permissible from a younger to an older person.

A further gambling tradition is that a winner must never remind a loser to pay a gambling debt. For this reason, scorekeepers have a direct responsibility to make sure that all players are informed as to the state of the score at the end of the game. If one is in the difficult position of being both a scorekeeper and a winner, one's duty as scorekeeper comes first, when others are involved. If, for example, the only loser has left the table, it becomes incumbent upon the scorekeeper to track him down and inform him as to the amount of his losses. When there are two scorekeepers, one a winner and the other a loser, the loser can more gracefully do whatever tracking down is necessary.

GAMBLING DEBTS

In spite of all the rules of good sense in gambling, there are some times when, through fantastically bad luck, one cannot settle a gambling debt immediately. If it is a small amount, one which may seem utterly inconsequential to one's creditor, it is better to delay payment without making any fuss about it. The purpose of this is not, of course, to avoid paying the debt, but only to spare one's creditor the uncomfortable knowledge that the money he has won is inconveniently difficult for the debtor to pay. If debtor and creditor often play together, the debt can ride until the next game when, it is to be hoped, the situation will have improved. In this case, the debtor can say cheerfully, at the beginning of the game, "I haven't forgotten that I owe you ———— dollars from the other night; let's put it on the score right now." If the situation hasn't improved, the debtor can wait and see how the evening's play turns out, balancing the old debt against any new gains. If he loses again, he should say, "I haven't forgotten that I owe you ———— dollars from the other night. May I pay it all together, and send you a check?" In any case, one should never play any game for stakes with a person to whom he owes money, without mentioning a previous debt and indicating an intention to pay it.

When debtor and creditor do not often play together—and particularly if they are acquaintances rather than friends—the situation becomes a little more difficult. If the sum is a small one, one can appear to ignore it until it is possible to pay it. Then an explanatory note can be written, enclosing a check. The classic excuse is that the debt had been forgotten until a written reminder was found. If, on the other hand, it is a considerable sum and there is no way of meeting it within a reasonable length of time, it is better to own up immediately, giving one's creditor some idea of the time in which it might be paid, the amount of the installments, etc. For example, if one owed twenty-five dollars, and if one were on a limited budget, one might require two or three weeks to make up the amount; but it could be done without fuss since the delay is not exaggerated. (The wisdom of gambling for money in such circumstances is another point—much more important, perhaps, than anything else we are discussing here, but not a lesson which can be effectively taught in a paragraph or two.) However, if one owed three or four hundred dollars or more, and if there were no prospect of being able to pay within a month or so, it would be better to write, or to go and see one's creditor, and explain. The letter might be as follows:

Dear Mr. Abbott:

I am very sorry not to be able to send at once the $375 I owe you. I've gotten in a bit of a jam at the moment, and I won't be able to do very much about it for another month or six weeks. By that time, everything ought to be in fine shape, and I expect it should be all paid up three months from now.

I enjoyed our game so much. My only regret is that I have had to bother you with these details.

Sincerely,
David Bartlett

The purpose of this is not only to acknowledge the debt, and to emphasize one's desire to pay it, but also to make the creditor feel that the difficulties are only temporary and that one's financial condition is not gravely embarrassed. The only possible answer is something like this:

Dear Mr. Bartlett:

Thank you very much for your extremely kind letter. I quite understand and hope you will not permit the situation to inconvenience you in any way. I so much enjoyed meeting you at Mrs. Baker's—what an agreeable evening it was! I hope we shall meet very soon again.

Sincerely,
Charles Abbott

Although it is true that one should never remind a debtor of a gambling debt, it is also true that the gambling code is based on a mutual acceptance of all its premises. Therefore, if one is quite sure that a debtor is presuming upon the flexibility of the code to avoid a just debt, well within the limits of his ability to pay, there are three possible courses open. None of these is advisable, perhaps, because they all contravene one of the primary laws: never to remind a debtor of his debt. But in extreme cases, they are permissible.

If a creditor has lost money to his debtor, at the end of a game he may say, "Am I wrong, or do you owe me something from the other night? We might balance them off." This is the mildest form of reminder, because it is contingent on the debtor's having won.

A slightly more forceful reminder—more forceful because it shows no regard as to whether or not the debtor has lost again—is to suggest that the debtor add his new losses to his old debt: "Why don't you just add this to our score of the other evening?" Even more forceful is the reminder at the beginning of the game: "By the way, don't you owe me ———— dollars from the other night?"

In extreme cases, and particularly if the debtor has been—or could again be— a guest in the creditor's house, one may send a letter such as this:

Dear George:

I did not like to mention it last night, but I wondered if you remember an evening we spent playing bridge at Mrs. Lane's a month ago. As far as I can remember, at the end of that evening you owed me $84. I should not be writing to you now except that, in thinking it over, I decided that I should certainly want you to write me if I had forgotten such a debt. Perhaps I am entirely mistaken about the whole thing. In any case, please let me know.

Sincerely,

Henry

A letter such as this should never be sent to someone who quite honestly may have forgotten such a debt. It is only a last recourse, to be used when one is almost certain that evasive tactics are being used by the other. The advantage of such a letter is that it enables a man to take a measure of his opponent. If he receives no answer or acknowledgment of this letter, he may or may not want to invite the other again to his house according to the strictness of his standards; but it becomes absolutely incumbent upon him never to subject other guests in his house to any game for stakes at the same table with this man.

The only possible answer to any of these reminders is the fullest expression of regret at having forgotten the debt and of gratitude for the reminder. Any suggestion of annoyance is bad taste, bad sportsmanship, and bad manners, even if one is justified in feeling that the reminder has been a little officious. This answer to the letter suggested above is an example of the right attitude:

Dear Henry:

I cannot tell you how grateful I am to you for reminding me about the $84 I owe you. I had a most uncomfortable feeling that there was some situation of this kind but I lost my little notebook the next day and have only been able to worry about it ever since. I enclose my very belated check with many thanks again for your kindness in reminding me.

As ever,

George

CHEATING

If one is a guest and notices that another guest is cheating, the most discreet thing to do, as a stranger among people who are old friends, is to retire from the game under some pretext or other. This is particularly true if the cheat is losing, there being somehow less moral obligation to protect the others from losing money they have won by gambling than there is to protect them from losing more than they have already lost through the sharpness of the cheat. If the host is a friend, one might go to him and explain the situation.

As a host, of course, one's responsibilities and duties are much greater. No one wants a scene, but on the other hand one cannot permit innocent people to be fleeced in one's house, as though it were a gambling hall. The best thing to do, if the cheat has lost money, is to stop the game, saying, "I think we've all had enough of this; let's settle up now." If the cheat has won, the only thing to do is to call the whole thing off. One can join the game, or watch it for a few moments, and then break in with some such phrase as this: "I think this game is getting a little bit complicated, and if none of you minds, I'd like to call the whole thing off." These are, of course, most extreme measures and must be used with a sense of proportion. No matter how large or how small the stakes actually are, if the sums involved could conceivably be of the slightest material importance to any one of the guests, one's duty as host makes one of these disagreeable measures necessary.

If one is neither a guest nor a host, but a member of some club or organization, and one notices that a fellow-member is cheating, the best thing to do is to take the cheat aside and by subtle stages approach the final point, which is that unless he stops cheating you will report him to the officers of the club. If the cheat is the guest of a member, one should speak to the one who is responsible for bringing him to the club.

16

Clubs

THE CLUBS we are discussing here are not those which one can join automatically, by virtue of one's profession, political or religious affiliations, occupation, or achievements. We are discussing clubs in which election on personal grounds is the only means to membership. And, although there are a dozen different kinds of clubs such as these, ranging from university and college clubs to country clubs and purely social clubs, there are certain unwritten rules and customs common to them all.

FOUR CUSTOMARY RULES

The first rule is that members and their guests treat the club as though it were a second home. A man invites his friends there and entertains them as he would in his own house; he rings for the stewards as he would for the servants in his own house. For this reason, the staff, or stewards, of a club are never tipped; although there is usually a fund, to which members subscribe at Christmastime, for presents to the staff. Exceptions to this rule are very informal clubs, among them country clubs or clubs in small communities, but these are definitely exceptions to a widely observed rule.

Another rule common to most clubs is that members sign for meals and services and pay for such meals at the end of the month, instead of paying cash on the spot.

The third rule is that one should never entertain at a club, except, perhaps, in a private room, a guest who might be unacceptable to the other members. In a business club, or a college club, for example, one could quite properly entertain any guest who is, or even might be, the graduate of a college, or engaged in a business similar to that of other members of the club. But it is wiser not to use a club to which members are elected on a social basis to entertain business acquaintances who would never presumably be elected members. There are two reasons for this rule. The first is that one should not put a guest in such a position. The second is that, as a member, one must accept the policy and rules of the club. If there are rules of which one does not approve, the moment to protest is when one is considering membership. After accepting membership there is nothing to do but comply with the club's regulations and customs, or resign.

The fourth rule is that one should never propose oneself as a member of a club. A newcomer in a community must wait until he meets several members, after which he can suggest, or hint, that he would like to join the organization. But he should never write the governors of the club or take any other such formal steps on his own initiative. Exceptions to this are informal country clubs in small resorts; one may often quite properly write to the secretary of such a club requesting membership. But if there is any doubt it is best to stick to the rule.

Because men take clubs more seriously than women do, this chapter is written from a man's point of view. The customs in both men's and women's clubs are, however, essentially the same, and the few changes necessary (as for example, in addressing a board of woman governors) will be found at the end of this chapter.

HOW TO JOIN

In most clubs, the procedure of becoming a member starts when a friend, who is already a member, suggests that you might like to join the club. You inquire concerning the initiation fee and dues, and, if they are satisfactory, your friend becomes your proposer, and finds a seconder. Governors and trustees are often not permitted to act as proposer or seconder.

They then write letters of proposal somewhat as follows:

To the Governors of the Blank Club:
Gentlemen:

It gives me great pleasure to propose for membership in the Blank Club my friend, Mr. Edward Adams of New York. He is a graduate of St. Andrew's School and Harvard University, a member of the Racquet Club in New York and of the National Golf Links on Long Island. He is married and lives at 129 East 69th Street in New York. He is a member of the firm (or "a partner in the law firm," or "associated with the law firm") of Davis, Harley and Stevens.

I have known him for a number of years, and believe that he has all the qualifications necessary to make him a desirable member.

Sincerely yours,
Frederic Lashley

The seconder's letter is much the same:

To the Governors of the Blank Club:
Gentlemen:

I am very glad to second Mr. Edward Adams, who has been proposed for membership in the Blank Club by Frederic Lashley. Mr. Adams is . . . , etc.

These two letters should be accompanied by at least two other seconding letters from other members of the club, a matter which is looked after by the proposer. As a rule, the proposer also arranges to have the prospective member meet as many governors, or members, as possible before his name comes up for election. On these minor points, however, customs and rules may differ. A member who for the first time is proposing a friend might do well to follow the procedure by which he joined the club.

As soon as a new member has been elected, he will be notified of his election by the secretary of the club, who will enclose a request for the amount of the initiation fees and dues. The initiation fee is payable at once while dues are, as a rule, payable quarterly or semiannually.

HOW TO PROPOSE A NON-RESIDENT MEMBER

As the word implies, a non-resident member is one who lives outside the city. Some clubs have a definite ruling as to how far outside the city limits a man must live in order to qualify as a non-resident. Since a non-resident member may be expected to use the club very much less than a regular member, his dues will, usually, be less. The letters of proposer and seconder are very much the same as those of a regular member. For example:

"It gives me great pleasure to propose for non-resident membership, etc."

CONDUCT AS A MEMBER

If a member has complaints to make, or suggestions which he feels would be valuable on such matters as food or service, he should write directly to the chairman of the house committee; on such matters as the heating, the telephone service, or repairs to the building or grounds, etc., he may write to the governors themselves.

To the Governors of the Blank Club:
Gentlemen:

I beg to advise you that on Saturday, August 12th, I tried to reach the club by telephone for half an hour without success. As this is the third such experience, I hope that you will give this your attention in order that the service may be improved.

Sincerely yours,
Peter Hartwell

Guests may be brought to the club by a member as often as the bylaws of the club may allow. Many clubs have "Visitors' Books" in the hall and, when guests are brought for a meal, members are expected to write their names and addresses in this book. This does not usually apply when guests are only invited for a drink at the bar.

PUTTING UP A FRIEND

The question of putting up a friend at the club for the night, or for a week, is a little more complicated. In the first place, as a rule, one should not put up a friend who is a resident of the same city; indeed, most clubs have rules against it. Granted that the friend is a non-resident, the usual procedure is to write to the secretary.

To the Secretary of the Blank Club:
Dear Sir:

I would like to put up my friend, Mr. James Carroll, of New London, for a guest privilege in the club for one week. I hope that you will be kind enough to issue him a membership card. His present address is the Grandston Hotel, Park Avenue, New York.

Sincerely yours,
Robert Crowley

Two weeks is usually the maximum guest privilege permitted; for longer periods, a temporary membership must be secured and dues must be paid. In this case, a letter must be written to the governors, substituting the words, "temporary membership" or "thirty-day membership," etc. Three months' temporary membership is usually the club maximum. The only exceptions made to this rule are in the case of distinguished foreigners, who are often allowed a free membership of six months.

A guest who is being put up at a club has all the privileges of a full member. He signs for all meals and services, and settles his bill before or after leaving. The member who has arranged for his guest privileges is responsible for his behavior in the club and for any debts he may fail to pay.

CONDUCT AS A GUEST

The customs governing the behavior of a guest in a club are exactly the same as those concerning his behavior in another man's house. Unless he has been "put up" according to the formal procedure, he must never give any of the staff an order; he must not take it upon himself to organize his own entertainments; he must not make a complaint about the service or anything else; and he must ask his host's permission to telephone, since he will have to give the member's name to the operator when he makes his call. In addition, he must be careful not to wander around, since many clubs have strict restrictions as to which rooms a guest may use.

HOW TO RESIGN

To resign from a club, one must write a letter to the governors, well before the time that the next dues are payable, giving some explanation for the resignation. The most usual letter is that pleading absence as an excuse.

To the Governors of the Blank Club:
Gentlemen:

I regret very much to inform you that I must tender my resignation as a member of our club. I shall be away from the city for so long that I will not be able to use the club save at the rarest intervals. I have greatly enjoyed my membership and hope you will believe how sorry I am to discontinue so many pleasant associations.

Sincerely yours,
Geoffrey Hoffman

COUNTRY CLUBS

The suggestions given above apply to pretty nearly all clubs, from the most strictly governed social clubs to the more liberal athletic and university clubs, in all matters not explicitly covered by the written bylaws of the club.

It would be impossible here to discuss all the variations that might apply to the different kinds of clubs, but it may be useful to suggest a few of the widely accepted customs concerning country clubs and such city clubs as maintain courts for squash or tennis. To members, these rules and customs will be familiar, but the following hints may be helpful to one who is to become a guest.

Golf Courses

In country clubs, it is the standard practice for guests to pay a special "greens fee" for the privilege of using the golf course. This, together with a standard payment to the caddy, may be settled for at once, or else charged to the member who has invited the guest in question. Tips to caddies are, in most clubs, optional. Guests should always offer to pay their hosts for greens fees and caddies, and the hosts usually accept. Other customs and courtesies of golf are discussed on page 81 in the chapter, "Games and Sports."

Tennis Courts

A charge for using the courts is made, but guests do not, inflexibly, offer to pay this charge as they do greens fees. A very common practice in all clubs where there are squash courts or tennis courts is for a member who wants to play to ask the professional in charge of the courts to make up a game for him. (See also "Tennis," page 82, in the chapter, "Games and Sports.")

WOMEN'S CLUBS

All the above suggestions apply equally to women's clubs, with a few necessary changes.

The first two are simple: In writing a board of governors, the salutation is "Ladies"; in writing the secretary, the salutation is "Madam."

The third change is a little more complicated. In proposing a friend for membership, the letter may differ quite a bit from that which a man would write. In a letter to the governors of a social club, the woman's maiden name, education, and any charitable or political activities would be included as a matter of course. Her parents would be mentioned if they, or their names, might be known to the governors; or, if not her parents, her husband. But if she were working, her job would be mentioned only if it were particularly interesting, or if she held an important position. In a letter proposing a friend for membership in a professional club, her college would be mentioned, but not, perhaps, her school. Her husband's work would be included if it might interest the governors, but her work and achievements would be covered in full. Both letters should include a few flattering remarks and mention of her membership in other clubs, particularly of the same kind as that for which she is now being proposed. Some clubs may want information in even greater detail, but these two letters are examples of the average:

Letter to the Governors of a Social Club

To the Governors of the Madison Club:

Ladies:

It gives me great pleasure to propose for membership in the Madison Club my friend, Mrs. Henry Goddard Adams of New York. Mrs. Adams, who was Mary Winthrop Mason before her marriage, is the daughter of Senator and Mrs. Hugh Mason of Massachusetts. She is a graduate of Farmington and Vassar and a member of the Vincent Club of Boston.

Mrs. Adams is exceptionally attractive and charming; she has wide interests in civic and charitable work, and has been doing volunteer work for the Red Cross and Sydenham Hospital ever since she moved to New York last year. She has many friends who are members, and I am sure she will be a most valuable addition to the club.

> Sincerely yours,
> Lucy Delafield Crowley

If the husband were to be emphasized instead of the parents, the letter might read, ". . . my friend, Mrs. Adams of New York. Mrs. Adams, who was Mary Winthrop Mason before her marriage, is the wife of Henry Goddard Adams who served as Assistant Secretary of State in President Blank's cabinet."

Letter to the Governors of a Professional Club

To the Governors of the Fennimore Club:

Ladies:

It gives me great pleasure to propose for membership in the Fennimore Club my friend, Mrs. Edward Beecher of New York. Mrs. Beecher, whose professional name is Sarah Underwood, is a graduate of Bryn Mawr and a full professor of anthropology at Barnard College. Her husband, Dr. Beecher, is Associate Director of Medical Sciences in the Rockefeller Institute.

Mrs. Beecher is a most attractive woman—young and very charming. I am sure that she would be a most valuable addition to the membership of the Club.

Yours sincerely,
Eleanor Woodrow Coolidge

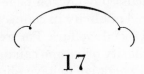

17

Personal Publicity

BEFORE WE DISCUSS the modern attitude toward publicity, it might be wise to define exactly what we mean. We are not discussing the publicity which men and women in business, in the arts, in professions, or in politics, must often accept or even seek, for professional or political reasons; the customs concerning this are a matter of business, professional, and political practice. Nor are we discussing the publicity which may appear in the news sections, the columns, or the editorials of newspapers and magazines. These are the province of freedom of the press and cannot, as a rule, be controlled by individuals. The subject of this chapter is the publicity in which the people involved, or their families, have obviously co-operated. Their co-operation is most obvious, of course, when they have allowed themselves, their house, or their family to be photographed; or when they have sent an announcement to the newspapers. For this reason, the first point in connection with all publicity is that one must be extremely careful about the integrity and responsibility of any publication before co-operating in any publicity. Otherwise, since one's co-operation is obvious, one will be blamed for any errors of taste of which the editors may be guilty.

The question that instantly arises is, What are the modern standards of taste concerning publicity? What publicity is considered dignified? What publicity can one seek and what can one accept? The answer is still based on the old-fashioned dictum: A woman's name should appear in a newspaper only three times—when she is born, when she marries, and when she dies. These three events were felt to be matters of record and factual information, rather than publicity. Publicity was considered ill-bred. Although the modern attitude is very different from this, traces of this dictum can still be found. It is still true, with one great exception, that the only way in which one should openly seek publicity is to send announcements of births and deaths, engagements and weddings to the newspapers. (These announcements are fully discussed below, on page 97.) The great exception is made in favor of organized publicity in connection with charitable institutions, civic projects, and social welfare. For example, as the head of the publicity committee of a charity drive one can quite properly badger publications for space. One may arrange to have photographs taken, or stories written, involving oneself or any co-workers, provided only that the purpose is to benefit the cause. As a member of any committee, especially as an important member, one should be willing to co-operate in all the dignified publicity which is usually involved. This is so accepted and so firmly grounded in public opinion that willingness to co-operate has become a matter of duty rather than choice. Very often, however, the judgment of publicity agents or even of the most responsible editors is not a sure guide in deciding what is dignified. Apart from the usual standards of common sense, there is only one reliable yardstick, and that is relevancy.

The best way to explain what is relevant and what is irrelevant is to give an example: In the society columns of a newspaper, announcement is made by the parents of the bride of the marriage of Miss Barker to Mr. Wilson. Apart from the bare facts sent by the family (see page 98) there are fuller details concerning Miss Barker and Mr. Wilson, which have been gathered by the society editor from newspaper files and from a conversation with the mother of the bride. Details concerning the bride's ancestry, the special decorations of the reception rooms, etc., are relevant. Details concerning the size of Mrs. Barker's house, the number of her household staff, whether or not she has a swimming pool or tennis court, are irrelevant and in extremely bad taste. Equally irrelevant, since this is a society page and not a legal review, are any details concerning scandals, law cases, or divorces in which members of the family have been involved.

If an announcement is being made of the remarriage of a widow or widower, mention of the previous marriage should be considered relevant, and the date of the death of the first wife or husband may also be given. In the case of divorcées, the previous marriage is also mentioned, and often the date of the divorce. After one has sent an announcement to a newspaper, if the society editor should telephone, one may quite properly give relevant information. If information of any other kind is asked for, one should refuse, adding a request that such details be omitted. Whether they will be or not, depends on the policy and integrity of the newspapers.

NEWSPAPER ANNOUNCEMENTS

In each column below are, first, the bare facts which the family may give in writing or on the telephone, to the newspaper. (Letters should be addressed to the society editor at the newspaper.) Following immediately after are details which society editors may want to include in a column with the family's announcement. Such information is never sent by the family, but it may quite properly be given at the request of the editor.

Births

(See page 612 for ways to announce a birth privately, and ways to avoid.)

Announcement Sent by the Family:

"Mr. and Mrs. John J. Morris of 333 East 57 Street, and Greenwich, Connecticut announce the birth of a son, Peter Lowell Morris, on July 7 at the Doctor's Hospital" (or . . . the birth of their second son and third child . . . etc.).

Information Given on Request:

"Mrs. Morris is the former Geraldine Perry, the daughter of Mr. and Mrs. Ian Perry of Edinburgh, Scotland. Mr. Morris, who graduated from the Harvard Law School this spring, is the son of Mr. and Mrs. George Edward Morris of Providence, Rhode Island" (or "Mr. Morris is a partner in," or, "associated with the firm of . . .").

The adoption of a child is not announced.

Engagements

Announcement Sent by the Family:

"Mr. and Mrs. George Edward Abbott of Farmington, Connecticut, announce the engagement of their daughter, Miss Isabel Greenway Abbott, to Mr. Charles Russell Polk, the son of Mr. and Mrs. Harvey Mansfield Polk of Cleveland, Ohio."

NOTE: If there are no parents to make the announcements, the fiancée's guardian or grandparents can do so, or her brother or sister. In the case of an older woman, this form is often used: "Announcement is made of the engagement of Miss ———, daughter of the late Mr. and Mrs. ———, to Mr. ———." If the fiancée's parents are divorced, this impersonal form often makes an awkward situation easier: "Announcement is made of the engagement of Miss Bridget Mary Jones, daughter of Mrs. Seaforth Jones of ——— and of Mr. Charles Hay Jones of ———, to Mr. ———." Or the announcement may be made in the mother's name only: "Mrs. Seaforth Jones . . . announces the engagement of her daughter . . ."

Information Given on Request:

"Miss Abbott is a graduate of Miss Porter's school in Farmington and of Bryn Mawr College. For the last year she has been working in the social service department of the Maternity Center. Mr. Polk is a graduate of Phillips Exeter Academy and of Dartmouth College. During the war he served as a Captain in the 102nd Division in France and Germany. Since then he has been associated with the General Electric Company."

Engagements of Young Widows

The engagements of older widows and divorcées are not usually announced. (See also note under "Engagements" above.)

Announcement Sent by the Family:

"Mr. and Mrs. Thomas Emerson Ashforth of 34 East 68th Street announce the engagement of their daughter, Mrs. William Wadsworth Warren, to Mr. Philip Dunbar Osborne, son of Mrs. Philip Pratt Osborne and the late Mr. Osborne of Detroit, Michigan. Mrs. Warren is the widow of the late William Wadsworth Warren and before her marriage was Miss Mary Elizabeth Ashforth."

Information Given on Request:

"Mr. Osborne was graduated from St. Mark's School, Amherst College, and the Yale Law School. During the war he served abroad as a captain in the American Field Service. He is associated with the firm of Milbank, Davis, Smith and Pearson."

Weddings

(See note under "Engagements" above.)

Announcement Sent by the Family:

"Mr. and Mrs. George Edward Abbott of Farmington, Connecticut, announce the marriage of their daughter, Miss Isabel Greenway Abbott, to Mr. Charles Russell Polk, the son of Mr. and Mrs. Harvey Mansfield Polk of Cleveland, Ohio. The wedding took place yesterday afternoon" (or "on October 14") in St. Bartholomew's Chapel in Farmington."

Information Given on Request:

Details as for engagement announcement on preceding page, above; also details concerning the wedding dress; the ushers' and bridesmaids' names; the place where the reception was given; any plans for the wedding trip; and mention of plans for the future. The standard wording is: "After a short trip to ———, Mr. and Mrs. Polk will live in ———."

Re-marriages

(Announcement of the wedding of a widow follows the form given above for the announcement of the engagement of a widow; the following form is for divorcées only.)

Announcement Sent by the Family:

"Mr. and Mrs. Cooper Halsey of Sheridan, Wyoming, announce the marriage of their daughter, Mrs. Halsey Burton, to Dr. Robert Briggs of Denver, Colorado. The wedding took place on July 12, on Mr. and Mrs. Halsey's ranch near Sheridan," or "in Mr. and Mrs. Halsey's house in Sheridan." (A phrase which should not be used is "Mr. and Mrs. Halsey's home.")

Information Given on Request:

"Mrs. Briggs, whose marriage in 1943 to Mr. Henry Grant Burton terminated in divorce in 1945, was the former Phyllis Jane Halsey. Dr. Briggs, the son of Mrs. Latham Briggs and the late Mr. Latham Briggs, served in the South Pacific during the war and has since been a member of the staff of the General Hospital in Denver."

Deaths

(See also page 143 in the chapter, "Funerals and Mourning.")

Announcement Sent by the Family:

"Gordon, George, on Sunday, August 14, at New London, Connecticut. Husband of Mary Rutherford Gordon, father of Isabelle Rutherford Gordon and George Gordon, Junior. Funeral at the Church of the Resurrection, Tuesday, August 16, at 10 A.M. Burial at Woodlawn Cemetery."

Information Given on Request:

It is difficult to give an example of the kind of information that may be given at the request of the editor, who will write the obituary. The activities of a lifetime vary too much to make one or two examples of the customary obituary notices useful. In any case, since such notices are printed separately from the death notices sent by the family, the family is not responsible for the material in an obituary. This material is often found in the newspaper's files; if not, the editor in charge will probably telephone and ask to talk to a member of the family for further details. Information on any of the following can be given: business or occupation at the time of death; philanthropies and civic work; place and date of birth, parents' names; education, clubs, societies; a brief review of any business, professional, military, or political career; marriage, or marriages; the names of the surviving members of the family.

SOCIAL NOTES

On the society pages of many newspapers there are often little notices such as these:

"Mr. and Mrs. Hampden Brown of Rutland, Vermont, are staying at the Hotel Plaza."

"Mrs. Henry Dunham entertained at luncheon yesterday at the Tuileries Restaurant for her sister, Mrs. Douglas Potter of Los Angeles, California. Guests at the luncheon were . . ."

These perfectly harmless little notices are not usually within the control of the people involved. Hotels and restaurants, eager for publicity, often send lists of their guests to the society editors, who choose for publication the names which seem the most newsworthy. Such notices should not, however, be sent to the newspapers by those concerned. In very big cities, if the society editor should telephone asking for a list of guests or other information, it is better to refuse any details. In small towns, where a list of guests might be interesting and recognizable to a greater proportion of the readers, such details are relevant, and therefore not bad taste.

Another social notice often seen in small town newspapers is the following:

"Mrs. John Terhune of Atlanta, Georgia, is visiting Mr. and Mrs. Charles Cook Calhoun at Apple Tree Farm."

This, too, is perfectly harmless and acceptable, since many readers may be interested.

MAGAZINE PUBLICITY

The question of how much publicity to accept from magazines is a delicate one. A great deal depends on the character of the magazine, not only as to its integrity and responsibility, but also as to its readership and distribution. If one is the head of a nation-wide organization, such as the Infantile Paralysis Campaign, one can quite properly accept publicity in any reputable publication, no matter how widely it is distributed. The cause requires mass support and anyone would be quite justified in seeking mass publicity. This does not mean, however, that one need allow photographs to be taken of every corner of one's house, or material to be written about one's family or way of life. In a widely circulated magazine, one might be shown at one's desk, in one's office, on the lawn of one's house, in the doorway, or even in the living room. But a full reportage, for which the house and the whole family are photographed, and in which one's way of life is discussed, can properly appear only in magazines which are specially designed for a public interested in such matters. Any woman's magazine would fall into this category, and this is not an arbitrary custom but a matter of taste and sense and, finally, of relevancy.

POSING FOR ADVERTISEMENTS

The practice of posing for advertisements in which one's name will be used to endorse a commercial product is a comparative newcomer to the field of personal publicity. It runs directly counter to the old-fashioned opinion that all publicity is ill-bred. And one might expect, since traces of that dictum can still be found today, that to pose for a commercial advertisement would be considered hopelessly bad taste. Actually, under certain conditions, the practice is now considered acceptable by all but the most conservative.

Those who are asked to endorse a commercial product usually belong to one of two major categories: Either their names are newsworthy and interesting to the public because of their family connections, or they have accomplished something which makes their endorsement of the product valuable, whether or not their names are known. In this second category belong all those whose profession makes them expert in their fields: the home-economics experts who endorse household appliances or supplies; the baseball and golf champions who endorse sporting goods; the long-distance swimmers who endorse cigarettes or bathing suits. All these, to some extent, are covered by the customs and ethics of business practice, and are not properly the subject of this chapter.

The first group—those who are asked to pose because their names are newsworthy—are the ones with whom we are concerned. The practice of posing and lending one's name for advertisements is considered acceptable for women of this group, from the post-debutante age onward, but not before. Since they are obviously paid to pose, the incentive is the money they will receive, rather than the publicity, and public opinion seems to regard this indulgently, in the light of a legitimate windfall. Perhaps this explains why the practice is not good taste for men of this category: Men are apparently supposed to have more reliable sources of income.

The second consideration is the kind of product which, according to the standard of modern taste, can properly be endorsed in an advertisement. With one exception, the general rule is that one should endorse only strictly impersonal products, such as food, soft drinks, and cigarettes, which are used both by men and by women. The exception is cosmetics which are designed to beautify. Perfume, cold cream, and face soaps are considered acceptable; others, such as deodorants and tooth powders, are not.

The next question is how, and how much, one should be photographed. The answer to this depends, of course, largely on the product. If one is endorsing a food, soft drink, or a cigarette, the advertising company will probably ask for a photograph taken in one's living room or dining room, showing one using the product. These photographs are considered acceptable and so are those less directly linked to the product, showing the endorser, in evening dress, perhaps, in a photograph obviously designed only to add a certain atmosphere to the page.

In cosmetic advertisements, there are often two photographs, one showing the endorser in evening dress, the other showing her at work. This custom has now become an accepted form. The photograph showing the endorser at work may even be considered desirable if it is charitable or social service work, in that such work indicates a sense of civic responsibility. One should avoid, however, any photographs showing one in the process of using or applying a cosmetic.

. The last question is what should be said in the text accompanying the photograph, and, again, relevancy is the yardstick. In an advertisement for a soft drink, there might be a phrase to indicate that the endorser entertains a great deal and very well. This would be relevant. In an advertisement for a cosmetic, her good looks would probably be mentioned in the text. In most advertisements, any details about her travels or accomplishments might be considered relevant because they suggest wider knowledge and experience, both of which enhance the value of her endorsement. Her husband's business connections, the size of his fortune, or hers, or any reference to a former marriage, are all irrelevant details and should be avoided.

Also to be avoided are such pretentious and commercial phrases as: "society leader"; "member of the smart" (or "social") "set"; "Social Registerite"; "exclusive"; "palatial country home"; "beautiful country estate"; "Park Avenue home." For the first four there are no possible substitutes, and the whole idea should be abandoned. The last three might read "big house in the country"; "lovely country place at . . ."; and "modern" (or "classic eighteenth century," or other) "apartment on Park Avenue." As a rule, advertising companies will submit proofs of the text with the photographs, and both should be carefully looked over.

PUBLICITY FOR ITS OWN SAKE

Publicity for its own sake is not always approved by good usage. And the way to decide whether or not to accept is to ask oneself, "Why am I considering accepting?" Suppose, for example, that a school official telephones the mother of one of the pupils, asking if the child may be photographed for a school circular or yearbook. If no names are to be used, or if the publication is to be sent to a few people only (perhaps the parents of the other pupils) then the child's mother may quite properly give her permission; her motive is obviously to help the school.

But if a magazine editor should ask to do "a story" about a young girl, complete with photographs of all her activities, a mother with good taste will never agree, because there is no obvious reason for her permission except her desire for publicity for her daughter.

It is perfectly good taste, and good usage, to allow a dignified "portrait" to be taken for an appropriate publication: a conservative newspaper, or a magazine directed to an appropriate audience. It is also good usage to permit a photograph to be taken for a very limited and specific audience. If the young girl is a wonderful golfer, for example, she might quite properly be photographed playing golf for a golfer's magazine. And it is just conceivable that there might be special circumstances, such as a serious sociological study, which could involve a very broad report of one's way of life without any suggestion of publicity-seeking or bad taste.

What immediately causes the accusation of bad taste is a private citizen's accepting publicity, not for the benefit of any worthy cause, not as a result of achievement in any recognized field, not as a duty attached to public or official life, but only for "fun" or for the sake of publicity. In such circumstances, the more detailed the "story" and the more intimate the details, the worse the taste. This is true of grown men and women, of young men, and particularly of young girls and children.

18

The Choice of Words

ONCE, when Bertrand Russell, mathematician, philosopher and Cambridge don, was asked which was correct, "None of them were able to deny it," or, "None of them was able to deny it," he answered, " 'None was' is right, of course; but who wants to be the kind of person who makes a point of saying, 'None of them was'?"

And in Lord Russell's answer lies the whole range of subtle shading between grammar and usage, between the impeccable pedant who firmly says, "To whom are you speaking?" and the blithely incorrect moderns who, with confident candor, say, "It's me." Some bad grammar is good usage; some phrases, although technically correct grammatically (for example, "I cannot attend the gathering at your residence") are appallingly bad usage. Perfection lies in a knowing mixture of the two. And to the uninitiated, the most maddening element in the whole question of good usage is the apparent senselessness of the choices, and the inconsistency of the points of departure.

There are, in fact, only three consistent bases for choosing one word in preference to another. The first mostly concerns writers and orators: Choose a word with a Saxon root in preference to one with a Latin root; for example, "shut" rather than "close." The second expresses the modern impatience with all pretentiousness: Always choose a simple word rather than an evasive, complicated euphemism; "come to" or "go to" rather than "attend"; "house" not "residence." And always use English words instead of flourishing an unnecessary foreign phrase. The third involves words called "commercialisms": Always use a simple or classic word rather than one which has crept into the language through business usage; "stockings," for example, is a better word than "hosiery."

Beyond these guides, there is only the arbitrary, random choice of modern taste, of a fashion in words which make up the almost-secret language by which strangers recognize each other as not "the kind of person who says, 'None of them was.' " Why is "sofa" part of this vocabulary, and why are "couch" and "davenport," definitely not? The only possible answer is, "Because."

It would be difficult to list all the keywords of this language. Fowler's *Modern English Usage*, published by the Oxford University Press, is a profound and impressive treatise—and most amusing—on the subject. Here, we can list only a few of the most objectionable words and phrases, most of them objectionable for esoteric reasons of taste rather than grammar. Further to complicate the matter, the taste is that of a relatively small group in the English-speaking world, and it can change very quickly.

MISUSED WORDS AND PHRASES

AFFAIR should not be used to mean "party," "dinner," or "dance." It is correctly used in other ways; for example, when it means "concern" or "business"; as, "It's a family affair," meaning the concern of the family only.

ALLOW ME should not be used by itself as a full sentence, as it is, regrettably often, by a man offering to do some small service for a woman. If a man wants to open a taxicab door or a restaurant door, he can do it in silence. If the woman seems to be embarking on a palpably impossible task, such as lifting a heavy bag, the man can intervene saying, "Let me do that," or, "Here, let me carry that for you."

AQUA should not be used to mean "aquamarine-blue." As in the case of turquoise, it is bad usage to say, "It was gray with a belt of aqua" or even "of aquamarine." Since both aquamarine and turquoise are the names of stones, it is more accurate to say "aquamarine-blue" or "turquoise-blue" and, though good usage does not necessarily follow either accuracy or good grammar, in this case they all agree. Further, aquamarine must always be pronounced with a good flat "a" as in "candy"—never "ah-qua."

ATTEND should not be used instead of "go to" or "come to." "Attend" is also wrongly used in the phrase, "She attended Westover School." Better phrases are, "She was a student at Westover"; "She studied at" (or "went to") "Westover."

BOY FRIEND should not be used instead of "beau." There is a further reach in which "boy friend" can be amusingly used—a sort of willful double-twist, implying much more than appears on the surface. "He was definitely not the boy-friend type" would suggest one who lacked a certain open or cozy quality.

BUFFET should not be used instead of "buffet supper" or "buffet luncheon." "She asked me to come to a buffet" is wrong because a buffet can only be: 1) the food set out on a buffet table; or 2) in a more technical and French sense, the sideboard or table on which such food is laid. Modern usage does, however, sanction such an abbreviation as, "Is it a regular dinner, or buffet?" Buffet is one of the few French words to which correct English usage gives its French pronunciation. The French "bu" sound is difficult in English, but "*boo*-fay" is better than "buff-*fay*."

CARE TO should not be used instead of "like to" or "want to."

CHAISE should not be used instead of "chaise longue." ("Chaise lounge" simply doesn't exist, either in French or English.)

CHIFFONIER should not be used instead of "bureau" or "chest of drawers."

CLASS should not be used instead of "kind." "They are the class of people" should never be used for "They are the kind of people."

CLASSY. See "high-toned" and "high-class." Where "classy" is used to mean "high-class," use "good." When "classy" means "high-toned," it should be forgotten.

CONTACT should not be used as a transitive verb; and the noun should be used less often than it is: "I must contact him" should be, "I must reach him." "He has lots of business connections" is better than ". . . business contacts."

CORSAGE should not be used instead of "flowers," or "bunch of flowers," or "flowers to wear," or "bouquet."

COSTLY should not be used instead of "expensive," in speaking of something that cost a lot of money. It is good usage to say "a costly battle"; but "a costly fur coat" is bad usage.

COUCH should not be used instead of "sofa."

CREAMER should not be used instead of "cream pitcher" or "cream jug."

DATE should not be used to describe an individual. "He's my date for tomorrow evening" is bad usage. "He's my beau for tomorrow evening" is correct. But it is good usage to say, "I have a date for tomorrow," meaning an engagement.

DAVENPORT should not be used instead of "sofa."

DEN (or STUDY) should not be used instead of "library."

DETECT should not be used instead of "notice" or "see" or "smell."

DINNER should not be used instead of "luncheon" or "lunch." Dinner is in the evening, except for Christmas dinner or Thanksgiving dinner or some other such institution which may take place at any hour of the day. Sunday dinner is definitely not included as an institution. "Come to lunch Sunday" is correct, even if there is only a cold meal in the evening; the fact that the heavier of the two meals is at midday does not mean that it should be called dinner unless local custom is definitely to the contrary. Purists insist that "luncheon" is the noun and "lunch" the verb and that, therefore, "the lunch was delicious" is wrong. At the moment, modern usage, though it leans toward this view, permits either. "Supper," which is technically a light late meal after dinner, is often misused to mean dinner, but this misuse is less offensive than the misuse of "dinner."

DISTINCTIVE should not be used instead of "original," "distinguished," "personal," or "unusual."

DOG should not be used instead of "hound," meaning one of the pack of hounds. "Dog" is correct in speaking of sporting dogs, such as retrievers and pointers, which hunt separately and not in packs. The only correct use of the word "dog" in connection with hounds is in making a sex differentiation: "The dogs are in this kennel, the bitches on the other side."

DO HAVE or "Do you have?" should not be used instead of "Have you?" "Do you have the time?" is appallingly bad. "Do" and "have" are often combined when "must" is implied. "Oh, do you *have* to go?" is perfectly good usage, although "Must you go?" would be better. They may also be used to-gether to imply custom—"Do you have much snow here in winter?"—or sometimes for emphasis.

DON'T HAVE should not be used instead of "haven't" or even "haven't got." "You haven't a moment to spare" is perfect. "You haven't got a moment to spare" is good usage. "You don't have a moment to spare" is a violation of the English language. As in the case of "do have," "don't" and "have" can be used together when compulsion is implied.

DRAPES OR DRAPERIES should not be used instead of "curtains." The excuse that "curtains" means thin organdy curtains and that "draperies" must be used for heavy curtains is not valid. If one means organdy or ruffled muslin curtains, one should say so. Anything that hangs by a window or between two rooms to screen one from another, is a curtain.

DRESSER should not be used instead of "dressing-table," "bureau," or "chest of drawers."

DROP should not be used instead of "come" or "stop." "Do stop in for a cup of tea" is better than "Do drop by" or "Do drop in."

ESCORT should not be used instead of "The man I was dining with" or, "The man who had taken me to the theater." "Escort" should be used only as a verb, and then it is es-*cort*, unless it refers to the guard that is given the central figure of a parade, pronounced *es*-cort.

ESTATE should not be used instead of "country place" or "place" or "house." In America, "estate" is good usage only when it describes the property (which would include all the assets, not only real estate) of someone who has died.

FABRIC should not be used instead of "material" or "stuff" unless one is speaking in a technical or poetic sense. "That dress is the most lovely fabric" is wrong. "The fabric of her life had worn thin" is right, and so is "This fabric has a tensile strength of fourteen pounds."

EQUALLY AS should not be used instead of "equally." "As," in this case, is superfluous and bad usage.

FELLOW or FELLA or FELLER should not be used instead of "beau."

FOLKS should not be used instead of "family" or "relatives."

FORMALS should not be used instead of "evening clothes." "We're going to wear formals" should be "We're going to wear evening clothes" or "We're going to dress." "A beautiful formal gown" should be "A beautiful evening dress." "Formal" is never used as a noun, but only as an adjective meaning "according to a written or unwritten set of rules."

FUNCTION should not be used instead of "party," "dinner," "reception," "musicale" or whatever.

FRAT should not be used as an abbreviation of "fraternity."

GEMS should not be used instead of "precious stones" or "jewelry." "She was covered with gems" is bad usage. A gem is 1) a technical word of jewelers, describing a flawless or particularly fine stone; or, 2) in modern usage, a word used to describe the best of its kind, the epitome of a particular category: "Among funny hats, this one was absolutely a gem," "What followed was a gem of double-talk."

GENTLEMAN should not be used instead of "man," in speaking of one's own friends or acquaintances. Exceptions to this rule are employers who use "gentlemen" in speaking of their friends to their employees. Employees also use "gentleman" when speaking to their employer of a friend of the employer. See the heading "Lady" in this list of words for a fuller discussion, as the same rules apply to both words.

GIFT should never be used instead of "present," except for stock phrases such as "gift certificate" which have a technical implication, or traditional phrases such as "the gifts of the Magi." "Wedding gift" and "Christmas gift" are wrong. A correct use of "gift" is in the sense of "talent": "She has a gift for mimicry" or "He is a most gifted musician."

GIRLS should not be used instead of "women" when those described are over 25 and obviously no longer girls. Four women, all lunching together and all over 40, are too often described as "girls." "I'm having a girls' luncheon" should be, in these circumstances, "I'm having some women to lunch."

GOOD FRIEND should not be used instead of "great friend." "He is a very good friend" is correctly used to describe a man who is especially loyal and understanding in friendship. "He is a

good friend of ours" is incorrectly used to describe merely a friend whom one often sees. A similar mistake is the use of the phrase, "a close friend": "An intimate friend" is correct.

GORGEOUS should not be used instead of "beautiful" or "magnificent" or "attractive." To use "gorgeous" correctly, the object described must be really gorgeous; that is, highly colored or brilliant; as, "a gorgeous sunset," "a gorgeous day." "A gorgeous fur coat" is bad usage and implies only that the fur coat struck the observer as being extremely expensive.

GOWN should not be used instead of "dress," except for "nightgown," "dressing gown" and "tea gown," which are correct. Nightdress is correct also, but a little quaint.

GRACIOUS should not be used instead of "very kind"; as, "your very kind letter," "your very kind invitation." Perhaps because of the modern antipathy to all forms of condescension, the word "gracious," with implication of a superior bending to an inferior, is now used only in a derisive sense, or in condemnation. "Oh, she was very gracious indeed" would not be a flattering remark. "She lives graciously" should never be used except deliberately to imply a rather laughable condescension.

HIGHBALL should not be used instead of "whiskey and soda," "rye and soda," etc.

HIGH-CLASS should not be used to mean "good" or "distinguished." "It was a high-class restaurant" is appalling. What this phrase usually means is, "It was a good, but very expensive restaurant," and there is absolutely no reason for not saying so. "High-class food" should be "good food"; "a high-class person" should be "a nice man" or "a distinguished man," or "an outstandingly good man." (See also the use of the word "person.")

HIGH-TONED. There is almost no permissible simile for this. "It was meant to be very high-toned" would be better as, "It was meant to be very smart." But the best mental usage would omit the whole idea.

HOME should be used less often than it is, to mean "house." This is perhaps the most important and most ill-used word. "Home" is incorrect when used to describe a building: "a beautiful home," "a country home," "your own home" are all wrong. "House" is the right word here. "Home" is correctly used when a preposition is used or implied: "at home," "going home," "home-grown," "of home," "homemade." "At your home" is wrong because "your" comes between "at" and "home"; "at your house" should be used instead. For the same reasons, "near home" is good usage, while "near your home" or "near my home" is not. The only exceptions are idioms as, "It's home to me"; "that remark hit home"; "that means home"; "this seems like home"; or clichés like "home, sweet, home." The word "home" means essentially something intangible. It cannot be used correctly to describe a building or furniture; it can be used correctly in describing an atmosphere; as, "It had a cozy, homelike aspect."

HOSE or HOSIERY should not be used instead of "stockings." There is absolutely no excuse for a commercial word such as "hosiery" in normal conversation. "Hose," of course, is just as bad.

HOSTESS-GOWN should not be used for "teagown."

JACKET should not be used for "coat" when speaking of men's clothes. Exceptions are dinner jackets, Norfolk jacket and hunting jacket. But always use "riding coat" instead of "riding jacket."

LADY. This is a very complicated and delicate word to use correctly according to the standards of modern usage. It is correctly used in speaking to porters or waiters, or others to whom a woman's name is of no interest or importance; as, "No, this bag belongs to the lady over there," or, "The oysters are for the lady." "Lady" is also used by employers, in speaking to an employee of their own friends, or an employee's friends. And, similarly, employees use "lady" in speaking to an employer about a friend of the employer; as, "The lady you were to meet for luncheon . . ." In speaking of a friend or a potential friend, the correct word is "woman." "She seems like an awfully nice woman," is good usage, while ". . . an awfully nice lady" is not.

There are, however, certain exceptions to this rule. The first is when you mean to describe a woman who has particular qualities of character, mind, or upbringing. A typical example of this would be: "Jane isn't at all kind, but she *is* a lady, so you're safe in putting that bore next to her at dinner; at least, she'll make an effort to talk to him." In other words, through training, Jane will recognize her responsibilities as a guest, and try to make the man feel at ease; Jane has a quality on which one can rely, even though, unfortunately, it is one of manner and not one of character. Or, "Mary may not know right from left, but she is a lady," would describe a woman whose training does not encompass the technicalities of social responsibility and behavior, but whose qualities are such that the word "lady" is needed to describe them.

Other exceptions are in speaking of older women, and to an acquaintance about an acquaintance. "The lady I sat next to at dinner at your house" is a better and more formal phrase than "the woman I sat next to." In speaking of a very much older woman, to whom respect is due because of her years, the word "woman" is not used with the word "old," perhaps because of the disrespect attached to the word "old," as in "just any old thing." In many phrases "old" is used casually: "A wonderful old lady," "a nice old lady" rather than "old woman." When the word "old" is used deliberately to emphasize the point of age, it is not necessary to say "lady"; "She is a very old woman" would be correct in this sense. The English title "Lady" is not, of course, involved in these rules.

LAVATORY should not be used instead of "bathroom."

LIKE should not be used instead of "as" or "as though" or "as if." "Like we were saying" and "like he was going" are appalling. "As we were saying" and "As though he were going" are correct. (See also "WAS" below.)

LOCATE should not be used instead of "find."

LOUNGE should not be used instead of "sofa" or instead of "the sitting room" or "living room" of a house. "Lounge" is properly used only as a verb. However, "the ship's lounge" or "the hotel lounge," although unattractive phrases, are essentially correct.

MAN should not be used to mean "beau." "Bring your man" is wrong, although "Bring your girl" is good usage. "Bring your beau" or "Bring a man" are right. "Man" instead of husband is in the category of "ball and chain": outmoded and unattractive slang.

MOTHER (or MOMMA) should not be used by a man in speaking to, or of, his wife. This belongs in the category of "Father" or "Papa" used by a woman in the same way, and "Junior" as a name for a little boy. These words are not only bad usage, but surely they also are psychologically unhealthy. They all indicate a relationship that is indirect and, so to speak, contingent. Why should a man address his wife through the children? And why should "Junior" be denied his individuality? "Brother" and "Sister" as nicknames seem to escape the curse of "Junior" perhaps because they imply a less egotistical attitude on the part of the adults who bestowed them on the children. None of this applies, of course, to the obviously correct phrase "your mother" or "your father" used by a parent, or others, in speaking to children.

"MR. JONES" should not be used instead of "Charles" or "my husband." No woman, unless she is very old, or very old-fashioned, should speak of her husband as "Mr. Jones" except to an employee or tradesman or to a stranger to whom she has never been introduced. If she is old enough to belong to the school which addressed a husband to his face as "Mr. Jones," that is another matter. "Charles" is used informally, whenever the husband would be recognized by that name; "my husband" is more formal and can be used with strangers to whom "Charles" might be equivocal. In the same way, a man should say, "Mary" or "my wife," not "Mrs. Jones."

NAVY should not be used instead of "navy-blue." "She was beautifully gowned in a navy sheer," should be, "She was beautifully dressed in a thin, navy-blue dress," or, "She wore a beautiful dress of navy-blue chiffon."

ONE HUNDRED FIFTY should not be used instead of "one hundred and fifty." This unfortunate little newcomer in the ranks of bad usage seems to have been born of the radio. "One fifty" is an abbreviation sanctioned by modern usage —"one hundred fifty" is not. For the same reason, "Nineteen hundred and nineteen" and "nineteen-nineteen" are both good usage but "Nineteen hundred nineteen" is not.

ODOR should not be used instead of "smell" or "perfume."

PARDON should not be used instead of "Sorry," "I'm sorry," "Excuse me" or even, "I beg your pardon." "Pardon me," like "Pardon my glove," is so famously bad that it has slipped into the language of satire. "Pardon" should not be used, either, by one who has misunderstood or failed to hear. "What did you say?" or, "I'm sorry—what did you say?" are the correct phrases here. Even "What?" is better than "Pardon?"

PARTY should not be used in the sense of "you and your party." "All of you," or "You and your friends," or "You and the others" are better phrases than "you and your party."

PEOPLE should not be used instead of "family." "How are your people?" should be, "How is your family?"

PERFUMERY is a word that should never be used as the plural of perfume. The correct word is "perfumes." Also correct, although markedly English, is the word "scent."

PERSON should not be used instead of "girl," "man," or "woman." Person is an indefinite term. "The person you were talking to on the telephone" is good modern usage, because the speaker does not know whether it was a man, woman, or child. "The person I was talking to" is bad usage, unless the speaker is being deliberately evasive. "Persons," in the plural, should always be "people" or, more formally, "those." "The persons behind me on the train" should be "The people behind me . . ." or, "Those who were behind me . . ."

PHONE should not be used instead of "telephone"—either as a noun or a verb.

PORTIERES should not be used instead of "curtains." This is a completely unnecessary Gallicism.

PRECIOUS should not be used instead of "wonderful" or "beautiful." "A precious baby," "a precious powder box" are both bad usage. "Precious" is correctly used with the word "stone" to describe jewels; as, "The window was full of precious stones"; or, in a further sense which is borrowed directly from the French, to describe an over-finicky intellectual or esthete; as, "He seems a little precious"; or an over-fine point; as, "I think that's a precious distinction between the two"; or something too self-consciously perfect; as, "The whole house was a little precious." Still another use of the word "precious" is sanctioned by modern usage—usually a willful exaggeration—as, "My address book is precious to me."

PREFER should not be used instead of "rather." "Prefer" should indicate a choice between two or more people or things. When it is used instead of "rather," it is not good usage. "I prefer not to" should be "I would rather not." "Of the two, I prefer Beethoven," would be perfectly correct. "Prefer" has a prim yet elaborate flavor and should really be avoided unless it is definitely necessary.

PROMINENT should not be used instead of "important," "well-known," or "distinguished."

QUICKIE should not be used instead of "quick drink." "Quickie" is objectionable not because it is slang, but because it implies a certain shame on the part of the speaker, as though to minimize the fact of drinking.

REALTOR should not be used instead of "real estate agent." Used in this way, it is a ridiculous euphemism, and its blood brothers are "mortician" for undertaker, "beautician" or "cosmetician" instead of "the girl in the beauty shop" or "beauty expert." Avoid them all.

RECALL should not be used instead of "remember."

REFINED should not be used instead of "well-bred" or "gentle" or "quiet." "Refined lady" should be "well-bred woman"; "refined voice" should be "a gentle voice"; "refined place" should be "quiet place" or even "attractive place."

REMAIN should not be used instead of "stay." "She remained with her parents" should be, "She stayed with her parents."

RESIDE should not be used instead of "live." "They reside in New York," should be, "They live in New York."

RESIDENCE should not be used instead of "house." "Residence" is correct only in an engraved invitation or when used by a domestic employee in answering the telephone: "Mrs. Jones' residence."

RETIRE should not be used instead of "go to bed" but it is correctly used to suggest backing away; as, "he retired in confusion."

RIDE should not be used instead of "drive." "It was a wonderful ride" refers, primarily, to a ride on a horse or any other animal. "It was a wonderful drive" means a drive in a car or carriage. The word "flight" must be used in connection with aeroplanes. The verbs "ride" and "drive" should be used in the same way as the nouns.

ROBE should not be used instead of "bathrobe," "dressing gown" or "wrapper." Nor should it be used to mean "motor rug."

ROSE should not be used instead of "pink" or "rose-red" or "rose-pink" or "rose-colored." "The walls are rose with a white border" should be, "The walls are rose-pink . . ." "Rose" is the name of a flower and it is bad usage to use the word "rose" by itself as a description of a color. (See also "Aqua.") If usage were consistent, which it is not, "lavender" would fall under the same rules. But for some reason, modern usage sanctions the word "lavender" without further qualification, as a description of color. To a lesser extent, "violet" also can be used by itself to describe a color. "Her dress was pale lavender with a violet sash," would be a perfectly acceptable sentence; whereas, "Her dress was pale rose with an aquamarine sash" definitely is not.

SELECT should not be used instead of "choose."

SETTEE should not be used instead of "sofa." "Settee," although not a word accepted by modern usage, has a rather attractive, old-fashioned flavor compared to such pretentious words as "davenport" or the Gallicism "couch."

SHADE should not be used instead of "color" unless it is really meant as a shade. "A beautiful shade of red" is correct, although "a beautiful red" is better usage. "That's a lovely shade" is wrong.

SHEER should not be used as a noun but only as an adjective. "Sheer material," "sheer folly," are good usages. "She wore a sheer" is not.

STATIONERY should not be used instead of "letter paper" or "writing paper." "Stationery store" or "stationer's" is correct.

STUNNING should not be used instead of "beautiful." "A stunning gown" is probably one of the worst phrases in the English language. "A stunning blow" is, of course, entirely correct.

SUITES should not be used instead of "sets" of furniture. A "suite" (which is pronounced "sweet") is a series, of connecting rooms, musical compositions, etc.

"TELL" GOOD-BYE should not be used instead of "say good-bye." "Tell him good-bye for me" is not as good a phrase as, "Say good-bye to him for me."

THEATER should not be used without being prefaced by "the": "I went to theater last night" is wrong; "I went to the theater" is right.

THOROUGHBRED should not be used instead of "purebred." A thoroughbred is a horse of an English breed first developed about 1725 in England. Every other animal is either "purebred" or not. A "thoroughbred sheep" or even a "thoroughbred Percheron," although permitted in a halfhearted way in the dictionary, are not phrases that show a sound knowledge of modern usage. "Purebred" or "pure-blooded" are correct.

TRICKY should not be used instead of "clever"; as, a "tricky idea"; or "attractive"; as, a "tricky dress." Both these phrases are wrong because modern usage sanctions the use of "tricky" only as meaning "wily"; as, "He seems too tricky"; or as meaning "difficult" or "complicated"; as, "It was a tricky problem."

TURQUOISE should not be used instead of "turquoise-blue," as a description of color. "Turquoise-blue trimming" is better than "turquoise trimming" unless it is actually trimmed with the stones. (See "Aqua.")

TUXEDO should not be used instead of "dinner jacket" or "evening clothes."

TYPE should not be followed immediately by a noun. "That's a nice type person," "useful type hat," are bad usage. "He's an extraordinary type,"

"That's the type of thing," are both good usage.

VAL should not be used to mean "Valenciennes" lace. A further unfortunate use of "val" is "Val-type lace."

VALISE should not be used instead of "bag" or "luggage" or "suitcase" because it is an unnecessary Gallicism.

VANITY should not be used instead of "dressing table" or "powder box."

"VERY" LOVELY should not be used instead of "very beautiful" or just plain "lovely." There seems to be absolutely no reasonable basis for the objection to the phrase, but it is offensive. A further point in connection with the word "lovely" is that "a lovely person," meaning a "gentle and lovable character," which was bad usage ten years ago, has now crept into the language and seems firmly lodged there.

WAS should not be incorrectly used instead of "were." Here, too, grammarians support modern usage. "If I was you" should be "If I were you," because the subjunctive is used "for a wish, volition, or condition [which is] improbable or contrary to fact." When the situation described is not in the definite past and is "contrary to fact"—a hypothesis, and not a statement of fact or possible fact—"were" must be used in place of "was" after the pronouns "I," "he," "she" or "it." "If it were wrong, he'd do it anyway," is a correct sentence. "If I was wrong, I'm sorry," is correct because the sentence admits the possibility of having made a mistake.

WEALTHY should not be used instead of "rich." The possession of a large fortune is still a rather delicate topic, it appears. Modern usage often cloaks it in a phrase: "They have lots of money," or "They're frightfully rich," or "They have an enormous income." But "They're wealthy people," or "They're very wealthy," is bad usage.

WELL-OFF should not be used instead of "comfortable." "They're very comfortably settled" is a modern substitute for the old-fashioned "well-off."

WRAPS should not be used instead of "coats," or even "things." "Wouldn't you prefer to drop your wrap in my room?" should be, "Wouldn't you rather leave your coat (or 'things') in my room?"

MISPRONUNCIATIONS

AVIATION is mispronounced "avviation." The *A* sound is long, as in "take."

BLOUSE is mispronounced "blowss" to rhyme with "mouse." It should be "blowz" to rhyme with "arouse." The French pronunciation "blooz" is old-fashioned.

BOUQUET is mispronounced "bow-kay"; "boo-kay" is correct. The first syllable should rhyme with "true."

BRASSIERE is mispronounced "brazeer"; "brass-yare" is correct.

CAVIAR is mispronounced "cah (or 'car')-viar." It should be "caviar" with a good flat clean "a" as in candy.

CHAUFFEUR is mispronounced "shofa." The correct French pronunciation is "show-*fur*" and this is correct in English also. To be entirely in accord with modern usage, the word "chauffeur" should be used only to describe a man who is employed to drive someone's private car; as, "The chauffeur of old Mrs. Barker's car."

CHIC is mispronounced "chick," instead of "sheek."

CHIFFON is mispronounced "shif-*fonn*." "Chiffon" is a French word and, the English pronunciation being not yet firmly established in good usage, it must still be pronounced in the French way. The only way to write the pronunciation in English is "*shee*-fong" but the ring of the "g" must be left out of the last syllable.

CHINESE is mispronounced "Chi-niece" instead of "Chi-knees."

CIGARETTE is mispronounced "*cig*-rette," instead of "cigar*ette*." All the accent should be on the final syllable; and there are three syllables.

DERBY is mispronounced "Darby" when it is used to describe a hard, Al Smith hat. "Darby" is the English pronunciation, correctly used in speaking of the great English horse race at Epsom Downs. A man's hard, round hat is called in England a "bowler" and, therefore, it is an absurd snobbism to say "darby hat," using the English pronunciation for a term the English themselves would never use. The race at Churchill Downs in America is the "Kentucky Derby," and a hard hat is a "derby," too.

DUKE is mispronounced "dook." The only correct pronunciation is "dewk" (see "new").

HEIGHT is mispronounced "heighth." The word ends in a clear *T* sound, not "th."

INTRICATE is mispronounced "intri-cate" instead of "*in*-tricate," with the first syllable heavily accented.

LINGERIE is mispronounced "lan-jer-ay" or "lon-jer-ee" in three long, terrible syllables. "Underclothes" is a good English word and should always be used instead of "lingerie." When one must say "lingerie" (for example, if a shop is called "The Blank Lingerie Shop") it should be pronounced in the French way, almost in two syllables and with a soft "g": "*lange*-ree."

MASSEUR is mispronounced "massewer" instead of "mass-*sir*."

MASSEUSE is mispronounced "mass-soose" instead of "masserz," with the *r* very lightly sounded. "Danseuse" and "chanteuse" often suffer the same fate; as do many others, such as "chartreuse," "diseuse."

NEW is mispronounced "noo." "New," "dew" and "avenue" should be pronounced "nyou," "dyou" and "avenyou." The same rule applies to "absolute." "Absolyute" is correct; "absoloote" is wrong.

OIL is mispronounced "erl." All "oi" sounds should be pronounced "oy" as in "boy."

PERFUME is mispronounced "per*fume*." The only correct pronunciation is "*per*fume," which is preferred in the dictionary; and, although "per*fume*" is given first as the pronunciation of the verb, usage leans toward "*perfume*" for the verb also.

PROGRAM is mispronounced "progrum." This is one of the most telling words in modern usage. "Progrum" is indefensible; "program" is correct, with a good flat "a" as in "gram."

SUIT is mispronounced "soot." It should always be "syout." (See "new.")

TOMATO is better pronounced "to-mah-to," as there is some logical support for this: It comes from the Spanish "Tomate" which is pronounced "tomah-tay." However, Webster calls "tomay-to" correct also.

VALET is mispronounced "val-lay" instead of "valet." When such a role exists, the man who fills it is called a "valet." The verb form, too, is good usage; as, "She valeted her husband like an expert."

It should be noted, however, that "ballet," most irrationally, does not follow this rule. It is pronounced "*bal*-lay."

VASE is mispronounced "vayss." "Vaze" is the correct modern usage. "Vahz" is a little old-fashioned.

19

Jobs

THIS CHAPTER is addressed to anyone who works in an organization, whether man or woman, as a volunteer or employee, full or part time. To the part-time worker, of course, fewer of the rules of manners will apply; fewer personal telephone calls, for example, will come in for one who works part time. But the underlying attitude of all workers should be the same: respect for superior officers, interest in the job, self-discipline in accord with the office routine, dignity, and self-respect. These can all add up to a pretty dreary whole if one does not add also a little charm and cheerfulness. But anyone who has ever worked in an organization knows that even a tight-lipped stoic is a more satisfactory co-worker, in the long run, than a gay rule-dodger who shifts work to others whenever possible and indulges in merry quips with outsiders at the expense of the organization's heads.

LOYALTY

The first point of manners and good taste is involved in this question of criticizing co-workers. Self-respect is intimately concerned with it. In every organization, there is a certain amount of conversation about personalities, and some of it will perhaps be criticism. Granted that such criticism stays within normal bounds and within the organization, it is not necessarily bad taste, although gossip is always an unwise practice. In criticizing co-workers to those outside the organization, however, bad taste enters at once, especially when the heads of the organization are being discussed. There are two explanations of this.

The first is that, in criticizing any co-worker, one is taking advantage of inside information not available to those outside the organization. The rule of good taste which prevents house guests from criticizing their hosts operates almost as imperatively here, as far as criticism on personal grounds is concerned. When it is a question of criticism on professional grounds, the rules of good taste are as strict as any professional code of ethics: One cannot, as a trusted member of the organization, take advantage of inside information for personal gain, even if the gain is nothing more than a moment's amusement with others. Criticism on ethical grounds redounds very much to the discredit of the worker himself. "If such are your associates," the listener feels like asking, "why do you work with them?"

The second explanation concerns criticism of the heads of the organization. Such criticism is in worse taste than any other not only because outsiders are more interested and more apt to remember what is said, but because the heads of an organization are responsible for its policy, and criticism of them therefore discredits the organization. Any worker who feels that the interests of his country are endangered by his chief's actions is in duty bound to report any facts he has to the proper authorities. But most criticism has nothing to do with patriotism.

SOCIAL LIFE AND OFFICE LIFE

Office routine has many rules quite different from the accepted ones of social usage, and many of them even run counter to the usual social forms. When people meet for dinner, the object is a gay and pleasant time, and other considerations must be subordinated to that end. But when people meet in an office, the point is to expedite the business at hand, pleasantly and agreeably, but most of all efficiently. The basic rule, and one of the soundest in all office practice, is that office life and social life must be kept apart. This protects employer and employee alike from the interference of business associations, which are not discretionary, with social relationships, which should be a matter of choice. The forms this rule takes in daily office routine, as compared to social usage, are these:

1. A senior officer does not rise for a junior, regardless of age or sex. The only exceptions to this are at the first interview (see page 114), and the final interview when the employee is leaving the organization.
2. A senior officer may ask his secretary to reach a junior officer by telephone without hurrying to be ready to speak to him or her at once. (See page 14, "On the Telephone.")
3. A senior officer must always be the first to suggest lunching or dining with a junior, unless a business luncheon or dinner is being planned.
4. A junior officer is free to consider all non-business invitations on a strictly social basis; in other words, if a senior officer says, "Would you like to dine and go to the movies next Thursday?", the junior is free to accept or refuse; and normal social usage is followed. However, should the superior say, "Could you dine to celebrate our chief's twenty-fifth anniversary here?", business considerations may enter and some form of office routine will probably prevail.
5. As a matter of general practice, presents are given to junior officers in many organizations on such occasions as Christmas or anniversaries. And in such

cases, of course, it is perfectly good practice to accept them with thanks. Presents from seniors to juniors for special reasons, such as the completion of long and particularly hard jobs, are also quite acceptable in most circumstances. (See page 63, # 3.)

But when the senior officer is a man and the junior a woman, it is sometimes wise to give the matter a little consideration. Should she feel that the present is a perfectly openhearted expression of gratitude, there is no reason to stand on ceremony. On the other hand, should she feel that the giver wishes to put her under obligation, as he might if the present were very expensive, then it is wiser to refuse with many thanks. If the alternatives are not clear, one may accept in a provisional spirit, leaving the perfume unopened for example, or the cigarette box unused. Then the present can be returned if later developments indicate that such a course is wise.

INVITING THE BOSS TO DINE

"Inviting the boss to dinner" is a classic American situation, discussed almost weekly on the radio and shown every day in the comic strips. It is presented, quite accurately and understandably, as a moment of considerable strain. Many suggestions concerning food and service have been made in the section, "Household Customs," and many would be useful on such occasions. Here we are looking at it from the office point of view.

The first point is that entertaining one's chief is an obligation only after entertainment on his part. In other words, he must do the inviting first, and the obligation involved is the usual one of social reciprocity. (See page 433, "Entertaining.") It is not, as it is so often mistakenly represented, the annual obligation of every young married man in the organization. Waiting for the chief's lead follows the traditional social practice, by which the older and more established members of the community take the initiative in calling on newcomers. Besides, it is immensely practical in this case because the junior officer is given a clearer idea of his senior's conception of the social relationship between them before inviting him to his house.

For example; if "dinner with the boss" was a family party, with children of all ages present and no outside guests, the situation is clear that "dinner for the boss" may be equally informal. On the other hand, if the dinner was quite big and elaborate, the junior should, within the dimensions of his pattern of living, give a dinner of equal ceremony in return. (This question of the relative versus the absolute return in hospitality, is discussed on page 433, as suggested above.)

BEING INTERVIEWED

In applying for a job, whether as a volunteer or employee, the wisest course is to think of the situation from the interviewer's side of the desk. Everyone wants an enthusiastic, intelligent, sensible, and attractive worker, who appears able to contribute something to the organization. No one, except in emergencies, will take on a dull, lifeless, untidy, and incoherent prospect, who cares only about getting a job as a practical necessity or "for something to do."

Seen from this perspective, most of the points become fairly obvious. One should know something about the organization one hopes to work for and, if one department seems particularly interesting, say so. One should be alert and polite, ready to answer, quick to apologize if one inadvertently interrupts, but not nervously overeager. The proper pattern of behavior in any interview such as this is the most formal one. One should say "How do you do?" or "Good morning," or "Good afternoon"—*not* "Hello"—and one should let the interviewer make the first gesture toward shaking hands. (See page 56, "Introductions, Acknowledgments, Greetings and Good-byes"; also pages 25 and 33, "Men's Manners" and "Women's Manners.")

In describing work one has done, it is better to say, "I enjoyed that work so much," than, "I was good at that work." The first shows an attractive zest for work; the second sounds boastful. If asked to do unfamiliar work, it is wise to be truthful and frank: "I've never done that work, but I'd be delighted to try it," or, "I've never done that work and I'm afraid I wouldn't be very good at it."

If asked why one left a previous job, frankness is the best unless an explanation would involve a loss of proper reticence; for example, "I enjoyed the work, but I wanted a better job," but not, "I had to leave because I wanted to go west to get a divorce." If there are such personal reasons, the standard expressions are, "There were family complications then," or, "For personal reasons I had to leave the city that year"; or, "I was ill and had to leave," but not, "I had to have my appendix taken out."

Finally, there is the matter of personal appearance. One should be neatly dressed, and well-groomed. One's clothes need not be markedly fashionable; in fact, the ideal is perhaps a tempered version of the current fashion. But they must be spotlessly clean, with shoes shined; in short, the general effect should be "neat, clean, and efficient-looking."

INTERVIEWING

In many ways, the one who is interviewing a prospective worker is under a greater obligation of courtesy and politeness than the one who is asking for a job. His is the dominant position and his responsibilities are therefore greater. The perfect attitude combines kindness, understanding, and common decency; condescension must be no part of it, and sharpness is out of the question. A pert remark on the part of the prospective worker is foolish, but sharpness on the interviewer's part is the height of bad taste.

When a man interviews prospective workers who are women or older men, he should stand to greet them. (See page 112, "Social Life and Office Life.") Whether one shakes hands or not depends on the circumstances. A woman interviewer should rise for an older woman, a contemporary, or a much older man; and those who have particularly good manners always rise. All prospective workers should be asked to sit down for the interview.

When the interview is over, the interviewer indicates as much with closing phrases to give the worker time to collect himself. If a job for the worker is doubtful or more than doubtful, there should be some indication that this is a special situation, that the special needs of the organization do not suit the worker. It should never be implied that the worker is inadequate to meet the organization's standards. In other words, the suggestion should be, "I am afraid this isn't quite what you would like," and not "I'm afraid you are not experienced enough for this organization." If the meeting has ended in engaging the worker, the interviewer should give some indication of pleasure; as "Thank you so much for coming in to see me. We'll look forward to having you here." If a job is not definite, the thanks must be stressed even more.

MANNERS TOWARD SENIOR OFFICERS

Good manners towards one's seniors in an organization must include a certain deference and respect. This does not mean that every assistant and every secretary should pop to her feet every time an older officer of the organization comes in. But it does mean that senior officers, whether older or younger, cannot be left to pull their own chairs forward, or stand without one. It means that juniors must rise to greet their seniors in the morning and to say good-bye to them in the afternoon. It means that juniors must rise to converse with a senior, if the senior is standing, and that they must wait for the seniors to make all overtures of friendship or informality. Such behavior does not, in any way, involve a loss of self-respect or personal dignity. Quite the contrary. Granted the proper spirit, it adds to the dignity of any worker, because it shows not only respect for the office and title, and for the organization, but also that the worker has a valuable knowledge of social usage and worldly ways.

OFFICE MANNERS

The following are rules of behavior for every kind of organization and are based on the facts of all office life. They are as valid for military personnel as they are for industrial workers, for ecclesiastical organizations as for the Red Cross.

1. Never make or encourage personal telephone calls, if you are sitting in an office with a senior officer. If a call should come in, it should be answered in a low voice and as briefly as possible. (In time, this rule may be relaxed a little; but it should never be forgotten.)
2. Never bring friends or family into any office in which there is a senior officer, except at his specific request.
3. Never ask the secretary or assistant of a co-worker, whether junior or senior, for help, without the co-worker's permission. In any emergency, if the co-worker is absent, one may ask the secretary for assistance and explain the situation to the co-worker later.
4. Never take a suggestion, a complaint, or an important piece of information over the head of a senior officer to an officer still higher in the organization. In other words, speak to your department head before speaking to your office manager or chief. Exceptions to this, of course, are in the case of serious complaints involving the immediate superior, or situations in which the good of the organization or a higher consideration demands discretion.
5. When possible, never shift the blame, even rightfully, to others. For example, if a superior asks rhetorically and in some irritation, "Why were those papers left here?" the best answer is, "I'm sorry," or "I'm not sure"; not, "Miss

Wyeth was supposed to put them away." If the matter is important, more searching questions will be asked and they will have to be answered truthfully. But it is bad taste and bad office practice to lay the blame on others, particularly if the guilty one is a junior officer.

6. Never discuss salaries.

7. Never discuss or make apparent the relative advantages of one's personal or social life.

TRAVELING

Traveling for business or official purposes, or for charitable enterprises, has become so common in America that an accepted pattern of behavior has grown up around it.

When a man is traveling with a woman assistant or secretary, the arrangements are made, as a rule, by the home office. The telegram for reservations should read:

HOTEL ASHTON
PARK PLACE, LOUISVILLE, KENTUCKY

PLEASE RESERVE TWO SINGLE ROOMS AND BATHS FOR MR. JOHN BRUCE, A PARTNER [OR A MEMBER] OF OUR FIRM AND HIS SECRETARY. WIRE CONFIRMATION.

BLANCHARD AND HITCHCOCK O WALL ST. N.Y.

The telegram should not read:

PLEASE RESERVE TWO ROOMS AND BATH FOR ME AND MY SECRETARY. HOPE YOU WILL TAKE CARE OF US. PLEASE WIRE CONFIRMATION.

JOHN BRUCE
BLANCHARD AND HITCHCOCK O WALL ST. N.Y.

The hotel will reserve rooms on separate floors, the correct and accepted practice. It is foolish and impractical to reserve rooms in different hotels for appearance's sake.

Train reservations are made in the same way. For overnight trips, reservations may be made on the same train, but in different cars. On short day trips and in airplanes, no special arrangements are necessary.

If a mistake has been made in filling the request for reservations, the senior officer should be the one who asks to have it rectified. For example, if the hotel has reserved adjoining rooms, the senior should ask for a room on another floor; as, "That will be very nice for Miss Wyeth, but I would like a room on a higher floor." If he fails to do so, the junior officer may take over if she feels that it would be wise; as, "Are those rooms on the court? . . . Then could I have an outside room on a higher floor, please?"

When work must be done on a trip of this kind, a sitting room is often reserved next to the senior officer's room, and the secretary comes there to take dictation or answer the telephone. At other times, she should stay on call, in her room, unless sure she will not be needed. On short trips, dictation may be given in the hotel sitting room, or garden, or even in the senior officer's room, but the secretary's room is never used for this.

The question is often raised as to whether or not a senior officer and his assistant or secretary should eat meals together, either on the train or in the hotel dining room. There is no rule on this point, but as a matter of general practice, the answer is "No." A business trip should be regarded as an extension of the usual office routine into another area, and not as a part of social life. If a lecturer and his assistant often lunch together when not on tour, they will of course continue to do so on a trip. But it is not necessary for an officer and his secretary, who usually meet only in business hours, to feel that they must take every meal together only because they are traveling. When there is work to be done, they will probably lunch together, but not otherwise.

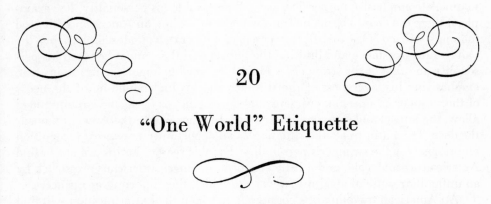

20

"One World" Etiquette

It would be impossible to learn every detail of all the social usages and customs of every country in the world. And even if it were possible, it would be unnecessary, because in any foreign city the code of manners outlined in this book is now accepted as the standard of the Western world. In the Orient, for example, among those accustomed to foreigners, a Westerner is not considered impolite if he fails to examine and discuss the markings on the bottom of his teacup. It is understood that such is not the Western custom. In a book of this size, it would be impossible to bridge the gap between the Western code of manners and the codes of other civilizations. But within our civilization, in Europe and in the Western Hemisphere, there are certain variations of custom and usage which it is useful for any American traveling abroad to know.

THE DIFFERENCES BETWEEN THE LATIN AND THE ANGLO-AMERICAN TRADITIONS

Before proceeding to specific details, we must discuss the greatest single variation in the manners of our Western civilization: the difference between the Anglo-American conception and the Latin conception. The basic philosophy that underlies American social customs is identical with that of the British Isles and Canada, and, for that matter, of Australia or any other country which was developed by the British. The Latin philosophy is dominant in France, Italy, Spain, and all the Latin-American countries. To divide Europe still further: The Scandinavian countries, northern Germany, and Holland are in the first group; Belgium, South

Germany, Austria, Poland, Czechoslovakia, Hungary, and the Balkans are in the second group. The basic difference between these two philosophies has many aspects—psychological, philosophical, social, and political. As far as manners and customs are concerned, the difference between the two philosophies might be expressed in a rough definition such as this: In the Anglo-American tradition, consideration for one's fellow man is expressed by respect for his rights; for example, the right to privacy when traveling in a public conveyance. In the Latin tradition, this consideration is expressed in respect for his personality. It is a point of manners, in our tradition, to minimize the trouble one has taken in performing a small service for a stranger; in the Latin tradition, it is a point of good manners to emphasize the service, as a tribute paid to his personality. For example, if there is a door to be opened or a window to be shut, an American with good manners will do it as casually as possible, deliberately underemphasizing the value of his assistance and limiting the impact and the contact between his personality and that of the stranger. A Latin with good manners springs to his feet, emphasizing his awareness of the stranger and his understanding of the needs of the stranger as a person, enjoying and developing, as far as the circumstances allow, the impact and contact with another. In other words, the American opens the door. The Latin treats the situation as an opportunity to express recognition and respect for the stranger's personality. For this reason, Latins are apt to find Americans casual, cold, and a little abrupt in manner. Americans are struck by an unfamiliar sense of assiduity, a warmth which they interpret as insincere.

An American traveling in a country founded on the Latin tradition will find his relations with others much easier and more pleasant if he remembers this point. It underlies many differences in custom and procedure; the question of the importance of shaking hands, for example. (See page 122 below.) It accounts for many small differences in business customs. In a shop in America or England, it is considered correct to go in and buy something, pay for it, and leave, with no more personal contact than, perhaps, a brief "Thank you" when the package and the change are handed over. In a Latin country, it is considered extremely rude and abrupt not to establish a personal contact first and at once, by saying not only, "How do you do?" but, "How do you do, Sir?" (or "Madam" or "Miss"). The ideal American business transaction is brief and to the point, with a minimum of fuss. The ideal Latin transaction is on a broader level; the point is not only the business at hand but also the mutual interchange of respect and recognition.

Such examples could be multiplied indefinitely, but it would be impossible to cover all the many ways in which the differences in attitude can be expressed. Some of the points discussed below are based on the difference in philosophy. Others are purely technical and have more to do with economics than philosophy. The technical details are useful, but not so important as the others. It may be useful, for example, to know that in some countries theater programs must be paid for. But it is important to understand and respect the differences between the philosophies of others and our own.

VISITING CARDS

In the British Isles, the customs concerning visiting cards are very much like our own; but in the rest of Europe and in Latin America, it is always wise to follow the formal suggestions on page 598. After a dinner party, for example, it is accepted as only normal politeness that guests should leave cards; flowers sent with a note or visiting card are not at all unusual.

When there has been a death in the family, friends and acquaintances are expected to go to the house and leave visiting cards during the usual hours: after lunch and before dinner; or they may sign in the register or book which is often kept in the front hall on such occasions.

AT TABLE AND AFTER

At table in Latin countries, all the women are served first, before the men, in the order of their precedence at table: the woman at the right of the host, then the woman at his left, and so on, ending with the hostess. After the women have been served, the men are served in the same way: the man at the right of the hostess, then the man at her left, ending with the host. After dinner or luncheon, the men do not separate from the women as they do in England and America. Instead, they all go in to the living room together. These procedures should always be followed when one is entertaining in Latin countries.

TIPPING

Americans traveling abroad are often and quite understandably confused by the whole question of tipping. In the first place, in many foreign countries tipping is expected for services for which a tip is never expected here; many of these are discussed under the different headings in this section. In the second place, the currencies are confusing. And finally, Americans often feel that a very much lower scale of tipping is customary in other countries. To some extent, it is true that in small villages and in out-of-the-way places abroad the scale of tipping is very much reduced; but in big cities, it is about the same all over the world. The tips of restaurant waiters are almost always determined by the amount of the check, according to the scale outlined on page 71. For other services, one can use basic costs, such as the price of food and hotel rooms, as a remarkably accurate guide. In a small country village, for example, where the most expensive hotel room costs $2.00 a day and the most expensive meal costs less than a dollar, porters, doormen, bootblacks, and hat-check girls, if there are any, will obviously not expect very large tips. In London and Paris, in Amsterdam and Rome, hotel rooms, food, and tips are all as high as they would be in the United States. With the differences of currency firmly in mind, one can use the scale suggested on page 68, keeping more or less the same relation between the basic costs and the tips. When the costs are very much lower, however, the scale of tipping must be adjusted upwards. And in every country, tips are usually given in round figures: 10¢ or 15¢, not 12¢ or 13¢.

Dinner or Luncheon in Holland and Switzerland

As a dinner or luncheon guest in a house in Holland or Switzerland, one is expected to give a tip to the household. The standard procedure in Holland is to leave the tip on the hall table, and the sum is a gulden from each guest, or each couple. In Switzerland, the tip is a franc from each guest, and it is given to the butler as one leaves the house.

At the Theater

On all the Continent of Europe, it is customary to tip the usher who escorts one to one's seat. This is done in movie theaters as well as other theaters, and the amount is scaled to the cost of the seats. For example, if two seats cost the equivalent of a dollar, the tip to the usher should be about 15¢. If two seats cost $3.00, the tip to the usher would be about 25¢.

In the British Isles, the ushers are not tipped, but one is expected to pay for the theater program; in movie theaters where there are no programs, there is nothing to pay for but the ticket.

ON THE TRAIN

In the British Isles, train tickets are taken up when one's destination is reached. The conductor punches the ticket on the train, as he does in the United States, but the ticket must be surrendered in the station at the end of the trip. This practice is standard in the British Isles and is followed in many countries on the Continent also. If one has followed the casual American custom of dropping the punched ticket on the floor, one can often explain one's way out of the situation, but it is much easier to hold on to the ticket and avoid the fuss.

In many trains in foreign countries, one cannot go into the dining car at any hour one chooses, as is usually the custom in the United States. Depending on the number of passengers, there is usually a set number of "services" at definite hours, when a table d'hôte meal will be served. As soon as one boards the train, it is wise to speak to the attendant and ask when the dining car will be open and what time each service will be. At the appropriate hour, a waiter from the dining car goes through the train calling out, "First service," or "Second service," and the passengers who are inscribed for that service make their way to the dining car.

IN HOTELS

One of the most important differences between American and foreign hotels is the institution of the concierge, known in England as the hall porter. This key figure in foreign hotel life has no American equivalent. From his desk in the hall, he controls all the details that can make one's visit pleasant or unpleasant. He is the one who arranges for theater tickets and hired cars; he is the one who accepts C.O.D. packages; he is the one who gives advice and counsel concerning trips, guides, picnics, tips, and all the other unfamiliar and necessary details. Even after one leaves the hotel, the concierge is still important because he will be the one who forwards (or does *not* forward) one's mail. In the hierarchy of tipping, the concierge receives about the same as the headwaiter. In the big hotel in a big city, if one's room has cost $6.00 a day, the tip to the concierge could be $2.00 or $3.00 a week, depending on the amount of work he has done.

In the British Isles and in some hotels on the Continent, there is another person who has no American equivalent and who is always tipped. This is the "boots." Men's shoes, and women's shoes, too, are cleaned not by the valet, but by a special boots-boy who picks up the shoes outside each room door every evening. If a set charge for this should be on the hotel bill, the "boots" is tipped according to the usual scale: the nearest equivalent in round figures to 5¢ or 10¢, depending on the expense of the hotel room. If (as is usual) there is no charge for shoe cleaning on the bill, the total amount is given to the boots.

In many countries, 10 or 15 per cent is added to the hotel bill for "service," but one must nevertheless give tips as well. Depending on the service, the usual amount of extra tipping totals about 8 to 10 per cent of the bill, divided proportionately according to the suggestions given in the chapter on tipping, on pages 65 to 74.

AT DANCES

In Latin countries, there is no cutting in. At the end of each dance, the music stops and the couples separate to find their partners for the next dance. Women who have no partners for the next dance can join another woman friend, or a group of friends; or they may be left alone—with a bow, and thanks for the dance.

THE PLACE OF HONOR

The matter of the "place of honor" is more important in foreign countries, particularly Latin countries, than it is in the United States. In almost every country—with the notable exception of Scandinavia, where the places of honor at table are to the left of host and hostess—the place of honor is at the right hand. But in Latin countries, a consideration of the place of honor extends far beyond the usual confines of the dining-room table. At the theater, in a conveyance, or in any public place, a punctilious Latin man will always sit to the left of a woman or of an older man. In a car, for example, the woman will sit at the right and he will go around the car to avoid stepping over her feet. When walking with a woman, in an open park or square, he will walk on her left, although in most countries men keep to the curb side of the sidewalk in the street. To a lesser extent, this courtesy is observed also by a younger woman toward an older one.

Among the most conservative elements of some of the more conservative Latin countries, there used to be a rule which showed how far this attitude can be carried. A man walking with his wife, or sitting in a restaurant with a "respectable" woman at his right hand, would never salute a friend unless the woman with him were also at *his* right hand, on the assumption that any woman placed at a man's left could not be respectable and could not be introduced to a respectable woman. Although this rule is now rarely observed, and in big cities, in cosmopolitan circles, and particularly among the younger generation may in fact be unknown, it has nevertheless left a very strong and easily recognizable mark. In Latin countries, where personal honor can be affected by the actions and respect—or lack of respect—of others, the place of honor has great significance. In other countries it is less important and, except in Scandinavian countries as mentioned above, the customs are very like our own.

INTRODUCTIONS

In Continental Europe and in South America, introductions are very much more important than they are in the Anglo-American tradition. In England, particularly, introducing is done as little as possible, and it is quite possible to spend an evening among twenty or thirty guests, without being introduced to more than half a dozen. Necessarily, under this system, one can talk to any other guest without introduction; but if the occasion should arise naturally in the course of the conversation, it is quite permissible to introduce oneself. This is not true, however, on the Continent, where self-introductions are considered very bad form. The Continental system demands that one must ask to be presented to older or ranking guests, if by any chance one's host or hostess has neglected to make the presentations. It is rude, for example, if an older woman or a bishop is present, not to ask to be presented. One need not ask the host or hostess to do this; anyone who has been properly presented can perform the introduction. Following this rule, all men *must* see that they are presented to all the women and to very much older or distinguished men; and younger women are expected to ask to be presented to older women. If there is no one who can perform the introduction—as, for example, if two guests who are unknown to each other should arrive early— according to the strictest Continental form they may introduce themselves if they are both men; but a man and a woman, or two women, should never introduce themselves to each other. (See also "Rising," page 57.)

SHAKING HANDS

An important point in the Continental system of introductions is that one must shake hands on arrival, when being introduced, and when saying good-bye. And one should say how-do-you-do and good-bye to *all* the guests, unless there is a special reason not to; as, for example, if one has been taken ill, or is leaving at an inappropriately early hour. As a week-end guest, one is expected to shake hands with one's host and fellow guests at least twice a day, every day: when one says good morning and again when one says good night. The importance of this matter of shaking hands cannot be overemphasized. It is considered extremely rude and casual not to follow the custom. Again, according to the protocol of introductions, the older, more important, or ranking guest offers his hand to a younger guest, and women offer their hands to men.

FORMS OF INTRODUCTIONS

No collective form of introduction is suggested here as it is used much less on the Continent than it is in Anglo-American society. If the late arrival is a very important guest, the others are brought up to be presented; if not, he is taken around the room and presented individually to each person.

The following Continental forms cannot be used in the English language. If the English language is used, the Anglo-American forms must be used (see page 58).

The Most Formal Continental Introduction

"Madame, voulez-vous me permettre de vous présenter Monsieur Cartier?"
Or, "Madame, permettez-moi de vous présenter Monsieur Cartier."

The name of the woman to whom Monsieur Cartier is being presented is not added at the end, on the assumption that she is so well-known that it is unnecessary. This form is used also, of course, when men are concerned; as, "Monsieur l'Ambassadeur, permettez-moi . . ." etc., or "voulez-vous me permettre . . ." etc., or "Excellence, . . ." Theoretically, therefore, this most formal introduction is used only when the personage to whom one is presenting a guest is of such importance that the mention of his name would be inappropriate. Practically speaking, it is made more widely applicable by the usual preliminaries, "Monsieur Cartier, will you come with me? I would like to introduce you to the British Ambassadress." Or by a request from Monsieur Cartier, "Will you present me to Cardinal Verdier?"

The Informal Continental Introduction

"Vous connaissez Monsieur Duval?—Madame Marsengo."

Or, "Monsieur Duval—Madame Marsengo." This is the most widely used form. It is important that the man's name be mentioned first.

ACKNOWLEDGMENTS

The classic acknowledgment, which corresponds to "How do you do?" is "Bon jour, Monsieur" (or "Madame") or "Bon soir, Madame" (or "Monsieur").

SAYING GOOD-BYE

The Continental tradition often demands a more formal and ceremonious leave-taking than the simple Anglo-American good-bye. Among friends one may say "Au revoir," for which the response is either, "Au revoir" or, "A bientôt." But with acquaintances one must use the more formal, "Au revoir, Madame," or "Bon soir, Monsieur." The most formal leave-taking might involve, on the part of the more important of the two people, "Au revoir, Monsieur; enchantée d'avoir fait votre connaissance," to which the response is, "Moi aussi, Madame; et j'espère vous revoir très bientôt."

HAND KISSING

The whole question of kissing hands is becoming very complicated. The old rule was that the men of all countries which belonged to the Latin tradition kissed the hands of married women (but never of young girls), instead of shaking hands. If foreigners would observe the rule, the situation would be simple; but some foreigners, who know that hand kissing is not an American custom, do not kiss the hands of American women. The result is that sometimes, expecting one's hand to be kissed, one offers a rather limp handshake with the back of the hand up instead of sideways. And at other times, not expecting one's hand to be kissed, one prepares for a rather hearty handshake, and the result is a struggle in which the foreigner's nose often gets bumped. Until foreigners make up their minds to one course or the other, all that American women can do is to be alert about it.

USE OF "MONSIEUR" AND "MADAME"

The repeated use of "Monsieur" and "Madame" in French conversation, without the surname, is always surprising to English-speaking people. But it is a fact that, except in informal conversation between friends, the omission of "Monsieur" or "Madame" is considered a rudeness. They need not accompany every statement, but they are liberally sprinkled throughout the conversation and are always used, except most informally, in saying good-bye. (See also pages 591 and 595 for French and Spanish "Forms of Address".)

INVITATIONS TO WOMEN

In Latin countries, a man does not, as a rule, ask a young woman whom he has just met to dine or lunch alone, as he does in Anglo-American countries. The usual procedure is for him to arrange a party of four or six people; and a woman or a young girl who is invited by a man to luncheon or dinner, or even to tea, will usually expect this arrangement. This applies not only, of course, to invitations to a man's house or apartment, but also to invitations to restaurants, cafes, night clubs, picnics, or whatever.

COMPLIMENTS

In Latin countries, a great many more compliments are given than in other countries. This does not mean that the compliments are insincere, but that Latin people express themselves more freely. After dinner, for example, compliments about the food are almost expected by the hostess. The host will be delighted with favorable remarks about the wine, and the whole tenor of such compliments is on a much fuller scale than it is in America. As a compliment to a woman from a man, "You are ravishing," is not at all surprising, nor is it necessarily a prelude, as it might be in this country, to a good deal more.

On the other hand, although compliments are so much a part of good manners, personal questions very definitely are not. Questions which are quite acceptable in the United States, such as, "Have you always lived in . . . ." or "Are you working in the . . . . company?" are not considered polite in foreign countries, particularly Latin countries. And any questions or comments concerning money are very bad manners.

DRINKING

A word must be said about the difference in the attitude of most foreigners toward drinking as compared to that of many Americans. In most foreign countries an appreciation of wines is one of the recognized amenities of living, and an art which is very much respected. The chief reason for drinking is an appreciation of flavor; in other words, foreigners drink for taste and not for effect. Those who drink for effect are regarded in the same light as a music lover would regard a man who likes music only because it helps him go off to sleep. Because this is their basic attitude toward the whole question of drinking, intoxication is an insult to the hostess and all her guests. To be markedly affected by alcohol is an embarrassing and unattractive breach of manners.

TRAVELING

When asking for directions or information, all requests should be preceded by "Excuse me." The question should end with "Please," and the answer must be received with "Thank you."

FUNERALS

In many Latin countries, especially in small towns, an attitude of respect is expected whenever a funeral procession goes by. Men take off their hats and stand quietly until the procession has passed. Women, too, must show their awareness of the procession by an attitude of silent respect. A hint as to whether or not this is expected is the behavior of other passers-by: If they are walking along without noticing the procession, one may do the same, but if they are all standing uncovered, one should follow their example.

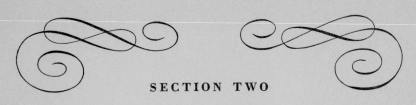

SECTION TWO

CEREMONIES AND EVENTS

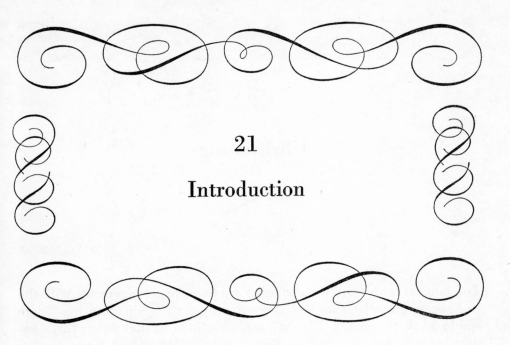

21

Introduction

WITH THE EXCEPTION of the last chapter, which is of patriotic rather than personal importance, the ceremonies and events which are discussed in this section are the milestones of a lifetime: christenings, engagements, divorce and separation, and funerals. Weddings are discussed in the next section, beginning on page 165. For events of such importance, it is difficult to prescribe a pattern of procedure which will apply to every conceivable set of circumstances. The suggestions given in this section are widely used and generally accepted, but they are always subject to modifications for special reasons. The important and unchangeable element in each procedure is the attitude from which it springs. Modern taste has very definite views on this subject, and these can be clearly and definitely set down. It is unimportant, for example, whether or not one decides to have a reception after a christening; but it is important that a christening be considered primarily a religious, rather than a social, event.

In the last chapter there is a full list of the customs concerning the United States flag, the ways in which it should be flown or hung, or handled. But in this too, the spirit is the important part. It would be impossible to list all the circumstances which might alter the usual rules in some minor way. The important thing is that the flag should not be handled carelessly. In each chapter of this section, the spirit will be found with the rules—either implicitly, as in the case of the last chapter, or explicitly as in the others.

22

Christenings

THE FIRST STEPS toward a christening are to make arrangements with the clergyman or minister for the ceremony, to ask the godparents to officiate and to invite the guests. We shall consider them in that order. Birth announcements are discussed on page 612 in "Cards"; and forms for the newspaper announcements are given on page 97, in "Personal Publicity."

THE AGE OF THE BABY AT CHRISTENING

The age at which a baby is christened depends somewhat on the religion of his parents. A Catholic baby is usually christened before he is a month old; a Protestant baby may be three, or even six months old, or, in certain circumstances, even older. For practical reasons the best ages are less than four months, or over three years. According to the law and custom of all three major denominations of Judaism, boys receive their names in a ceremony which usually takes place at home, eight days after they are born; girls are named in the temple or synagogue on the Friday evening or Saturday morning after their birth.

ARRANGEMENTS WITH THE CLERGYMAN

In both Protestant and Catholic churches, the baby may be baptized either in the morning or in the afternoon; after the regular Sunday morning service, or in the afternoon at a special service, or during Evening Prayer. If any special decorations are wanted for the church, these are discussed at the first meeting with the clergyman, but usually, if anything, there are only a few vases of flowers or a few potted plants in the baptistry.

The clergyman is not given his fee at this first meeting, nor is his fee ever discussed with him. The very sound rule concerning the amount of the fee is that it should be commensurate with the scale of the christening. If a big luncheon or a tea with many guests is to follow the christening, the clergyman's fee might be fifty dollars, or even a hundred. As a rule, it is fifteen to twenty-five dollars and, for very small christenings, five to ten. A contributing factor in deciding whether to choose the higher or the lower amounts in each bracket is whether or not one is a regular member of the congregation; those who support the church throughout the year might choose the lower, and others the higher, fee. The fee is given the clergyman in cash, in a closed envelope, by one of the parents, usually when the completed forms necessary for the parish records are being given to him.

If one is planning any reception after the ceremony, the clergyman—and his wife, if he is married—must be invited.

ASKING THE GODPARENTS TO OFFICIATE

There is no form for inviting a friend to be godparent for one's child. In fact, the only invitation which would be entirely outside the form would be one which attempted to be pompous or elaborate. As a rule, godparents are intimate friends or members of the family, and the best and most natural invitation is face to face: "We're planning to christen the baby in the next week or so, and Bobby and I hope so much that you will be his godmother." The only possible answer to this is to accept. One cannot refuse to be godparent, and parents must, therefore, be sure to ask only intimate friends who will gladly accept the responsibility. As a rule the godparents are of the same faith as the parents; when there are differences of faith, it is wise to consult the clergyman before asking anyone to serve as a godparent.

If one of the godparents is away, the invitation is sent by letter or telegram. Godparents who must be absent from the ceremony can be representd by proxy. The usual number of godparents is two godfathers and a godmother for a boy, two godmothers and one godfather for a girl; but this is a minimum and there may be more.

PRESENTS FROM THE GODPARENTS

Each godparent should send a christening present to the child, and the traditional present is one made of silver. Silver porringers and mugs were the classic presents of our mothers' and grandmothers' days; but these are better and more useful: a set of silver knife, fork, and spoon in small sizes; or an old silver tumbler-cup, which may be used for the baby's pins or for short-stemmed flowers (later on, of course, for cigarettes); or a small tray of old silver, which will be useful for a lifetime. Presents other than silver are: the beginnings of a pearl necklace, to which the godparent will add each year until his goddaughter is eighteen; bonds or an endowment insurance policy. The ideal christening present is one which is lasting, which will still be useful to the child when he grows older, or which he can give later to his children.

When one gives a present of old silver, it is becoming customary not to engrave it. The traditional form, if one wishes to engrave silver, is:

To
Mary Marshall Thatcher
January 15th, 1948
From her godfather
Richard Bull

If the present is not engraved, it is usually sent with a card either to the baby

—"To Mary Marshall Thatcher with love, from her godfather, Richard Bull"—or to the mother—"Dear Dorothy, this brings much love to Mary Marshall from her godfather, Yours, Dick." The first package would be addressed to the child in care of its mother; the second to the mother, herself.

INVITATIONS TO THE GUESTS

As in the case of invitations to the godparents, invitations to a christening should be most informal. A letter might read:

Dear Mab,

The baby's being christened at the Church of the Resurrection next Wednesday, the fifteenth, at a quarter past twelve, after the morning service.

Bobby and I hope so much that you and Henry will come and bring the girls, and that you will all lunch with us afterwards.

Affectionately,
Dorothy

A telegram contains exactly the same information in an abbreviated form. The telephone invitation sent through a servant is, "Mr. and Mrs. Thatcher would like to know if Mr. and Mrs. Post and the young ladies could come to the baby's christening at the Church of the Resurrection on Wednesday, the fifteenth of January, at a quarter past twelve o'clock, and if they could lunch with Mr. and Mrs. Thatcher afterward."

DRESSING FOR THE CHRISTENING

For his christening every baby wears his finest clothes, usually (although not, of course, necessarily) a long white dress and a fine coat and bonnet of white or pink or blue. The coat and bonnet are taken off just before the ceremony. The parents, the godparents, and the guests dress exactly as they would for Sunday church.

THE CEREMONY

The baby's coat and bonnet should be off and the baby in his godmother's arms before the clergyman reaches the baptismal font. Then, without hurry or delay, the three godparents go up to the font with the baby. His parents and the other christening guests stand nearby during the ceremony. At the appropriate moment, the clergyman will take the baby from his godmother's arms and return him to her again when he has been baptized, but the godmother must hold him until the ceremony is over, when he is given back to his mother or nurse.

The godmother is the one who answers the clergyman when he asks for the child's name. She should make a point of speaking very clearly, and mentioning only the "given" names, never the family name. At one christening, the child might have been named "John Richard Brown Junior Brown" had it not been for the presence of mind of the clergyman, who ignored the godmother's answer, and baptized the baby properly, "John Richard."

AFTER THE CEREMONY

When the ceremony is over, the godparents, parents, and all the guests either return to their places in the church, if the christening took place during a service, or leave the church, if the christening was held after a service or in a special service.

There is no special protocol of departure from the church, although the parents and child usually precede the others of the christening party in order to arrive first at the house. Once there, the child stays downstairs for a while to be admired and then is taken to the nursery. The parents receive their guests as they would at any informal luncheon or tea party. Toasts to the child's health are proposed by the godfather either at dessert, if there was a luncheon, or when tea is almost over if there was a tea.

There is no other ceremony connected with christenings, but it might be useful to give a few suggestions concerning the food.

LUNCHEON AFTER THE CHRISTENING

Since christenings may take place either in the morning or in the afternoon, they may be followed either by a luncheon or by tea. At teatime, no matter how many guests one plans to invite, one provides only tea food, of a more or less elaborate kind (see below). The luncheon may be either seated or stand-up. There are only two traditional items common to both forms of entertainment, the wine and the cake, which are discussed below.

A very formal and elaborate seated luncheon would consist of four courses at most: soup, or an entrée; a main course; salad; and dessert. Three courses are, however, more common, and on such an occasion the first would probably be an entrée rather than soup.

TEA AFTER THE CHRISTENING

If the baby is being christened in the afternoon, there need be only tea food at the reception afterward. So many suggestions are given on page 318, in "For an Afternoon Reception," and on pages 318 and 319, in "For Everyday Tea," that there is no need for further ones here. If there are many guests, the dining-room table will have to be used, and the tea tray will be set there. For fewer than ten or twelve guests, the usual tea table is set in the living room.

THE WINE AND THE CAKE

The only two traditions of a party after a christening are the wine and the cake. The cake is usually white all through, with white icing. It is often decorated with a garland of white sugar flowers, although the baby's initials and the date, which used to be on all christening cakes, are now sometimes left off.

The wine is usually champagne or champagne punch, although any other wine punch can be substituted. Caudle cup, the old and traditional drink, is unheard of nowadays. At a seated luncheon, champagne is poured into champagne glasses, as it would be at dinner. At a buffet luncheon, a tray, with bottles, bucket, and champagne glasses is put on the sideboard. Champagne punch is not usually served at a seated luncheon; at a buffet luncheon it is put in a punch bowl, on a tray with punch glasses and a ladle. A wine cup is served in tall glasses at a seated luncheon, in punch glasses at a buffet meal.

At teatime, the champagne or punch is served as soon as tea has been served. If the food is on the dining-room table, the tray will be set on a sideboard, as at luncheon. At a small tea party, when tea is served in the living room, the tray is brought in there and the host serves it as soon as the guests have had their tea.

There is only one more point that must be made in connection with the drinks served after a christening; whatever they may be, they should not be emphasized, or served in such a way as to turn the event into a cocktail party. Although it is true that whiskey, gin, and other very strong drinks are not so fitting a sequel to a festive religious ceremony as wine is, nevertheless the important point is not what drink is served, but how it is served. Whiskey and soda is often given to the guests who do not drink champagne, and cocktails may be served before luncheon or late, after tea. But it is always true that any undue emphasis on drink is unattractive and essentially bad taste at a christening.

CHRISTENING AT HOME

There was a time when, as far as church regulations permitted, babies were christened at home rather than in church. Except for medical reasons which might make a house christening necessary, this custom is a somewhat unfortunate one, in that it subordinates the religious ceremony to the entertainment which usually follows. Now, with greater good taste, the importance of the church sacrament is stressed, and a christening at home is rare unless the baby is exceptionally delicate, or unless one of the parents is unable to leave the house.

If the christening must be held at home, a room, usually the living room, is arranged for the ceremony. Flowers for the vases are a matter of choice; light colors are, of course, the most appropriate and all the flowers should be in vases, not in "arrangements" or sprays. A special table must be fixed for the font. As a rule, a small, oblong table—not too low a table—is put in front of the fireplace or in some other focal point of the room. For an elaborate christening it may be covered with a white damask cloth which hangs to the floor, and on a winter afternoon it is often set with candles. At a simpler ceremony, the table is often bare. In either case, there must be a bowl which is used for the baptism. This bowl is usually made of silver, although crystal or china could be used also, and it must be about ten inches in diameter, at least. The only kind of bowl which must never be used is one which even remotely suggests either a finger bowl or a punch bowl. If they are becoming to the shape of the bowl, flowers may be laid around its base like a flat garland. Baby's breath, bouvardia, lily of the valley, or any other rather delicate white flower would be the best.

House christenings may be held in the morning, but are oftener in the afternoon. The guests should arrive at the house a few minutes before the hour set for the ceremony, and they are received by the baby's parents as at any other informal tea. The godparents and the minister wait until all the guests have arrived and then they come into the room, the clergyman first, the godmother next, carrying the baby, and the other godparents following. The guests stand aside to let them reach the font and the ceremony begins.

After the ceremony, as after a church christening, the baby stays in the living room for a moment or so and then is carried away to supper and bed.

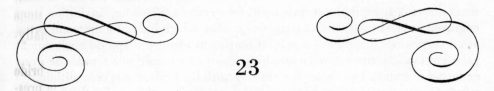

23

Engagements

THE ONCE INEVITABLE financial discussion between the father of the bride and the prospective bridegroom is as much a thing of the past as the father's speech about honorable intentions which was always delivered during the nineties as soon as a young man had called three times. The custom today is that the two principals make up their minds first, and the bride tells her parents about the engagement afterward. On the other hand, it must be made clear that although a financial discussion is no longer essential, there is obviously no reason to avoid one if it seems indicated. In today's very pleasant custom, such discussions are always quite natural and informal, and they may be opened either by the fiancé or by the father of the bride.

Once this little preliminary is over, the engagement can be announced to the rest of the family, and the moment for engagement presents has arrived. (See below.) The old-fashioned custom, which demanded that the groom's family make a formal call on the fiancée, has been abandoned in favor of more normal ways of entertaining such as at a dinner, tea, or luncheon. There is perhaps only one more thing that need be mentioned: the attitude of the engaged couple toward each other. Ideally, it is halfway between the two extremes of surprising coolness and embarrassing warmth. The perfect attitude for a fiancé expresses attentive and enthusiastic affection. The perfect fiancée has a similar but less jubilant aspect: more friendly and more reserved. These ideal creatures, firmly lodged in the minds of all romantics who see an engaged couple, are perhaps what makes the engaged state a peculiarly difficult one. But too wide a deviation from these models will be considered bad taste, not by a romantic only, but by any sensible onlooker.

ENGAGEMENT PRESENTS

It is a widely held tradition, although not a very old one, that the bridegroom give his prospective bride a ring as an engagement present. This is often chosen by the engaged couple together. A ring set with a diamond was very definitely the fashion in the early part of this century; but various factors, including economy and the trend toward wearing very large stones, nipped this fashion in the bud before it ever became a binding tradition. Perhaps this needs explanation: "A binding tradition" in this sense is one that cannot be broken without causing some surprise. It would be surprising if, for example, a wedding invitation were engraved in bright red; but an engagement ring which has not a diamond is not at all surprising. Some have a special sentiment about a diamond engagement ring; but modern rings may be anything, from an emerald to a topaz, one stone or cluster of stones. The choice lies entirely with the bride. Some untraditionally-minded brides would rather have a bracelet, or earrings, than a ring.

The only other people, beside the fiancé, who usually give presents to the bride are the parents and immediate families of the bride and groom. And these presents, unlike that of the groom, are purely a matter of inclination and have nothing to do with custom. An affectionate note from the groom's mother to the bride is indispensable, if she lives at any distance from the bride and cannot see her often; but nothing else is absolutely necessary. (See page 545 for a suggested note.) Distant relatives and business acquaintances do not, as a rule, send any engagement present other than flowers; but this, too, is a matter of inclination and, if they should, it would be a lovely surprise.

ANNOUNCING THE ENGAGEMENT TO THE PUBLIC

The Traditional Procedure

The only way to make a correct public announcement of the engagement is in the public press, in this accepted form: "Mr. and Mrs. George Edward Bourne of 127 East 69 Street announce the engagement of their daughter, Miss Ann Stuyvesant Bourne, to Mr. George Baker Ellis, the son of Mr. and Mrs. William Livingston Ellis, of Sand's Point, Long Island, New York."

There are no other accepted ways of announcing an engagement to the public. It is permissible, however, to allow the society editor of the newspaper to which the announcement is sent to fill out the column with further details about the engaged couple, their education, parents, accomplishments, and any bits of family history the editor thinks interesting. This column is often accompanied by a photograph of the fiancée, and it is perfectly proper, if the editor asks for the photograph, for the bride's mother to give one, and to furnish any other suitable information the editor asks for. (A discussion of the information considered suitable for the occasion will be found on page 96 in the chapter, "Personal Publicity"; examples of announcements are on page 97.)

Permissible Departures

If the bride's parents are dead, her engagement may be announced by her older brother or sister, by her grandmother, uncle, or any other relative, following the form given above: "Mrs. Henry Worthington Bourne . . . announces the engagement of her granddaughter, Miss Ann Stuyvesant Bourne . . ." etc. See page 97 in "Personal Publicity" for the proper form when the bride's parents are divorced or separated.

It is quite wrong to send out engraved or printed announcements of the engagement or for the family of the groom to make the newspaper announcement. And in no circumstances should the bride's mother send an unsolicited photograph to the newspaper.

To Family and Friends

There is no set form for the announcement of an engagement to the immediate family or to friends. It would, of course, be very unkind to allow old friends or relatives to receive their first news of the engagement through the newspaper announcement. Letters should be sent to all of these by the engaged couple or by their mothers. A telegram or even a telephone call would do, if the time were short, but they should be notified. Intimate friends and members of the immediate families will probably know all about it through the usual grapevine of rumor, but if by any chance the whole thing has been a well-kept secret, they may be notified in any way one chooses.

CANCELING THE ANNOUNCEMENT OF AN ENGAGEMENT

If the engagement is already announced in the newspapers, and the bride changes her mind, a second announcement must be sent to the same newspapers. A little delay in sending the second notice would probably be wise, in view of the bride's variability. This second announcement follows closely the form of the first: "Mr. and Mrs. George Edward Bourne of 127 East 69 Street announce that the engagement between their daughter, Miss Ann Stuyvesant Bourne, and Mr. George Baker Ellis, has been broken by mutual consent."

ENGAGEMENT PARTIES

Since only family and friends are apt to be invited to an engagement party, there is no conventional form. Modern usage has, however, made some changes in the old customs. The old-fashioned engagement party, with elaborate and amusing arrangements for announcing the news, has become more or less a thing of the past. There is no reason *not* to have one, as fancy and original as you choose, but there is certainly no reason to feel that one *must* have one in spite of inconvenience or expense. It would be a good idea, if one were planning to give a party in any case, to announce the engagement on the morning of that day. The fiancée could wear her ring for the first time, there could be toasts and speeches and general jollity, without all the fuss and pretentiousness of planned effect, to say nothing of the danger of jokes that are meant to be funny and don't come off. Needless to say, the parents of the engaged couple should all be present, if they live in the same town or near enough to come in conveniently.

Whether one entertained in the afternoon or in the evening—at tea, at dinner, or in the late evening—would be entirely a matter of convenience. (See pages 318 to 334 for suggestions for food for tea, dinner, or supper.) It might be impossible to invite to dinner all the members of the families and all the friends who would have to be included. In that case, a small dinner party, with other guests invited "to come in after dinner," would probably be best.

TOASTS

The ability to make a graceful toast, a witty after-dinner speech, was a talent much admired and assiduously cultivated among the men of the past generation. Such is, unfortunately, no longer the case. The temper of the times is not adapted to the leisurely savoring of a well-rounded sentence. Writers and speakers are geared to deliver a smash opening phrase, rather than a carefully built up climax, as though modern audiences needed to be bludgeoned into listening or reading.

But there are still moments when some kind of toast must be made, and a dinner party on the day an engagement is announced is certainly one of them. In this case, the father of the fiancée is the one who should propose the toast. "I am very happy to announce the engagement of my daughter Ann to George Ellis, and I ask you to join me in a toast to them both" would be a rather formal beginning, but an easy one for a father who hates public speaking. "I am sure it will be no surprise to any of you, but on this day Ann and George were formally engaged to be married, and I think we should mark the occasion with a toast to them both, their good health, their good fortune, their happy marriage," is said by a more fluent father, in case George has been an ardent beau for a long time. Longer and funnier toasts can easily be imagined, and certainly they would be a great addition to the dinner party. The only dangers lie in trying to make an amusing toast if one is not practiced in the art, or in making a joke at someone's expense. On such an occasion, kindness, good will, friendliness, and jollity are much more important than wit. Even a rather old-fashioned toast, referring to "our new son," would be better than a painful wisecrack.

SHOWERS

After the engagement has been announced, it is the custom in some parts of the country, although not in New York, to give a "shower" for the bride. To these parties, usually given in the afternoon in the house of the bride's best friend, only women are invited and usually only friends of the bride's age. Since each guest is supposed to bring a present, only fairly intimate friends should be asked.

There are many different kinds of showers, among them kitchen showers, linen showers, stocking or lingerie showers. Any very elaborate way of setting out the presents should be avoided and so should elaborate or fancy foods. A big tea table in the living room or, if the living room is too small for all the presents and the guests and tea, a tea tray on the dining-room table is all that is necessary at an afternoon party of this kind. (See page 318 for suggestions about the food and page 289 for the ways to serve it.)

24

Divorce and Separation

No MATTER how one looks at divorce and separation, they are two of the saddest factors in modern life. Their growing number in America is an appalling record of failure. If the divorced people recognize the sadness of their failure, the sorrow is explicit; if they take marriage lightly, the failure is in our culture and the tragedy is perhaps even greater. Whatever one's personal feelings may be, the whole approach of modern social usage to the question of divorce and separation is based on the acceptance of this truth: that divorce is a public confession of failure, and so it is the height of bad taste to celebrate it with "freedom parties" or any other kind of jubilation. As far as casual acquaintances and the public are concerned, the matter should be treated with the utmost dignity, reticence, and reserve. All the accepted customs listed below are based on this approach.

SEPARATION

When two people are separated, whether informally or legally, it is customary for the husband to leave home: to move to his club, a hotel, or his family's house. The wife should never be the one to leave, except in extraordinary circumstances. If she has behaved outrageously, in such a way as to make a public scandal, he might be justified in asking her to leave his house; or, if the situation is impossibly difficult for the wife, and the husband refuses to leave, she might be justified in taking the classic step of "going home to mother." As a rule, however, it is the husband who moves out.

The Wife's Part

The wife:

continues to wear her wedding ring;

continues to be addressed as "Mrs. Charles Jones";

    (not "Mrs. Seaforth Jones"; see below)

forwards whatever mail comes for her husband to his club or hotel;

regrets automatically all formal invitations issued jointly to her and her husband;

informs casual acquaintances, tradesmen, etc., *when asked,* that her husband can be reached at such and such address or telephone number.

The Husband's Part

The husband:
>   never issues any formal notice of the separation; specifically: not a little newspaper announcement, "My wife having left . . ."

All these customs having been adhered to, a reconciliation would be perfectly easy and unembarrassing. The husband returns and there is nothing to retract or undo; there are no burnt bridges. On the other hand, if a reconciliation is impossible, divorce proceedings can start quite properly from this point.

DIVORCE

After a woman is divorced from her husband, her status is completely changed; legally, of course, and to some extent socially, as well. In foreign countries, the social effect of divorce is much greater than here. It should be noted that the divorce is a fact, and that the following steps should be taken only after the final decree has been handed down; *not* when the divorce proceedings are initiated.

A Woman Who Is Divorced

The woman who is divorced
>   wears her wedding ring and engagement ring if she wants to. Divorcées with children often prefer to.
>   is addressed as "Mrs. Seaforth Jones"—"Mary Seaforth," for example, having been her maiden name—not as "Mrs. Mary Jones." If, by an unfortunate coincidence, her former husband's Christian name was Seaforth, she would call herself "Mrs. M. Seaforth Jones" after her divorce. (See also page 602 in the chapter, "Cards.")
>   sends no notice of any kind to any newspaper.
>   notifies shops and trades people with whom she has charge accounts that there is a change in the charge address, as follows:

>   Black and Company
>   Fifth Avenue at Fiftieth Street
>   New York 20
>   New York
>   Dear Sirs:
>   Please change my charge address on your records from Mrs. Charles Jones, 120 East 67th Street, New York, New York, to Mrs. Seaforth Jones, 8 East 64th Street, New York, New York.
>
> Yours truly,
Mary Seaforth Jones

A Divorced Husband

The divorced husband makes no formal announcement, and takes no steps other than those suggested in the event of a separation.

Whatever the private turmoil and unhappiness may have been, these few changes are the only ones that divorced people may exhibit to the public. The only question that remains, as far as the public is concerned, is how they will act when they meet: in the lobby of a theater, in the paddock at a race meet, in a new friend's drawing room. The answer is, though they may pretend not to see each other in a public place, they must at least say how-do-you-do in a friend's house, no matter how bitter the feeling between them. As guests in a house to which they have both—although perhaps most tactlessly—been invited, they must subordinate their private feelings to their responsibilities as guests. It might be better to nod a greeting in the theater lobby, especially if there were friends who might notice a willful coldness; but there is no obligation to speak except as guests in the same house.

As for the other extreme, the divorced couple who dine gaily and repeatedly together in all the most conspicuous places, nothing could be more questionable from the point of view of good taste. If there are business matters to discuss, or questions concerning the children, they should meet in the daytime. They could meet for tea, at the woman's house, or for luncheon in any restaurant which has a business-like rather than a purely social atmosphere. Or, if the divorce was most unfriendly and relations are strained, they may prefer to meet in a lawyer's office. The point is that they should never look as though they had just met for a jolly good time.

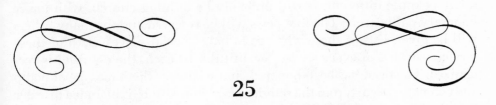

25

Funerals and Mourning

IN EVERY FAITH, funerals are largely governed by religious tradition and rule, but there are always a few details which are left to the discretion of the family. This chapter is designed to cover the points which are not matters of religious custom, and a description of the different religious services and practices is included only because it may be helpful to those who will go to funerals of different faiths.

Before taking up the details, however, a few words must be said about funeral arrangements as a whole. Anyone who is responsible for funeral arrangements wants to be sure that the ceremony will be beautiful and fitting in all its details. In the Protestant and Reformed Jewish faiths, great latitude is often given to the wishes of the family in choosing the texts and the hymns for the funeral. But even in Roman Catholic funerals, where most of the ceremony is a matter of religious rule, there are still decisions which must rest with the family. It is sometimes difficult for those who are grief-stricken to remember or consider such details, and they are set down here in the hope that such suggestions will be useful at such a sad and difficult time.

The first point is that a funeral should, as far as possible, reflect the character and position and personality of the one who has died. If he had always led a very quiet life, very much confined within a small circle of family and friends, a funeral in a small church, or chapel, is the most fitting and appropriate. There need be no pallbearers, no lists of seating arrangements. The few ushers will be members of the family and friends, to whom all those at the funeral will be known. If the family can choose the text and hymns, they will make their choices to reflect the character and tastes of the one who has died. The funeral of one who has lived in a wider circle, who has many friends and business acquaintances, and who has given a great deal of his time to important charitable work will necessarily be quite different. It will probably be in a big church, with many honorary pallbearers. The first pews will be reserved and the many ushers will be given lists of those who are to have special places. Both of these services can be, in every sense, "beautiful." In each, the essential is recognized. The dead has been honored, and whatever there may be of pomp and ceremony, apart from the religious ceremony itself, is included in order that the funeral may reflect as far as possible the life, the quality, and the achievements of the one who has died.

ARRANGING FOR THE FUNERAL

The first step is to talk with the clergyman or minister to decide on the day and hour of the funeral service. The clergyman and sexton will also be able to advise the family about an undertaker. Then the death notices can be sent to the newspapers.

A word must be said here, however, about choosing the coffin. At such a difficult moment, it is often hard to decide details such as these, especially since the decision is usually made by someone other than the one closest to the deceased. Elaborate coffins are not necessary or even especially to be desired. Solid mahogany is very beautiful but very expensive; a simple coffin of plain wood will do quite well. No considerations as to whether or not the coffin will look expensive should ever enter. Far better from every point of view a simple coffin than a pretentious one, or one which will subject the family to any financial strain. When a man has died, the family usually brings to the undertaker a dark-blue or black suit, such as might be worn for church on Sunday; or it might be a cutaway, instead. When a grown woman has died, the family brings a long-sleeved dress, ankle-length with a high neck; often with a high, surplice closing. The best colors are pale and subdued: beige, grey, lilac or even a light, soft blue, but not red or orange or such bright colors, and rarely black. For a young girl, white or light blue is often chosen. For children, a dress or suit such as would be worn to church on Sunday.

FLOWERS AT THE DOOR

It used to be the custom to hang flowers and ribbons or crape by the doorbell after a death in the house. This custom began, it is said, in the days when doorbells were literally bells hanging at the front door. During an illness the bell was muffled, so that the patient should not be disturbed; and, when he died, dark cloths were hung to indicate the mourning of the household. This changed, in time, to flowers and ribbons, hung as a symbol of the family's mourning—white for the young, purple for older people—from the day of the death until the day after the funeral. Today, when many more die in hospitals than at home, the custom has almost been abandoned. Those who find comfort in it may, of course, follow it. The flowers are hung just below the doorbell by the front door, whether out of doors at the door of a private house, or indoors at the door of an apartment.

DEATH NOTICES

Death notices follow the traditional form:

Clayton—John Willard, on June 20, 1948, husband (or beloved husband) of Mary Gardener Clayton, and father of Agnes and John Willard Clayton, Jr. Funeral at Grace Church at 3:00 P.M. Thursday.

In death notices the most important relationship must be given precedence. In the death notice of a man this is the order: "......... husband of ...., father of ...., son of ...., brother of ...." That of a woman follows the same order: She is first a wife, then a mother, then a daughter and then a sister. Other relationships are not given, and as a rule not more than two are mentioned. Death notices are telephoned or sent by mail to the newspaper by members of the family, or, if there is no family, by the one who is closest to the deceased. If there is no immediate family, the notice is sent to the newspaper by an executor, or by the one in charge: "Clayton, John Willard, on June 20, 1948, husband of the late Mary Gardener Clayton, and son of the late Daniel Lloyd and Esther Willard Clayton. Funeral at Grace Church at 3:00 P.M. Thursday."

If the dead had many friends or relatives in another city, to this notice can be added the phrase, "Baltimore papers please copy," or "San Francisco papers please copy." If the funeral is in a country town, train arrangements are added: "Funeral at St. Mark's Church, Somerton, Connecticut, at 11:30 A.M. Train leaves Grand Central Station at 10:15." When the funeral service is held at one place and the burial at another, the notice reads: "Service at .... Burial at ...."

If the family prefers a small funeral, the words "Funeral private" may be substituted for those concerning the funeral arrangements, and the only ones who will come to the funeral are those whom the family will have notified privately. If the family prefers not to have flowers sent, the following may be added to the death notice: "It is requested that no flowers be sent," or "Please do not send flowers." (In certain faiths, flowers are forbidden, so this request must always be obeyed.) Very often the notice reads: "It is requested that no flowers be sent, but that donations be given, instead, to a worthy charity." Or this form may be used: "It is earnestly requested that no flowers be sent. Instead, friends may send a donation to the . . . . (the name of the charitable organization) at . . . . (the address) in the name of . . . . (the deceased)." Such notices are becoming more and more the custom, and the last is often used when the deceased was particularly interested in a specific charity. Sometimes these requests are made under instructions left by the deceased, but often the family decides that such a tribute to the one who has died is better than a great quantity of flowers, which can last only a short time. When such a request has been made, /there are no flowers in the church other than a pall or wreath sent by the immediate family, and one or two sprays sent by other members of the family.

OBITUARIES

Obituaries are written by the newspaper editor in charge of that department and are never sent by the family, although it would be perfectly correct, should the editor ask for information, for a member of the family to supply any details concerning the life, the work, or the achievements of the person who has died. If the newspaper wants a photograph, the family may quite properly forward one; but, as in the case of the obituary itself, a photograph should never be sent unless it is requested by the newspaper. (See also page 98, in the chapter, "Personal Publicity.")

FLOWERS

At the time of a death, before or after the funeral, flowers are often sent to the family of the one who has died. The only exceptions are Roman Catholic and Orthodox Jewish families. The note or card which accompanies them may be written in terms as intimately sympathetic as the relationship warrants. To an acquaintance, a visiting card should be sent with the engraved name struck out in ink, and some such message as this:

> Dear Mrs. Clayton:
> These flowers bring you all my sympathy.
> Affectionately,
> Margaret Cutting

Flowers sent to the church (see "Church Arrangements" below, for rules and customs of the different faiths) carry with them a visiting card or a florist's card, with the name of the sender—as, "George Hart" or "Mr. and Mrs. Douglas Davis"—but no message. The envelope is addressed as follows:

> The funeral of John Willard Clayton, Esq.
> Grace Church

When flowers are sent directly to the cemetery, the envelope enclosing the card is addressed according to this form:

To the funeral of
Colonel Edward Adams
3:30 P.M., Tuesday, March 18th
Care of the Superintendent of the Cemetery
Arlington, Virginia

Friends often send, instead of flowers, contributions to the institutions and charities in which the deceased was particularly interested. The family should receive a notice from the organization; as, "A contribution has been received from Mr. and Mrs. Henry St. George in memory of Mr. John Willard Clayton." Thank-you letters should be sent by the family for these, as well as for flowers. (See page 152 below.)

MASS CARDS

Mass cards are Roman Catholic in origin, but they are often sent by non-Catholics also to the widow or another member of a Catholic family, at the time of a death or on the anniversary of a death. Basically, a mass card is a statement, signed by a priest, that a mass will be said for the repose of a soul. Among Catholics they replace flowers, which the Church considers symbols of happiness and joy. To get a mass card, it is necessarily only to ask a priest for one. Differences in religion do not enter; non-Catholics, as well as Catholics, may ask that a mass be said for anyone who has died, no matter in what faith. It is customary, as in most religions, to make an offering to the church at that time, usually at the time of asking for the card.

BEFORE THE FUNERAL

In some families and communities, it is customary for friends and members of the family to call at the house, or mortuary chapel, where the body is lying until time for the funeral. The coffin is left half-open, surrounded with flowers and sometimes candles. In other communities, such visits are not customary and some families prefer that no visits be made. In these cases, if the body is in a mortuary chapel, the doors are closed, with a sign which reads, "Family only." In a private house, if visitors are expected to visit the body, there is always a member of the family who will receive visitors and invite them to do so. If not, visitors can speak to the member of the family in charge and leave their cards for any member of the family who may have been unable to receive them.

CHURCH ARRANGEMENTS

Church arrangements differ according to each religion. The Roman Catholic funeral mass is always held in the morning; Protestant services, although usually also in the morning, may be in the afternoon as well. At a Roman Catholic funeral, no flowers are permitted in the church except for the pall of flowers which covers the coffin and is usually sent by the family. Flowers may be sent, however, to the funeral parlor, or to the church, to accompany the coffin to the cemetery.

In Protestant churches an embroidered or brocaded pall belonging to the church is often used, and it is permitted to send as many flowers as the family or friends desire. Some member of the family should always be at the church, to make a list of the flowers and to supervise the placing of the bouquets. The list should be as detailed as possible so that thanks can be written "for the beautiful roses" rather than "flowers." Bouquets from intimate friends and members of the family should be nearer the coffin, or in a more central position, than those sent by distant relatives and acquaintances. In Orthodox synagogues, no flowers are permitted and no flowers should be sent either to the synagogue or to the house. Reformed temples, like the Protestant churches, permit any quantity of flowers, but Conservative synagogues may follow either the Orthodox or the Reformed rule, so it is wise to ask some member of the family whether or not flowers may be sent.

The undertaker and sexton arrange for all the physical details of the burial, including the hearse and the automobiles which may, if necessary, be hired to take the family to the cemetery.

MUSIC AT THE FUNERAL

The Roman Catholic mass for the dead may be a Low, a High, or a Solemn Requiem Mass; in other words, a Low Mass, which is read, or a chanted mass with music. In many Protestant churches, however, and in many Jewish temples and synagogues, wide latitude is given the family in the choice of music which will be played at the service. The hymns, certain prayers, and the music before and after the service are often chosen by the family in consultation with the clergyman and organist. The following music is approved by most Protestant clergymen:

"Prelude and Angels' Farewell" from *The Dream of Gerontius* by Edward Elgar

"Largo" by Handel

"All Flesh Doth Perish" from the *Requiem* by Brahms

"Give Rest O Christ" (Contakion, Keiff Melody) by Parratt

"Come, Sweet Death" by Bach

"Souls of the Righteous" by Noble

"I Heard a Voice from Heaven" by Goss

"I Know that my Redeemer Liveth" by Handel

"In Paradisium" by Mulet

"Death and Resurrection" by Langlais

"Funeral March" by Dierne

"Funeral March" from the Piano Sonata in A Flat, Opus 26, No. 12, by Beethoven

"Dead March" from *Saul* by Handel

March in B Flat by Schubert

PALLBEARERS AND USHERS

Traditionally, pallbearers were necessary for every funeral to carry the coffin to the church and finally to the grave. In our days, the coffin is usually carried by members of the undertaker's staff, and pallbearers are only "honorary." They are usually chosen among the friends, family, and associates of the one who has died, and they should all be men. Furthermore, according to Christian tradition, honorary pallbearers serve only at the funeral of a man. Jewish custom permits pallbearers for both men and women. The customary number is six or eight, four being the usual minimum and ten the maximum. The widow or parent may ask the pallbearers to serve; but as a rule this is done by another member of the family: a brother, son, or cousin who has taken charge of the funeral details. Incidentally, one cannot refuse, if one is asked to be a pallbearer; the only excuse is illness or absence.

As a rule, at all services, the pallbearers sit in the front pews across the main aisle from the family. When the coffin is carried into the church after the congregation is seated, the honorary pallbearers march up the aisle, two by two, just in front of the coffin. At the end of the service they march down the aisle, again just in front of the coffin.

When the coffin is in place before the congregation comes in, the pallbearers usually march down the aisle just before the family is seated. At the end of the service, if the coffin is carried from the church, the pallbearers precede it down the aisle. If not, they march down the aisle just after the family has gone into the vestry. And as a rule they drive to the cemetery ahead of the hearse.

Apart from the fact that they march with the coffin, and the fact that, unlike the rest of the congregation, they usually go to the cemetery, honorary pallbearers have no function. If they have come from a distance, they often go to pay their respects to the family, either before or after the service, but otherwise they are only asked to serve as an honor to the dead and in recognition of their relationship with him. At a big funeral, it is fitting that such recognition be made publicly, but at small funerals, pallbearers are rare.

Ushers, on the other hand, are a part of almost every funeral. As in the case of pallbearers, they must all be men and they should all be friends or members of the family, rather than members of the undertaker's or sexton's staff. Ideally, they should represent all the relationships and interests of the dead. Alphabetical lists, showing where each person is to sit, are comparatively rare today, except at official funerals; and it is most helpful to have ushers who will be able to recognize as many of the people as possible. As explained below, the decision as to where each person is to sit now depends mostly on his own good sense and tact, but ushers can do a great deal to minimize the danger of important and intimate friends sitting in the back through their own modesty. When there are no honorary pallbearers, the ushers sit opposite the family and they often march up the aisle (two by two as the pallbearers do) just before the coffin is brought in, or just before the family comes in from the vestry. At the end of the service, after the coffin has been carried from the church, or after the family has gone into the vestry, they again march down the aisle while the rest of the congregation is still seated.

SEATING ARRANGEMENTS

At most Protestant funerals, the immediate family occupies the first pew at the right of the main aisle: at the right, that is, facing the altar. (In Jewish temples, the family sits on the side nearest the vestry door.) At all but the biggest funerals, the members of the family are the only ones who sit in a special pew; and as a rule they enter the church from the vestry, after everyone else has been seated. The church doors are opened as soon as the coffin is in place, usually about half an hour before the ceremony is to begin; the ushers take their places at the door, and escort the people up the aisle as they arrive. At the end of the service, the family leaves by the vestry. When there are pallbearers, the first pews across the aisle from the family are reserved for them. If a great many people are expected, the first three or four pews on both sides may be "seated." The ushers will have short lists of the names of the family, the most intimate friends, the wives of the pallbearers, and any others who should be given special places.

At Roman Catholic funerals the family sometimes sits at the right and sometimes at the left. The procedure, which is followed also at some Episcopal funerals, is that the congregation is seated before the coffin is brought into the church. The coffin, preceded by any honorary pallbearers, is carried up the main aisle and set down in front of the altar. The family follow it up the aisle, the closest members first, and take their places in the front pews. At the end of the service, the coffin is carried down the center aisle, again preceded by the pallbearers and followed by the family.

Orthodox Jewish synagogues never permit a casket to be brought within the doors, so Orthodox funerals are usually held in funeral chapels. The Orthodox rules which forbid men and women to stand together, and forbid men to remove their hats, apply only to synagogues. At a service in a funeral parlor, husband and wife stand side by side and men take off their hats.

At smaller funerals of all faiths today, since the ushers have no seating lists, the question of seating usually depends upon the tactful decision of each individual. Relatives or intimate friends may quite properly sit near the front of the church on the center aisle; those who know the family less well will seat themselves toward the back. In every case, of course, any suggestions or hints given by the ushers must be observed. Special pews may have to be kept for a group of colleagues or business associates. Nothing is more unfortunate than to give the impression of rushing to the first pews, only to be moved back by the usher. A woman does not take an usher's arm at funerals, as she does at weddings. An usher escorts her up the aisle, but does not offer his arm.

A rule which is followed at funerals of all faiths is that no one should leave his place in the pew until the immediate family and all the pallbearers have left the church. Some members of the family always follow the coffin to the cemetery, and, sometimes, before getting into the waiting automobiles, they greet the friends who have lingered by the church door. A few years ago, many funeral processions followed the old custom of drawing the shades in the automobiles following the coffin, but this is now entirely a matter of choice.

AT THE GRAVE

At the short ceremony in the cemetery, there are usually only members of the immediate family, a few of the most intimate friends, and the pallbearers, if any. For a small simple funeral, no special arrangements are necessary in the cemetery. At bigger funerals, there is sometimes a tent by the side of the grave.

The ground around the grave is covered with a grass carpet and the flowers, which have been brought with the funeral procession, are put around the grave by the undertaker's staff.

OFFICIAL FUNERALS

Military and naval funeral regulations are extremely explicit. Although at Protestant and Reformed Jewish funerals the usual latitude is given the family in the choice of texts and hymns, all such details as the procession up the aisle, the seating arrangements, and all the other details are a matter of strict protocol and are in the hands of the chaplain and the commanding officer.

FUNERALS AT HOME

When the funeral service is to be held at home, a room must be especially arranged for the ceremony. As a rule, the biggest room is chosen and the furniture is removed or pushed against the walls. The coffin is put wherever it seems most fitting or most convenient: usually at one end of the room, or in a bay window. Small chairs, facing the coffin, can be set in rows. For a Protestant or Reformed Jewish service, the coffin is covered and surrounded with flowers. At Orthodox Jewish funerals, it is customary not to have flowers. Some members of the family should always be downstairs to receive those who have come to the funeral; but as a rule a widow or mother stays upstairs until it is time for the service. Then she takes her place in the front row of chairs nearest the coffin, the minister comes in, and the service begins. When the service is over, the family follows the coffin to the cemetery, and the other people leave also.

Sometimes, particularly if the service is held in a country house, luncheon or tea is given to those who have come to the funeral. Again, a widow stays upstairs and sees only one or two of the guests who go especially to visit her.

THE CLERGYMAN'S FEE

In almost every faith it is customary to give a fee to the clergyman who performs the funeral service. This may be given in cash in a closed envelope, or a check may be sent with a letter after the funeral. The letter should be written by the nearest relative of the one who has died and should include thanks to the clergyman and a word about the service. ("The service was such a comfort to us all . . .") Mention of the enclosed check may be made in the letter ("I enclose a check which I hope you will use in any way you see fit, with many thanks again . . .") although many, especially women, make no mention of the check at all. The letter should be written by hand on personal or "house" writing paper, not on business paper.

The amount of the fee, as usual, depends on the elaborateness of the service and whether the giver is a regular supporter of the church. If there were many choir boys and special music, a regular member of the parish might send 50 or 75 dollars; someone not a member of the church, perhaps 100 dollars. If the service was very small and simple, the fee might be 10 or even 5 dollars. The average fee is 25 dollars.

CLOTHES FOR THE FUNERAL

No matter how one feels about mourning, or how relaxed the rules governing mourning may be, it is extremely bad taste for women who are intimate members of the family to wear anything but black at the funeral. This need not mean full mourning—black gloves, black stockings, etc.—but it does mean all-black clothes, even for those who do not believe in mourning at all. Others may wear anything they please, although dark colors are naturally more appropriate; but the women who will sit in the front pews should all be dressed in black. Black crape, or crape-bordered chiffon veils, may be worn by any women members of the family, although they are now rarely worn except by the widow, mother, sister, or daughter of the dead person. (See also "Mourning Clothes and Materials" below.)

Masculine members of the family may wear "morning coats," with striped trousers, black waistcoats, and black four-in-hand neckties (see page 617 in the chapter "Men's Clothes," for details). Now, more often they wear dark-blue, black, or even gray suits with white shirts, black neckties, socks, and shoes and, with a dark-blue or gray suit, a mourning-band on the left arm. Others dress as they would for Sunday church but with dark neckties and socks. Ushers and pall-bearers need not necessarily be dressed exactly alike unless they are to march up the aisle together. At very big funerals, they may wear morning coats, but at almost all funerals now, dark-blue or black suits, with black ties, white shirts, and black shoes and socks are the rule. For both men and women, of course, military or naval uniform overrides all the usual rules.

VISITS OF CONDOLENCE

A visit of condolence always used to be considered one of the obligations of friendship and, to some extent, a social obligation also. In the 1920's and 1930's, the tendency was to abandon the practice on the grounds that one should not intrude during a time of mourning. Now, the whole question has resolved itself on a very sound basis: One does not make a visit of condolence as a matter of social obligation but only as an evidence of friendship. Those who are in deep mourning often have little heart for the activities which used to fill their days, and a visit of condolence, prompted by affection, can be a great comfort.

A day or so after the funeral, friends telephone the house and leave a message asking if they may call at such and such an hour, or at some other time which might be more convenient. If one is really not able to receive visitors, a member of the family should telephone and explain, thanking the friend; or a letter of thanks may be written, explaining the situation. Very intimate friends often call without advance notice and, if one is out or unable to receive them, they call again the following day. The essential point is that friendship and true affection must be the basis of any call at such a time.

LETTERS OF CONDOLENCE

There is probably no letter more difficult to write than a letter of condolence. In these days, when letter writing is an art reduced to a vestige of its former splendor, most people find it extremely difficult to begin suddenly to be articulate on paper, to express adequately the sorrow and sympathy they feel and, in some measure, to comfort the one who mourns. And besides, a feeling of diffidence sometimes makes one hesitate to write, especially to acquaintances. Actually, neither of these considerations should stop one from writing. It cannot be over-emphasized that, to those who are in deep mourning, answering letters of condolence and receiving visits of condolence are often the only really comforting activities. The bases for writing a letter of condolence are much broader than those for making a visit of condolence. Respect and obligation are valid grounds, as well as affection and friendship. A letter to an acquaintance will naturally be more reserved than the letter one might write to a friend, but it is always kind to write one. A letter of condolence to a friend is one of the obligations of friendship.

Letter to an Acquaintance

Dear Mrs. Elliot,

I was so sorry to hear of your sad news. I am writing to send you all my sympathy, remembering the many happy days we spent together at Nantucket. I hope so much that we shall meet very soon; and if there is anything I can do for you here, please do let me know.

Affectionately,

Mary Thayer

Thursday
July 21st

To a Business Acquaintance

Dear Mrs. Chambers,

I was so sorry to read your sad news in this morning's newspaper. At such a moment, I know that there is very little anyone can do to help, but if there should be anything, I hope you will let me know. In any case, I send you all my deepest sympathy.

Sincerely,

Mary Thayer

Thursday
July 21st

To Friends

A letter of condolence to a friend will usually be more warmhearted and fuller than the examples given above. The important thing, at such a moment, is that the two friends should feel a shared burden of sorrow; that the sincerity and depth of the friendship should be made plain. Anything one truly feels can be written; if one is crushed or heartbroken, one may say so. But the quality of the friendship, the reserve or reticence of the friend to whom one is writing, must always be the determining factor in deciding how emotional the letter will be.

The ideal letter of condolence has a traditional form: first, an expression of sympathy; as, "I was so sorry to hear of your father's death"; second, an observation or a passage to convey the writer's interest either in the dead person, or in the one to whom the letter is addressed; as, "I remember so well your father's kindness to us during that dreadful summer of 1942 when . . ."; third, some expression of comfort; as, "I know it must be a help to you, in these days which are so sad for you, to know how many people will miss him . . ."; and, finally, a last word of affection and sympathy.

151

ANSWERS TO LETTERS OF CONDOLENCE

The important thing about answers to letters of condolence is not their length, or even their content, but the fact that they *must* be written. No one who takes the time and trouble to write a letter of condolence should fail to receive an answer. And unless there is the excuse of extremely frail health, even the deepest grief is not a valid reason for avoiding the responsibility of writing. Answers should always be written by the one who received the letters of condolence, or at least by a close member of the family. Except in most unusual circumstances, it is incorrect to have them answered by a secretary. A few words will do if there are many letters to answer, or in cases of ill health or extreme age.

Dear Mrs. Thayer,

Thank you so much for your sweet letter. I am most grateful for your sympathy.

Affectionately,
Margaret Elliot

Sunday
    July 24th

or,

Dear Mrs. Thayer,

Thank you very much indeed for your kind letter. At such a time, the sympathy of friends means so much. I hope I shall see you very soon.

Sincerely,
Margaret Elliot

Sunday
    July 24th

or,

Dear Mrs. Thayer,

Thank you so much for your sweet letter of sympathy about Bobbie. It is all so awful that I can't yet fully take it in, or begin to understand why.

I hope I shall see you this summer.

Always affectionately,
Margaret Elliot

Sunday
    July 24th

As far as possible, no matter what one's feelings may be, a letter of condolence should always be answered in the spirit in which it was written. An emotional answer to a formal note is out of place; a reserved and markedly reticent answer to a warm outpouring of emotion may have the cold effect of a rebuke.

THANK-YOU LETTERS FOR FLOWERS

Like answers to letters of condolence, letters of thanks must be written for flowers sent to the house or to the church, or for contributions sent to charities in memory of the deceased. The letters should always be written by the widow or parent of the person who has died, or by a close member of the family. Letters written by a secretary, engraved cards, and all other such impersonal ways of thanking people are not correct. Even the briefest note is better than none:

Dear Mrs. Thayer:

Thank you so much for the beautiful flowers. It was very kind of you to send them.

Affectionately,

Margaret Elliot

Sunday
July 24th

The more usual, slightly longer version is, of course, much better:

Dear Mrs. Thayer:

Thank you so much for the lovely roses you sent me (or, if the flowers were sent to the church, "for sending the lovely roses"). I can't tell you how pleased and how touched I was by your thoughtfulness—nothing is more comforting than to be reminded of the sympathy and affection of friends.

I shall look forward to seeing you very soon. Perhaps you would telephone and come for tea?

Many, many thanks again,

Affectionately,

Margaret Elliot

Sunday
July 24th

MOURNING WRITING PAPER

The custom of using black-bordered writing paper during the time of mourning is, like other mourning traditions, observed less strictly today than it was thirty or forty years ago. For those who still believe in mourning, however, it is a cherished and most comforting tradition. Writing paper should to some extent reflect the personality and circumstances of the writer, and mourning paper certainly conveys a sense of sorrow and loss, so much so that it should never be used by anyone who is not in mourning, even if a long period of mourning has just ended. Today, the black border has grown somewhat narrower than it used to be; now it is usually only a sixteenth of an inch instead of a quarter of an inch wide; and all-white paper is used more than before. But it is still true that no one who goes into mourning at all would consider using colored paper, or white paper with a colored monogram, after a death in the family.

Mourning paper for men is very simple: all white, or white with an address or initials engraved in black. Mourning paper for women may be all white with a black monogram or address, white with a black border, or pale gray with a black border and a black-lined envelope. Black-bordered paper is not correct, however, in business correspondence. Personal letters to tradesmen or shops are not, strictly, "business correspondence"; they can be written on mourning paper, on plain white paper, or on ordinary post cards. Men and women in business use the firm's writing paper; and no matter how highly colored it may be, it is perfectly correct for business correspondence. (See also page 529, "Writing Paper.")

MOURNING

Mourning has two main purposes or functions, one personal and the other social, one to protect the mourner, and the other to honor the dead. There used to be a third also: to emphasize the importance and prestige of the family; but this has, happily, almost entirely disappeared. Every society has developed some way of marking the solemn fact of death, and even the most primitive has usually evolved a pattern for the behavior of the family of the dead. In our own civilization thirty or forty years ago, the pattern was strict and rigid: How one should behave, what one should wear, how long one should mourn, were all covered by a minutely detailed code. Today, such a code does not exist. Individual choice and feeling are given much more scope than ever before. When one sees a recently widowed woman in a beige suit, the reaction is no longer, "Shocking, heartless creature!" but rather, "She does not believe in mourning"—an observation that carries no suggestion of criticism.

One of the few elements in mourning that has remained constant is that women are still the predominating and decisive influence in determining what the period and degree of mourning shall be.

BEHAVIOR DURING MOURNING

Basically, mourning has two outward manifestations: behavior, which is by far the more important; and material things, such as clothes, writing paper, and jewelry. What determines how one behaves in mourning is a delicate fusion of three elements: respect for the dead, respect for the feelings and opinions of others, and one's own feelings. We cannot here discuss deep personal sorrow; etiquette is concerned with relations with others, not with the way in which one resolves a heavy individual problem. But before we consider the behavior of the chief mourner, we might discuss the attitude of other members of the family, of friends, acquaintances, and strangers.

Out of common decency and kindness, as well as good taste, the first duty of everyone concerned should be to make an effort to understand and sympathize with the behavior of anyone who has lost a parent or a child, a husband or a wife. Lack of taste and imagination are painfully obvious in criticisms of anyone who may be stunned by grief. Open criticism is deplorable, but there are more subtle ways also of showing bad taste. If the widow is in deep mourning, for example, it would be extremely bad taste for other women of the family to wear bright colors or to go to dances a few weeks after the funeral. If the widow does not believe in mourning, it would be an evidence of great understanding and sympathy should her mother and sisters-in-law moderate a little their own attitude to suit hers. Family misunderstandings should not be made public at such a moment, either by direct criticisms, or indirectly, by pointed differences in actions or behavior. And certainly if members of the family must so subordinate their grief to that of the widow, the sorrow of friends and acquaintances confers no right of criticism of any kind.

All this kindness and consideration impose an additional responsibility on the chief mourner, whose actions and attitude will to some extent influence what others will wear and how they will behave. The very fact that everyone acknowledges a duty to refrain from criticism means that one must behave as well as one possibly can. One may not believe in mourning, one may even consider it wrong to wear black clothes, but one cannot ignore the opinions and feelings of others.

Peculiar behavior, or any behavior that departs widely from the normal, can shock other people, or it can hurt them. Naturally, very few of us want to do either, and the purpose of this discussion is to set down the shape and the extent of current public opinion on this subject. To begin with, people are more apt to be shocked or hurt by what one does than by what one wears. Because so many have held as a principle that it is undesirable to wear mourning, the hitherto rigid code has been broken. But gay, insouciant behavior is another matter. If one disapproves of black clothes for mourning, one may wear colors the day after the funeral without incurring any justifiable criticism. Colored clothes may easily cover deep sorrow. But even the most generous-minded will find it hard to believe that the one who chooses to go to dances, night clubs, or dinner parties really feels very sad. Anyone who was fond of the dead will be hurt; more casual observers will criticize.

Those who find this attitude unfair, or believe that it shows courage to dine out in the face of sorrow, should perhaps reconsider the whole question of courage. It is certainly a virtue, and much to be admired, when it subordinates individual feelings to the common good, to responsibilities toward others, or to some great or worthy purpose. It is courageous to continue one's philanthropic work immediately after the funeral, to keep one's regular hours in a hospital or kindergarten. It is courageous, also, to carry on with unheroic household tasks, to keep one's children happy. But it is evasion, rather than courage, when in such circumstances one goes to a dance to avoid loneliness or sorrow for oneself only.

Aside from the fact of shocking others or hurting their feelings, there are considerations of social tact and fitness. A widow in deep mourning could quite properly go to a small dinner party of four or six people, where presumably everyone would understand and share her feelings. But at any big dinner party, most of the guests would arrive expecting a gay and happy time—an attitude which the widow could scarcely be expected to share. If they laugh loudly in the face of her obvious grief, they feel callous; they subdue their mirth and the widow must become uncomfortably aware of her dampening effect. The whole evening becomes a painful and difficult situation which could easily have been avoided.

Naturally, very little of this applies to a stranger in a strange community. If a relative in a distant city has died, one can wear mourning or not, dine out or stay home, without running any risk of hurting or shocking other people, or making them uncomfortable. Life in a community imposes other duties and responsibilities. Every death is new and different, and circumstances alter each case. It has been wisely said that no man dies once and in one way only, but, instead, once and in *many* ways: in all the different facets of his life and of his relationships. And this is what the chief mourner must remember. Personal feelings and prejudices should be so patterned as to allow others, as far as possible, to express their sorrow in whatever way they find most comforting.

(See also "A Wedding in Time of Mourning," page 190.)

Traditional Rules

According to the customary and extremely sensible rule, no one in deep mourning should go to the following:

Dinner parties of more than eight people.
Fashionable restaurants, especially in the evening.
The opera, particularly in a conspicuous box.
The theater, especially in the evening, movie theaters excepted.
Races, or any big organized sports meetings, especially indoor events such as prizefights.

And this rule still holds *if* one is dressed in deep mourning. Half mourning or semi-mourning does not look strange or incongruous in places normally associated with gaiety, but deep mourning most definitely does.

THE PERIOD OF MOURNING

Thirty or forty years ago, the length of the mourning period and the materials that were considered correct for mourning were part of a widely accepted pattern, so well established, in fact, that it was considered shocking and extremely bad taste when the pattern was departed from. As we have said, this is no longer true. Although many adhere to the traditional form, and even more accept the modern modification of that pattern, some do not believe in mourning of any kind. Mourning black is mandatory only for the funeral itself, where colors worn by intimate members of the family would still be conspicuous and, therefore, bad taste.

Traditional Periods of Mourning

The following used to be the strict pattern for the length of the mourning period in Britain and the United States. Mourning in Latin countries is two, sometimes three, times as long. (See "Mourning Clothes and Materials" below for explanations of the terms, "full mourning" and "half mourning.")

Two years' mourning: one year of full mourning, one year of half mourning; for husband, wife, father, mother, son, or daughter.
One year's mourning: six months' full mourning, six months' half mourning; for a grandfather, grandmother, aunt or uncle (by blood), brother or sister.
Three months' mourning: one month's full mourning, two months' half mourning; for first cousin, uncle or aunt (by marriage), niece or nephew.

Contemporary Periods of Mourning

Although, as we have said, mourning is now largely a matter of individual choice or feeling, there are still so many people who accept the following pattern that it may be considered modern social usage:

Six to twelve months' mourning: either full mourning or half mourning; for husband, wife, mother, father, son or daughter.
Three to six months' mourning: either full or half mourning; grandfather, grandmother, aunt or uncle (by blood), brother or sister.
One to two months' half mourning: for all other relatives.

MOURNING CLOTHES AND MATERIALS

Mourning clothes for women, in the strictest interpretation, mean black clothes in certain specified materials, and with few exceptions, nothing but black clothes. Beige stockings cannot be worn as mourning in the city (see "Country Mourning" for country customs) and neither can beige gloves nor gold jewelry. Summer clothes follow rules of their own, and clothes for active sports follow those governing mourning for men (see below). The one rule that must govern all mourning is that it must not be too conspicuously "smart" or too obviously in the latest fashion.

Here follows a list of materials and accessories that may be worn in the deepest mourning, together with a list of those which are incorrect.

Correct	*Incorrect*
Dull materials, such as wool, jersey, cotton, linen, silk, rayon, tulle, and chiffon.	Glossy materials, such as velvet, lace, satin, taffeta, and some silks.
Black furs, such as fox, astrakhan, and the traditional mourning fur, sable. (Although sable is not, of course, a black fur, it has been considered correct for mourning for many years.)	All light furs, brown furs, mixed furs (such as silver fox), and even black sealskin.
Pearls, jet, black onyx, or lacquer; and a few touches of silver, such as a silver clasp on a purse, or a silver pin. The only accepted gold is a gold wedding ring, which, of course, need not be taken off.	All colored stones, diamonds, all gold jewelry and any touches of gold, such as a gilded clasp or chain.
Dull braid or soutache.	Sequins, even if black, and all other shiny decorations.
Dull straws or felts for hats; horsehair hats.	Shiny straws or hats made of any of the materials listed above.
Ostrich feathers.	Cock feathers, even black ones, and all other feathers, except ostrich.
	Patent leather, or any other kind of shiny leather.
Dull leathers, such as kid or suède.	All natural flowers, and all imitation flowers made of "incorrect" materials.

THE WIDOW'S BONNET AND VEIL

The black crape bonnet, the heavy black veil of crape or crape-bordered chiffon, and black-bordered handkerchiefs have almost disappeared from the contemporary scene. All three are still perfectly correct, but for some reason—perhaps because they do not seem to fit modern life—they are seldom seen. Most widows, and many other women, wear black veils for the funeral service, and some widows (particularly older women) continue to wear a black veil for a few months; the bonnet, however, is a thing of the past. Veils are now worn with any narrow-brimmed hat, thrown back from the face, and falling about ten or twelve inches down the back. The only rule concerning veils is that they must be worn with the correct mourning; a black, crape-bordered veil should never be worn with bright jewelry or colored stockings.

COUNTRY MOURNING

In the country, the rules governing mourning for women are much less strict than in town, particularly in the matter of daytime and sports clothes. As we have said, clothes for active sports are governed by the rules for men's mourning (page 159), but women's daytime clothes fall into somewhat the same category. For example, it would be perfectly correct for a woman in the deepest mourning to go walking in a heavy brown tweed overcoat with a black armband. Heavy walking shoes and the stockings worn with them need not be black, and even heavy tweed suits in a neutral color would be considered correct for all but the deepest mourning, provided they were worn with a black armband and a plain white blouse. Evening clothes, clothes for Sunday or for church should, of course, be all-black or all-white.

MOURNING FOR CHILDREN

In modern life, children are not usually put into any form of mourning until they are ten years old. Before this time, if a parent or grandparent has died, little girls might at most wear only white or pale mauve dresses, or gray flannels, for a short time; but black armbands or any other form of conventional mourning are seldom seen. Boys under ten years old, after a death of a parent or grandparent, usually wear the same little gray flannel suits or gabardine shorts that they normally would, but bright neckties and brightly colored sweaters might be left aside for a month or so. After the age of ten or twelve, boys follow the rules governing mourning for men, which are much less strict than those for women. Girls from ten to eighteen (or until their families consider them grown up) are usually dressed in a modified form of half mourning. In summer, their dresses could be white, pale gray, or mauve. In winter, they should wear gray flannels or tweed suits in neutral colors, with black armbands. Girls young enough to wear, ordinarily, flat-heeled oxfords should not wear black shoes, but older girls of sixteen or seventeen should have black accessories.

SUMMER MOURNING

In summer, all-white clothes are considered deep mourning, just as all-black is, provided that the correct materials and accessories are used. A white chiffon evening dress, for example, worn with white slippers and stockings, would be just as deep mourning as a black chiffon dress with black slippers and stockings. All-white clothes, are, however, impossible in a city, except in the evening, but since all-white and all-black are interchangeable as far as mourning is concerned, it would be perfectly correct to wear all-black in the daytime and all-white in the evening.

HALF MOURNING

Half mourning, technically, is any combination of black with white, or white with black. A white collar on a black dress, white gloves with a black suit, a black ribbon on a white hat—all these mean half mourning. In addition, half mourning includes all shades of gray and purple, from pale dove gray to dark gray, from pale mauve to purple. When mourning lasted a year or so, gray and mauve were often worn in the last month or six weeks; in these days of shorter mourning, they are less often seen.

It is still true, however, that colored jewelry and all the other incorrect mourning materials and accessories should not be worn with mourning of any kind, even half mourning.

SEMI-MOURNING

Semi-mourning is a modern development which, technically, is not mourning at all. It is worn after the death of an intimate friend or a distant relative, and by many of those who do not believe in official mourning. In semi-mourning, one wears beige stockings, colored or gold jewelry, and black, white, or black-and-white clothes. No attention is paid to correct or incorrect materials, and no special pattern of behavior is observed. In the country, one wears beige or gray suits with white blouses and brown accessories. The whole point of semi-mourning is not to appear to be in mourning, but to avoid bright colors.

MOURNING FOR MEN

In the United States, as in Great Britain, it is not customary for men to go into deep mourning as they do in Latin countries. A black armband, white shirts and handkerchiefs, black neckties, socks, and shoes are considered deep mourning.

After an active sport such as tennis, when normally they might have worn a brightly colored sweater, men should wear a white sweater instead. For golf, thin gray flannel or gabardine trousers would be perfectly correct, with a white shirt, and a black necktie. Polo coats, or any other overcoats which are worn after exercise, should have black armbands and, of course, no one in mourning should wear brightly colored scarves or socks; neutral colors, such as gray and beige, are best.

For shooting, no mourning is necessary, because shooting requires special clothes which are basically informal, and besides, they are usually neutral in color. The only exception might be for driven-bird shooting, where ordinary tweed coats are worn. In such a case, the coat should have a black armband.

For riding and hunting, both men and women should wear a black armband on all riding coats, and on all overcoats worn with riding clothes. The only exceptions are "hunting pink," which may be worn quite correctly while in mourning, or black riding habits on which, of course, a black armband would be superfluous. Black four-in-hand neckties are worn with tweed riding coats, instead of colored ones.

26

Flying the Flag

THE FOLLOWING RULES and customs connected with the flag of the United States are gathered from various sources. Some are official, others civilian in origin, but all are commonly accepted as standard usage.

WHEN THE FLAG MAY BE FLOWN

Between sunrise and sunset out of doors—every day, but especially on the following days:

The day a president of the United States is inaugurated.
February 12, Lincoln's Birthday.
February 22, Washington's Birthday.
April 6, Army Day.
April 14, Pan-American Day.
Second Sunday in May, Mothers' Day.
Third Sunday in May, "I-Am-An-American Day."
May 22, National Maritime Day.
May 30, Memorial Day. Flag at half-staff until noon; at full staff from noon to sunset.
June 14, Flag Day.
July 4, Independence Day.
August 19, National Aviation Day.
First Monday in September, Labor Day.
September 14, Anniversary of the writing of "The Star-Spangled Banner" in 1814.
September 17, Constitution Day.
Last Sunday in September, Gold Star Mothers' Day.
October 12, Columbus Day.
October 27, Navy Day.
The day of election of a president of the United States.
November 11, Armistice Day.
Thanksgiving Day.
Not in rainy or stormy weather, except for a special reason.

THE POSITION OF THE BLUE FIELD

The blue field is always uppermost, whether the flag is flown from a staff or hung against a wall. The blue field is downward only as a signal of distress.

The blue field is always nearest the point of the staff, whether the staff is upright, or hanging horizontally, or at an angle, from a building.

The blue field is always at upper left when the flag is hung against a wall (at the left, that is, from the point of view of one who is facing the wall), and this is true whether the flag is hung horizontally or vertically.

The blue field faces north or east when the flag is hung between two buildings or across a street: north in an east-and-west street; to the east in a north-and-south street.

WITH OTHER FLAGS

On a staff with another emblem or pennant, the United States flag is flown above any other.

With one other flag, on crossed staffs against a wall, the United States flag is at the left as one faces the wall, and the staff of the United States flag is over the other.

With other American flags—e.g. flags of States, cities, or associations—in a decorative grouping of flags, the flag of the United States is in the middle, on a staff longer than the others. Flags of foreign nations are not adapted to an arrangement of this kind because international custom holds that one country's flag should not, in peacetime, fly above another's.

With flags of other nations, hung or displayed from a balcony or window, the United States flag is at the left, as seen from the street. The staffs should be of equal length.

With other flags, both American and foreign, in a row of vertical flagstaffs, the United States flag is at the left as seen by one facing the row of flags. When the United States flag is flown out of doors with the flags of other nations, the United States flag is raised first and lowered last. The staffs should all be the same height and the flags about the same size.

With other flags, both American and foreign, hung against a wall, the United States flag is at the left, as seen from the audience.

IN A PROCESSION

With one other flag, the United States flag is always at the right as seen from the marching column.

With two or more other flags, the United States flag is in front of the center of the line of other flags.

It is never carried flat, or horizontally, but only on a staff.

ON AN AUTOMOBILE

The flag is flown on a small staff fixed at the right end of the front bumper, as seen from the driver's seat, within the line of the mudguard. The staff should be long enough so that the flag clears the radiator hood. Or a small flag may be flown from the radiator cap.

ON A PLATFORM

The flag flies from a staff at the speaker's right as he faces the audience.

IN CHURCH

Within the chancel, the flag flies from a staff at the clergyman's right as he faces the congregation.

Outside the chancel, the flag is at the clergyman's left.

ON A COFFIN

The flag lies with the blue field at the upper right, over the body's left shoulder. A flag-covered coffin should be carried foot first. The flag is never lowered into the grave.

IN TIME OF MOURNING

On a stationary staff the flag is flown at half-staff, not a literal "half," but far enough down from the point of the staff so that the effect is obtained without putting the flag too near the ground or the building. The flag is raised to the top of the staff before being lowered to the half-staff position and, again in the evening, the flag is raised to the top before being taken down.

When carried, the flag is flown from the top of the staff, as usual, but with mourning streamers of black ribbon tied at the point of the staff.

BUNTING

Bunting is hung horizontally with the blue stripe at the top; vertically, with the blue stripe at the left as seen from the audience.

GENERAL RULES

1. The flag should be raised fairly quickly, and lowered slowly.
2. It should never be allowed to touch the ground or the water.
3. It should never be draped, nor tied with ribbons or bunting. The flag should always hang free.
4. It should never be used as part of a costume, or embroidered on scarves, handkerchiefs, etc.
5. Lettering should never be placed on the flag, and neither should it be flown from a pole to which any advertising is fastened.
6. It is never dipped to any person or any other flag.
7. The flag should never be used or stored in such a way that it may easily be damaged. If a flag has become very much worn, it should be burned or otherwise carefully destroyed.

SECTION THREE

WEDDINGS

27

Introduction

IN ACCORDANCE with history and tradition, and in complete accord with the facts, marriage is the single most important event in a lifetime. The interests of the community and of nature fuse at this moment, though they so often conflict during the rest of man's life, and every society, even the most primitive, recognizing the importance of marriage, has clothed it in customs which, to them, seemed both beautiful and significant.

In modern weddings there is an extraordinary complex of inherited ritual, most completely exemplified, of course, in big and elaborate weddings. But even in the simplest wedding there are certain customs that must be observed, some because they are beautiful and romantic, others because they involve social and economic factors. If the first are left out, no serious breach of etiquette is involved (they are described on pages 167 through 186). But to omit the second group would show a complete lack of interest in, or knowledge of, accepted customs.

The two wedding customs that should be observed are:

Neither the groom nor his family should issue the invitations and announcements, nor give the wedding.

Neither the groom nor his family should pay the expenses of the wedding.

Both of these are soundly based on the theory that the bride's parents are responsible for her until she leaves their house with her husband, responsible for her financially and morally. Under this convention, the financial responsibility is her father's, the moral, her mother's. And because, happily, morals are universally held to be more important than finances, the bride's mother is the more important of the two. In case of divorce between the parents, for example, it would be quite wrong for the bride to be married from her father's house, and to have him be the one who gives the wedding reception. Only flagrantly and openly scandalous behavior on the mother's part warrants her being ousted from her place in the wedding and, if such were the case, and the bride had been living with her grandmother, it would be better that the wedding be given by the bride's grandmother than by her father. Whether or not there had been a scandal, had the bride been living with her father—or with an older, married brother—he, of course, would give the wedding and issue all invitations and announcements in his name.

The only possible exceptions to the rule that the groom's family must not give the wedding are caused by unusual circumstances which are well known to the community or easily explicable. For example, a bride whose parents are foreign residents might be married in her mother-in-law's house, particularly if the parents of bride and groom were friends. The implication to be avoided is that a bride for some ulterior motive wishes to be married in the groom's house in preference to her own.

ESSENTIALS OF A WEDDING

Both simple and elaborate weddings are described further on in this section, but certain elements are indispensable to every wedding, which is more than just a marriage. A marriage can be performed quite simply in a judge's or registrar's office, or, better, in a church empty of all but the clergyman, the couple, and the two witnesses; and the bride and groom can leave together, with only the clergyman's blessing. But this is not, according to Webster or any woman's conception, a wedding.

To all weddings, the following are essential: 1. a religious ceremony; 2. a father, brother, uncle, cousin, or other male relative, to give the bride away; 3. a best man for the groom; 4. at least one attendant for the bride; 5. a bouquet for the bride; 6. a ring for the bride. And, if possible, 7. a reception, no matter how small, which need only entail a wedding cake and a drink in which to toast the bride.

Such a wedding, provided that the inflexible rules concerning invitations and announcements were followed, would be in every sense perfectly "correct." It might lack some of the beauty that ritual and wedding dress, flowers and music, can give to the ceremony. It might lack some of the gaiety of waltzes and wedding guests, but it would be completely in accord with modern social usage. And, if it were full of a warm spirit of affection and love and kindliness, it would be a far more pleasant occasion than a cold wedding of the most elaborate perfection.

In fact, the main thing to avoid in weddings is elaborate perfection at the expense of anything else. Better a small reception, in a house familiar through long association to the bride, than a large reception, brilliant with flowers and thronged with guests, in surroundings which mean little to the bride. And better the simplest of weddings than one which might impress the guests as a financial strain on the bride's family. Nothing could be less in the temper of the times. The days of "show" are happily over. Exhibitions of wealth are not in fashion. And, if fashion is to be considered at all in a matter of such deep concern, it would be far more fashionable to have a wedding less expensive than one could quite easily afford, than a wedding obviously out of proportion to one's usual way of life.

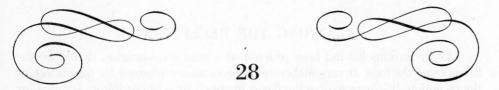

28

Preparations for a Wedding

RESERVING THE CHURCH

As soon as the engagement has been announced and before the wedding invitations and announcements can be ordered, the bride's mother must consider the date and the hour of the wedding and speak to the clergyman about reserving the church. (The contribution to the clergyman is given by the groom; see page 232.)

THE DATE AND HOUR OF THE WEDDING

The hour for the ceremony varies in the different sections of the United States. In the East and North most weddings, both formal and informal, take place either in the late afternoon, about half past four or five o'clock, or at noon (more usual for Roman Catholic weddings). In the South and West, perhaps because of the climate, weddings are in the evening, usually at eight o'clock. These are the traditional hours for weddings, and to depart too widely from the hour that is customary in any community is apt to raise many questions about procedure from guests, caterers, and all the others concerned.

The date or season for the wedding is entirely a question of church procedure, and personal convenience. The most formal wedding is one given in a big church, in a big city, during the "season" and not during Lent. The season varies in different cities. In New York it is traditionally during the months between the opening of the Metropolitan Opera and the first day of Lent; in New Orleans and Galveston, it is from late November until Mardi Gras, the Tuesday before Ash Wednesday. But, though these are traditional "seasons," there is, of course, no reason not to have a most formal wedding at any other time of the year, except during Lent when festive religious ceremonies accord badly with the church calendar.

Once these matters are settled, and it has been decided where the reception will be, the wedding invitations and announcements can be engraved, and the family can consider the less technical preparations for the wedding, which are discussed immediately below. See pages 199 to 217 for information about ordering invitations and announcements.

PLANNING THE RECEPTION

The invitations having been ordered, the next consideration should be the flowers and the food. If very elaborate decorations are planned for the church or the reception, it is wise to give the florist as much time as possible to arrange for the proper flowers; and one should also notify the caterer who will furnish the tables, waiters, food, and all the other essentials for the wedding breakfast. It is an important point of manners and procedure that the proper church authorities be consulted before making elaborate arrangements for church decorations. For the sake of example, we shall imagine that the bride and her mother have decided to have a big wedding in a large church at noon. (Church decorations, music and seating plans, are discussed on pages 176 to 179.)

In planning the reception the first question is always the hour set for the wedding. If the wedding is to be at noon, it must be followed by a fairly substantial meal, whether seated or not. If one decides on an afternoon wedding, one may have a seated meal which is like a supper, although it is rare nowadays, or a buffet meal. (Menus for the afternoon wedding reception will be found on page 192.) Our bride having decided on a most formal wedding at noon, plans will have to be made for a seated wedding breakfast. If there is to be dancing, this is the time to reserve the orchestra (usually not more than four or five players unless the reception rooms are very big). Since the wedding reception is to be given at home, no rooms need be reserved in a hotel. (The decorations for the reception rooms are discussed on page 172.) All these arrangements are made more or less simultaneously, but we shall discuss the wedding breakfast in detail first.

THE WEDDING BREAKFAST

As we have said, food for the wedding reception is of two main types: 1. a three- or four-course luncheon which is served after a noon wedding, and 2. buffet refreshments. (The first is described below, the second on page 192. The setting of a buffet tea table is shown on page 254.) Basically, the origin of both is the same: the feast to celebrate a joyful and important event, a custom long antedating the Christian era. In the early days of man's struggle with nature, food and wine in plenty were almost a miracle; dinner parties—those modern shadows of the ancient feasts—were unheard of, and feasts were rare events in the lives of all but the kings. For a wedding, however, every family summoned all its resources. Goats and kids were slaughtered, and the best wine was set aside in its bulging skins. A feeling of great and unaccustomed joy prevailed; feuds were forgotten; the feasting began.

Little of these early festivities is still apparent, perhaps, in the physical aspect of a wedding breakfast or buffet, but there is still much of the same spirit—or should be. An ample feeling of warmheartedness and affection, of gaiety and all-cares-forgotten should be the subtle flavor that permeates all the food and drink the wedding guest will be given.

MENUS FOR THE WEDDING BREAKFAST

For a wedding such as the one we are describing, a caterer is always necessary. Even the biggest and best furnished house can scarcely be expected to have enough chairs, tables, glass, china, linen and silver for two or three hundred guests. The caterer sometimes provides the champagne also, in addition to the food. But the long, elaborate menus of wedding breakfasts of twenty years ago are no longer fashionable. For a winter wedding at high noon and one, as we said, of the most elaborate kind, four courses would be the maximum. (At a formal wedding, if the menus are written formally, the French names, which are given in parentheses after each dish below, should always be used on the menu cards; a fuller description of some of these dishes will be found on pages 308 to 338 in the chapter "Fashions in Food," rules for the writing of menus on pages 270 to 272.)

Green turtle soup (Tortue verte)
Roast turkey (Dindonneau rôti)
String beans (Haricots verts au beurre)
Cold Virginia ham (Jambon de Virginie en gelée)
Romaine salad (Salade de romaines)
Ice cream with ginger (Glace Manchu)

Consommé (Consommé Brunoise)
Crabmeat Newburg (Crabe à la Newburg)
Breast of guinea hen (Pintadeau rôti)
Green salad (Salade verte)
Strawberry mousse (Mousse aux fraises)

Both these menus are the longest and most elaborate one would possibly find in normal society today. Much more common, even for a formal breakfast, are menus such as these:

Consommé
Squabs en casserole (Pigeonneaux en casserole)
Peas (Petits pois)
Vanilla ice cream (Glace vanille)

Consommé Madrilène
Virginia ham (Jambon de Virginie)
Russian salad (Salade Russe)
Ice cream (Glace pralinée)

In the last menu, the ham may be served either cold or hot and eaten on the plate with the salad. The salad might be a plain mixed green salad, instead of vegetable salad. If the day is a little warm, any of the soups suggested in these four menus can be chilled. At a wedding breakfast, the soup is always served in cups. In hot weather, the menu might be:

Melon (Melon)
Breast of chicken (Suprême de volaille)
Endive salad (Salade d'endives)
Orange Ice (Granité à l'orange)

Or one might have hot soup, followed by cold Virginia ham, salad, and ice cream. Coffee in small cups should be served at the end of the breakfast.

A seated breakfast does not, of course, *necessarily* follow a noon wedding. One might have a seated bride's table and buffet refreshments for the parents and the guests. Or one might have buffet refreshments for everyone. Six simple menus

169

are on pages 193 and 194, with suggestions as to how they may be used for breakfasts.

THE WEDDING CAKE

The wedding cake is the one indispensable of the wedding reception. At small weddings, punch may be substituted for champagne, and a gramophone or radio can even take the place of an orchestra, if the bride will have music; but there must be some kind of wedding cake, with a white icing. In the North, the traditional wedding cake is made like a heavy fruit cake, with a great many raisins and very little batter. In the South the "bride's cake" is white all through. At very big weddings, the cake is two or three tiers high, often topped with a decoration such as a tiny bell or a bouquet of orange blossoms. It always has white icing, and it always occupies the middle of the bride's table. If there is to be no seated bride's table it is set in the middle of the main buffet table.

THE BRIDE'S TABLE

At a seated wedding breakfast there are usually only two large tables, one for the bride and groom and bridal party, the other for the parents. If it is convenient and if the room is big enough, it is an attractive custom to have both these tables in the same room so that the parents of the bride and groom and their friends can join in toasts to the bride.

The bride's table must always be covered with a white cloth, preferably a white damask cloth, since lace and lace insertions are now somewhat out of fashion. The wedding cake is set in the middle of the table as the principal decoration, with secondary decorations of white flowers; on a long table, for example, there are often low bowls of flowers at each side of the cake halfway between the cake and the ends of the table; on a round table, there may be a garland of flowers around the cake. The rest of the table is set as it would be for a formal dinner (see page 481) with the necessary glasses and silver, but naturally without the candlesticks that are used at dinnertime.

Seating the Bride's Table

If a seated breakfast is planned for the reception, the seating of the bride's table should be as follows:

The bride and the groom together at one end; or in the middle of the table, an arrangement becoming more and more common. It is attractive and practical as well, since the cake is thus directly in front of the bride and groom.

At the right of the bride, the best man.

At the right of the groom, the bride.

At the left of the groom, the maid of honor.

Bridesmaids and ushers alternating around the table.

MENU CARDS AND PLACE CARDS

Menu cards for the bride's table and for the parents' table are specially made for the occasion. They are the usual size, about 4½ by 6 inches, of pure white pasteboard with a beveled silvered edge. The bride's initials, intertwined with those of the groom, are engraved in silver at the top of the menu. Sometimes there are only two initials: those of the bride and groom's first names; or, more conventionally, their last names. But four initials, in a cypher or a monogram, are also used: the bride's first and last initials and the groom's first and last initials. Although it used to be the fashion to print the entire menu in silver, this is no longer done. The menu is written out, in ink and by hand, as it would be for a dinner party. At a big elaborate wedding, the French words are used as they would be at a formal dinner. At simpler weddings, English is used. The menus can stand in little silver holders or lie flat on the table, one at every third plate.

Place cards, silver-edged and monogrammed like the menu cards, should be at each place except those of the bride and groom, the names written by hand and in ink. At a very elaborate and formal wedding these place cards will probably have been written by a secretary and will read, "Miss Alcott" or "Mr. Lord." At less formal weddings, the bride often writes these cards herself, in which case "Jessica," or "Robert," would be perfectly appropriate. (See pages 487 to 490 for formal usage concerning place cards and menus; pages 270 to 274 for the simpler forms.)

THE PARENTS' TABLE

The parents' table is decorated exactly like that of the bride except, of course, that there is no wedding cake. In place of the wedding cake, there might be another bowl of flowers or, if the parents' table is smaller than the bride's, there might be only one bowl of flowers. The only other difference between this table and that of the bride is that at a formal wedding the place cards must be written as they would be for a dinner party ("Mrs. Haight," "Mr. Flagg.") First names and nicknames, which might be written on the place cards at the bride's table, should never be found here. As usual, there are no cards at the hosts' places.

Seating the Parents' Table

The seating at the parents' table is arranged as follows:

The parents of the bride facing each other at each end of the table, or across the table from each other.
At the right of the bride's mother, the father of the groom.
At the left of the bride's mother, the officiating clergyman.
At the right of the bride's father, the mother of the groom.
At the left of the father, the wife of the clergyman, if he is married, or any other important woman guest if he is not.
Members of both immediate families and intimate friends around the rest of the table.

In case there is not room at the parents' table for both families and all the friends they would like to include, the bride's mother can preside at one table, the bride's father at another. The father of the groom sits at the right of the bride's mother; the groom's mother, at the right of the bride's father; etc.

ONE TABLE FOR BRIDE AND PARENTS

At many small weddings the bride's table and the parents' table are combined. This is particularly sensible and practical when the bride has only one bridesmaid. The best arrangement of the seating is this:

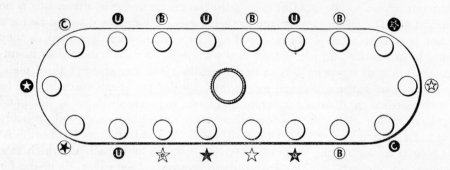

BRIDE'S AND PARENTS' TABLE COMBINED

☆ *Bride*
★ *Groom*
❶ *Bride's father*
✪ *Bride's mother*

✿ *Groom's father*
✪ *Groom's mother*
✪ *Maid of honor*
★ *Best man*

Ⓒ *Clergyman*
Ⓒ *Clergyman's wife*
Ⓑ *Bridesmaid*
Ⓤ *Usher*

At a small wedding, when the bride has only a maid of honor and the groom has only a best man, friends will replace the ushers and bridesmaids shown in this diagram.

TABLES FOR THE GUESTS

When the bride and groom and their parents are all seated, there must be enough small tables for all the guests. These tables are set for four or six people, usually with a white cloth, white flowers, and menu cards, but never place cards. Otherwise, these tables are set with silver and glasses exactly as they would be for any luncheon or dinner; and at a most elaborate wedding, the guests might be served. (Usually of course, the guests fetch most of their own food from the buffet table, even when the bride's and the parents' tables are served. See page 193 below.) If the dining room is very large, a few small tables may be put there with the bride's table and the parents' table. But as a rule, the small tables have to be put in another room. At a country wedding when the bride's table and the parents' table may be on a terrace, the guests' tables, each with a round umbrella awning, may be set on the lawn around or below the terrace.

DECORATION OF THE RECEPTION ROOM

If the wedding is being given in a big house or apartment, all the reception rooms are thrown open and filled with as many flowers as the bride's mother likes. Unless the wedding is tiny, there should be at least one room for the breakfast and another for the receiving line; otherwise, the traffic jams of guests become impossible. If there is to be dancing, the receiving line stands in the room which has been prepared for that purpose. The orchestra plays very softly in one corner of the room, or in the hall, while the wedding guests are being received.

Except for the room in which the receiving line stands, there are, as we have said, no special floral decorations. White or light flowers may be chosen for the vases, but otherwise (except for the necessary removal of some furniture) the rooms will look as though ready for any big dinner party or reception. The background of the receiving line, however, needs special consideration. A screen of vines, or a bank of ferns or flowers, flat against the wall, are the traditional (if unimaginative) arrangement. The most attractive and newest arrangements are simpler: a curtain of white or some light color, or even a strong color that goes well with the colors chosen for the bridesmaids' dresses, a Coromandel lacquer screen, or the bare wall if it is prettily paneled or papered. The essential point is that the background should be neither confusing nor too conspicuous.

BRIDESMAIDS, PAGE BOYS, AND FLOWER GIRLS

While the bride's mother is busy with these details, the bride is making her decisions about an important part of every formal wedding: her bridesmaids. The tradition of having bridesmaids or attendants for the bride is rooted deep in the culture of all Europe, and even back of that in the pagan rites of the Mediterranean world. They were intended originally to help the bride in the literal sense: to arrange her veil and wreath, to help her dress; and, symbolically, also to epitomize the virginal state from which the bride was now departing. For this reason, in the strictest of old-fashioned weddings only unmarried girls could be bridesmaids. Today it is quite usual in even the most conservative and formal weddings to have married friends or relatives as bridesmaids or as matron of honor.

It is, of course, a great compliment to be asked to be a bridesmaid and, therefore, if the groom has a sister of a suitable age, she should be asked, even if she is a comparative stranger to the bride. Traditionally, a marriage should be almost a merger of the two families. Such was the purpose of the marriages between royal houses. To ask the groom's sister to be a bridesmaid is one of the ways of emphasizing the relationship.

There is no set or required number of bridesmaids. For the very largest wedding there might be twelve or none at all. More than twelve would be overwhelming! At every wedding, however, even if the bride is being married in a registry office, she should have at least one attendant: a friend or sister for a marriage at a registry office; a maid of honor, a page boy, or a flower girl for a wedding in church or at home.

In America, it is less usual than it is abroad to have small children as bridal attendants. But this is only a question of choice. There is no reason not to have a page boy or a flower girl as the bride's single attendant, or a pair of them, or to add one to the full number of bridesmaids. It is, in fact, an extremely attractive custom, and one that might well be more popular. Page boys and flower girls sometimes carry the bride's train, one holding each corner, but usually they march in front of the bride in the wedding procession, the flower girls carrying a tiny bouquet, the page boys carrying nothing at all. The custom of having the page boys sprinkle rose leaves on the floor, before the feet of the bridal party, has been discarded and should not be followed unless the whole setting of the wedding is intentionally picturesque. The only rule, as far as child attendants are concerned, is that they should be definitely small, especially the boys. Most boys over six will hate a velvet suit, and most girls over ten, in these vitamin-conscious days, are too big not to be a bit gawky.

All attendants, small or full-grown, should be notified as soon as possible of the date of the wedding, and although the bride's mother is the one who does all the rest of the inviting, it is the bride who asks her friends to be her bridesmaids. If any of them lives at a distance, visits will have to be arranged for fittings for her dress. (The bridesmaids pay for everything they wear for the wedding, although everything is chosen by the bride. Brides should be careful, therefore, not to choose an expensive model for the bridesmaids' dresses. See page 231 for a complete list of who pays for what.) And for the bridesmaids who live out of town, accommodations must be arranged by the bride's mother, either in her own house or in the house of a friend. If by any chance it should be impossible to find a place for the bridesmaids to stay, the bride's mother could take rooms for them in a hotel, but she should arrange to have a married woman stay in the hotel with them.

Lately, it has become the fashion for the bride and her bridesmaids to dine together on the night of the groom's "bachelor dinner" (see below). This dinner is usually given at the bride's house, or in the house of any relative or friend. It is not, however, as much a part of the wedding custom as the bachelor dinner, and many brides don't bother with it at all. If such a dinner is given, this is the moment for the bride to give the bridesmaids their "bridesmaid presents" (page 175).

USHERS

Ushers are to the bridegroom exactly what bridesmaids are to the bride. In earlier days, they were called "groomsmen"; and in feudal Europe they assisted the bridegroom in the pranks that were part of the rather coarse wedding customs of the day. Now, happily, there are no such pranks, unless they take place at the groom's bachelor dinner, which is given a night or two before the wedding. If the groom or his father belongs to a man's club, this dinner is usually given there; if not, in his own house or in a hotel. Unlike the bridesmaids, who often give individual presents, the ushers always band together to give the groom a joint present, in which the best man can join or not, as he chooses. Standard presents are a silver cigarette box or tray, inscribed with all the signatures. This is presented to the groom at the bachelor dinner, accompanied by endless toasts and responses.

The ushers are, by custom, the best friends of the groom, the best man being his brother, or the bride's brother, or anyone else who is close to him. The functions of ushers are described on pages 178 to 183; the functions of the best man are more subtle and more personal. He is the one who is responsible for seeing that the ushers are all properly dressed and in order, for getting the groom to the church on time, for calming his nerves, for presenting the ring at the right moment during the ceremony. He is the groom's support and mainstay on an occasion which most men find peculiarly nerve-wracking—perhaps because most men lack the sense of drama that most women seem to be born with.

THE WEDDING RING

Surprisingly enough, wedding rings are very much subject to change in taste and fashion. Only two customs concerning them have remained constant: The first is that the bride must have a ring; the second, that the groom always pays for it. Otherwise, wedding rings have rounded the full circle of taste, from the broad gold bands of our grandmother's day to the tiny platinum circlet of the thirties and back again to the broad and often decorated band which is in fashion now. But no matter what the fashion, a bride who plans never to take off her wedding ring should hesitate before choosing a very elaborate and conspicuous one. Tastes do change, and although gold is now considered becoming to almost any stone, a time may easily come when a wide gold band would be difficult to wear on the same finger with another ring. If one is considering sentiment, tradition, and the highest standards of taste, a plain yellow-gold wedding ring, only moderately wide, is probably the best.

As a rule the bride and groom go together to the jeweler to choose and fit the wedding ring. The ring is often engraved on the inside with the initials of the bride and groom and the date: "A.S.B.—G.B.E., April 4th, 1948," the bride's initials coming first, or "G.B.E. to A.S.B. . . ." When the engraving has been done, the jeweler will send it to the groom's house or to that of the best man.

Although it is not a tradition in America that men wear wedding rings, there is no reason not to do so if one wants to. A man's wedding ring should always be plain gold and neither conspicuously big nor too fragile, although it is better to err on the small rather than the large side. The groom's ring is chosen, fitted and engraved in the same way and at the same time as the bride's. And, just as her ring is a present from him, so his ring is a present from her.

PRESENTS FOR THE BRIDESMAIDS AND USHERS

According to a long tradition, the bride gives identical presents to all her bridesmaids and a slightly different present of the same kind to her maid of honor. These presents should be lasting—not, for example, something like perfume—but there is no other rule concerning them. Many brides give presents such as little gold plaques that can be worn on a charm bracelet, or little silver trays that can be used for pins or cigarette ashes, as both of these can be engraved with the date or with the initials of the bride and groom. It is an attractive idea to give something that can be so engraved, to commemorate the occasion, and there are dozens of other suitable presents. But as there is no tradition to follow, the bride can give anything she chooses.

In exactly the same way, the groom gives presents to each of the ushers—cuff links, money clips, ash trays, leather jewelry boxes marked with each usher's initials—anything durable and generally useful. These presents can be given to the ushers at the bachelor dinner, a box at each place. In addition, of course, the groom gives the ushers their gloves and neckties for the wedding, but these are not really presents and should not be treated as such. Usually, the best man or the groom has them sent directly to each usher's house from the shop.

THE WEDDING REHEARSAL

A rehearsal of the wedding procession and of a few of the points of the ceremony is a necessary preliminary to any wedding except the smallest and simplest, when a few words of instruction from the clergyman are enough. As a rule, before a big wedding, the rehearsal is held in the church a day or so in advance. All the bridesmaids and ushers should be there, as well as the bride and groom and the bride's father. The clergyman explains the procedure and each one, except the bride, takes his place, acting out the clergyman's instructions exactly as they will on the wedding day. Traditionally, the bride does not act her own role, but watches carefully the friend or relative who substitutes for her.

Everything should be explained and practiced until each is able to take his part smoothly and effortlessly.

CHURCH DECORATIONS

For all formal weddings, whether they are given in the afternoon or in the evening, the church may be as much or as little decorated as the bride's parents desire. White flowers on the altar, white flowers tied in bouquets or sprays and set in the windows, white flowers in small bunches tied with white ribbons to the pews—all these, with the lights and candles and the music, can make a magnificent setting for the wedding ceremony. If the church is very large, so large that all the wedding guests could not possibly fill it, the pews on each side of the main aisle are often roped off with white satin ribbons so that the families and all the wedding guests will surely have their proper seats. These ribbons are arranged in such a way that the ushers can unhook them to allow each guest to go in, and hook them up again as soon as the guest is seated. They serve as a warning to innocent bystanders and uninvited guests, of whom there are always a great many at a large church wedding, that these pews are reserved for those who have been invited. Another frequent custom at large weddings is that of stringing a long white satin ribbon across the pew entrances on the main aisle, just before the wedding procession starts. Two ushers, one on each side, walk down the aisle unrolling the ribbon which other ushers hold on spools at the back of the church. If this system is used, the hooked ribbons are, of course, unnecessary. The reserved part of the church can be roped off with white ribbon down each side aisle, and ushers, standing at the foot of the main aisle, warn off the unknowing and merely curious.

It used to be accepted that a carpet for the aisle of the church was a necessity for any except the smallest church wedding. And often there was a carpet, or a carpet and canopy, between the edge of the sidewalk and the church door. The latter are rare, nowadays, but a carpet for the church aisle is still often used.

The usual arrangements are these: A carpet, usually either plain carpeting or drugget, is laid when the church is decorated, or a canvas is unrolled just before the bridal procession starts, after the bride's mother is seated. This canvas, like the ribbons described above, is unrolled by two ushers, from a spool. Sometimes the spool is unrolled from the back of the church, sometimes from the steps of the chancel. Both kinds of carpeting are left down until all the guests have gone from the church.

CHURCH MUSIC

Music played at church weddings is sometimes the one false note in a beautiful ceremony. Too often music that should be heard only at the reception is played in church, especially before the actual ceremony begins. The most common of these pieces, basically unfit for a sacrament of the church, are "Because," "I Love You Truly," "Oh, Promise Me," Schubert's "Serenade," Wagner's "Liebestod," Liszt's "Liebestraum," and the "Meditation" from *Thaïs*.

The following music is approved by even the most strict church standards:

Before the Ceremony

BACH, J. S.
Air in A minor (from Toccata and Fugue in C major)
Air from Suite in D for Strings
Arioso in E flat (from Book of Airs, pub. by Boston Music Co.)
Largo from Fifth Violin Sonata (Book of Airs)
Sarabande from Sixth 'Cello Suite (Book of Airs)
Siciliano from Second Sonata for Flute and Clavier (Book of Airs)
Chorale Preludes:
All praise to Jesus' hallowed Name (Gelobt seist du)
Blessed Jesus, at thy word (Liebster Jesu)
Jesu, joy of man's desiring
Lord Jesus Christ, be present now (Herr Jesu Christ)
O thou, of God the Father (Herr Christ)
Salvation now is come to earth (Es ist das Hier)
BATTISHILL
Andante in A major (Twelve Short Pieces, pub. by Novello)
BOËLLMANN
Carillon (Douze Pièces, pub. Leduc)
BONNET
Romance sans paroles (pub. Leduc)
BRAHMS
My inmost heart rejoiceth (Herzlich thut mich erfreuen)
BUXTEHUDE
From God I ne'er will turn me (Von Gott will ich nicht lassen)
CLÉRAMBAULT
Prelude in D (Anthologia Antiqua, pub. J. Fischer & Bro.)
COUPERIN
Soeur Monique
CROFT, WM.
Andante and Allegro Maestoso (pub. Hinrichsen, London)
FRANCK
Cantabile

GIBBONS
Fantasia in C major—Andante
Fantasia in C major—Allegretto (pub. J. & W. Chester, Ltd.)
HANDEL
Aria from the Tenth Organ Concerto
Arioso in D major (A Book of Classical Airs, pub. G. Schirmer)
Sarabande from Oboe Concerto (A Book of Classical Airs, pub. G. Schirmer)
JONGEN
Chorale (pub. Durand)
KARG-ELERT
How bright appears the morning star (Wie schön leuchtet)
MENDELSSOHN
Andante religioso from Sonata No. 4
OLDROYD, GEO.
Liturgical Prelude No. 2 (Oxford)
PURCELL, HENRY
Prelude in G (pub. in Bonnet Historical Organ Recitals. Vol. 1)
Trumpet Voluntary
REGER, MAX
Gott des Himmels und der Erden
RHEINBERGER
Monologue No. 5
Monologue No. 11
STANFORD, C. V.
Andante tranquillo (pub. with Six Short Preludes and Postludes by Stainer & Bell)
Prelude on an Irish Church Melody (pub. ditto)
Prelude on "The King of Love" (St. Columb, pub. ditto)
TARTINI
Adagio cantabile (A Book of Classical Airs, pub. G. Schirmer)
VAUGHAN WILLIAMS, R.
Prelude on "Rhosymedre" (pub. Stainer & Bell)
WIDOR, C. M.
Adagio from Symphony No. 5
WOOD, CHARLES
Psalm XXIII (pub. Stainer & Bell)

The Processional and Recessional

The Bridal Chorus from Wagner's *Lohengrin* and the Wedding March from Mendelssohn's *Midsummer Night's Dream,* although conspicuously secular music, are both approved by most modern churchmen. If the Lohengrin Chorus is not approved for the processional, a hymn such as "Praise, My Soul, The King of Heaven," "The Voice That Breathed O'er Eden," "The King of Love My Shepherd Is," is sung by the choir or played by the organ instead.

The Organist

Any music played in the church is usually, of course, played by the regular organist of the church. Should the family want to ask another organist to play, the regular organist must be consulted first, and the invitation must be given through him. As a rule, the regular organist is given his standard fee, whether or not he plays for the ceremony. The amount of the fee varies in different churches and different communities; the bride's family can ask the sexton, or the organist himself, how much it is.

29

Procedure of a Wedding

So FAR we have considered only the preparations for a very big formal church wedding. Now, we come to the procedure for the wedding day. While the bride is dressing at home, the bridesmaids arrive at her house all dressed for the ceremony. The groom, always faithfully accompanied by the best man, goes to the church where he sits, in nervous anticipation, in the vestry with the clergyman. The guests start arriving at the church promptly, since they know the doors will close only a minute or two after the hour set for the wedding, and the ushers, who have arrived at the church at least half an hour before the appointed time, start showing the guests to their places.

SEATING IN THE CHURCH

At all weddings, large or small, in a church with a center aisle, the family of the bride is seated on the left side, the family of the groom on the right. At the biggest, most elaborate, and most formal weddings, the ushers are sometimes given typed alphabetical lists of the guests, with notations as to where they are to be seated.

In making the lists, care should be taken to give each member of the family his proper place. If the bride's mother cannot make out the lists herself, the task should be delegated only to someone who knows all the guests well. An usher meets each guest at the door of the church, asks the guest for his name, consults his lists, and escorts him to the proper seat.

However, such lists as these—like elaborate and formal weddings in general— are not very much in the temper of the times. Much more frequent are smaller and more informal weddings, where there are no lists and no set order of precedence for the guests. Even "pew cards" which, when lists were first discarded, were often enclosed with the invitation to the wedding, are scarcely seen any more. (The forms for pew cards are on page 209.)

Even at a very big and fashionable wedding, the seating of guests is a much more informal matter today. If the usher knows that the guest is an intimate friend or a member of the family, he will take him to the proper pew. If the usher does not know the guest, as is often the case, he asks, "Where would you like to sit?" The guest answers, "On the bride's side, please. I am a cousin of the bride." Or, "On the groom's side. This will be splendid." In such a case, of course, wedding guests must always take a seat a pew or two back of the one to which, had there been pew cards, they might have been assigned. Otherwise, when older relatives arrive, those who seated themselves in the forward pews may have to be asked to move back—an unfortunate maneuver in a crowded church.

At all weddings where there are ushers, guests should wait at the back of the church until an usher comes to escort them to their seats. If the guest is a woman, the usher offers his right arm, held out in a bent position. The woman guest puts her hand on the inner side of his arm—not lightly on the outer side, in the minuet position, as one sometimes sees. A man guest does not, of course, take the usher's arm, but walks beside him. When couples arrive together, the woman takes the usher's arm and the man follows behind, unaccompanied. The bride's mother is the last person to be seated. She is escorted down the aisle by the head usher, the groom's mother having just preceded her. The groom's mother also is escorted by the head usher, her husband following alone. The church doors should be closed and no one seated after the bride's mother has taken her place. If a canvas carpet is used, it is unrolled at this moment—see page 176 above.

When the Church Has No Center Aisle

When the church has no central aisle, the family of the bride sits at the left side of the right hand aisle, the family of the groom at the right of the left aisle. The right aisle is used for the procession to the altar and the left aisle for the return procession.

THE WEDDING PROCESSION

Before the groom's parents and the bride's mother are seated, the bridesmaids should all have arrived at the church. The ushers are assembled in the vestibule where the head usher joins them and the procession can start. At the sound of the Wedding March, the clergyman, followed by the groom and his best man, come out of the vestry. The clergyman stands on the steps of the chancel, facing the congregation; the groom, with the best man behind him, stands at the end of the aisle, at the right, and at a right angle to the pews, but usually with his head turned to the door of the church, so he can see his bride coming up the aisle.

The ushers march in pairs, each pair four to six feet from the next. In a very big church, they may be eight or nine feet apart. Ideally, they would all be identical in size, but since this is not likely, they are matched in pairs of more or less the same height, the shorter pairs going down the aisle first. At the end of the aisle the pairs divide, each usher on the right going to the right side of the church, each usher on the left going to the left. In a small church or chapel, they line themselves up along the wall or, if there is room, in front of the choir stalls in the chancel. If the church is so large that no guests are seated in the side sections, the ushers can stand in front of these sections facing the altar.

The bridesmaids follow directly after the ushers, about eight feet behind them and, like the ushers, in pairs four to six feet apart. At the steps of the chancel they divide in the same way as the ushers. If there is room for both the bridesmaids and the ushers in the chancel, in front of the choir stalls, the bridesmaids stand in front of the ushers. In a smaller church, there might be room in the chancel for the bridesmaids only. In a very small chapel, too small to allow many bridesmaids to stand in the chancel, the bride will probably have only a maid of honor.

There is a new way of arranging the procession, by which the bridesmaids wait to start down the aisle until the ushers have taken their places at the far end of the church. But the first procedure outlined here is traditional and more usual.

The maid of honor comes next in the procession, walking alone about eight feet behind the last pair of bridesmaids. Then, at the same distance, come the page boys or flower girls, unless, of course, they are carrying the bride's train. The maid of honor waits at the foot of the chancel steps on the left, directly opposite the best man, and, like the best man, she faces sideways to the congregation.

At the end of the procession, again at a distance of about eight feet, behind

THE WEDDING PROCESSION

☆ Bride
★ Bride's father
Ⓕ Flower girl or page boy
✭ Maid of honor
Ⓑ Bridesmaid
Ⓤ Usher

the maid of honor or the flower girls, comes the bride, leaning on her father's right arm. When they reach the bridegroom, her father stops, and the groom comes forward to join her. Bride and groom take one or two steps forward together and stand before the clergyman. Then the maid of honor and the best man turn to face the altar. If there are page boys or flower girls, they stand by the bridesmaids during the ceremony.

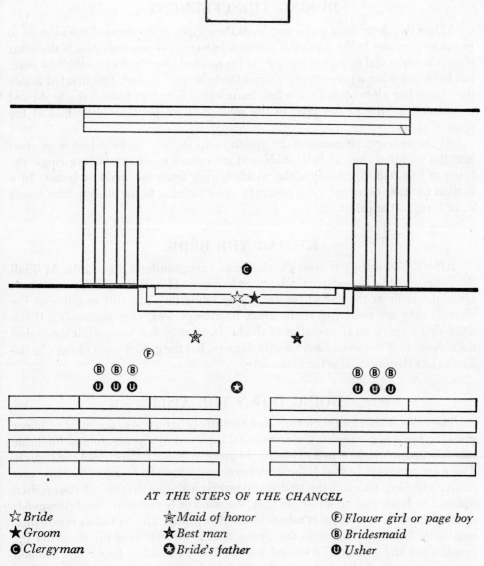

AT THE STEPS OF THE CHANCEL

☆ *Bride*	⚝ *Maid of honor*	Ⓕ *Flower girl or page boy*
★ *Groom*	✦ *Best man*	Ⓑ *Bridesmaid*
Ⓒ *Clergyman*	✪ *Bride's father*	Ⓤ *Usher*

If the entire ceremony will take place at the chancel steps, all except the bride's father —who goes to his pew after giving the bride away—keep the positions shown in this diagram. In any case, the bridesmaids, the ushers, and the flower girl, having taken these places, will stay where they are.

GIVING THE BRIDE AWAY

When the clergyman asks, "Who giveth this woman to be married to this man?" the bride's father steps forward and, taking his daughter's right hand, gives it into the clergyman's hand. He then goes back and takes his place next to his wife in the first pew on the left. In Roman Catholic weddings, the father leaves the bride when the groom joins her at the end of the aisle. He then genuflects, enters the pew, and takes no further part in the ceremony.

DURING THE CEREMONY

When the clergyman turns and leads the couple to the steps of the altar or to the prie-dieu, the bride takes the groom's left arm. When they reach the altar steps, she turns and gives her bouquet to the maid of honor who, like the best man, has been following a pace or two behind the bride and groom. The maid of honor then takes her place opposite the best man, about four feet behind the bride and groom and a little to the side, in the same relative positions they had at the chancel steps.

At the appropriate moment the groom turns slightly and the best man gives him the wedding ring. If both bride and groom are to wear wedding rings, the bride at this moment receives the wedding ring from the maid of honor. In a Roman Catholic ceremony, the best man gives the ring to the acolyte who hands it, in turn, to the priest.

KISSING THE BRIDE

After the ceremony is over, the clergyman congratulates the couple. At small Protestant weddings and particularly at house weddings, the groom sometimes kisses the bride at the end of the ceremony while they are still standing at the altar. If they are receiving at the altar, he always does. (See page 191.) If the officiating clergyman is a relative of the bride, he may kiss her just at the end of the ceremony if the groom has already done so, but the groom must always be the first to kiss the bride after the ceremony.

GOING DOWN THE AISLE

The bride and groom then turn and face the congregation, the maid of honor gives the bride her bouquet, the recessional is played by the organ, and the bride takes the groom's right arm and begins the procession down the aisle of the church. There are two ways in which the bridal procession may be formed after the ceremony. The first, which is the traditional one, is a simple reversal of the original order: The bride and groom come first, the maid of honor next, the bridesmaids in one group, followed by the ushers in another group. The best man meanwhile goes with the clergyman into the vestry, where he retrieves his own and the groom's hat and gloves. The second way is that the maid of honor and the best man, arm in arm, follow immediately after the bride and groom, with the ushers and the bridesmaids paired off, arm in arm, coming after. This is a modern development and is not approved by many of the clergy.

The head usher comes back up the aisle to fetch the bride's mother, who is the first after the wedding party to leave. She walks down the aisle, arm in arm with him, her husband following. Another usher takes the groom's mother down the aisle in the same way, but the other relatives leave their pews without waiting for a special escort. No guests, however, should ever leave their pews until the immediate members of both families have reached the vestibule. Once the families have gone, there is no reason for the other wedding guests to stand upon the order of their going. The church can be emptied as it would be after any other ceremony, without regard to whether one person has been nearer the front pews than another.

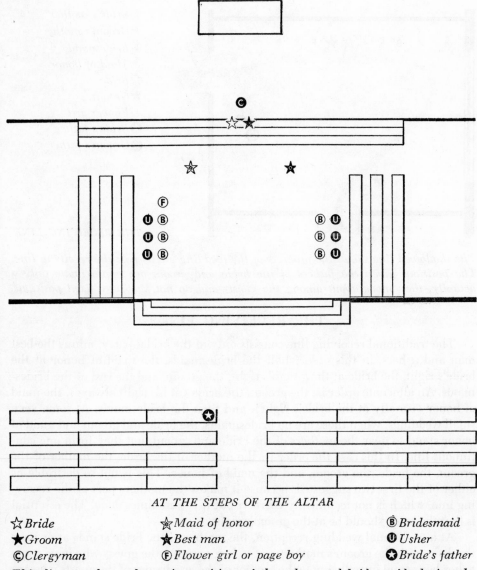

AT THE STEPS OF THE ALTAR

☆ *Bride*   ⭐ *Maid of honor*   Ⓑ *Bridesmaid*
★ *Groom*   ★ *Best man*   Ⓤ *Usher*
Ⓒ *Clergyman*   Ⓕ *Flower girl or page boy*   ✪ *Bride's father*

This diagram shows alternative positions of the ushers and bridesmaids during the ceremony. When there is room within the chancel, they may go directly to these places, instead of standing outside the chancel as shown in the diagram on page 181, "At the Steps of the Chancel."

183

THE RECEPTION AFTER A FORMAL CHURCH WEDDING

Outside the church, automobiles will have been waiting for the bridal party and the other members of the family, automobiles that belong to the family or which have been borrowed or rented for the occasion. The star figures of the reception—those who will stand in the receiving line—will, therefore, arrive at the house well before the other guests. If the house of the bride's parents is very small and the wedding is very large, it may be necessary to give the reception in the entertaining rooms of a hotel, but, if possible, this should be avoided (p. 166).

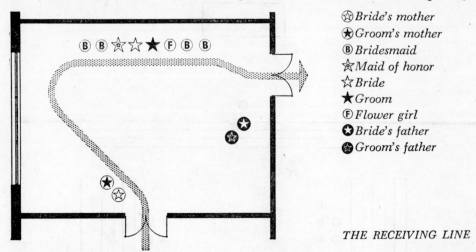

⊗ *Bride's mother*
★ *Groom's mother*
Ⓑ *Bridesmaid*
☆ *Maid of honor*
☆ *Bride*
★ *Groom*
Ⓕ *Flower girl*
✪ *Bride's father*
✪ *Groom's father*

THE RECEIVING LINE

The shadowed line shows the progress of the wedding guests past the receiving line. The positions given the fathers of the bride and groom are approximate only— actually, they move about among the guests and do not keep any fixed positions.

THE RECEIVING LINE

The traditional receiving line consists only of the bridal party, minus the best man and ushers, in this order: half the bridesmaids, the maid of honor at the bride's right, the bride at the groom's right, the groom, and the rest of the bridesmaids. An alternate order is: the groom, the bride (at his right always), the maid of honor (usually at the bride's right), and then the bridesmaids. At some very small weddings, when there are no bridesmaids, the bride and groom and maid of honor stand so near the mothers of the bride and groom that they form one continuous line. In this case the order is: the mother of the bride, the mother of the groom, the bride, the groom, and the maid of honor. This is not so desirable as either of the first two suggested, because it makes the mothers part of the receiving line, which is not technically correct; but it is sometimes done. The essential is that the bride should be at the groom's right.

At a traditional wedding reception, the mother of the bride stands at or near the door, with the groom's mother next to her, greeting the guests who have come to her house and introducing to the mother of the groom any of the guests who are strangers to her. (See page 58 on "Introducing.") The two fathers, meanwhile, are circulating around the rooms or standing not far from their wives; but not *beside* their wives except possibly the groom's father, who may not know many guests.

As soon as the bridal party arrives, they should take their places. According to the custom of formal weddings, a butler standing near the door asks each guest his name and announces it clearly, so that the bride's mother and the bride can both hear it. But it is a custom with no basis other than convenience and at small weddings can quite easily be dispensed with.

Receiving a Stranger

If a guest who may be a stranger to the other guests arrives, the bride's mother, as hostess, should delegate a friend or a member of the family to take care of him and introduce him to a few of the others. If she fails to do this, the stranger may, as always, talk to any of the other guests who look congenial. (See page 59.) But as a rule, a guest who arrives at a wedding reception as a total stranger leaves shortly after going through the receiving line.

The point of going to the church, not difficult to do by oneself, is to witness the ceremony; and the point of going to the reception is to greet the families of the bride and groom, and to wish the bride and groom good luck. There is no need to stay after this has been done.

THE WEDDING BREAKFAST

After a formal church wedding, such as the one we have been describing, the wedding breakfast should be served as soon as the first guests arrive from the church. When they have greeted the bride's mother and have "gone down" the receiving line, the guests find places for themselves at the little tables that have been set for them. They should be served as soon as they sit down or very shortly afterwards. The bride and groom and their parents, however, must wait until it seems that the last guests have arrived. The mother of the bride is the one who decides when this moment has come and then they all go in to the bride's and parents' tables. (Menus are on page 169.)

CUTTING THE CAKE

At a seated wedding breakfast such as this, the bride cuts the cake, with a certain amount of ceremony, at the end of the meal. The groom stands beside her, and their parents and friends gather round to watch. At military or naval weddings, the bride cuts the cake with her husband's sword. This cake is eaten at the table, with the ice cream. As soon as those in the bridal party have finished their coffee, and the inevitable toasts, they go in to the dancing.

TOASTS

Whether or not there is a seated bride's table, the first toast is always a toast to the bride, proposed by the best man. There are other attractive customs, such as a toast to the bride's mother, proposed by the groom; toasts to the bridesmaids, etc., but the best man's toast to the bride is, even more than a custom, a rule.

DANCING AFTER THE WEDDING

By tradition, the bride and groom dance the first dance together and, for a minute or two at least, alone—usually to the accompaniment of pleasantly embarrassing applause from all the guests. Then all the guests join the dancing, the father of the bride dancing first with the groom's mother, and the bride's mother with the father of the groom. The dancing may last an hour or so, while the bride chats with the guests and dances with them. Then some guests may start to leave and the bride will consider her departure also.

GOING AWAY

After the cake is cut and the last toast is drunk and the last waltz is played, the bride goes upstairs to change her clothes. On the stairs, she stops to throw her bouquet to her bridesmaids clustered among the wedding guests below; and the one who catches it will of course be the next to be married. If the bride is married in an apartment, she can throw her bouquet from the doorway. The groom, too, goes to his room to put on his traveling clothes, while the guests wait around downstairs to see the couple off. The parents often go upstairs at this point—the bride's mother always does—to say good-bye to their children privately. By tradition, the bride and groom should meet at the top of the stairs and come down together, preceded by the bride's mother and all the bridesmaids who have gone up to help her dress. Pausing for a moment to kiss their parents good-bye again, they run out to the motor that is waiting at the door, while the guests who are lined up on each side pelt them with confetti and rice. This is one of the oldest of all the wedding customs; rice is the symbol of fertility and for thousands of years has been used at weddings to wish the couple the blessing of "many sons."

In the raccoon-coat-and-rumble-seat days of the 1920's, it was very much the fashion to decorate the "going-away" motor with signs reading "Just married," with old shoes, and tin cans tied on long strings to the back bumper. The ushers attended to all this—a relic, perhaps, of the Mittel-Europa pranksters. Nowadays, after a wedding in a big city, it is more usual to tie only one old shoe, for luck, to the back bumper, and let it go at that.

THE WEDDING TRIP

The ideal wedding journey, in almost every American girl's imagination, starts in a car at high speed, continues in a rapid succession of boats, planes, and trains, and ends with the groom carrying her over the threshold of her new house. And if there are bread, salt, and a Bible on the hall table, the picture is complete. Modern grooms, alas, often have little time for travel, but the wedding trip still has certain traditions that should not be relinquished. The first is that the bride and groom should start off alone in the motor—alone at least except for a chauffeur or taxi driver; and, if they are continuing by train or boat, they should still be alone. If it should be necessary for some of the ushers or guests to take the same train from the city, this rule is not so strict that the bride and groom must go to any great lengths to avoid them. But if it can be arranged otherwise, so much the better. The newly married couple, sitting surrounded by jolly friends in the train, certainly has no part in the traditional picture; it lacks romance and, to a slight degree, good taste.

The second custom that should not be given up, because it is so attractive, is the one of the groom carrying the bride over the threshold. Ideally, the bride's new house should be ready for her when she returns from her journey, and her husband should carry her in when she enters the house for the first time as a married woman. But if everything cannot be ideal, if the bride has been working for days to get the house in order, as is often the case, then on the day the house is finally ready to live in, her husband should be there to carry her over the threshold the first night they spend under their own roof.

There is no need, however, to bother about a wedding journey if it seems at all inconvenient or expensive. The bride and groom can merely motor from the reception to their new house and settle down. In fact, this is much more in accord with the most ancient wedding customs, when the bride was carried off, by mock force or real, straight from her father's house and her mother's protection to the house of her husband. Wedding journeys were first in fashion during the Renaissance; but weddings are much older than that.

SOME NECESSARY VARIATIONS IN THE TRADITIONAL PROCEDURE

All of the foregoing is predicated on a single wedding, not a double one, and further, on the bride's having two living parents who are not divorced. Double weddings are discussed below, on page 188. We shall consider first the marriage of a bride whose parents are divorced, and of a bride whose father has died.

If the Bride's Parents Are Divorced

If the bride's parents are divorced, her mother usually gives the wedding and the reception. (The matter of invitations and announcements is discussed on pages 199 to 217.) Some changes are also necessary in the procedure of the wedding day. As a rule, if the father is alive, he gives his daughter away even though he may not go to the reception after the wedding. On the day of the wedding, just before the ceremony is to begin, the bride's father comes to fetch her at her mother's house. He waits in the motor at the door, only sending up word that he is there. At the church, the usual procedure is followed except that the bride's father, instead of going into the first pew at the left with the bride's mother, sits in the second or third pew during the ceremony. If the divorce has been a difficult and unpleasant one, or a very recent one, the bride's father often does not come to the reception. But, particularly on such a day, every effort is usually made to overlook and forget past difficulties, and the bride's father comes to the reception as one of the most important guests. He does not, however, sit at the parents' table or in any way act as host. During the ceremony he sits with his wife, if he has remarried, in the third pew on the left. If the relations are extremely friendly, his new wife may even come to the wedding reception, although this is not a traditional procedure.

If the bride's mother has remarried, her husband sits with her during the ceremony in the first pew at the left of the aisle. At the wedding reception after the ceremony, he acts as host and takes over the role of the father of the bride.

If the Bride's Father Has Died

If the bride's father has died, a brother, uncle, or some other male relative usually gives her away. If there are no near relatives of suitable age (twenty-one years old would be the minimum), the bride can be given away by an older man who is an intimate friend of the family. In some cases, when the bride's father is dead and her mother has been long remarried, the bride is given away by her stepfather. It is against good usage for a bride to be given away by her mother or any other woman.

Double Weddings

Double weddings are not a very usual practice but there are, nevertheless, a few accepted customs which have grown up about them. They are a departure from the usual practice and, as a rule, there is usually some special reason, such as a blood relationship, to explain them. (In some faiths, there *must* be such a reason.) The most usual double weddings are those of two sisters, or of a brother and sister, or two girl cousins who have been brought up together, or who are intimate friends.

When two sisters are being married, the elder takes precedence over the younger throughout the ceremony. It is she who comes first up the aisle on her father's arm, her younger sister following with a brother, or another male relative, or the head usher. The father gives both his daughters away, the elder daughter first, then the younger. The bridegrooms stand at the head of the aisle, as usual at the right, with their best men behind them, the bridegroom of the elder sister nearer the congregation. During the ceremony the elder sister is at the left and the younger at the right. The vows are repeated separately and, when the ceremony is over, the elder sister goes first down the aisle, followed by the younger. Very often, the sisters have joint bridesmaids, half of whom are special friends of one sister, and half of the other. The ushers, also, are divided in this way; but each bride should have a maid (or matron) of honor, and each groom should have a best man. The order of the wedding procession is as follows: the ushers; the bridesmaids; the maid of honor of the elder sister; the elder bride and her father; the younger bride's maid of honor; and, finally, the younger bride. When the younger sister has a separate group of bridesmaids, they follow immediately after the elder bride and her father, just before the second maid of honor.

Unless the families of both grooms are to share the first pew at the right, the order of precedence of the wedding ceremony is usually followed. In other words, the family of the groom of the elder sister sits in the first pew, the other family, in the second pew.

At the wedding reception the receiving line is made up, as usual, of the bridesmaids, the maids of honor and the brides and grooms. The elder sister comes before the younger sister in the receiving line but the traditional order should be followed: the bride at the groom's right always, and the maid (or matron) of honor at the right of the bride. At the door, the mother of the bride stands first in line with the mother of the elder sister's husband next to her, and the mother of the other groom beyond.

When the brides are not sisters the question of precedence is more complicated. In church, the best precedence to follow is that of age. The older bride comes first up the aisle, as she would if the brides were sisters. The mothers of the brides sit together in the first pew, the older one nearer the aisle. At the wedding reception the same order of precedence is followed in the receiving line. If the wedding reception is being given in a club or hotel, the older mother stands first in line at the door, with the mother of the other bride and the mothers of the grooms beyond her. If it is given in a private house, the mistress of the house comes first in line.

There are many other possible combinations of relationship in double weddings, each bringing its own complications of seating and procedure. But these two examples will serve as the point of departure in making the arrangements. See also the examples of invitations to a double wedding given on page 207.

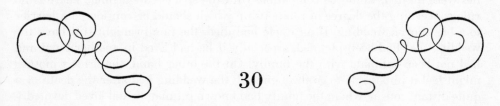

30

The House Wedding

THE HOUSE wedding has a host of advantages and only two disadvantages, one major and one minor. The major disadvantage is that one misses the spiritual significance and beauty of a church ceremony; the minor one is that all the wedding guests are automatically invited to the reception. One is committed, so to speak, to a reception as large as the number of guests one invites to the ceremony. The advantages are that it can be very much less expensive; that one can have a tiny wedding without feeling forlorn in an almost empty church; that one eliminates the bother of cars to and from the house. There is another element, too, in favor of a wedding at home: the reassurance for the bride of being married in a place she loves and knows so well; a feeling of continuity as she comes down the familiar stairs in her wedding dress, for the last time as an unmarried girl, and repeats the familiar words of the service in the living room she has known since childhood.

In some cases, for example, in a wedding between two people of different faiths, church regulations prohibit a church ceremony, and a house wedding is mandatory. Weddings in hotels should be avoided, if possible, and a registry office scarcely permits a real wedding.

Although the bride is often married at home when the family wants the wedding to be small and somewhat informal, a house wedding can, of course, be as large and as elaborate as any other. Any religious ceremony in a house will always lack some of the formality and solemnity of a church ceremony, but there is no reason not to have as many guests as the house will hold.

A WEDDING IN TIME OF MOURNING

Contrary to a fairly widespread belief, mourning does not rule out the possibility of a church wedding. In the case of a death in the family, it might not be very good taste to have a very big, formal church wedding, unless the relationship were so distant that a certain indifference might not be thought lacking in respect. But a small church wedding, and a reception to which only the immediate families were invited, would be compatible with the strictest mourning. There is no rule concerning the degree of relationship which should be considered a barrier to a big church wedding. If an uncle had died, the family might still have the wedding that had been planned, especially if he had lived in another town and had not been intimate with the family. On the other hand, the bride's mother might feel it impossible to go through with the wedding just after the death of a quite distant cousin, whom the family had known intimately and loved devotedly for years. The point to be considered is not, however, only one of affection. Out of respect for the dead, one should not do anything that others might consider unfeeling or disrespectful. And if there has been a family feud, certainly this is not the moment to make it plain. But family mourning does not demand a wedding at home.

THE FORMAL WEDDING AT HOME

As an example of a big house wedding, let us imagine a wedding in summer in the country, at five o'clock in the afternoon. All the windows and doors are open; the rooms full of flowers; small tables, with umbrellas shading them, are set out on the lawn under the trees. The bride's table is on the terrace, under a big awning, where a floor has been laid for dancing. The orchestra of five men, dressed in short, red Hungarian jackets, is indoors, in the living room which has been arranged as a chapel. At a quarter to five, the first guest arrives. These are the mechanics behind this well-planned scene.

ARRANGING THE LIVING ROOM FOR THE CEREMONY

The first step is to move all the furniture, or as much of it as possible, out of the room. Sofas and big chairs are pushed along the walls at the end of the room, away from the place where the ceremony will be held. There should be a few rows of small, straight, "caterer's chairs," not necessarily for all the guests, but for the immediate families and for elderly relatives and guests who may not want to stand all through the ceremony. An aisle should be marked out, either by edging with chairs, or by ribbons strung from one little stand to another, from the door to the place where the bride and groom will stand for the ceremony.

As a rule, the best place for the ceremony is the end of the room farthest from the door. If there is a fireplace in the middle of this wall, it may be necessary to cover it in some way in order to eliminate a confusing background for the ceremony. A screen may be used, or curtains may be hung from the molding, if no mantel shelf interferes, but often nothing is needed except a few plants or vases of flowers tall enough to mask the hearth opening. A word of warning must be said, however, against "florist's pieces" or trellises of flowers, particularly paper flowers. Florists' arrangements can be beautiful but they must be very skillfully done. Vases of simple flowers are much more appropriate and usually make a much better background for a ceremony at home.

Against this background, there is usually a long, narrow table or altar, arranged according to the clergyman's directions. And directly in front of this, allowing enough room for the clergyman to move around in, is the place where the bride and groom will stand. Two prie-dieux for the bride and groom are often used in Episcopal and Roman Catholic weddings. These may be as elaborate or simple as you like. Plain red velvet and dark wood are the most usual, perhaps, but for a summer wedding it would be much prettier to cover them with white satin and decorate them with a little knot of white flowers at each end of the arm rest.

When all this is done, and big bowls and vases of flowers have been put on tables in front of the open windows and around the walls, the room is ready.

SEATING THE GUESTS FOR THE CEREMONY

Since most of the guests are not seated for the ceremony, there is very little of the formality of precedence that there is in a big church wedding. The immediate families of the bride and groom are put in the first rows to the left and right of the aisle, just as they are in church (see page 178), and a few of the oldest guests are given seats, through kindness and not for reasons of protocol. Beyond that, all the rest of the guests fend for themselves. The ushers are not given lists, but they should stand near the front door to show any stranger where to go.

As soon as the guests have arrived, the families take their places in the chairs up near the altar, the groom's mother goes up the aisle with her husband, and last of all, the bride's mother comes with a male relative, or the head usher. Then, when the clergyman, the best man, and the groom have taken their places, the orchestra starts playing the wedding march. The bride arrives.

THE WEDDING PROCESSION AND THE RECEIVING LINE

Except that ushers should not be included, the wedding procession follows the same form exactly for a house wedding as for a church wedding—bridesmaids first, then the bride and her father. Just as in church, the groom and the best man stand near the altar, at the right side of the aisle, with the best man just behind the groom. The first chair at the left side of the aisle is kept for the bride's father, or whoever is to give her away.

At house weddings, however, there is no procession down the aisle, as there is in church, unless the receiving line is to form outdoors or in some other room. Usually, the bride and groom just stand together at the altar, with the brides-maids, and the guests come up to congratulate them without any of the fuss and formality of a butler to announce their names. In this case, the groom *must* kiss the bride at the altar as he must always be the first to kiss the bride after the ceremony. (See page 182, "Kissing the Bride.")

If only a few people have been invited to the ceremony, and many more are expected to come to the reception, it might perhaps be easier to receive on the terrace or in some other room. In that case, the bride and groom followed by the bridesmaids go down the aisle directly to the place in which they will receive and the guests follow in any order they choose. After this the form given on page 184 is followed for the receiving line.

OUTDOOR WEDDINGS

The procedure of outdoor weddings is substantially the same as that of any wedding at home. The place where the bride and groom will stand during the ceremony, the aisle and the chairs for the guests, are all arranged in exactly the same way. And, as always, the bride and groom may receive without moving from their places, or they may go to some more convenient spot.

THE WEDDING RECEPTION

At afternoon weddings, particularly after a wedding and reception at home, there is often no seated bride's table. At small receptions there may be only one buffet table and when all the guests have been received, the bridal party joins the guests there. With the bridesmaids and ushers, their parents and friends around them, the bride and groom stand together while the bride cuts the cake. After the first piece has been eaten by the bride and groom, everybody else has a piece and the toasts begin. Then the dancing starts just as described on page 185. If a member of the family has just died, there should, of course, be no dancing. There might be music, played softly during the reception, but no dance music should be played unless the bride and groom have a sentimental attachment to a certain song.

At a very large reception, all the food probably could not conveniently be put on one table with the wedding cake, even if there were many waiters to replenish the dishes as they were emptied. In this case, and at the big country wedding we have imagined, the guests sit at small tables. Some wait on themselves, but many are served by the waiters who bring plates with the portions already served. The guests begin eating as soon as they have been "through" the receiving line, before the bride and groom can possibly leave it. They help themselves to whatever they like on the buffet table, and seat themselves at one of the small tables, or wherever seems convenient. Then as soon as the receiving line breaks up, the bride and groom will follow the guests' example, going to a small table which, although not set as a dining-room table would be, has been specially arranged for them with the wedding cake and white flowers. Here, food will be brought to them either by the waiters or by the ushers or other guests. Or if the menu is long enough to warrant a served and seated meal (two courses) there may be seated tables for the bridal party and the parents.

If there is not enough room for small tables, the wedding cake and the food for the bridal party may be put on a buffet table separate from the rest of the food, or even in a different room, in order to avoid confusion and crowding.

MENUS FOR THE WEDDING RECEPTION

At an afternoon wedding reception, a buffet tea is usually served. Dinners are now given only for some special reason; as, for example, after a country wedding held so far from town that guests can hope only for a very late dinner, if any. The food may be served or the guests may help themselves, whichever is more convenient for the hostess.

Tea

At wedding receptions, when there is a buffet tea or a buffet meal, waiters may bring served portions to any guest who has not served himself: little plates with a selection of sandwiches at a tea for example, and plates of ice cream. Although this method of service is not approved for other entertaining, it is often done at informal weddings, particularly country weddings where the small tables may be some distance from the buffet table.

In this case, the little tables are not set with glasses or silver and they may have a cloth or not, depending on their surface. The waiter brings a napkin and the necessary silver with each plate. Champagne, or punch, and coffee are served already poured, from large trays. The idea behind this arrangement of the service is obviously not that the guests are being served according to any form, but only that tables are there for their convenience and that waiters will help the younger men guests in seeing that everyone is fed.

The food usually provided at modern afternoon receptions is extremely simple. Whether there are three hundred guests or thirty, this is often the menu:

> Tea or coffee, or both
> Sandwiches
> Little cakes and cookies
> Punch or champagne
> Ice cream or water ice (This is sometimes omitted.)

The cakes are small and easily eaten in a bite or two. "Madeleines" are perfect. The sandwiches might be made of brown and white bread with cream cheese, or white bread with finely sliced chicken, smoked turkey, paper thin Virginia ham, or pâté de foie gras; or in summer: cucumber, watercress, or tomato. They should be very small and thin, square, oblong or triangular. Others may be made of thin white bread, spread with plain sweet butter, cream cheese or cress, and made into little rolls.

If one wants to serve a little more food than this, one of these three menus might be used for a late afternoon reception:

Cold turkey and tongue	Pâté de foie gras (or eggs) in aspic *
Celery and apple salad	Plain salad
Water ice	Ice cream
Tea, coffee and cakes	Tea, coffee and cakes

> Chicken (or lobster, or shrimp) salad
> Ice cream in individual molds
> Tea, coffee and cakes

With hot soup added, and tea omitted, one of these menus might also be used for a simple buffet breakfast in hot weather.

* With eggs in aspic a dressing of mayonnaise mixed with Roquefort cheese is often served.

Dinner

The menu of a dinner should always include one hot dish, even if it's only soup, unless the weather is tropically hot. If there is to be a buffet dinner with little tables for the guests, one of the menus suggested on page 169 could be used, with the first course omitted. And for any buffet meal, whether dinner or breakfast, one of these:

Timbale of sweetbreads and mushrooms   Lobster Newburg
Ham mousse and celery salad   Asparagus (hot or cold)
Meringues with ice cream and coffee   Puff-paste with ice cream and coffee

Creamed chicken with a border of peas
Tomato aspic with lettuce
Ice cream in individual molds, cakes and coffee

If there is to be a seated dinner (or a seated breakfast) one of these three menus might be used, with the addition of soup, hot or cold, at the beginning of the meal. Or, for an elaborate seated dinner, one might use one of the menus suggested on page 169 for a formal seated breakfast. (But if there are menu cards, as there well may be at a seated meal, the simple lists given here cannot serve as a model—the general rules of menu writing are given on pages 271 to 272, special suggestions for wedding menus, on page 170.)

THE BUFFET TABLE

The most convenient and the most usual place for the buffet table is, of course, the dining room. But this is purely a matter of convenience and, if any other room would work out better, that is the place to put the buffet table. It is rarely wise however, if a great many guests are expected, to put the table up against the wall. The best arrangement is to leave a space behind the table so that it is readily accessible from the pantry from which the waiters can circulate, replenishing the platters of food, bringing extra hot water for the tea, and so on.

The dining-room table is pulled out to its greatest length, and covered with a white damask cloth which falls to the floor. At a very large reception, of course, one table may not be enough and a second table (a caterer's table perhaps) will be needed for the guests' food. As in the setting of any buffet tables (see page 262 and diagrams, pages 254 and 263) balance and even spacing are the first principles. If there is to be but one buffet table, the wedding cake is set in the middle with a bowl of white flowers at each side of it if there is room. If there is not room for a bowl of flowers, the cake may be ringed with a flat garland of white flowers and green leaves. Little glass tubes of water hidden by the leaves will keep the flowers fresh. At an afternoon reception in winter, when it is dark and the lamps are lighted, the table may also be set with candelabra. At one end of the table is the tea tray, and at the other end, the coffee tray. An urn may be used for the coffee. (See page 261 in the section, "Setting the Table.") Spaced evenly are the platters of food, the stacks of plates and napkins, and the clusters of silver. As a rule, it is wise to have two platters of each dish on the table so that the guests will not have to wait too long to serve themselves. For a buffet breakfast, a tray set with soup cups and an urn of hot soup will replace the tea tray or, if the table is not big enough at any reception, the tea and coffee, or the bouillon and coffee, may be set on a side table.

If there are two buffet tables, or if the wedding cake is set on a small table specially arranged for the bridal party, the ice cream usually occupies the middle of the guests' table. The rest of the food on the guests' table is arranged as described above.

Champagne or punch is always on a table by itself except at the very smallest wedding, where it may be set on the main buffet table, balancing the tea tray. The guests will help themselves to the champagne or punch, but a waiter should be nearby to bring fresh bottles and glasses. Other waiters may circulate among the guests with trays of filled glasses, or with bottles of champagne wrapped in napkins from which the guests' glasses can be refilled. If punch is served instead of champagne, the waiters may carry pitchers from which to refill the guests' glasses. And there should always be some non-alcoholic drink in addition to the champagne or punch—hot tea or coffee in winter, iced tea or fruit juice in summer.

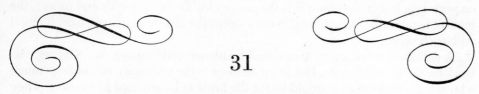

31

The Formal Evening Wedding

THE EVENING wedding is firmly a part of the tradition of the Southern states, and of those Western states which were explored, developed, and settled by Southern pioneers. In the days of horse and buggy, weddings usually took place in the house, rather than in church, because the plantations were so big that each one was far from the other, and the church was miles from them all. A wedding in those days was a magnificent, party-like occasion, with candlelight and bare shoulders and the house crowded for weeks before. And, although many Southern weddings nowadays take place in a church, and although some—particularly in the Southwest—are given in the afternoon, the typical Southern wedding still retains some of the evening party flavor.

THE CHURCH CEREMONY

Exactly the same preparations for a wedding prevail in both North and South, so that all the suggestions given on pages 165 to 178 apply equally here. Invitations, church decorations, and seating are all the same, but from the moment the first guest crosses the threshold of the church, the major differences become obvious. In the first place, it is eight o'clock or half past eight, and all the women guests are in full evening dress. The dress that was perfect for Charleston's Saint Cecilia Ball, for example, would be just the thing to wear to a big wedding at Saint Philip's. Some of the older women have little jackets, or a lace or tulle shawl; some of the young girls have bare shoulders with only a little ruffle covering the upper part of their arms. In Episcopal churches, all their heads are covered, with a bit of tulle, a flower arrangement, or a tiny linen square which has been given them at the door. Only in winter do they wear evening coats or jackets.

The men guests are in dinner jackets, with stiff-bosomed shirts and the usual black tie. But the bridegroom, the best man, the ushers, and the bride's father are all resplendent in white tie and tails. The mothers of the bride and groom are almost always dressed a little more conservatively than the rest of the women guests, with covered arms and a moderate décolletage. The bride dresses exactly as she would for a formal wedding in the North; so do the bridesmaids, except that they may have shorter sleeves and a slightly deeper décolletage.

The wedding procession of an evening wedding follows the form described on page 179, but in the South it is the custom for the bridesmaids and ushers, the maid of honor and the best man, to come down the aisle arm in arm, a bridesmaid with each usher.

A definite part of every traditional Southern wedding are the Negroes who work for the bride's family. Not to invite them to the ceremony would be as much a breach of etiquette as it would be for the bride to be married in trousers. They come as a matter of right, and no Southern woman in her senses would forget to include them.

THE WEDDING RECEPTION

The receiving line, the decoration of the rooms, the procedure of the reception in the South, all follow the pattern described on pages 184 to 186. The differences are that there is rarely a seated wedding table, but only a buffet table set with a white cloth, candles, white flowers, dishes of candy, decanters of wine and wine glasses, and the wedding cake, called in the South the bride's cake. In Charleston, one of the most tradition-minded Southern cities, this cake is always a fruit cake with almond paste and a very elaborate white icing, but without any little figures; in other Southern cities, the traditional bride's cake is white all through.

The sandwiches and the champagne or punch, which are the only other things served at most receptions, are never set on the big buffet table. Young friends of the bride pass the sandwiches around to the guests; older friends of the bride's mother serve the punch, of which there are usually several bowls in different parts of the reception rooms. Butlers and waitresses do not appear except to remove glasses and plates and bring fresh ones. Whether or not there is dancing, the whole reception has the flavor of an evening party which is a family matter, in which no caterer has any part. In the most conservative parts of the South, the reception is always given in a house or in one of the old "halls," with cake and sandwiches all made in the house of the bride's mother or in those of her friends; in other parts of the South, in recent years, a great many wedding receptions have been given in clubs; in which case, of course, the food is provided by the club's staff.

When there is no dancing, receptions after an evening wedding usually last only about an hour or so, depending on the number of guests and the time it takes for them all to pass the reception line. As in the North, the wedding guests start eating and drinking as soon as they have congratulated the groom and kissed the bride, and the wedding party joins them as soon as the last guest has been welcomed. The bride cuts the cake, and after a few moments of toasts and general conversation, she and the groom go to change into their traveling clothes. On their way to the door, they are pelted with rice, as at all other weddings, though never, in the South, with confetti. As she drives away from the candles and the flowers and the gaiety of lights in the darkness, every Southern bride—if she thinks of it at all—wonders how Northern women can possibly want anything as unromantic as a wedding in the broad light of day.

32

Small Weddings

WE HAVE considered so far only the most elaborate and formal weddings— all held at different hours of the day, but all on a scale that has become less usual than it used to be. All three are, however, good examples of their kinds, examples that can be scaled down to fit any house, any purse, or any heart's desire. It might be useful to consider here a small wedding, held in a small house or apartment, and in the late afternoon because an afternoon wedding can be the easiest and least expensive.

AFTERNOON WEDDING AT HOME

The preliminaries may be exactly like those of an elaborate wedding: newspaper announcements of the engagement, engraved announcements of the wedding sent in the name of the bride's family, arrangements with the clergyman, etc. This has been described on the preceding pages. Or the bride may decide not to have engraved announcements (see page 217, "Informal Announcement of a Small Wedding") and, if the ceremony is to be in a church, to have only a few white flowers in the church. Whether the marriage is religious or civil, the bride may perhaps be married in a short dress (see page 222) and the only expenses for the reception are the wedding cake, punch, tea, a few sandwiches, and one or two bouquets of flowers. The dining-room table, pulled out to its greatest length, is brought into the biggest room, pushed against a wall and covered with a white cloth. A mirror back of the table, reflecting the cake and the flowers, adds greatly to the effect. The cake is set in the middle of the table, the tea at one end and the punch bowl and glasses at the other. Plates of sandwiches are spaced evenly between, with stacks of little tea plates and napkins. On a large table, white flowers are put in low bowls near the cake. If the room is big enough, no furniture need be moved; in a very small apartment, some of the furniture will undoubtedly have to be taken away, but it is not necessary, or even desirable, to make the rooms as stiffly bare as they would be for a formal reception.

At such a wedding there is no receiving line. The parents of the bride and groom greet the guests just as they would at any other time, and so do the bride and groom, although they stand always together, as they would not usually do at a tea party. As soon as all the guests have come, the bride cuts the cake, and the toasts begin. After a little while—a shorter time, naturally, than at a big reception where there are many guests to see—the bride and groom decide to leave. The parents and friends go out to where the motor is waiting, and pelt the bride and groom with rice and confetti, and the wedding is over. Wedding announcements, or letters written in advance, are sent off the same day, and the bride has had a happy, joyful wedding, "correct" in every detail, and a pleasant memory forever.

SECOND MARRIAGES

A second marriage for a man does not in any way affect the ceremony. If he is marrying a young girl, she can wear the longest train and the whitest veil, and be married with the utmost pomp and circumstance, provided, of course, that church regulations permit such ceremony. But it is equally plain that a second marriage for a woman can never be like her first. The long wedding dress, the veil, and a big church wedding are out of the question. She can have as large a reception as she chooses, but a small wedding and reception such as we have outlined above would probably be more appropriate.

Announcements of the engagement are not sent to the newspapers, unless the bride is a very young widow. The remarriage of a divorced woman, or of an older woman, is always less elaborate than that of a young widow. Engraved wedding invitations and announcements, which are perfectly proper in the wedding of a young widow (see page 207), are quite out of place in these weddings. These can be as solemn and as happy occasions as any other marriage, but they necessarily lack some of the joyful spontaneity of a young girl's wedding.

33

Wedding Invitations and Announcements

WEDDING invitations and announcements are sent to a wide circle of the family, friends and acquaintances of both the family of the bride and the family of the groom. They are stiff with tradition, governed by inflexible forms. Their purpose is to announce an important family event, or to invite a guest to witness it, and there is very definitely a right or wrong way to go about it.

The first rule that covers both invitations and announcements is that both should be sent in the name of the bride's parents; or, if her parents are dead, by other members of her family, by her friends, or even by herself. They should never, in any circumstances, be issued by the family of the bridegroom. Nor should an invitation or announcement ever be sent to the immediate family of the groom. His parents, and any brothers and sisters who are living in the same house, should presumably have been fully and more intimately informed of the impending event. Ideally, the invitations should be mailed to arrive at least two or three weeks before the wedding, so it is usually wise to order them a good two months in advance.

MAKING UP THE INVITATION LIST

The lists of those who are to be invited are made up by the mother of the bride and the mother of the groom. As a rule, the bride's family invites more guests than does the groom's, and the great majority of the guests may be their friends if the groom's family lives far away.

If the wedding is to be very big and elaborate, the bride's family usually engages a social secretary who will address and mail the invitations. There is a special consideration involved here, because the handwriting used is a matter of form. See page 200 below.

Invitations to the wedding should be sent not only to all the family and friends who might conceivably be able to come, but also to friends who live so far away that they could not possibly make the journey. In fact, if it is to be a small wedding, invitations might be sent to a great many distant friends and relatives, while every name on the list of neighbors will be carefully thought over and anxiously weighed. An invitation to a wedding is more than it seems on the surface: It is an indication of affection, a way of showing one's friends that they are important enough or close enough to share in one of the major events of family life. An invitation to a wedding is a compliment, a traditional one that follows traditional forms.

THE TRADITIONAL PAPER AND SIZE;
ENVELOPES AND ADDRESSES

The most conservative and traditional paper for wedding invitations is a heavy, white or faintly cream-colored paper known technically as vellum, or "kid finish." This paper may have a raised frame or "plate mark" on the first page, enclosing the message, but the plain, flat sheet is more often used. The traditional paper is a double sheet, about 5 by 7¼ inches, which is folded across its length and enclosed in two envelopes.

It is a rule that all engraved wedding invitations should be addressed by hand, and the handwriting a social secretary uses is also a matter of form.

This is an example of the outer envelope, which should always include the full name:

Mr. and Mrs. Douglas Delano White

352 Clinton Avenue

Des Moines 13

Iowa

THE OUTER ENVELOPE OF A FORMAL WEDDING INVITATION

When many guests are invited, and a secretary will address the envelopes, this formalized handwriting should be followed as closely as possible. When there are fewer guests, and the bride or her family writes the addresses, there are no rules except that the spacing should follow this general form.

A joint invitation may be sent to two members of a family living in the same house, although the best practice is to send a separate invitation to each married couple and to each separate guest. (See also "Forms of Address," page 555.)

To a couple with one daughter, the envelope might be addressed:

Mr. and Mrs. Douglas Delano White
Miss Monica White

To a brother and sister:

Miss Brooke Adams
Mr. Charles George Adams (or "Charles George Adams, Esq.")

The inner envelope, although sometimes left unaddressed, according to the modern practice, in the conservative tradition is always addressed:

Mr. and Mrs. White

The flap is not sealed, and it should not even be gummed.

Permissible Modern Variations

It is perfectly correct in modern usage to deviate slightly from traditional form in the weight of paper used. A lighter weight paper in the same kid finish or a lighter weight glazed paper are both correct in these days of air mail. A modern innovation which became popular during the wartime paper shortage is a small, double sheet, about 4½ by 6 inches, sent in one envelope instead of the more conventional two. If the smaller size is used, it is not folded and is slipped sideways into an envelope of the same size.

LETTERING

The most conservative lettering for a wedding invitation is script, but the modern favorite is shaded antique Roman. London script, or shaded modified Roman lettering, is also often used. Novelty lettering should be avoided. Unless a shortage precludes the use of copper engraving plates, all wedding invitations and announcements, like all formal invitations in the third person, *must* be engraved—never printed—and they must be engraved in black. Examples of the four accepted letterings are on page 202. The complete wordings, which, for convenience' sake are all shown in Waverly, the text type of this book, are given on pages 203 to 208; but it must be emphasized that any of the four styles of lettering illustrated on the next page may be used.

COATS OF ARMS AND CRESTS

Since there is no college of heralds in the United States, there is no authority to decide who has the right to bear a coat of arms. Most Americans who use a coat of arms do so only if their ancestors had an unquestionable right to it.

If by long custom a family has established a tradition of using a coat of arms, it is embossed without color on wedding invitations and announcements. The invitation illustrated on page 202 shows where it should be placed. There are, however, two important technical rules: First, on an important document such as

Mr. and Mrs. George Edward Bourne

request the honour of your presence

at the marriage of their daughter

AN EXAMPLE OF SCRIPT, WITH A COAT OF ARMS

Mr. and Mrs. George Edward Bourne

request the honour of your presence

AN EXAMPLE OF SHADED ANTIQUE ROMAN LETTERING

Mr. and Mrs. George Edward Bourne

request the honour of your presence

AN EXAMPLE OF LONDON SCRIPT

Mr. and Mrs. George Edward Bourne

request the honour of your presence

AN EXAMPLE OF SHADED MODIFIED ROMAN LETTERING

a wedding invitation or announcement, the full coat of arms should be used (i.e., the crest, shield, and motto); second, a coat of arms cannot be used by a woman and should never appear on invitations or announcements sent in a woman's name only. American custom has to some extent sanctioned the use of a crest by a single woman. But a crest, without the shield and motto, should be used only on menu cards, place cards, and writing paper; never on wedding invitations and announcements. And, in any case, its use by a woman is not correct according to the strictest opinion. The only heraldic device which according to all the authorities a widow or an unmarried woman can always use is the lozenge. A lozenge is a diamond-shaped device on which a family shield is engraved. An unmarried woman uses her father's shield only. A widow uses her father's shield and her husband's; the lozenge is divided in half vertically, and the husband's shield is impaled at the left, the father's at the right.

TRADITIONAL WORDING OF A WEDDING INVITATION

This is the traditional form, evolved in the days when divorce was unheard of, when every bride's parents had the same name as her own:

Mr. and Mrs. George Edward Bourne
request the honour of your presence
at the marriage of their daughter
Ann Stuyvesant
to
Mr. George Baker Ellis
on Wednesday, the third of March
at four o'clock
Saint Thomas Church
New York

Note that the phrase, "the honour of your presence," must be used whenever one is issuing an invitation to a religious ceremony, and tradition demands the old-fashioned spelling, "honour." "The pleasure of your company" is correct for the invitation to the reception. (See page 210.) The hour is written out in full, as shown; if the ceremony is to take place at the half hour, the form is "at half after four o'clock." The quarter hour is not a traditional time for a formal ceremony. The address of a very well-known church is not given. If the city is very large, and the church is not well known, the address of the church should be engraved directly under the name:

Church of the Resurrection
115 East Seventy-fourth Street
New York

In an engraved, formal invitation or announcement, particularly a wedding invitation or announcement, it is best to avoid the use of numerals as far as possible. But, since many addresses would be inconveniently long if entirely written out, some abbreviation is often necessary. The best usage permits numerals for the number of the church (or house), if it is a long one, with the number of the street written as shown immediately above. If the first number is short—"Ten" or "Thirty," for example—it, too, is written out.

"R.s.v.p." is never engraved on invitations to a church ceremony, and such invitations need never be answered. The forms for invitations to the wedding of a minister will be found on page 213 and for the wedding of a military or naval officer on pages 214 to 216. According to the traditional form, "junior" is always written out in full, and is not capitalized.

. . . .
to
Mr. George Baker Ellis, junior

"II" or "III" is engraved in numerals after the name:

. . . .
to
Mr. George Baker Ellis, II

Permissible Modern Departures

It has become somewhat the fashion to omit the "Mr." before the bridegroom's name, a permissible but very informal custom. Another less desirable departure from the conservative pattern is to engrave "junior" as "Jr." This is not too incongruous in upright modern lettering, but neither of these new fashions should be used when script, which is very conservative, has been chosen.

Other changes are the use of the phrase "half past," instead of "half after," and the omission of the word "on" before the day of the wedding. Although "on Wednesday, the third of March" is better usage than "Wednesday, the third of March," "on" is occasionally omitted. A further change is that weddings are now sometimes held at the quarter-hour, particularly in the country when the quarter-hour fits better with the local train schedule. The wording is "at quarter past . . ." or "at quarter before . . ." But like other innovations, these look less well in the traditional script than in the other letterings.

VARIATIONS OF THE TRADITIONAL WORDING

1. When the bride's father is dead and her mother has not remarried, the invitation reads:

Mrs. George Edward Bourne
requests the honour of your presence
at the marriage of her daughter
Ann Stuyvesant
etc.

When the bride's mother is divorced, and has not remarried, the first line includes her maiden surname. For example, had Mrs. Bourne been born a Woodward, the first line of the invitation would read: "Mrs. Woodward Bourne." The rest of the invitation follows the above example.

2. When the bride's mother, whether widowed or divorced, has remarried:

> Mr. and Mrs. Henry Harrison Slater
> request the honour of your presence
> at the marriage of her daughter
> Ann Stuyvesant Bourne
> etc.

If the family prefers, the invitations may be issued in the mother's name only; as,

> Mrs. Henry Harrison Slater
> requests the honour of your presence
> etc.

A third form uses the phrase ". . . at the marriage of Mrs. Slater's daughter . . ." but this is not so desirable as the first.

3. When the bride's parents are separated but not divorced, the invitations are often engraved in the traditional form, ignoring the fact of the separation.

4. If the bride's father is a widower, invitations are naturally sent out in his name only, as they are when the bride's mother is a widow, not remarried. (See example 1.)

5. If the bride's mother is dead and her father has remarried:

> Mr. and Mrs. George Edward Bourne
> request the honour of your presence
> at the marriage of his daughter
> Ann Stuyvesant
> etc.

This form may also be followed if the bride's parents have been divorced in such circumstances that the bride has always lived with her father. (See also page 165.)

6. If the bride's brother is giving the wedding, both parents having died:

> Mr. George Edward Bourne
> requests the honour of your presence
> at the marriage of his sister
> Ann Stuyvesant
> etc.

7. If the brother is married, the bride's last name is given, to avoid confusion, because the same form might be used if the bride were the sister of Mrs. Bourne; as,

> Mr. and Mrs. George Edward Bourne
> request the honour of your presence
> at the marriage of their sister
> Ann Stuyvesant Bourne
> etc.

8. If the sister of the bride is giving the wedding:

Miss Agnes Ripley Bourne
requests the honour of your presence
at the marriage of her sister
Ann Stuyvesant Bourne
etc.

9. If the sister of the bride is married:

Mr. and Mrs. Albert Johnson Miller
request the honour of your presence
at the marriage of their sister
Ann Stuyvesant Bourne
etc.

10. If the wedding is being given by an aunt, an uncle, or a grandparent, the relationship is given:

Mrs. Henry Worthington Bourne
requests the honour of your presence
at the marriage of her granddaughter
Ann Stuyvesant Bourne
etc.

or "Mr. and Mrs. . . . ." at "the marriage of their . . . ."

11. If the wedding is being given by other relatives, the relationship is not explained; the invitation reads as it would if the wedding were given by friends of the bride:

Mr. and Mrs. Richard Doubleday Willys
request the honour of your presence
at the marriage of
Miss Ann Stuyvesant Bourne
etc.

12. If the wedding is being given by the family in the house of friends:

Mr. and Mrs. George Edward Bourne
request the honour of your presence
at the marriage of their daughter
Ann Stuyvesant
to
Mr. George Baker Ellis
on Wednesday, the third of March
at four o'clock
at the residence of
Mr. and Mrs. Richard Doubleday Willys
2554 Marlborough Street,
Boston

13. If there are no relatives or intimate friends, the bride may send out the invitations herself:

The honour of your presence
is requested at the marriage of
Miss Ann Stuyvesant Bourne
to
Mr. George Baker Ellis
etc.

14. When there is to be a double wedding—and the brides are sisters:

Mr. and Mrs. George Edward Bourne
request the honour of your presence
at the marriage of their daughters
Ann Stuyvesant *
to
Mr. George Baker Ellis
and
Frances Butler
to
Mr. Henry Symonds Addington, junior
etc.

When the brides are not sisters, but cousins:

Mr. and Mrs. George Edward Bourne †
and
Mr. and Mrs. James Stuart Lacy
request the honour of your presence
at the marriage of their daughters
Ann Stuyvesant Bourne
to
Mr. George Baker Ellis
and
Mary Allen Lacy
to
Mr. John Robert Carpentier
etc.

15. Engraved invitations are not always sent for the marriage of an older widow, but there is no question of bad taste in this case, as there is in the case of divorcées. But if the bride is a very young widow, engraved invitations may be sent in the traditional form or any of the permissible departures from that form.

* The name of the elder sister is given first.
† There are several ways of deciding which parents shall be listed first on the invitations. When there is little or no difference in the brides' ages, the names are often listed alphabetically and that order is used in deciding all matters of precedence. When the reception is given in the house of one of the families, rather than in a club or hotel, the hosts' names are sometimes listed first, on the theory that the same order should be used for all the engravings, and that, as hosts at the reception their names look better at the head of the invitations to the reception. Any considerable difference in age—either between the brides or their families—is usually accepted as the most valid deciding factor, and precedence is given to the older ones. (See also page 188, in the chapter "Procedure of a Wedding.")

The only change is that the name of her first husband is added to her baptismal names; the modern tendency is to use the parents' name as a middle name, but this form is technically the only correct one:

Mr. and Mrs. George Edward Bourne
request the honour of your presence
at the marriage of their daughter
Ann Stuyvesant Wheeler
etc.

16. If a widow is giving her own wedding, the invitation reads:

The honour of your presence
is requested at the marriage of
Mrs. Henry Hudson Wheeler
etc.

If the bride prefers, the third line may read, "Mrs. Ann Bourne Wheeler." The form, "Mrs. Ann........" is never a desirable one, but in this case many women prefer to break that custom rather than to use their first husband's name on a wedding invitation.

17. If the bride is a divorcée, engraved invitations are rarely sent. In fact, unless the circumstances of the divorce were most unusual (if the divorcée were very young, for example, and the conditions of the divorce entirely in her favor), engraved invitations would be in questionable taste. The marriage of a divorcée should be a small and quiet ceremony, but if one particularly wants to send engraved invitations, form 15 suggested above may be used. Or, if the bride is giving the wedding herself, this is the form:

The honour of your presence
is requested at the marriage of
Mrs. Bourne Wheeler
to
Mr. George Baker Ellis
etc.

INVITATIONS TO A HOUSE WEDDING

Invitations to a house wedding are engraved exactly as are invitations to a wedding in church, except, of course, that the address of the house will be substituted for that of the church. The last two lines of all the examples given here, instead of reading,

Saint Thomas Church
New York

would include, perhaps, the name of a country house:

The Fields
Ridgefield, Connecticut

or, if the wedding were to be given in

a large city:

127 East Sixty-seventh Street
New York

or, if the wedding were given in a small town:

114 Cherry Lane
Rocky Hills, New Jersey

TRAIN CARDS

When a wedding is being given in the country, an extra card, showing train and transportation arrangements for the guests, may be included in the envelope with the invitation. In former times, special trains were often chartered for a big wedding; today, this is a rather unusual procedure. Trains on the regular schedule, arriving at convenient times before and after the wedding, are listed as follows:

Train leaves Pennsylvania Station at 2:30 p.m.
Arrives Somerton at 3:40 p.m.
Train leaves Somerton at 5:40 p.m.
Arrives Pennsylvania Station at 7:00 p.m.
Train leaves Somerton at 7:10 p.m.
Arrives Pennsylvania Station at 8:20 p.m.

If a special train has been arranged for, the card should read:

A special train will leave
the Pennsylvania Station
at 2:30 p.m.
and, returning, will arrive in New York
at 7:30 p.m.
Please present this card to the conductor

These cards always used to be engraved on stiff card (two-sheet or three-sheet board), in the same color and finish as the invitations and in the same lettering. When there is a special train, this is still done; but when the regular trains are used, the train card is often more businesslike: small, dead-white, with block letters and simple numbers. A train card should be about 4¼ by 3 or 3½ inches and it should never be embossed with a crest, even if the invitation has one. Guests need not, of course, buy a railroad ticket for a trip on a special train; this card is all the ticket they need.

CARDS OF ADMITTANCE TO THE CHURCH
AND PEW CARDS

For a very large and elaborate wedding, cards of admittance to the church are sometimes—but rarely now—enclosed with the invitations. They should be engraved on stiff card of the same color and finish and in the same lettering as the invitation. They should be about 3½ by 2½ inches and, again like the train card, should never be engraved with a crest. The most usual form is:

Please present this card
at St. Thomas Church
on Wednesday, the third of March

If the guests are to be assigned to special pews, "Pew No. ...." is engraved in the lower left-hand corner. The number of the pew is written in by hand.

Another way of assigning guests to a special pew is to enclose the visiting card of the mother of either the bride or the groom with "Pew No. 7" or "Pew No. 4" written in the upper left-hand corner. Those who have received visiting cards from the bride's mother will, of course, be seated on the bride's side of the church; those with cards from the groom's mother, on the groom's side.

Cards of admittance and pew cards should be brought to the church by the wedding guests. The card of admission is shown to those who stand at the door of the church and, like the pew card, is given to the usher. But, as we have said, these cards and the big weddings which made them necessary are now very rare.

INVITATIONS TO THE RECEPTION

All the guests who are invited to the ceremony are not necessarily invited to the reception. Sometimes the determining factor is the degree of intimacy: Casual acquaintances, and business friends of the bride's father or of the groom, are often invited to the church and not to the reception, particularly if the bride is married in a big church. Or else the space available may decide the lists of guests. If the bride is married at home, in a small drawing room arranged as a chapel, there may be only a few guests at the ceremony and many more at the reception. The greatest compliment that can be paid a guest is to be invited to both.

There are four ways of sending an invitation to a wedding reception.

1. To include the invitation to the reception in the wording of the invitation to the ceremony, when all the guests are invited to both church and reception:

Mr. and Mrs. George Edward Bourne
request the honour of your presence
at the marriage of their daughter
Ann Stuyvesant
to
Mr. George Baker Ellis
on Wednesday, the third of March
at half after four o'clock
Saint Thomas Church
and afterwards at
127 East Sixty-seventh Street
New York

R.s.v.p.

The more conventional "The favour of a reply is requested" may replace the commonly used "R.s.v.p." in all invitations to the reception.

2. To include in the envelope with the wedding invitation a stiff card (two-sheet or three-sheet board) about 3 by 4 inches, or a little smaller than half the wedding invitation, when more guests are expected at the ceremony than at the reception. This card should be in the same color and finish as the invitation, and engraved in the same lettering, but even if there is a crest on the invitation, there should never be one on a card of this kind.

Mr. and Mrs. George Edward Bourne
request the pleasure of your company
on Wednesday, the third of March
at five o'clock
127 East Sixty-seventh Street

R.s.v.p.

An alternate wording which may be used is:

The pleasure of your company
is requested at the reception *
after the ceremony
at
127 East Sixty-seventh Street

   R.s.v.p.

3. To send to those guests whom one does not want to invite to the ceremony a separate invitation to the reception only. This should be engraved on paper of the same size and kind as a wedding invitation, and sent in the same way (see pages 200 to 202 for suggestions about paper, size, lettering, etc.).

Mr. and Mrs. George Edward Bourne
request the pleasure of your company
at the wedding reception of their daughter
Ann Stuyvesant
and
Mr. George Baker Ellis
on Wednesday, the third of March
at half after four o'clock
127 East Sixty-seventh Street
New York

   R.s.v.p.

Or this form may be used—extremely polite, but rare:

Mr. and Mrs. George Edward Bourne
request the pleasure of
the company of
Mr. and Mrs. Howard   (*written by hand*)
at the wedding reception of their daughter
Ann Stuyvesant
etc.

4. To send a small invitation card to the ceremony with a big invitation to the reception, when a great many people are to be invited to the reception and very few to the church. The first part of the invitation to the reception is similar to example 3, above. When the reception is given in the rooms of a hotel, or a club, the second half reads:

and
Mr. George Baker Ellis
on Wednesday, the third of March
at half after four o'clock
Ballroom of the Madison Club
120 East Sixty-seventh Street
New York

   R.s.v.p.
   127 East Sixty-ninth Street
   New York

* Or, "at the wedding breakfast."

The enclosed card, which is similar to the small reception card in example 2, reads:

Mr. and Mrs. George Edward Bourne
request the honour of your presence
at the marriage ceremony
at four o'clock
Church of the Incarnation
Ten East Sixty-fifth Street

The variations to be used in the case of divorced parents, etc., follow the forms given for wedding invitations on pages 204 to 208.

TRADITIONAL WORDING OF A WEDDING ANNOUNCEMENT

When the wedding has been very small, and the families' friends are very many, engraved announcements may be sent to all but the most intimate friends, who, if they were not invited to the wedding, should be informed by letter or telegram. If the wedding has been very large, announcements will be needed for less intimate friends or for business acquaintances whom one might not know well enough to invite to the ceremony. (See also "Newspaper Announcements," page 98.)

Except in the case of business acquaintances, who are thus made privy to a part of one's family life, a wedding announcement is not, in itself, a compliment. It is merely a notice of an important family event, and an indication that the bride's family wishes you to be informed of it. It follows a rigid form, very like that of the wedding invitation. This is the traditional wording:

Mr. and Mrs. George Edward Bourne
have the honour of announcing
the marriage of their daughter
Ann Stuyvesant
to
Mr. George Baker Ellis
on Wednesday, the third of March
One thousand, nine hundred and forty-eight
Rumson, New Jersey

Note that the second line, instead of reading "have the honour of announcing," may read "have the honour to announce . . ."

Permissible Departures

The name of the church may be added and the year may be written out according to the more modern and less traditional form, as follows:

Nineteen hundred and forty-eight
The Riverside Church
New York

Another departure from the conventional pattern is the use of a brief "announce" in place of the phrase "have the honour . . ." It is not so graceful as the other two forms, and it should never be used when it might be construed as evidence of family disapproval.

VARIATIONS OF THE TRADITIONAL WORDING

Variations within the traditional form follow the examples given for wedding invitations on pages 204 to 208. When the bride's parents are divorced, for example, the announcements are sent in her mother's name only, if the bride lived with her mother, just as the invitations are (see example 1, page 204). Announcements of a double wedding may be sent jointly, in the form of the invitations, or separately with no mention of a double ceremony, according to the standard form.

The only major differences in the forms of announcements and wedding invitations are in the case of a wedding given by the couple themselves. The invitations are shown on pages 207 to 208 (examples 13, 16 and 17). The wording of the announcements is as follows: . . . .

Miss Ann Stuyvesant Bourne
and
Mr. George Baker Ellis
announce their marriage
on Wednesday, the third of March
Nineteen hundred and forty-eight
The Riverside Church
New York

or,

Mrs. Henry Hudson Wheeler
and
Mr. George Baker Ellis
etc.

or,

Mrs. Ann Bourne Wheeler
etc.

or,

Mrs. Bourne Wheeler
etc.

PAPER, LETTERING, ADDRESSES

The suggestions for the paper, lettering, addresses, coats of arms, and the sizes of wedding invitations, given on pages 200 to 202, should be followed also in the case of wedding announcements. The only difference is that announcements should be mailed the day after the wedding has taken place.

INVITATIONS AND ANNOUNCEMENTS FOR THE MARRIAGE OF A MINISTER

If a minister is being married, his name is written on the wedding invitations and announcements as follows:

. . . .
Ann Stuyvesant
to
The Reverend Thomas Waterman Pyle

INVITATIONS AND ANNOUNCEMENTS FOR NAVAL AND MILITARY WEDDINGS

Reserve officers of the Army and officers of the Naval Reserve use their military and naval titles only when they are on active duty. When a military or naval title is used, whether the officer is in the regular Army, Navy, or Reserve, the line directly under his name is engraved in a type smaller than that used for the rest of the invitation. No abbreviations are ever correct.

Military Titles

There are two correct ways of engraving an Army officer's name on a wedding invitation or announcement. The first is:

....

to
Percy Clark Allen
Lieutenant, United States Army

The second form is:

....

to
Lieutenant Percy Clark Allen
United States Army

These forms are used also by Reserve officers on active duty with the necessary changes, as follows:

....

to
Percy Clark Allen
Lieutenant, Army of the United States

or,

Lieutenant Percy Clark Allen
Army of the United States

The branch of service may be engraved on the wedding invitation and announcement as shown in the examples which follow; or it may be omitted. It is out-of-date to mention the officer's regiment; and since a wedding invitation is not an official document, Army custom does not differentiate between a first and second lieutenant.

....

to
Lieutenant Richard Spooner Desmond
Air Corps, United States Army

....

to
Captain (or Major) Richard Spooner Desmond
Infantry, United States Army

....

to
Lieutenant Colonel (or Colonel) Richard Spooner Desmond
Quartermaster Corps, United States Army

214

. . . .
to
Brigadier (or Major or Lieutenant) General Richard Spooner Desmond
United States Army

. . . .
to
General Richard Spooner Desmond
United States Army

or,

. . . .
to
Percy Clark Allen
Lieutenant, Ordnance, United States Army

. . . .
to
Percy Clark Allen
Captain (or Major), Field Artillery, United States Army

. . . .
to
Percy Clark Allen
Lieutenant Colonel (or Colonel), Corps of Engineers, United States Army

. . . .
to
Percy Clark Allen
Brigadier (or Major or Lieutenant) General, United States Army

Again, for Reserve officers, the phrase "United States Army" is changed to "Army of the United States."

If the father of the bride is an Army officer, the first line of the invitation and announcement reads as follows:

Major General and Mrs. John Ward Lowe

Naval Titles

In wedding invitations and announcements for officers of the Navy, the forms for the regular Navy and for the Naval Reserve are exactly the same except that in the case of Reserve officers, the phrase "United States Naval Reserve" must always be substituted for "United States Navy." The following example shows the form for the wedding of an officer in the regular Navy; if he were in the Naval Reserve, the line under his name would read, "Ensign, United States Naval Reserve:"

. . . .
to
George Albert Patterson
Ensign, United States Navy

The correct titles, which are followed by a comma, are: "Ensign," "Lieutenant, junior grade," "Lieutenant," "Lieutenant Commander," "Commander," "Captain," "Commodore," "Rear Admiral," "Vice Admiral," and "Admiral."

As in the case of Army officers, if the father of the bride is a Navy officer, the first line of the wedding invitation and announcement would read:

Lieutenant Commander and Mrs. Forrest Martin

"AT HOME" CARDS

When engraved wedding announcements are being sent, "at home" cards are often enclosed in the same envelope. These are like a very large visiting card. They are engraved on heavy card (two-sheet or three-sheet board) of exactly the same color as the wedding announcement, in a size about 4 by 3 inches. Following the modern tendency to avoid the words "at home," the best form is as follows:

Mr. and Mrs. George Baker Ellis

110 East 67th Street
After the fifteenth of March · · · · · · · New York

An alternate form is a small card, like a visiting card, which may be enclosed with the announcement. This card reads:

After March 15th
110 East Sixty-seventh Street
New York

INVITATIONS TO A SMALL WEDDING

For a very small, informal wedding, no engraved invitations are necessary. If the bride is married in her mother's living room, for example, with no guests other than the few the room can hold, formal invitations would be absurd. A note, a telegram, or even a telephone message, would be a perfectly proper invitation, with the proviso that the invitation is sent by, or on behalf of, the mother of the bride. The same principle applies both to the verbal invitation to a small wedding and to the formal, engraved invitation: The bride's parents, family, or even friends, must be the ones in whose names the invitations are issued. (See pages 204 to 208 for suggestions in the case of divorce, remarriage, etc.) If it were a verbal invitation given by telephone, for example, by the sister of the bride: "Mother has asked me to tell you that Evelyn and John are being married, very quietly, here at the house on Wednesday afternoon. She hopes so much that you and Uncle George and the twins will be able to come. The wedding is at half past four, and she would love to have you stay for tea afterwards."

Telegrams, too, should be sent in the name of the bride's mother: "Evelyn and John being married very quietly at the house Wednesday afternoon at four-thirty. Hope you and George and twins will surely come. Love, Marian."

A short note would be more polite than either of the above invitations, particularly to the older members of the groom's family, who may well be almost strangers to the bride's mother:

Dear Mrs. Howard:

John and Evelyn are being married, very quietly, here at the house, at 2360 Pine Street, next Wednesday afternoon. George and I (or more formally, "My husband and I") hope so much that you and Mr. Howard and Annabelle will be able to come. The ceremony will be at half past four and, though there will not be any reception, we shall count on your staying on to have tea with us afterwards.

Sincerely,
Marian Byrd

The address need not be repeated, of course, if the letter is written on paper engraved with the house address.

INFORMAL ANNOUNCEMENT OF A SMALL WEDDING

No matter how small or how informal a wedding has been, the most formal engraved wedding announcements may be sent to family, friends, and acquaintances. Perhaps, indeed, if the wedding has been small, there is all the more reason to send them. (See page 212 for the correct form.) If the bride's family should, however, wish to avoid the expense of engraved announcements, an announcement may be sent to the newspapers, following the form given on page 136 for the engagement announcement, but substituting the words, ". . . announce the marriage on the third of March of their daughter, Miss Ann Stuyvesant Bourne, to . . ." (See pages 95 to 98, in the chapter, "Personal Publicity.")

But if this procedure is followed, notes should also be written by the bride's mother to all her relatives and friends, and by the groom's mother to all *her* relatives and friends, expressing their pleasure and happiness in the marriage. Otherwise, the newspaper announcement might be construed as an expression of family disapproval of the match.

To announce a marriage by writing a personal letter is, in every sense, just as "correct" as it is to send an engraved announcement—and, also, of course, more flattering. The only drawback is that it is obviously impossible to send as many. There is no set form for such a letter, but there are three elements that should be included: first, and most important, the pleasure of the bride's mother in the marriage; second, if the bride's parents would normally have sent engraved announcements, some explanation, if only by inference, as to why this was not done; third, some expression of the affection or respect which causes the letter to be written, since a letter is not the usual or formal way of announcing a marriage.

ANSWERING INVITATIONS TO WEDDINGS AND RECEPTIONS

Engraved invitations to a church ceremony do not require an answer. But when one is invited both to the ceremony and to the reception, or to the reception alone, an answer is usually requested and must be sent. Although the answer is not, of course, engraved, it follows the form of the engraved invitation. It is written on personal or "house" writing paper (see page 528, "Writing Paper"), with or without an engraved crest, monogram or address, and it must be written by hand. The correct wording is given below. (See page 519 in the chapter "Invitations, Acceptances and Regrets," for a facsimile of a written acceptance.)

Mr. and Mrs. Douglas Delano White
accept with pleasure
the kind invitation of
Mr. and Mrs. Bourne
to the marriage of their daughter
Ann Stuyvesant
to
Mr. George Baker Ellis
on Wednesday, the third of March
at four o'clock
Saint Thomas Church
and afterwards at
127 East Sixty-seventh Street

An older wording reads as follows:

. . . .
take pleasure in accepting
the invitation of
. . . .
to be present at the marriage of their daughter

Accepting an Invitation to the Reception

Mr. and Mrs. Douglas Delano White
accept with pleasure
the kind invitation of
Mr. and Mrs. Bourne
to the wedding reception of their daughter
Ann Stuyvesant
and
Mr. George Baker Ellis
on Wednesday, the third of March
at half after four o'clock
127 East Sixty-seventh Street

An alternate but less desirable form for answering these invitations is:

Mr. and Mrs. Douglas Delano White
accept with pleasure
the kind invitation of
Mr. and Mrs. Bourne
for
Wednesday, the third of March
at four o'clock

218

Regretting an Invitation

Exactly the same form is used to regret as to accept an invitation, with two exceptions. The second and third lines read, "regret that they are unable to accept . . . the very kind invitation of . . ."; and the hour of the ceremony and the exact address of the church, if it should be given, are omitted. There are sound reasons for both of these changes. If one cannot accept the invitation, it is more polite to stress the kindness of those who have sent the invitation; and if one cannot come, obviously there is no need to repeat the exact hour, a detail in which accuracy would be important only if one planned to be present.

Answering Invitations to Small Weddings

When an invitation is sent by letter, it is always more polite to answer by letter, rather than by telegram or verbally. And such letters need not, of course, follow any set or formal pattern. When an invitation is sent by telegram, one may answer by telegram, although a letter would be more polite, if there is time.

RECALLING WEDDING INVITATIONS

Sometimes, even after the wedding invitations have been issued, changes have to be made. The wedding may have to be postponed if the bride or groom is ill; or, if an important member of one of the families has died, the plan for a big wedding will have to be given up; or the bride may have changed her mind. No matter what the reason, it is always difficult and a little awkward to recall a wedding invitation, or send a notice of postponement, and certainly it is not a step that should be lightly undertaken. The form, however, is quite simple:

Mr. and Mrs George Edward Bourne
announce that the marriage of their daughter
Ann Stuyvesant
to
Mr. George Baker Ellis
will not take place

Or, if the wedding is to be postponed:

Mr. and Mrs. George Edward Bourne
announce that the marriage of their daughter
Ann Stuyvesant
to
Mr. George Baker Ellis
has been postponed from
Wednesday, the third of March
until
Wednesday, the twenty-fourth of March
at four o'clock
Saint Thomas Church
New York

219

Or, if the invitations must be recalled because a member of the family has died:

Mr. and Mrs. George Edward Bourne
regret exceedingly
that owing to the recent death of
the mother of Mrs. Bourne
the invitations to the marriage of their daughter
Ann Stuyvesant
to
Mr. George Baker Ellis
must be recalled

All these may be engraved in a lettering like the one used for the invitation or, if there is no time for engraving, they may be printed in a type which resembles one of the standard letterings for engraving. (These are shown on page 202.) When the wedding is to be postponed, the announcements are sent on paper of the same size, weight, and finish as the invitation. When the invitations are recalled without postponement, a stiff white pasteboard card is often used instead.

34

Dressing for the Wedding

THE CUSTOMS governing dressing for a wedding are based on tradition and fitness—tradition as far as the bride is concerned, fitness for everybody else. As the central figure in the pageantry of a wedding, the bride dominates everyone else; if she dresses in a certain way, the groom, the ushers, and bridesmaids, and everyone else must follow. Here follow the traditional form, and the permissible modern departures from that form.

TRADITIONAL DRESS FOR THE FORMAL DAYTIME WEDDING

What the Bride Wears

A white dress. In winter, of silk, satin, lace, velvet, taffeta, chiffon, tulle, or faille. In summer, any of these except velvet and, in addition, organdy, dotted swiss, embroidered muslin, piqué, or linen.

Wedding dresses are now more or less floor length; but this is not inherently a matter of tradition, but of fashion. During the late 1920's, brides wore dresses to the knees. As a rule, a wedding dress is as long as an evening dress.

A white veil. Long or short, made of tulle, lace, chiffon, or organdy; or a head-dress without a veil. The essential is that the bride's head be covered for any religious ceremony.

White suède gloves are very often worn with short sleeves. Some churches have regulations concerning the length of sleeves and the depth of the décolletage. If there is any question, consult the clergyman who will perform the ceremony. In any case, very short sleeves, worn without gloves, and a low décolletage would be in very bad taste.

White silk or satin slippers.

For the trip to and from church, the bride wears a cape or a stole over her dress, unless the weather is warm.

What the Bride Carries

A bouquet of flowers or a white prayer book.

What the Bridegroom Wears

A black or dark Oxford-gray cutaway coat.

Black and gray striped worsted trousers.

A wing collar.

A light gray silk ascot tie or a light gray silk four-in-hand tie.

A double-breasted waistcoat of buff-colored woolen or, in summer, white linen.

A stiff white shirt.

Buff-colored spats, or white linen spats; to match waistcoat.

Black silk socks.

Plain black shoes with black soles. Pale soles, upturned while the bridegroom is kneeling, are a discordant note.

A boutonniere: a white carnation or any other simple white flower.

For the trip to and from the church, the bridegroom, best man and ushers wear silk hats and pearl-gray mocha gloves, and carry walking sticks. A fuller description of the cutaway is given on page 617 in the section concerned with men's clothes.

What the Best Man Wears

Exactly what the groom wears.

What the Ushers Wear

Exactly what the groom wears, except that they may wear a less formal fold collar and four-in-hand tie. Their gloves, neckties, and spats may differ a little from those of the groom and best man. Ushers should all be dressed exactly alike and, to insure this uniformity, gloves and neckties are given them by the groom. (See page 175, "Presents for the Bridesmaids and Ushers.")

What the Maid (or Matron) of Honor Wears

A dress exactly the same color as the bridesmaids', in a slightly different model; or a dress of the same style in a different color. Headdress, slippers, and gloves like the bridesmaids' (see below).

What the Maid of Honor Carries

A bouquet or spray of flowers that may differ slightly from those of the bridesmaids.

What the Bridesmaids Wear

Dresses exactly alike, of the same length as the bride's.

Hats, caps, or garlands of flowers, but not usually veils.

Slippers or sandals such as would be worn in the evening.

What the Bridesmaids Carry

Bouquets or sprays of flowers carefully chosen to look well with their dresses.

What the Flower Girls Wear

Dresses that will fit harmoniously into the color scheme of the wedding procession, in a style suitable to their age. ("Kate Greenaway" is a favorite.)

Ballet slippers, or little, flat leather slippers.

Little caps or garlands on their hair.

What the Flower Girls Carry

Small bouquets of flowers adapted to their size.

What the Page Boys Wear

Trousers of velvet, silk, or linen, long or short, sometimes with a short jacket to match and usually a frilly blouse.

Flat buckled slippers, or flat shoes of colored leather, and white socks.

What the Father of the Bride and the Father of the Groom Wear

Exactly what the groom wears, except that their neckties and spats need not match anyone else's.

What the Mother of the Bride and the Mother of the Groom Wear

Long-sleeved afternoon dresses of the most elaborate kind. These are either street-length or floor-length, unless floor-length dresses are as impossibly outmoded as they were in the 1920's. But never black.

Hats or turbans of the most formal afternoon or evening type.

Gloves of any color but black, long enough to meet the sleeves.

Light, high-heeled afternoon shoes or slippers.

Flowers, usually orchids, gardenias, or camellias, and usually pinned at the shoulder or waist; or flowers pinned to their pocketbooks.

A fur piece if they want to.

What the Men Guests Wear

Dark suits.
Stiff collars.
Black shoes.
Black socks.
Dark blue and white, or gray and white, neckties.
White shirts.

Older men may wear cutaways as do the groom and the father of the bride, or striped trousers with a short black coat. (This is fully described on page 618.) But, except at very big or official weddings, most of the men wear dark blue suits.

What the Women Guests Wear

Formal, street-length dresses or afternoon suits; black, if need be, but gay enough not to be confused with mourning.

Light, high-heeled afternoon shoes.

A gay, "dressy" hat.

A fur coat or jacket, or an afternoon coat, in cold weather.

Gloves of any color.

This is the most formal and conservative way of dressing for a wedding, honoring the ancient tradition that, if the bride wears a long wedding dress and veil, the groom *must* wear a cutaway. Uniforms, of course, transcend all these purely civilian customs. Modern usage has, however, made some changes in the old form— changes which, at certain times and under certain conditions, have come to be accepted as perfectly correct.

PERMISSIBLE DEPARTURES FOR THE BRIDE

For a civil ceremony, the bride wears a street-length dress and a hat, in any color except black. If the ceremony takes place in her own house, she may wear a hat or not, just as she pleases.

For a second marriage, the bride does not wear a wedding dress or veil, but may wear an elaborate afternoon dress, of street length, or a floor-length dress, hat, and flowers as suggested for the mother of the bride in the lists above.

For a wedding at home, or a very small church wedding, if she wishes not to wear a long wedding dress and veil, the bride may wear an elaborate street-length dress in any color except black, in any material suited to the season: velvet or satin in winter; thin silk or printed silk in summer. She can wear a hat, or a headdress of flowers, tulle, or feathers. She does not carry a big bouquet with a short dress, but may wear flowers on her dress.

For the most formal wedding, instead of the traditional white, her wedding dress and veil may be one of the palest pastel colors: ice-blue, pale pink, pale celadon-green or cream color; or gold-and-white or silver-and-white brocade.

PERMISSIBLE DEPARTURES FOR THE MEN IN THE WEDDING PARTY

When the Bride Wears a Full Wedding Dress and Veil

For a very small, very informal church wedding, the men of the wedding party and the fathers of the bride and groom may wear dark blue suits, stiff white fold collars, white shirts, black shoes and socks, light gray silk four-in-hand neckties. They should *never* wear tails or dinner jackets for an afternoon wedding.

For a very small wedding at home, they may dress as they would for the very informal church wedding (see directly above).

For a small country wedding, in church or at home, dark blue suits are also permissible.

For an outdoor wedding, in the country in summer, they can wear dark blue coats and white flannel trousers.

For all weddings, the groom, ushers and best man can dispense with a walking stick.

When the Bride Wears a Short Dress

For a second marriage, the men may wear either cutaways or dark blue suits, because the bride's short dress is not a matter of choice. In other words, the bride is wearing a short dress and a hat for reasons of custom, not because she wants a small or informal wedding. Therefore, the men may dress as formally as they choose.

For all other weddings, they should wear not cutaways but dark suits, as suggested above for the very small, very informal church wedding.

DEPARTURES TO BE AVOIDED

These are two examples of mistakes which should be avoided:

A big church wedding, with the bride in full wedding dress and veil, and the groom in a dark suit, a light suit, or anything except a cutaway or a uniform.

A wedding in which the groom wears a cutaway, the father of the bride a dark suit, the best man a business suit, and the ushers white jackets—or any other mixed combination of clothes. The men must be dressed as though they all regarded the ceremony in the same light.

DRESSING FOR THE EVENING WEDDING

For an elaborate evening wedding, all the men in the bridal party wear full evening dress, just as they wear formal afternoon dress for a daytime wedding. The fathers of the bride and groom too should wear white tie and tails. Guests are free to choose whichever they prefer. An older man or a member of the family might wear full evening dress; others, particularly the younger men, will wear dinner jackets and black ties. (See page 619 for a fuller description of men's evening clothes.)

This is the traditional form for evening weddings, but at very small simple weddings, even though the bride were wearing a veil and a long wedding dress, the men might wear dinner jackets. They never look as well as they do in tails, but if the wedding is small and informal enough, it is often done.

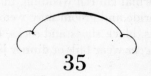

35

Wedding Presents

THERE ARE no rules at all concerning wedding presents. To begin with, a wedding present is not an obligation for each guest who accepts an invitation to the wedding or reception. Great friends and, of course, members of the family give presents. Others need not. The bride's parents often, but not always, give their daughter silver. The groom, more often in the old days than now, gives his wife a piece of jewelry. But wedding presents are not bound by any traditions that one must observe, and if the bride wants most of all a horse or a Frigidaire, there is no reason—except perhaps a financial one—for her not having it. ("The Trousseau," pages 227 to 231, and the chapters "Linen," pages 377 to 381, "Silver," pages 382 to 392, "Glass," pages 392 to 402, and "China," pages 403 to 422, suggest many presents suitable for a bride. Anniversary presents are listed on page 64.)

EXHIBITING THE PRESENTS

Exhibiting the wedding presents used to be one of the indispensable customs connected with weddings. Days before the wedding, long tables were covered with white damask cloths in a room specially cleared for the purpose, and the wedding presents were all laid out for the guests to see. Indeed, at very large receptions, there were often plainclothes men keeping watch. All this may still be done, and sometimes is; but happily one of the old customs is being discarded, that of putting by each present the card of the donor. The theory of this custom was quite innocent and simple: to identify each present and the person who gave it; but in practice, it often resulted in invidious comparison and, though one still sees it occasionally, the modern trend is more and more against it. When presents are exhibited, white cloths are still used, because they are the best background.

"WHAT DOES SHE WANT FOR A WEDDING PRESENT?"

It is a very sound idea, if the bride can bring herself to it, for her to make up her mind in advance about the kind of house and china and furniture she likes best. If she has decided that she likes French Provincial, for example, it would be perfectly easy for her and her parents—and a great help to their friends—to answer the eternal question, "What does she want for a wedding present?" with, "Oh, anything French Provincial, or anything that would go well in a French Provincial house." Then, if the friends have any imagination, the bride will receive breakfast sets of Sarreguemines china, French pottery, lamps, dark walnut or French silver trays, instead of a heterogeneous collection of Anglo-Americana which will take a long time to assimilate or exchange.

And one last word on the subject of wedding presents: The bride *must* write a letter herself, by hand, to each person who has sent her a present. The only possible excuse for a dictated, typewritten letter would be some crippling accident, such as a broken hand. After a very big wedding, when the bride may have received as many as a thousand presents, a little printed card may be sent by the secretary, just to give notice that the present has arrived, but this *must* be followed by a letter from the bride.

THANK-YOU LETTERS FOR WEDDING PRESENTS

There are a hundred variations of the thank-you letter; but that one must be written to each person who sent a present is, as we have said, one of the strictest rules in all wedding etiquette. Except for unusual circumstances, all the letters should be written by three weeks after the wedding. Those that go to intimate friends need no form: "Darling Aunt Katherine, That was a marvelous idea— George and I simply adore the rug. Will telephone you as soon as we're settled— a thousand thanks, Ann." But more formal acquaintances and, especially, members of the groom's family, need a different kind of letter. To the great-aunt of the groom who has sent a check as a wedding present:

Dear Mrs. Ellis,

Thank you so much for your wonderful wedding present and for your sweet letter (or, if the letter has been formal rather than affectionate, "for your very kind letter.") Ever since they arrived, George and I have been making plans— to get a sofa for the living room, or a dining-room table, or to get nothing just now, but start a travel fund for the future! Our only disappointment is that you will not be able to be here for the wedding—but George has promised me a long week end trip sometime in May or June and, if we can possibly get as far as Natchez, we shall hope to see you. In any case, I'll write you as soon as we have any definite plans, or a house of our own, in case you might be in the East and be able to stay with us.

So many, many thanks again for all your kindness. George joins me in sending our best love.

Affectionately,

Ann

To a great friend of the bride's mother:

Dear Mrs. Hatch,

I can't tell you how delighted I am with the lovely little table! It's absolutely perfect and I can't wait to get settled and see it in its proper place. George likes it as much as I do, and he says it looks exactly like the kind of thing you would have chosen.

I don't know when we'll finally be able to move in. Mother has been marvelous, but I never realized how difficult it was to set up housekeeping. A cup of tea, however, can always be managed—even on a packing case—so I hope you will come and have one with us very soon.

It was sweet of you to send us such a lovely present—thank you so much again from both of us.

Affectionately,
Ann

To a friend of the groom's parents:

Dear Mrs. Sedgewick,

Thank you so much for the beautiful plates. Blue has always been my favorite color and the flowers are just the ones I hope to find for the dining-room chintz.

Mr. and Mrs. Ellis will be in Boston next week. If only George and I were coming—so that we could all meet!

So many thanks again from both of us for your lovely wedding present.

Sincerely,
Ann Bourne Ellis

To a casual acquaintance of the bride's parents:

Dear Mrs. Carroll,

Thank you so much for the lovely candlesticks you and Mr. Carroll sent us. It was so kind of you to think of us.

We have already moved in—a minor miracle which was accomplished almost singlehanded by Mother—and the candlesticks look beautiful on the dining-room table.

So many thanks again to you and Mr. Carroll from us both.

Sincerely,
Ann Bourne Ellis

Note that the full signature, "Ann Bourne Ellis," which is used only for formal or very businesslike correspondence as a rule, is suggested for all thank-you letters except those going to intimate friends or members of the family. A friend of the bride's mother, who has always thought of the bride as "that nice child of Eleanor Bourne's," might not recognize her in the signature "Ann" or "Ann Ellis."

36

The Trousseau

In its most strict and traditional interpretation, the trousseau should include clothes for the bride and all the linen that the bride will need for her new house: sheets, pillowcases, blanket-covers, towels, table linen, and even kitchen dish towels, in sufficient quantity to last for a great many years. And in our grandmother's time, trousseaux were like this. They lasted a lifetime and even more: dozens of sheets, all beautifully monogrammed; dozens of face towels, fringed and embroidered; and at least a dozen white damask tablecloths, in different sizes.

Modern trousseaux are rarely like this, and if they were, modern linen closets could not hold them. But there is an irreducible minimum. Every bride should have enough linen to start housekeeping with—and a little lavender to put on her shelves! The following list covers the absolute minimum; a fuller discussion of the subject is on page 377 in the section, "Furnishing a House."

LINEN FOR THE BRIDE

Bed Linen

8 sheets for a double bed; or 12 for two single beds. (Twelve is the minimum if there are only two beds in the house. But if there are other beds on which the same kind of sheets will be used, the *minimum* is four sheets to a bed.)

8 pillowcases; or 12 for single beds.

3 blanket-covers of silk or thin muslin; or 4 for two single beds.

3 quilted mattress protectors; or 4 for two single beds.

Bath Linen

8 bath towels.

8 face cloths.

4 bath mats.

12 large face towels of linen or terry cloth.

6 small linen hand-towels, for guests.

Kitchen Linen

12 linen dish towels for glass and fine china.

12 heavy dish towels for pots and pans.

12 dish cloths.

Table Linen

This is listed last, not because it is not important, but because it is the most complicated of the lists. Personal tastes do not enter into the other lists, but table linen is open to many whims. If one did not want to bother with linen mats or tablecloths, one could buy cork, straw, cellophane or mirrored mats, and the minimum list would read as follows:

12 large dinner napkins, about 24 inches square.

12 smaller napkins for luncheon or breakfast, about 15 inches square.

12 very small napkins for tea or breakfast in bed.

If one likes linen mats, to the above irreducible minimum should be added:

3 sets of linen mats for luncheon, small dinners, and every day.

1 set of linen mats for parties.

Further suggestions for the budget buyer are on page 378, followed by specific details concerning mats, sheets, and all the rest of the linen. But certainly the best advice to a bride who is buying a trousseau is to buy it from a well-established and reputable shop and to plan carefully ahead. Too many brides have bought peach-pink sheets, only to find a few years later that they really would have preferred candy-pink or white. The safest course is to buy white sheets and towels, and to think a long time about any colors. The same is true, of course, of table linen. White is the safest unless the bride has definitely decided on a color scheme, and has irrevocably committed herself to it by buying a lot of china that cannot be returned!

MARKING THE TROUSSEAU

By the principle that rules the whole wedding tradition, all the bride's linen and silver should be marked, if at all, with her maiden initials. In the matter of the trousseau, there is an even more practical reason for it: Earlier generations of women worked for years, almost from the time a daughter was born, to prepare the linen against her wedding day; and, obviously, it was impossible to know the groom's last name. Cynics have suggested a modern reason, too—the eventuality of divorce—but anyone who marks a trousseau with this in mind should clearly not be getting married. (See page 426, "Furnishing a House," for further suggestions and examples of monograms.)

SILVER FOR THE BRIDE

Silver is discussed more fully on page 382 in the chapter, "Furnishing a House," where there are many suggestions which might be helpful in choosing presents. Here, where we are concerned only with brides, we will give a minimum list of absolutely necessary silver. All of it is flat silver, because china, glass, and wood can easily and inexpensively be substituted for other household goods and chattels often made of silver, from pepper pots to candelabra. These are discussed in detail under the headings, "Glass," "China," and "Wood" on pages 392 to 423.

This list is predicated on the assumption of a household of two in which never more than two guests will be entertained at the dining-room table. If one plans to have dinner parties of six or eight people, the list will have to be increased proportionately.

8 teaspoons. A double number of teaspoons is suggested because they are among the most useful pieces of silver.

4 dessert spoons.

4 large, oval-bowled soupspoons. If one plans to serve soup at dinnertime in widemouthed modern bowls and not in plates, one would buy four extra dessert spoons, instead of these soupspoons. Otherwise one must manage to have the dessert spoons washed between the soup and dessert courses.

4 demitasse spoons.

1 gravy ladle.

4 serving spoons. Very big oval-bowled soupspoons can be used as serving spoons, so these two categories can to some extent be interchanged. Every hostess, however, needs at least four spoons, and four forks, too, that can be set aside for serving—one for the meat dish; one for each vegetable dish; and one for the dessert. Or, one for the first course, if it is not soup; one for the meat platter, which in this case will hold the potatoes also; one for the veg-

228

etable dish; and one for the dessert.
4 dessert forks.
4 large forks.
4 serving forks. If the large forks are a good size, they can be used as serving forks (see the note concerning serving spoons directly above).
4 large steel-bladed knives.
4 smaller knives, often silver-bladed.
4 butter knives.

Actually, this list can be reduced still further. One can leave out the four demitasse spoons and buy, instead of silver ones, little modern chromium spoons or any small old-fashioned ones. If the spoons are old, they need not match one another; odd sets are extremely attractive. One could also buy glass-handled, chromium-bladed butter knives—very small and less expensive than silver. In a pinch, one might even omit butter knives, and plan to serve buttered toast, or rolls that are split and buttered; or slices of French or Italian bread lightly toasted and eaten without butter.

For buffet suppers, the bride can buy an inexpensive set of chromium knives and forks and spoons. The most attractive have handles made of bamboo or walnut. Although a set such as this is not, of course, as durable as solid silver, it is practical enough because it is used only occasionally. And if the bride should suddenly inherit a big set of silver, she can always use the chromium set for picnics or for a summer house.

GLASS FOR THE BRIDE

The following minimum list of glass is not in any way a full guide. Suggestions concerning the best designs for glass and advice on buying will be found on page 392. Here we give only a minimum list to show which shapes and sizes can be interchanged and which cannot. As in the case of the silver list, the numbers are predicated on the assumption of a household of two, with provision made for serving two guests at the dining-room table—and for a little breakage.

6 water glasses for the table. These glasses should be stemmed, with a capacity of about 10 or 11 ounces.

6 wineglasses, stemmed, holding at least 3 to 5 ounces. The standard wineglass has a rounded, tulip-shaped bowl; but many very beautiful matched sets are made with pointed or squared bowls throughout.

6 sherry glasses, stemmed, about 2 ounces. The standard sherry glass has a pointed bowl; although in a matched set, the bowl may be rounded or squared. In a matched set, the distinguishing feature of the sherry glass is that it is very much smaller than the wineglass.

12 cocktail glasses, stemmed or not, about 3 to 4 ounces, with round, pointed, or squared bowls; but not a tulip-shaped bowl.

Note: Cocktail glasses and wineglasses can often be used interchangeably. Almost any wineglass that is not too big, and which is not made in the classic tulip shape, can quite easily be used for cocktails. A very big sherry glass, too, could be used for cocktails, but it must hold at least 2½ or 3 ounces. The essential point is that cocktails must not be served in a glass obviously designed only for wine or only for sherry; sherry should be served in glasses which at least suggest the classic sherry shape and size; and wine should not be served in a glass so small that it is quite clearly meant only for sherry. While we are on the subject, we might mention a point which is discussed more fully on page 392: many modern sets of glass are made in different sizes for different wines, but earlier glassmakers did not make such subtle distinctions. The best wineglass for the budget buyer who plans to serve only one wine at a time is a plain, rounded glass—either old or new—which can be used for any wine, except champagne or sherry, which is served at the dining-room table.

12 whiskey-and-soda glasses, straight-sided, with no stem or pedestal foot, with a capacity of *at least* 12 ounces; 14 is ideal. These can be used for iced tea and all other long drinks. Although they are really too big for water served in the living room, they would be better for this purpose than a stemmed water glass, which should be used only at the dining-room table.

6 fruit-juice glasses, straight-sided, without a stem or pedestal foot, usually a 4- or 5-ounce replica of the whiskey-and-soda glass. These are a budget compromise between the standard 6-ounce breakfast-juice glass and the 3- or 4-ounce glass for tomato juice served in the living room before meals. They are used for both purposes.

And perhaps, also:

6 liqueur glasses, stemmed, holding about an ounce.

6 tumblers, straight-sided, without a stem or pedestal foot; often, but not necessarily, a 7- or 8-ounce replica of the whiskey-and-soda glass; used for serving water after meals. Many of these are not as well-designed as the glasses for fruit juice. If so, it is wise to buy more expensive tumblers for serving water in the living room. Stemmed glasses should not be used for this.

6 finger bowls.

This list covers the minimum requirements of a small household, granted the usual ways of entertaining. If one wanted to cut it down still further, the categories which could be most easily eliminated would be the finger bowls and the sherry glasses. Finger bowls are not necessary for informal entertaining and neither, of course, are sherry glasses. Instead of serving both sherry and cocktails, one might serve tomato juice and cocktails instead, eliminating sherry entirely. On the other hand, if one wants to serve old-fashioned cocktails, six old-fashioned glasses will have to be added to the list, since no other glass can be substituted for this purpose. We have not included champagne glasses in this minimum list; but, of course, if one wants to serve champagne, champagne glasses must be added also.

It is wise to remember that although inexpensive plain glass can be very attractive, inexpensive monogramming is *always* a mistake. It can turn a simple glass into a pretentious object which bids for attention, without quality to sustain it.

CHINA FOR THE BRIDE

This minimum list, like the other lists in this section, is predicated on a household of two, with a maximum of four people at the dining-room table at any one time. Like the other minimum lists, it is not a full guide to buying. See also page 407, "Buying China on a Budget"; and, for more detailed discussion of the subject, read the whole chapter on china, pages 403 to 422.

6 big plates for the main course.

6 butter plates.

12 medium-sized plates. A double number of these is suggested because in any three-course meal they will have to be used twice: for the first course and for dessert.

6 cups and saucers for afternoon tea.

2 extra-big cups for morning coffee. These, used every day, will help keep the set of teacups intact.

2 cereal bowls. These should be used only for morning cereal and are not needed unless one plans to have cereal.

6 demitasse cups and saucers.

1 coffeepot.

1 teapot.

1 sugar bowl.

1 cream pitcher.

1 large-sized cream pitcher, or jug, which can be used for hot water, hot milk, or maple syrup.

6 soup cups and saucers.

6 soup plates.

Or, to replace both the last two,

6 widemouthed soup bowls.

Since this is a budget list, on the assumption that there will not be silver serving dishes:

1 large, oval serving platter for roasts.

1 smaller, oval serving platter for chops or fish.
1 round serving platter for cakes or pies.
2 vegetable dishes.
1 deep bowl for serving desserts. This could be of glass.
1 sauceboat, or a china bowl which can be used for serving hot sauces and gravies. Glass can be used for cold sauces.

With the addition of six more big plates for the meat course and six more demitasse cups and saucers, this list could serve for a two-course buffet supper for twelve people. A breadbasket and a salad bowl are not listed because a wicker breadbasket and a wooden salad bowl are more practical. In fact, unless the china is very beautiful, a wicker breadbasket and a wooden salad bowl are not only more practical but in better taste as well.

Very useful dishes for small households are casseroles which can be used for cooking as well as serving. Inexpensive china plates can be extremely attractive, whereas platters, bowls, and other more "decorative" pieces in the same design are often extremely unattractive. If such is the case, it is much better to use brown earthenware casseroles or even glass ovenware. The plainer and more functional it is, the better. One can also, of course, use copper for cooking and serving; but copper, though very good-looking, is not inexpensive. (See "Ovenware Used for Serving" on pages 424 to 426.)

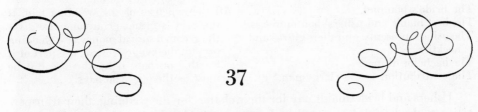

37

Who Pays for What

CURIOUSLY ENOUGH, the question of who pays for what in connection with a wedding is not a matter of who is most generous, nor of who has the most money. There is a very definite tradition that must be followed. First and most important, the bride's family must pay for the wedding, all the costs of the reception, every stitch of the bride's trousseau and all her clothes, including her going-away clothes. If the bride is an orphan, her relatives, her friends, or even she herself, can pay for all this; but there is no permissible departure from the rule that the groom or the groom's family must have no part in it. The groom can give the bride jewelry before their marriage, but he can give her clothes and furs only after she is his wife. (There is an old Spanish custom, said to be Moorish in origin, that exemplifies this: A bracelet is the classic engagement present, and a fur coat the classic wedding present.) Apart from this principle, all the other customs concerning money matters are technicalities.

WHAT THE BRIDE'S PARENTS PAY FOR

Engagement announcements in the newspapers.

Wedding invitations and announcements.

The flowers in the church.

The fees for the sexton and for the organist. The bride's parents can discuss with the clergyman the question of how much to give (and the church organist is paid even if another is asked to play).

The bridesmaids' bouquets and presents for the bridesmaids.

The bride's wedding dress, clothes, and linen.

All the expenses of the reception: food, flowers, music, champagne, and cars for the bridal party from the house to the church and from the church to the reception.

There the bride's family stops, and from the moment she leaves her parents' house, the groom takes over.

WHAT THE GROOM PAYS FOR

The engagement ring.

The wedding ring.

The marriage license.

The bride's bouquet.

The best man's and ushers' boutonnieres.

The ushers' presents, and their gloves and neckties.

The bachelor dinner.

The contribution to the clergyman.*

The automobile in which the bride and groom leave the reception—if it should be necessary to hire one.

All the expenses of the wedding trip. If the bride's father or anyone else gives the groom a sum of money as a wedding present, he can, of course, use part of it for this purpose if he chooses. But he must be the one who pays.

Ushers and bridesmaids pay for their clothes for the wedding, their transportation to the bride's house and back home again. Naturally, if one of the bridesmaids lives at a great distance and hasn't very much money to spend on such trips, and if the bride's family wants to and can easily afford it, there is no reason why they should not pay for the bridesmaid's traveling expenses. But, unless there is some special reason, they are not bound by custom to offer to pay.

* The amount of the contribution, which is always given enclosed in an envelope, should never be discussed with the clergyman. The best man, or the groom, gives it to the clergyman at some time before the day of the ceremony. A special appointment can be made for this unless an occasion arises naturally. The amount of the contribution should always be commensurate with the total cost of the wedding. For the most formal and elaborate wedding given in a big church during the season with lavish decorations of flowers and a reception for several hundred people, the contribution to the clergyman might be $500 and should not be less than $100. For a big but less elaborate wedding, when there will be a reception for a hundred guests or so and when the decorations are more moderate, the sum might be $50. For a very small wedding, such as the one described on page 197, $5 or $10 would be the just amount.

SECTION FOUR

HOUSEHOLD CUSTOMS

38

Introduction

"THE HOUSEHOLD" can be a very big phrase. "The house" is a shell. "Home" may be one room, where a bachelor hangs his hat. But "household" means a unit, a group of people joined together, living under the same roof. It includes the house and the family and all those who live in the house. And it means a unit which prospers—or fails—by the same stroke of fortune.

Apart from the material or economic bases of the household, and essentially far more important than any physical factors, is its spiritual foundation. A sense of duty, responsibility, and justice is the rock on which it is built; respect and affection and love give it life. From these spring the benefits of family life which sociologists (and criminologists, too, for that matter) find so important to society. And these, combined with contemporary standards of taste and good sense, are the source also of most of the housekeeping customs and traditions which modern usage still holds valuable and good.

"A well-run house" might only mean that all the physical standards had been met. It would certainly mean a clean house and a tidy one. It would probably mean that details (flowers, for example) were always properly attended to. But "a well-run household" describes a much more important accomplishment. It implies an atmosphere of happiness; or satisfaction and comfort, at least. It enters immediately into the realm of the spirit.

In this section a great many details of the physical and practical aspects of housekeeping are minutely described. All of them can contribute toward the achievement of a well-run house and—granted the right spirit— a well-run household. But all of them together are not worth a fraction of the principles and the warmth which they are designed to express.

The biggest practical considerations in running a household are the arrangements for food and drink. The kitchen stove has often been called the heart of a household, but so far as etiquette is concerned, certainly the dining-room table is one of its key points. As though to prove this, our civilization has developed the simple acts of eating and drinking into a most complicated ritual of setting and serving and menu planning. Year after year, one little detail has been added to another, and we are now faced with an elaborate complex of customs almost accepted as rules.

Of course, all of these customs, practical or aesthetic as they may be, have to do with the art, rather than the essentials, of living. It is agreeable to know them, but we could change every one of them without losing a single value of any importance. What is important about them is that, like all manners, they are an expression not only of consideration for others but also of one's own conception of behavior and good taste. For these reasons, they must be part of a way of life, and not a part-time attitude or an act. To have one way of living for "company" and another for family life is a form of pretentiousness that is psychologically unsound and socially unwise. Very few people can carry off the hypocrisy involved in such pretentiousness; there is something unsure, unrelaxed, and ill at ease in their manner that is death to a dinner party. And, more important, such a false-front atmosphere is an extremely bad one in which to bring up children.

Naturally, this does not apply to details. This does not mean the best china and the most delicate glass will be used every night for the children's supper, or that one must not use paper napkins for a family luncheon if one uses linen napkins for a dinner party. But it does mean that the family should maintain a certain standard as a matter of principle, and quite apart from the opinions of others; it means that children should be taught to tidy up in time for meals; that the family should gather in the living room beforehand and all go together into the dining room; that no one should read at the table, with perhaps the classic exception of breakfast newspapers, or be allowed to argue too loudly, or slip down in a chair, or behave otherwise than he would if guests were there.

This question of attitude is the most important, but there are minor manifestations of a pretentious double standard. For example, if the mistress of the house usually serves the family from dishes placed in front of her at the table, it would be a pretension on her part to feel obliged to hire a waitress every time there were one or two guests for luncheon. Bigger luncheon parties or formal dinners obviously demand an elaboration of the normal routine, since few modern households are so constituted as to be able to handle within the usual framework any considerable number of guests. When one is giving a dinner party, it is quite natural to hire a butler or an extra waitress for the evening, but it is unsound and unwise to do so just because one guest is coming for dinner. It smacks of the desire to create a false impression concerning one's way of life.

Honesty, simplicity, and unpretentiousness are the very basis of the modern attitude toward all our inherited social customs. However complicated the superstructure may seem—and eating is admittedly surrounded with elaborations—it is in this light that all the old rules must be considered. In the matter of food and drink, two complementary sets of customs have been evolved: one dealing with how to consume them, the other with how to present them. To be brief, there are table manners which have been discussed on pages 50 to 55, in the section "Manners," and table customs, which we shall consider here.

Table customs may be considered under three main divisions. The first is setting the table and the second is serving the food; both of these are a matter of rules, technicalities, and mechanics, adaptable to a wide variety of occasions, but basically slow to change. The third division deals with the kind of food and table arrangements which modern taste approves, a subject open to great and sudden change in taste and fashion. Two other topics complete this section: the organization of the household staff, which begins on page 348, and the matter of differences in the degrees of formality which, since it is a basic consideration, follows immediately here.

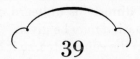

39

Three Degrees of Formality

BEFORE DECIDING how the table is to be set, or which pattern of service is to be followed, one must have a clear idea of the elements involved and of their total effect. Setting and serving, which are matters of convention, express different degrees of formality, just as table decorations, which are aesthetic, express different conceptions of beauty. For this reason, before discussing the technicalities of setting and serving, we must consider the differences in the degrees of formality.

In order to bring clarity to a subject which is full of vague and subtle shades of meaning, the words "informal," "semiformal," and "formal" are used to describe the three most definite classifications. They are, in a way, the only signs on an otherwise unmarked scale which covers the whole range of possible dinners and luncheons, from the simplest family dinner of four to the most elaborate dinner of thirty. But it must be emphasized that, with the possible exception of "informal," these phrases are never used in conversation or in invitations. In communities where dressing for dinner is the accepted custom, the invitation is phrased as, "George and I wondered if you and Dick could come to dinner Tuesday night," and that is understood to mean evening dress, whether the dinner is to be "informal" or "semiformal." If dressing were the custom and guests were nevertheless to wear day clothes, the hostess would explain in some such way as, "We're not dressing, because I thought we would go to the movies afterwards." In communities where dressing is not the custom, the standard invitation is given and is understood to mean day clothes; when the hostess wants to make an exception, she explains, "We're dressing because it's Helen's birthday."

The only time the word "informal" is used is when the invitation is much less formal than the guests might think. For example, if one were giving a dinner for a very important man, a high official of Church or State, one might say, "Come to a very informal dinner we are giving next week for the President and his wife"; so that the guests will know that, although the dinner is being given for such a personage, dinner jackets will be worn, and not full evening dress, as they might think. The phrase, "Come to a semiformal (or 'formal') dinner" is unheard of. When the guests are to wear white ties, an explanation may be given: "We're going afterwards to the dance and George is on the committee, so it has to be white tie."

The outline which follows may be used either for family meals or for entertaining. The formula includes guests for each one only because all the details can thus be mentioned. For family meals, of course, the points concerning the guests are irrelevant.

WHAT MAKES A DINNER INFORMAL

These are the hallmarks of an informal dinner:

1. Guests are usually invited verbally, either face to face or by telephone. (See pages 501 to 503.)

2. Guests and hosts may wear either evening dress, or day clothes, depending on local custom or the hostess' decision, but men and women *must* dress with equal formality. If the women are in evening dresses, the men wear dinner jackets; if the women wear afternoon dresses, the men wear dark blue suits. (See page 617 in the chapter "Men's Clothes.")

3. The table is set more or less simply, depending mostly on the menu. (See page 257, "The Informal Dinner Table.")

4. The food consists, as a rule, of not more than two or three courses. (See page 321.)

5. The service may vary between one extreme and the other. For the purposes of this book we have called "informal" any service in which the family or their guests co-operate. But although every dinner with informal service must be called informal, not every informal dinner must be served informally. For ex-

ample, if six or seven people are dining together before going to a hockey game, and if there are two people waiting on table, the service may be as complete as that of the most formal dinner; but, the dinner is most definitely informal because hosts and guests are in afternoon clothes, the food and table arrangements are simple, and the invitations were given verbally. On the other hand, an elaborate buffet dinner, where there may be twenty guests in evening clothes, is always informal because the service is not handled completely by the staff. (Buffet meals and other informal patterns of service are discussed in detail on pages 297 to 298 and 280 to 284.

6. The hour might be any time between 6:30 and 8:00 P.M.

WHAT MAKES A DINNER SEMIFORMAL

These are the hallmarks of a semiformal dinner:

1. The guests are invited by telephone, by letter, or by a partially engraved invitation. (This invitation is shown on page 514; it is always answered in writing; see page 518, "Accepting All Invitations in the Third Person.")

2. The men wear dinner jackets and black bow ties (see page 619), and the women, evening dresses.

3. The table is set as described on page 259 in the section, "Setting," either with a cloth or with mats.

4. The menus, if there are any, are written either in French or in English. (See page 272 for the English form, and page 488 for the more elaborate French pattern.)

5. Place cards are written as a matter of convenience only, without unnecessary formality. (See page 273, "Place Cards.")

6. There are usually three or four courses; five, at most. (See page 321.)

7. The service follows the standard procedure discussed on pages 284 to 287.

8. Local custom not being to the contrary, the standard hour is 8:00 P.M.

A semiformal dinner is probably the most comfortable, the most practical, and the most pleasant way of entertaining. The hostess is free to choose any kind of food that makes a good menu. The guests will be waited on, and neither they nor their hosts will co-operate in the dining-room service.

WHAT MAKES A DINNER FORMAL

Formal entertaining is so rare in America—and in other countries, too, for that matter—that, with certain exceptions noted below, all the details concerning it are discussed in a separate chapter beginning on page 477. These are, however, the hallmarks of a formal dinner, in the very strictest interpretation of "formal":

1. Invitations are sent in the third person, and the guests answer in writing. (See pages 514 and 518, "Invitations, Acceptances, and Regrets.")

2. Men and women wear full evening dress. (See page 619 for a description of a man's clothes.)

3. Each man guest is given a card in the hall, to tell him who his dinner partner will be. (Page 478.)

4. The guests are announced by the butler as they come into the drawing room. (Page 479.)

5. Each guest goes arm in arm with his assigned dinner partner into the dining room. (Page 480.)

6. The table is covered with a cloth and set with candles and flowers. (Page 481.)

7. The menu is written in French. (Page 487.)

8. The place cards are written with the names in full. (Page 490.)

9. The food is chosen in accord with certain traditional French rules, and there are usually six or seven courses. (Pages 484 to 487.)

10. The service follows a formal pattern. (Pages 483 to 484.)

11. Except for a special reason, a formal dinner is always given either at eight or at half-past eight.

As a rule, at a formal dinner there are apt to be at least sixteen people. Although they used to be given in very big cities, both in America and abroad, as a matter of course during the "season," they are now extremely rare and are usually given only on some special occasion, or for official reasons. It would be a great mistake, in a community where such entertaining is not customary, to give a formal dinner for no reason at all. In wartime, or in times of widespread distress or suffering, it is bad taste to entertain so elaborately unless official duties make it necessary.

40

Setting the Table

STARTING WITH the bare surface of the dining-room table, one's first step in setting any table is to decide whether one wants to cover it with a table-cloth, or to set it with the more usual, more practical, modern mats. Under a cloth, there is either a blanket felt or a stiff felt board, cut to fit the table. Under the mats, there are usually smaller mats, to protect the table from hot plates. Whichever one chooses, the following irreducible minimum is added for any seated meal: a centerpiece, unless the table is really too tiny;

pepper and salt within reach of every guest; a water glass, a napkin, and a fork and knife at each place. In addition, for every meal except the most informal, a place plate is set at each place. (This is the standard American practice, but many follow the English custom and never have a service plate.) The size of the knife and the design of the fork depend a great deal on whether one's silver is American or imported, old or new (subjects that are fully discussed, together with china, glass, and table linen, on pages 377 to 422). But for a seated meal there should be a knife, even if it is superfluous as far as the menu is concerned.

Apart from all considerations as to what makes a table beautiful, this technical foundation is the basic pattern which may be adapted to all eating at the dining-room table, from a family breakfast to the most elaborate dinner party. Before we consider each separate kind of meal, it might be useful to set down the primary rules which govern all elaborations of this pattern.

RULES FOR SETTING THE TABLE

The basic rule of conventional setting is that everything on the table must be symmetrically placed and balanced: the centerpiece in the middle, and other decorations spaced from it. This is the traditional rule, and it may be set aside only for valid practical or aesthetic reasons. For example, when a table is placed against the wall, the centerpiece is put close to the inner edge of the table near the wall, not in the middle, although still halfway from each end. Or to achieve a special effect, the centerpiece may be set deliberately off center in order to accord with the plan. But as a rule, the centerpiece, as the name implies, belongs in the middle of the table. The eye expects to find it there, and any deviation from the conventional plan must be readily and unmistakably clear.

For example, let us consider one of the traditional table arrangements for a dinner of four to eight people, using a centerpiece, four candlesticks, and four pepper pots and saltcellars.

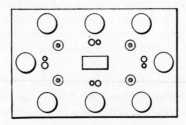

A TABLE SET FOR EIGHT

In this and the next two diagrams, the large circles around the edges of the table represent the plate at each place. The oblong in the middle of the table is the centerpiece, and the four circles with the black centers are four candlesticks. Salt and pepper are represented by the four pairs of small circles between the candlesticks, with the pepper pot to the left of the saltcellar. This table is set for eight people; if there were four, the places to the right and left of both host and hostess would be removed.

If one has a centerpiece and two candelabra, the table is arranged as follows:

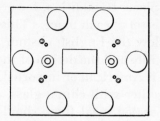

A TABLE SET FOR SIX, WITH TWO CANDELABRA

In this diagram, the circles between the centerpiece and the plate at each end of the table represent the candelabra. The pepper and salt are set on an angle to the edge of the table, rather than parallel with it, the pepper pot nearer the centerpiece, the salt cellar nearer the table's edge.

On a small table, decorations other than a centerpiece and candles are unnecessary. On a bigger table, two plates of fruit or candy are often put halfway between the candelabra and the place plates at each end of the table.

A very long table might be arranged as follows:

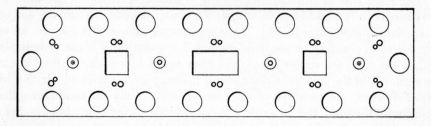

A TABLE SET FOR EIGHTEEN

Down the middle of this long table, starting from the plate at the end, are: a candlestick or small candelabrum; a bowl of fruit or flowers, or some other table decoration smaller than the main centerpiece but chosen to look well with it; a tall candelabrum; the centerpiece; a second tall candelabrum (a twin of the other); a decoration exactly matching the other; and, finally, a candlestick or a small candelabrum which is a pair with the one at the other end. All the pepper pots and saltcellars, except those in the four corners, are set parallel to the table edge; those in the corners are set at an angle, as shown also in the diagram immediately above this one.

As this diagram shows, everything on the table except the centerpiece is one of a pair or one of a set of four, so that each half of the table is a twin of the other. And everything is spaced *exactly*, according to a readily understood symmetrical plan.

In the same way, place plates are evenly spaced, one at each end (or two, if the table is wide enough and extra guests make it necessary), and the other place plates down each side. The ideal space allotted each guest is two feet, measured from the middle of each place plate; guests are thus near enough to chat easily, and far enough apart to be served comfortably. The last place plate on each of the long sides of the table should be not less than eighteen inches from the end of the table, again measured from the middle of the plate.

The "Dummy" Place

In setting a table for more than four people, only the number of places needed should be set at the table. Five, for example, are placed as follows: one at each end; one exactly halfway down one side; and two on the other side, each one halfway between the middle and the end of the table. But for fewer than four, there are variations. When there are two, a place is usually set at each end of the table; or at a very big table, set informally for two, the second place is sometimes set at the host's right instead. When there are three people, a place may be set at each side of the host, or at each end and one side of the table. Or one may follow the conventional, formal system, which was often used for two and always for three, of setting four places at table—the necessary ones complete with water in the glasses (and, at luncheon, butter on the plates) and the other one or two set as a dummy place. (See also Rules 4 and 5 below concerning the question of pouring the water or putting butter on the plate before the guests come to the table.) This "dummy place" system was standard in old-fashioned conventional households, but modern usage tends towards the simpler and more practical method of setting only the necessary number.

Menu cards and place cards are not necessarily a part of every table setting. For this reason, and because they are surrounded by a rather long set of customs and rules, they are discussed separately at the end of this chapter.

Place Setting

The other six rules of setting are more cut and dried. (See diagrams in "Serving," pages 282, 283, 286, and 287; and "Formal Entertaining," page 482.)

1. Knives and spoons are at the right of the plate, the knife nearest the plate with the cutting edge toward the plate, the spoon next. Even at the most elaborate dinner, no more than three knives should be set at each plate at the beginning of the meal. If, by any remote chance, a fourth is needed, it is brought when the plate for that course is brought; fruit knives, of course, come in on the fruit plate. A further point in connection with knives is that they are often put on the table as a matter of form, even if they are not to be used. Salad is never cut with a knife, but a knife is traditionally put opposite the salad fork. Not all fish and entrée dishes need knives but, according to the most formal practice, a knife should be in place for each of them. Modern usage, however, has made a few changes in this rule: a fish knife always, but a salad or entrée knife may be left off if it is patently unnecessary. This is not according to rule, but is done every day.

2. All forks are put to the left of the place plate (this is the plate which is set at each person's place at the table before the meal begins) with only one exception, the fork for oysters or clams. This fork, which is small, long-handled, and short-tined, is placed to the right of the spoons, either parallel to them, or at an angle with the tines resting on the bowl of the soup spoon. (This is shown in the diagram on page 482.) And, as with knives, never more than three forks should be put at the left of each place. If more are needed, they are brought later and put in their proper places at each place just before the course is to be served.

3. All implements for eating are placed in the order of their use, the ones first to be used farthest away from the plate. This is a rule without exception, no matter how strange or unaesthetic the arrangement may appear. It does not extend, however, to dessert spoons and forks, or fruit knives and forks; after the

table has been cleared, these are brought in on the dessert plate and on the fruit plate, spoon to the right, fork to the left, and fruit knife to the right, fruit fork to the left. (See "Serving," page 279.)

4. Glasses are placed off the upper right-hand corner of the place plate, a north-easterly location by compass. If there is more than one, the water glass should be to the left of the other and slightly higher; that is, farther away from the table edge. This is the basic pattern for all the glasses that may be used at the biggest dinner party. A second wineglass should be placed at a point to make a triangle, the long side of which is nearest the plate. The glass for a third wine is put to the right of the first wineglass and slightly below it. (See diagram of formal place setting in "Formal Entertaining," page 482, and diagrams on pages 258 and 259.)

As a rule, in America water glasses are filled before the guests come into the dining room. According to the most formal procedure, however, water glasses are not filled until the guests are seated; but this custom is rarely observed.

5. Butter plates are essentially informal and are not used for big dinner parties. A butter plate is set to the left of the place plate, far enough away to clear the forks conveniently, far enough away from the edge of the table to bring the top of the butter plate approximately in line with the top of the place plate. This is the standard, conventional place for the butter plate, but it may be altered to fit the circumstances. At an informal luncheon, for example, a covered cup of soup might be set on the place plate before the guests come into the dining room. In this case, the napkin would have to go to the left of the place plate and the butter plate would necessarily be farther from the table edge. Or if the napkin were on the place plate, on a round table it would probably be necessary to put the butter plate nearer the edge of the table, where there would be more room.

The butter knife should never be placed among the other knives and spoons at the right of the place plate; instead, it should lie across the upper third of the butter plate, in line with the edge of the table, the blade pointing to the left, the handle near the place plate, and the sharper edge of the blade facing toward the center of the butter plate.

Round butter balls formed with wooden paddles or curls of butter are usually put on the plate before guests come into the dining room. As in the case of water, the most elaborate service demands that butter be served after the guests are seated; but, again, this is in no sense a rule. (See also page 337, "Butter.")

6. The correct place for the napkin is on the place plate. The napkin may be folded in any number of ways. The easiest, particularly with a large napkin, is to fold it down to about ten or twelve inches square; a third of this square on each side is then folded under, making a somewhat flattened cylinder. This cylinder lies down the center of the place plate, at right angles to the edge of the table. The napkin best adapted to the cylindrical fold is a big dinner napkin with a monogram in the very middle. Smaller luncheon napkins, which often have embroidery or a monogram in one corner rather than in the middle, are folded another way: First make a square, then a triangle, with the decorated point at the apex; fold under the other two points, making a shield shape; and put the napkin in the middle of the place plate with the decorated point towards the edge of the table. To a good English butler, these two extremely simple ways of folding a napkin might seem as primitively plain as the scale to a musician; butlers used to enjoy pyramid effects, with napkins standing, and often concealing a bun. Nowadays,

however, the pyramid is disappearing and the two systems described above are used everywhere: the cylinder for even the most formal dinner, where the biggest dinner napkins might be used, and the shield shape for any smaller napkins. There is only one advantage to the butler-beloved and bun-concealing convolutions of the standing napkin, and that is that this system puts a roll of bread right on the table at the beginning of the meal. A roll can be put inside a cylindrical or shield-shaped fold, but the standing napkin and the roll are an almost inseparable pair. This is the simplest way to fold a standing napkin: Make a square about nine or ten inches across, then a triangle, tuck one point of the triangle inside the other and fold the points down, so that one lies just a little above the other, until the top one is left pointing straight up.

Whenever a tray or a table is set with food on the place plate, the napkin is put to the left, near the fork. (See diagram, page 258.)

Practices to Be Avoided

It is not good usage to set any dining-room table with cups for coffee or tea, except at breakfast. Standard practice is to serve small cups of coffee after luncheon and dinner. The tray is described below on page 260; the service on page 293. Unless it is iced, tea should not appear at lunch time at all. If one of the guests particularly wants a big cup of coffee or tea with luncheon, this rule will, of course, be broken. (The service is discussed on page 304, "Hot Drinks.") It is also entirely wrong to set any table with little side dishes for vegetables. All vegetables served with meat should be eaten from the same plate. The only exception is salad, which is sometimes, informally but quite properly, eaten from a plate at the left of the main plate with the main course.

Tomato juice should never be made the first course of a meal at the dining-room table except at breakfast, when it is sometimes a substitute for orange juice. At luncheon or dinner time, it should be served in the living room before the meal begins. Fruit or vegetable juices, served as such and not made into soups or long drinks, do not belong on the dining-room table. Cut-up fruit is a dessert.

SETTING A TRAY

There is only one rule that applies to all trays, and it is set down here only in order to avoid endless repetition in the rest of this chapter. With three exceptions, a tray that is used to carry silver, glass, or china should not be covered with a cloth or a lace paper doily. A single glass of water, for example, is brought on a bare tray; cocktails and coffee and tea are served on a bare tray. The three exceptions are breakfast, luncheon, and dinner trays, which are treated as miniature dining-room tables. These are, by tradition, covered with a linen cloth but even here, especially for breakfast, modern usage sanctions an uncovered tray.

The silver and china are set on the tray exactly as they are at table: glasses to the upper right, butter plate to the left, etc. (See also "Breakfast in Bed," page 246.)

ARRANGING OPEN PLATES AND PLATTERS

Food which will be taken and eaten in the fingers should always be served on a doily-covered plate or platter. Old-fashioned doilies were made of lace, or lace-edged linen; modern ones are usually made of lace paper. Exceptions to this rule are such foods as olives and nuts which, although eaten in the fingers, are exempt because they are served in bowls. Cakes are served with at least two or three slices already cut (at big parties, the whole cake may be cut), and with a silver knife or an old-fashioned silver "cake server" slipped between or under the cut slices. A wire cake cutter, useful though it may be, should stay in the pantry.

ARRANGING COVERED DISHES

Hot food served with tea or cocktails is served in a covered silver "muffineer," which has a compartment for hot water; no doily is necessary. When it is served in a big silver vegetable dish, as it often is at big receptions, the bottom of the dish is often lined with a folded napkin. When it is served on china plates, with or without covers, it should lie on a paper doily. Covers for hot food served on china or silver plates are usually made of china, or chromium, or silver; a china cover should match the china plate. Covers for food which is not hot or heated, as, for example, a cake, cookies, or sandwiches, are usually made of transparent plastic, often chromium-edged. These are particularly useful when one is serving food out of doors.

This completes the primary rules of setting. But it is only the theoretical outline, the skeleton on which the simplest tray or the most beautiful table setting is built. Now we come to the practical application of these rules, and to their correlated subjects: the courses, the wines and other drinks that have become customary for each different food occasion.

BREAKFAST

There are all sorts of breakfasts: real breakfasts, such as breakfast in bed, breakfast at the dining-room table, or breakfast in the garden; and pseudo breakfasts, such as hunt breakfasts, wedding breakfasts, and that modern invention with the horrid name of brunch. Wedding breakfasts are discussed separately, on page 168. We shall start, as most people do, with breakfast proper.

Breakfast in Bed

Breakfast in bed is not, as the movies would have us believe, exclusively a super-luxurious pleasure of the pampered. For certain temperaments it is almost a necessity, and the proof of that is that there are thousands of hard-working unpampered women who would rather prepare their own trays and carry them back to bed, than eat with less comfort and trouble at the dining-room table. Furthermore, when there are guests in small households, trays are sometimes immensely practical: no waiting to set the table for lunch, no crumbs on the dining-room carpet, and no serving beyond the one trip to the bedroom.

Setting the breakfast tray follows the same basic rules as setting the table: cup to the right, knives and spoons to the right, forks and butter plate to the left. The tea or coffeepot should be in the upper right-hand corner of the tray, with the hot-water, or hot-milk pitcher beside it. Sugar and cream, pepper and salt, go in the middle, across the top of the tray; jam or honey in the upper left-hand corner; toast in a rack, or folded in a little napkin on the butter plate or, if there is room, on an extra plate. Eggs or cereal should be in a covered dish in the lower middle of the tray; fruit juice or berries wherever there is room. The napkin, which is usually very small—about the size of a tea napkin—is usually put at the left side of the main dish. A very pretty addition to any breakfast tray is a tiny vase of flowers; but be sure that it is a solid one that doesn't tip over easily. All breakfast trays, except those especially designed to be bare, should be covered with a tray cloth, which often may be bought in a set with two little napkins to match. One may also use, instead of a cloth, one of the big cellophane mats especially designed for trays. But a linen cloth is the standard.

A TRAY SET FOR BREAKFAST

Breakfast trays vary as much as breakfast menus, and this diagram is only a suggestion —not a limiting pattern. For the sake of example, it is set as follows: across the top, from the left, flowers; pepper and salt; sugar and cream; hot milk or hot water. Below the flowers is the plate of toast, and below this, the butter plate with its knife and the napkin. Above the fork is a jar of marmalade or jam; above the knife, fruit juice. Eggs and bacon are in the covered dish in the lower middle of the tray; the cup, with the coffee or tea pot above it, at the right. If it were necessary to put cereal on the tray, as well as eggs, the flowers would be taken away, and the jam jar would go above the toast. A bowl of cereal, with a small under plate, would be set above the fork. When there is less on the tray—when only coffee, hot milk and sugar are needed, for example —the dishes at the right all move up a bit. The cup is a little farther from the lower edge of the tray; the coffee pot (which should always be next to the cup) is almost in the upper right hand corner of the tray, and the hot milk is next to it, at the top edge of the tray. In setting a tray, a great deal naturally depends, also, on the size of the china and the proportions of the tray. This diagram shows only the basic plan.

As for the tray itself, there are three main types: the tray with folding legs; the absolutely flat tray; and the tray with open wicker-basket ends, which hold the mail and a newspaper.

Breakfast-tray china is discussed, together with other china, on page 409, "China for the Table."

Breakfast in the Dining Room

For breakfast in the dining room, the table is set as a luncheon table would be, except that a coffee or teacup is put at the right of each plate. (See the diagram of a luncheon table, page 250.) A glass of fruit juice may be set above the cup, but there need be no water glass. Spoons for cereal or fruit are put in the proper order beside the knife. As a rule, breakfast is not—and should not be—served, as luncheon or dinner is served, and the setting reflects the rule.

Perhaps the most formal breakfasts ever known were those of the Edwardian period in England, when guests helped themselves from sideboards loaded with heavy copper burners supporting dishes of hot porridge, eggs, bacon, finnan haddie, kippered herring, or even lamb chops. Smaller editions of the old-fashioned burners are still used in some houses, and they are most practical, particularly when there is a very big house party, or a very big family. Failing a burner, the coffee and hot milk, the toast, and all the rest of the breakfast are set on trays on a sideboard. Or a small tray with the coffee and hot milk is put at one end of the dining-room table, another tray with a big bowl of porridge or a covered dish of eggs at the other end of the table, and the toast is put in a breadbasket which is passed around.

Still a third system—an attractive old-fashioned one, and immensely practical—makes use of the "Lazy Susan." This is a big tray that revolves on a solid base and is set in the middle of the table; everyone helps himself, and there is no bother of passing plates from one to another. All these arrangements presuppose a fixed hour for breakfast and a number of prompt guests. But even if each late arrival has his breakfast separately, the table is set in exactly the same way. (For differences in the service see page 288.) On the breakfast table there are often jars of jam, honey, and marmalade set together on a tray, or separately, each on its plate, but, most jellies, except guava jelly, are considered accompaniments to meat and should not be served at breakfast. None of these should be served in its own jar, unless the jar is exceptionally attractive. (Several marmalades, for example, and many kinds of honey come in very attractive crocks.) As a rule, jams and marmalades should be put into bowls or jars of glass or china, each one with a little plate under it, and a spoon next to it. And there should always be, of course, flowers or a pretty centerpiece in the middle of the table.

Breakfast Out of Doors

For breakfast out of doors the table is set as described above, the only differences being matters of taste rather than custom. For example, butter balls are not as practical out of doors as indoors; it is better to give each person a tiny covered crock of butter, brought fresh from the icebox and set directly above each butter plate. Covered dishes such as jam jars and sugar bowls are a necessity out of doors. But, apart from these minor details, breakfast tables are all alike.

Pseudo Breakfasts

America's Saturday-night tradition has evolved its own form of Sunday pseudo breakfast, which is often—although it never should be—called "brunch." The same pattern is used for the breakfasts meant in the invitation, "Come in for something afterwards," which are given after almost any form of early-morning outdoor exercise—duck shooting, turkey shooting, hunting, or anything else.

These pseudo breakfasts follow the traditional English hunt-breakfast arrangements: burners and big covered dishes on the sideboard for hash or scrambled eggs, ham or bacon, sausages, kedgeree or any other such solid foods; a big tray with a coffee urn, sugar, cream, and hot milk. The coffee urn is more practical than a pot when there are so many guests, as the burner keeps the coffee hot and obviates the necessity of filling and refilling the pot.

The table is set exactly as for any other breakfast, with cups instead of water glasses; but there should be a big tray on another sideboard with whiskey and soda, plain water, ice, perhaps a pitcher of orange juice, and many big glasses. (Tumblers are better than stemmed glasses for this purpose.) This is the basic pattern for all pseudo breakfasts. Whether it is a hunt breakfast or breakfast-luncheon, such a meal is based on the assumption that the usual breakfast hour has passed and that no one has had a real breakfast. If it is very cold, and everyone has been out of doors for a long time, the traditional drink is sherry, served in the living room before everyone goes into the dining room to eat. Whiskey and soda is the traditional post-hunt breakfast drink.

The kind of food that should be served at these breakfasts has already been indicated immediately above. Any sturdy breakfast dish may be served, but it is wise to have a choice of several. Porridge or cereal is not usually served; waffles or pancakes would be excellent except that they present a problem of timing; desserts such as ice cream are incorrect, but it would probably be a good idea to have a bowl of berries or stewed fruit or something of the kind. Wedding breakfast food follows its own rules; see page 169 for suggestions.

LUNCHEON

According to the widely accepted table customs of our day, luncheon and dinner are the only two meals which are ever completely served. Of the two, luncheon is the more informal. As evidence of this are the facts that, even at the most elaborate luncheon, butter plates and ashtrays, cigarettes and matches, which are incorrect at a formal dinner, can be a perfectly correct part of the table setting; and that soup in plates—a more formal way of serving than in cups—is not usually served at luncheon.

For luncheon, the table is set according to the basic pattern on the next page.

The Informal Luncheon Table

The most informal luncheon table may be covered with a cloth, or set with mats, perhaps of heavy linen or straw. If the service is informal, the food for the first course is often put on the table before the guests come in. Decanters of red wine or bottles of white wine, with a breadbasket of wicker or straw, are very often part of an informal table setting, to say nothing of the almost inevitable ashtrays and cigarette containers. (See the diagram on page 259, "A Place Set for Dinner," and the text and diagrams on page 282, in the chapter, "Serving.")

The Most Elaborate Luncheon Table

The most elaborate luncheon table, according to modern usage, is the most bare. For luncheon on Christmas Day or Thanksgiving Day, the table may be covered with a cloth, and with a beloved clutter of turkeys or reindeer. But apart from such holidays, according to the customs of modern entertaining, the table is usually uncluttered. It is not covered with a cloth but usually set with mats of linen or, for a very elaborate luncheon, with mats of linen and lace. Under lace mats, or any mats with open-work insertions, there should be a small mat of dark felt as nearly as possible the color of the table top, the object being to emphasize the delicacy of the material. If the mats are solid linen or linen with a lace border, small white pads should be used to make the linen look even

A PLACE SET FOR LUNCHEON

At left are the butter plate and knife, the entrée (or fish) fork and the meat fork. In the middle is the place plate, with the folded napkin on it. To the right are the meat knife and entrée knife and, above, the water glass and the smaller glass for wine. If soup were to be served, instead of an entrée (or fish), the small fork and knife would be removed. The spoon—a teaspoon is best—might be set on the table to the right of the meat knife; or it might be brought in on the saucer back of the cup, with the handle to the right. If no wine is served, the wine glass is omitted. The arrangement of cigarettes is shown in the diagram on page 259.

whiter. Runners matching the mats are now somewhat out of fashion, and the centerpiece is usually set on the bare table.

Outline of the Menu

Food for luncheon is treated in detail on pages 312 to 317, but an outline of the menu is included here, since it will be needed in setting the table. The most common modern luncheon, neither the most elaborate nor the most informal, has three courses: soup or an entrée, a main course, usually meat, and a dessert. This is the "basic" luncheon, the framework to which other courses can be added and from which some things may be stripped away. Very often there are not more than two courses: in winter, a good big casserole dish and dessert; in summer, hot meat with a salad instead of a vegetable, followed by fruit. Or one might have a hot first course and end with salad and cheese. At a most formal luncheon, one might have four courses: soup, meat, salad, dessert; or better, an entrée, meat, salad, dessert. Five courses are unheard-of at lunchtime. (See page 313 for suggestions concerning specific dishes.) And incidentally, contrary to restaurant usage, an "entrée" is technically a prelude to the main course, not the main course itself.

Wines at Luncheon

Wines, and the foods to which they are best suited, are fully discussed on pages 334 to 336; the serving of wines, on page 300. Here, we shall consider only the ways in which the general rules concerning wines apply to luncheon. In the first place, since luncheon is basically much more informal than dinner, a traditionally formal wine such as champagne would be out of place except for wedding breakfasts or other equally special occasions. Second, and for the same reason, two wines are the most that should be served as a rule: sherry with the soup, followed by a white or red wine; or white wine with the entrée followed by a red wine. One wine, however, either red or white, is much more usual. Finally, very heavy white and red Burgundies are not usually served, not only for the very practical reason that they are too rich for any meal in the middle of the day, but also because their full-bodied character is wrong for the kind of food one is apt to serve.

AFTERNOON TEA

The most usual way of serving tea is in the living room at about five o'clock in the afternoon. This involves, first of all, a tea table which should be covered with a cloth, and a tea tray which should be set according to a standard pattern. The most traditional way of serving tea implies a cloth of fine linen, lace, or organdie, with little napkins to match; thin china cups and plates, and a tea set complete with a teakettle. There are, however, simpler systems that involve none of these; both the elaborate and the simpler methods are outlined below.

The Tea Tray

The tea tray is usually made of silver, wood, painted "Tole" or Mexican tin; and, unlike the tea table, should never be covered. The basic purpose is to make a self-contained unit. The traditional method—and, if there are more than a very few people, the most practical—is to set an alcohol burner and kettle at the center back of the tray, with a teapot conveniently in front of its spout; cream pitcher, sugar bowl, and plate of lemon to the right; tea caddy to the left. Back of the tea caddy there is often an extra bowl of silver or china into which the remains of each guest's first cup of tea can be poured. The tea strainer lies across this empty bowl when the tray is brought in, unless it has a special stand of its own, which is placed to the left, beside the caddy. Teacups, saucers, and plates are arranged on the tea tray as follows; first, the plate, on top of the plate a small folded napkin, then the saucer, cup, and spoon. If all of the teacups cannot fit conveniently on the tea tray, the remainder can be brought in with the first platters of food, and set around the tray and on the tea table. Butter knives, if there is to be jam or honey, are put on each plate under the edge of the saucer. Such a tray is shown in the diagram of a tea table on page 253.

This system, which is the traditional English one, is not a timesaver or worksaver. It demands a shining metal kettle, whether silver or copper, and someone with time enough for polishing. It is most attractive, and perfectly correct always, but it is practical only when there are several people to be served, and a ready supply of boiling water is a necessity.

A simpler system is to use a china tea set and to have the tea made in the kitchen. The tray is set with the teapot, a jug of hot water, cream, and sugar, very much as a breakfast tray would be. Tea plates and napkins are often stacked separately, with all the butter knives lying on the top napkin and a napkin between each plate. If there is room, cups and saucers should be stacked in pairs, two cups on two saucers, but if there is not, the saucers are stacked by themselves; the teacups are stacked in pairs, but only in pairs lest they topple over.

A SIMPLE TEA TRAY

This tray is set for eight people. At the left is the stack of butter plates and napkins, with the eight butter knives on top. Next to these, across the top of the tray, are the big bowl into which the dregs of the first cups of tea may be emptied, the sugar bowl, the cream pitcher, the hot water jug and, finally, the tea pot. The slices of lemon and the tea strainer are near the sugar and cream; the cups and saucers, stacked in pairs with their spoons, take up the rest of the tray. The food may be set around this tray, or on another table conveniently nearby.

(In the section, "Furnishing a House," tea sets are discussed more fully: china ones on page 420, silver ones on page 390.)

The Tea Table

The most practical tea tables are big enough to accommodate not only the tea tray, but also the extra plates, a platter of sandwiches, a jar of marmalade or jam, etc. Those designed for this purpose are usually folding tables, planned in height for the average living-room chair; but any table of a convenient height and size can be used. If it is not big enough for both the tea tray and the food, the food can be put on a separate table. The customary one is a little three-legged, three-tiered stand set beside the tea table.

Traditionally, the tea table should always be covered with a cloth. The usual way of serving sandwiches and cakes is from a flat china or silver plate covered with a paper doily. The last generation used doilies of lace or fine linen, but these are becoming rare. About a quarter of each cake is cut in slices, and a silver knife is left between two of them so that guests can cut the rest for themselves. There should be a supply of small forks (dessert forks) for any cake which has a soft icing.

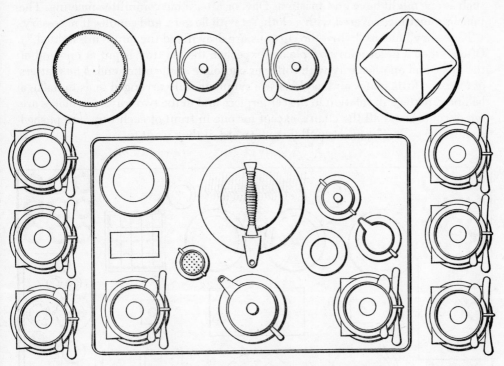

THE TRADITIONAL TEA TRAY AND TABLE

This diagram shows a tea table set for eight in the traditional way. Three cups, each stacked with its own spoon, saucer, napkin, butter knife and plate, are at the right and left of the tray, on the table; at the upper left is a platter of cookies or cake; in the middle, between the cake and a plate of napkin-covered toast in the upper right corner, are two jars for jam or honey. The tea tray is at the lower edge of the table, with the kettle at the back and the tea pot directly in front of it. Sugar and cream (the sugar to the left of the cream) and slices of lemon are set to the right of the kettle; the bowl for the dregs, oblong tea caddy, and a strainer to the left. A cup, arranged like the others, is set in each lower corner of the tray.

Tea in the Dining Room

Sometimes it is more convenient to have tea served in the dining room—a custom which is followed on the Continent and in Scotland. The dining-room table, in this case, is treated as though it were an enormous tea table; no places are set and each guest pulls his chair up to the table himself. The tea tray is put at one end of the table, where the hostess will sit; the food, the jam, the little plates, and napkins in the middle. This is a practical idea if there are many guests and a small household staff, because everyone goes back to the living room as soon as tea is over and the table can be cleared without ceremony whenever it is convenient.

Afternoon Reception

As described above, tea in the dining room is most informal, but this system can be elaborated to fit the most formal afternoon reception, or a big tea party such as one might have on Christmas Day, or after a big committee meeting. The table is sometimes covered with a cloth, set with flowers, and candles if necessary. ("Necessary" means "when the curtains are drawn and the lamps are lighted.") Often, when a great many people are expected, the tea tray is put at one end of the table, and another tray with coffee or chocolate at the other end. The platters of food, the little plates and napkins, are symmetrically arranged so as to make a balanced pattern in relation to the centerpiece and to the two trays. No places are set, of course, and all the chairs, except for one in front of each tray, are pushed against the wall. The guests pull them forward, if they want to.

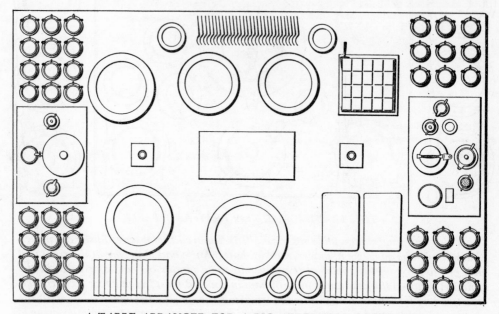

A TABLE ARRANGED FOR A BIG AFTERNOON RECEPTION

In this diagram, a tray for coffee or chocolate with cups beside it is set at the left end of the table, a tea tray and cups at the right. Between these, across the top, are a stack of tea plates, dessert forks (for a sticky cake) and more plates. Below these, a plate of small cakes, two of cookies, and a square cake. Across the middle of the table are a candelabrum, centerpiece, and a second candelabrum (but if there is still daylight other decorations replace the candelabra). In the row below these are two platters of sandwiches and two oblong covered dishes for toast or muffins. And, finally, across the near edge of the table, tea napkins, four stacks of little plates, and more napkins. But this is only one of the many possible ways of arranging such a table. There might well be only one plate of cookies, one of sandwiches and one cake. In warm weather, cold drinks might replace the coffee tray and cups. The fundamentals, which are common to all well-arranged buffet tables, are a pattern somewhat like this one, and an overall effect of symmetry and design.

This diagram may be used as a pattern for a table at a small wedding reception. The tea and coffee services will stay as shown in the diagram; but ice cream or sherbet may replace the cookies. Dessert spoons will then be needed as well as dessert forks, and large forks and spoons to serve the ices. If salad were to be served, a big platter of salad could replace the big round dish of sandwiches, and the necessary forks and plates would be put near by. Although a great many cups and saucers may be put on a table of this kind, there is often not room enough for all the plates, especially if ices are served, as well as cakes and sandwiches. High stacks of plates are ugly and too many small stacks look like a china shop. It is always wise to arrange beforehand to have extra plates, napkins, forks, etc., brought as they are needed.

High Tea

The only difference between high tea and everyday tea is that high tea is served at a later hour—at six or half-past instead of five—and there is heavier food and more of it. (See page 319.) Tea may be served either in the living room or in the dining room as described above. At high tea, a tray of whiskey and soda is usually set on a side table, since dinner is presumably still quite far in the distance.

Food at Teatime

There are three different kinds of tea food, so distinct in character that they are almost like the courses of a meal. First, there should be something hot; then, something bland and fresh; and last, something sweet. The essential thing about all tea food, with few exceptions, is that it is eaten with the fingers. Salads and desserts that require spoons and forks are not correct at tea time except at wedding receptions, which follow their own rules. (See page 192, "Menus for the Wedding Reception.") Suggestions for food served at tea time are on page 318.

"Nursery Tea"

One reason, perhaps, that tea is not served more often is that it involves a complicated ritual and food which, although simple in itself, requires a certain amount of preparation. For an informal tea in the country, for tea out of doors, or for any tea at which there are children, an elaboration of the English system of nursery tea is most attractive, and very much simpler. Nursery tea is always served at a big table, indoors or out of doors, anywhere that there is a table big enough to pull chairs up to. For such a tea, however, a very beautiful or elaborate dining-room table would probably be covered with a plain sturdy linen cloth. On the tea tray at one end of the table is a big earthenware teapot, an earthenware water jug, cream pitcher, and sugar bowl. The tea tray itself, instead of being made of silver or painted tin, is plain wood or bright Mexican tin. The little plates are earthenware, the napkins heavy linen or even paper. And opposite the tea tray, at the other end of the table, there is a big pitcher of milk and a tray of glasses. In the middle of the table, there is a big jar of plain honey or strawberry jam, a wooden board with a loaf of bread and a kitchen bread knife on it, and a covered glass dish of butter. This is the only time butter is brought to the tea table; otherwise, everything that *is* buttered is prepared in the kitchen before being brought in. "Nursery tea" has nothing to do with little tidbits of sandwiches or paper-thin slices of bread; the emphasis is on simple goodness and plenty. If strawberries or cherries or peaches are in season, there could be a bowl of these on the table, and a big platter of oatmeal cookies, gingerbread, or sponge cake.

Other Teas

All tea parties other than those described above could not really be called "tea." Russian tea at midnight, and Arabian tea served in glasses after meals are not part of the usual pattern of life in America. But there are many days during the hot American summers when hot tea is unbearable, and when "Come to tea" means something quite different from the accepted tea-tray-and-tea-table system.

The tea tray in this case is any big tray that one might use for drinks. There is a big bowl or thermos of ice, tall glasses filled with ice, mint, and tea, and a big extra pitcher of cold tea. Cold tea is best when it is made earlier in the afternoon; after it has cooled it is mixed with a little orange and lemon juice, carefully strained through muslin, and put in the ice box. For a very big tea party, it would be wise to have a pitcher of fruit juice as well, and a few bottles of ginger ale and other soft drinks. This tray can be set anywhere, indoors or out, on a tea table or any other table. No effort is made to approximate the usual tea pattern, except that the food is somewhat the same. The first "course" of hot tea food is eliminated, but there are the usual sandwiches, slices of plain buttered bread, and cookies. In the extreme heat, heavy cake would be unappetizing. The food is brought on a separate tray with the usual tea plates and little napkins.

COCKTAILS

A generation or so ago, cocktails were a dashing American innovation, half gin, half vermouth, and not very cold. Today, they are served in almost every quarter of the world, in so many different combinations that their simplest description now is, "a short, strong, iced mixture of two or more ingredients, at least one of which is highly intoxicating." These are the times when cocktails are served: before luncheon; late in the afternoon, when tea has been over for quite a long while; and just before dinner. And never at any other time. They are served in small cocktail glasses, except for "old-fashioneds," which are served in small heavy-bottom tumblers, and champagne cocktails or frozen daiquiris in saucer champagne glasses. (For suggestions concerning glasses, see page 397, "Cocktail Glasses.")

The Cocktail Tray

At formal dinners, the cocktails are mixed in the pantry, and each cocktail is specially poured for each guest. The tray is, therefore, set with empty cocktail glasses, empty sherry glasses and a few filled glasses of tomato juice. At big dinners of eighteen or twenty there are often two different kinds of cocktails, one whiskey, perhaps, and the other gin. When the service is less formal, the cocktails are often served in filled glasses. (See page 291, "Cocktails.") If there is room, the cocktail napkins are neatly folded into triangles around the edge of the tray; if not, they may be put around the edge of the tray on which the first dish of cocktail food is served. The shaker and the plates of food are taken back to the pantry, and the butler or waitress comes in again with a freshly filled shaker and plates of food.

At less formal dinners, the cocktails may still be mixed in the pantry, but the cocktail shaker will be set on the tray, which is left in the living room.

The customary way of setting a cocktail tray, however, is neither of these. It is predicated on the host's mixing the cocktails himself, in the living room, and it is designed to make the tray a complete and self-contained unit. The tray is set with a bowl or thermos of ice, the cocktail shaker, the necessary glasses and bottles, or decanters. Besides the usual cocktails, it is well to have tomato juice cocktails, or sherry. One kind of intoxicating cocktail is enough for the usual dinner of eight or ten people. The "what'll-you-have?," professional barman, approach is extremely bad taste. (See page 292, "Cocktail Parties.") Cocktail food is served on silver or china plates, on a lace-paper doily; nuts and olives in small bowls of glass or silver.

Cocktail Parties

At very small cocktail parties, no special table setting and arrangements are needed as the host can serve at informal ones and a butler at formal ones. For more than a very few people, however, it is usually more practical to set the food on a big table as it would be for an elaborate afternoon tea. (See page 263.) The dining-room table may be covered with a cloth and set with the platters of food, flowers, and if necessary candles. Small plates, such as one uses at tea time, are not necessary at a cocktail party, but there should be cocktail napkins. If the table is bare, the napkins are often put on a flat plate; if it is covered with a cloth, the napkins are arranged so as to form a part of the pattern.

It is rarely practical to put the drinks on the same table as the food. They should go on the dining-room sideboard, or on a separate table: soft drinks on one tray, whiskey and soda on another, filled cocktail glasses on the others, unless they are to be served. (See "Serving," page 292.) More than two kinds of cocktails— one gin and one whiskey, or one gin and one rum—are never necessary except for the very biggest parties of fifty or sixty people. The most one should serve in a private house would be three kinds: Manhattan, Martini, and Old-Fashioned, or Martini, Bacardi, and Manhattan. More than this puts an unattractive emphasis on drink.

DINNER

Dinner is the most widely variable of all our meals. It may be as informal as a farmhouse supper, or it may embody all the most formal traditions and ritual of serving and table setting that our civilization has evolved. Almost every kind of china and glass, food and wine, that there is in the world can be used at one time or another for dinner. (See also page 481, "Setting the Formal Dinner Table.") The diagram at the foot of page 259 shows the basic setting for a four-course dinner—soup, meat, salad, and dessert—and two wines. The essential differences between a place set for dinner and one set for luncheon are that butter plates and teaspoons, which are standard at lunch time, are used only at informal dinners.

The Informal Dinner Table

For the informal dinner table, there are few limitations. The table might be set with a cloth, of white, pale pink, pale blue, or cream-color, and the finest china and glass; or it could be bare except for a mat under each plate and set with peasant glass, pottery, the casserole containing the main course, the decanters of wine, and the breadbasket. There is a further deviation from the formal pattern which, although it transgresses the basic rules for setting given on page 243, would be correct for a table such as the one we have just described. The dessert fork and spoon are put across the top of the place plate at the beginning of the meal, parallel to the edge of the table, the fork below the spoon with its handle to the left, the spoon above with its handle to the right—a system which is particularly useful if the food is being served by the hostess from platters placed in front of her.

A PLACE SET FOR AN INFORMAL THREE-COURSE DINNER OR LUNCHEON

This setting makes it possible for the hostess to serve the dessert directly from the platter to each plate, without bothering about the dessert forks and spoons. (See also text and diagrams in "Serving," page 282.) To simplify still further, the butter plate and wineglass may be omitted and, if the menu is two courses, the teaspoon, also. The teaspoon is shown here for an imaginary first course of soup, which will be served in little covered bowls or casseroles, and set at each place before anyone comes to the table.

At a table such as this, there might be plain hearty dishes, the kind that are called coarse by people who don't like them; and although there might be as many as three courses, since the decanters and much of the food is on the table, the service would probably be of the simplest kind. On the other hand, if a pale cloth or fine mats were used, there would be more delicate, more subtly flavored dishes, and the service might be either partial or complete. The essential point is this: As far as the table setting is concerned, for an informal meal any table setting within reason can be considered correct if it goes well with the food.

Outline of the Menu

The menu of an informal dinner is given here because it may be useful in setting the table. As a rule, there are three courses: 1. soup, 2. meat, and 3. dessert; or, 1. fish, 2. meat, and 3. dessert. Or, there may be only two courses, perhaps a casserole dish served with or without a salad, and dessert; or, a main course followed by salad and cheese.

Further suggestions for the food will be found on page 321, for serving coffee on page 293, for the coffee tray on page 261. Cigarettes will have been on the table throughout the meal; arrangements for this are described on page 262.

The Semiformal Dinner Table

Since many of the formal rules and technicalities (such as "No cigarettes on the table") are ignored in setting a semiformal dinner table, the degree of formality depends upon subtleties of choice and taste. One may have a tablecloth or not, one may decide to put cigarettes on the table or to keep them away; as soon as one departs from the formal pattern, the question of formality or informality becomes one of degree. The only thing that is important is to be consistent in choosing china, glass, and silver that go well with the food.

Setting the table for an elaborate semiformal dinner, where a cloth is to be used, begins as follows: The table is covered with a thick pad or blanket of felt, cream-colored or white so that it will not make the tablecloth look dark. Over this comes the white or pale-colored damask cloth, which should, if necessary, be ironed on the table, so as to remove all the creases. The centerpiece, candlesticks or candelabra, pepper pots and saltcellars follow. (See diagram page 242.) On very long tables, there may be two smaller bowls of flowers or fruit, and one or two plates of candies, matching the centerpiece, spaced evenly between the centerpiece and each end of the table; but the many extra little dishes of bon-bons and vases of flowers, which were once considered essential, have now become rare.

Less elaborate tables are usually set with mats as luncheon tables are; but rarely, as luncheon tables are, with butter plates. The rest of the table is set as described above, with flowers and candles. But on this, the more usual modern dinner table, there are almost inevitably cigarettes and ashtrays which ought to be within reach of each guest. There are several ways of arranging the cigarettes on the table, the technicalities of which will be found on page 262 of this section. The only system that must be avoided is to have one or two big boxes of cigarettes which are to be passed from one guest to the other. (See also "Cigarettes and Cigars" on page 295 in the chapter, "Serving.")

A PLACE SET FOR DINNER

This is set for an informal or a semiformal dinner, with cigarettes and a packet of matches directly above the plate. The meat fork and salad fork are at the left of the plate; salad knife, meat knife and soup spoon at the right. Two wines are to be served —sherry in the glass nearest the soup spoon, red or white wine in the glass directly above this. (Or white wine in the lower wine glass, red wine in the upper.) The dotted line represents a place card, which is not needed at small dinners (see page 273).

Outline of the Semiformal Dinner Menu

The structure of a semiformal dinner which, as we have said, may be formal in every sense except the most strictly technical, is usually composed of four courses, as follows: 1. soup, 2. fish, 3. meat, and 4. dessert; or, 1. soup, 2. meat, 3. salad, and 4. dessert; or, 1. oysters, 2. soup, 3. meat, and 4. dessert. Or, less conventionally: 1. fish, 2. meat, 3. salad, and 4. dessert.

At most, it might be composed of five courses; as, 1. soup, 2. fish, 3. meat, 4. salad, and 5. dessert; or, 1. oysters, 2. soup, 3. fish, 4. meat, and 5. dessert; or, 1. oysters, 2. soup, 3. meat, 4. salad, and 5. dessert.

Menus for a semiformal dinner are on page 321; serving coffee, on page 293; setting the coffee tray, below, and on the next page.

WINES AT DINNER

Wine is more important at dinner than at any other time of day. At dinner time, no wine is too heavy since there is presumably plenty of time for digestion and full appreciation, even if the meal is short and informal. (All the customs concerning the choice of wines and liqueurs are described on page 334, the serving details on page 300.) All that need be said here is that, although it is true that wine should be served at every dinner party, and that at dinner the greatest variety of wines may, if one wants, be served, one should not apply the full, formal theory of serving a different wine with every course unless the rest of the dinner, from food to table decorations, is equally formal. If one were serving a very informal dinner of two or three courses, it would be disproportionate to serve two or three wines; one wine would be much better, unless the guests were making a special point of winetasting.

Dinner is the only meal at which champagne may always be served. Abroad, it is treated as a dessert wine which, at a formal dinner when different wines have been served with each course, appears only with the dessert. In America, however, at any but the most formal dinner, when champagne is served at all it is often the only wine; and it may appear with the meat course—or even the soup.

Liqueurs are not often served after an informal dinner; but at a formal dinner they follow the coffee almost as inevitably as the coffee follows the dinner itself. (See "Serving," pages 303 to 304.)

COFFEE

In America, coffee is not generally served at any odd hour of the morning, afternoon, or evening, as it used to be in Vienna and still is in Brazil. It is sometimes served at an afternoon reception at the same time and in the same way as tea, but usually it is served only at breakfast and after meals. Iced coffee is sometimes served at luncheon in tall glasses (see "Non-alcoholic Drinks at the Table," page 304); hot coffee, according to the strictest usage, is never served in large cups at luncheon or dinner, but only in small cups after the meal is over.

The Coffee Tray

The question of how the coffee tray is set depends largely on how the coffee is to be served. (See text on serving coffee, on page 293.) As a rule, the cups and saucers with a little coffee spoon on each saucer are toward the front of the tray, the cream jug and sugar bowl with the sugar tongs or scoop at the center back. Sometimes, particularly if the tray is round, the sugar and cream are in the middle surrounded by the cups. If the coffeepot is to be on the tray, as it is when the hostess serves the coffee herself, it should be at the center back, with the sugar and cream at each side of it.

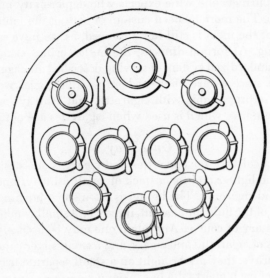

A TRAY SET FOR COFFEE SERVED AFTER DINNER OR LUNCHEON

This shows how a tray is arranged when it is to be set down before the hostess, who will pour the coffee herself. The sugar bowl is at the upper left, with the tongs; the coffeepot is at the top, with the cream to the right of it. Two cups are stacked at the lower edge of the tray, to show how it is done when the tray is crowded. Single cups, each with a demitasse spoon, fill the rest of the tray.

The tray may be made of almost any material, usually silver, wood, or painted tin. The cups may be old or new, of earthenware or porcelain; the only thing that they should not be, perhaps, is glass, which somehow makes coffee seem much less appetizing. The coffeepot may be china, matching the cups, or silver; the sugar bowl and cream jug may be china or silver or glass. China is, of course, most practical as well as attractive; but different patterns of china should not be used on one tray, unless, for example, the coffeepot, cream jug, and sugar bowl match, with the coffee cups in a somewhat similar or subordinated pattern. (See page 411, "Furnishing a House," for a detailed discussion of this.)

At buffet meals, hunt breakfasts, or at any time when a coffee urn is used, the tray is set on a sideboard or at one end of the dining-room table. The urn should be at the center back, sugar on the left, cream jug on the right, with the cups and saucers filling the rest of the tray.

There is only one thing more that must be said about after-dinner or after-luncheon coffee: It must be very hot, very strong, and very richly flavored. The sugar should be either white lump sugar, white crystals, or brown crystals; never granulated or powdered.

CIGARETTES AND CIGARS

The whole subject of smoking at table with food is colored by the nineteenth century theory that all women hate the smell of tobacco and particularly cigars. The most conventional and formal customs concerning smoking stem directly from this theory, but these customs are now followed only by the most tradition-minded, and by gourmets and wine experts who deplore any mixture of food or wine with tobacco. The more modern custom of setting the table with cigarettes at the beginning of the meal is still not approved, as we have said, for the most formal entertaining. At formal dinners, the butler brings cigarettes on a tray, according to the standardized system of serving described on page 295, "Cigarettes and Cigars." Here, since we are concerned only with settings, we will discuss the different ways of setting a table with cigarettes and ashtrays, and the arrangement of the cigarette tray which is used when cigarettes are not put on the table.

On a Tray

The most practical tray for cigarettes and cigars is one designed especially, with a place for the lighter and for a stack of small ashtrays and with compartments for cigars and cigarettes. The lighter is often spirit-burning but, for purists who find the smell of the fluid unpleasant, it may be a small candle or taper. These trays are not necessary of course. Any plain one may be used instead, with open boxes or little trays of cigarettes and cigars, and a small silver candlestick. If there is no room for ashtrays, they are brought on a small separate tray, and one is set down at the right of each guest who has taken a cigarette.

When cigarettes are offered after the meat course, as they usually are, cigars should not be included on the tray; the cigar compartment is filled with extra cigarettes. When the tray is brought at the end of dinner, the cigars replace these cigarettes, since the women will presumably be leaving almost immediately.

On the Table

These are the three most common ways of arranging cigarettes on the dining-room table: Little boxes of china or lacquer—or anything else that looks well with the rest of the table setting—are set between each two guests, near an ashtray with matches or a lighter. Or there may be small open urns of glass or silver, or small china cups, filled with cigarettes and treated as part of the table decorations. These should be within reach of every guest, but not necessarily between each two, with ashtrays and matches at alternate places. The third way is to set a small ashtray at the left of each guest, a little above the butter plate on a luncheon table, or above each guest's plate with two cigarettes across the upper rim and a very small packet of matches in the middle.

No matter how informal the luncheon or dinner, cigars should never be put on the table until the women have left the room, and then only after an informal dinner when the host will have taken charge of the matter. (See page 295, "Cigarettes and Cigars.")

BUFFET MEALS

The problem which buffet meals were designed to solve is that of too many guests: either too many guests for the dining-room table, or too many guests for the available household staff. Service is fully discussed on page 297. Here we are concerned mainly with the table, which may be arranged to solve the problem from either point of view. The first object in setting the table for a buffet meal is to put all the food in one convenient place, usually the dining-room table or a big dining-room sideboard—so that the guests can wait on themselves as quickly and as easily as possible. The second object is to arrange the platters of food, the plates, napkins, silver, and whatever else may be necessary, in an attractive symmetrical pattern, so that the whole looks fresh, inviting, and appetizing. Since buffet meals —whether luncheon, dinner, or late supper—are more informal than any others, we might first discuss how tables may be arranged to solve the problem of too many guests for the dining-room space.

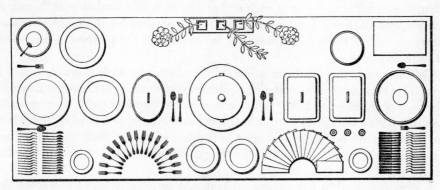

A BUFFET TABLE

Across the top of the table are the sauce for the dessert, a plate of cakes or cookies, space for flowers or candelabra, a cheese, and crackers for the cheese. In the next row, the dessert, more cookies, a dish for vegetables or rice, the platter or casserole containing the main course, dishes of toast and rolls and, at the right, the bowl of salad. Across the lower edge of the table are the forks and spoons for the dessert, the dessert plates, the forks for the main course, the plates for the main course, napkins, salad plates with pepper and salt above them, butter knives for the cheese and forks for the salad. But all this must be used as a general guide, not as a fixed pattern. The arrangement will have to be changed to fit each menu.

The Most Informal Buffet Table

Whether indoors or outdoors, the table for a buffet luncheon would probably not be covered with a cloth. It is usually pushed up against a wall, with the platter of the main course set in the middle of the table. In front of this is a stack of plates with the necessary number of forks. Although knives must be a part of almost every other table setting, they should not be put on a buffet table unless they are going to be used. The forks are neatly arranged, often in a fan-shaped pattern (see diagram above), half of them on each side of the stack of plates; or all on one side, balanced by the napkins neatly folded on the other. The stacks of plates need not match each other, but all the plates in any one stack must be the same design; and the same is true of the silver. On one end of the table is the salad bowl with its plates and forks; and at the other end, the dessert, flanked by the dessert plates, forks, and spoons, and, perhaps, a plate of cakes. If a cheeseboard is used, it should be put to one side of the salad bowl, with crackers beside it or balancing it on the other side. As a rule, cheeses served on a board should be put directly on the board, not on a doily. If a single cheese, particularly a very runny one, is served on a plate by itself, it can have a doily underneath it. Cheese bought in a crock may be served in the crock; all other cheeses should be carefully unwrapped. Flat platters or baskets of bread, rolls, and crackers are placed at intervals along the table, the important point being to produce a pleasing over-all effect of patterned symmetry. If the table is wide enough there might be a bowl of flowers or fruit back of the center dish; but decorations are not necessary and unless there is plenty of room they often give an unpleasant effect of overcrowding.

Another arrangement, which is practical when there are many guests, is to leave the table in the middle of the room so that the guests can move freely around it. Duplicate platters are put at each end and at each side—salad at each end, for example, and the main course at each side. The platters for the main course are taken away while the guests are eating the salad, and the platters of dessert are put in their places.

Coffee, water, and whatever other drinks one might wish to serve should be set on trays on a sideboard: water in a pitcher, without ice, on the same tray with a thermos of ice and tumblers; tall glasses and whiskey and soda; beer; or coffee in an urn with a burner to keep it hot, sugar and cream, and cups. If there is no urn, coffee should be brought in later as it must, of course, be hot. Wine should be served on a separate tray with its own glasses: red wine in a decanter, white wine iced and left in its own bottle.

A very informal buffet supper table would be exactly like this except that candles would be necessary, both on the sideboard and on the main table.

A More Elaborate Buffet Table

For a more elaborate dinner, the table is covered with a fine damask cloth, and set with fine china and glass. Instead of being served in earthenware casseroles, the food is set on big platters of china or silver; but, though the details vary, if any buffet meal is entirely unseated and unserved, with the guests perched around on any available furniture, the pattern will always be more or less the same. The great drawback to this form of entertaining is that it is an untidy business. If there are a great many guests, they will overflow from the dining room into the living room; they will set down glasses on small tables or on the floor, plates balanced precariously on napkin-covered knees. A partial solution, if there are not too many guests, is to clear away some of the ornaments from the small tables, or to put extra little tables beside the chairs. If possible, it is best to avoid all such novelties as cafeteria trays, or plates especially made to hold food and a glass. Unless the food is to be served—or at least eaten—outdoors, or unless all the arrangements are most informal, these trays and plates have a rather unattractive cafeteria character.

Seated and Semi-Served Buffet Meals

The best development in the field of buffet meals has been the seated buffet luncheon or dinner. The guests are seated at small tables, either in the dining room or in any other room near by, usually in both. The tables are almost always card tables, covered with a cloth and set exactly as they would be for any other seated meal, except that the formality of a place plate is usually omitted. Salt and pepper should be on each table and perhaps a decanter of wine, an ashtray and cigarettes. At buffet dinners, there is a candlestick or a small candelabrum on each little table, if the room is dark; but there is usually not enough room for flowers. (If there are flowers, they should be in a sturdy, heavy-bottomed little vase.) The food is put on one big table, as before, with whiskey and soda and extra bottles or decanters of wine on the sideboard or on another table. The guests wait on themselves.

Another way of arranging a seated buffet meal is to have two or three fairly large tables, set as formally or as informally as one wants. If the problem is a shortage of staff rather than a shortage of space, the guests may all be seated at the dining-room table. The food is put on the sideboard and the guests wait on themselves.

Seated buffet meals such as these are very often "semi-served." The guests choose their own food from the buffet table but, as soon as they leave the table, the butler or maid takes away used plates. The first course is set on each little table or on the dining-room table, if the guests are to sit there, before the guests come in. If the first course is a creamed fish or something of the kind, it may be put on each table in a casserole or a burner. If it is soup, it may be put in covered cups at each place or, at a big table, the hostess may serve from a tureen into the plates set in front of her. No arrangements are necessary for the coffee, since it will be brought directly from the kitchen. For further details, see "Semi-Served Buffet Meals" under "Serving," page 298.

The Food for Buffet Meals

The classic buffet meal has three courses: a hot first course, which is usually the main one: salad with cold meat or cheese; dessert and coffee. Since the main problem connected with buffet food is how to keep it hot, the first course is often the only hot one, except in summer when there might be nothing hot but the coffee. There is no reason, however, apart from the convenience of the usual pattern, not to vary it in any number of ways. See page 329 for suggestions concerning the food.

SUPPER

Perhaps, before we describe the different kinds of supper tables, it might be wise to define exactly what we mean by supper. We do not mean a children's supper, when the table is set with glasses of milk and butter plates; we mean those suppers which are an adult way of entertaining other adults late in the evening, when the dinner hour has long since passed. These fall into three main types: supper after the theater or movies; supper at a dance, or a large evening reception; and supper after a big dinner party. This last is so simple that it often resembles crackers-and-milk at bedtime rather than supper; but, essentially, they are all suppers because they are served at supper hours and for supper reasons. Because it is the simplest, we shall start with after-dinner supper first.

After-Dinner Suppers

If food is to be served late in the evening, after a dinner party, a table is often put at one side of the living room, or in the hall immediately outside the living room. The tea table may be used for this purpose, covered with a cloth, set with plates of food and with the tray of drinks. After an elaborately served dinner, when some of the guests are playing cards in other rooms, the food is served to them there by the butler or footman; after a simple, informal dinner, the food is usually not served at all. As soon as it is set out, or after it has been served once, the guests will wait on themselves.

The plates of food are set exactly as they are for tea, with little paper doilies. After an elaborate dinner, when only small sandwiches will be served, nothing more is necessary. If there are to be hard-boiled eggs, or cheese and crackers, there should be a stack of plates and little napkins, both tea-size. If hot coffee, hot soup, or hot chocolate is to be served, an urn may be set in the middle of this table with cups around it: teacups for coffee or chocolate, soup cups for bouillon. Or else the soup may be served in a tureen, the hot chocolate and hot coffee in pots. Suggestions for the food will be found on page 332.

Supper after the Theater

Supper after the theater or opera may be an elaboration of the simple after-dinner supper described immediately above; or it may be a buffet meal, seated or not, like one of those described on pages 262 to 265 of this chapter; or it may be a short but elaborately served and seated supper at the dining-room table, very like a semiformal dinner (see page 259). The choice of the food will determine how the table is to be set: whether with a coffee urn and plates of sandwiches; or with plates of food and a casserole and burner; or with a centerpiece, glasses, place plates, and all the usual paraphernalia of a seated meal. The choice of which kind of supper to have is entirely free except that the seated supper at the dining-room table should only be served when one is sure that all the guests have had nothing earlier except high tea, or coffee and sandwiches, or something of the kind. Suggestions for the food for these three different kinds of suppers are on page 332 to page 333.

Supper at Dances

At a small dance, particularly a dinner dance, a buffet table is set in the dining room, as it would be for a buffet dinner. One should make sure, however, that every guest can sit while he eats. When there are more than a very few, the best solution is usually to set up small tables in the dining room and in any rooms conveniently near by. These, covered with a cloth, need be set only with candles or flowers, not necessarily with glass or silver.

At large dances, when a great many people have been invited to come after dinner, the supper arrangements must be more elaborate. Instead of a buffet table, from which the guests will choose their own food, there will be a regular supper of two or three courses, served directly from the kitchen. There should be enough small tables so that all the guests can be seated simultaneously. These tables may be set as for a dinner or, more simply, only with candles or flowers. At a supper such as this, the silver for each course and the napkin can be brought in on each guest's plate. Besides these small tables for the supper, there is often a big buffet table with such food as sandwiches, small cakes, cheese, and crackers. After supper is over, the guests will help themselves from this table until it is late enough for scrambled eggs to be served. This buffet table would, of course, be

266

covered with a cloth and decorated with flowers and candles, as any other buffet table would be.

At a big ball, when some of the guests may have official positions, a seated and served supper is sometimes planned. The table is set as it would be for a formal dinner, covered with a cloth (never with mats) because a served and seated supper follows the formal pattern in almost everything except the menu. In certain circumstances, one might combine a seated supper and a buffet supper. The older and more important guests might be seated, and served at a table in one room; the younger people could help themselves from a buffet table in another.

At a dance or reception it is always wise to have the drinks on a table separate from the food. At a small informal dance, when the food is on the dining-room table, the drinks are put on large trays on a sideboard or—and this is really more attractive and more practical—on a separate table. At bigger dances, they are often served from trestle tables which should, of course, always be covered with a cloth. If there is punch, the bowl should be set in the middle of the table with small punch glasses around it. Other drinks, with the necessary glasses, can balance each other at each side of the punch bowl. (See page 333, "Supper at Dances.")

PICNICS

There are two large branches of the family of picnics: one, the simple basket-sandwich-and-thermos kind; the other, the elaborate grouse-and-white-wine kind. The distinguishing mark of the second is that it is served and of the first that it is not. The elaborate picnic is one in a thousand not only because it means a lot of work and planning but also because it is possible only within a limited radius of one's source of supply. It is impossible for traveling, pointless very near the house, but ideal for its true purpose: to bring food—the delicious kind of food that is impossible for a simple picnic—to a prearranged place for a fairly large group of people. Apart from this one kind of picnic occasion, the simple picnic is the only answer.

Simple Picnics

By simple picnics we do not, of course, mean a shoe-box picnic such as any ten-year-old might, and probably does, prepare for himself a dozen times in the summer. The picnics described here are all planned for entertaining, rather than for convenience, and presuppose a certain number of guests, whether a dozen or only two or three, whom one wishes to entertain as agreeably and as attractively as possible.

Even when narrowed down this far, the simple picnic has several variations ranging from the traveling picnic to the clambake. The traveling picnic, as the simplest, comes first.

Traveling Picnics

A traveling picnic is based on the assumption that one is making a trip through country which, as far as food is concerned, is a desert. Everything one might conceivably need for the luncheon should be in the picnic baskets, from pepper and salt to water. The first requisite is a good basket, and among baskets by all odds the smartest—and, unfortunately the most expensive—are those made of smooth, brown luggage leather, shaped like boxes. Beautifully fitted with brass locks and hinges, these baskets are full of sandwich boxes, plates, and cups (sometimes chromium boxes and china plates and cups, but usually all of white enamelware), and small knives, forks, and spoons of chromium or silver. The perfect companion for such a picnic basket is a thermos case which holds two or three large thermos bottles, and is made of the same leather with the same locks.

The major drawback of these baskets, aside from their expense, is that they are extremely heavy to carry. But, otherwise, they are all plus; they last from generation unto generation, solving the picnic problem year after year. Imitations of these baskets made in cheaper lighter leather are undesirable, but there is another kind that is much less expensive and almost equally attractive. These are made of wicker, either plain (very inexpensive) or fitted (a little more expensive). Plain ones can be fitted with white enameled boxes which have clamp-on lids, the kind that are used in ice boxes for vegetables, or with any other eminently washable and dustproof container. Plates and cups can be made of enamelware or sturdy earthenware; knives, forks, and spoons, of bamboo-handled chromium. The thermos-case companion for such a basket might be covered in canvas or duck, or any other plain heavy material, in dark brown, dark green, dark blue, tan, or gray.

No matter how simple the picnic, quite big linen napkins are much more attractive than paper ones. But whether paper or linen, they must be big enough to cover the lap. Motor-rugs to sit on and a heavy, sturdy tea cloth, on which the containers or plates of food can be spread, add considerably to a picnic's charm. Another very useful thing is an extra bottle of water which can be used to rinse out the glasses and cups. To be avoided are paper cups or composition cups, which almost inevitably give soup and coffee a peculiar taste, and, above all, any picnic system which is built on the principle of "we can burn it up right there." Aside from the fact that disposing of used paper cups, plates, and napkins is neither an attractive sight nor an attractive idea, there is the danger of starting an uncontrollable fire. Beyond this, there is the rudeness inherent in any such misuse of the property of another. When one is traveling, there is not time to stay and watch the last spark and ember, and carelessness in such matters is bad taste as well as dangerous. To leave papers, eggshells, or any other debris is, in the words of the little boy in the cartoon, "unethical and lousy."

Food for Traveling Picnics

Food for these picnics is all of the self-contained, eaten-in-the-fingers kind. Knives and forks are not needed; and spoons only for coffee or soup. The standard menu is a hard-boiled egg, sandwiches, and a banana, but even the simplest picnic can be a little gayer than that. Hard-boiled eggs can be deviled, put together again, and wrapped separately in twists of waxed paper. Sandwiches, all neatly cut and trimmed, should be varied enough to seem like the course of a luncheon at home: first, something solid, such as ham, ham and cheese, beef, chicken, lamb or tongue; then something fresh such as cream cheese, watercress, tomato, sliced radish, or cucumber; finally, something sweet, such as Bar-le-Duc, jam, or marmalade. As variations, instead of meat sandwiches, there might be cold croquettes of creamed minced meat or chicken; or tiny cold broiled lamb chops with all the fat carefully cut away; or cold broiled or fried and skinned chicken, cut in conveniently small pieces. Dry sandwiches can be neatly stacked in a container lined with waxed paper, and passed from hand to hand in the container, but "wet" or creamy sandwiches should all be separately wrapped in waxed paper. One great trouble with picnic sandwiches is that, too often, too little imagination is shown in choosing the bread. French or Italian bread is excellent with meat or jam; black bread or pumpernickel with cheese; brown or raisin bread with cream cheese; thin slices of rye bread, buttered, with thin slices of Gruyère cheese and a little mustard. Or there could be a really good cheese cut in thin slices, to eat with crackers at the end of the meal, with the coffee.

Fruit is often difficult. Oranges, peaches, plums, and pears are juicy and messy. Tangerines are better, but best of all are cherries, or a big bunch of grapes which can travel, bedded in cotton or tissue paper, in one of the containers. Excellent, too, are the very small tomatoes—yellow or red, round or oval—which can be eaten in one bite.

As for drinks: Granted three thermos bottles, the most usual in hot weather are water, hot coffee, and milk or fruit juice. If there are no children at the picnic, it might be water, hot coffee, and iced white wine, or even cocktails, such as Martinis. In cooler weather, there should be two hot drinks, a clear soup and coffee, and one cold drink, perhaps a white wine or cider. Red wine is not advisable for a picnic because the sediment rises when it is bounced around; sherry, whiskey, or brandy may be carried in a separate flask.

Cooking Picnics

Cooking picnics are quite unlike traveling picnics. The point is the picnic, not a farther destination. There is no feeling of hurry, and, of course, the rule against fires does not apply because there is plenty of time to ask the owner's permission, and there is plenty of time to make sure that the fire has been properly put out.

It is true of all cooking picnics, whether a clambake in Maine or a barbecue in the South, that those are best which are most carefully planned ahead of time. It is perfectly possible to start out all together, hoping to find adequate firewood on the spot and planning to do all the cooking together; but it is much wiser and much easier to send someone ahead to get everything started. It is also true that glasses, china plates and cups, and big solid napkins are the only ones that are really satisfactory. Finally, as at all picnics, everything must always be as neat as on a man-of-war. The great trouble with picnics is that they often have a slightly grubby aspect. If anything must be kept cold in a pail of ice, the ice should be scrupulously clean and look it. The pail should be new and shiny, or painted, or made of some attractive material such as wood. Adults, particularly women, should not be asked to drink out of bottles. Everything should look, and be, clean and fresh and attractive.

Beyond this it is impossible to make rules for cooking picnics. Each one follows a law of its own, a purely sectional law based on the specialties of each of the different sections of the United States. Quite unlike traveling picnics, which follow a sort of international custom, cooking picnics are as native or local as a country dance, and whatever is done in each section by the majority of the "natives" is correct. Cooking picnics can be beautifully and elaborately done with tables, lanterns, hurricane lamps, and a big buffet table, just like a buffet supper out of doors. Or they can be whittled down to a fire on the beach, with a few steamer rugs spread on the sand. The point, and the fun, is to cook the food on the spot, whether it is quail grilled with bacon in the Southeast, barbecue in the Southwest, brook trout baked in a mud casing in any fishing region, clams steamed in seaweed on the Maine coast, or hamburgers anywhere. But it is also, of course, perfectly possible to precook a big casserole dish, such as baked beans, and only reheat it out of doors over the fire.

Served Picnics

The served picnic is not, of course, served as a meal at home would be, but it differs radically from anything that might be called a simple picnic in that all the food is handled by members of the household staff and not by the hosts or guests. In England and Scotland, where these picnics were most elaborately done, they were usually given at a prearranged place in the middle of a day's shooting. Hampers of food, and elaborate leather picnic-baskets were brought by the butler or first footman, dressed in his morning livery. The beaters or gillies helped in setting up the folding tables on which some of the food was laid out; the old coaching tables were perfect for this purpose. Guests stood, or sat around on shooting sticks, steamer rugs, or folding chairs. They helped themselves to all the food, but bottles were opened for them, and all the used plates were whisked out of sight by the manservant. In the more modest, and more modern, version of this system, the food is prepared and carefully packed at home, brought to the rendezvous by the chauffeur or by anyone else who can drive, and set up and arranged by the hostess and some of the guests.

Food for Served Picnics

At a served picnic the food is very like that which is served at a buffet luncheon. In cold weather, hot soup is brought in big thermos bottles, and served in cups. Big widemouthed thermos jugs are used for a second hot course, such as curried eggs with rice, creamed chicken, hash or croquettes; and for a cold third course of some salad such as cole slaw, or celery and apple.

The drinks are almost equally elaborate; iced white wine, cocktails, sherry, whiskey and soda—any of these, and more, are not only possible but probable at a picnic of this kind. The point of such a picnic is not to serve the guests in a formal way, which would be ridiculous out of doors, but to have someone to take care of all the usual picnic chores, from arranging the food to gathering up the used plates.

MENU CARDS FOR MEALS AT HOME

The Cards

For informal meals at home, one may use any of these three standard kinds of menu cards: an old-fashioned china stand, which can be washed and used over and over again; or a plain white menu card of stiff pasteboard; or a decorated pasteboard card. For informal meals in the country, some families have white cards engraved in color with their crest or coat of arms, or with the name of their house, but the standard menu card which is used for semiformal dinners and for all formal entertaining is never decorated in colors. It is a pure white or cream-white card of the best quality (four-sheet board is now customary), about 4 by 5½ or 6 inches, with a gilded or silvered beveled edge. This means that the card is gilded in its thickness, as the page of a book might be; there should never be a border of silver or gold on the face of the card. It may be decorated with the family crest or coat of arms embossed in gold or silver, to match the edging, at the center top. Or, in the house of a widow or an unmarried woman, it can be embossed with a lozenge. (See page 201, in the chapter "Weddings," for a detailed discussion of heraldic devices used by women.) If the family has no coat of arms, a monogram may be embossed on the card instead, although the very strictest opinion holds that one should use a heraldic device or nothing.

For special occasions, such as a wedding anniversary, menu cards can be especially decorated with the initials of the married couple intertwined at the top of the card, in place of the coat of arms, and with the dates of the marriage ("1897-1947") directly underneath the initials. For a wedding anniversary dinner, menu cards are usually embossed in silver, in memory of the menu at the wedding breakfast (see page 170).

Writing Menus

A menu may be put on the table for any meal, no matter how formal or informal. In a private house, or even at a banquet in a hotel, the basic rule is that the list of courses must always be either engraved (this is done, of course, only for the most elaborate occasions), or written by hand. Whether engraved or written, the following rules can be used for all menus:

Unless one is entertaining royalty, the word "Menu" heads the list of courses, by itself, on one line directly under the crest or coat of arms, or at the center top of the card. When one is entertaining royalty, the line under the crest reads "Dîner" (or "Déjeuner" or "Souper") "de Leurs Majestés" (or "Altesses").

Only one dish is written on each line.

Each line is centered on the menu.

Only the first letter on each line is capitalized, except for personal or proper nouns, or adjectives derived from personal or proper nouns. This is the opinion of one very strict French school; another, with equal vehemence, holds that an impression of over-all symmetry is more important than any technicality such as this. Those who follow the second school of thought often capitalize the first letter of each word, except for "the," "of," and other articles and prepositions.

Each course is separated from the next by a line space, or at most by a little dot or asterisk.

The vegetables and sauces that are served with any course, unless they are on the platter with the course, are also listed under that course. The sauce is on the second line, the potatoes on the next, any other vegetable on the third. Any sauce or vegetable is written in smaller writing under the main dish of each course. Or, in the case of sauces, if the course is a short word like "Asparagus," the sauce may be written on the same line: "Asparagus, Hollandaise sauce."

The cookies or the cake served with the dessert are listed in writing smaller than that used for the dessert itself.

The following must never appear on any menu: appetizers, toast, bread, rolls, etc., pickles, relishes, jellies, etc., fruit, candy, coffee, drinks; except at public banquets when wines may be listed opposite the food.

Beyond this point, menus must be considered in three categories: menus for informal meals at home, which are discussed here; menus for formal or official meals in a private house, which will be found on page 487; and menus for public banquets on page 489. Menus for semiformal meals may be written according to the informal pattern given here, but at a big elaborate semiformal dinner they will probably follow the traditional French samples shown on page 488.

Menus for informal meals at home may be written either in English or in French, either on one of the old-fashioned washable china stands or on the usual menu card. (See page 270.) The menu is written in black pencil on a china stand, in black ink on a menu card.

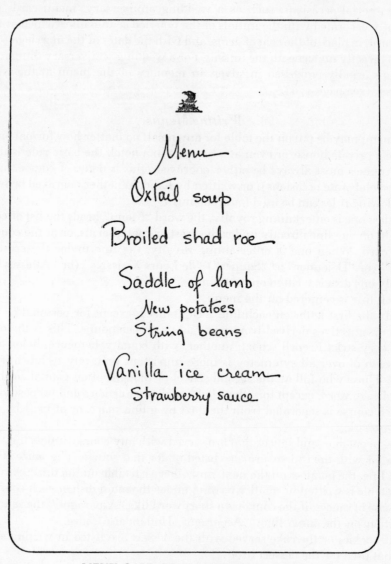

Menu

Oxtail soup

Broiled shad roe

Saddle of lamb
New potatoes
String beans

Vanilla ice cream
Strawberry sauce

MENU CARD OF AN INFORMAL MEAL

The crest shown on this card is embossed in gold but, as suggested above, no decoration is necessary.

On the Table

The menu card may be held in a stand, or it may lie on the table: one in front of the hostess, one in front of the host, and one or two placed at regular intervals down each side of the table. This is not a rule, however, and at informal meals there is often only one menu in front of the host.

PLACE CARDS

Place cards are necessary as a matter of custom on all formal tables and as a matter of convenience when there are more than eight guests. When there are very few guests, it is quite easy for the hostess to direct each one to his place at the table, but this is always an informal and, if there are more than a few guests, necessarily a slow and cumbersome system.

The Cards

Like menu cards, place cards are made of heavy card, about 2 by 2¾ or 3 inches. They may be either white or cream-white but, if there are menu cards on the table, the place cards should be made of exactly the same pasteboard. If the menu card has a beveled edge, silvered or gilded, the place card should also. And if the family crest or coat of arms is embossed on the menu card, the place card may also be decorated in the same way, although this is a matter of individual choice, and not a rule. Some hostesses approve the use of a coat of arms on the menu, but consider it unnecessary on a card as small as a place card.

Because they are so practical, place cards are often used when there are no menu cards. In this case, the heavy pasteboard cards described above may be used or, since there is no menu card that need be matched, one may use lighter, paper cards, in a dull or glazed finish. These are usually about 2 by 3¼ inches, and they are often made with narrow border of silver or gold instead of a beveled edge. They also may be embossed with the family crest or coat of arms.

Another type is the folded place card, of medium-weight paper about 3 by 3¼ inches, folded in half, with the name written across the lower half. These cards too, are often edged with a narrow silver border, but they are rarely decorated. No fancy or colored place cards should ever be used except for public banquets or special occasions. In a pinch, it is better to use the back of a visiting card than it is to use a would-be funny innovation.

Writing Place Cards

At informal meals, place cards are a practical convenience only, and need follow no special set of rules. First names or nicknames can be used if all the guests are friends. But strangers, squinting anxiously to make sure of their dinner partners' names, should be given more help than "Kitty" or "Sister": "Mrs. Herrick" and "Miss Paton" would be more practical. There is no set custom concerning the handwriting or anything else.

At a semiformal meal, place cards are still a matter of common sense and convenience, rather than form. As explained on page 237, "Three Degrees of Formality," the difference between semiformal and informal entertaining is often nothing more than a technicality of service. With common sense as the guide, therefore, at a small semiformal dinner there would probably be no place cards at all; at a big dinner of friends, the place cards would be written informally as shown here; at a big elaborate dinner, they might be written according to the formal pattern described on page 490.

A PLACE CARD FOR AN INFORMAL MEAL

This card is decorated with a crest, to match the menu card but, as we have said, no decoration is necessary.

On the Table

Place cards are laid on top of the napkin, which is folded on the place plate. If the napkin has been folded so as to stand up, the place card is put in front of the napkin, leaning against it. Or else the place card may be laid flat on the table, above each place plate. Folded place cards stand on the table, directly above the place plate.

41

Serving

It might be wise to make it clear, at the beginning of this section on serving, that serving customs are among the least important of those which are connected with food and drink. It is impossible to call anyone civilized who has boorish table manners, no matter how perfect his dinner, or how perfectly served. On the other hand, of course, thousands live extremely well, and in every sense in a most civilized way, with a part-time maid or none at all. The traditional ways of serving food can be adapted to a staff of any number from one up. The only thing that is really unfortunate is to have a staff, of whatever size, which does the wrong things.

The first essential of good service is that it be quick, silent, and unobtrusive. Whether a household staff consists of one person or ten, no matter what meal it may be, this principle always holds true.

The second essential of good service is that, as far as possible, each guest should be given individual attention and a free choice. With the best service, for example, drinks are poured for each guest under his supervision, not brought already poured; food is not portioned, but instead the guest is allowed to help himself from the platter or bowl. This is a subtle but very important point, and it applies to all service no matter how large or small the household staff.

For the purposes of this section, the standard household divisions will be used. "Butler" means whoever is in charge of the pantry and of waiting at table; "footman" refers to anyone who is second to the butler in the same department. (Other household duties which have nothing to do with the serving of food are discussed in "The Household Staff," page 352.) Obviously, in modern America, only one-tenth of one per cent of the houses have a butler, and even fewer, a footman; but, if there is a part-time "general" who covers every household department from the kitchen and dining room to the upstairs, the customs that govern her serving and waiting on table are based on the departmental system described above. In other words, if she leaves the kitchen to bring in a glass of water, she should follow the rules laid down for such service. In households without a maid, these rules do not, of course, apply. Suggestions for these will be found beginning on page 445, "Entertaining Without a Maid."

ESSENTIALS OF ALL SERVICE

Before we consider the different customs attached to each food occasion, we might set down the few basic rules that apply to all serving.

First, anyone who waits on table or brings food out of the kitchen must be dressed in the conventional way. (See "The Household Staff," pages 352 to 354.)

Second, nothing is ever given or taken directly from the guest's hand to that of the butler, or vice versa. For example, a telegram is brought on a tray; a glass of water must be brought on a tray and the empty glass received on a tray, which the butler holds in his left hand. This is a convention so firmly established that a tray must often be carried even when it is useless; for example, if a second round of cocktails is being served in the living room by the butler, he brings the shaker in on a small tray which he continues to hold in his left hand while pouring with his right. It extends even beyond the direct hand-to-hand situation. For example, at the dining-room table, when the butler brings a glass of milk, even though it will not be handed to the guest but set directly on the table, it must be brought on a tray.

Third, the mistress of the house should never be the first to be served unless she is alone with her husband and children. (The procedure to be followed at the dining-room table is discussed below, beginning on this page, "Essential Rules of Dining-Room Service.") Anything served in one's house, whether in the living room or anywhere else, should be offered first to the oldest or most important woman guest. This rule applies also when no women are present; everything should be offered first to the man at the host's right, on the assumption that he is the most important guest.

Fourth, with very few exceptions, notably soup, no food should be brought in from the kitchen on the plate from which it is to be eaten; no portions, that is, should be served in the kitchen. Whether the food is to be served at the dining-room table or elsewhere, there should be a bowl, serving dish, or platter, from which each may help himself. Exceptions other than soup are such shellfish as oysters or clams on the half shell; sea-food cocktails, which are to be eaten at the beginning of the meal; melon, grapefruit, papaya, or any other such fruit served in large sections either at the beginning of the meal or as dessert. (Note that, when such fruit is cut up and served as a dessert, it should not be portioned.) Food which is cooked in individual dishes, such as eggs cocotte, shirred eggs, and French custards (or "pots de crème") are served from a large flat platter when they are cold; when they are hot, unless they are served on little dishes or ramekins which have a handle, for practical reasons each dish is usually brought to the table on each person's plate, already served. (See also "Serving Water" and "Wine and Other Drinks," on page 300.)

Fifth, second helpings of any food, except soup and those dishes which are "portioned" before serving (as noted immediately above), may be offered at any meal. At all informal and semiformal meals, second helpings are so customary as to be almost mandatory; at the most formal dinners, when there is a long menu of six or seven courses, the platters of food are usually offered only once. At cocktail parties and afternoon receptions, food may be served any number of times.

Last, without exception, no butler or maid should ever remove used plates by the "stacking" system: one on top of the other, with silver pushed off to one side or piled on the top plate. At teatime, and after an informal dinner when coffee has been served to the women in the living room, saucers may be stacked in order to facilitate removal, but the cups never should be. The rule should always be observed, but particularly at the dining-room table. It does not, however, apply to a host or hostess who is entertaining without a maid. At informal meals, at teatime, and at buffet meals, clean plates may always be brought in a stack if the guests are to help themselves, or if the hostess is to serve.

ESSENTIAL RULES OF DINING-ROOM SERVICE

The service of luncheon and dinner are exactly alike and, in spite of all the variations that modern life has made necessary and modern usage has made permissible, it is a very definite and traditional one.

Here follow the rules that govern all seated meals at the dining-room table. The specific application of these rules to semiformal and informal entertaining will be found below on pages 280 to 287. Formal entertaining is described in a separate chapter beginning on page 477, and a definition of that makeshift phrase "semiformal" is given on page 239.

The first rule of all serving at the dining-room table is that all food is offered to each guest at his left hand at a conveniently low level. The platter or serving dish should rest on a folded napkin on the flat of the butler's left hand; he should never grasp any serving dish by the rim. Ideally, the butler's right arm is close to his side, or slightly behind his back; but, in practice, in informal service he often carries a dish in each hand to expedite the service. Both are correct, but the first is used for all formal entertaining. A large serving spoon and fork should be on each serving dish, face down, with their handles toward the guest.

A WAITRESS SERVING AT TABLE

This shows where the waitress should stand, and the conveniently low level at which all serving dishes should be held.

The mistress of the house is never served first at table unless she is alone with her husband and children, or with women members of the family who are younger than she. At table the classic order of service is as follows: the woman at the right of the host, the host, the woman at his left, and so on clockwise around the table. Less customary, but also good usage, is the system of serving counter-clockwise, always beginning at the host's right. According to a very old-fashioned custom, the service should alternate—one course clockwise around the table, the next counterclockwise, etc.—so that the same man is not always the last to be served, but this is rarely observed except at formal dinners. At dinners of twelve or more people, when two or more services are needed (i.e. two complete sets of serving platters and dishes), the system is elaborated as follows: At a dinner of twelve to sixteen people, one service starts with the woman at the host's right, the other with the woman just beyond the hostess's right, each going clockwise around the table. When there are three services, for eighteen or more people, one service starts with the woman at the right of the host and is offered to the next six or seven to her left. The next service starts where this one leaves off and so on around the table. There are only three principles that must be observed whenever more than one service is necessary:

First, the serving should be synchronized so that each platter is offered at one end of the table at the same time that its twin is offered at the other end.

Next, the hostess should never be the first to serve herself from a platter.

Last, platters of food should be offered first to women, and it is an unbreakable rule that the woman at the right of the host should always be offered an untouched dish; but at times it will be found more convenient to begin one of the other services with a man. For example, when there are fourteen people, the man at the hostess's right will be the first to be served at that end of the table; when there are twenty, one service will begin with the man at the hostess's left.

According to the American rules of service, no place at table—that is, the space directly in front of each guest—should ever be empty, except for that short moment immediately before dessert is served, while the pepper, salt, crumbs (and at luncheon, butter plates too) are being removed. English rules sometimes ignore place plates, so this rule does not apply to those who follow the English custom until the soup plate has been brought. When the guests come into the dining room, at each place there should be a place plate; with very elaborate service, this place plate is removed and replaced by another one, hot or cold, depending on the course, as soon as all the guests are seated; at simpler meals, a cold first course is eaten on the place plate, or the soup plate is set on it. Used plates are taken away from the left of the guest by the left hand of the butler, and replaced immediately by a fresh plate which he holds in his right hand.

There is a further rule—an old one—which must be discussed at this point although it is followed only at the most elaborate dinners by the most protocol-conscious hostesses: A plate with food on it, e.g. soup, must never be set in front of a guest as a replacement for one which has had food on it (e.g. oysters). In other words, according to the most strict, old-fashioned system of serving, the oyster plate should be taken up and a clean plate should replace it at once. Then, when all the places have been so cleared, the soup may be brought and set on the clean plate in front of each guest. This system should still be followed if one is entertaining officially or very elaborately, but it would be foolish to pretend that it is observed—or even known—in the great majority of well-run American households.

No soup plate should ever be set directly on the mat or tablecloth unless one is following the English custom of omitting a place plate. In this case, the soup plate may be set directly on the cloth or mat. The most strict American service demands that a soup plate with a larger plate underneath it be set down together to replace the place plate; with less elaborate service, the soup plate is set on the place plate as soon as the guest puts his napkin on his lap. Similarly, at luncheon, a soup cup and saucer should be set on the place plate, or brought on another larger plate, if the place plate is to be taken away. The only exceptions to this rule would be rare or exotic china soup plates, which cannot be happily combined with any other: some Chinese porcelain, for example, or high, thick Lowestoft "hot-water plates"; with these, an underplate could be omitted. This rule applies also to plates of oysters or clams on the half shell, although the practical element of melting ice would make an underplate necessary, quite apart from any rule.

A very fine point of service, rarely observed, is that the soup plate may be removed first, by itself, without the underplate. Celery and olives are then served and subsequently the underplate is taken away and replaced by the plate for the next course. Usually, of course, if celery and olives are served, they are served with the soup, not after it.

The butler or first waitress, or whoever is head of the pantry department, always serves the more important dishes such as the meat, salad, or desserts. The footman or second waitress follows after him, with auxiliary dishes such as the sauce or vegetables. The only exception to this is in very big houses, at very big dinners, when the butler acts only as general of his staff; he directs, but serves nothing except the wine, and sometimes not even that.

Plates are removed in the order of service, when all the guests have finished eating. The proper system is as follows: The butler brings the fresh plate in his right hand, removes the used plate from the guest's left side, and sets the new plate down immediately and still from the left side. See also page 285, where there is a discussion of when to remove the plates.

This is the standard system but, for informal entertaining, if it is necessary to expedite the service, the butler may take up a second used plate on the first trip back to the serving table or pantry, and bring two fresh plates on the next trip. This is, however, an informal system and a slight transgression of the rules, because it leaves a guest's place empty for a short while. (See pages 285 and 286, "Semiformal Luncheons and Dinners" for a further discussion of this.)

When two plates—a meat plate and a butter plate, for example—are removed at the same time, the smaller is taken up first, with the left hand, and then transferred to the right hand. In this way, the left hand is free to take up the meat plate.

Crumbs may be removed either with a folded napkin or, if there is a tablecloth, with a special scoop. Standing to the left of the guest, the butler brushes them off onto a small tray held just below the table edge. At dinners, where there are no butter plates, large pieces of the roll, or sometimes the whole little roll, are often left on the table. These may be removed first, before the crumbs are taken away, by the footman or second waitress with a fork. Place cards are scooped or brushed into the plate with the crumbs. Place card holders are neither fashionable nor necessary, but if they are used they are removed with the saltcellars.

Everything except the glasses, the table decorations including ashtrays and, unless there is a tablecloth, the place mats, should be taken off the table before the dessert is served. This does not, of course, apply to decanters of wine, which at an informal dinner may stay on the table throughout the meal; but, even at informal dinners, it does include the pepper and salt, the breadbasket, and unused knives and forks, and anything else of that kind. Sherry glasses are often, according to strict English practice, taken away also at this point.

There are two ways of bringing the finger bowl to the table, both perfectly correct, one more formal than the other. The simpler system is as follows: After the table has been cleared, the dessert plate is brought in with the finger bowl on it, and with a small lace or linen doily under the finger bowl. Sometimes, the finger bowl has a small matching plate of its own, which can be used instead of a doily. But a paper doily must never be used; better none than one of paper, and many think none is best of all. On the dessert plate, also, are the dessert spoon and fork, the spoon to the right of the finger bowl and the fork to the left. According to the more formal system, each dessert plate is brought with only the fork and spoon on it; the finger bowl is brought on a second plate, after the dessert plates have been taken away. If fruit is to be served, this second system is much more practical, because the fruit knife and fork can be put on each side of the finger bowl. As a rule, of course, for informal entertaining, no finger bowls are used. The dessert plate is brought with the fork and spoon on it, and nothing follows.

There are two ways of arranging the service of candy at the end of a meal. The first and less formal, which is followed in the great majority of American households, is to have a butler or waitress take from the middle of the dining-room table the candy dishes that have served as decoration throughout the meal. The candy is served in the usual way and replaced on the dining-room table. The second system is to have separate candy dishes which are brought from the pantry or serving table and offered to each guest. This system is followed at formal dinners and at elaborate semiformal dinners, whether or not candy dishes are part of the table decorations.

NECESSARY NUMBER FOR WAITING ON TABLE

Before we consider the application of these rules to the various kinds of service, it might be useful to discuss the ratio of household staff to the number of those at the dining-room table. Happily, the days have passed when for every dinner a flock of extra footmen was hired, not only for the ostensible purpose of waiting on table, but also to impress the guests with the size of the establishment. Under present standards, except for the very rare rigidly formal dinner, it is entirely a question of how many guests there are, how many courses there are, and how many are needed to make the service go quickly and smoothly. (The formal dinner is described in detail on pages 478 to 490.) It is axiomatic that the better the service, the less the guests will notice it. If plates are quickly removed and if there is no waiting between courses, guests will probably be unaware of the fact; if there are long waits, they will be conscious of them.

The rule of thumb prescribes for semiformal entertaining one footman or waitress for each six or at most eight people at the table; at dinners of more than ten, one service (i.e., one complete set of serving dishes) for each eight guests. These very rough estimates are open to a great many variations; for example, one service and two waitresses would be ideal for a semiformal dinner party of ten people; two waitresses and two services, for fourteen; two services and perhaps a butler and two waitresses for sixteen. Two services, or perhaps three, and three or four waitresses could do very well for eighteen or twenty people.

INFORMAL LUNCHEONS AND DINNERS

The question of what makes a meal formal or informal is fully discussed on page 237 in the beginning of this section. The differences that arise from such subtleties as table decorations or the menu have nothing to do with serving, which is our immediate concern. For example, there might be a most informal luncheon with an arrangement of courses quite different from the formal pattern, and still, if there were no more than eight people, with two waitresses, the service might be exactly like that of the most elaborate dinner. The primary point is that informal service means service that is not taken care of entirely by the staff, as it is at a semiformal meal. For the purposes of this section, therefore, we will describe the service of informal meals from the point of view of a shortage in the household staff, in order to show the widest permissible deviations from the traditional pattern.

As we have said at the beginning of this chapter, the ideal service is quick, silent, and unobtrusive, but it is obvious that, with a shortage of domestic help, service can no longer be ideal. There often comes a moment, which varies with the training and speed of each maid, when the delays are noticeably uncomfortable. Certain motions must be eliminated—the least important, naturally, first. This is a progressive list of suggestions.

First, finger bowls may be brought on the dessert plate, not on a separate plate; or, which is much more usual, they may be omitted entirely.

Next, the waitress may carry two serving dishes at once.

Third, the plates may be removed as described in paragraph 2 on page 279.

Next, the wine may be set on the table and passed from hand to hand; one bottle at each end if there are nine or ten people, a single bottle for five or six. The men often fill the women's glasses.

Fifth, bread, as well as wine, may be set on the table and passed from one person to another.

Last, the first course may be set at each place on the table before the family comes into the dining room. The difficulty here, of course, is that most food should not be portioned or served in the kitchen. This is discussed under the general rules that govern all serving at the dining-room table (paragraph 3, page 276) where exceptions to the rule are also given. Any one of the exceptions could be useful here and besides, at such an informal meal as this, covered bowls of soup are both acceptable and practical.

These suggestions, which may, of course, be used for dinner as well as luncheon, will have done away with at least half a dozen trips around the table. If the waitress still cannot manage to make the service quick enough, service can be whittled down still further. The one maid can limit her activities to the following: bringing the platters of food and a stack of clean plates directly to the hostess, who serves from her place at table; removing used plates; and clearing the table of crumbs, salt, pepper, and bread before the dessert. This method is particularly useful when one person is responsible for the cooking as well as the serving. A play-by-play description of such a meal comes next.

If anything more must be given up, the meal should be turned into a buffet meal. If the waitress is to appear at all, she must remove the plates and do it in the proper way. She should never resort to such timesavers as stacking the plates or removing them from the right, or leaving the crumbs on the table. If for any reason one prefers a seated meal to a buffet, and such service as this cannot be arranged for, it is better for the hostess to handle all the serving herself. The basic outline suggested on page 445, "Entertaining Without a Maid," could be used in this case, with the difference, of course, that the hostess need not do the cooking.

With One Maid

When there is one maid, and only one, it is not usually practical to follow the standard service described on pages 276 to 280. A very sensible pattern has been evolved whereby the hostess serves from casseroles or platters set before her, and the maid does nothing more than bring the food and take the used plates away. As though to corroborate the saying that it is the details that are really important, this service is completely different from the others in all its major aspects, and resembles the usual routine only in the minor ones. The customs and usage of this form are not at all new, but in the last five or six years in the United States they have assumed a quite definite pattern. Given the right attitude on the part of the hostess, given the right food, china, and general surroundings, it often has more charm than the stiffer, more formal one; at its best, it has a flavor of warm hospitality, a particularly pleasant atmosphere of old-fashioned bounteousness.

There are, of course, a few minor drawbacks to offset the many advantages of this form of entertaining. Without practice, it is not easy to manage for more than six or eight people; it is not very quick, and it requires a certain amount of co-operation from everyone at the table. Let us imagine, for example, a two-course luncheon for six people. A well-trained maid can very often manage to cook and serve for six, but well-trained maids are not always easy to find, and even the best do not always enjoy the dual role of cook-waitress.

At a luncheon such as this, there is usually no place plate, but only a napkin, at each place. The casseroles or platters of food are brought in either before or after the family have come in, and set on the table in front of the hostess, just off the upper edge of her place mat. Then, the stack of heated plates is brought and set at the hostess' place. If there were three courses, with a first course of melon or soup, it would be set at each place before the meal was announced, unless the hostess particularly wanted to serve the soup herself from a tureen. Wine and bread are on the table and are passed from one to another, the bread going to the right, the wine for the sake of convenience to the left.

After the hostess has filled the plates, they are

THE HOSTESS' PLACE, WHEN SHE IS TO SERVE

Across the top of this diagram are the wine decanter and the oval breadbasket, but these positions must not be considered fixed—if there is a host, as well as a hostess, these can be more conveniently put at his end of the table. Below them are the serving fork and spoon, and the casserole or platter for the main course. Dessert fork and spoon, as suggested on page 258, are above the stack of plates for the main course. The butter plate and knife and the wineglass are optional.

passed from one to another and, regardless of age or sex, the woman farthest from the hostess is usually served first. The best way is to start the first plate down the left side of the table, so that the woman at the host's right will receive it; the host gets the second plate, the woman at his left the third, and so on. Second helpings are managed the same way: The plates go up to the hostess and back again, without regard to any order other than speed in eating.

As soon as the first course has been eaten, the hostess rings. She should have an electric buzzer attached to the table, or a little handbell set on the table. She should never have to get up to ring, and calling is disturbing. The maid removes the plates from the left in the usual way but, instead of taking one at a time, she takes two on each trip to the serving table or pantry. This is done also when there are three courses not only because the luncheon is informal but also because, under this system, the rule against leaving a place empty does not hold. As soon

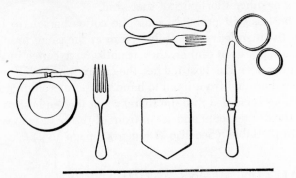

as the plates and the casserole or platters have been removed, the maid takes away the pepper, salt, breadbasket, and crumbs. The dessert and then the dessert plates are brought and the hostess serves as before. Finger bowls are omitted entirely and, when dessert is finished, everyone goes into the living room for coffee. Or, if she wants to have coffee at the table, the hostess rings again when the

A GUEST'S PLACE, WHEN THE HOSTESS SERVES

At such an informal meal, no place plates are necessary, and the napkin lies directly on the table as shown here. There are only two courses and, to simplify further, at dinner the butter plate and knife may always be left off.

guests have eaten their dessert; the platters but not necessarily the dessert plates are removed, and the coffeepot is brought on a tray, with empty cups, sugar, and cream. This is set down before the hostess, who pours each cup after inquiring as to the guests' preferences in the matter of sugar and cream.

This way of entertaining may be used either for luncheon or for dinner, either for two courses or for three. Two courses are naturally easier; and, if the maid feels the slightest strain, it is better to have two courses smoothly served than three with a struggle. (Entertaining without a maid is described on page 445, in the chapter "Entertaining.")

With One Waitress for Eight

Having considered the one-maid meal, it might be useful to describe a luncheon or dinner for eight people, with one person to wait on table and another in the kitchen. Quick service is impossible, even though the meal is kept to three courses. As we have said, the first course may be on the table before the family and their guests come in to the dining room; but if it is served, it should be according to the usual rules of dining-room service. Wine and bread may also be on the table and, as described above, the wine bottles, or decanters, and the breadbasket may be passed around the table. When possible, the waitress carries two serving dishes at once; at the meat course, for example, she may be able to manage no more than the meat platter on the first round, but on the second round, she carries a vegetable dish in each hand. If the meat is a roast, the potatoes are put on the meat platter and the waitress makes a second round with the green vegetables in one hand, and sauce or jelly in the other. It is good usage to present matching vegetable dishes or two sauces, or sauce and jelly, together on a small tray; but if a vegetable and a sauce for the meat are served simultaneously, they should be served in separate hands, not on the same tray. Another very good way of quickening the service is to have the meat and both the vegetables served on the same platter, in the French fashion. See page 310 for suggestions concerning the food which is best adapted to this. The six service-saving suggestions on page 280 may all be followed for a meal of this kind, but as suggested there, the maid should never resort to plate stacking or other short cuts of that kind.

After such a meal, the hostess will probably pour the coffee herself in the living room. At a luncheon, the men leave the dining room at the same time as the women; but when there are guests at dinner, they usually have coffee in the dining room. (See pages 293 to 295.) The host fetches the cigars for himself and his guests, and the box is passed around from hand to hand. If there are liqueurs, one tray with bottles and glasses is carried into the living room for the hostess to serve; another is brought to the dining room and set in front of the host, who will serve the men from his seat at the table. (See also "Liqueurs," page 303.)

SEMIFORMAL LUNCHEONS AND DINNERS

The essential point of the service of a semiformal meal is that convenience and practicality are all-important. The only considerations are that the service should not be too slow, and that those at the table should not concern themselves with it in any way. This marks the difference between semiformal service and formal service, for which the number of footmen is prescribed; and the difference between semiformal and informal entertaining, when guests and hosts may co-operate to some extent in the service. To show exactly how the rules of service are applied to semiformal entertaining, we shall give a step-by-step description of a dinner party for ten people. It can equally well, of course, be used as a pattern for a semiformal luncheon. A diagram showing the progression of the service of such a dinner is on pages 286 and 287, following.

With Two Waitresses for Ten

For such a dinner party, there will probably be one service and two maids, or a butler and a waitress. The table is set as shown in the diagram on page 259 if for dinner, or on page 250 if for luncheon. The dinner menu has four courses: soup, meat, salad, and dessert. When the guests come into the dining room, the headwaitress or the butler is standing behind the hostess's chair, the second waitress at the other end of the room, ready to push in the chair of the woman who will sit at the host's right. As each woman sits down, the waitress pushes in her chair or, if the waitress is busy at the other side of the table, the woman's chair will be pushed in by one of the men who is sitting next to her.

As soon as the guests are all seated, the waitresses go quickly into the pantry to fetch the soup. Since this is a semiformal—not a formal—dinner, the soup plates will probably be set directly on the place plate, although at an elaborate semiformal dinner the formal pattern might be followed. The service begins with the woman at the host's right and proceeds clockwise around the table. If the waitresses are well trained, there is no reason why they should not bring a plate of soup in each hand. This system greatly expedites the service; there is nothing against it except the danger of spilling the soup, although some of the most particular hostesses do not approve. The headwaitress then pours the wine, usually sherry, and the second waitress brings the toast, usually Melba toast.

One of the features of ideally good service is that there should always be a waitress in the room. If anything is needed—a whiskey and soda for one of the guests who has refused wine, for example—the hostess need only turn to the waitress and ask. If this cannot be arranged, the alternative is to have a small electric buzzer. There is one kind that is attached underneath the table edge; another, that is put under the carpet in front of the hostess's chair. Small hand-bells of silver or glass are also very practical, but they are better for informal entertaining.

There are two schools of thought on the matter of removing plates. One holds that no plate should be removed until all the guests have finished eating; the second, which is followed at all big, formal dinners, demands that each plate be taken away as soon as the guest has indicated that he has finished. The guest does this by putting his knife and fork, or spoon, across his plate as described on page 51 in the chapter "Table Manners." The first system is the most widely used in the United States and, certainly, it is the more attractive of the two because it avoids any suggestion of rushing the guests through their food. Sometimes, if one or two guests are eating a little more slowly than the others, the hostess may nod to the headwaitress to indicate that she can start taking the plates away. The slow guest will be skipped in the order of removal and his plate will be taken just before the hostess' plate which is always the last. But the service of the next course must never begin until all the guests have finished with the earlier course and have been given new plates.

The standard system for removing plates is described in paragraph 6, page 278, but there is a variation of that system which is particularly useful for semi-formal entertaining. It is less conventional and more efficient than the standard practice and is now perfectly acceptable in modern usage: The second waitress follows the first one with a large tray holding the new plates; removing the used plate with her left hand, the first waitress replaces it immediately with a new one; putting the used plate on the tray the second waitress is holding (but never "stacking" it), she takes a second plate, and so on.

To return to our sample dinner: The soup plate and place plate are removed together, and the heated plate for the meat course is set before each guest. The headwaitress comes in first, bringing the platter of meat, the second waitress following with the gravy or, if there is no gravy, with the vegetables. The vegetables may be served in any one of four different ways. If the potatoes are on the meat platter, as they often are, for example, with roast beef or roast lamb, the second waitress will bring only the green vegetable in a serving dish on her left hand. The second system is that the two vegetables are served in matching vegetable dishes on a small tray which the waitress holds on her left hand. The third way is for the waitress to hold a vegetable dish on each hand, offering first the potatoes in her left hand, then the other vegetable in her right hand. This last suggestion is more practical if the table is crowded, with one guest sitting very near the next. The final alternative is the least practical, although technically the best service: one trip with the potatoes only, and a second with the other vegetables.

As soon as the meat and vegetables have been served, the headwaitress pours the wine, usually a red or white wine. But, as we said on page 260, if champagne is to be served at all, in most American houses it is served from now on throughout the meal. The second waitress follows with rolls or buttered toast.

When the guests have finished, the meat plates are taken away, salad plates are brought, and the salad is served exactly as described above. At most semi-formal dinners today, cigarettes and ashtrays are set on the table, so that no service of cigarettes is necessary. If not, cigarettes are often offered to each guest as soon as his meat plate is removed and before the salad is brought (see page 295 in this section). Again, as in the case of the meat course, the first waitress carries the first and most important of the dishes: the salad, if salad and cheese are to be served; the cold meat, if meat and salad are to be served. In the following diagram there is a fork only for salad, because, although a salad knife is traditional, modern custom often omits it. But, if cold meat were served, a knife would be needed.

There is a change in the routine of serving at the end of the salad course, or at the end of any course that immediately precedes the dessert. The salad plates are removed, and the place in front of the guest is left empty until salt and pepper, unused silver, crumbs—everything but the glasses and table decorations—have been taken away. The dessert plates are then brought, each with its dessert spoon and fork and—since this is a semiformal dinner—each with its finger bowl and doily. The headwaitress brings the dessert, the second waitress any subsidiary dishes such as sauces, cookies, or cake.

The hostess decides when it is time to leave and shepherds the women guests out of the room. Coffee is served to them in the living room and to the men in the library or at the dining-room table. The service of coffee and cigars is discussed on pages 293 and 295 of this section; liqueurs, on page 303; after-dinner service is described on page 296.

As suggested above, this description of the service of a semiformal dinner may, with a few changes, be adapted to the service of luncheon. To begin with, there is a change in the menu. Although a four-course luncheon is possible, three courses are more usual: an entrée, or soup in cups; main course; and dessert.

The changes in the service are that the butter plates, which are always used at luncheon, are taken away with those of the main course; and coffee is served to the men and women together, in the living room. The differences in the setting reflect these changes. To the diagram below, for example, butter plates should be added, and the soup spoons should be omitted. Teaspoons may be brought on the saucer, with the soup cups. If an entrée is to be served, a small fork is set outside the dinner fork and a small knife outside the dinner knife; the salad fork, of course, is removed.

A PLACE SET FOR A FOUR-COURSE DINNER

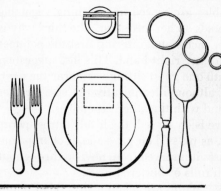

This place is set for a four-course dinner consisting of soup, meat, salad, and dessert. (See also the diagram on page 259, where an alternative arrangement of the wine-glasses is shown.) Starting at the left, at the table's edge, are the meat fork, the salad fork, and the place plate, with the napkin and the place card (represented by the dotted lines); then, the meat knife and soup spoon. Above the plate are two cigarettes on an ash tray with a paper packet of matches next to them. To the right are the glasses for water, wine and sherry.

THE GUEST IS SERVED SOUP

*THE GUEST IS ABOUT TO BE
SERVED MEAT*

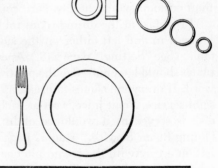

*THE GUEST IS ABOUT TO BE
SERVED SALAD*

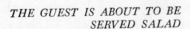

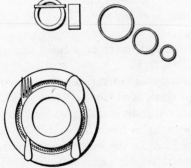

*THE GUEST'S DESSERT PLATE IS
PUT BEFORE HIM*

*The finger bowl, with a doily under-
neath it and the dessert fork and spoon
beside it, has just been brought in on the
dessert plate. No fruit is to be served.*

287

FORMAL LUNCHEONS AND DINNERS

See the chapter "Formal Entertaining," which begins on page 477.

BREAKFAST

The service of breakfast is always informal, with the exception, of course, of wedding breakfasts. A butler wears his morning clothes, maids their morning uniforms, whether breakfast is to be served in the dining room or to the family in their rooms.

Breakfast in Bed

After knocking, the waitress or lady's maid brings in the breakfast tray with the front of the tray away from her body so that the tray can be set down directly without being twisted. Ideally, the maid should then ask, "Will Madam ring when she is finished, or should I come back in about twenty minutes?" In practice, maids are often too busy for this and the tray is left until the room is made up. Few men like breakfast in bed, but those who do are served by the footman, if there is one, the butler or waitress if not.

Breakfast in the Dining Room

The descriptions of service which follow set forth some of the accepted customs of serving breakfast, presupposing a number of people and a staff to wait on them. Households which have no staff, or households where there are several children, will devise their own patterns; but these informal ways are personal rather than customary and here we are concerned only with customs.

Breakfast at the dining-room table should not be a served meal. The food is brought in and left either on the sideboard, on burners, or on the dining-room table. (See "Setting," page 248.) Apart from this, and from the fact that the used plates should be removed to the pantry, there is no service in the usual sense of the word. If everyone comes to breakfast at the same time, there might be a sort of semi-service. Fruit juice is set at each place, before the guests come in, the main dish is served as it would be at luncheon or dinner (see "Essential Rules of Dining-Room Service," rule 1, page 277), the pots of coffee and hot milk are left on a tray with the cream pitcher and sugar bowl, either on the dining-room table or on a sideboard. Toast is left in a rack over a burner or in a covered dish, either on the table or on a sideboard. Like waffles or anything else, according to rule, toast should not be made at the dining-room table. The only other service that is permissible at breakfast is to have the butler or waitress serve each guest with coffee from a tray, but breakfast should never be a fully served meal, as luncheon or dinner is.

If breakfast is to be served in the dining room at varying hours, to guests who may not want to come down at a fixed time, food can be left on a sideboard as discussed above or each guest can be served individually. A small tray with the coffee, hot milk, sugar and cream is brought in fresh for each one; and a little covered dish of toast is set down before him. In the most formal household, the butler would inquire as to how each guest liked his eggs cooked and, with the exception of boiled eggs, would serve them on a small platter from which each guest would help himself. In less elaborately run houses, the eggs are often brought in on the plates from which they are to be eaten, and set down before the guest.

Pseudo Breakfasts and Wedding Breakfasts

Pseudo breakfasts can be completely served. When they are, like wedding breakfasts, they follow the rules for served meals, given on pages 276 to 279. Otherwise, the service is like that of buffet meals. (See pages 297 to 299.)

LUNCHEON

See "Informal Luncheons and Dinners," page 280, or "Semiformal Luncheons and Dinners," page 284; and the chapter, "Formal Entertaining," page 477.

TEA

The serving of afternoon tea is based on one major premise: The mistress of the house must pour the tea herself. Only in the movies are overdressed butlers seen consistently and quite mistakenly serving the tea. Whether one follows the simple system of having tea made in the kitchen and brought in in the pot, or the more elaborate routine of kettle and tea caddy, it must be the hostess who gets the tea from the pot into the cup. Only at very large afternoon receptions should this rule be broken. If about sixty or seventy people are coming, it will obviously be too difficult for her to welcome them all and pour the tea as well; in this case, women friends or relatives often take her place at the tea table. But only on very rare occasions, such as an afternoon wedding reception when the hostess is expected to stand in a receiving line, should this task be performed by a member of the staff.

Afternoon Tea

The most usual way of serving tea is at home in the afternoon with a relatively small number of people. The standard system, which can easily be handled by one maid is as follows: The waitress or butler brings the tea table, sets it up in front of the hostess, and covers it with a tea cloth which she carries on her arm. Then she brings the tea tray, set with cups, teapot, etc. as described on page 251. The kettle is not usually brought at this time as it would make the tray too heavy but it is brought on the third trip, with the plates of food. The waitress lights the burner under the kettle, leaves the room, and does not come back until she is rung for, or until tea is over.

The tea is taken away in the same progressive stages but in reverse order. The waitress first gathers up the teacups and the little plates; if the rule against stacking is strictly followed, this may mean that several trips will have to be made, but modern usage sanctions a certain latitude in this respect. The saucers, but not the teacups or tea plates, can be stacked one on top of the other, provided that it is done unobtrusively and quietly. After the teacups have been gathered up, the food is then taken away. For convenience, plates of cakes or sandwiches can be carried out on the tea tray, but if possible all the food should be removed before the tea tray leaves the room. Only the tea table and cloth should remain to be taken after the tea tray is gone.

When there are two or three to serve the tea, the steps are exactly the same: On the first trip, the butler, carrying the tea tray, follows the footman or waitress who carries the tea table and cloth; on the second trip, the butler brings the kettle, followed by the footman who carries the food. Their roles, too, end at this point, until it is time for the tea to be taken away.

Deviations from this system are sometimes necessary under certain circumstances. For example, when the hostess is entertaining very much older women, for whom it would be more comfortable to be able to sit down uninterruptedly, or when it would be difficult for the hostess herself to wait on the guests, she can pour the tea and give it to the butler or waitress who stands waiting by the tea table. In this way the cups, and after them the food, can all be served. An even wider deviation is permissible when, for example, the hostess and her guests are playing bridge and when there is not time for her to leave the bridge table. In this case, the tea tray is brought in the usual way; the waitress pours each cup of tea and sets it down with a little plate on a small table beside each guest, or between each two guests. The waitress then serves the food from the left, as she would if the guests were seated at the dining-room table. Either of these suggestions is an exception, however, and the standard system should be followed as a matter of rule.

Tea in the dining room needs no service of any kind. The tea tray, which is set exactly as for tea in the living room, is put on the table before the guests come in and, unless something is needed during teatime, the maid need never appear. As soon as tea is over, everyone goes back to the living room and the tea-things are cleared whenever convenient.

AFTERNOON RECEPTIONS

At a very large afternoon reception, tea is often served at the dining-room table rather than in the living room. Suggestions for the technical details of setting the dining-room table will be found on page 254.

Before the guests come into the dining room, the tea tray should be set on the table with the kettle in place, the water boiling, the plates of food on the table, and a dining-room armchair drawn up to the tea tray. If it is impossible for the hostess to take the time to pour tea herself, as it probably will be at a large reception, one of her friends or some woman member of the family can take her place. As a rule, those who want tea will come up to the person sitting in front of the tea tray and ask for it, but it is perfectly correct for the butler to ask any of the guests if they would like tea, and to fetch it for them. The butler may also offer plates of food, although the most usual procedure is for the guests to help themselves from the plates on the table. In any case, whether the guests help themselves or not, the butler or waitress should be there to remove used cups and plates as soon as they are set down, to bring fresh ones, and to keep the kettle and cream jug filled.

If there are to be a hundred or more guests, as at a wedding reception or a political meeting, the tea is poured and served by the butler and footman or waitress. This is not always true in the South, where the fine points of hospitality are a matter of great pride, but it has become very much the custom in the North and East. The best way to arrange the service for so many guests is to have two services of tea, or perhaps one of tea and one of coffee. One is set at each end of the table, and the butler and footman or waitress stand beside each one to do the serving. Plates and cups should be removed as soon as they are used; the food may be passed around or left on the table so that each guest can help himself.

COCKTAILS

No matter what the time of day, whether it is before luncheon, in the late afternoon, or before dinner, there are only four ways of serving cocktails. Each is as correct as the other; the one to choose is the one which best accords with the rest of the service.

Serving Cocktails before Meals

The most informal kind of cocktail service is to have a big tray, with all the necessary ingredients on it, brought into the living room before the guests arrive. This tray is left either on a side table or on a special folding table which has been set up for the purpose. And as far as service is concerned, if there is no cocktail food other than a dish of nuts or crackers, there is nothing more to be done. The host mixes the ingredients in the shaker, adds the ice, shakes the cocktails, pours them, and hands one to each guest. He then offers the cocktail food, and the tray is left until the guests have left the room. (See also "Entertaining Without a Maid," page 445.) This system of service is often used whether or not there is a maid. But when there is a maid, she often brings the cocktail food after the guests have arrived. After offering it to each guest, she sets it down on the table with the cocktail tray. If any of the cocktail food is hot, this is almost a necessity.

Another, slightly more formal, way of serving cocktails, is to have them mixed in the kitchen and brought into the living room in the shaker, on a tray with the requisite number of empty glasses. The butler or waitress asks each guest if he wants a cocktail, and pours it. The guest then takes the glass from the tray, and the cocktail shaker is left on the tray in the living room, so that the host can refill the glasses. Cocktail food is brought and served by the butler or waitress in the same way and then it, too, is left so that guests can help themselves.

At very big dinner parties, where two kinds of cocktails are often served, more or less the same system is followed. The most elaborate service is as follows: The butler comes first with a small tray, holding one of the two cocktail shakers, the footman or waitress follows with a tray of glasses, the other shaker, and perhaps a sherry decanter. The glasses should all be empty, except those for tomato juice cocktails, which are already poured. The butler asks each guest what he wants— "Martini, Manhattan, or sherry, Sir?"—and, taking the proper glass, pours the drink for each guest, and offers it to him on the small tray. All this is obviously a time-consuming system and therefore at very big dinners, cocktails are often poured in the pantry. The tray of filled cocktail glasses is then brought into the living room by the butler.

In either case, the cocktail food is offered to each guest as soon as he has been offered a cocktail, and the cocktail tray and the food are taken back to the pantry, where the shakers are freshly filled and the platters of food are rearranged. After an interval of five or ten minutes the butler brings the cocktail shaker back on a small tray to refill the glasses, the footman or waitress again following with the food. If two kinds of cocktails have been served, it will of course be necessary for the butler to bring two cocktail shakers on the tray. The glasses are always left to be collected until the guests have left the living room.

Serving Cocktails in the Late Afternoon

In the late afternoon, cocktails are usually served in the first two and more informal ways described above. The cocktails may be mixed in the pantry or in the living room, but, in any case, the platters of food are left in the living room after the waitress has served them once. The system which is often used before a formal dinner, whereby the food is always taken back to the pantry as soon as it has been served, is rarely followed in the late afternoon.

Cocktail Parties

Serving at cocktail parties, when there are a great many people, has one major pitfall that must be avoided: the barroom or hotel touch of having a white-coated waiter who looks like a barman, cornered behind a drink-loaded table that is all too obviously a trestle table covered with a cloth. The most attractive cocktail parties, and those which are best served, are those that depart the most widely from this. If there are only a few people, the host can mix and serve the cocktails as described above. The only difference is that there will be more people, more cocktails, more cocktail food. At a very small, formal cocktail party the cocktails are mixed in the pantry and brought in with the cocktail food as they are before a formal dinner. The only difference here is that the butler or waitress will have to serve them repeatedly instead of only once or twice. It will be necessary, also, of course, to collect used glasses as soon as they are set down. But otherwise there need be no changes.

At informal cocktail parties or when there are too many guests, as there almost invariably are, to make either of these systems feasible, the cocktail food can be set out on a big table, usually the dining-room table. Whiskey and soda, ice and glasses, are on another table or the sideboard, together with trays holding glasses of tomato juice, a decanter of sherry and sherry glasses. The cocktails, which cannot be left standing in the shaker because they become warm or watery, are served by the butler as they are before a formal dinner.

At the biggest cocktail parties, however, none of these ways of serving cocktails may be efficient enough to provide quick and continuous service. A satisfactory way is to have big trays of poured cocktails brought in from the kitchen. These can be set down on a table from which the guests will help themselves, on the assumption that at such a big cocktail party they will not be left long enough to get warm. If two kinds of cocktails are to be served, both should be on the tray at the same time: Martinis, for example, on one side, Bacardis on the other. The butler can go later among the guests with a small tray and two cocktail shakers, offering to refill any glasses that may be empty, while the footman brings in fresh trays of cocktails for later arrivals. The guests will help themselves to whiskey and soda, tomato juice, and sherry from the sideboard.

Any of these systems is attractive and obviates as much as possible the danger of the barroom touch. This touch will, however, quickly be introduced into any one of them by an overemphasis on the number and variety of drinks. Two kinds of cocktails, besides whiskey and sherry, are suggested not only because they make the problem of serving easier but also because a great variety of assorted drinks does not belong in a private house. At the very biggest cocktail parties there might be three kinds, but there should never be more.

Another detail that can suggest the barroom is the way the servants are dressed. Ideally, they should be dressed in the standard afternoon clothes (described on pages 252 to 254) whether one has a single waitress or three waiters hired from the caterer. But if this is difficult, as it sometimes is with waiters, they may wear white coats with colored collars and braid, such as those worn by stewards in men's clubs. Waitresses, whom one can usually find much more easily than waiters, often have their own plain black afternoon uniforms which are almost always perfectly all right.

It might also be useful here to outline the number of waiters or waitresses needed for cocktail parties of different sizes. Quite apart from any question of preparing the food and arranging the table and the trays, if one plans to have the cocktails and food served as they are before a formal party, two waiters will be needed for twenty or thirty guests. If the food is left on the table, and no service is needed other than to replenish the platters as they are emptied, two could serve forty or fifty guests; and this proportion remains stable for any greater number. All these figures mean, of course, the number of waiters free to stay in the dining room or living room and wait on the guests; as we have said, they do not allow leeway for the behind-the-scenes work that must be done in the kitchen: washing the glasses, mixing the drinks, preparing the food, etc.

DINNER

See "Informal Luncheons and Dinners," page 280, or "Semiformal Luncheons and Dinners," page 284, or the chapter on "Formal Entertaining," page 477.

COFFEE

There are two ways of serving little cups of coffee after meals, and both are equally correct although not equally formal.

At the Table

The first, which is often used after informal meals in America, is to have the coffee served at the table, while all the guests are still seated. There are several ways of doing this. The most elaborate version of this informal service is as follows: The butler holds a small tray to the right of each guest, or slightly back of each guest if the chairs are close together; on this tray there is one cup, sugar and cream and a coffeepot. He asks each guest, "Coffee, Madam (or "Sir")? Sugar and cream?" and pours a cup for each guest, setting it down at the right hand. Taking another cup from the big tray of cups carried by the footman, he proceeds thus, clockwise around the table. A slight variation of this is for the butler or waitress to fill each cup as the tray is presented at the left of each guest. The guest then takes as much sugar and cream as he wants and takes his own cup from the tray. A third way, which is really contrary to the theory of good service but is accepted usage in America, is to have the cups filled with coffee in the kitchen, and to have the tray set only with the filled cups, the sugar and cream; the butler offers the tray to the left of each guest who takes his sugar and cream and sets his cup down at the right of his plate. Still another way, feasible only at small, very informal luncheons and dinners, is to have a tray with the coffeepot, cream, sugar, and empty cups set directly before the hostess; the hostess asks each guest whether or not he wants sugar and cream and the filled cups are taken around by the waitress or passed from one guest to another.

In the Living Room

After a semiformal or a formal dinner, coffee is not traditionally served at table. The French custom is that men and women have their coffee together in the living room, but the English custom of serving the women in the living room and the men in the dining room or library has become standard for all entertaining in America except the most informal. Soon after the women have left the dining room, the coffee is brought in to them. The most formal version of this system—and the one usually followed if the service has been elaborate—is that the butler or first waitress carries a small tray with the sugar, the cream, one cup, and the coffeepot. The footman or second waitress follows with a tray of empty cups. The butler goes first to the most important woman guest, saying, "Coffee, Madam?" and offering the tray. He fills the cup; the guest helps herself to sugar and cream, and takes the cup. A slight variation of this is to have the sugar and cream on the big tray with the empty cups. The butler inquires as to each guest's preference, pours the coffee, puts the cup on his small tray and offers it to the guest.

BUTLER SERVING COFFEE AFTER LUNCHEON OR DINNER

This diagram shows the formal service of coffee, after meals, in the living room.

The second way of serving coffee in the living room is managed by the waitress or butler alone. All the cups—five are usually the maximum possible—and the sugar and cream are balanced on a tray on one hand. The coffee is poured from a pot held in the other hand, and each guest helps himself to sugar and cream.

Still a third way—but, again, somewhat contrary to good service—is to have the butler bring a tray of filled cups, with the sugar and cream; each guest helps herself. Finally—and this is probably used more than any other—the complete coffee tray, with empty cups, coffeepot, sugar and cream, is brought in and set down on a low table in front of the hostess. (See diagram, page 261, in "Setting the Table," for the arrangement of the tray.) After asking each guest what she likes in the way of sugar and cream, the filled cups are passed to the women by the hostess, or each guest comes up to take her cup for herself.

Coffee for the Men

In the dining room, where the men have been left behind, coffee is served before the women have been given their coffee in the living room. The dining-room service parallels that in the living room; for example, if the more formal version has been used in the living room it should be observed in the dining room, too, the butler coming first with the tray holding an empty cup, sugar, and cream, and the coffeepot, the footman following with the extra cups. The only difference between coffee service in the dining room and in the living room is that the host rarely pours the coffee himself; even when the hostess is to serve the coffee in the living room, the maid may serve the men first. When there is no maid, coffee may be served at the table by the hostess, before the men and women separate; or, if men and women are not to be separated, it is served in the living room. If liqueurs are to be served, they are brought before the coffee cups are removed (see page 303, for suggestions concerning the service).

Coffee after Luncheon

These are the ways that coffee is usually served after dinner. At luncheon, or at the most informal dinners, where there are only one or two guests, the men often go into the living room with the women. In this case, of course, if coffee is served at the dining-room table, there is no difference in the service. If it is served in the living room, the only difference is that the host and the men guests may fetch the cups of coffee for the women, if the hostess is serving the coffee herself.

CIGARETTES AND CIGARS

Almost the only time it is necessary to serve cigarettes and cigars is at the dining-room table. This follows a standard pattern, even though it has become more and more the custom to set the table with cigarettes and ashtrays at the beginning of the meal—a new and somewhat informal custom which obviates any necessity for service. At semiformal dinners, the butler brings a tray of cigarettes at the end of the meat course. When each guest has lighted his cigarette, the butler sets an ashtray at his right. (See page 262 for details concerning the arrangement of the tray.) If there is no room on the butler's tray for ashtrays, they are brought on a small separate tray by a footman. A still more formal pattern permits the butler to offer guests cigarettes and cigars only at the end of the meal. If the dinner has followed the usual Anglo-American custom of separating men and women as soon as dinner is over, the tray is brought by the butler immediately after the fruit while the women are still at table. Sometimes only cigarettes are passed while the women are still at the table, and the cigars are brought in their boxes after the women have left the room. If the dinner has followed the strictly formal French custom—rare in this country—no cigars or cigarettes are passed at the table, the men and women have their coffee together in the living room, and the butler brings cigarettes and cigars together on the tray as soon as the coffee has been served.

The only other time cigars might be offered to the guests is when they are playing cards and do not want to leave the table. In this case, the butler brings the box of cigars on a tray, together with a cigar cutter and matches, or a small lighted candle. As soon as the guest has taken his cigar and lighted it, the butler takes the tray away unless he is told to leave it by the host. Otherwise, cigars are usually kept in humidors in the library and offered by the host to his guests. Guests are always expected to help themselves to cigarettes from the boxes which are scattered in almost every room of a modern house.

AFTER-DINNER SERVICE

After any meal, except the most informal, service very often does not end with the coffee and liqueurs. After a very formal dinner of an official or semi-official nature, there is little other service because guests are not expected to stay very long. The only service is that used ashtrays are taken away from time to time, and fresh ones are brought, and the guests are given water or fruit juice. This is done as follows: the butler or footman brings a small tray with a stack of clean ashtrays, picks up the used ashtray, puts it on his tray (without stacking), and replaces it immediately with a fresh ashtray. This is done as soon as liqueurs have been served, and repeatedly thereafter. About half an hour later, when the service of liqueurs is over and the liqueur glasses have been collected, small tumblers of water or fruit juice are brought on a large tray. The standard juices are orange or grapefruit. Some of the glasses should be filled with still water and ice, some with still water without ice, others with fruit juice, others perhaps with soda water, ice and a twist of lemon peel. After the stiffest formal dinners, there might be no service other than this.

In America, such rigidly formal entertaining is rare. After an elaborate dinner, in addition to the above service, champagne or whiskey and soda, or both, may be served. (See suggestions on page 302, "Wines Not Served at the Table," and "Mixed Drinks Not at the Table.") This service may begin very shortly after the men have rejoined the women in the living room. For example, if the men had been left in the dining room—as they usually are at American dinners—liqueurs would have been served to the women in the living room immediately after the coffee. Water would have followed about half an hour later, whether or not the men had come into the living room. Water is usually served again, just after the men have come in, or about twenty minutes after the first round, or the service of whiskey and soda or champagne can start at this moment. The first round of water glasses is usually collected also. Fifteen minutes later, the second water glasses are collected and, if champagne is being served, the butler brings a bottle to refill the glasses. As always, any guest who refuses champagne is offered whiskey or brandy and soda instead. At about eleven or half past, plates of small sandwiches may be brought, served to the guests, and left on a side table or, more formally, carried back to the pantry. (Suggestions for the sandwiches will be found on page 332, "Fashions in Food.") Champagne must be brought a second time, if it is served at all, but it is not usually offered more than three or four times, at about fifteen-minute intervals. After an interval of at least twenty minutes or half an hour, the food may be served a second time, and even a third time if the guests stay long enough. At the end of such an elaborate evening, the butler and the footman (or waitress) and the lady's maid should always be waiting to help the guests with their coats and to see them out the door.

A simpler and much more usual form of after-dinner service is as follows: Tumblers of water are brought after the liqueur glasses have been collected. As soon as these glasses have been taken away, a tray of drinks is brought and set on a table at one side of the room. Guests help themselves and there is no service other than changing ashtrays, until about eleven or shortly after, when plates of sandwiches may be brought in. The food may be served once, and left on the side table near the drinks, but often it is not served at all. It is set on the table from which the guests will help themselves. The maid may wait up to help the guests into their coats, but not necessarily.

At informal dinners, there may be no service at all once the coffee cups have been removed and the tray of drinks has been brought. If liqueurs have been served, the maid will have to take away the glasses, but liqueurs are not always part of an informal dinner. There is usually no food after a small, informal dinner, but if it is a late evening of bridge, food may be brought and left on the same table as the drink tray. (See "Suppers" in the chapter, "Fashions in Food.")

SETTING UP CARD TABLES

Card tables should be set up while the guests are at dinner and at an elaborately served dinner when there is no shortage of staff this is inevitably the procedure. If not all the guests are playing, the tables should be set up, not inconveniently near one another, in a separate room. If there is a library as well as a living room, card tables can be arranged in the library before the guests arrive. But they should not be set up in the living room before dinner, except in a very inconspicuous, out-of-the-way corner.

If tables are to be put in the living room, and if there is no way of doing this during dinner, they may be set up while the women are taking their coffee. At informal dinners, the host very often does this himself, after he and the other men have come in from the dining room.

In any case, each table should have two packs of cards, score cards, and sharp pencils. It is also a good idea to set a small, extra table between each two guests, for drinks, ashtrays, etc. Finally, if food or drink is to be served, the players may be served at their tables.

BUFFET MEALS

As we have said, buffet meals are designed to solve the problems that arise when one invites too many guests, whether it is a matter of too many guests for the available space at the dining-room table, or too many guests for the available household staff. Setting the table is fully discussed beginning on page 262. Here we are concerned only with the details of service, which fall into two categories: the absolute minimum, which is practically no service at all; and the semi-served meal, which is a recent and extremely practical innovation.

Unserved Buffet Meals

The principle of unserved buffet meals is that all the food, even the coffee, is in the dining room before the guests come in; the guests help themselves, and put their used plates on a sideboard or on an extra table in the dining room. Used plates are not attractive and every effort should be made to have them taken away to the kitchen. If there is a waitress, she should not pile one plate on top of another when she is doing this. Whatever plates have been stacked by the guests can be removed in a stack, but the waitress should do no stacking on her own.

Semi-served Buffet Meals

For a semi-served buffet when small tables are set up for the guests, many hostesses choose a first course that can be set on the tables before the guests come into the room. As soon as this course is eaten, the used plates are taken away as they would be at a seated informal dinner, while the guests help themselves to the second course from the buffet table. After the second course the plates are again removed, and this procedure is followed throughout the meal until the guests have eaten their dessert. Then the coffee tray is brought with coffee cups, sugar, and cream, and a cup is poured for each guest. With this system, there need be only one maid to fourteen or sixteen guests, and it is particularly useful when the problem is one of space. It might be, for example, that one's dining room was too small for a dinner party of sixteen, even though one had the requisite staff to wait on table. The seated, semi-served buffet, with small tables in the dining room and in the hall near by, is ideally suited to answer this problem.

Another very practical variation of the semi-served buffet meal has been evolved to solve the problem of a dinner of twelve or so, with one maid. The main course with the salad, if there is salad, is put on a long table near the dining-room door. A stack of plates comes first, the platters of the main course next, and any sauces or extra dishes after. Each guest, as he comes in, takes a plate, helps himself and goes to his place at the dining-room table, which is set as it would be for a served dinner except that wine, and bread perhaps, is on the table. Each guest fetches his own second helpings; but the plates are removed and the dessert is served as at a completely served dinner. The hostess pours the coffee herself, in the living room afterwards. Since the great virtue of this system is that no one need get up more than once (for a second helping), two courses, or a main course with salad eaten simultaneously, are better than three.

SUPPERS

We have already described on page 265 the three main kinds of suppers: supper after the theater; supper at a dance or evening reception; and supper late in the evening, at the end of a large dinner party. The service of this last has already been discussed above, under "After-Dinner Service." Here we are concerned only with the service of the other two.

Supper after the Theater

For a simple supper after the theater, the movies, or the opera, there need be no service at all, since sandwiches, hot soup, and other such foods can be set on the sideboard in the dining room. If such a table is set up in the living room, a maid will be needed to take away cups and plates. Although the food that might be served at such a supper is as simple as that which is served late in the evening at the end of a very large dinner party, it should not be served unless there are so many guests that such service is necessary for convenience' sake. It would be out of proportion and somewhat absurd, for example, if six or eight people were coming back from the theater, to have such food served, or to have the maid do anything more than bring the food and set it out on the table. If, however, it were a very large reception given after an opening night, or in honor of an author after his lecture, it would be perfectly proper to have a maid or butler serve the plates of food and tray of glasses filled with champagne or punch. If any guest refuses the drink that is offered, the butler or waitress should suggest some other drink, such as whiskey and soda, fruit juice, or something else.

At such a large reception, the ashtrays would be emptied at frequent intervals, as they are after a dinner party. If there were only six or eight people—and particularly if they were all friends—the maid would not usually be kept waiting, and the host or hostess would empty the ashtrays instead.

A slightly more elaborate supper is served exactly as a buffet dinner would be. The only differences are in the choice of food, which is discussed on page 332 and served as described on page 297.

The most elaborate after-the-theater supper is like a dinner in every way except that the menu is a little different and much shorter. The guests are seated at the dining-room table and served as they would be at any other meal. The question of how formal the service may be is a matter of choice. If the table is set in a formal way, the service should be equally formal. (Setting is fully discussed on pages 257 to 259, and serving, on pages 284 through 287. Ideas for the food will be found on page 333.) As we have said before, a seated supper at the dining-room table would be given after the theater only if one were sure that none of the guests had had an earlier dinner.

Supper at Dances

If one has decided to have a served and seated supper, for which the table will be set as for a formal dinner, the service will naturally follow the pattern used for such a meal. A buffet supper is, however, much more usual. The service of a buffet supper, such as one might have at a dinner dance, is as follows: If there are forty or fifty guests who will help themselves from the platters set on the buffet table, there should be at least two or three waiters to carry away used plates, to replenish the platters of food, empty ashtrays, bring fresh glasses, etc. Another will be needed, all through the evening, to serve the drinks.

At large dances, when a great many people may have been invited to come in after dinner, and when a more elaborate supper will have been planned, more service will be needed. In the first place, if there are a hundred guests or more, it will be impossible for them to wait on themselves. There should always be enough small tables so that all the guests can find a seat and be served. For example, if there are a hundred guests, there should be a dozen small tables with eight places at each, and at least a dozen waiters. At a very elaborate party, these tables could be set and served as at any dinner. The simpler and more usual way is to cover each with a cloth, decorate it with flowers, and bring the silver with each course. For example, if the first course were bouillon, a large plate would be brought with the napkin folded along one side; on top of this a saucer, cup and spoon. At such a supper (as at a wedding reception) the portion can be brought on the plate; so, if the second course were curry and rice, or lobster Newburg, this would be put on the plate, with a fork and toast or a roll. Ice cream or sherbet, often in a mold, is brought the same way: on a plate with a spoon. Coffee is served already poured in cups, on a tray with sugar and cream. The punch or champagne is served already poured. Any guest who refuses it is offered one of the other drinks suggested on page 333, "Supper at Dances."

After supper is over, five or six waiters will still be needed to serve the drinks and to tidy up the small tables. If there is also a buffet table, they will replenish the platters of sandwiches; and if it is a very late party, bring scrambled eggs and soup or coffee later on.

SERVING WATER

The customs attached to the serving of water are widely different from those of other drinks. Water is the only drink which, whether at the dining-room table or in the living room, can *always* be poured before it is served. As we have said, on page 244, in the chapter "Setting the Table," under the most elaborate system of service, water is not poured until the guests are seated at the dining-room table. But, as a matter of widely accepted practice, the water glasses are usually filled before the guests come into the room, and refilled from a pitcher as soon as any considerable quantity has been drunk.

Water served in the living room is brought in filled tumblers on a small tray; stemmed water goblets belong only on the dining-room table. It is perfectly correct, of course, to leave a pitcher of water in the living room or hall, on a tray with empty glasses, but whenever a guest asks for water, except in the dining room, it may always be brought already poured in a tumbler on a small tray.

SERVING WINE AND OTHER DRINKS

In this section we shall not discuss the customs governing the choice, storage, and icing of wines and liqueurs (for these see pages 334 to 336) but only the service as performed by the butler or waitress, or by the host, himself.

To Decant or Not to Decant

As a preliminary to serving, the first question is whether or not a wine should be decanted. (See pages 400 to 401, in the chapter "Glass," for a discussion of the various kinds of decanters.) The rule is that red wines, which are apt to have a good deal of sediment, should be decanted; that white wines, spirits, and liqueurs may be decanted if one wishes; that sparkling wines, such as champagne and sparkling Burgundy, must never be decanted. Only the third clause of this rule is inflexible. In practice, any of these except the sparkling wines may or may not be decanted, depending on the wine itself and the occasion on which it is to be served.

This is the way it works out. Very formal hostesses usually stick to the rule about red wines, leave white wines in their bottles, and decant spirits and liqueurs because they don't like the bottles. Very informal hostesses often decant both red and white wines when they are giving a dinner party, because the wine is set on the table and decanters are prettier than most bottles. When they are giving a small luncheon they often leave the wine in the bottle. Whiskey and other spirits, and all liqueurs, they leave in the bottle both at dinner and lunchtime. Great wine connoisseurs, or those who serve great wines, usually wince at the thought of decanters and everything is left in its bottle ("a beautiful sight" is their feeling).

A good common-sense practice is to have the red wine decanted and the white left in its bottle, if it is to be served by a waitress or butler. Liqueurs, which may be served in a set of small matching decanters, and spirits, which are served in bigger decanters, are often left in the bottle as a time- and work-saving custom.

Wines at the Table

There has always been a little confusion as to whether or not wineglasses should be taken away when a new wine is poured. This is sometimes done at special wine-tasting dinners, but in a private house no wineglass except the sherry glass is taken away before the end of the meal. And even this is not usually done unless many wines—three or four—are to be served. When there are three or four wines, the sherry glass is taken away after the salad plates, when the pepper and salt are removed.

No wine should be poured until everyone is seated at the table and until some food, whether oysters, soup, or an entrée, has been served. The traditional procedure is as follows: About a tablespoonful of each wine, as it comes with each course, is first poured into the host's glass, on the theory that he will taste it to determine whether or not it is corked or in any way unfit for his guests. He may or may not observe the formality of tasting it; if he does, the maid or butler waits for his approving nod; if he does not, the wine is poured without further ceremony. Standing to the right of each person, the maid or butler fills each glass about two-thirds full, full enough not to look niggardly, not so full as to spill easily. Very fine wines, and particularly Burgundies which are served in larger glasses, are often poured not more than half full, to allow room for the wine to "breathe" and for the bouquet to be appreciated. The question of whether the wine is to be iced or not, and the choice of wine for each course, are not relative to this section, which covers service only. (The ways in which wine is chosen and treated are on page 334, "The Choice and Handling of Wines and Liqueurs.") In any case, care should be taken not to allow a drop to fall on the table or to run down the side of the bottle; a slight twisting motion is often used to catch the last drop. Once the ritual of the host's sample has been dealt with, the order of the service of wine is as follows: the woman to the right of the host, then skipping the host the woman to his left, and so on around the table, ending with the host.

This is the traditional procedure for fully served meals. The custom for informally served meals varies; the host may pour a little into his own glass and taste it before serving the others; or he may fill his neighbor's glass and then pass the bottle on around the table to his left. When there are more than six or seven at table, it is wiser to have two decanters or bottles on the table, one at the host's end and the other at the hostess's. In this way, the hosts can be sure that each glass will be filled whenever necessary.

In theory, wineglasses are filled at the beginning of each course and should be refilled as often as they are empty, until a new wine is brought for a new course. Some years ago, it was the fashion to simulate complete indifference and lack of interest in the procedure, with the result that at the end of the dinner there were usually several full glasses of wine at each place. Today, it has become the custom to indicate that one does not wish to have his glass filled, and whoever is pouring should be on the alert to notice the smallest gesture of refusal on the part of the one who is being served. The refusal of one wine should not, however, be taken as a blanket refusal of all wines. The same wine should not be offered a second time to a guest who has refused it once, but each wine in succession should be offered, even though earlier ones have been refused.

Wines that are to be served with ice and soda water at the dining-room table follow the customs concerning other mixed long drinks. See page 303.

Wines Not Served at the Table

Most wines are served in the dining room, but sherry, champagne, and wines that are to be mixed with seltzer, or in a punch, are often served in the living room.

Sherry: Sherry may be brought in already poured, on a tray with the cocktails. Or according to a more formal system of service, it may be brought on a tray with empty glasses, and poured by the butler for each guest. Or it may be left in the living room, on a tray with empty glasses and a covered dish of crackers, to be taken in the late afternoon. Sherry may either be decanted or left in the bottle, but decanters are usually prettier. See page 396 for an example of a sherry glass.

Champagnes: Champagne may be served in the living room throughout the evening after a very formal and elaborate dinner, or on such occasions as a dance or a wedding reception. In either case, a tray of empty glasses with the bottle of champagne is brought in by the maid or butler, who offers it in turn to each guest, pouring the champagne from the bottle held in the right hand. After a suitable interval the maid returns carrying a smaller tray of glasses on her left hand, for the guests who may have refused the first time, and a bottle in her right hand. Those guests who accepted champagne on the first round will have their glasses refilled; others who may have refused the first round will be able to accept the second. At very big dinners, the most elaborate service follows the usual pattern: The butler first, with a small tray and one glass, the footman next with a big tray of glasses, and perhaps a second bottle of champagne. Another way of serving champagne which is essentially not as good service and is more usual at a wedding reception than after a dinner, is to have the butler bring in a tray of filled glasses, which he presents to each guest. Unless one likes the deep champagne glass described on page 396—and they are comparatively rare in America—wide, stemmed champagne glasses should always be used, except at a very large reception, when small, straight-sided tumblers are more practical. Champagne bottles are always opened in the pantry if the butler is to serve the champagne. If there is a buffet table (as there is, for example, at a dance) from which the guests will fetch their own glasses of champagne, the bottles can be opened by the servant at that table. Champagne bottles are often wrapped in a napkin before serving, but connoisseurs insist that the best practice is to fold the napkin in a narrow band, which is held like a strap along the length of the bottle, between fingers and thumb. If champagne is served in a punch, it is treated as other wines are; see immediately below.

Wines: Wines, especially white wine, may be served in hot weather in the living room, or out of doors, in tall glasses with ice and soda water and fresh mint. This is a newly developed custom, and one that is not, obviously, very much approved by wine connoisseurs. Wine that is used in this way should never be poured before it is served; the best way to serve it is to have a tray with glasses full of ice and sprigs of mint, and with bottles of wine and soda water. A butler or maid may pour the wine and water under directions, but usually each one waits on himself.

Champagne, also, is sometimes served this way. But it is always a waste of any good vintage, whether a still or sparkling wine.

Punch: Punch is often made of wine or champagne, mixed with fruit, fruit juices, soda water, or other drinks. It may be served, already poured, in little punch glasses at receptions, or it may be put in a big bowl on the sideboard with the empty punch glasses around it and left for the guests to help themselves. (Punch glasses are shown on page 398.)

Mixed Drinks at the Table

At the dining-room table, whiskey and soda has become an almost standard drink for those who cannot, or do not, drink wine. Even the approach to the serv-ing of whiskey has been standardized. At small, informal meals when there is a shortage of staff, or no staff, it is always wise to leave a tray on the sideboard with glasses, soda, an extra pitcher of water, ice, and whiskey. When a guest refuses wine, he can be offered whiskey and he or the host will take care of the service. At small dinners where there is a staff big enough to do all the service, the host or hostess should ask any of the guests who may have refused wine if he would like to have whiskey; and order it for him. At large dinners, this duty falls on the maid or butler. In any case, this is the standard procedure of formal service: The bottle or decanter is brought on a small tray, with a newly opened bottle of soda, and a glass with two or three pieces of ice in it. The maid or butler stands to the left of the guest, and pours the whiskey into the glass after drawing the guest's attention so that he may indicate when enough whiskey has been poured. The maid or butler then takes a step back, and, having filled the rest of the glass with soda, sets it down at the guest's right hand. Or, more informally, the guest may take the glass off the tray and set it down with the other glasses at the right of his plate. Although whiskey and soda is the drink most often offered to a guest who has refused wine, milk, one of the cola drinks, or brandy and soda are sometimes offered instead. If the guest has refused champagne, he is often offered claret or Burgundy, or whiskey and soda.

This method of serving is followed for serving any special requests on the part of the guests. For long drinks served to each guest as part of the hostess's plan, a slightly different system would be used. For example, suppose one has planned to serve iced white wine with mint to all the guests. The tall glasses are set at each guest's place next to the water glass, with nothing in them but ice and mint. As soon as the first course has been served, the maid or butler goes around the table, standing to the right of each guest, with a tray bearing the wine and soda water in the left hand. The wine is poured first, according to each guest's signal as to amount, and then the glass is filled with soda water. Very light white wines are sometimes served in this way without soda water.

Mixed Drinks Not at the Table

If whiskey and soda and other mixed long drinks are served in the living room, the procedure outlined above may be followed. The less formal and more usual way is to put a tray on a side table so that the guests can help themselves. If after a more formal meal one of the guests is playing bridge and asks for a whiskey and soda, or any other long mixed drink, the standard table service is followed. Otherwise, the maid or butler may bring it already poured, although this is not in the tradition of the best service.

Liqueurs

Liqueurs are served only after meals, and usually only after dinner, in the dining room, living room, or library.

At informal meals, liqueurs are served by the host or hostess, from a small tray set beforehand with glasses and bottles.

There are several patterns for more formal service. If coffee has been served at the table, liqueurs are brought after the cigars and cigarettes have been passed, and served in the order of precedence that has been used throughout the meal. The formal system is used only when men and women have separated to have coffee. The butler comes first with a small empty tray followed by a footman who carries a big tray with bottles, decanters, and glasses; going first to the woman who sat at the host's right he says, "Brandy, crème de menthe, or Cointreau, Madam?" (there are usually two or three different kinds of liqueurs; see page 336). Taking the appropriate glass and decanter from the footman's tray, he pours each glass on his small tray to order. A less elaborate system is to have the butler bring everything on one tray, and pour with one hand while he balances the tray on the other; but this cannot be done if there are many glasses and decanters. A still simpler system is to have a tray brought to a low table in front of the hostess, so that she may serve her guests.

If the women are being served their coffee in the living room, liqueurs are brought to them there, immediately after the coffee and before the coffee cups are taken away. If it is a very large dinner, two separate trays of liqueurs will probably have to be arranged in order to avoid delay. The men are served their liqueurs in the dining room, after they have been given their coffee and cigars. In every case, liqueurs are served as described above. The trays are set the same way, and the same procedure is followed.

Non-alcoholic Drinks at the Table

If iced tea, iced coffee, or a fruit drink is to be served, filled glasses may be set on the table next to the water glass before the meal. Or, empty glasses, or glasses filled with ice only, may be set at each guest's place, and the drink poured when guests have been given the first course. At informal meals, when hosts and guests co-operate in the service, the pitcher and necessary extras, such as cream and sugar, may be set on the table and passed from one to another. At less informal meals, the drink is poured as wine is, by the waitress or butler. If iced tea is to be served, for example, it is poured from a pitcher by the waitress, who stands to the right of each guest. Lemon and sugar are then brought on a separate tray and offered to each guest from his left. Milk or soft drinks are brought in already poured in the glass, whenever a guest asks for one of them, but they should not be planned for all guests, except children, as a matter of course.

Non-alcoholic Drinks Not at the Table

Any of these drinks, when they are served away from the dining-room table, may either be poured and served in the glass, or brought in a big pitcher and set on a tray with empty glasses, with sugar, cream, lemon or whatever else is necessary. Milk is not usually left to stand in a pitcher unless it is to be taken late at night, in which case the pitcher must be covered.

Hot Drinks

The service of tea and coffee has already been described on pages 289 and 293, but it might be useful here to bring up the question of serving tea and coffee at the dining-room table. Although, as we have said, it is not in accord with the best usage to serve these with meals, if the hostess knows that one of her guests likes tea or coffee, she will always suggest it to the guest and arrange that it be served. When there is a maid, the most usual system is that she brings a small tray with an empty cup, the coffee or teapot, sugar bowl, and cream pitcher. She asks the guest how many lumps he likes, and pours the coffee and cream under his direction, standing at the guest's right hand meanwhile. When this is done the maid sets down the cup. Or else she may stand at the guest's left, while the guest helps himself to coffee, sugar, and cream, and takes the cup himself. If a second cup is wanted, the maid should bring in the coffee or teapot on a tray with the sugar and cream, fill the cup from the right, and serve the guest with sugar and cream from the left. When there is no maid, the hostess may arrange a special tray, perhaps with a small thermos jug, so that she can easily fetch it for the guest as soon as it has been suggested. Hot drinks served late at night or at buffet suppers are a question of presentation rather than service and will be found on pages 264 and 266, in "Setting."

SERVING SPECIAL DISHES

Most of the good cookbooks give minute descriptions of the ways in which game, terrapin, and other such foods should be cooked. But there is a gap that needs to be filled in here with a brief outline of the ways in which they should be served. (See also "Special Customs and Techniques," page 54, in the chapter, "Table Manners.")

It might be wise, however, to point out that although these are called "special dishes," we do not mean to imply that they need be considered suitable only for formal entertaining. Woodcock or terrapin might be one of the six courses at a formal dinner, or the focal point of a most informal dinner of two courses. Oysters may be served to two or twenty.

Oysters and Clams

Oysters and clams may be cooked or raw. The ways of cooking are described in every cookbook, so that a brief outline of the ways of serving them raw is all that is necessary here. Oysters or clams are served on the half shell, as a first course before the soup, on a bed of cracked ice. A little cup of cocktail sauce can be embedded in the ice but a simpler and more formal way of serving them is with nothing more than a section of lemon. Little trays of horse-radish, tabasco sauce, and oyster crackers should never appear at the dinner table; they belong only in restaurants. Small oyster crackers, if one wants them, may be served in the breadbasket, as toast is served with the soup. The traditional wine is a dry white Burgundy.

Caviar

Caviar may be served in three ways on

three different kinds of occasions: on small pieces of toast as a cocktail food before luncheon or dinner; in a bowl before dinner or at buffet suppers; or as a first course, also in a bowl, at a dinner.

When it is served as a cocktail food, caviar is spread thickly on small pieces of toast (one- or two-bite size). These pieces of caviar-covered toast may be edged with the chopped white of hard-boiled eggs and sprinkled with the yolks of hard-boiled eggs. Segments of lemon are put between the pieces of toast, around the platter, so that guests can put a little lemon juice on the caviar if they want to. At very large cocktail parties, or before a large dinner when there are a great many people to be served, the segments of lemon are usually omitted. The hard-boiled egg is always optional.

When caviar is served before a small dinner party or at a buffet supper, it is set on a tray with toast, chopped hard-boiled egg, and onion. The details are as follows: Since caviar should be very cold, the best way to serve it is in a "double bowl," a large glass bowl, lined with ice, with a smaller glass bowl for the caviar inside it. These glass bowls are set in the middle of the tray; at the left is a plate of white toasted bread, the traditional accompaniment, and a stack of small tea plates and little knives; at the right a silver dessert spoon and little glass dishes of finely chopped onion, egg white, and egg yolk, each with a small teaspoon. There should also be a plate of halved or quartered lemons; the sections of lemon may be covered with a little strip of muslin which is knotted at the top, but, unless everything is extremely elaborate, this will smack a little of the very expensive restaurant. The purpose of the muslin is to catch flying drops of juice—obviously not a vital necessity. Before a small dinner or at a very simply served buffet supper, caviar may be presented in its own crock, but never in a tin or jar, fresh from the icebox and very cold. In this case, the little bowls of onion and egg could be omitted and the caviar could be served with toast and lemon only.

At a dinner, caviar is served in a bowl. Although attractive, a double bowl is not necessary because the caviar has come fresh from the icebox and will not be left standing, as it is on a buffet table. Each guest will help himself, first to the caviar and then to the toast which follows on a tray with sections of lemon, and little bowls of finely chopped onion and hard-boiled egg. Since caviar is eaten on toast, and spread on the toast with a knife, a small silver butter knife should be set at each place at table, outside the soup spoon.

Pâté de Foie Gras

Pâté de foie gras may be served on toast at cocktail parties or with cocktails before dinner; with toast or biscuits, in a crock or mold before an informal dinner or at a buffet supper; and with the salad, as one of the courses of a formal dinner. If it is served on toast as a cocktail food, pâté de foie gras need only be spread quite thickly. As in the case of caviar canapés, the toast should be cut in small pieces so that each can be eaten in one or two bites.

Before a small dinner or at a buffet supper, pâté de foie gras is served on a small tray, in its own earthenware crock, on a china or silver plate, with a silver knife beside it (a butter knife, or a very small luncheon knife). Beside this plate, on the same little tray, is a plate of toast or crisp, mild-flavored crackers. If the pâté has no crock of its own, it is molded into a form (a custard cup would do as a small mold) and put on a small plate with a paper doily and a knife, or on a bigger plate with a knife and the crackers or toast neatly arranged around it.

With the salad course at a dinner, pâté de foie gras is often served in a ring mold of mild-flavored aspic, or in a plain mold, garnished with aspic. A plain salad, or an endive or escarole salad follows. It is also used as a salad course with breast of chicken. The cold chicken breast is lined with pâté de foie gras and covered with a chaud-froid sauce. (See page 486.)

Terrapin

This should be treated as a fish course in any long dinner menu, but like any fish it may also be the main course of an informal meal. Terrapin is served from a tureen or deep platter and is eaten with a dessert fork, or any fork that is used for fish. It may be eaten either from a fish plate or from a soup plate; a soup plate is customary at a buffet dinner. When a soup plate is used, guests are always given a soup spoon as well as a fork. Vegetables or potatoes should not be served with terrapin. The only traditional accompaniment is toast. A white Bordeaux is the best wine.

Wild Duck

There are so many different theories and tastes in the cooking of wild ducks, as of any game, that the first prayer of every hostess who receives a present of game is that the donor will not have to be invited to eat it. Anyone who does a lot of shooting has his own theory as to how "gamy" and how raw the meat should be, and nothing is more distressing than to see the expression that indicates a feeling that "my beautiful ducks are ruined." In this indefinite realm of personal likes and dislikes, there is no absolute criterion of perfection in cooking that will please everybody. The customs of presentation are blessedly definite.

All the various members of the wild duck family, and in fact, all dark-fleshed game and waterfowl, are presented as follows: one, or if there is room, two birds to each platter; the flesh carved but put back on the carcass; nothing else on the platter except the thin natural juice of the meat and a little cress or parsley. Currant jelly, which often accompanies duck, is served separately on a tray immediately following the duck with (optional) a sauceboat of gravy made from pressing the carcass of another duck. This gravy should never be mixed with flour. The most usual accompaniments to wild duck are wild rice and creamed, or buttered, cooked celery. Or, hominy or hominy soufflé and peas or string beans. A heavy red Burgundy is the customary wine.

Grouse, Pheasant, etc.

This includes all the white-fleshed upland and forest game birds, except the very small ones. They should be roasted; one or two, or as many as possible without crowding, should be served together on the platter, the flesh carved and replaced on the carcass, surrounded with dried, browned, bread crumbs. At big dinners, it is more practical to serve breast of pheasant only; these are cut away from the carcass, and arranged neatly on a platter with the bread crumbs. Immediately after this platter should follow a tray with currant jelly, a sauceboat of creamed, bread-crumb sauce and (optional) another sauceboat of dried browned bread crumbs. Traditional accompaniments are wild rice with string beans or buttered broccoli; or rice croquettes and peas. The wine may be Burgundy or claret.

Snipe, Woodcock, etc.

This includes the smaller game birds, such as quail, which may be broiled or roasted. When roasted, these birds are served whole, without carving, because they are so small that at least one is necessary for each guest. Snipe and woodcock are served whole with the heads left on, and the long beaks folded back either into the breast (woodcock) or under

the wing (snipe). All of them may be served on toast spread with a paste made of the giblets; or the platter may be edged with small diamonds of the same toast. Traditional accompaniments are wild rice or hominy, and currant jelly; Burgundy or claret. The best vegetable is one with a mild flavor such as string beans or peas.

Venison

The most usual cuts are venison steaks, served as beefsteaks are, and haunch and saddle of venison, which are roasted, carved, and served like a "standing" roast beef or saddle of lamb. The traditional accompaniments are a Cumberland sauce (melted currant jelly, raisins and thin gravy); or a Madeira sauce of thin gravy and Madeira wine. The customary wine is Burgundy.

Suckling Pig

Suckling pig should be served whole, carved, with the head left on and with a small raw apple in the mouth. Traditional accompaniments are applesauce or roast apples, or red cabbage cooked with apples. The wine should be a heavy red Burgundy.

Plum Pudding

Plum pudding is the traditional Christmas dessert; often, in America, served with ice cream. It should be presented on a round platter of silver or china, covered with brandy which is lighted at the last moment so that the dish is brought into the room flaming. Sometimes it is decorated at the top with holly, but only real holly should be used, never an imitation. If ice cream is to accompany it, it should be served on a separate platter immediately following the plum pudding. Another custom—but one that is not always followed—is to have a small decanter of brandy passed around from hand to hand at the table so that each guest can pour a little more over his plum pudding.

42

Fashions in Food

THIS CHAPTER and the next have nothing to do with rules. They are designed to provide the pleasant flesh for the grim but necessary skeleton of rules and customs given in the other chapters about setting and serving, very much as the smile and the friendly glance are designed to lend charm to the empty formula of "How do you do?" In earlier chapters, we have set down the bare outlines of menus, and the mechanics of table settings; now, we are concerned with good food and pretty tables.

Although they are inextricably bound together, food and table accessories are separated briefly here for convenience's and clarity's sake. And because taste changes, and the delight of one generation becomes the bane of the next, we shall discuss them both from the point of view of contemporary taste. Food, as the most important, comes first. Table settings are in the next chapter.

PLANNING THE MENU

Planning a menu is not an easy job. In the first place it is extremely difficult to be imaginative about food seven hundred or more times a year. Or, if one has inexhaustible imagination, it is not always easy to make it march smoothly with such vital considerations as households and budgets. And, finally, when one has had nearly a lifetime of practice, it is sometimes true that one has lost touch with contemporary taste. Just as some women become wedded to a certain way of doing their hair, evolved when they were successful young wives or even debutantes, so do they become wedded to certain ways of planning a menu, certain ways of considering food. "Soup, meat, green vegetables, potato, and dessert" is their conditioned reflex to the prospect of a family meal; "a roast" is their automatic reaction to the idea of giving a dinner. To fall into this attitude is admittedly a temptation: one has acquired platters, serving dishes, and table ornaments which suit this kind of food (they are, of course, by far the easiest to acquire); one is used to a certain pattern and there seems little reason for the effort needed to change it. But the reason is big enough: it is the pleasure of one's family, one's friends, and one's guests. And the effort should be made.

The first change in fashion, as far as food is concerned, is that menus are shorter—shorter and, in comparison to old-fashioned menus, funnier. One needn't *always* start dinner with soup; one can end dinner with salad and cheese; one can almost entirely dispense with the rigid rules that governed our grandmothers' menu planning. Only one factor remains constant: the system of following one kind of flavor with another kind of flavor, one food value with another.

START A MENU HERE

The proper system of menu planning is based on principles as physically sound as a child's craving for sweets. The dreariest treatise on the laws of nutrition and the most lyric gourmet's eulogy about that little filet of sole both add up to the same thing: Man needs certain fuels and nourishment, and he can get them either by following a theoretical blueprint or by following his own instinctive taste. An extremely interesting experiment proving this theory was conducted with a group of one-year-old and two-year-old children. They were offered food of all kinds at each meal and allowed to choose. Some ate nothing but sweets for days on end, one nothing but bananas, but at the end of a year every child had chosen for himself a fully balanced diet. In other words, whether one approaches the matter from the point of view of a dietitian, a baby, or a gourmet, the results are almost the same.

A long menu which skillfully alternates one flavor with another, encouraging and stimulating the appetite, will almost automatically meet all nutrition needs. A short menu must go more directly to the point and satisfy the instinctive taste which clamors most loudly for attention: the craving for the full, rich taste of meat, or, as nutritionists say, some "protein-rich meat substitute." Because this is true, the protein dish is the main course of any meal and other foods must be subordinated to it. The fact that the French have long called this "la pièce de résistance" does not make it any less compellingly or scientifically true. In the same way, one instinctively rejects the idea of a heavy sweet as a first course, and one is instinctively unsatisfied by a completely fat-free diet. It is not necessary, although some find it agreeable, to know about the numbing effect of sweets on the taste buds, or that certain vitamins are fat-soluble only.

THE PERFECT MENU

The perfect menu must include these essentials: a good strong, full flavor, whether meat, fish, or cheese; a rich, creamy food, whether a cream soup, a creamed vegetable, cheese, butter, or a rich dessert; a sharp, thin clean taste, whether vegetable, salad, or fruit; the solid neutral taste of potatoes, rice, wheat, or some other grain; and a sweet taste. One can achieve this by having the nightmare meal suggested by one professor of nutrition as perfectly balanced: a peanut-butter sandwich on whole-wheat bread, a raw tomato, and a glass of milk. (All that is missing is a piece of candy-coated chewing gum as a sweet!) Or one can have a decent meal: a good meat stew with vegetables, a plain fresh salad, and crème brûlée.

The variations on this theme are infinite. The sweet can supply the thin clear taste, as in a compote of fruit; or the creamy, the neutral, and the sweet elements may be combined as in rice pudding. Or the meat can be made the one creamy dish by being hashed or creamed. In long menus, of course, the craving for protein can be satisfied more than once and in a variety of ways: in a strong clear soup; a fish; a heavy meat; and cold meat, or pâté de foie gras with the salad. Short menus give it only one chance.

Less important than taste in planning a menu but still considerable are color, texture, and temperature. All three embody perfectly simple principles—an all-white or all-pink dinner, no matter how subtly planned as to taste, is monotonous to look at, and the eye can have an important role in encouraging or discouraging appetite. For example, a dark meat may be served with a light vegetable such as cauliflower, but chicken should not be accompanied only by white vegetables; tomato soup, salmon, and strawberry ice do not make a good menu. Texture, or form, has a lesser effect, but it is still a fact that chopped meat, creamed spinach, mashed potatoes and applesauce are less appealing than York ham and creamed spinach, with new potatoes in their jackets, followed by baked apples with cloves. Temperature is even simpler and more obvious: cold foods are less formidable than hot ones to an appetite almost satisfied; a cold dessert must be the last in a series of heavy rich courses, a hot one will bolster a light meal. Hot weather demands cold food—one reason why a traditionally formal dinner is difficult in summer—and even at an informal meal in winter some mingling of hot and cold food is more appetizing than an all-hot menu: meat, salad, and a hot dessert; or hot soup, hot meat, and cold dessert; but rarely three hot courses. And of course hot means *hot*, and cold—except for salad or cold asparagus—means icy fresh. Finally, two dishes cooked in the same way should not follow each other on the menu. Sauté fish should not precede sauté chicken, for example; a creamed fish would be better.

These five principles of menu-planning are more needed now than ever. The old rigid pattern almost imposed recognition of them and now that the form has been broken it is vital to understand the spirit. That many Americans do not was proved by the great number of ill-fed young men, rejected by the Army for malnutrition, whose families had more than adequate incomes. The loaded farmhouse tables of nineteenth century America may have been a hit-or-miss approach to nutrition, but the can and opener are apparently not an infallible way to good health or good eating.

For a variety of reasons, some economic, some social, long menus are not the fashion of our times. They exist, but they are not new and have none of the characteristic modern attitude toward food. This attitude is best exemplified by the two or three course meal, by the leaning toward hearty, more "peasant-like" dishes. Inevitably, it is matched by a new preference for plain linen over lace, plain silver over decorated silver, flowered or simple china rather than heavily gilded china. Ways of arranging a table are suggested in the next chapter, beginning on page 339. Here, having discussed the point of view from which menus are planned, we shall consider suggestions for each course of luncheon and dinner, for tea and buffet meals.

A MENU WHEN THE STAFF IS SMALL

Every menu must, of course, be planned with the service in mind. There is food which is perfect for a buffet dinner and impractical for a seated dinner; for example, curry with all its condiments when the staff is barely adequate and pressed for time. And there is food which is perfect for a seated dinner, and impossible for a buffet dinner; squabs, for example, when plates will be balanced precariously on the guests' knees. But when the staff is small and one wants a completely served, seated meal, wise and careful menu-planning is more important than ever. It can make all the difference between a smoothly served meal and a long, difficult, and disjointed hour.

This menu, for example, is badly chosen for a dinner when one waitress is serving ten people, or two waitresses, sixteen: soup, with croutons or cheese served separately (one extra trip); meat, with gravy and jelly (another extra trip); two vegetables, each served separately, one with a special sauce (three extra trips); dessert, with sauce and cookies separately served (two extra trips). These six unnecessary circuits of the table, caused by careless menu-planning, can almost bring a dinner to a standstill.

This menu is a good one: soup or fish; meat, with the vegetables around it, served on a big platter; dessert, complete in itself (no cookies are necessary). There are so many soups that can be served in one trip that it is unnecessary to discuss them here. Many are listed on page 322. Fish may be served in various self-contained dishes also. These are listed on page 314, page 322, and page 485. Egg dishes, and other first-course suggestions for luncheon, are on page 313. Desserts, too, are easy to choose with quick service in mind. The key to a successful menu for a dinner or luncheon of this kind is the main course.

The essential thing is to plan the main course to present everything, meat and vegetables, together. The easiest way to do this is to have a casserole dish or stew. Even better, perhaps, are dishes which present the vegetables on the platter with the meat. Roast potatoes served with roast lamb, beef, fowl, or veal are the classic example, but one can go much further than this. For example, on the platter with boeuf à la mode one can put all the vegetables: neat little clumps of onions, carrots, string beans, and potato balls. On a platter with filet mignon or a filet of beef, one can put artichoke hearts, peas and mushrooms, leaving only the potatoes to follow. Noisettes of lamb can be served on a big platter with grilled tomatoes and potato balls, and tiny beets or peas. Around a small rump roast of veal, roast potatoes may alternate with neat bundles of string beans. But it must be emphasized that whenever this is done, it must be done neatly, even artistically. The platter must never look overcrowded or messy.

LIST AND SEQUENCE OF COURSES

As will be seen from the dinner and luncheon menus which follow, there is a traditional progression of courses. The list of all the courses which is given at this point is not, of course, a suggested menu for any one meal but only an outline to show the relation of one course to another. The rules of menu-writing are on pages 270 to 272.

Hors d'oeuvres: Hors d'oeuvres, which are essentially an exaggerated form of cocktail food served at the table, are a first course served only at luncheon, or at the most informal dinner. They are followed by meat or fish, never by soup.

Soup: Soup is traditionally the first course of a dinner, unless it is preceded by oysters or clams on the half shell, caviar, or some special dish such as smoked salmon. In America, it is also very often the first course at luncheon.

311

Entrées: An entrée is, theoretically, only an introduction to the more substantial part of the meal. At old-fashioned formal dinners, it was a light meat course served after the fish. Today, as the first course of a luncheon, it often consists of gnocchi, or eggs in some form, a risotto, or perhaps soft-shelled crabs.

Fish: Fish, which is traditionally a second course following immediately after the soup, may also be a first course, preceding the meat course; or a main course at informal meals, following the soup at dinner, or an entrée at luncheon.

Meat: Meat is usually the main course, and usually hot; but cold meat may also be served with salad, after a meat course or, informally, after a main course of fish.

Salad: Salad is the course which traditionally follows the meat course. But plain lettuce may also be served with a hot meat; or, in very hot weather, a more elaborate salad may even be the main course, between a hot entrée and an iced compote of fruit. But no salad should ever be served, as it sometimes is in American hotels, at the beginning of the meal.

Cheese: When cheese is served at the dining-room table, it belongs with the salad, unless one has decided to follow the very sound French bourgeois custom of ending the meal with cheese, fruit, and coffee, all served more or less simultaneously. Cheese and pears, or apples, are delicious together. Cheese and crackers, or cheese with thin slices of bread, may be served with a salad course at a buffet dinner or luncheon; or late in the evening, after a dinner party; or, in very small pieces, as a cocktail food.

Dessert: Dessert is the last course of the meal and can be followed only by fruit or, in the English tradition, by a savory. Although twenty years ago it would have been unthinkable to end a meal without a sweet, it is now somewhat the fashion to omit dessert entirely, and many an informal meal ends with salad, cheese, coffee, or with raw fruit which is left whole and not prepared as a dessert.

FOOD FOR LUNCHEON

No fashions in food have changed more radically in the last few years than the fashions in food for luncheon. In 1920, no luncheon was really *anything* unless the food was complicated and unless, above all, it looked complicated. Today, one might almost say that it does not matter what the food is, so long as it does *not* look complicated. For example, sweetbreads are broiled instead of being cut up, creamed, mixed with mushrooms and stuffed into a pastry shell, as they used to be. Salads are usually tossed around in a big bowl, instead of being carefully and elaborately set in a pinwheel design on a flat platter. Desserts may still take hours of careful simmering and measuring, but they bear no resemblance to the "cute" or "pretty" little birds-nests and flowers of those days.

There are two reasons for this. One, which applies to all food, is that in America informal entertaining has increased to such a point that probably not more than one per cent of all entertaining could be called formal. The second, which applies more specifically to luncheon, is that the nineteenth century fable that women have no appetite has at last been laid to rest. Under the burden of this tradition, women pretended that they had to be tempted by dainty foods: tiny steps for tiny appetites. "She eats like a bird" was a compliment. And since most luncheons at home were women's luncheons—American men, perhaps in self-defense, having taken to lunching near their offices—food for luncheon became a matter of pastry shells, cream sauces, and spun sugar, often pink and white, always "dainty." The only shadow that remains of this unhappy conception of the feminine constitution are the "Green Luncheons" for Saint Patrick's

Day or the "Red Luncheons" for Saint Valentine's Day, which so often are suggested to four women who gather for an afternoon of bridge. It is probably unnecessary to warn our readers against these unfortunate ideas; the fact that such luncheons are never served when men might be present is adequate warning. The attitude that produces them is an affront to the goodness of food, which should be chosen and planned only according to the principles of gastronomy and nutrition. Luckily, very little of the food eaten in America is planned to fit a "story"; perhaps there are a few children's parties given on Washington's Birthday where cherries and tiny chocolate hatchets are set around the ice cream, but these are beside the point. To decorate one course in order to amuse a group of children is quite different from coloring the whole meal in order to impress a group of adult women. Food should never be "angled"; potatoes should never be dyed with spinach juice to make them green for Saint Patrick's Day. Food should be treated with respect and, fortunately, it usually is.

As we have said on page 250, where the outline of a luncheon menu is given, the basic modern luncheon has three courses. This is often cut down to two courses, sometimes enlarged to four, but the form remains more or less the same: something light to begin with, a sturdier second course, and dessert. From this basic pattern the first course can be taken away; or to it can be added a fourth course of salad. Here are suggestions for each course.

First Course

In America, soup is very often the first course, although this is not a tradition of French cooking and therefore is not a custom that should be followed at the most formal luncheons. If soup is to be served at luncheon as the first of the usual pattern of three courses, it should always be served in cups. Any soup can be served that goes well with the rest of the menu. Several soups are suggested on page 485, "Formal Dinners," and on page 322, "Semiformal Dinners," any one of which could be useful at luncheon. If the usual three-course pattern is not being followed, one might serve one of the "meal-in-itself" soups suggested, on page 329, for buffet dinners. For example, one might have a bouillabaisse followed by salad and cheese; or a crab gumbo served with a plain salad on a separate plate, followed by dessert.

In the French tradition, the first course is often eggs in some form, hot or cold. For warm weather: cold, soft-boiled eggs, cooked only until firm enough to peel, chilled, set on a bed of watercress and lightly covered with mayonnaise into which a little cress has been mixed; or cold poached eggs, with a slice of tomato and a slice of ham underneath, crossed leaves of fresh tarragon on top, covered with a mild aspic and served on a bed of shredded lettuce; or cold soft-boiled eggs, chilled whole in a ring or bed of aspic, served with mayonnaise. Hot egg dishes, for cold weather, are: hard-boiled eggs cut up in a rich cheese sauce, baked and served in little brown earthenware casseroles; baked or shirred eggs with chicken livers, "au beurre noir," cooked and served in glazed white ovenware dishes; a really good omelet, almost liquid inside its thin skin, flavored with fine herbs or cheese, or, for a more elaborate luncheon, a timbale with mushroom sauce.

Other first-course dishes are a cheese soufflé; gnocchi with butter and grated cheese or with "sauce Mornay" (a cheese sauce); a risotto, with chicken livers or truffles, served with grated cheese. For an elaborate luncheon, sauté soft-shelled crabs with a little fried parsley and lemon; raw smoked Parma ham with slices of melon or pear; smoked salmon served with olive oil, capers, and lemon; "Clams Southside," a wonderful hash of minced clams, served with toast; clams or oysters on the half shell; coquilles St. Jacques; crabe ravigote, which is cold crab meat mixed with mayonnaise, stuffed back into the crab shells and topped with grated egg yolk; hors d'oeuvres. The list is as wide and as long as one's taste and experience. Many Americans like to start luncheon with fruit—a melon or grapefruit, served plain, in the rind—but fruit cup and fruit juices should be avoided. (See page 245.)

Main Course

The second course is, as a rule, the main one of the luncheon. The most usual combination, except in warm weather, is some kind of meat or fish, a green vegetable, and potatoes. But this need not be as humdrum as it sounds. For example, one might have chicken or duck, or squab cooked in a casserole with peas, served with new potatoes in their jackets; or one could have hash, or a meat pie, either of which may be made with potatoes, with another vegetable served separately. If one has had a substantial first course, the second course could be broiled shad with the roe and sections of lemon, served with creamed spinach. Or a simple meat with some vegetable such as cauliflower polonaise; okra or zucchini squash, sliced and sautéed; acorn squash, halved and baked with butter; leeks or Jerusalem artichokes, boiled and buttered or creamed; halved tomatoes, sprinkled with herbs and broiled with a dab of butter; eggplant, sliced and fried, or chopped and simmered with tomatoes and a little garlic. Or one might adopt the French custom of serving a plain green salad on the same plate with almost any plain broiled or roasted meat: chicken, veal cutlets, lamb chops, or squabs.

Excellent main courses for an informal two-course luncheon are Cassolette Toulousaine, a wonderful dish of bean and duck, and Arroz Valenciana, rice cooked with saffron and a little garlic, full of chicken, clams, artichoke hearts, and peas. Either of these, followed by a plain salad, cheese, fruit and coffee would be a complete meal.

In warm weather, an excellent luncheon is a first course of cold eggs or cold soup, a plain hot meat with a green salad, followed by a simple dessert of fruit. Or, instead of hot meat and salad, one might have a simple hot fish, such as filets of sole meunière, served with cold sliced tomatoes and cucumbers. Another plan is to reverse the order and have a hot first course—a cheese soufflé, a risotto or hot eggs—followed by a cold main course. Cold meat and salad are the most usual but there are also brook trout, served whole with fresh tarragon in aspic, with a plain salad; cold salmon or halibut, with mayonnaise or sauce verte and a salad of lettuce, tomato, and hard-boiled egg.

Dessert Course

The third and last course of modern luncheons is very often some kind of fruit, fresh or stewed: fresh berries with sour cream; stewed berries or apricots with "coeurs à la crème" which can be approximated by making a mold, or small molds, of cream cheese mixed with cream; pears cooked in honey, or in port wine, with grated orange peel; rhubarb cooked with strawberries; peaches cooked with cherries; dried apricots, figs, and prunes, cooked together with raisins, served hot or cold, with or without sour cream, in an earthenware casserole. Other than fruit, the most usual desserts are crème brûlée; Bavarian cream; or an old-fashioned deep-dish pie, served hot or cold, with cream; gingerbread, hot, with lemon sauce, or a bitter chocolate sauce. For an elaborate luncheon on a special occasion, such as a birthday or christening, one would probably have ice cream or an ice. See page 486 for suggestions.

With any of the desserts suggested above, except the pie and gingerbread, one might have plain sugar cookies, or toasted angel-food cake, or chocolate leaves, or French "sablé" cookies, or Scotch shortcake; or, with a very plain fruit dessert, a rich beautiful cake.

Menus

The first four menus may be used for informal luncheons; the rest, either for luncheon or for an informal dinner. At dinner time soup may be added to any of the menus which lack soup:

Chicken livers broiled in bacon jacket, or en brochette with mushrooms
Small baked potatoes, or hashed in cream
New beets

Apple pudding with raisins, walnuts, hard sauce

Cold meat cuts
Sauté eggplant and tomatoes,
sliced and cooked with oil
Corn bread

Fresh pears poached in lemon peel syrup;
or grapefruit Jello smothered in grapefruit, orange
slices and juice, and strawberries

Shrimp bisque

Eggplant and tomatoes baked with bacon
curls in French earthenware casserole

Alligator pear and grapefruit salad

Risotto with chicken livers
Mixed green salad, Brie cheese
Marquise Alice (a cold chocolate soufflé)

Casserole of chicken cooked slowly in stock with finely-sliced bacon, onions, leeks, carrots, mushrooms, peas, string beans, or any available vegetable except the cabbage family; some sherry
Boiled white or brown rice

Apple strudel, cream

Curried shrimp, served with boiled white rice, grated fresh coconut, fried finely shredded onion, sliced cucumber in French dressing, dried chopped peanuts, and hot popadums (popadums are a thin wafer imported from India)

Tomato and lettuce salad, well tossed

Pineapple ice and vanilla ice cream mold
Wafers or cake

Crab or shrimp gumbo with rice
Breadsticks

Escarole, endive, and chicory salad
Liederkranz cheese

Cold lemon soufflé

Kidney Tourbigo (lamb kidneys, chicken livers, tiny sausages, and mushrooms)
Mashed potatoes or brown rice
Whole broiled tomatoes

Fruits rafraîchis au rhum
Chocolate nut roll

Fish pudding
Baked whole tomatoes with tufts of bacon
and Major Gray's Indian chutney
Thin, crisp corn bread

Papaya cubes or rings, marinated and chilled
in fresh lime-juice syrup
Old-fashioned coconut layer cake

Home-made sausage meat, grilled
Baked potato or purée of potatoes, or brown
rice (or pancakes and maple syrup for luncheon only)

Raw spinach salad with cottage cheese and French dressing

Dried figs or dates, apples, tangerines

Pâté Maison *   Hard rolls

Veal à la Grecque
Sauce with tomatoes and peppers
Brown rice

Watercress and lettuce salad

Maple nut cake

* For dinner, instead of the pâté serve soup or a fish mousse.

Cream of curry soup

Broiled filet of sole or pompano, tomato
and cucumber
Bermuda potatoes
Broccoli with lemon butter

Soufflé Grand Marnier (or orange with peel)

FOOD FOR TEA

As we have said on page 255, there are three different kinds of tea food, a little like the courses of a meal: something hot, something bland and fresh, and something sweet. And all this must, with very few exceptions, be eaten with the fingers. Because food for an afternoon reception is in some ways more limited than the food for other teas, we will start with afternoon receptions first.

For an Afternoon Reception

For an elaborate tea, the hot food should be "self-contained": tiny beaten biscuits, sliced, filled with marmalade, and toasted; biscuits filled with hot creamed chicken; tiny doughnuts, very crisp, with no sugar; rusks, halved or quartered, buttered and very hot; small, very thin, slices of bread rolled up with thin slices of cheese and toasted until the cheese melts; Scotch oatcakes; quartered English muffins; or buttered toast, made of French or gluten bread, Irish soda bread or egg bread. It is always wise to have something very simple in each "course" at any large reception. Any or all of these should be buttery and piping hot.

For the second "course": sandwiches of cream cheese and chopped olives, or pâté de foie gras, cucumber or tomato; or thin small slices of white bread, rolled around watercress, or watercress and cream cheese, with little tufts of watercress sticking out each end; or sandwiches of very thin rye bread with sliced radishes; and, always, plain sandwiches of bread and butter. The only important thing about all these sandwiches is that they must be small, not bigger than two good bites. They can be oblong or round (cut with a small cookie cutter) and the crusts should never be left on.

If the desirable flavor for the first course is hot spiciness, and for the second crisp freshness, for the third it is richness: a big chocolate cake with dark, half-bitter, chocolate icing, or a plain cake made in six or seven very thin layers with the dark chocolate between and on top; an incredibly rich cocoanut cake, with white icing almost an inch thick; devil's food or angel cake; a plain pound cake; brownies or chocolate leaves; the little French cookies called "sablés"; Scotch shortbread; sticky macaroons; spice cookies; and, as usual, plain, thin sugar cookies. All cakes and cookies must be as sweetly rich as possible or as their characters allow, and it is better to serve one or two which are really up to the mark than a wider variety of mediocrities.

At a very large reception, in addition to the tea, one might serve coffee or chocolate. Suggestions for the service and the setting are on page 289 and page 251.

For Everyday Tea

Of course, everyday tea is never like this. In fact, unless there were to be at least twenty or thirty guests, it would be extremely bad taste. For three or four guests, one should rarely have more than one hot thing, one kind of sandwich, and one sweet thing. For a dozen or so, perhaps two of each kind.

The hot food for everyday tea might consist of any one of those suggested for the afternoon reception, with the possible exception of the chicken-filled muffin. In addition to these, there is the whole field of toast and muffins, jams, honeys, and preserves which are impossible for big receptions. Nowhere, perhaps, is less imagination shown than in the usual choice of jam or honey for tea. So often, there is nothing to choose from except a crock of plain marmalade and a jar of plain thin honey; and in view of the variety in honeys alone, this can only be laziness or lack of interest. For example, besides the usual amber-colored clover honey, there is the dark richly flavored buckwheat honey; there is honey in the comb; there are the tupelo and acacia honeys; there are the almost solid cream-colored or white honeys; and there is a wide variety of foreign honeys. Marmalades are less varied, but still too few seem to know that there are marmalades made not only of oranges but also of kumquats or limes. Besides honey and marmalade, there are guava jelly, and damson jam, and a wonderful beach plum jam from Cape Cod; there are all sorts of elderberry, blackberry, raspberry, and strawberry jams, although these can be disappointing and should only be bought if they are especially good; and for those who like very sweet things, there is maple butter, which is made of pure maple sugar. All these are delicious with any kind of toast or English muffins, but in small households neither toast nor muffins is a practical suggestion. Instead, it is much easier to serve something that need only be heated in the oven or briefly under the broiler, such as Holland rusk, French croissants or brioches, Swedish wafers, or flat bread, scones, corn bread, flat wheat biscuits or cassava biscuits.

After the hot food there could be any of the sandwiches suggested on page 318, or very thin open slices of buttered bread. When bread is served this way at tea, the crusts are left on, the slices are served whole, or cut in half lengthwise. Sweet things are correspondingly simple: at most, there might be one large cake and a plate of plain cookies. Less usual, but delicious at teatime, are strawberries, in the Rupert Brooke tradition. They are served in a big glass bowl, washed but not hulled, with granulated or powdered sugar. Eaten in the fingers with a dip into the sugar between bites, they are the perfect ending for tea.

For High Tea

The classic English trademark of a high tea is a soft-boiled egg, but in the United States there are more apt to be, in addition to any of the usual, everyday tea food, one or two of the following hot things: little grilled sausages, eaten on toothpicks; or grilled sardines on toast; or tiny codfish balls; or chicken livers wrapped in bacon; or bacon sandwiches made by opening one side of a piece of toast and filling it with bacon. There might be open sandwiches of turkey, chicken, or smoked turkey, sprinkled with coarse, freshly ground pepper; sandwiches of guava jelly and cream cheese. And any amount of cakes and cookies. To end up with, there might be strawberries, cherries or grapes.

A simple "nursery" tea, ideal for the country or if there are children, is discussed on page 255.

FOOD SERVED WITH COCKTAILS

Cocktail food, like tea food, is always eaten in the fingers. Reduced to its minimum, it can be nothing more than a dish of salted nuts, such as one might have with a very late afternoon cocktail, or with a cocktail served before a very informal luncheon. This is brought in on the tray with the cocktails. At its maximum, cocktail food can approach the dimensions of a Swedish smörgasbord. Cocktail food can be hot or cold, simple or rich; the only kind which should be avoided is the kind one finds in bars and restaurants: canapés overdecorated with little squiggles of mayonnaise, or with slices of egg cut to look like daisies. These are unattractive because they are too elaborate, but such barroom simplicities as popcorn, pretzels, and peanuts are not much better. The best cocktail nuts are the macadamian nuts from Hawaii, hard to find but delicious, or cashews or pecans. All of these should be heated a little before they are served. Instead of pretzels, there are dozens of different kinds of crackers that are more attractive, some made with cheese, some with soya flour. All should be crisp and hot, and with a salty or piquant flavor.

Before Dinner

For the usual dinner of eight or ten people, the cocktail food could be a choice of one or two of the following: nuts or crackers; ripe or green olives; little pickled onions; slivers of raw carrot; little cauliflower tops served on a flat plate with a bowl of mayonnaise in the middle (these should be soaked in a bowl of ice water, with a little vinegar and salt, for several hours beforehand); potato chips, served plain and hot, or with a bowl of softened cream cheese mixed with chives; anchovy filets—not paste—on toast; slices of smoked salmon on toast, served on a flat dish with pieces of lemon; hot grilled sardines on toast, served like the smoked salmon with lemon; celery stalks stuffed with a Roquefort cheese mixture; small crackers spread with American cheese, toasted until the cheese melts; small round pieces of toast covered with a hot cheese mixture which puffs up like a tiny soufflé. In addition to these, there is a whole family of cocktail foods served on toothpicks: cooked shrimps, cold and speared with a toothpick, to be dipped into a little bowl of mayonnaise or Russian dressing; bacon wrapped around olives; very small pork sausages; very small, very hot, codfish or cheese balls. These cheese balls, called Délices d'Emmenthal, are about the size of an olive; the larger versions, about the size of the usual codfish cake, are an excellent first course for luncheon. Cocktail food, except for hot things, should be neatly and symmetrically arranged on flat china or silver dishes with doilies. Hot things can be served either on a flat plate, or, better, in a covered silver dish with a hot-water compartment.

At Cocktail Parties

Food for cocktail parties is merely an exaggeration of the usual cocktail food described above. In addition to that already suggested, there might be caviar or pâté de foie gras and a few fairly substantial sandwiches. Open sandwiches, of smoked turkey or pheasant, or plain turkey or chicken, would be the best. See pages 305 and 306 for the service of pâté de foie gras and caviar.

FOOD FOR DINNER

Fashions in food for dinner have changed much less than those for luncheon. Thirty years ago, menus of eight or ten courses, punctuated by sherbets between two heavy meats, had already been abandoned. But in late years the spirit has changed. Then the emphasis was on ostentation. The food was heavy and elaborate; and it was almost more important that it should look monumental and imposing than that it should be delicious. It was designed to show that it had been cooked by an expert chef, because twenty years ago a vestige of the old tradition still lingered—the tradition that made dinner parties an opportunity to emphasize, through the number of guests, the number of servants, and the number of courses, the family's position and prestige. None of this is any longer true. At one dinner party in a thousand there might be seven courses; there are sometimes five; but usually, even at quite elaborate big dinners, there are not more than four. And if the old pattern of the menu has been retained, it is partly from habit, partly because it is sensible and good, and not because it is impressive.

A perfect example of the change of attitude is in the choice of food for dinner parties. Thirty years ago, almost every dinner of more than ten people was automatically formal, and so there developed the tradition of "party food." If an important guest were coming, even to a small dinner of eight or ten people, no hostess of those days would have dreamt of serving anything as "unrefined" as chicken pie; the elaborate silver, the bonbonnières and cake baskets that were used for entertaining almost demanded fancy food. Today, silver of that kind is not in fashion, and though it is still true that a strictly formal dinner follows certain traditional rules and demands food as delicate in its way as the china and glass that will be used, fancy food has been abandoned with the bonbonnières. In choosing food for a dinner, aesthetics are important: the harmony of china, glass, linen, silver, flowers and food. Practicality is important, in that certain dishes which are possible for four people are impossible to serve to ten or twelve. But the snobbish question of whether or not food is "refined," or whether or not it will be impressive to the guests, is no longer a consideration.

For an Informal Dinner

The food for an informal dinner has more variety than any other; there is no dish too informal and none too elaborate. The customs and traditions of formal entertaining make certain dishes impractical or unsuitable; the problem of keeping food hot limits the choice of dishes for buffet meals—but here there are few rules and few such problems. For example, an informal dinner might start with caviar, proceed with paper-thin veal cutlets and a plain lettuce salad, and end up with any dessert, from stewed fruit and cake to vanilla ice cream with powdered chocolate. Or it could start with a big fish stew, followed by salad and cheese, and end with fruit and coffee. The less formal the dinner, the wider one's choice. The only limitation of an informal dinner is in the number of courses: two courses are not unusual, three are standard, and four would be the maximum. And if there were four, the dinner would probably be "informal" only from the point of view of service. For this reason, although informal dinners constitute ninety-five per cent of all entertaining, we are not listing specific suggestions for the different courses. Any of the foods suggested for luncheon, dinner, and buffet meals would be appropriate for an informal dinner, provided only that one observed the basic system of menu-planning and that the table appointments were in harmony with the food. These must be chosen with a consistent point of view.

For a Semiformal Dinner

"A semiformal dinner" is a fairly elastic phrase and it might be useful to set down, right at the beginning, exactly what we understand it to mean. The most salient feature of a semiformal dinner, as differing from a strictly formal or an informal dinner, is the service. ("Serving" is fully discussed on page 284; but see "Three Degrees of Formality," page 237.) It is more difficult to give a formula for the food, but it might be roughly summed up as follows: It differs from the food for an informal dinner in that there are at least three courses and that they follow the classic progression; it differs from a rigidly formal dinner in that there is a very wide choice in the kind of dish that can be served. The usual semi-formal dinner has three courses: soup, meat, and dessert; or fish, meat and dessert. A more elaborate one might have four courses: soup, fish, meat, and dessert; or soup, meat, salad, and dessert; or fish, meat, salad, and dessert. The most elaborate—but this would be very rare—might have five.

Food for each course is suggested under each of the separate headings which follow below, but there are one or two suggestions which do not fit into any of the categories and which must be discussed here. For example, if one has decided to have three or even four courses and not to have soup, the fish course could quite well be oysters, clams, caviar, smoked salmon, smoked brook trout, or any such semi-fishlike delicacy, instead of one of the more usual hot fish dishes. In small houses, a cold fish course such as one of these, although it may be expensive, is apt to be practical from the point of view of service and kitchen arrangements. When it is followed by a hot meat course and dessert, or a hot meat course, salad, and dessert, only one course of the meal need be carefully timed in the cooking and carefully kept hot in the serving.

The usual courses are listed under their five separate headings, but it must be emphasized that five courses are most unusual. Three, or perhaps four, should be chosen among them according to the outline suggested above.

First Course

Soup, hot or cold, depending on the season; thick or thin, depending on the rest of the menu. If the soup has been preceded by oysters, or particularly caviar, and is to be followed by a heavy creamed fish, one of the thin soups suggested on page 485 would be advisable. Among the more substantial soups are curry soup, which is basically a creamed chicken soup with curry powder, and which can be served either hot or cold; potato soup, served hot with milk and leeks (potage santé) or cold with cream and chopped chives (Vichyssoise); boula gratinée, which is a combination of turtle and pea soup with cheese-topped whipped cream on it, or just plain pea and turtle soup mixed; bilibi, which can be approximated by mixing chicken broth and clam juice with cream; a plain pea soup made of dried peas, and flavored with a ham bone; tomato soup, thin and clear, spiced with lemon and sugar; Scotch barley broth, almost like a new soup when served with a slice of lemon; onion soup, served in the French way with slices of fried bread and grated cheese (this verges on the informal); black bean soup, served with a thin round slice of lemon in it; broccoli soup; watercress soup. According to the conventional rules, all hot soups are served in plates, at dinner, and all cold or jellied soups in cups, but many hostesses serve cold soups (not jellied soups) in plates. Avoiding the conventional, one may serve all soups in widemouthed modern soup bowls, which are really oversized cups. Dessert spoons should be used with these.

Fish Course

Fish, hot or cold. Any of the fish dishes suggested on page 485 for the strictly formal dinner could be served. In addition, there is plain broiled shad roe with

322

lemon; any fish—filet of sole, trout, bass, rock fish—"sauté à la meunière" (sautéed in butter, flavored and served with lemon); striped bass à l'Orientale (a spicy tomato sauce); soft-shelled crabs with tartar sauce and lemon; broiled swordfish; fish mousse—delicious with a cream sauce but best with a lobster sauce; any fish with a white wine sauce; or, perhaps the best of all, clams Southside, a creamed hash of very finely chopped clams, served with toast. In fact, the only fish dishes that would not be appropriate for a dinner of this kind would be those such as fish stew, which are usually served in the deep casserole in which they are cooked. Any plain broiled or sautéed fish may be accompanied by sliced tomato and cucumber, which are served immediately after the fish, followed by the bread. (But this is "may," not "must.") The bread may either be sandwiches in very thin slices (a slice of white bread, a little butter, a slice of brown bread); or else it may be cut so as to make a single slice in a brown and white checkerboard pattern. Or one can skip the tomato and cucumber slices and serve little cucumber sandwiches. (Informally, of course, no special bread is ever served with fish.)

Main Course

Meat, always hot. There are all the meats suggested on page 485 and many more besides: filet mignon; Chateaubriand (or any other) steak; roast beef; roast veal; roast loin of pork; roast Virginia ham; roast chicken; roast turkey; roast duck; roast pig; roast goose; tongue with Madeira sauce; chicken with a sauce made of sherry, chicken broth, mushrooms, and cream; boeuf à la mode, a delicious French version of beef pot roast. Filet mignon and Chateaubriand steaks are often served with sauce Béarnaise, which is brought in a sauceboat immediately after the meat. Lamb is sometimes served with mint sauce or mint jelly, as well as the usual gravy; the best way is to have a tray brought immediately after the meat with a flat glass dish of jelly and a sauceboat, or two sauceboats, one with mint sauce and the other with plain gravy, each with its ladle. The details concerning the ways of serving game will be found on page 306 to page 307.

As for the vegetables, those most often served are peas, string beans, lima beans, broccoli, creamed spinach and, particularly with filet of beef, artichoke hearts with sauce Béarnaise. And one can also use any of those suggested on page 486, for the formal dinner. In addition to one of these vegetables, there are always potatoes or rice. Wild rice with wild duck, and chopped cooked celery. (See page 305, "Serving Special Dishes.") Any of the potatoes suggested on page 486 could be used and, in addition, there are roast potatoes, mashed potatoes, and French fried or matchstick potatoes.

Salad Course

Salad served on a flat dish, round or oval, is more formal than a salad served in a deep bowl. Therefore, if the dinner has been fairly elaborate, one of the salads suggested on page 486 would be advisable. Or, perhaps, a cold string bean or asparagus salad, served in a bed of small lettuce leaves on an oval platter. For less formal dinners, any of the usual salads could be served—plain lettuce, tomato, vegetable, raw spinach—in a deep wooden, china, or glass bowl. If the salad is served in this informal way, cheese and crackers may be eaten with it; one kind, or two or three different kinds, of cheese on a wooden cheese board, or on a round plate with a paper doily. There should be a small knife, silver or steel, for each kind of cheese. A wonderful cheese, if only one is to be served, is a whole Brie or Camembert. If there are to be two or three kinds, a big segment could be cut from the whole cheese and served with another which is completely different in flavor, such as Edam, Gruyère or Roquefort. (See also "Cheese," page 331 of this chapter.) If possible, it is better to avoid the kind of cheese that comes in small individual portions or segments; but, if these are used, they should always be unwrapped before being served. The crackers, which should be heated, may be served in any breadbasket, or on a round flat plate on a paper doily or—and this is perhaps the most attractive of all—in a straight-sided, three-inch deep, oblong silver platter. At more formal dinners or at large ones, a cheese board is apt to be impractical, and crackers or little cheese straws called "pailles parmesan" are more usual. When served by themselves with a simple salad, the crackers are often covered with melted cheese or with a mixture of cheese and egg that makes a tiny soufflé on each one. With any but the simplest salad, biscuits are usually served, crisp, hot and plain. The best ones are almost without flavor except for a mild saltiness.

Dessert Course

On page 486, there are suggestions for desserts for a more formal dinner, any one of which could be useful here. Others are crème brûlée; a mold of wine jelly with whipped cream; halved pears, cooked in port wine with orange peel, and symmetrically arranged in an overlapping pattern in a glass or crystal dish; whole sections of orange, peeled, skinned and very cold, flavored with kirsch and grated peel, and served in the same way as the pears; deep dish pies; tarts; shortcakes. With any of the elaborate desserts suggested on page 486, the same petits fours might still be served. With the simpler desserts, however, there could be any kind of cake, small or large, and the more simple the dessert, the richer the cake.

Menus

The following menus, some fairly elaborate and others more simple, show the wide variety of food that can be served at a dinner of this kind:

Mushroom soup, thin and strong

Roast stuffed squabs or roast quail
Wild rice   Peas

Mixed green salad, cheese soufflé

Hot sliced oranges, with grated rind, sprinkled
with a little burning brandy
Vanilla wafers

Fish chowder gumbo

Grilled chicken
Plain salad with French dressing

Chocolate roll, hot chocolate sauce, or strong
coffee jelly with eggnog sauce

Terrapin stew, Baltimore style,
or a fish mousse

Roast boned leg of veal
Whipped sweet potatoes (very light,
whipped a long time)
String beans, not cut or sliced, but whole,
in neat little bundles

Orange ice and coffee ice cream mold
Small sweet wafers

Thin potato soup

Wild duck, black currant jelly
Wild rice or fried hominy

Apple and celery heart salad

Apricot soufflé with hot apricot sauce

Mixed soup (¾ fresh clam-juice, ¼ fresh
spinach-juice), seasoned to taste

Roast pheasant or guinea hen
Purée of chestnuts
(Serve pheasant or bird nestled in brown crumbs
and fine fat raisins)
White bread sauce, currant or grape jelly

Alligator pear and grapefruit salad
with cheese biscuits

Pineapple sherbet with chocolate leaves

Chinese tomato soup, "Egg Drop"

Poulet Chasseur

Baked Idaho potatoes   Green beans

Baked Rome Beauty apples
with apricot glaze, cream

Cheese soufflé, or boula-boula (half fresh
pea purée and half rich turtle soup)

Stuffed mackerel or stuffed bluefish
Potato strings, or French fried potatoes

Salad

Baked fresh pears or peaches

Crabmeat with Russian dressing

Squab en casserole with mushrooms served
on green noodles

Artichoke, or fresh asparagus with
sauce vinaigrette

Black cherry tarts (rum flavored)

Plain or creamed mushroom soup

Broiled sirloin steak
Broiled whole tomatoes with a dash of Major
Gray's chutney on top
Scalloped baked potatoes

Green salad, Oka cheese

Fruits rafraîchis au rhum
Vanilla wafers

Consommé (clear beef, or veal, with sherry)

Breast of guinea hen on Virginia ham
Wild rice and mushrooms
Braised endive or lettuce

Meringue with crushed fresh raspberries

Clams on half shell, or oysters on
half shell, or clear turtle soup with sherry
Celery, carrot sticks, etc.

Roast duckling with orange sauce
Orange potatoes
Green peas

Chicory, lettuce, and beet salad

Apricot Flan

Clam broth with cream

Roast loin of pork
Purée of sweet potatoes
Red cabbage and applesauce mixed

Deep-dish pie of mixed preserved peaches,
apricots, and sliced oranges

Purée St. Germain (cream of pea soup)

Birds (quail, woodcock, and small game)
Purée of celery root
Samp, plain boiled or fried

Artichokes Hollandaise

Tangerine sections in sherry
Plain poundcake

Purée of spinach or carrot soup

Fried chicken, pan gravy, green peas
Spoonbread, plain, or with spiced
peaches or apricots, or
Sweet potatoes with apple and banana, Hawaiian

Green pepper, tomato, and lettuce salad

Chocolate rum mousse

Fresh tomato soup with chives

Calves' liver sauté
Baked Bermuda onion rings
Scalloped baked potatoes

Field salad with sliced beets

Prune soufflé

Chinese watercress soup, "Egg Drop"

Roast leg, or saddle, or rack, or crown of lamb
Mint sauce, green peas
Parsley potatoes, or pan roast or French fried potatoes

Mixed green salad, Camembert cheese

Strawberry Flan

Chilled tomato soup

Beef Strogonoff, or steak-and-kidney pie
Plain boiled potatoes and braised carrots

Mixed salad greens

Apple strudel, or apple meringue

FOOD FOR BUFFET MEALS

For buffet meals, as for any other, the old rule "a little more food than just enough" is still in force. But at buffet meals, if it is broken, it is more obvious. If there is too much or too little food, it becomes immediately obvious, since all the food is laid out to be seen. And too much food is worse than too little. Unless there are a great many guests, there should never be more than one or two different kinds of meats sliced (unless they are all on a platter together), or more than one salad. For twelve guests, one big, whole turkey would obviously be more than enough, and it would be bad taste to have a Virginia ham and roast beef as well. If there were sixty guests, however, turkey, ham, and roast beef would be better and more sensible than the three or four turkeys which, from the point of view of quantity alone, would be needed.

As we have said on page 265, in the chapter "Setting," the classic buffet meal has three courses, of which the first is usually the hot one: hot soup in a tureen, or a solid hot dish, kept hot in a casserole or on a burner; cold meat or cheese with salad; and dessert. But, just as there is no reason apart from convenience to cling to this pattern of courses, so there is no reason to have three courses instead of two. One might have, for example, a big casserole of chicken with potatoes, peas and mushrooms, and for dessert crème brûlée with stewed cherries or fresh raspberries. Or, one might have crab or shrimp gumbo with rice followed by a plain salad, cheese, and coffee. Therefore, the following suggestions, although listed as soups, hot dishes, cold dishes, etc., can be juggled around to fit any kind of pattern.

Soups

As a practical matter soups, other than "meal-in-itself" soups, are not a good choice for buffet meals. But if one wants soup, these points may be helpful. If there are a great many guests, jellied soups are not a wise choice unless the guests are seated, because the filled cups cannot be stacked and take up too much room on the big buffet table. Cold soups can be served in a tureen, at the point where they begin to thicken, and before they turn to jelly, but cold soup which never even approaches the jelly stage is better: for example, curry soups, vichyssoise, bortsch, or, for the more catholic taste, a cold Spanish soup called gaspacho. If the weather is no problem, one of the usual hot soups could be served in a tureen. Some are suggested on page 322, others on page 485, any one of which would be useful here as a first course.

Soups served with rice and any of the following "meal-in-itself" soups could be the main course of a simple buffet luncheon or dinner; Hochepot Normande, which is a shin of beef slowly and gently cooked with leeks, potatoes, peppercorns, and bay leaves, and served in a tureen with slices of the meat and the vegetables (this is eaten in big soup plates, and a knife, fork, and spoon are necessary); bouillabaisse, a French stew of almost every kind of fish, based on lobster, flavored with saffron and garlic (this, too, in soup plates with a dessert fork and spoon); crab or shrimp gumbo, which should be eaten in soup plates and served in a tureen or chafing dish, with separate dishes of dry, firm rice near by. Any of these soups would be excellent followed by a plain salad and cheese, and dessert. Or oyster stew, rich with oysters, accompanied by big crisp soda crackers; this to be followed by cold meat and salad, and dessert.

Hot Dishes

The most usual hot dish is probably baked beans, curried shrimp, or chicken à la King, but these are more interesting: clams Southside, a creamed hash which should always be served with a platter of crisp toast beside it; lobster or crabmeat Newburg, also accompanied by toast; kedgeree, a baked fish dish; creamed halibut or sole Mornay; risotto with chicken livers, mushrooms, and truffles; creamed chicken hash, finely minced, served with rice or small, very hot beaten biscuits; chicken Tetrazzini, which is cooked with noodles and mushrooms in a cream sauce (for such a meal, the chicken should be cut into small pieces); a really good curry of lamb or chicken, with Bombay duck, grated cocoanut, chutney, and rice; a big shepherd's pie; roast beef, or corned beef, hash; Swedish meat balls, served with string beans; chicken and oysters in a casserole; fish mousse, with cream or lobster sauce. Any of these would be delicious and most practical for a "stand-up" buffet, because none of them needs a knife and any of them can be eaten, so to speak, with one hand.

If the guests are seated at little tables, with knife and fork at hand, one's choice is infinitely wider: a big Virginia ham, with Cumberland or Madeira sauce and creamed spinach; "Noisettes d'agneau," the solid meaty part of a French lamb chop served on an artichoke heart, and accompanied by creamed mashed potatoes; roast beef; roast leg of lamb; roast pig; roast loin of pork; or a roast turkey, stuffed with oysters and served with creamed celery.

Cold Dishes

The most frequent cold dish is a platter of sliced meat, all of one kind, or mixed: ham, roast beef, roast turkey, roast lamb, tongue, roast chicken. More original are French lamb chops, with all the fat carefully trimmed away; or breast of squab, carved and served as breast of chicken would be; or breast of guinea hen. Smoked turkey or pheasant, or Virginia ham, can be served standing (on the carcass), or sliced and arranged on the platter garnished with lettuce and aspic or parsley. The only meats that should be avoided are those that look as though they belonged in a store window: square, pallid slices of ham, liverwurst, salami, bologna, or sausage. If there is no time to order or cook special meats, cheese is better than any of these.

Cold fish dishes are too often overlooked: salmon, halibut, brook trout, or a cold shellfish, such as lobster or crabmeat. Some of these are suggested on page 485 in the sections dealing with fish and salads for a formal dinner. For a buffet luncheon, whether simple or elaborate, cold eggs would be an excellent first course in summer. There are several suggested on page 313. And, besides, there is avocado, which could be used here either as a first course or as a salad. Another way of serving eggs as a salad course for a buffet would be hard-boiled in an aspic, with sliced tomatoes, lettuce, and mayonnaise.

Salads

For simple buffet luncheon or dinner, or whenever cheese is to be served, the best and most practical salads are the simplest. Served in a deep bowl of wood or china, mixed with a good French dressing, they are usually made of lettuce (the best and most useful kind is the green Boston lettuce), either plain, or combined with watercress, raw spinach, endive, or chicory. Another very good plain salad, particularly with Roquefort cheese, is chopped raw spinach, garnished with lettuce. If it is not served with the cheese, this spinach salad is delicious mixed with a little chopped bacon. Other salads not designed merely as a foil for cheese are: cold corn salad, which is boiled corn stripped from the cob, cooled, mixed with French dressing and served plain or with a border of lettuce; string bean, beet, carrot, pea salad, each by itself with lettuce, or mixed in a vegetable salad; raw chopped celery and cold raw cauliflower salad (only the very tenderest tips of the cauliflower should be used). One of the best of all simple salads is tomato and lettuce, but too often this means pallid slices of unripe tomato drenched in vinegar with a large unyielding leaf of iceberg lettuce. All tomatoes used for salads should be fully ripe, and the small round or oval tomatoes should be used as well as the usual big ones.

For a more elaborate buffet, salads are often served on a flat platter as at a formal dinner. Any one of those suggested on page 323 would be helpful here, but there are simpler varieties of the same type: a ring of tomato aspic surrounded with lettuce and filled with chopped celery and apple, which is mixed with a light mayonnaise; or hard-boiled eggs in aspic, with a cream sauce of Roquefort cheese; or cole slaw; or potato salad, particularly good with cold roast beef.

Cheese

Nowhere, perhaps, is a great variety of cheeses more attractive than on a buffet table. A cheese board is put near the salad at one end of the table, each cheese neatly separated from its neighbor, each with its own knife. (See page 263 in the chapter "Setting the Table.") On such a board there might be one, or any number, of the following: Edam, Roquefort, Gruyère, Liederkranz, Gorgonzola, Bel Paese, Gouda, Brie, Camembert, Stilton, Cheddar, "California Jack," Oka, Argentine Blue. Besides these, there is a whole new family of smoked cheeses, many of them made in Wisconsin, which also supplies some of the best American Brie and Camembert. Another way of serving cheese, instead of having so many on one board, is to have one large round Brie or Camembert on a plate or board by itself; balancing this, on the other side of the salad bowl, a round tray with little crocks of such special cheeses as Cheddar or Stilton in wine.

Desserts

For a simple buffet luncheon or dinner, the variety of desserts is endless. In summer: a big iced watermelon cut so that sections of the meat are free from the rind but are left on the rind in more or less the original shape; cut up fresh fruit with kirsch, berries with cream, or any of the other desserts suggested on pages 314 and 324 for luncheon and dinner. For the most elaborate buffet, perhaps one of the desserts suggested on page 486 for the formal dinner. In winter: a big hot compote of dried fruit served in the casserole in which it was cooked; pies of any kind; a big tray of éclairs and little tarts, but not too many: otherwise there is danger of suggesting a French restaurant.

FOOD FOR SUPPER

As outlined on page 265 in the chapter "Setting," there are three kinds of late suppers—supper after dinner, supper after the theater, and supper at dances. The simplest of these is after-dinner supper.

After-Dinner Supper

Late in the evening, after a dinner, food is very often brought into the living room. (This is described from the point of view of serving, on page 298; from the point of view of arranging the table, on page 266.) The only exception might be a stiffly formal dinner, after which the guests are expected to go home before any further nourishment will be needed. After a fairly elaborate dinner of five or six courses, only simple sandwiches will be served: round or oblong, but always small and thin, usually with the crusts cut away. These sandwiches are made of white bread and butter, or very finely sliced chicken, cream cheese, chutney, pâté de foie gras, or smoked turkey. Or they can be made of brown bread and cream or Swiss cheese. For a dinner of twelve, there should be two plates of sandwiches of at least two different kinds.

After a shorter dinner, the food will be more substantial than this. In addition to the sandwiches there might be any one of the following: hard-boiled eggs, chilled, peeled and served in a bowl on a bed of shredded lettuce (small plates, pepper and salt, and napkins are needed for these as they are eaten in the fingers); pâté de foie gras and biscuits, served as described on page 306; a cheese such as Edam, Oka, Gouda, or Gruyère with biscuits and very thinly sliced buttered rye bread with the crusts left on. With this food, hot soup or hot coffee, or sometimes hot chocolate is served. In many ways, soup is the best, because hot coffee is not always very popular late at night, and chocolate is rich.

Supper after the Theater

If a few friends are coming back for supper after the theater, or after a hockey game, one might have a supper such as the one described immediately above: soup, cheese, eggs, and sandwiches. In addition, if one wanted a little more than this, one might have very finely sliced sausage, with biscuits or buttered bread; open sandwiches of turkey or chicken; a hot covered dish of very small sugared doughnuts; broiled sardines on toast; hot melted cheese on toast; hot Russian pastries, called piroshki, stuffed with chopped meat; or very small beaten biscuits, split and filled with chopped bacon or minced chicken.

Any food more elaborate than this is a buffet meal. For a simple buffet supper, which may be served either in the dining room or in the living room, one might have one of the following dishes: a cheese fondue; kippered herring or finnan haddie; very small meat balls; délices d'Emmenthal, which are delicious croquettes made of melted Camembert; codfish cakes and bacon; sliced hard-boiled eggs in a cheese sauce; or—the old standby—scrambled eggs and bacon. With this, soup or coffee, thin half-slices of buttered rye and brown bread, toasted French or Italian bread and some mild sandwiches such as plain butter or cream cheese.

A more elaborate buffet supper would, of course, be set up in the dining room. If a great many people are expected, it would be more practical to arrange little tables as described on page 264 in the chapter "Setting." If there are fewer guests, no arrangements are necessary other than to put the food on the dining-room table. For a supper such as this, one might have oyster stew, Virginia ham and salad, and very small tarts of wild strawberries or apricots; or soup, a creamed fish such as clams Southside or lobster Newburg, salad and cheese. For the most elaborate supper, one might have caviar and champagne, a thin hot consommé, pheasant, guinea hen or grouse with celery and apple salad, and coffee. For further suggestions, see pages 329 through 331.

If one is sure that all the guests have had no dinner and nothing more substantial than soup and sandwiches, or high tea, one might have a short served seated supper at the dining-room table. This would be particularly appropriate for official guests or older people who might not enjoy a buffet meal. It is usually served to a relatively small number of people, perhaps eight or ten. A supper such as this could start with a hot thin soup, followed by a creamed dish, such as lobster Newburg or creamed chicken, cold meat, salad, and an ice. Or one might have a hot cream soup, such as lobster bisque, cold meat, and salad, and a big hot compote of fruit. Or, oysters or caviar; hot roast squabs or squab chickens, served with a plain lettuce salad; and ice cream. This supper is served exactly as any seated meal is served at the dining-room table. The important point of difference between this supper and any dinner is that the pattern of hot meat served with hot vegetables is never followed. With this in mind, one might substitute many of the dishes suggested between pages 322 to 324, and 485 through 487.

Supper at Dances

At a small dinner dance, there is often a buffet supper instead of the more elaborate served supper. A buffet table is set in the dining room, with all the food on it so that the guests can help themselves. There should be at least one or two hot dishes, and a cold dessert. For example, in summer, one might have cold soup; a hot dish such as creamed chicken or turkey with rice, or lobster, crabmeat, or shrimps with toast; and a water ice. Or: a hot soup; cold meat, or ham or chicken mousse, or an aspic of eggs, ham, chicken or pâté de foie gras, with salad; and a water ice. In winter: hot soup; one of the usual hot creamed dishes, or terrapin (but this is wildly expensive, of course); and ice cream. Or, particularly for younger people, one might have a simpler supper of two courses: scrambled eggs with sausage or bacon, and muffins or rolls; or chipped beef in cream; or sliced hard-boiled eggs with sauce Mornay; or codfish cakes and bacon; and ice cream with cookies or little cakes.

At a big dance, where there will be many guests who were not entertained at dinner, the supper is usually served directly from the kitchen, with the guests seated at small tables. The most usual menu is one of three courses, as suggested immediately above. The dessert can be as elaborate as one wishes; ice cream is better in winter, water ice in summer. (Suggestions for both will be found on page 486.)

Supper at a dance is usually served at about midnight or half-past twelve, but the food need not end with supper. When the supper itself is finished and the tables have been cleared, sandwiches, cheese and crackers, and small cakes are often set on the buffet table near the drinks so that the guests can help themselves from time to time. If the dance lasts until very late, till four o'clock in the morning or later, hot coffee, chocolate, or soup is often served with scrambled eggs and bacon, or sausages.

At all dances there should be at least two non-alcoholic drinks as well as the others. Milk, a cola drink, ginger ale, and orangeade or lemonade are the most usual; and at a very big dance all of these might be served. The classic drink for a dance is champagne or punch, either a champagne punch or a wine punch. At a dance where many older people are expected, whiskey and soda may be served; as a rule it is not set out with the other drinks, but brought especially by the waiters.

THE CHOICE AND HANDLING OF WINES AND LIQUEURS

Too much has been written about wines being "correct" or "incorrect." The fable of correctness was born of common sense and familiarity, fostered by a cabal of enthusiastic experts who have zestfully explored all the subtleties of wine drinking, and accepted by the great majority who have less time to spend on the palate. The majority accepted it because they agreed with its conclusions. Without bothering about the intricacies of the vernacular, they agreed that a dry white wine tastes better with fish, and that red Burgundy tastes better with red meat; and these have come to be called "correct." The recommendations given below are based entirely on this democratic process of judgment; the majority of guests at any dinner will concur in this opinion; and it has been the majority vote for so long that it has become the custom.

Custom permits a different wine with every course, on the assumption that each wine is peculiarly well-suited to one special flavor. In theory, therefore, the number of wines is limited only by the number of courses, but good taste imposes certain restrictions to the application of this theory. At the most elaborate and formal dinner possible, the theory may apply in full as is shown on page 489, where a different wine is suggested for almost every course. But for a most informal dinner, only one or two wines should be served, even if there are three courses. ("Serving Wines" will be found on pages 300 to 304; the proper glasses are shown on pages 394 to 398, in the section "Furnishing a House.")

Sherries

Sherries are "fortified" wines and, therefore, unlike other wines, can be left almost interminably in a decanter without spoiling. There are three main types of which the most useful is the medium dry:

Amontillado: Very pale, very dry, best when served cold instead of cocktails.

Medium dry: Light brown, best with soup and between meals. Excellent when chilled and served cold before meals.

Heavy, semi-sweet: Only good if of excellent quality, served at room temperature, with strong clear soups. (This is usually called "Oloroso.")

White Wines

There are four main types of white wine, of which the most useful are Rhine wines and white Burgundies. White wines should be served cold and are not necessarily decanted, because white wine has no sediment. They need be opened only a short time before serving. If any is left over, it is usually still fresh and good the next day. Suggestions are given concerning the food to which each wine is specially suited, but any of these except the sauternes may be served throughout an informal meal. In storing all wine, the bottles should be laid on their sides—not standing—because the cork will shrink, in time, if it is dry.

Rhine wine: Very light, good with fish and oysters, particularly good in summer, and the best wine to be mixed with seltzer and mint in a long glass (although this is a wasteful use of any really good wine).

Bordeaux (the "Graves" type): Good with fish, light meats such as veal, poultry; a most useful wine.

Burgundy, including Chablis: Drier than Bordeaux, good with fish or poultry. A dry white Burgundy is the customary wine for oysters, clams, or caviar.

Sauternes: A white Bordeaux, sweeter than any of the other three and less useful. In France, it is served as a dessert wine.

Red Wines

Of the two main types of red wine—Burgundy and Bordeaux, or claret—the more useful is claret. Like white wine, red wine should be stored on its side, because the cork shrinks, in a cool, even temperature; but it is always served at room temperature. Old wines, which have a great deal of sediment, are brought up from the cellar a week before serving to stand before being decanted. (Experts often decant old and rare wine in the cellar, but see page 300 for a discussion of the question of decanting.) Wines with less sediment need less care but all except the youngest red wine should be very carefully decanted about two hours before serving and left in the dining room. To be at its best, the wine should be drunk the day it is decanted. As in the case of white wines, specific courses are suggested, but any red wine may be served throughout the meal, provided only that it is suited to the main course.

Claret (red Bordeaux): The classic accompaniment to the main meat course.

Burgundy: Dry, heavy wine, excellent with game, heavy meats, and cheese. At old-fashioned formal dinners it was served with game, immediately before the dessert and champagne, and just after the meat and claret. Now, it is rarely served in the same meal with claret, but it often replaces claret when game or beef is served.

Other types of red wine are Rhône wines and Italian wines. All are used and treated as a claret, and are especially good at luncheon. Sparkling Burgundy is a wine not admired by connoisseurs. If it is served, it is only at dinner. It is iced like champagne and served with the main course. Like champagne, it is not decanted and it must be drunk as soon as it is opened.

Champagne

There are two kinds of champagne, of which only one, the golden, need be considered. The other, champagne rosé, is extremely rare. Champagne can be dry (brut), semidry, or sweet; Americans usually like dry champagne best. It must be served very cold, left in a bucket of ice so that the ice comes in contact with the sides of the bottle for several hours before it is served, or put next to the freezing compartment in the icebox a day ahead of time. If the time is short, a way of icing it more quickly is to twirl the bottle in the ice, so that the wine at the center of the bottle gets to the outside and cools more quickly. A little salt in the ice speeds the process. It must be drunk as soon as the bottle is opened, since it will go flat in a very few minutes. Champagne is never decanted but poured directly from the bottle into the glass.

After-Dinner Wines

In England, where a savory was often served after the dessert, the tradition of after-dinner wines flourished. There are several kinds that are served at the end of the meal: Malaga, port, Madeira, Tokay; but by far the most popular is port. All these wines are served at room temperature, either in decanters or in their own bottles, before the coffee, liqueurs, and cigars. All are fairly sweet and very heavy. None of them is customary in the United States, although port is becoming more popular than it was. It is served at the dining-room table, in small wineglasses which are brought just before it is to be served. And it is *always* served clockwise.

Liqueurs

Liqueurs are served after dinner is over, just after the coffee. They may be poured from decanters or from their own bottles. The five most usually served in the United States are these:

Brandy: Served in small liqueur glasses, or, as experts prefer, in very large rounded glasses with a short-stemmed foot. (These are called "balloon" glasses; see drawings on page 398.) If the brandy is especially fine, these large glasses are sometimes warmed by burning an inferior brandy in the glass before pouring the liqueur brandy into it.

Crème de Menthe: This liqueur can be either white or green; when it is served in glasses filled with crushed ice, the glasses must be bigger than those used for brandy or chartreuse (see the diagram on page 397).

Cointreau: Served at room temperature, in small liqueur glasses.

Chartreuse: Served at room temperature, in small liqueur glasses.

Fruit brandies: The most common are cherry and apricot brandy; served at room temperature, in small liqueur glasses.

Punches

Punches have two main family lines, hot and cold. The most common hot punches are hot mulled or spiced wine (usually claret), hot buttered rum and hot whiskey toddies. These should be mixed in a china or silver bowl, and, by preference, should be served in long glasses with stands or holders, or in china mugs. They are, of course, winter drinks, for special occasions.

Cold punches fall into two categories: those mixed with milk or cream, such as eggnogs, which are cold but not iced; and those mixed with water or wine, which are served with ice. Eggnogs, the traditional drink for winter holidays, are served from a punch bowl of glass, china, or silver. The standard drinking glass is a round punch glass or a silver goblet. Iced punches, which are served at dances and wedding receptions, are mixed in the bowl with a big block of ice. The traditional punch glass (see example on page 398) is the best, but sometimes a small tumbler is used instead. The most usual punches are those with a wine base, either champagne or still wine, mixed with soda water or fruit juice.

MINOR NOTES
Bread and Rolls

Slices of American bread, cut off the loaf, neither toasted nor halved and served by themselves, are a dreary part of too many meals. Most American bread (both the nutritionists of the U. S. Department of Agriculture and gourmets agree on this) was not worth eating before it was enriched. Even now it is rarely as good as French or Italian bread, both of which are very easy to find in most American towns. Thick slices of either of these, plain, heated or toasted, are delicious for luncheon or with an informal dinner menu. When the menu is longer, these are often served: toast with the soup, often Melba toast; brown and white bread with fish (see "Fish Course," page 322); and, with meat, toast or rolls (small glazed rolls, Parker House rolls, or French croissants); with the salad, toasted hot saltines or cheese straws. For luncheon when there will be butter plates, half-slices of some special bread, such as gluten bread or a specially good whole-wheat bread, may be served in the basket with toast and rye crisp or thin wheat biscuits or Melba toast, etc. Flat breads, muffins, popovers, Southern biscuits, beaten biscuits, English muffins, are all good for luncheon. All rolls and toast should be served hot or at least warm. It is not good usage to set the table with bread—or anything except butter and a knife—on the butter plates.

Butter

There are several ways of serving butter, of which the most common is certainly to put a butterball or a curl of butter on each butter plate before the guests come into the dining room. The systems are as follows:

The most elaborate, old-fashioned system was to leave a butter plate, like a water glass, empty until the guests were seated at the table. The butler then went around the table from place to place and, standing to the left of each guest, put a butterball on each plate, using a small pointed fork. The tray, balanced on his left hand, held a glass dish of butterballs, sometimes deep enough to contain a few pieces of ice, also.

Another way is to set by the butter plate a small covered crock filled with butter. This system, which originated in France, is particularly useful for luncheon out of doors.

Third, on the tray with the breadbasket, or on a small tray held in the other hand, or offered immediately after the breadbasket on a second trip, the butler offers a little glass dish of butterballs. If a deep dish is used there are often pieces of ice among the butterballs. The serving implement is a small pointed fork. This system may be used also with a big mold or print of butter, which is offered on a flat glass dish with a small silver knife or butter knife. The most attractive mold for this is half-pound size, with a design such as a wheat sheaf on the top.

For informal entertaining, the butter may be set in a glass dish on the table. A covered dish is best and the butter should be worked into butterballs or else molded, as suggested immediately above. If there are butterballs, a deep dish which is big enough to hold pieces of ice also will make the butter look fresher.

To be avoided are squares of butter cut from the standard, quarter-pound bars, which are often put on butter plates; also standard bars set on the table or offered whole.

337

Celery, Pickles, Preserves, etc.

No part of entertaining twenty years ago was more unfortunate than that which fell under the popular misapprehension that one could not entertain without following through on the last detail of the dinner party routine. This was expressed in the feeling that one *must* have certain "accessories," such as celery and olives with the soup. If one likes celery and there is beautiful fresh celery on the market, or, if one has found some specially good big olives, there is no reason not to serve them with the soup. But nothing could be worse than pallid, stringy celery or small insipid olives served only for the sake of custom. This same spirit is true all down the line. Melba toast is good with soup, and it is a custom besides. But to serve Melba toast, good, bad or indifferent, only because it *is* a custom is entirely out of the spirit and fashion of our times. Similarly, except at the most formal dinners, there is no reason not to serve a specially good pickle, if one happens to like it; or very small fresh scallions, or strips of carrot. Whatever it is, it must be served for its own sake, because it is good and not because one feels that guests might expect it.

Soup

There seems to be a superstition that clear soup is served only in cups, and that thick soup is served only in bowls or plates. Where and how it developed is a mystery, because it is utterly unrelated to any fact. Cups are used at luncheon, no matter what the soup. Plates are traditional for serving hot soups at dinner, whether thick or clear. Jellied soups are served in cups. And apart from the sensible custom of serving a clear soup rather than a thick one when there are many courses, there are no other rules concerning the service of soup.

Fruit Cup

Fruit cup should not be used as a first course at luncheon or dinner. Cut-up fruit, which must always be fresh and raw, is a dessert only. The only exception might be some fruit such as cut-up oranges and bananas, served at breakfast time. Melon or papaya cut in big sections (quarters or halves) or grapefruit cut in halves, with the rind left on, may be served either as a first or last course.

GLOSSARY

For those who dine often in restaurants, the following short glossary may be useful:

à la Russe: this means a dish combined with Russian dressing (roughly, mayonnaise sauce with ketchup).

à l'Espagnole: like "Napolitaine," this means a dish combined with tomatoes and usually garlic. If it is a rice dish, it means that the rice has been cooked with saffron.

à l'Orientale: usually a dish cooked with tomatoes and many spices.

au gratin: a dish that has been sprinkled with grated cheese and put briefly under the broiler so that the cheese melts. Sometimes, also, the dish is made with a creamed cheese sauce, but *au gratin* means that grated cheese has been sprinkled on top.

Bercy: white wine and shallot sauce.

Bisque: a cream soup of shell fish. *Bisque d'homard* is cream of lobster soup. *Bisque d'écrevisses* is cream of shrimp soup.

Chantilly: a dish combined with whipped cream.

Chivry: a dish, usually meat, garnished with artichoke hearts.

Compote: cooked fruit.

Cressonnière: a dish combined with watercress.

Florentine: a dish combined with spinach, usually creamed spinach, and very often with cheese as well.

Jardinière: a dish that is garnished with vegetables, usually peas, carrots, string beans, and artichoke hearts.

Macaroni au gratin: this usually has cheese mixed in the sauce all through the dish, as well as grated on the top.

Macedoine: cut-up fruit which is served as a dessert and often flavored with kirsch or Cointreau.

Meunière or *à la Belle meunière:* a dish cooked in butter, usually served with a slice of lemon.

Minestrone: this is an Italian vegetable soup with a meat stock base.

Mornay: this is a cream sauce highly flavored with cheese.

Napolitaine: tomatoes, and often garlic.

Nesselrode: a dish, usually a dessert, with chestnuts or purée of chestnuts.

Petite marmite, Henry IV: this is a clear meat soup served with many cut-up vegetables in it and often shreds of meat.

Pilaff or Pilaw: a rice dish in which the rice has been cooked, or at least heated, with oil.

Potage: this is an unclarified soup, usually creamed, often made with potatoes.

Purée: literally "mash." Mashed potatoes are *Purée de pommes de terre.* On French menus, it is often used in the name of a soup, *Purée St. Germain,* for example.

Rafraîchi: usually "fruits rafraîchis," literally "refreshed." As a rule, it is cut-up, raw fruit, iced and sometimes flavored with kirsch ("Fruits rafraîchis au Kirsch") or rum ("Fruits rafraîchis au rhum").

St. Germain: peas—usually it's pea soup: *Purée St. Germain;* but it can also mean a purée of peas: *Emince de volaille en bordure St. Germain* is chicken hash with a border of purée of peas.

Soupe à l'onion au gratin: this is onion soup covered with croutons of bread, sprinkled with grated cheese, and put under the broiler.

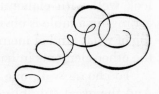

43

Fashions in Table Decoration

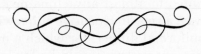

ARRANGING a table is, without doubt, a minor but most neglected art. And, like all arts, it demands an understanding of one's medium, and a conception which one wants to express. The medium is, of course, the china and glass, linen and silver, wood and fruit and flowers which make the finished table. But, before we go any further, it might be wise to set down the prerequisites which are the basis of all successful tables. The first is an evident interest in the job, a desire to create a beautiful and pleasing whole which is obvious in the care and originality with which everything for the table has been chosen. One of the minor but most immediate evidences of a lack of interest is a pallid "set" of china, one of those which "goes with everything" and carries on interminably and drearily throughout the meal, course after course. Unless the set is magnificent or, in itself, an object of great beauty, a different pattern for each course is much more attractive. (For further suggestions, see page 403, "Furnishing a House.")

Granted an interest in the matter, the first consideration in decorating a table is that everything on the table must be subordinated to the food. And, fundamentally, this means subordinated to the menu, because very few dishes have such definite character of their own that they can impose their personality on the whole menu. For example, one might have a saddle of lamb at the most informal dinner, or at the most formal dinner. If it has been preceded by three courses, and is to be followed by two more—according to the pattern of the most formal menu—the table will have to be arranged formally. On the other hand, if it is preceded by soup and followed by dessert, the table can be set in almost any way one fancies. Only a few dishes, notably the heavy stews and such soups as bouillabaisse and Hochepot Normande, impose their own limitations; partly because of their innate character, partly because the serving dishes they demand do not look well with elaborate china and fine linen. The first step, then, in arranging a table is obvious interest and thought, and a clear understanding of what kind of menu one has constructed. The second step is to choose the other elements in harmony with that menu.

To choose well, one must understand the character of each element. And the great stumbling block here is a tendency to confuse the cost or rarity of an object with its character. Queen Anne's lace is a weed, but it is also a delicate and beautiful flower and can be used with a light flower, such as sultana or candytuft, to make a beautiful centerpiece. Kale is an inexpensive vegetable, and not even a very popular one; but, as a centerpiece, the mauve-pink and pale-green colors and the fine texture of the leaves are perfectly suited to almost any china or glass except the most delicate. In the same way, a very inexpensive china with a delicate pattern could be used for a semiformal dinner, for which a much more expensive china with a coarse, peasant pattern would be far less appropriate; thin, inexpensive napkins of Swiss cotton could be used for an elaborate women's luncheon, whereas heavy linen napkins with peasant embroidery, which might be much more expensive, would be used only for the most informal entertaining.

Some people have a flair for recognizing the nature of inanimate objects; others have to learn it through experience, interest and study. A safe rule of thumb is that it is better to mix elements of the same type from different countries than it is to mix different types from the same country. It is better, for example, to put flowered English china, of the category we have called "American or English cottage," on a French Provincial fruit-wood table, than to put heavily gilded Sèvres porcelain on that table. The deciding factor in determining the character of an object is sometimes the degree of culture or sophistication of the civilization which produced it. Peasant glass from Mexico can combine very well with peasant china from Italy or Czechoslovakia. Or the determining factor may be the period in which the object was made: Bristol and Waterford glass go better with Meissen than with early English pewter. An understanding of these two points—the character of the menu and of the table arrangements—makes an expert craftsman, one who knows his tools. But artists have something more.

Artists have, above all, an idea to express, imagination enough to visualize the finished whole, and taste enough to carry it out well. The factor that makes arranging a table an art, although a minor one, is that it is a medium of expression. And, as in all minor arts, the fashion changes constantly. The tables of thirty or forty years ago, so poignantly described in the Patty Fairfield series, were considered beautiful, with all their little pierced baskets of bonbons, their trailing fronds of asparagus fern. To us, they seem to have fallen miserably between an effort to be refined and an effort to be sumptuous. But they were considered both fashionable and aesthetic in their day.

Modern tables, if one can find a least common denominator for so heterogeneous a group, strike for a certain crispness of outline, a neatness and simplicity that would have been called bare and plain by the past generation, and will perhaps be called plain and bare by the next. The contemporary bugaboo is overornamentation, and useless, irrelevant, elaboration. Modern taste leans toward the heavier, sturdier and simpler, and away from the lighter, the more delicate, and the more elaborate. The passion for collecting Lowestoft china, which began in this country in the 1920's, is a perfect example of this trend. Lowestoft used to be considered a little coarse, just as a wooden salad bowl was unheard-of except for picnicking in the country. The first break in this consistent trend toward simplicity is the very new fad for Meissen china.

Modern taste has evolved many ways of expressing this trend toward simplicity. But there are six, each quite different from the other, which are immediately recognizable as types. Broadly speaking, with infinite variations, they can be identified as follows: French Provincial, American or English cottage, Eighteenth Century English; modern—usually Swedish or American; peasant—of any country; and the new Middle-European, as expressed in the rococo swirls of Meissen and Berlin china. Many tables, of course, do not fit into any of these categories. Some seem to be lacking in any cohesive idea—if one had to find a phrase for them, it might be "the New-York-apartment look"—a dark table covered with a filet lace cloth or set with filet lace mats; a dozen roses, always pink; chased glasses, wishfully ornate; modern silver with a single initial, wildly elaborate; and too small, flimsy napkins. Other tables are extremely beautiful, expressing subtle and original conceptions which spring from none of the usual parent-ideas. But for some reason, whether because the kind of china and glass that is sold today fits into these categories, or because these patterns, so often repeated, spring first to the mind, these six ideas are the most popular.

Before we make specific suggestions for formal and semiformal meals, it might be useful to explain these six ideas a little further.

FRENCH PROVINCIAL

French Provincial means, usually, a bare fruit-wood table, with mats of straw or fairly heavy linen, often colored, and linen napkins. A china-vegetable centerpiece; an old brass scale, balanced with fruit, is an excellent centerpiece, too. At night, candlesticks of china or plain heavy glass. At luncheon, little earthenware butter crocks, cream-colored or pale gray-blue. China saltcellars and pepper pots, or wooden salt and pepper mills; plain heavy glass ashtrays or, more typical, china ashtrays in the shape of lettuce leaves or grape leaves. A wicker breadbasket; a wooden salad bowl; fruit-wood trays. Brown earthenware casseroles; china platters—white inside, brown outside. Pottery in light colors, or fine china; but never the kind of very fine porcelain that is heavily banded in silver or gold. Any flat silver not too primitively heavy or too ornate. Any glass of a simple design, not cut or very elaborately chased, nor too starkly modern.

AMERICAN OR ENGLISH COTTAGE

American or English cottage means, usually, a bare table of mahogany, pine, cherry, or maple (these last three are more difficult and limiting than mahogany: see the next paragraph below); mats of plain mediumweight linen, or old-fashioned crocheted or embroidered doilies, and plain linen napkins; or linen mats with a colored border of crochet, and napkins to match. A china tureen, covered, or filled with simple garden flowers, such as lilac or bleeding heart, or orchard fruit; and, at night, plain silver or china candlesticks. Silver or china saltcellars and pepper pots; china ashtrays in a simple flowered pattern (old miniature samples of Wedgwood or Staffordshire plates would be ideal for this). A simple silver breadbasket; a glass, china, or wooden salad bowl; painted tole trays. China platters and serving dishes; flowered china, or dimmed old-fashioned luster. Any simple flat silver except one with a markedly modern design. Any glass that is neither massive, nor modernistic, nor ornate.

The advantage of a plain mahogany table over a table of cherry, maple, or pine is that mahogany gives one much greater latitude in choosing table ornaments. The following, for example, are apt to look well on mahogany, and not as well on the other woods: very fine linen, such as organdie; fine china, and china in neutral colors such as Wedgwood "Queensware"; glass candlesticks or china candelabra; glass ashtrays.

CLASSIC ENGLISH

Classic English suggests a mahogany table, with star-shaped mats of very fine stiffened twine, or very small square mats of hemstitched Irish linen, or round linen mats with a border of some fairly heavy lace such as point de Milan; napkins of plain damask, or matching the linen mats. A centerpiece of Waterford glass, or a silver tankard, or an Early American silver bowl; candlesticks of a heavy glass such as Steuben, or Waterford, or small Queen Anne silver candlesticks, or silver candelabra, or crystal candelabra with prisms in a heavy glass such as Waterford. Saltcellars of silver or a fairly heavy china such as Lowestoft. Steuben glass ashtrays and urns for cigarettes. A silver breadbasket, or a round Early American silver "barber's bowl"; a salad bowl of dark wood or china; silver trays; silver platters and serving dishes, unless one has platters to match the china. Fairly heavy china: Lowestoft is ideal for this kind of a table, but black and white Creil, old Leeds or Wedgwood (the cream-colored Queensware) could also be used. Pistol-handled knives and rattail spoons and forks, or a heavy simple silver in an Early American design. Solid heavy glass, unless one has a simple, round, stemmed glass that can go on almost any table.

MODERN

Modern usually means a table of pale wood, glass, or painted wood, although it could also be mahogany. Mats of cellophane, mirror, plastic, or cork, or linen with a tiny lamé thread. Napkins of a fairly heavy linen, rarely damask, and often colored. A centerpiece of straight-sided glass or silver, filled with fruit or flowers, such as gladioli, anemones, or hyacinth. Candlesticks in geometric shapes made of glass, mirror, wood, or pottery, or silver; saltcellars and ashtrays of these same materials and these same geometric shapes; or wooden salt and pepper mills. A breadbasket of wood, china or silver; a salad bowl of wood or glass; wood, silver, or glass trays, silver or china platters and serving dishes. Modern pottery or china, rarely decorated except with lines or circles and made in shapes which, as a rule, carefully avoid the classic. Flat silver that is sharp-edged, clean-lined, rarely ornamented; or extravagantly elaborate silver such as agate-handled knives and forks with plain silver tines and blades, or chrome knives and forks with wooden handles. Glass in geometric forms, often cones, or round glasses set on squared stems.

PEASANT

Peasant means, usually, an oak, walnut, or unvarnished pine table; not an elaborately carved Italian or Spanish oak table, unless the carving were of a rough peasant kind. No mats at all, or mats of straw, or mats and napkins of heavy coarse linen, often striped or brightly colored, or embroidered Greek, Czechoslovakian, or Italian peasant linen. A centerpiece of pottery, or pewter, or a wooden bowl, filled with marigolds or zinnias, or with a bold fruit such as apples, pomegranates, or cherries; or a tin centerpiece, of Mexican or Navajo Indian design, for candles and flowers. Candlesticks of glass, wood, pewter, pottery, or a Mexican tin. Pewter or pottery saltcellars, or wooden salt and pepper mills. A wicker breadbasket, or a wooden breadboard set on the table; wooden salad bowl;

wooden trays; earthenware casseroles and pottery or pewter platters and serving dishes. Pottery or china with a primitive pattern, usually in bright colors. Plain heavy silver, or modern knives and forks of chrome and wood. Peasant glass in bright colors, or any plain glass that is not too delicate or too modern.

MIDDLE-EUROPEAN

Middle-European means, usually, a mahogany table with round doilies of fine, fairly heavy linen, lace-edged or embroidered, and napkins to match. A centerpiece of china or glass with hothouse fruit or fairly delicate fruit such as peaches, pears, apricots, nectarines, or grapes; or flowers such as roses, dahlias, peonies, auratum or regal lilies. Candlesticks or candelabra of china or silver; or elaborate glass candelabra such as Bristol or Bohemian, white or colored. Salt-cellars of silver, china, or glass of the kind suggested above. A very elaborate silver breadbasket, or a round shallow china bowl; a glass or china salad bowl; silver trays; silver or china platters and serving dishes. China of a fine quality, usually decorated with a pattern of flowers; the candelabra and centerpiece designed in richly elaborate curves, often decorated with cupids, flowers, and human figures in high relief. Most typical, of course, are such chinas as Meissen, Vienna, Saxe and Nymphenburg, but Capo di Monte can also be used to produce the same effect. Extremely elaborate silver decorated in relief, which would look badly with many other kinds of china; or any simple silver except one that is markedly modern. A heavy, elaborate glass, such as Bristol, Baccarat, or Bohemian, cut, etched and decorated as extravagantly as one desires (the best shape is a round one); or Venetian glass, gilt-edged or plain; or a simple unobtrusive stemmed glass without decoration and with a rounded bowl.

FOR AN INFORMAL TABLE

As described above, the six parent types of tables are all suited to informal entertaining; or, with the exception of the peasant table, to semiformal entertaining. The peasant table can be adapted for semiformal meals but, unlike the others, it cannot be used for a formal dinner without losing its essential character. To make the peasant table suitable for semiformal entertaining and to make the others suitable for formal entertaining, the following changes will be necessary:

FOR A SEMIFORMAL TABLE

Peasant

The peasant table should be covered with a cloth of damask or fine linen. China should be used instead of pottery; and the more delicate the pattern, the better. Suppose, for example, that one had candlesticks, glasses, and a glass bowl in emerald-green Czechoslovakian or Mexican glass. One could cover the table with a cloth of palest shell pink damask, and fill the bowl with pink carnations as a centerpiece. With sapphire-blue glass, one might use a pale blue cloth; with amber glass, a cream-colored cloth; with red glass, pale pink. Glass saltcellars, matching the rest of the glass, should be used rather than the wooden mills; a shallow glass or china bowl, rather than a wicker breadbasket; a glass salad bowl rather than a wooden one, and china serving dishes rather than pottery or pewter. Pewter serving dishes or platters might be a discordant note if the whole table were set as described above, with glass candlesticks and centerpiece. But a whole set of old pewter—centerpiece, candlesticks, and place plates—would be beautiful on a pale pink damask cloth and, in this case, one would, of course, use pewter serving platters also. For such a dinner, one would use plain heavy silver, rather than the chrome and wood knives and forks which are also suggested as typical of a peasant table.

FOR A FORMAL TABLE

French Provincial

The French Provincial table should be covered with a cloth, a white damask with no pattern or, at most, a very simple one. The same glass candlesticks that are used for informal and semiformal entertaining could be used here; the same china or glass saltcellars, china platters and serving dishes. Instead of a wicker breadbasket, a shallow china bowl. A centerpiece and plates of flowered Chantilly, Sèvres, Creil, or Bow china. Black and white Creil would be beautiful with dark red roses; with another china one might use any fairly delicate rosy-red flower, or a thick pale flower, such as camellias or magnolias.

American or English Cottage

The American or English cottage table should be covered with a white tablecloth in a simple Irish damask pattern of ferns or roses. The silver candlesticks, saltcellars and breadbasket suggested on page 342 could be used, and the china platters and serving dishes. As a centerpiece, one could use an old tureen of heavy silver or Sheffield plate, with stock in pale colors, or columbine, and old luster plates; or, if one had a centerpiece and plates of some china such as Chelsea, one might use white ruffled petunias, or small single dahlias.

Eighteenth Century English

The Eighteenth Century English table is covered with a white damask cloth patterned in any of the classic designs of Irish linen. The napkins are usually very large—at least 24 by 24. One could use either silver candelabra, or crystal candelabra with prisms and drops; silver or cut-glass saltcellars; silver platters, serving dishes and breadbasket. The centerpiece could be made of silver, of Bristol cut-glass or of Waterford glass, with hothouse grapes, white roses, pale pink peonies, delphinium, camellias, or bouvardia. The china could be Lowestoft or any of the more elaborate English chinas, as Worcester, Derby, Minton or Bow.

Modern

The modern table should be covered with a white cloth, with no pattern other than a broad border-stripe or band. Candlesticks and saltcellars of glass, mirror, or silver; silver breadbasket, platters and serving dishes. China should be used, rather than pottery; but a white cloth, *not* one of the brightly colored ones. Any of the modern chinas with a silver border, a monogram or some such simple decoration, would be suitable. The centerpiece could be glass or silver; the flowers, lilies, gardenias, tulips, anemones, or poppies.

Middle-European

The Middle-European table should be covered with a white damask cloth, elaborately patterned. The most typical pattern would be one of those so usual in German linen: a hunting scene, a landscape with figures. China candelabra, or glass candelabra, as suggested on page 344. Silver or glass saltcellars, silver platters, serving dishes and breadbasket. The centerpiece, which often matches the china candelabra and is usually extremely ornate (see page 344), can be a large group of figures, or a covered dish, or an urn which is not only too ornate for further decorations or flowers but is often not designed to hold them. In a centerpiece of glass, flowers or fruit could be used; in a red and white epergne, for example, hanging bunches of white hothouse grapes with white-fleshed peaches. In a red and white glass bowl, white roses, white anemones, and white tulips with the petals curled back to show the dark centers.

ORIGINAL CENTERPIECES

All of these tables, with the possible exception of the Middle-European which is still very new, are in the accepted fashion of the day. All of them are fairly foolproof. But it may be objected, with a certain amount of justice, that none is strikingly original. Experts in arranging centerpieces go farther afield in choosing flowers and decorations, even though many of them still base their tables on one of the parent-ideas suggested here. They use unexpected vegetables: wheat, oats, pea-vine, tomatoes, kale, and even parsley (which is beautiful in a cream-colored or white china bowl, starred with little, single, clove-pinks). Or eggplant, red cabbage, and pink camellias on a wooden board. Or odd, unpretty flowers, such as jack-in-the-pulpit—especially good with pussy-willow on a modern table. In winter, when flowers are scarce, china or glass figures are used as a centerpiece; a glass bowl, or a low round glass vase, filled with water and marbles and set on a mirror. Shock-glass mirror, by the way, is not only cheaper than plate glass but also does away with the faintly clinical aspect that plate-glass mirror sometimes has. Or one can use a few flowers in combination with other things to make a centerpiece: roses stuck into big pieces of branch coral, or among bunches of grapes. For a modern table without flowers, big hollow balls of colored glass, heaped like fruit in a shallow bowl; or jagged lumps of melted glass (giveaways from bottle factories) piled like huge raw aquamarines on mirror.

For a special occasion there are all sorts of fantasies impossible for ordinary entertaining: tall, many-branched candelabra with some of the candles removed and replaced by small tight bunches of flowers, and with bows of ribbons trailing to the table; or candelabra tied with stiff bows of wide ribbon to stand high among the candles; or short wide candles crowded in a shallow silver bowl and ringed with flowers; or old-fashioned cut-glass epergnes, each set with a few of these short candles ringed with fruit. Or, a wide shallow bowl with flowers floating on the water, and tall candles rising out of the water among them. Or—but this is possible only for a modern table—there are even such extravagances as that suggested by a New York decorator: big lumps of hard coal set on mirror, with gardenias or camellias among them.

Having said all this, there are two points that must be made clear. The first is that these six classifications, with all their detailed suggestions, should not be treated as watertight compartments. Certain kinds of china, silver, and glass are suggested in order to show which is most typical of each category but, of course, there are many more which will do quite as well. Nor need any one of them be restricted to the category for which it is suggested. In the case of china, the determining factor should be the texture and the pattern. For example, very early soft-paste Sèvres, with a scattered pattern of flowers, could be used on an American Cottage, French Provincial, or Eighteenth Century English table, for any meal. In the same way, a very fine high-glaze Sèvres, with no decoration other than a gold band and a monogram, could be used on a completely modern table. A fuller discussion of silver, glass, linen, and china, which might be useful in choosing table decorations, is on pages 377 to 422 in the chapter, "Furnishing a House."

The second point is that none of this is set down as the beginning and end of all beautiful tables. Although it is true that many kinds of table arrangements which were considered fashionable ten or fifteen years ago (such as, for example, the heavily magnificent Italian or Spanish) are now no longer in fashion, it is obviously even more true that a beautiful table of any kind is still beautiful. The change lies in the fact that tables which fall short of the beautiful, if directed toward the Italian or Spanish conception, are unappealing to the contemporary eye; a table based on any one of the six ideas we have suggested here may fall far short of perfection and still satisfy modern taste.

All these admonitions will be useless if they are constructed as the end rather than as the beginning of the subject of decorating a table. As in everything else, imagination is a vital factor. One must not get stuck in the rut of a successful combination which becomes, and amazingly grows to look like, an automatic reflex to the word dinner. Further, with imagination there must be discipline. If one has a beautiful possession—a bowl, a tureen, a pair of candelabra, or even one candelabrum—the table should be built around that. One must learn to take trouble to find china and linen that will heighten the effect of the centerpiece, and one must learn to resist the pressure of emergencies and great bargains that don't fit in. In the end, the woman who decorates her table most successfully is probably one who can do all this, who can improvise and experiment—and who enjoys every minute of it all.

MINOR MEMOS

Ashtrays and Cigarette Boxes

It might be useful to list a few of the ways in which ashtrays, cigarettes, and matches are most attractively presented on the dining-room table. The first consideration, of course, is the type of glass, silver, china, and linen one plans to use. The simplest system, and one which goes well with almost any table arrangement, is to put two cigarettes across one half of a small crystal ashtray and across the other half a small paper match book (white or a pale color is best for most tables). These are set to the left of each guest, above and to the left of his plate; or directly above the plate.

There are, of course, many other ways of arranging cigarettes, a little more complicated than this, but more interesting, and more directly suited to each kind of table. For an Eighteenth Century English table, with Lowestoft china and a heavy glass such as Waterford, old English snuffboxes, painted or lacquered, would be most attractive for the cigarettes; for the ashtrays, small round ones of heavy glass or flat ones of plain silver; paper-covered matches, with plain or monogrammed covers, or small old silver fishes made over into lighters. With a more finely glazed china such as Derby or Worcester, little urns of silver or crystal would be better than the lacquered boxes; for a French Provincial or a cottage table, old china cups without handles. For a modern table, there are little silver or mirrored matchboxes, but, as a rule, since it is almost impossible to find matchboxes and lighters that are in the spirit of the rest of the table, it is better to use the plainest paper-covered book matches.

Butter Plates

Butter plates are often a problem. They rarely match the bigger plates, except in the none-too-desirable "sets," and it is hard to find pretty ones that are unobtrusive enough to look well with many different patterns. For a fine, high-glaze china with a white background, a plain small modern butter plate, white, with a high glaze, is the most practical. Silver butter plates would look equally well, but they are very expensive and a bore to clean. For the heavier chinas, an off-white plate is best. Beleek, in a plain pattern, is very useful. Lowestoft is almost impossible to combine successfully with other chinas. Fine ones make its lemon-peel texture look coarse. Earthenware is out of place. The best solution at luncheon is to use Lowestoft only for dessert. Dinner, of course, is no problem, since butter plates are not used. (See also pages 401 and 413 in the chapter, "Furnishing a House.")

44

The Household Staff

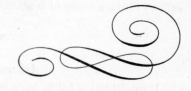

"THE HOUSEHOLD STAFF" may seem a rather quaint phrase, in these days when a part-time general houseworker is often the best one can hope for; but it is used purposely to avoid the word "servants." Before we consider duties, clothes, manners, or anything else, we must go into the subject of terminology, which in a subtle way can influence one's entire thinking. "Servant" is no more necessary to describe one who is doing household work than "female" is necessary to describe a woman, girl, or child. There may be butlers and footmen, waitresses and parlormaids, cooks and kitchenmaids, ladies' maids and valets, chambermaids or housemaids and laundresses—but they need not be lumped as "servants." And if they are, they don't like it. "The household staff" is the traditional phrase, and "the staff" is the traditional abbreviation. But in America, many find "the staff" a little prim. Instead, "the household" is often used and it can always be used when there is a staff of three or more. When there are one or two, they are referred to by name, or specifically by occupation; as, "The cook and the new waitress are coming down tomorrow," for example; or, "The cook and the new maid . . ."; or even more simply, and more usually, "The maids." And a word must be said here about the modern use of the word "maid." It is certainly not in the tradition of housekeeping in great houses, and it is often frowned on by purists for that reason; but it is so apt and so useful that it seems foolish, now that ladies' maids are so scarce, to keep it only for them. Without the contraction "maid" one would often have to use such cumbersome and roundabout phrases as "chambermaid-waitress"; and certainly when there is a general houseworker the only short alternative is "the cook" or "the maid." So much for the terminology from this point of view.

THE BASIS OF GOOD HOUSEKEEPING WITH A STAFF

The only sound foundation for a satisfactory relationship between employer and employee is mutual respect. It has been said that this relationship is "mutually degrading," and necessarily so. But nothing could be further from the truth. No one who understands how to run a house well could ever make such a remark. There are two ways of looking at the question of domestic service and neither has anything to do with degradation. One, the traditional English and Continental point of view, is that domestic service is a career. Boys start as apprentice footmen and hope to become that powerful and respected figure, a butler. Girls start as kitchenmaids or housemaids and look forward to being heads of their household departments. That is the European point of view. The other, which is the old-fashioned American point of view, is that domestic service is a form of "helping." One is paid, of course, as one is for any other form of honorable and respected work, but it is not necessarily a lifetime career. Young girls and widows, and others with no immediate and heavy family responsibilities, help those who have big houses and many outside responsibilities. It is no accident, but rather an accurate reflection of the reality, that the American word for "household staff" always used to be "help."

The only attitude which can possibly make such a relationship degrading is one which springs from a misapprehension of these facts. The relationship of master and slave is, perhaps, mutually corrupting—if not degrading—but when the relationship between employer and employee is based on mutual respect, as it should be, it can be most rewarding and satisfactory. Ideally, this respect is tinged with warm mutual regard, and with equal solicitude for the other's welfare and happiness. Ideally, too, it is always conducted with a certain amount of reticence and formality.

Another vital factor in running a household well is a clear understanding of what the employer and employee should be able to expect from each other. An outline of the traditional duties of members of the staff will be found below, but modern households rarely follow more than a shadow of the traditional pattern. From a practical point of view, as every employer and employee knows, it would be impossible to set down a list of rules for any subject as changeable as modern housekeeping. Standards of work, time off, and wages all vary from community to community, and it is always wise to observe the prevailing customs. Whatever the customs, however, no household is really well run unless these general principles are followed: Employees who live in the house are never expected to work all day; if they are on hand from breakfast-time until after dinner, they obviously must rest and relax for at least two or three hours in the afternoon. Those who are employed by the day, however, are expected to work steadily for the specified number of hours, with an hour out for lunch or dinner. Those who come for a few hours are expected to work right through, unless their hours stretch over lunchtime or dinnertime .

These are not new customs, but in old-fashioned households there was also a rule that the household must have an attractive, comfortable room in which to entertain friends. And although modern households of one or two often prefer smaller quarters, with less to clean and more time off instead, the attitude behind this rule should not be abandoned. It has always been the duty of the mistress of the house to see that the rooms of the staff are attractive, comfortable, and cheerful. With every generation the standards have happily risen, but still it is axiomatic that no woman who really lives well, and with completely good taste, has ever neglected this point. Solicitude for the welfare of the household is one of the marks of those who live *well*, as compared to those who merely live extravagantly or fashionably. These are the cornerstones of good housekeeping.

From a practical point of view, the first point and the one to which all other practical considerations must be subordinated, is that the house must be clean. No matter how big or how small the staff, the first mark of a well-run house is cleanliness, not elaborate service. Far better a house which is shiningly clean, where the service is sketchy, than one where the service is punctiliously complete and the corners are dusty. It cannot be overemphasized that cleanliness is the prime consideration in working out the routine of household duties. We come now to their traditional divisions.

THE TRADITIONAL DEPARTMENTAL SYSTEM

Working Departments

Since it is true, as we have said, that few modern households follow more than a shadow of the system outlined below, it may seem strange that it has been included at all. There are two reasons why. The first is that it might still be of practical use to a few readers who are starting official life, or a life in which a large household is still customary. The second and more important reason is that, although there are great differences between the traditional system and its modern interpretation, the simpler system is nevertheless based on the more elaborate one. Whether one is the employer or the employee, an understanding of the basic idea is immensely valuable. It is impossible to understand clearly the shape of the shadow if one has never heard of the substance.

All households with a staff of three or more are divided into these departments:

1. The kitchen department.
2. The pantry department.
3. The upstairs department.

In very large households there are also:

4. The laundry department. (This will not be discussed below because the duties are obvious.)
5. The valeting and maiding department (consisting of a valet and lady's maid).
6. The outdoor department (consisting of chauffeurs, gardeners, etc. Only the chauffeur need be considered here).

Nurses, Secretaries, etc.

These are the six "working departments" of the household. In addition, there is another category which includes companions, private or social secretaries, tutors, governesses, and registered nurses. Their special duties are obvious and do not lie within the scope of this book, but perhaps it would be wise to mention that all are professionals and should be treated as such.

They eat with the family at the dining-room table or on trays in their own rooms, which are guest rooms, but never with the household staff. They are treated by the staff as guests of the family, and they are not in any way involved in the regular departments of the household.

This is an outline of the specific duties of each of the working departments, and the clothes which are traditionally worn:

KITCHEN DEPARTMENT

Duties

The kitchen staff is expected to cook for the family and the household, and to wash the dishes after the household's meals. (The other members of the staff are sometimes asked to take their used dishes to the kitchen sink.) It is also expected to keep the entire back of the house clean, except for the household's bedrooms. Each one is expected to take care of his own bedroom. In very big households, a kitchenmaid may take charge of the cook's room, just as one of the chambermaids takes care of those of the butler, lady's maid, valet, and housekeeper. But this is an almost hypothetical case, since households of this size are exceedingly rare. The head of the kitchen department is, of course, the cook.

Clothes

There is no uniform for members of the kitchen staff. The white or light-colored dresses which a cook and kitchenmaid wear, or the white coats worn by a chef, may be supplied either by the staff or by the mistress of the house.

PANTRY DEPARTMENT

Duties

The pantry staff, whether it consists of a butler and footman, a waitress and parlormaid, or one waitress, is expected to take care of the following: serving the family and their guests; setting and clearing the table; washing the dishes after family meals; polishing the silver; arranging the flowers; answering the telephone and doorbell; taking care of the dining room, the living room, and library, and all the downstairs halls in the front of the house, and the front stairs up to the first floor. And "taking care" means not only cleaning but also constant tidying up: ashtrays emptied and cleaned, sofa pillows plumped, shades drawn in the evening, etc., so that the rooms always look as though they had just been "done." In households where there are footmen, the junior member is often responsible for cleaning the brasses and tending the fires all over the house; and when there is no valet he cleans the shoes of the family and their guests.

A member of the pantry staff is expected to be "on duty" from after luncheon until half-past nine or ten o'clock—which means dressed in afternoon clothes ready to answer the telephone or doorbell. (See also the sections "Entertaining," pages 433 to 522, and "Serving," pages 274 to 307, for more detailed descriptions on the duties of the pantry staff.) Unless there is a valet, the pantry staff also takes care of the valeting of the family and their guests. This practice is based on the old theory that only a man can press a man's clothes properly; but in smaller households today, if the valeting is done in the house, it is done either by the pantry department or by the upstairs department.

At the head of the pantry department is the butler who, in very large households, has a very important position. In America, where housekeepers are even more rare than butlers, butlers often engage and dismiss all the rest of the staff.

Clothes for a Butler

Note: it is a primary rule of appearance that butlers and footmen must be clean-shaven. Traditional and formal dress:

Morning:
1. A dark sack suit
2. White shirt
3. Stiff fold collar
4. Black four-in-hand tie
5. Black shoes
6. Black socks.

Luncheon time, afternoon, and teatime: (This is not worn in the evening.)
1. Black dress coat (the same as that worn in the evening; see below—or, to be most technical, a cutaway coat)
2. Gray-and-black striped trousers
3. A black double-breasted waistcoat, stiff white shirt, stiff white wing collar (or, less formally, a fold collar), and black four-in-hand tie; or black bow tie with wing collar
4. Low black calf oxford shoes and black socks.

Dinner and the evening:

1. Stiff-bosomed white shirt, wing collar, small gold studs (as small as collar buttons)
2. White bow tie
3. Black waistcoat and tail coat
4. Black trousers without braid or stripes
5. Black shoes and socks.

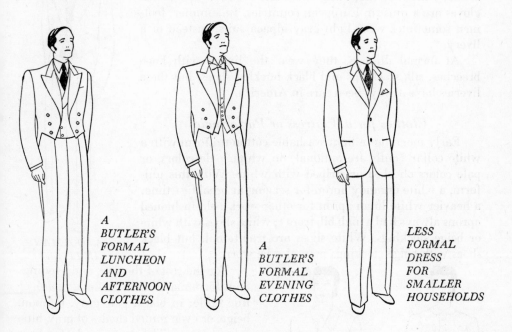

A BUTLER'S FORMAL LUNCHEON AND AFTERNOON CLOTHES

A BUTLER'S FORMAL EVENING CLOTHES

LESS FORMAL DRESS FOR SMALLER HOUSEHOLDS

Less formal variations (black calf oxfords and black socks are also standard with all of these):

Afternoon and Evenings: Gray-and-black striped trousers with a short black single-breasted sack coat, black waistcoat, soft white shirt and stiff fold collar, black four-in-hand tie; or

Less formally, a black alpaca coat with striped trousers worn with a soft white shirt, black waistcoat, semi-stiff collar, black four-in-hand tie.

Hot weather: Gray alpaca coat (with three buttons) with black trousers with soft white shirt and collar, black four-in-hand tie; or

White linen or duck double-breasted coat worn with black trousers, white shirt and collar and black four-in-hand tie. (This may be worn both afternoon and evening.) Another very good white coat is white linen or duck with black, or colored, collar and cuffs, which may be solid colors—the "house" color— or striped like a footman's waistcoat. This coat is worn with black trousers and, for evenings, a wing collar and bow tie; or, for afternoons, a fold collar and black four-in-hand tie.

353

Clothes for a Footman

Morning, afternoon and informal evening livery: (Note that footmen's clothes are always called "liveries.") A dark broadcloth tail coat, usually dark green, dark maroon or dark blue, with silver or brass buttons, perhaps embossed with the family crest or a monogram; trousers to match; striped waistcoat, usually yellow, black, and white, with buttons to match those on the coat; stiff white shirt and collar; white bow tie; black shoes and socks. White cotton gloves are a must in European countries. In summer, footmen sometimes wear light gray alpaca suits, instead of a livery.

At formal dinners, they wear the livery with knee breeches, silk stockings and black buckled shoes, but these liveries have always been rare in America.

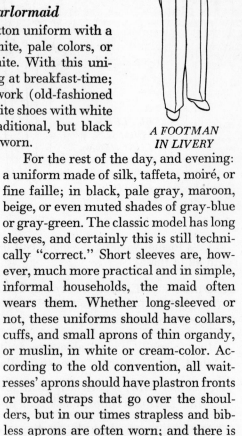

A FOOTMAN IN LIVERY

Clothes for a Waitress or Parlormaid

Early morning: a light washable cotton uniform with a white collar (cuffs are optional) in white, pale colors, or pale colors checked or striped with white. With this uniform, a white organdy apron for serving at breakfast-time; a heavier white linen apron for other work (old-fashioned aprons always had a high bib front); white shoes with white or beige stockings. White shoes are traditional, but black shoes with beige stockings may also be worn.

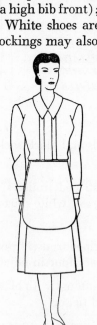

A WAITRESS OR PARLORMAID IN MORNING UNIFORM

A WAITRESS OR PARLORMAID IN AFTERNOON AND EVENING UNIFORM

For the rest of the day, and evening: a uniform made of silk, taffeta, moiré, or fine faille; in black, pale gray, maroon, beige, or even muted shades of gray-blue or gray-green. The classic model has long sleeves, and certainly this is still technically "correct." Short sleeves are, however, much more practical and in simple, informal households, the maid often wears them. Whether long-sleeved or not, these uniforms should have collars, cuffs, and small aprons of thin organdy, or muslin, in white or cream-color. According to the old convention, all waitresses' aprons should have plastron fronts or broad straps that go over the shoulders, but in our times strapless and bibless aprons are often worn; and there is also the fashion, new for waitresses, of wearing a small black taffeta apron with no straps other than those which tie around the waist. This apron is often velvet-bound and really very attractive. Black shoes and beige stockings are standard. Caps have almost disappeared, except for those worn by highly-trained maids—and on the stage or in the movies. If there are two maids, they are always dressed alike.

UPSTAIRS DEPARTMENT

Duties of a Chambermaid

To clean all the front of the house upstairs—halls, bedrooms, bathrooms, and sitting rooms. To take care of mending the linen; to draw the shades in the evening; turn down the beds after the family has dined (i.e., take off the bedspread and put it away, and turn a corner of the top sheet and blankets back over the blanket cover); fill thermos jugs and cracker jars in each bedroom; wash the bathtub and tidy the bathroom, bringing fresh towels if necessary, whenever the bathroom has been used. According to the highest standards of housekeeping, each bedroom and bathroom should always look as though it had *just* been prepared for the occupant.

In smaller households, the chambermaid may also help the waitress at table and take afternoon "duty" in turn with her. In the very biggest households, especially in England, there are several "housemaids," and the head housemaid is responsible for maiding the guests.

Clothes for a Chambermaid

These are exactly like the clothes a waitress wears. In the morning any light-colored (striped, checked or plain, but not dotted) washable cotton uniform with either short or long sleeves, with white collars and cuffs and white cotton broad-cloth aprons. White shoes with beige or white stockings; or, perhaps, black shoes and beige stockings. In the late afternoon and evening, a dress like the waitress', but never an apron with shoulder straps except in the dining room.

Duties of a Lady's Maid

To take care of the clothes of the mistress of the house and, in most households, those of any grown daughters and of any women guests. (In the very biggest households, as we have said, the head housemaid takes over all the duties of a lady's maid as far as guests are concerned.) A good lady's maid washes and presses all fine underclothes and blouses; she takes care of all packing and unpacking; she knows how to do light dress-cleaning and all fine sewing. Apart from these basic duties, she also carries in the breakfast tray, if breakfast is being served upstairs to the mistress of the house or her guests. (See also "Serving" on this point.) She draws the bath for them before dinner; lays out the evening dresses and the dressing gown and bedroom slippers; gets the evening bag ready with a fresh handkerchief and, in the most consummate maiding, prepares the dressing table as follows: powder box open with the powder puff at hand; the lipstick open, screwed up, and ready for use; mascara and rouge and any other make-up that is used prepared on the dressing table, ready to use. As soon as the guests have left their rooms or have gone down to dinner, she goes into each room to tidy it, putting away hats and bags, taking away dresses to be pressed, underclothes and stockings to be washed, shoes to be cleaned. Then at night, when the bed has been turned down, the lady's maid lays the dressing gown on a chair near the bed, or in the dressing room, and puts the slippers immediately in front of the chair. The nightgown, which according to the best standards of maiding should be fresh, or at least pressed, every night, is folded neatly on the bed on the part of the sheet which is turned back over the blankets.

When there are guests for dinner, the maid should be on duty to help the women guests with their coats.

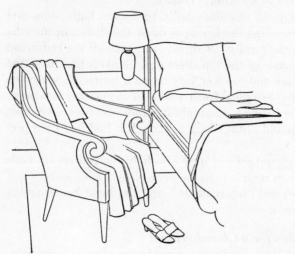

A BED TURNED DOWN FOR THE NIGHT

This shows a woman's bedroom, with her dressing gown on the armchair by the bed, and her slippers in front of the chair. The nightgown is folded neatly on the turned-back corner of the sheet.

Clothes for a Lady's Maid

In winter, dark silk dresses—not uniforms—with long sleeves, with or without thin white collars and cuffs. In the evening, long-sleeved black silk dresses. In summer, or in hot climates, dresses in light colors but not prints, unless it is a print with a very small regular pattern. These dresses should always be simply cut, on a shirtwaist pattern or with a plain V or round neck.

In the evening, even in summer, ladies' maids often wear black silk or taffeta dresses. But the small black silk aprons which, unlike a parlormaid's apron, never had a plastron front or shoulder straps, are now less worn than they were. When traveling with the family, they are expected to wear simple clothes of the most conventional kind. They must always wear a hat out of doors, for example, in dark colors, usually dark blue or black.

Duties of a Valet

(Note: Like the butler and footmen, a valet should be clean-shaven.)

To take care of the clothes of the master of the house, and those of any grown sons or any men guests. The valet does for the men exactly what the lady's maid does for the women. (See above.) As in the case of a lady's maid, in the very biggest households, he may valet the owner only; guests are then valeted by the first footman. In smaller households, the butler performs the valet's duties.

Opposite is one of the standard ways of laying out a man's clothes.

Clothes for a Valet

The valet never wears anything but a dark blue or black suit, with a soft white shirt and stiff white collar, or, less formally, a soft white collar; a black four-in-hand tie; black shoes and socks. In some houses, valets are asked to serve at big dinners and, if so, they usually wear a footman's livery.

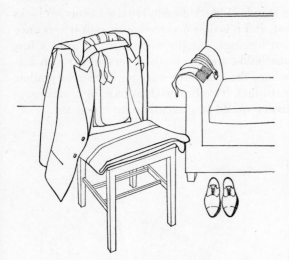

A MAN'S EVENING CLOTHES ARRANGED ON A CHAIR

The dinner jacket is hung over the back of the chair, and the trousers are folded on the seat. On top of the dinner jacket are the shirt and necktie, and on top of these the underclothes. Socks and garters are hung over the arm of the sofa, and shoes are set conveniently in front of it.

OUTDOOR DEPARTMENT

The only one whose duties and clothes need be discussed is the chauffeur.

Duties of a Chauffeur

To drive the family and their guests, run errands, and usually, to keep the car clean and in order.

Clothes for a Chauffeur

(Note: Like other male members of the staff, the chauffeur should be clean-shaven.)

The most formally dressed chauffeur wears breeches, cut very like riding breeches, high-laced shoes with leggings or puttees; and a coat that buttons high up under his chin like U. S. Army uniforms in the first World War; and, always, black leather gloves. The edge of a stiff white collar should be just visible above the collar of the livery. This used to be called the "French livery"; another version had a high V-neck and was worn with a plain black four-in-hand tie. Winter liveries are made of wool, usually in black, maroon, dark blue or bottle-green. The color depends, traditionally, on the "family" color, which is used also for the footman's liveries. The liveries and the automobile are often the same color. Over the livery, in very cold weather, there is a long, double-breasted overcoat of the same material, which often has a fur collar, usually astrakhan. In summer, the chauffeur wears a livery cut in the same way as the winter livery but made of black or dark-gray alpaca. All liveries and overcoats have plain buttons of the same color as the cloth, or silver buttons which can be embossed with the family crest. A chauffeur's cap, in the same material and in the same color as the livery, with a patent-leather visor, completes the costume. If there is a footman, who sits in front next to the chauffeur, he is dressed exactly like him.

Less formally, and much more usually, winter and summer, a chauffeur wears a very dark gray or black double-breasted suit, with a black four-in-hand necktie, a white shirt, black shoes and socks. And, always, the traditional chauffeur's cap and gloves of black. In winter, the standard black double-breasted overcoat looks much smarter than a plain overcoat, and it is now accepted, although it was once thought impossible to wear without leggings. Leggings are worn in only a few very big and departmentalized households, and the modern version is much better suited to modern households where the chauffeur may perform many other duties besides those of a chauffeur. In fact, for a butler-chauffeur, or a gardener-chauffeur, the full old-fashioned livery would be pretentious and foolish.

A CHAUFFEUR IN A SMALL HOUSEHOLD—SUMMER

A CHAUFFEUR IN A SMALL HOUSEHOLD—WINTER

TRADITIONAL PHRASEOLOGY AND MANNERS OF THE STAFF

Before setting down the traditional phrases and manners used by members of the household, we must emphasize, as we have in other sections of this book, that such phrases as "the butler" must not always be taken literally. Butlers are rare in American households, but in those which follow the traditional pattern, the forms used traditionally by butlers are followed by the waitress or whoever is performing the butler's traditional duties. And it is in this sense that we use the phrase in this section. In describing telephone conversations, for example, "the butler" means the member of the staff who is using the telephone and we use the word "butler" because answering the telephone is traditionally the responsibility of that department. In the same way, we use "chauffeur" to describe the one who is driving. Whether "the chauffeur" is actually a handy-man-gardener, or whether "the butler" is a part-time maid, is beside the point.

Forms and Titles of Address

These titles, or forms of address, are used by members of the household staff when speaking to, or of, members of the family and their guests:

In speaking to, and of, the mistress of the house—"Madam."

In speaking to the master of the house—"Sir," and of him—"Mr. . . ." ("Mr. Brownlow," for example. The old-fashioned custom of speaking of the master of the house as "The Master" is rapidly disappearing everywhere, and has always been rare in America.)

In speaking to, and of, young unmarried daughters of the house, first names are used with the title "Miss"—"Miss Mary," for example, not "Miss Brownlow." (See also the note concerning children below.)

In speaking to, and of, young sons of the house, first names are also used— "Master Robert," for example, not "Master Brownlow." (See below.)

In speaking to married daughters of the house and any married women guests —"Madam" or, to avoid confusion, "Mrs. . . ."—"Mrs. Scott," for example.

In speaking to, and of, unmarried women guests, last names are used with the title "Miss"—"Miss Bruce," for example.

In speaking of any married women guests or members of the family— "Mrs. . . ."

In speaking to, and of, older sons of the house, and sometimes close relatives of the family, the first name is used with the title "Mr. . . ."—"Mr. Edward," for example.

In speaking to older men guests—"Sir"; and of them, "Mr. . . ."—"Mr. Harrison," for example.

In speaking to, and of, children who are guests in the house, the first names are used with "Miss" and "Master"—"Miss Rosalie," for example, and "Master George." (Very often, nicknames such as "Nikki" are used and almost invariably a standard nickname such as "Betty." "Master Nicholas" and "Miss Elizabeth" would be extremely formal.)

In speaking of guests in a group, the phrases "the ladies" and "the gentlemen" are used—for example, "the ladies have arrived and are in the drawing room, Madam," or "The gentlemen are in the library, Sir."

In speaking of young friends of the family, the phrases "the young ladies" and "the young gentlemen" are used—for example, "the young ladies are expecting Miss Rosalie at four o'clock, Madam." ("The young ladies" can also be used in speaking of the daughters of the house as a group, just as "the young gentlemen" can be used in speaking of the sons.)

A further point which was always observed in old-fashioned, well-run households but which is somewhat overpunctilious in small, modern households, is that the mistress of the house, a woman guest, or any woman other than a young girl, is always addressed in the third person. For example, "Would Madam like tea now?" (and not, "Would you like tea now, Madam?") or, "May I have the keys to Madam's luggage?"

The standard forms of greeting are "Good morning," "Good afternoon" and "Good evening," followed by the titles of address outlined above.

The First Rule of Manners

A primary rule of manners is that no member of the household should ever call to a guest or a member of the family. If the door is closed, he should come to the door, knock, wait to be told "Come in," and deliver the message. When there are a great many guests in the room, and it would be difficult for the hostess to hear a knock above the noise of conversation, he knocks as a formality and enters without being asked to. If there are only one or two people in the room, he need approach only within normal speaking distance; if there are many guests, the correct procedure is to approach as unobtrusively as possible and deliver the message in a very low voice. (See also "Relaying Messages," below.) This applies not only to the pantry staff—which is, of course, responsible for bringing messages to the hostess—but to members of other departments also.

On the Telephone

The conventional form used by members of the household in answering the telephone is, "Mrs. Blank's residence"; or, when "residence" is too exaggerated a word, "Miss Blank's apartment." Some employers, however, dislike both of these, and the phrase, "This is Mrs. ......'s house" is used instead. "Hello" is not, according to tradition, a proper form.

The following telephone conversations are examples of the phraseology a trained butler uses. The first is between the butler of a sample hostess, "Mrs. Bradley," and her friend, "Mrs. Ewing."

"Mrs. Bradley's residence," says the butler, answering the telephone.

"I'd like to speak to Mrs. Bradley, please," says Mrs. Ewing.

"May I ask who's calling, please?" asks the butler.

"This is Mrs. Ewing."

"I'm sorry, Madam is not at home. Would Madam like to leave a message?" the butler asks.

"Would you please ask Mrs. Bradley to telephone me as soon as she comes in," answers Mrs. Ewing.

"Very good, Madam," says the butler.

"Thank you," says Mrs. Ewing.

"Thank you, Madam." (Note that "goodbye" is not used in this case.)

If Mrs. Bradley is in, after Mrs. Ewing has answered the butler's, "May I ask who's calling?" with "This is Mrs. Ewing," the butler then says, "Just a moment, Madam, please. I'll see if Madam is in," and the "Thank you's" go on from there.

Messages of Acceptance or Regret

"Mrs. Bradley's residence," says Mrs. Bradley's butler, answering the telephone.

"I'd like to leave a message for Mrs. Bradley, please," says the voice at the other end. "Mr. and Mrs. Ewing will be delighted to dine with Mrs. Bradley on Monday, the seventh of September, at eight o'clock."

"Very good, thank you," says Mrs. Bradley's butler, or "Very good, Madam, thank you" if he has reason to believe Mrs. Ewing is speaking.

"Thank you," says the other; and the butler, again "Thank you"—or "Thank you, Madam."

This form is followed also in regretting, with the necessary changes in wording. The standard excuses given by a butler—or to a butler—are "Mr. and Mrs. Bradley are very sorry they will not be able to accept Mrs. Ewing's invitation for dinner (or "to dine") on the seventh of September because they expect to be away." Or, ". . . because they have a previous engagement" or, "owing to the illness of . . ." (See also page 16, in the section, "Manners.")

A Message of Invitation

In receiving a message of invitation, a butler repeats all the pertinent facts, so that there may be no mistake in the day or hour. For example:

"Mrs. Ewing's residence," says Mrs. Ewing's butler.

"Would you take a message for Mrs. Ewing, please," says Mrs. Bradley's butler. "Mrs. Bradley would like to know if Mr. and Mrs. Ewing could dine on Monday, the seventh of September at eight o'clock."

"To dine with Mrs. Bradley on Monday, the seventh of September at eight o'clock," repeats Mrs. Ewing's butler, "Very good—thank you."

"Thank you," says the other.

Other Messages

In giving or receiving any other messages, the forms suggested above are followed. But in receiving any unusual message, or any message where accuracy is important, the butler should repeat the essential points, as he does in receiving a message of invitation. For example, if a friend of his employer's should telephone saying that she will "meet Mrs. Bradley as arranged," the butler need say nothing more than "Very good, Madam. Thank you." But if she should give a more complicated message it must be repeated, ". . . to meet Mrs. Bradley at the Tennis Club, instead of the Library."

Relaying a Message

The correct form for delivering a telephone message to the mistress of the house is: "Mrs. . . . . . . would like to speak to Madam on the telephone," or, "Would Madam speak to Mrs. . . . . . . on the telephone?" If a message has come for one of the guests, it should be brought first to the hostess. For example: "Mrs. Stevens is wanted on the telephone, Madam," or, "A message has come for Mr. Stevens on the telephone, Madam." If necessary, the hostess will then direct the butler to the guest, "Would you tell Mr. Stevens, Parker, please." Usually, of course, "Mr. Stevens" will have overheard the original message and this second step will be omitted. The point is that the butler should inform the mistress of the house first. When he has found the guest, the butler says, "Mrs. . . . . . . would like to speak to you on the telephone, Sir," or, "Mrs. . . . . . . has left a message for you, Sir, asking you to telephone her whenever convenient."

Announcing Meals

Announcement that dinner—or luncheon, or tea, or anything else—is ready should be made as unobtrusively as possible. In theory, it may be made from the door of the living room, in a voice loud enough to attract the hostess's attention. In practice, the hostess usually keeps her eye on the door and the butler need only murmur, or make the announcement in a normal speaking voice. Some hostesses prefer that the butler come straight to them, and this also is good usage. The classic forms are: "Luncheon is served," "Tea is served" (if it is served in another room), "Dinner is served"; or, if it is a late supper, "Supper is served." Another correct form, derived from the French, is, "Madam is served."

At the Table

When the butler offers alternatives to guests who refuse wine the phrases he uses are fairly stilted and he avoids the directness of "Do you want . . ." Instead, he uses the standard "Would you like . . . ," or, "Would you care for . . ." For example, "Would you care for claret, or whiskey and soda, Sir?"; or, "Would Madam like anything else?"

In the Living Room

If cocktails are being served before dinner, or if water, fruit juice or champagne is being served after dinner, the butler need say nothing unless the guest fails to notice the tray. For instance: "Would Madam care for a cocktail?" or, "Water, Sir?" The same form is used if guests are playing cards: "May I bring you a whiskey and soda, Sir?"

At the Door

A butler should open the front door briskly and alertly and with a hospitable manner. In other words, he should open the door wide, and step aside, so that the guests need not sidle by him. He says nothing unless the guest speaks to him first, but when the guest—as he should—has said, "Good evening," the butler answers, "Good evening, Madam," or "Good evening, Sir." If the guests seem in doubt as to where to leave their coats, the butler uses phrases such as these: "May I take Madam's coat?" or "Will Madam leave her coat upstairs, please?" "May I take your coat, Sir?" If the guests seem in doubt as to where to find the mistress of the house: "Madam is in the drawing room; this way, please." If a guest arrives unexpectedly asking to see any member of the family, this is an example of the standard forms: The guest says, "Good afternoon. Is Mrs. Cane at home?" The butler asks, "May I ask who's calling, please?" or, "Who shall I say is calling, please?" "Mr. Bartlett," answers the guest. "Will you please wait here, Sir," says the butler, showing him into the living room or library, "and I'll just see if Madam is in." If the visitor has come for business reasons, the butler usually asks him to wait in the hall.

When the visitor leaves, the butler should stay at the door until the visitor is some distance away. For example, if the visitor has an automobile waiting at the door, the door should be held open until the guest has driven away. In apartment buildings, the butler should ring the elevator bell for the guest, step back to the door and hold it open until the guest has gone down.

Visiting Cards

When a guest calls and wishes to leave his card, the butler should receive it on a small tray; he should never take it directly from the guest's hand. For example, after the preliminaries described immediately above, the butler might say, "I'm sorry, Sir, but Madam is not at home." "Oh, very well, in that case, I'll leave my card," says the guest, getting out his card. The butler turns to the

362

hall table, where a small tray is usually conveniently kept for this purpose, and holds out the tray so that the guest can put his card on it. Still holding the tray, he opens the door and, in answer to the guest's "Thank you," says "Good day, Sir" or "Good day, Madam."

The Manners of a Chauffeur

This is the formal little routine of manners for a chauffeur: He stands by the door of the car, holding it open, when anyone gets in, except when a footman or doorman is there. Unless he has been given orders by the passenger, he asks for orders as soon as the passenger is seated. ("Where to . . . ?" is the phrase used, followed by the standard form of address, as suggested on page 359 above.) When the order has been given, he touches his cap as he says, "Very good . . . ," again using the standard form of address. Then he closes the door and takes his place at the wheel. The perfectly trained chauffeur does this briskly and neatly, and always goes around to the door near the wheel; he does not slide across the front seat. If orders are given him while he is driving, he nods without turning his head and again says, "Very good . . ."

In cold weather, the chauffeur stands by the door holding the motor rug folded over his arm. (It should not, incidentally, be called "the robe.") When the passengers are seated, while he is being given his orders, he puts the rug over their knees. This used to be the footman's job, just as it used to be the footman's job to open and close the door; old-fashioned chauffeurs never left their place at the wheel. Now that footmen have almost entirely disappeared, the chauffeur has taken over. Other ways of handling the motor rug are these: It is folded in convenient vertical pleats, on the far side of the back seat and, when the passenger is seated, the chauffeur draws it across his knees; or it may be tucked along the motor-rug cord, so that the chauffeur can lift it back over the passenger's knees as soon as he is seated.

Once arrived at his destination, unless there is a footman or doorman, the chauffeur again opens the door for those getting out and closes it after them. At restaurants and shops where there are doormen, he need not leave his place; although chauffeurs who are driving very old ladies often help them to the door of the shop, and hurry forward to help them from the door into the car. Finally, a chauffeur must never smoke on duty.

FORMS USED BY EMPLOYERS, GUESTS AND MEMBERS OF THE FAMILY

Forms of Address

The forms used by guests and members of the family in conversation with members of the household staff are as follows:

In speaking to the butler, valet, or chauffeur the last name is used. If his name is George Hardy, for example, he is called "Hardy," not "George."

In speaking to other members of the staff, first names are used, with the possible exceptions of the cook and the lady's maid. An English or Scottish cook may prefer to be called "Cook" or, if she is married, "Mrs. . . . . . ." according to the British custom. An English or Scottish lady's maid is addressed in England by her last name, and may prefer it; "Parkinson," for example, not "Mary." Children's nurses are not included in this outline, but while we are on the subject it might be useful to add that, as a rule, any British nurse will expect to be addressed as "Nannie" or "Nurse"; governesses are called "Miss ......": "Miss Wheeler," for example; "Mademoiselle" if French; or "Fräulein" if German.

In speaking to the staff about employers, older women members of the family, and guests, last names are used with "Mrs.," "Mr.," or "Miss."

In speaking of young, unmarried daughters of the family, first names are used; for example, "Has Miss Rosalie come in yet, Hardy?"

In speaking of young sons, first names with "Master" and in speaking of older sons and male relatives, first names are used with "Mr."; "Master Robert" and "Mr. Edward," for example.

In speaking of guests in a group, the phrases "the ladies," "the gentlemen," "the young ladies," and "the young gentlemen" are used. The two last can also be used in speaking of the children of the house.

In small households, employers and guests use these same forms with these exceptions:

In speaking of daughters under fifteen and sons under eighteen, first names are used alone; "Has Rosalie come in yet, Agnes?", for example.

In speaking of the children of the house or their guests, the phrase "the children" is used instead of "the young ladies," etc.

Introducing Members of the Staff

Members of the household staff are not, as a rule, introduced to guests or members of the family, but there are occasions when a sort of quasi-introduction is easy and natural. This is particularly true in American households, where the employer-employee relationship is not always a stiffly formal one.

Except for special reasons, members of the household are never introduced to guests who have been invited for a meal only. But when guests are apt to be in the position of giving orders, as week-end guests often are, some form of introduction is indicated. The easiest vehicle for this is a sentence indicating the service a guest may expect. For example: "I have to go to a meeting now, but I'll be back at six and Agnes will give you tea," or ". . . Agnes will be here if you need anything." To a newly-arrived week-end guest the hostess might say, "Agnes will unpack for you." The essential point is that in a sentence directed to the guest in the maid's presence, the hostess has drawn the guest's attention to her and mentioned her name. It is not necessary for "Agnes" to know the guest's name at once, because she can always use "Sir" or "Madam."

These quasi-introductions are completed when the guest turns to the maid with a nod and smile, and a phrase such as, "That will be splendid, Agnes, thank you." The maid answers with a smile, "Thank you, Madam," or "Thank you, Sir." The guest does not shake hands.

Introducing Employees of Long Standing

When an employee has been in the family a long time, a more definite form of introduction is used, emphasizing the affection the family feels, without necessarily using any elaborate or fulsome phrases. For example, when an intimate friend or relative arrives, the hostess might make the introduction as follows:

"Aunt Margaret, this is Agnes, who takes care of us all"; and, turning to the maid, "Mrs. Weldon will be staying a week, Agnes. Isn't that wonderful?" or, "Aunt Margaret, this is Agnes, whom you've heard so much about. Mrs. Weldon will be living in New York now, Agnes." Mrs. Weldon's acknowledgment is, "Well, I'm so pleased to see you, Agnes. I have indeed heard so much about you." Agnes answers, "Thank you, Madam." And a pleasant conversation often follows. During an introduction such as this, the guest usually shakes hands with the maid.

Introducing New Members of the Staff

When an employee has just entered the household, a quasi-introduction to members of the family is sometimes necessary. The following examples will give an idea of the very elastic form. To her husband, the mistress of the house says, "This is Norah, who just arrived today." The husband answers, "Oh, how do you do, Norah?" and the maid says, "Thank you, Sir"; or, less formally, "How do you do, Sir?" To a grown child, the mistress of the house says, "This is Norah. I don't think you've been here since she came," and, turning to the maid, "Mrs. Pyne (or Miss Rosalie or Mr. George) is my daughter (or son), Norah." Children are introduced with a phrase such as, "Say 'How do you do, Norah?' Jimmy. He's a big boy for five years old, don't you think, Norah?" After such an introduction, it is not customary to shake hands.

What to Avoid

No guest or member of the family, except a very small child, should ever be introduced to the employee. "This is my husband, Norah," or "This is my daughter, Miss Rosalie, Hardy," is impossibly wrong.

45

Smaller Households

IN ALL HOUSEHOLDS where there are fewer than three members of the staff, the departmental system must be discarded. There are three key household departments, kitchen, pantry and upstairs; and, when there are only two people, one of them, at least, must bridge the gap. Inevitably, this means that the list of duties will be cut down. And usually it means that the formality customary in large households will be somewhat relaxed. The two questions that instantly arise are, "How far is the list of duties cut down?" and, "How much of the formality is relaxed?" Phraseology and manners, which are the vehicles of formality, are discussed further on page 368. Here, we shall discuss the household routine.

A STAFF OF TWO

When the household staff consists of two members, these are the usual arrangements: There is a cook and waitress-chambermaid; or there is a cook-waitress and chambermaid-maid; or a cook-waitress and chambermaid-laundress. If the staff is a married couple rather than two maids, the wife usually acts as cook-chambermaid, and the husband as butler-houseman, butler-chauffeur, or butler-gardener. The question of how much work is done obviously can never be exactly delimited. It depends on the needs and circumstances of each household, and on the inevitable personal element. The essentials are that the house be clean and that the meals be cooked; and beyond that point we must turn to examples.

Our first is a small, modern house with a family of three and a staff of two very well-trained maids. The entertaining is carefully planned and organized in advance, and averages one dinner and one luncheon a week, and two guests for one week end each month. The cook helps the chambermaid-waitress with the downstairs rooms, alternates with her in taking afternoon duty, and performs all the waitress' duties on her day off. The waitress carries out the duties of the pantry and upstairs department according to the strictest traditional standards (see page 352) except for the maiding and valeting department. Maiding and valeting are cut down to this: packing and unpacking for her employers; laying out nightclothes (dressing gown, bedroom slippers, and nightgown or pajamas); pressing dresses and suits occasionally—not as a matter of course. The waitress substitutes for the cook on her days off, the cook having prepared most of the food beforehand.

In such a household, the waitress—and, when she is substituting for the waitress, the cook also—will dress according to the descriptions given on page 354, in the most conventional way.

When the family and the house are bigger, or when the maids are less well-trained, the picture changes a little. Our second example is a family of four in a larger, less modern house. There is still a cook and a waitress-chambermaid, because this is by far the most usual division in households of two. There is a good deal of impromptu entertaining and, although most of it is fairly simple and involves only the children and their friends, it nevertheless means a good deal of work. The cook can do little more than the cooking and the cleaning in the back of the house. On the waitress' days off, the meals are buffet meals; the beds may be turned down, but the cook does no other chamber work except to draw the shades. She may lay out the nightclothes, but that is all.

The waitress' upstairs and maiding duties are cut down as follows: She does no pressing, packing or unpacking; she cleans all the rooms and bathrooms, but the children make their own beds except when the linen is changed. The waitress goes upstairs only twice a day: to clean in the morning and to turn down the beds in the evening, and any other tidying up in between is done by the family and their guests; she may lay out the nightclothes, fill thermos jugs and draw the shades in the rooms of the employer's guests, but not in the children's rooms. Her pantry duties are cut down by eliminating afternoon and evening duty, by eliminating between-meal service and between-times tidying-up in the living rooms. She cleans the rooms in the morning and tidies them once again, before dinner. All unnecessary pieces of silver are put away, and the meals are short, so that there are fewer dishes to wash. But apart from these points, the pantry duties are carried out in full. When the cook is not there, she substitutes for her. And all meals are served according to the standard pattern described in the chapter, "Serving," beginning on page 274.

In such a household, the cook always wears a plain white short-sleeved dress. The waitress wears a white or light-colored short-sleeved uniform in the morning and sometimes, particularly in the summer, at lunchtime also. A colored dress is better at lunchtime (see page 354, where a full description of the classic morning uniform and aprons is given). In the evening, she will probably dress in the traditional way.

HOUSEHOLDS OF ONE

When there is one maid it is, of course, even more necessary to strip down to essential duties. The following outline is based on the premise of a family of three, and it should be feasible even when there are house guests, and even if the maid is not especially well-trained or quick. The cooking is taken for granted; and it is probably unnecessary to suggest that the most be made of such time and worksavers as two-course meals. (On pages 310 to 317 there are many suggestions which may be helpful in this connection.) Maiding and valeting duties are eliminated entirely. Upstairs she does nothing more than clean once a day, make and turn down the employers' and guests' beds, and make the children's beds once a week. Her pantry duties are arranged as follows, with the washing up and setting the table taken for granted: The downstairs rooms are cleaned in the morning and tidied again before dinner; luncheon is a buffet meal, with the table set as usual, but with all the food on the sideboard (the maid may come in once, to take away used plates or bring the coffee, but there is no service other than this); dinner is served, if possible, but if there are too many at table to make this feasible, the hostess does most of the serving from her place at table. (This is described in detail on page 281, in the chapter, "Serving.") The mistress of the house takes care of all minor, between-time details, such as tidying up the living room, arranging the flowers, emptying the ashtrays, plumping the sofa pillows, etc.

Whether there are guests or not, this system can work extremely well, but it might be helpful to examine one or two points in detail. Two questions often asked concerning the times when there are week-end guests are, "What is the best way of arranging breakfasts?" and, "What is the best way of arranging the service of drinks?" The answer to the first is quite simple. Depending entirely on the convenience of the household, breakfast can be served either in the dining room or on trays. Guests who like to get up for breakfast may eat with the children in the dining room at a set hour; but, as suggested on page 246, under "Breakfast in Bed," in small households—and particularly for one or two guests—breakfast trays often are the more practical and convenient system.

Arranging the drinks takes a little more organization. In small households, the indispensable object, and the key to the whole system of drink-serving, is a large, very good ice thermos. This is brought in by the maid just before luncheon, on a big tray with tomato juice, sherry, glasses, a cocktail shaker, and any cocktail ingredients or food. During luncheon, she takes away everything except the thermos (and, in winter, the sherry might be left also) and brings a pitcher of water, tumblers, and tall glasses, and any bottles of soda, whiskey, or ginger ale which will be needed during the afternoon. From that point until dinnertime, the drinks are the responsibility of the hosts. Just before dinner, the maid takes away the entire tray, and starts off fresh. The cocktail tray is brought with the shaker, fresh ice, glasses, cocktail ingredients, and food. Once more, during dinner, she comes to take away the cocktail things and bring the glasses and drinks which will be needed after dinner. And that is the end of her responsibility.

As every good housekeeper knows, no matter how clever one may be in organizing the work and planning the menus, guests in households where there is one maid always mean extra effort for her. This must be compensated for by arranging extra rest for her, and extra time for the thorough cleaning which is impossible while guests are there. Very competent hostesses and very quick, well-trained maids might be able to manage more of the fine details of good service: The guests' nightclothes might be laid out for them, for example, and even the packing and unpacking might be arranged. But, on the whole, this schedule is both practical, and good, and satisfactory all around.

PHRASEOLOGY AND MANNERS

In some small households, although the duties are inevitably fewer than they would be under the traditional system, the attitude of formality may be exactly the same. When the maids are highly trained and employers are accustomed to formal service, both employers and employees often feel much happier and more at ease in an atmosphere of formality. In most small households, however, particularly in America, the pleasant, old-fashioned word "help" describes the employer-employee relationship much more accurately than does "the household staff." Employees who are not highly trained usually feel no urge toward elaborate formality. And certainly, when the "staff" consists of one or two devoted women, or one maid who comes to work on a part-time basis, the formal attitude of rigid correctness is, and should be, very much relaxed.

That there is often a difference between the attitude of these employees when there are guests, and when they are alone with the family, is undeniable. And this is not necessarily an unpleasant manifestation of "false front" living, or hypocritical company manners. The traditional forms of address and the traditional pattern of manners are a means of conveying respect. And mutual respect should always exist between employer and employee. But a certain easy understanding, which might surprise guests and make them feel uncomfortable, is perfectly proper in private, and is entirely compatible with mutual respect. In many a small, well-run household, a maid will call out, "Telephone," if she is in the middle of cooking; and the employer, understanding the exigencies of the situation, will run to the telephone without a thought about the maid's manners. But when there are guests, the same maid might very well take pride in appearing properly at the door to say, "Madam is wanted on the telephone."

The private informalities of such households are understood, and there are, of course, no rules to cover them. As in any other relationship, the exact terms cannot be legislated. But it is nevertheless true, as every wise and experienced housekeeper knows, that a household cannot function well without certain minimum standards. (Minimum standards of service at the dining-room table are an example of this point; they are given on pages 280 to 281.) The shadings of manner which become possible, once one departs from the customary pattern, do not lend themselves to exact definition, and the suggestions given here should be regarded as examples of the permissible departures, rather than a full list of rules or forms. They are, however, exact examples of a form which is widely followed in households where the maid feels incapable (or embarrassed, as many Americans do) when faced with the stiffer and more elaborate forms.

Forms of Address

The maid may address her employers and their guests by their last names: "Madam," for example, becomes "Mrs. Thatcher"; "Sir," "Mr. Thatcher." Small children are addressed by their first names only—"Rosalie," for instance instead of "Miss Rosalie"—and the third-person form of address is never used. On the other hand, children over fifteen should be addressed in the traditional way, and guests should always be referred to as "the ladies," "the gentlemen," or "the guests"; never as "your friends."

On the Telephone

If the maid cannot become accustomed to answering with the formal "Mr. ....'s residence," she may say "Hello." The stiffness of such phrases as "Very good, Madam" becomes, "Yes, thank you, Mrs. ...." as it does in direct conversation.

Relaying Messages

In relaying messages, the maid will use "You" or "Mrs. ...." instead of "Madam"; "Mr. ...." instead of "Sir." But she should still bring messages to the hostess first.

Announcing Meals

In announcing meals the maid will use the simpler form, "Luncheon (or tea or dinner) is served," not "Madam is served."

At the Table

At the table and in the living room, both before and after dinner, the maid will avoid the stiff forms of "Madam" and "Sir" suggested on page 362 above. Instead, she will use such phrases as, "Will you have a cocktail?" or, "Water?" The phrase, "Do you want . . ." should, however, be avoided.

At the Door

At the door, the maid should present the same brisk, alert, and hospitable impression as that suggested on page 362. The phraseology may be changed in the usual way—"You" or "Mr. Bartlett," for example, instead of "Madam" or "Sir" —but the manner should be the same. In accepting a visiting card, too, the phraseology may be simplified, but not the manners. Every maid should receive a card on a tray and not in her hand. A tray must be used also in bringing water and other drinks (see page 275).

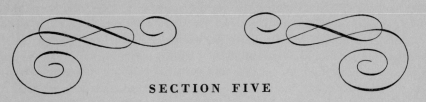

46

Introduction

AT FIRST GLANCE, furnishing a house might not seem to involve the question of social usage. One might think that there would be no considerations other than aesthetic standards—or, at most, fashions in decorating. And further, one might also think that "furnishing a house" meant only buying furniture, and that all the smaller household belongings were exempt. But as soon as one realizes that a room with furniture exactly like that in a museum can be entirely wrong as a place in which to live, one begins to see that there is some element in furnishing a house that stands over and above the highest and most erudite artistic taste. In such a room, the furniture itself is obviously beyond reproach; the mistakes are in the details. There are all kinds of beautiful houses and all kinds of ugly ones. Taste has an infinite number of facets. But there is one element in furnishing a house which makes even an ugly room home-like and which marks a beautiful room as belonging to someone who knows how to live well.

The element that is never sufficiently emphasized—the overriding imponderable without which the perfect Chippendale room is wrong as can be—is easy familiarity. A room should look as though the owners were completely familiar and at home with everything in it. If there are beautiful Chippendale tables, for example, in such a room they will hold a low and not too perfect vase of flowers, a family photograph, or a lamp with a shade not too obviously fresh from the hands of the decorator. This is a subtle and most important point because it implies a sense of values. It suggests a recognition of the fact that the most beautiful Queen Anne desk is built only to be used, and that family affection is a more important consideration than whether or not the picture frame is of the period. The weakness of many beautiful rooms is that they look as though their owners were overwhelmed by them.

373

Rooms furnished more simply may have this same weakness, but the difficulty of finding well-designed inexpensive furniture often involves another danger: pretentiousness. In a pretty room, there may be the most inexpensive new tables, but they will be frankly new, not painted with a dark stain to look old, not loaded with fake carving or plaster, not covered with ashtrays of imitation crystal and lamps of imitation porcelain. The curtains will draw across the windows—good, honest, full curtains, not skimpy ones hanging abortively at each side. Or else there will be no heavy curtains, and only crisp, clean little curtains of organdy, or plain Venetian blinds. In a well-furnished room—from the point of view of good taste— there can be nothing sham. When good articles on decorating urge the abolition of junk, that is what they mean. They don't mean, "Throw away that Victorian table; this is a French room." They mean, "Throw away those tables and chairs made without integrity or honesty, those pretentious and badly made objects that make the room look as though it were trying to seem more valuable and more beautiful than it is."

The easiest way, of course, to furnish a house well is to get a really good decorator who understands the basic rule of unpretentiousness and understands that you appreciate it too. Too many good decorators can make technically "correct" rooms that are almost embarrassingly inappropriate for their owners. Wise owners never allow a decorator to pretend anything for them; if they don't hunt or shoot, they don't let the decorator give them a library full of self-conscious leather chairs, gun racks, Munnings reproductions and sporting prints. If they don't like reading, they have no library at all; but, instead, a few shelves of books for guests in the upstairs hall. If the house is small and simple architecturally, they never let the decorator try to arrange a "grand" room, with rich materials and elaborate valances over the window; and they never—although this is beside the point—have a bar complete with bar stools, etc.; nothing could be worse, except perhaps a "rumpus room" for adults.

This is the sum of all wisdom in furnishing a house: never pretend to anything. The list of desirables and undesirables, which is added below, may be useful to those who are furnishing a house without benefit of a decorator. But these are details. "No pretense" is the nub of the matter. As a wise and witty Frenchman once said, "Show me a man, and I will tell you what he is; if he is too subtle for this, show me his wife; if she has acquired too much polish to be quickly identified, show me his house. Here, one can never be fooled."

47

Decoration

OUT OF DOORS

WE CANNOT here give a list of major mistakes in the outward setting of a house. In any case, if they are major, it would take an architect or a landscape gardener, or both, to correct them. Both of these, happily, are trained to avoid mistakes. Nor is it possible to say what is desirable; too many elements such as real estate values, surroundings, etc., are involved. But we can give an absolutely ironclad list of some of the smaller, would-be decorative things that are undesirable.

Outdoor Decoration

Mirrored spheres, large or small, on pedestals or otherwise.

Colored figures, in any material, especially ducks, cats, dwarfs, and Mickey Mouses. The only exceptions are painted iron jockeys by the front door—all right in any really non-suburban countryside.

Outdoor fireplaces, built to show. For anyone who loves to cook outdoors, such a fireplace can be built to fit unobtrusively into a stone wall, or a corner of a terrace. Built in this way, to fill a need as inconspicuously as possible, outdoor fireplaces are perfectly all right. They are a nightmare when they are big and bold and prominent, built not only to fill a need, but also to emphasize that this is a place in the country, that these owners are outdoorsy, country folk. It is no accident that all the big bad fireplaces are found on suburban properties, built so close to one another that neighbors can hear the meat sizzling. Under these conditions, these are bad because they are pretentious.

Superfluous stonework. Almost any stone wall, path, or step that fills a need is attractive and good, provided that the basic design, the type of stone used, and the sizes of the stones, are fitted to the proportions of the job and the character of the landscape. But the most beautiful wall, built for no other obvious reason than to satisfy the owner's need to embellish his property, can be glaringly bad taste. There are too many small places crowded and cluttered with paths, walls, sundials, and birdbaths; places that would be restful and beautiful under a small green blanket of lawn, with a fringe of flowers.

Would-be-Tudor mullioned windows, a very Tea-Shoppe touch.

INDOORS

Like the list of undesirable outdoor decorations, the following lists of indoor objects cannot be complete. There are so many well-made, unpretentious pieces of furniture, so many simple, attractive lamps and rugs and knickknacks that no list could possibly contain them all. All we can do is to suggest the type of thing, small and large, which is apt to be attractive in most houses, and the type that most definitely is not.

Walls and Ceilings:

Desirable:

Smooth plaster, plain or painted
Rough fieldstone or brick, plain or painted, only when these are part of the construction of the house, never artificially to achieve a rugged or rustic effect

Undesirable:

Quaint touches of plaster, fake ceiling beams, rough antiqued effects
All kinds of artificial paneling, especially plaster carving
Paper which imitates tapestry
Fake fireplaces filled with a fake coal fire, lighted by electricity
Built-in bookshelves with glass or wire-mesh doors
Rooms separated by curtains or so-called portières, instead of doors

Floor Coverings:

Desirable:

Plain carpeting, in a solid color
Needlework rugs
Oriental rugs, if they are really good ones
Savonnerie or Aubusson rugs
Felt carpeting, very inexpensive, in any neutral color
Rag rugs, for a child's room in the country
Old Brussels carpets
Cotton string carpeting or rugs
Straw matting

Undesirable:

Two-tone carpeting
Imitation Oriental rugs
Rugs with a pile patterned in uneven lengths unless they are the very best

Furniture:

Desirable:

Well-constructed, honestly built furniture of any period or style except a pretentious one

Plain overstuffed sofas and chairs, with no wooden border; feet which are plain cubes of wood, or hidden by a ruffle
Tables made of old painted tin trays on a modern stretcher base
Tables made of old or antiqued mirror

Undesirable:

Spring-filled sofa or chair cushions. Inexpensive kapok is better; down or feathers, best
Overstuffed sofas and chairs with stripes of imitation-carved wood running up the arm from the ornate, imitation-antique feet
Heavy golden oak furniture
Cheaply made modern carving which imitates classic antique designs
Imitation-antique painted furniture
Tables with long, spindly legs and tops made of glass

Lamps:

Desirable:

Lamps of almost any well-made, honest materials—china, porcelain, glass, silver, pottery—almost any except an imitation of something better or more expensive

Undesirable:

Imitation-antique bronze lamps, with a false green patina
Ornate, imitation-porcelain lamps
Lamps with cheap and elaborate jade finials
Lamps with tassels on the light cord

Lampshades:

Desirable:

Plain lampshades of white or cream-colored parchment paper
Paper lampshades with polka dots, rosebuds, or some such simple design
Opaque paper lampshades, painted in a solid color

Undesirable:
Paper lampshades with cheap prints
Paper lampshades made to look like old parchment manuscript
Lampshades of glass, such as the old-fashioned ones with iron rims

Knickknacks:

Desirable:
Small glass ashtrays, expensive or cheap, round or square, but always plain
Odd saucers of Lowestoft china, or any pretty antique china or earthenware, used as ashtrays
Old china cups, old wooden or china boxes, or modern glass boxes (these can be very inexpensive) used to hold cigarettes
Good modern crystal ashtrays and cigarette boxes; some of the most attractive are engraved with the owner's initials

Undesirable:
Table lighters made in the shape of airplanes, scotties, etc.
Ornate, imitation crystal or cut-glass ashtrays
Ashtrays on stands, no matter how well made. These, like a bar, belong only in a club, or in a smoking car
Metal ashtrays that work on the "push-it-down-and-forget-it" principle, with a trap
"Pop up" cigarette boxes of the kind that are meant to be funny or sporty. (These are often decorated with a scotty or nude.)
Silk squares on tables
A shawl on the piano
Badly made artificial flowers
Obvious and crude imitations of valuable old china figurines

Materials:

Desirable:
Chintz, linen or cotton
Mattress ticking
Monk's cloth
Really good silk damask
Plain quilted cotton
Real leather; cowhide, Morocco, or any other
Cotton or linen in a simple weave such as herringbone, shantung, etc.
All silks and satins of a good quality

Undesirable:
Jacquard tapestry upholstery
Plush and, in a country house, all velvet except a sturdy cotton velveteen
Imitation leather of any kind
Coarse filet net for curtains

This is a short list of only a few of the most obviously desirable and undesirable household objects. The rest of this section will cover a few other categories, such as china and silver, in greater detail.

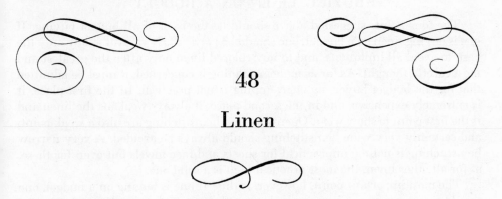

48

Linen

ADVICE TO those who are buying linen can be reduced to four or five very simple points. The first is that the only really good buy is the very best quality. Like flat silver, household linen is used every day, unremittingly. Even the best pieces of china or glass can have a short and violent end, but linen is usually the victim of a grinding process of slow attrition, and the better the quality, the longer its life will be.

The second point is to avoid buying any imitations; specifically, imitation lace and all imitations of fine embroidery, whether they are made by machine or coarsely made by hand. This does not, of course, include peasant embroidery, which may be coarse but is never imitative. It most emphatically applies to any coarse embroidery which pretends to make a piece of linen look "fine."

The third point is to avoid any funny or would-be-cute ideas for marking linen. The rule of thumb is that most linen should be marked with a monogram or initials or not at all. This rule applies specifically to all linen that will be used in the dining room, in the owners' bedrooms and bathrooms, and in the bedrooms and bathrooms of the guests and of any grown-up members of the family. The usual marking is the monogram of the mistress of the house. (See page 426 for suggestions concerning monogramming.) And, although bath towels, facecloths and bath mats can very well be monogrammed with machine embroidery, it is usually better that the other linen be monogrammed by hand. Beach towels, nursery linen, and all the kitchen linen may be marked in any way one fancies—by machine or by hand, with a single initial or with several—but, still no "cute" ideas.

Finally, there is the question of color, which is a question of taste rather than of an accepted standard. All that can be said is that, although it is widely acknowledged that white linen is by far the most satisfactory in the long run, colored linens tempt the buyer and are bought, day after day, year after year.

BUYING LINEN ON A BUDGET

The four points suggested above should be the basis of all budget buying. If one is buying linen on a budget, one should be particularly careful to buy only the best, to avoid all imitations, and to buy colored linen only after the greatest and most careful thought. As far as monogramming is concerned, it must be admitted that for the budget buyer, monogramming is not practical. In the first place, it is extremely expensive, and in the second place, it always weakens the linen and is the first point to show wear. Openwork and hemstitching are also a weak point, and certainly very wide hemstitching should always be avoided. A very narrow hemstitching is not too impractical for sheets and face towels but even for these, as for all other linen, the most practical hem is a solid one.

The most important point, however, is this: If one is buying on a budget, one should never try to use linen as a decorative note. This is particularly true of table linen, and the warning is particularly appropriate because so many pretty and colorful sets are made for the table. Linen requires maintenance—expense, if one is sending it to a laundry; and time and trouble, if one is to do it oneself. Colored linen mats and colored linen pieces for the middle of the table are often very pretty, but it is much wiser to buy small straw mats which fit snugly and functionally under the plate and to put any extra money into colorful table decorations of china. The main purpose of a mat under the plate is to protect the table from heat and wear. If a table top is as shiny and as immaculate as it should be, one needs nothing more than a simple, practical mat which will do the job. Perhaps the best choice would be a very small, round straw mat, smaller than the plates, which could be used for luncheon and very informal dinners. For other entertaining, the most practical mat is one made of a stiffened, crocheted string in a round or star-shaped openwork design. Although neither of these is really washable, both are so small that no food is ever spilled on them. In addition to these, as suggested in the budget list on page 227, there are also mats of cork, cellophane, and mirror, which are practical and usually very good-looking. There are also mats of linoleum, eminently practical but, unfortunately, not easy to find in good designs. In the budget list on page 227, we have suggested as a minimum twelve large dinner napkins and twelve smaller luncheon napkins. The wise budget buyer will buy all these in the very finest, strongest linen, pure white with plain rolled hems. Both sizes can be bought in a solid length of linen (the design is woven into the damask at regular intervals) and the wisest buyer will cut and hem the napkins herself. Tea and breakfast napkins need not be quite so sturdy; an embroidered hem or even a narrow border of hemstitching is not too impractical.

Percale sheets and pillowcases of a good quality are certainly the best for the budget buyer because, although fine linen is equally long-lived, it is much too expensive for most budgets. Linen face towels are not, however, comparatively so much more expensive than cotton ones and so good linen is the best buy for these.

LIST FOR LINEN

The following list includes only table linen, and linen for the bedroom and bathroom. In it, the characteristics which are considered desirable for each, according to the generally accepted standard of taste, are briefly discussed. Household linen, such as dishtowels, is not included, because it is governed by purely practical considerations. And no numbered lists are given, because the needs of each household will vary—but there is a budget minimum list on page 227.

Bath Towels, Bath Mats, etc.

Bath towels are often sold in a set with a bath mat and facecloth, and sometimes with smaller towels which are meant to be used for the hands and face. Such sets are often extremely good-looking and if the budget is no consideration, they are not impractical. In a small household, however, it is better to stick to the essentials and these are the essentials:

A bath mat, at least twenty-four by thirty-six inches, so thick that it does not wrinkle easily under the feet nor soak through with any normal amount of water.

Bath towels, at least twenty-four by forty-two inches, thick, springy, and closely woven. Many bath towels are bigger than this minimum size and they are perhaps better so; but better a small towel of good quality than a bigger one that is loosely woven and becomes soaked immediately.

Facecloths, at least ten inches across, of the same quality as the bath towel.

Linen face towels are made in two sizes and in two kinds of linen. (Smaller replicas of the bath towel are now made, to be used for the face and hands. But a linen face towel is the accepted standard, and even if one prefers toweling for oneself, there should always be at least one linen towel in case a guest should come.) The average size for a face towel is about twenty-two by thirty-six inches. Old-fashioned ones were much bigger. The average size for hand towels is about fourteen by twenty-four inches. Both sizes are made in standard white linen toweling (huck and birdseye linen are two classic examples), and the smaller size is made also in thin handkerchief linen. In well-run old-fashioned households, there were always two kinds of towels on each towel rack: bath towels and big face towels on the rack by the bath tub, face towels and hand towels on the rack by the wash basin. Handkerchief linen towels are much newer than the others. They are often elaborately embroidered, or lace-edged, and are made in many colors. The best of these are very beautiful and very expensive, but as a matter of good taste, a plain white towel of good quality with a simple hemstitched border, is equally desirable. Dark colors and funny, or pretentiously elaborate, decorations should be avoided.

Blanket Covers

From an aesthetic as well as from a practical point of view, there should be a blanket cover on every bed. A blanket cover is put over the blankets, with the top sheet turned back over it. It is left on at night when the bedspread is taken off. They should be made in light, thin, washable materials, in white or pale colors. Very good inexpensive ones are made of thin muslin, dotted swiss or seersucker. Expensive ones are made in silk or satin, often beautifully monogrammed or embroidered, sometimes with insertions or edgings of lace.

Cocktail Napkins

Cocktail napkins are about five or six inches square, or sometimes four by six inches; they are the only napkins that need not be square. The best are made of very fine linen with no decoration other than fine drawn work, hemstitching, lace or embroidery. There are a great many that are decorated with designs of cocks or cocktail glasses or other appropriate emblems; but, although these may seem amusing to start with, they are tiresome in the long run. Cocktail napkins were not suggested in the budget list because there are so many very practical paper napkins which, if the paper is of a good quality, are most adequate substitutes.

Sheets and Pillowcases

The most desirable qualities in a sheet are purely functional. A sheet must be big enough—amply big enough—for the bed, and it must be smooth and pleasant to the touch. From a practical point of view, almost every expert will agree that the higher the thread count per square inch, the longer the sheet will last. From an aesthetic point of view, the very strict rule is this: no fancy work, no colors, no ornamentation unless it is of the very highest quality. A simple cotton sheet is in better taste than a linen sheet with coarse embroidery or, worse still, imitation lace.

Pillowcases should match the sheets. They may be the usual oblong shape and design, or they may be "French" pillowcases: square or sometimes oblong, with a border flounce and buttons at the back.

Tablecloths, Mats, and Napkins

For various very practical reasons, tablecloths are no longer used very much, but unlike many other old-fashioned household standbys, they are now unusual rather than unfashionable. If one likes tablecloths, there is no reason, except a practical one, not to use them. The tablecloths that accord best with modern taste are these: white ones in damask of the best quality, woven in a plain banded design or in one of the traditional and elaborate patterns; fine damask in pale colors—shell pink, baby blue, dove-gray or cream colors—woven in a plain banded design; linen tablecloths in white or light colors, usually with a simple, fairly heavy embroidery. Italian and Czechoslovakian linen are the standard examples of these. There are also—but these are now extremely rare—magnificent tablecloths of very fine embroidered linen with insertions and borders of beautiful lace (Milan lace, for example, or Point de Paris or Binche); and—even more rare—tablecloths made completely of lace. But unless these are really magnificent, they should be avoided; the coarse lace tablecloths, such as those made of filet lace, which were fashionable twenty years ago, are not admired today.

When a tablecloth is used, the napkins should match unless the cloth is made entirely of lace, in which case the napkins should be made of white damask, plain or edged with lace to match. They should always be square and, for luncheon, not smaller than fifteen inches across; for any dinner except a very informal one, they should be at least twenty-four inches square. As suggested in the section "Buying Linen on a Budget," the most practical napkin is of perfectly plain damask of the finest quality without any decoration whatever. If one is not considering the practical aspects alone, there are many very beautiful designs: fine drawn work and embroidery, appliqué, "shadow-work," and lace. Many of these designs are made on fine handkerchief linen; but any napkin that is to be used for dinner, or for any meal which a man is expected to eat, should not be too delicate.

Table mats are usually sold in a set with an equal number of napkins and a runner or mat for the middle of the table. Although these sets are comparatively new, the center mat or runner has already become a little out of fashion, since a centerpiece is usually put on the bare table. From a practical point of view, it is best to choose linen mats of a very fine quality, with simple embroidery or a very narrow hemstitched border. Open-work and cut-out designs, however pretty they may be, are far from practical. From an aesthetic point of view, it is best to avoid dark or very brilliant colors and, as suggested at the beginning of the section, all imitation laces and coarse embroideries. Linen mats are made with all the decorations of embroidery and drawn work suggested in the paragraph immediately above, and there are also modern designs which combine linen with threads of cellophane, silver, and gold. Most of these are very good-looking, but equally expensive and are sold with napkins very slightly decorated to match. Other mats are made entirely of lace or of silk threads woven with gold and silver; they should be used with plain damask napkins.

Tea Cloths and Napkins

Tea cloths and napkins are often sold in sets—one tea cloth with six, eight, or twelve napkins—but a great drawback of these sets is that the tea cloth is very apt to be too small. Since a tea cloth is not used for the tea tray, but only for the tea table, it must be very big. Fifty-six inches across, square or round, should be the absolute minimum, and over sixty inches is usually much more satisfactory. The most practical tea cloth is made of damask, with a rolled hem or, at most, a narrow border of hemstitching; and this is the most practical design for the napkins, too. To be even more practical, it must be admitted that a tea cloth is not absolutely necessary. It is a pretty custom, but, if the tea table is beautifully shiny, a cloth is not considered necessary today, as it was in our mothers' time. Apart from any budget considerations, there are many extremely good designs for tea cloths and napkins, and a certain amount of whimsy and fantasy, which would be most unattractive in other linen, is quite permissible here. This is true also of tray cloths; see below. If they are well-executed, embroidered or appliqué designs of flowers or animals can be charming, especially as a present for a young bride. More conservative, of course, are designs of drawn work or fine embroidery, and appliqué lace.

Tray Sets

A tray set, consisting of a tray cloth and two small napkins, is used whenever breakfast, or any other meal, is served on a tray, when one napkin is used to wrap the toast in. But in these one finds all the same drawbacks and advantages as there are in tea cloths with napkins. The recurrent difficulty is to find a cloth that is big enough; the constant advantage is that there is a multitude of attractive and amusing, as well as simple, designs. Fine organdy, or handkerchief linen embroidered or appliquéd with bunches of flowers, drawn work, openwork, laces and hemstitching—all these are charming on the breakfast tray. For other meals on trays, the same tray cloth may be used, but a bigger plain white napkin should be used with the tray cloth for luncheon and for dinner. More practical, of course, than any of these delicate and fragile cloths are simple cloths in fine damask, embroidered with a monogram or left without any decoration other than a narrow band of hemstitching. Even more practical is the tray which needs no tray cloth at all. One of the best trays is made of Mexican tin, bright and shiny and unmistakably clean, and yet decorative enough to be attractive.

49

Silver

WHEN THE MOMENT comes to buy—or, better still, to be given—silver, there are several principles that should be kept in mind. The first is that there is no better advice than the old cliché, "The best silver to buy is the best one can afford, or even a little better than one can afford." Solid silver, well made, is a many-sided investment. It is beautiful and durable and, as far as flat silver is concerned, it is irreplaceably practical. The second point —a restraining one—is that with all its virtues of beauty, durability, and intrinsic value, a lot of silver means a lot of unremitting work. Silver that cannot be kept clean should be put away; dirty silver conspicuously lacks decorative value and does not suggest scrupulous housekeeping. The second principle, then, is to buy only what one can reasonably expect to be able to use and maintain.

The third point is that plain silver is more practical and easier to clean than silver which is heavily embossed, chased, or repoussé. And apart from this purely practical consideration, plain silver accords better with the modern taste for simplicity. There are, of course, many very elaborate pieces of silver which are extremely beautiful; but, as a rule, ornate designs and florid shapes are more difficult to handle than simple ones, and are less apt to fit comfortably into modern decoration. Whether one plans to buy plated or sterling silver, plain silver in a simple shape is usually the wisest choice.

The fourth cardinal principle is that, in the long run, solid silver is a better buy than plated, especially in pieces which will be handled often. Big pieces, such as trays and platters, are often made of plate; but flat silver, cream pitchers, pepper pots, and saltcellars of solid silver are more practical than those made of plate. Further, if plate is used for any dish which is to hold milk or acid foods, such as applesauce or cooked fruit, it must be replated as soon as it shows signs of wear. The copper or base metal which shows through the plating looks particularly badly in this case, although on such pieces as trays, candelabra, and centerpieces, it often has a certain charm.

A final point—and a very important one—is the marking of silver—but this is fully discussed in the chapter, "Monogramming," in this section.

FLAT SILVER

In choosing flat silver, the wisest course is to buy solid silver, and to limit as far as possible the number of pieces which have only one use. If one is buying a magnificent set of old English or Early American silver, these limitations will be imposed willy-nilly, because our ancestors never found it necessary to buy ice cream or bouillon spoons. Most of us, however, are *not* buying magnificent old sets of flat silver, and so we are free to choose exactly what we need. The following lists are drawn up not only on the basis of practical necessity but also on the basis of modern taste and usage. It is not only most practical to use teaspoons for soup served in cups, but it is also, most definitely, better usage. No figures are given in the following lists because the numbers one decides to buy will be largely a question of how big the household is and how much one expects to entertain. A minimum list for a bride, or for anyone who is starting housekeeping, will be found on page 228 in the section, "Weddings." This is a list of all the desirable kinds of flat silver.

Spoons

Teaspoons (about 5½ inches long): for all soup served in cups; for tea; for grapefruit or melon; for custard served in cups; for eggs served in cups or ramekins; for serving jam or honey at teatime; for serving jelly at the table; for serving sugar, unless one has a sugar shaker, whenever loose sugar is needed.

Dessert spoons (about 7 inches long): for cereal, for desserts, for soup served in widemouthed bowls.

Soup spoons (about 8½ inches long): always oval-bowled, for soup served in plates. If the soup spoons are very large, they are also used for serving.

Demitasse spoons (about 4 inches long): for small cups of after-dinner, or after-luncheon, coffee. These, like serving spoons and other pieces of silver which are not put together at a place at table, are often not part of the main set.

Serving spoons, unless the soup spoons are big enough: Serving spoons, which are usually from 8½ to 9 inches long with a long bowl, often do not match the rest of a set of flat silver; old serving spoons which are usually about 9 inches long with old silver forks of the same size, make wonderful, not-too-expensive wedding presents.

Forks

Large forks (about 8 inches long): for the main course of luncheon or dinner. If they are big enough, they can be used as serving forks.

Smaller forks (about 7 inches long): for salad, for dessert, for fish, for the main course (e.g., eggs and bacon) at breakfast, or for an entrée before the main course at luncheon.

Serving forks—unless the dinner forks are so large that they can be used as serving forks: The usual size is about 8½ or 9 inches long. (See "Serving spoons," above.)

Oyster forks (about 5½ or 6 inches long): for oysters or clams on the half shell.

Fruit forks (about 7 inches long): small and narrow, used only for fruit. These are somewhat special and are really necessary only for formal entertaining. For semiformal entertaining, cherries or grapes which need no knife and fork can always be served; for informal entertaining one can, if necessary, use a dessert fork and the silver-bladed knife suggested below under "Knives."

Knives

Large steel-bladed knives (about 9½ or 10 inches long): for the main meat course of luncheon or dinner.

Smaller silver-bladed knives (about 8½ or 9 inches long): for the entrée, for fish, for salad. In a pinch, these can be used for fruit (see "Fruit forks," above). Also used for eggs at breakfast.

Butter knives (usually about 7 or 6½ inches long, but often smaller): usually silver-bladed, used on the butter plate at luncheon, and on the tea plate at teatime.

When the budget is limited, these are sometimes not part of the set; the best odd ones are chrome-bladed and very small, about 5 inches long, with glass handles.

Fruit knives (about 8 inches long): small, usually silver-bladed. These are not an absolute necessity. (See note concerning "Fruit forks," above.)

Necessary Also

Sugar tongs: Sugar tongs are necessary for serving lump sugar with tea and coffee. If one prefers crystallized sugar instead of lump sugar for coffee after meals, one will need a scoop also. Crystallized sugar is not used for tea.

Gravy ladle: A gravy ladle is necessary for sauce or gravy served in boats or bowls. It is often not part of the set, but, although sauceboats are often not made of silver, a silver gravy ladle is very useful.

Desirable Additions

A large ladle: to be used for serving punch, or soup in a tureen.

A very long-handled serving spoon and fork: for serving salad in a big bowl; a wooden spoon and fork can very well be substituted for these.

Grape scissors: to cut small clusters of grapes from the main bunch, when grapes are served at table.

Fish knives (about 8½ inches long): may be used with matching forks, but the standard silver-bladed knife is equally correct.

Fish forks: These are roughly the same size as the smaller forks in the standard list; they are nice if the budget permits.

Iced-tea spoons (about 7½ to 8 inches long): These have a small oval bowl and a very long handle, which is practical when iced-tea is served in a very tall glass. When the glass is not too tall, dessert spoons are sometimes used instead.

FLAT SILVER

This is a complete set of flat silver. Left to right: sugar tongs; gravy ladle; serving fork; serving spoon; soup spoon; meat knife; entrée (and fish and salad) knife; meat fork; entrée (and fish and salad) fork; dessert spoon; teaspoon; after-dinner coffee, or demitasse, spoon; butter knife; fruit fork; fruit knife; oyster fork. The bracket includes the nine most useful pieces, a group which can, under certain conditions, serve for a complete and most elaborate meal. The first condition is that the soup spoon must be big enough—as it is in many sets of silver—to be used as a serving spoon. (The meat fork, even in the set shown here, is almost as big as a serving fork, anyway.) The second condition is that the menu must be planned with the limitations of these nine pieces in mind: no gravy, that will need to be served separately in a sauce boat; no fruit other than cherries, or small clusters of grapes, which need no fork and knife; no oysters or clams on the half shell. Instead of lump sugar, for which the tongs would be necessary, crystallized sugar can be served with the small cups of coffee; and for crystallized sugar, although a scoop is customarily used, a demitasse spoon can always be used instead.

Nutcracker: Nutcrackers are not often necessary, but when one is needed, the standard old-fashioned kind shown here is always better than any modern gadget.

Tea strainer: A tea strainer is a necessity if one plans to serve tea, unless one has a strainer which fits the spout of the teapot. There are many other good designs besides the one shown here; some are all silver with a little clip that fits over the edge of the cup, instead of a handle; many have stands.

A silver scoop for removing crumbs from the table is not shown below, because, although these are attractive they are a little archaic; a folded napkin is customary nowadays.

The drawing below shows the best designs for the desirable additions to a set of flat silver.

DESIRABLE ADDITIONS TO A SET OF SILVER

Left to right: punch or soup ladle; serving spoon and fork for salad; fish fork and knife; grape scissors; nutcracker; tea strainer; iced tea (or coffee) spoon.

OTHER SILVER

The following are listed without regard to anything other than alphabetical order. The question as to which is the most useful is one that is decided on different grounds in each household.

Ash Trays

Silver ashtrays for the dining-room table should be made of solid silver, not plate, because they are handled a great deal and must be cleaned repeatedly. (Whether or not silver is a practical material for ashtrays is another matter.) Very small old silver plates with beaded or gadrooned borders make good ashtrays; so do old, miniature "pap bowls" or boats. The best design for modern silver, however, is a simple one: a flat tray, round, oblong, or square, with no decoration unless it is beautifully executed. Ashtrays for the dining-room table should be a set, unless they are obviously old or rare. In any case, the designs should not be conspicuously different and the trays should never be conspicuously big. The best ashtray for the dining-room table is never very noticeable.

Bowls

See "Serving Dishes" below.

Breadbaskets

Three of the best silver breadbaskets are these: an old-fashioned, oval breadbasket with sloping sides; a shallow, round silver bowl; and a fairly deep, straight-sided oblong dish. The last has become fashionable comparatively recently. Baskets that are definitely not in fashion are the ornate "cake baskets" of the nineteenth century, usually made on a pedestal base with a jointed handle—and usually made of wildly convoluted plate.

Candelabra

Candelabra are often—in fact, usually—made of plate. There are no special points concerning the design of candelabra except that, as a rule, the best design is the standard one: a solid base, and a stem long enough and strong enough, both practically and aesthetically, to support the branching arms. A good rule of thumb is that fairly tall, heavy candelabra are more attractive than short or light ones. A flimsy design is unfunctional; a truncated design, with heavy, branching arms springing directly from the base, is often very ugly.

Candelabra for the dining-room table are usually bought in pairs. Single candelabra are used on sideboards and tables in the hall or living room. For a small dining-room table, particularly a round one, one might buy a single candelabrum lower than the average ones, with arms on four sides rather than the conventional two. A pair of candelabra with arms on three sides, although designed for mantelpieces or for tables flat against the wall, can also be used on the dining-room table, conventionally spaced at equal distances from the centerpiece or, less conventionally, set back to back in the middle of a small table. The only thing to avoid is candelabra that are too tall for the table. For many modern tables, candlesticks are better.

Candlesticks

Like candelabra, the best candlesticks are apt to be fairly substantial ones, with a strong stem and sturdy base. Heavy plate is better than thin light silver, which is flimsy and looks it. This does not mean that one must automatically choose large and imposing candlesticks of Sheffield plate, because certainly nothing is more beautiful than candlesticks of eighteenth century English silver, which are almost never more than a foot high. But it is nevertheless true, both from a practical and an aesthetic point of view, that one must avoid any design which seems to have a weak point: generally, an over-narrow waist, or a flimsy lightness where the stem joins the base. Since they have no branching arms, however, the best design for candlesticks is not necessarily a tall one. There are many short candlesticks in old and modern silver which are strong enough in design to support long candles. And candles must be long enough to bring the light above eye-level.

Candlesticks for the dining-room table are usually bought in sets of four but, since old sets are comparatively rare, two pairs of the same height and the same general type are often used together. When the table is long and four candles are not enough, a shorter pair of candlesticks may be added, one at each end of the table.

Very small candlesticks (less than five inches high) are used as cigarette and cigar lighters. A single one is brought on the tray with cigarettes at the dining-room table. Or one might have several, not necessarily matching, which will be set on the table between each two or three guests after the meat course.

Centerpieces

Like candelabra, centerpieces are often made of plate. The most practical, because one need not always buy flowers for them, are those which have covers. These are some of the best designs: a tankard, with or without a matching plate underneath it; a covered urn with handles; a round or oval tureen; a covered vegetable dish with feet (the best of these are often old Sheffield plate). As a rule, it is wise to avoid any very tall, narrow design; broad, substantial lines make a better focus point in the middle of the table, no matter what size the table may be. On a small table, a very tall centerpiece is impossible; and even on a long one, it is not usually entirely satisfactory. On a small table, one may use a covered sauce tureen. There are many lovely old ones, often with a matching underplate.

Cigarette Boxes

Cigarette boxes for the dining-room table, like all silver that is handled a great deal, should be made of solid silver, not plate. Modern boxes are best when they are made of plain silver, ornamented only with initials, a cipher, a monogram, or a crest. Other very pretty ones are old and quite small, and were designed originally for snuff. These hold only a few cigarettes, but one box between each two guests is plenty for the dining-room table.

Cigarette Lighters

It is very difficult to find good modern designs for silver cigarette lighters which are to be used on the dining-room table. The only really good design which is easy to find is the old Dutch design of a flexible fish with the lighter machinery hidden inside the hinged head of the fish. Failing this or some other familiar design, matches are better than most silver cigarette lighters. Table lighters made in the shape of airplanes or cocktail shakers should be avoided.

Cigarette Urns

Small silver urns or cups are most attractive cigarette containers for the dining-room table. Some of the best designs are these: a Georgian urn with a pedestal foot, with or without handles; a straight-sided cup or beaker, usually without handles; a U-shaped cup, also without handles. All of these are about as deep as a cigarette is long, or perhaps a little less deep. All these are old designs which have been reproduced repeatedly, in the nineteenth century as well as the twentieth, in solid silver and in plate.

Cocktail Glasses

Cocktail glasses are sometimes made of silver, although many purists insist that silver is never as good as glass. If one decides on silver, it must be solid silver. A stemmed design might seem, at first, the most practical; but a design which is so frankly an imitation of a design for glass is not the best for silver. The best-looking silver cocktail glasses are short and squat with, at most, a small pedestal foot.

Cocktail Shakers

Glass cocktail shakers will always be the first choice of many, but if one decides to have silver, the best design is a simple one with straight sides and a strong handle. Cocktail shakers that taper toward the bottom are top-heavy and impractical; elaborate decorations are out

of place, and hammered silver should be avoided. One of the best designs is a modern adaptation of an old flagon.

Coffee Sets

Coffee sets consist of three pieces: a coffeepot, a cream jug, and a sugar bowl. Besides these, one will need either a pair of sugar tongs or a scoop as suggested on page 384; but neither of these is part of the set. Modern silver is usually sold in matching sets of three pieces, or sometimes three pieces and a tray, but one can quite as well make up a set from old, unmatched pieces. One should avoid, however, mixing markedly different styles and periods and, above all, different scales. If one has a good sense of scale, one can often find an odd coffeepot which will look very well with the sugar bowl and the cream pitcher of one's tea set. But it is essential that they be small enough not to dwarf the coffeepot.

As we have said in the beginning of this section, simple designs and simple shapes are much more in accord with modern taste than florid and ornate ones. And this is even more true of a coffee set than it is of a tea set. The five pieces of the tea set, massed together on the tray with the big kettle, can to some extent impose their own nature. The three pieces of the coffee set cannot do this, and ornate coffee sets should, therefore, be avoided. Particularly to be avoided are modern reproductions of old ornate designs. The painstaking workmanship which made the original a work of art is usually not evident in modern reproductions. Simple designs are by all odds the best.

Coffee Urns

Coffee urns are useful if one plans to give a great many buffet suppers and luncheons, and they are ideal when one is entertaining without a maid. They are often made of plate, with a cover and spigot, an alcohol burner, and a stand. The best designs are classic and simple—a cover that opens easily for filling, strong handles that look sturdy enough to carry it by, and a stand designed only with its function in mind.

Failing a coffee urn, one can often buy burner-stands for one's coffeepot, a very practical arrangement if the coffeepot is a good, big size.

Ice Thermos Buckets and Ice Tongs

Ice thermos buckets are often made of plate; tongs are more practical in solid silver. The two best designs for silver ice thermoses are these: a classic Georgian wine cooler design; and a modern straight-sided cylinder, as functional as a drugstore ice-cream container, and rather like one.

Mustard Pots

Mustard pots are made both in plate and in silver, usually with a glass lining. The standard design is round, with straight sides and a flat lid which is notched for the spoon. They usually do not match the pepper pots or saltcellars. At informal meals they are set on the table; otherwise they are offered to each guest on the tray with the sauce or other condiments just after the meat is served. One mustard pot, therefore, is usually enough for each household—two would be a maximum. Mustard spoons are like salt spoons in shape, but often a little bigger.

Pepper Pots

Pepper pots should be made of solid silver, because plate is impractical for anything which must be handled and cleaned so often. There is little that need be said about the design because few designs for pepper pots are very bad. As always, on principle, one should avoid pretentious gilding, flimsy or peculiar shapes, and elaborate details which will be difficult to clean.

As a rule of thumb, one needs a pepper pot and a saltcellar for each two people at table, although one set for each three is often enough. On a long table, all the pepper pots and saltcellars used need not match one another; the four most elaborate sets are used at the four corners of the table, smaller and less elaborate ones in between. Four pepper pots and saltcellars are the most useful number; two of each are a minimum.

Saltcellars

Since salt is a corrosive deadly to silver, saltcellars are often made with glass linings. The great disadvantage of glass linings is that they break and are often extremely difficult to replace. On the other hand, it is a great relief not to have to empty the saltcellars every time they are used, a task which must be done if they are made entirely of silver. Glass-lined saltcellars are often made with sides pierced to show the glass lining, which is usually either white or dark blue. One of the best old designs is a boat-shaped top with a single pedestal foot. The best modern ones are simpler, oval or round, with straight sides and four very short straight feet.

Solid silver saltcellars have the great practical advantage of durability together with, as we have said, the disadvantage which lies in the fact that they must be emptied and rinsed after every meal. Some of the best designs are these: a boat-shaped bowl on a single pedestal foot; a small, fat little bowl with a pronounced bulge and three very short curved legs; a trencher with solid sides and a depression for the salt, all made in one piece. These come in almost any shape: round, oblong, oval, or square. For suggestions concerning the number of saltcellars one might need, see the second paragraph under "Pepper Pots" above.

Salt Spoons

A small, broad or round bowl, a short handle, and a simple, unornamented design are the only things necessary in a saltspoon except that, like all frequently handled pieces of silver, it should be solid silver. The maximum decoration is a small, beaded edge along the handle and a monogram, or initials.

Serving Dishes

Bowls: Silver bowls are among the most beautiful of all pieces of silver, and a round, shallow silver bowl can be among the most useful. It can be used at the dining-room table for serving bread, rolls, toast, and cookies, and for serving desserts. Filled with flowers or fruit, it can be used as a centerpiece on the dining-room table, or as a decoration in the living room or in the hall. Or it can be left empty and shining, as a purely decorative object, with nothing to distract the eye from the beauty of its metal and its line. Bowls which serve all these many purposes must, of course, be well-designed. The best are solid silver with a broad, flat bottom and softly flaring sides. Less useful, because they cannot be used for serving bread, are deeper silver bowls which often have a pedestal foot and are used for serving desserts. Bigger, deeper bowls, about ten inches across and six or eight inches deep, are used for salad and very big ones, often plated, are used for punch or as a decoration on a sideboard or a hall table.

Fruit dishes, etc: Silver dishes for fruit and candy are often so decorative that it is hard to say whether they should be considered primarily as serving dishes or as table decorations. Three of the best designs are a shell shape, a shallow boat shape, and a flat round platter shape. The shell-shaped dishes come in many sizes, from three to nine inches long, which are perfectly suited to nuts and candies and which can be used both for serving and as a table decoration. The shell design is an old Georgian one, often copied most successfully in modern silver. It is without pretensions but it is limited in scope and rarely as interesting as either the boat shape or the round flat platter shape. Both of these last are made in old or modern silver, with or without a pedestal foot. The boat-shaped ones are from six to fourteen inches long. There are bigger ones, too, but they are used primarily as centerpieces, or as decoration for a sideboard, and can be used for serving only at buffet meals. The round platters come in every size, from six to eighteen inches in diameter.

The smaller round dishes are used for candies or small fruit; as, cherries, strawberries, etc. They often have a pedestal foot about three inches high, and are used not only for serving but also as part of the table decorations. Among the most beautiful of these are the old, flat church dishes called tazzas, often so beautiful that they are used without candies or anything else, purely as decoration. In the bigger sizes, many of the round dishes have only a vestigial pedestal foot, often not more than half an inch high; these are often used with fruit as a centerpiece or, on a very big table, as auxiliary decorations flanking the centerpiece.

They are also very useful for serving cakes, cookies, and sandwiches. In design, they differ from platters in that they have no rim, and in that they often have wide borders of a most intricate openwork pattern. Such elaborate ornamentation is not usually attractive in a small plate. The dishes used for candies, for example, are best when they are solid from rim to rim.

But in a big plate, twelve inches or more in diameter, it can be extremely beautiful. One should be careful, however, not to choose an openwork design which looks flimsy in comparison with the solid center of the plate.

The boat-shaped dishes are best used for serving candies or nuts, or as auxiliary table decorations. The bigger ones, as we have said, are often used as centerpieces.

Platters: Platters for serving are often made of plate, not because plate is the most practical (the plating wears off, and food and worn plate are never a good combination), but only because platters are so expensive in solid silver. Perhaps the soundest course is to have solid silver for a small platter which will be used every day and to have plate or china for the bigger platters which will be used less often. In very big households, where big dinners of many courses are given, two or even three sets of platters of assorted shapes and sizes would probably be necessary; but for smaller and more usual households, the following is a useful set:

A small oval platter about fourteen or fifteen inches long: This can be used for meat or fish for four people and for a molded dessert for any number up to eight.

A big oval platter about eighteen inches long: This can be used for big roasts, for cold meat for buffet meals, etc. Platters in this size are sometimes designed especially for roasts with a gravy well at one end, and often a "tree" design leading into the well. These are a convenience as far as serving roasts is concerned, but such platters are not basically practical in a small household, because one cannot use them for any other food.

A round platter about twelve inches in diameter: This is used for serving pies, cakes, or cookies, and for serving any food in a round mold or ring; as, salad desserts, entrées, etc. It is useful, also, for serving small quantities of meat for one or two people; two lamb chops, for example, served with mashed potatoes, might look better on this round platter than on the oval one.

There are many designs for the borders of platters, but these are among the best: plain reeded borders; classic Chippendale borders; beaded borders (these are not particularly beautiful but they are very unpretentious and very good for a plated platter); gadrooned Georgian borders; and elaborate borders of grapes and leaves, like those so often found on old Sheffield plate.

Sauceboats: Sauceboats are not handled very much so they may be made either of plate or of silver. The most beautiful, of course, are heavy silver, solid and big; but whether one buys plate or silver, whether the sauceboats are large or small, the design should always be fairly substantial and heavy. The classic sauceboat design has a handle and three feet, and a lip for pouring. But earlier designs, which have been very successfully copied, have neither handle nor lip; these are unnecessary anyway, now that we use a gravy spoon. Essentially these early sauceboats are widemouthed bowls, usually oval. If the budget is no problem, it is always best to have a pair of sauceboats, because two sauces served on the same tray should be served in matching sauceboats. For each sauceboat or bowl, a ladle is, of course, a necessity. The best are made of solid silver, with a short curved handle, a broad full bowl, and no ornamentation other than a monogram or initial.

Vegetable dishes: Vegetable dishes come in many sizes and shapes, in solid silver and in plate, and almost all of them— except those which are either flimsy or pretentiously overornamented—are good-looking. The most usual, perhaps, are oblong, without feet and with a deep cover which is used as a second vegetable dish. Such oblong dishes, or oval ones of the same kind, are probably the most practical because two can be set side by side on a tray to expedite the service at table. A round vegetable dish is less practical from this point of view, but, like many other vegetable dishes with covers, especially big ones, it can very well be used as a centerpiece.

The ideal number (and the best wedding present) is a pair of vegetable dishes; however, one vegetable dish, with a cover that can double as a second one, is enough for most households.

Sugar Shakers

Sugar shakers are not handled as often as pepper pots and other small pieces of silver, because they are used only when loose sugar is needed at the dining-room table. They can be made, therefore, either of plate or solid silver; and better a good solid piece of plate than a flimsy piece of thin silver. In design, a sugar shaker is like a very big pepper pot and, as in the case of pepper pots, the designs of sugar shakers are seldom very bad. Whether one chooses a design with a pedestal base or with small feet, the functional requirements seem to impose their own very sound limitations. "Novelty" shapes, gilding, and heavy decoration should be avoided.

One sugar shaker is usually all that will be needed in the average household. Away from the dining-room table—on a breakfast tray, for example—loose sugar is usually served in small sugar bowls, with a spoon; berries, or other such fruit, are rarely served at tables so large that two services will be needed.

Tea Sets

A silver tea set is undeniably a very fine possession, and one that is pre-eminently in the heirloom category. Undeniably also, it is a luxury and not a necessity. It can easily be replaced by china; and china, although less durable, is certainly easier to handle. Granted, however, that one has decided to invest (because it is an investment) in a silver tea set, certainly it should be solid silver. Unless a plated set is rarely beautiful, it is better to buy china than to spend an always considerable amount of money on something which has all the disadvantages of silver and few of its virtues. The only exception to this might be a plated teakettle, which could be used with a china tea set on the few occasions when a great many guests make the ready supply of boiling water a practical necessity. If one is buying a plated kettle on this premise, it should be of extremely simple design and shape, so that it will subordinate itself to the china.

In this section we have so often stressed the virtues of simple designs and simple shapes, that it is almost a relief to be able to relax some of these strictures here. Certainly modern taste and decoration lean towards simplicity rather than elaboration; and certainly silver—clean silver— is so beautiful in itself that it does not really need ornamentation. But it is true, nevertheless, that a degree of ornamentation which would be ugly on flat silver, or on small isolated pieces of silver, can look very well in a tea set. Perhaps this is because the repetition of any design, in such big, rounded pieces of silver, gives the design a certain authority. In any case, whatever the reason, good taste and modern usage do not impose the limitations on tea sets that they do on other silver.

Tea sets need not, of course, always be bought as a whole. One can make up a tea set of old silver provided only that all the pieces are in scale and that they look well together. The wisest course is to decide at the very beginning which piece is to dominate the set: the teakettle or the teapot. If the teapot is the more interesting of the two, the teakettle should be as simple as possible, and vice versa. Modern tea sets, of course, come in matched pieces; but, old or new, a complete tea set consists of the following: a teakettle with an alcohol burner and a stand; a teapot; a cream pitcher; a sugar bowl; a pair of sugar tongs; a tea strainer; a tea caddy; and a bowl into which the dregs of the teacups can be emptied. In making up a set of old pieces, a silver porringer might be used as a bowl for the dregs; or a china bowl which matches the teacups. Tea caddies and strainers are often not found in modern sets, but they are necessary. An old, very plain, caddy goes well with almost any other silver; or, as in the case of the bowl, one can use china. Strainers are very easy to find in the standard and most useful design: a silver strainer with a fairly broad edge and an ivory or wooden handle. Old strainers often have a special holder or stand.

Tea Trays

Tea trays are discussed under "Trays," immediately below.

Trays

Trays, particularly large trays, are often made of plate. A big tea tray, for example, is rarely solid silver. The designs of the borders are very like those of platters but often more elaborate. The Georgian gadrooned border may be combined with a shell design or with a Chippendale design, and sometimes with a combination of both. The "grapes and leaves" pattern usual on oval Sheffield platters is found broadened and elaborated on Sheffield tea trays. Since the center of the tray is always plain, an elaborate border is attractive, although, of course, there is always the difficulty of cleaning. The only designs to avoid are etched designs, often not very well executed, which spread from the border over the center of the tray. Failing the finest workmanship, the design should be as simple as possible, and confined to the border.

Four trays are a useful number for any household in which there is not an extraordinary amount of entertaining, and these are the most useful sizes, not counting borders:

A tray about eight inches in diameter: to be used for receiving cards in the front hall; for bringing one or two glasses of water; for carrying a small decanter and one or two liqueur or sherry glasses.

A tray about thirteen inches in diameter: to be used for serving for four people; for serving iced tea and other drinks; for serving cocktails at small dinners, and liqueurs at bigger ones.

A tray about eighteen inches in diameter: to be used for serving after-dinner coffee for twelve people; for serving cocktails, long drinks, and liqueurs.

A tray about twenty-four inches long and sixteen inches wide, with handles: to be used as a tea tray; as a cocktail tray, when the cocktails are mixed in the living room and space is needed for the ice thermos, the shaker, the bottles, etc.; and as a drink tray for informal entertaining, when the tray is set down and the guests help themselves.

The last point is whether the tray should be round, square, oval, or oblong, and the answer is that, except in the case of the biggest tray, which should be oval or oblong, it doesn't really matter. The two smallest trays—the eight-inch and the thirteen-inch—are usually square or round. The eighteen-inch tray might be any of the four shapes.

Water Pitchers

Glass water pitchers are so practical that silver cannot be considered the ideal material for this purpose. Although they are used at every meal and are thus in constant danger of being broken, glass water pitchers can usually be replaced at a not too considerable expense. Therefore, both from the point of view of aesthetics and common sense, a silver water pitcher must be scrupulously clean and very beautiful; a water pitcher of even faintly moth-eaten plate is conspicuously impractical and unattractive. Granted, then, that the water pitcher is to be made of solid silver, there is little to fear as to the design. The two most usual designs for silver water pitchers are those which have a pedestal foot and those which have not. Some are all curves, some are octagonal or hexagonal. Whichever one chooses is entirely a matter of taste.

50

Glass

THERE ARE two methods of buying glass. The first is to buy a matched set, either old or new, of one design; and the second, to buy unmatched groups, mostly old, of various designs. The aim of the first is the classic ideal, a complete set of beautiful glass; the aim of the second is interesting decoration, and sacrifices the classic ideal to that end. The truth is that, if a set of glass is less than beautiful, nine times out of ten the classic ideal should be abandoned; the tenth time is a rigidly formal dinner, when a complete set, even if not very interesting, would perhaps be more in keeping. If one is going to make an art of housekeeping, the second method is by far the more easily rewarding and interesting of the two. The variety of the designs of the water and wineglasses is not a drawback but, on the contrary, an evidence of taste and imagination. Nor is this method, as one might think, necessarily an expensive one; time and interest and, above all, taste are more than adequate substitutes for money. But it does demand a lot of time, and a lot of interest, and a great deal of taste and discipline. One must resist a "perfect find," if it is out of scale with other glasses that must be set on the table at the same time; one must resist designs which have so much character that they would clash with the others.

In starting such a collection of glass, it is wise to proceed very slowly at first. The first point is to decide which kind of glass one likes best: a heavy, sculptural type—Waterford, for example; a light, delicate one, such as Baccarat or Venetian; a heavy cut glass, such as Bristol or Bohemian; or a light etched glass—Bristol and Bohemian are outstanding examples of this type, too. Having made this decision, the first glasses to buy are those for water. It is wiser to use the water glasses as the standard, both as to design and scale, because they are bigger and more important than any of the others. It is wise, also, not to buy colored water or wineglasses, except those for Rhine wine. Unless they are exceedingly interesting or rare, all the glasses of any one kind should be the same: all water glasses, for example, should match one another, and so should all white-wine glasses, etc.

Buying glasses in a matched set is, of course, the more usual and the easiest way. The relative sizes of the glasses are carefully proportioned, and the time and trouble involved are as nothing compared with the piecemeal method. Because glasses are so easily broken, and because a matched set of table glass *must* match, there are two sound maxims for buyers: First, find one that is guaranteed as open stock; and second, buy extra water glasses and, if one plans to serve wine often, extra wineglasses, too.

This is not the place for a treatise on glass and its different formulae, but it is useful to know the difference between ordinary glass and fine glass (crystal). Almost all glass is made with a basis of silica, usually sand. To this base many ingredients are added; but the main ones, in all common glass, are soda and lime. The distinguishing ingredient of fine glass is potash, which replaces the soda. In fine English and Irish glass, and in most American crystal, potash is also used, but lead replaces the lime. The distinguishing feature of lead glass is that it has a fiery sparkle, particularly in cut glass, which other glass lacks. It is heavier than other glass and, when it is struck, it rings like a bell. Like all crystal, it is clearer and more brilliant, and more expensive, than ordinary glass, but it is also tougher and less liable to chip.

As for designs, the most perfectly useful is the simplest: a plain, rounded bowl, a plain stem, and a plain base. Made in fine, thin crystal, this design is beautiful in itself, because it is entirely functional. Wine connoisseurs prefer it to all others; and, besides, it has the great virtue of looking well with almost anything else that will be put on the table. Unfortunately, however, this design is not always successful in inexpensive glass. A little working of the stem is often a more satisfactory way of handling a material which is not brilliant in itself and which may have a few flaws and imperfections. The only designs which must be scrupulously avoided are those which count on cheap engraving or cutting to conceal these imperfections, or those which strive for originality by twisting the shape of the bowl out of all resemblance to its functional purpose.

The following lists make no attempts to be all-inclusive. The first of the two is a list of drinking glasses, showing the classic shapes and sizes which have long been accepted as correct for each kind; all the suggestions that we have given here concerning design apply in general to this list. In the second list, there is a discussion of the other glass, apart from drinking glasses, which is often found in American households.

DRINKING GLASSES

Drinking glasses fall into two main categories: table glasses for wines and water served at the dining-room table; and other glasses, such as whiskey-and-soda glasses, which may or may not be used at the dining-room table. In many American households, glass is accumulated by an accretion of wedding presents, Christmas presents and, too often, unthought-out emergency buying. Such a system scarcely permits an over-all approach to the question, but if one takes a long view, certainly the best advice to anyone who is starting from scratch is to spend a relatively greater proportion of the glass budget on table glass and a smaller proportion on other glasses. Table glasses are seen in a group, as a whole; they are empty when the guests come into the dining room, and their quality and decorative value can do much to add or detract from the aesthetic appeal of the table as a whole.

The second point is to avoid overspecialization. Bars and hotels may have a special glass for almost every different drink, but in a private house such specialization is not necessary or even desirable. The following list of glasses may seem long enough to contradict this statement, but it must be emphasized that they are a maximum. Very few households serve all the different drinks for which these glasses are necessary, and most housewives take advantage of the many double- or triple-purpose glasses which are accepted as in good usage. As a rule, specialization reflects a special interest or taste of the owner. In one household, for example, there may be many different wineglasses, but only one glass for all long drinks, from beer and whiskey to milk and iced tea. In another, there may be only one or two wineglasses but there may be a pointed glass for beer, a big, straight-sided glass for whiskey and soda, and a still bigger one for iced tea. A list of the drinks for which each glass can be used is given with the illustration of each glass. A last word of advice to anyone who is starting housekeeping is to begin by buying glasses which have multiple uses and to specialize later on.

TABLE GLASSES

Everything to do with wine drinking has suffered from the theorizing and, above all, the vocabulary of wine connoisseurs. Stiffly clasped in erudite verbiage, the whole subject of wine drinking has, quite artificially and completely unnecessarily, become formidable to the layman. The following diagrams of table glass show how simple the subject can be. Some of the glass is inexpensive and some of it is extremely expensive, but none of it is contrary to the very highest standards of generally accepted usage. Great wine connoisseurs might prefer a slightly deeper glass, or one less deep. Like every other subject, the further reaches of wine drinking are complicated by violent disagreements of the greatest experts. One school of beer drinkers may hold that a pointed glass is best, and another that beer *cannot* be drunk in a glass without a handle. But anyone, expert or not, will admit that the following types, sizes, and shapes are among those accepted by modern usage.

A final word: Connoisseurs feel strongly that a big wineglass, half full, is better than a small one. But usage approves both.

FOR WATER AND ONE WINE—
MATCHED GLASSES

The line drawn across each glass shows the level to which it should be filled. In this drawing, the wineglass is a big one, and is only half full. It may be used for serving any wine at table, except champagne or sherry.

The diagram directly below and the one on the preceding page show glasses that may be used when only one wine is served. The following diagrams show the relative sizes and shapes of glasses when more than one wine is served.

FOR WATER AND ONE WINE —UNMATCHED GLASSES

The wineglass in this drawing, because it is not very big, is filled almost to the brim.

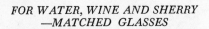

FOR WATER AND TWO WINES— MATCHED GLASSES

This drawing shows the relative sizes of glasses for water, red wine and white wine, and the levels to which each is filled.

FOR WATER, WINE AND SHERRY —MATCHED GLASSES

In this set of glasses the sherry glass is made in the rounded, Spanish shape; the classic pointed sherry glass is shown at the top of the next page.

FOR WATER AND TWO WINES —UNMATCHED GLASSES

The glass at the right is used only for Rhine wine, or "hock." The traditional hock glass has a pale green bowl and it is the only colored wineglass which connoisseurs approve.

FOR WATER AND TWO WINES —UNMATCHED GLASSES

The glass at the right is the standard pointed glass for sherry. The glass in the middle might hold either red or white wine.

When red and white wine are served, the red-wine glass is bigger than the glass for the white wine. For those who want to serve every possible wine:

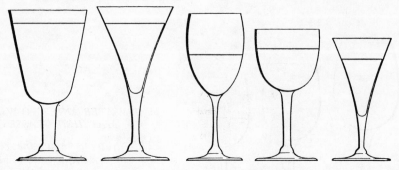

A SET OF UNMATCHED GLASSES

Next to the water glass, which is at the extreme left, is a deep pointed glass for champagne—a design which is found in many old glasses and in many foreign glasses both old and new, and one which is preferred by many connoisseurs. The big wineglass to the right of this champagne glass is half-filled with red Burgundy or claret; the smaller wineglass next in line is almost full, and may be used for any white wine. The pointed sherry glass completes the group.

A SET OF MATCHED GLASSES

Left to right: water glass; saucer champagne glass—the standard champagne glass in America; big glass for red Burgundy; smaller glass for claret; still smaller glass for white Bordeaux or white Burgundy; Spanish sherry glass. In modern times, claret and red Burgundy are rarely served at the same meal and all these glasses are not, therefore, shown as a set which may be used together at one place at table. Both glasses are included to show the small differences in size and shape—differences so subtle that they are interesting only to a connoisseur.

OTHER GLASSES

Beer Glasses

The glass that is best and probably the most often used for beer is the standard straight-sided whiskey-and-soda glass, which holds about twelve or fourteen ounces. Although they are not recommended for every household, and not shown here, two other glasses are often used by "beer specialists": a tall pointed glass with a pedestal foot, which usually holds about twelve ounces; and a broad, short glass (the classic "stein") with a handle, which holds about ten or twelve ounces. The first can be used for peach *bolle* also.

Cocktail Glasses

In a private house, every cocktail, except a frozen daiquiri, an old-fashioned, or a champagne cocktail, may—and, in fact, should—be served in the same kind of glass. Many of these are stemmed, others are not; their capacity is usually about three to four-and-one-half ounces. In some households, tomato and other fruit-juice cocktails are served in short, unstemmed glasses, and other cocktails in stemmed glasses. But this is entirely a matter of taste. Either of the following designs may be used:

TWO DESIGNS FOR COCKTAIL GLASSES

Champagne cocktails and frozen daiquiris are served in "saucer" champagne glasses like these:

GLASS FOR CHAMPAGNE COCKTAILS AND FROZEN DAIQUIRIS

Old-fashioned cocktails are served in straight-sided, heavy-bottomed glasses, with a capacity of seven to nine ounces. Glass muddlers are needed, also, and the best are plain, heavy enough to be sturdy, with a ball end and little ornamentation. Flimsy, fancy muddlers should be avoided; colored plastic muddlers belong only in bars and restaurants. This is the standard old-fashioned glass:

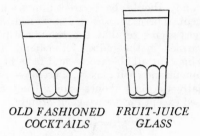

OLD FASHIONED COCKTAILS   *FRUIT-JUICE GLASS*

Fruit-Juice Glasses

The great American custom of drinking fruit juice at breakfast has fathered a very useful modern design—a straight-sided, five or six ounce fruit-juice glass. These can be used also for serving fruit juice at dances or after dinner in the living room.

Liqueur Glasses

There are four different types of liqueur glasses of which only two are really necessary; the other two are for brandy connoisseurs. The first is a small glass, usually stemmed, which holds about an ounce or an ounce and a half. If there is a matched set of table glasses, this glass sometimes belongs to the set. This can be used for any liqueur, including brandy, except a liqueur such as crème de menthe, which is served with crushed ice. This is an example of the standard design:

STANDARD GLASS FOR LIQUEURS   *CRÈME DE MENTHE FRAPPÉ*

Crème de menthe frappé needs a bigger glass: about two and one-half to three ounces to accommodate the crushed ice. This glass is shown on the preceding page.

For brandy connoisseurs, there are balloon-shaped "brandy warmers" in two sizes. The first, if filled, would hold about four ounces; the second, about seven or eight ounces; but, of course, only an ounce and a half or, at most, two ounces of brandy should be poured into each of them. These glasses are designed with short stems so that the brandy can be warmed in the palm of the hand. This brings out all the aroma and taste of the liqueur and such glasses, therefore—especially the bigger ones—should never be used except for a very good brandy.

TWO BRANDY GLASSES

Punch Glasses

The standard punch glass is used, as a rule, only at dances or at big receptions in the afternoon or evening. It holds about four to five ounces.

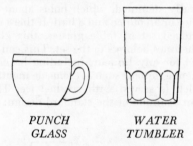

PUNCH GLASS   *WATER TUMBLER*

Water Tumblers

Straight-sided tumblers are always used for serving water, except at the dining-room table; and some use them at the dining-room table for breakfast also. The standard size holds about seven ounces although, if one wanted to specialize, one might have slightly smaller glasses for water served after meals in the living room, and slightly larger glasses for water served at other times.

Whiskey-and-soda, Iced-tea Glasses, etc.

Big straight-sided glasses are used for all long drinks. For iced tea and iced coffee, a very big sixteen-ounce glass may be used, but, as a rule, the fourteen-ounce size shown below is used for everything from milk, ginger ale, iced tea and iced coffee to whiskey and soda, beer, and Tom Collinses.

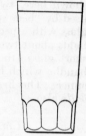

GLASS FOR WHISKEY AND SODA AND OTHER LONG DRINKS

OTHER GLASS

Ashtrays

Ashtrays used on the dining-room table should be very small, not more than about three or four inches in diameter; and, unless they are very old or rare, they should all match one another. One of the best designs is round and heavy, with no angles at all, and only a shallow, sloping depression toward the middle. Another is oblong and very shallow, like a tiny, flat tray. Both of these are absolutely simple, without ornamentation of any kind, except, perhaps, a monogram or initials. Other good modern designs are square or oblong with narrow bands, or other simple designs, as decorations. Among the best old designs are those made in nineteenth-century American pressed glass: wheat, crossed swords, patriotic figures, etc. which are very easy to find and usually very inexpensive. Designs which should be avoided are those with depressions on the lip or border, and with special wells for matches, which suggest smoking cars and restaurants.

Bowls

Glass bowls are used both as serving dishes and, when they are filled with flowers or fruits, as centerpieces. Since they are never empty, they need not be of a very fine quality. But if the glass is not very good, it should be absolutely plain, without any pretentious ornamentation of any kind. The best assortment of sizes would be the following:

A shallow bowl, not more than two or three inches deep: This may be used for serving any of the carefully arranged fruit desserts, such as sliced oranges, or compote of pears. It is used also to hold flowers, such as camellias or gardenias, which lie flat on the water.

A bowl about five or six inches deep: This is used for serving other desserts, such as berries or a cherry compote.

A bowl about eight inches deep: A larger replica of the five-inch deep bowl. This is used at buffet meals, when there are a great many guests; or, with the smaller bowl, it can be used to serve iced desserts. The bigger bowl is lined with ice and the smaller bowl is set inside it. Both of these deep bowls are also used to hold fruit or flowers; the bigger is often used for salad, too. But glass is not at its best as a container for anything hot.

Candelabra

Crystal candelabra, with their branching arms and classic prisms, are among the most beautiful of all objects made for the house; and cheap glass imitations of these candelabra are, beyond any doubt, among the most dreadful. That the beautiful ones should be extremely expensive is a disheartening truth, but it is no reason for being discouraged into buying inexpensive imitations. Between the two extremes, there are hundreds of extremely good old designs, and many modern designs, which pretend to nothing and copy nothing. Cut glass and prisms must be of the finest quality; glass which does not aim at such brilliance need not be so fine. Among the very attractive old and less expensive candelabra are those made of white glass, usually ornamented with round drops and scrolls of faded gold. Others are made of colored glass, in beautiful jewel-like colors and in a wonderful, unexpected, shocking pink. The best modern designs are completely functional, with no straining after imitation-antique nor exaggerated cubism.

Candelabra for the dining-room table are usually designed to hold three candles, with one arm branching off at each side of the center candle. As a rule, they are sold in pairs. Candelabra for the mantelpiece are designed with arms on three sides; and, others, originally meant for a table in the middle of the room, have arms on four sides. Both may be used as a centerpiece on a small table. The mantelpiece candelabra are set back-to-back in the middle of the table.

Candlesticks

Everything that has been said in the foregoing paragraph about candelabra applies, to a lesser degree, to candlesticks. Because the design limits the scope, the most magnificent candlesticks cannot be quite so magnificent as candelabra can be, nor can the most dreadful candlesticks be quite so dreadful. Between the two extremes of the very best and the very worst, there are a great many good designs for candlesticks—even more than there are for candelabra. The only designs that are apt not to be very good are those for inexpensive modern glass. Some of these are bad because they are grossly inadequate imitations of designs which were meant for glass of a fine quality; others are bad because their simple lines, although in accord with the modern fashion for simplicity, show too plainly the coarseness and the dullness which are the great drawbacks of all glass of inferior quality. Modern designs for fine glass are usually brilliantly successful; and most of the old glass, whether of good quality or not, has charm and great decorative value. Glass was a very good medium for earlier designers, who had no inhibitions as to ornamentation. Good glass shone in their hands, and the dullness of poor glass was concealed. This very exuberance of design and color is sometimes, however, difficult to combine with modern decoration. It is wise, therefore, to give classic or simple glass as a present, letting each one choose more elaborate pieces for himself.

Four candlesticks are the standard number for the dining-room table, and they should be a set. It is more difficult to combine two pairs of glass candlesticks than two pairs of silver ones, which have at least a standard medium in common. Pairs are used on console tables and mantelpieces, single ones on small tables. Single candlesticks of an interesting design, or small candelabra, make excellent presents. They are extremely decorative and they give a lovely light without all the ugly fuss of trailing wires.

Centerpieces

The great drawback to glass center-pieces is that, although beautiful ones are magnificent, the inexpensive ones are often not even pretty. Unadorned, inexpensive glass is rather dull all by itself, and pretentious, badly made ornamentation is even worse. As suggested in the paragraph concerning glass bowls, an inexpensive glass bowl filled with flowers or fruit can be a perfect centerpiece. But any centerpiece which can never stand on its own is scarcely worthy of the name. So from now on we shall discuss only those which can be used without flowers, or any decoration other than their own, no matter how expensive they may be.

For a small table, some of the most attractive glass centerpieces are these: a bowl with or without a pedestal foot, in clear or colored glass; glass figures—one or more, depending on the size—perhaps combined on a mirror plaque; glass fruit or flowers in a glass bowl, or arranged on mirror; an old cruet stand, either all glass or with silver mountings. On a larger table, a bigger bowl of the kind suggested above could be used, but the cruet stand would probably be too small. One might have a glass epergne which is now, after an eclipse of twenty years, again somewhat in fashion.

Cigarette Urns

Small glass urns are the most practical containers for cigarettes on the dining-room table, because, like silver, they go well with almost any china; and, unlike silver, they need no polishing. In inexpensive glass, the best are made in a U-shaped design or in the classic Georgian urn shape, without handles. Some of these are of clear glass; others, very satisfactory and very inexpensive, are made of modern white milk-glass. In fine glass, the best designs often have handles, and, sometimes, cutting or other elaborations.

Cocktail Shakers

Glass is the ideal material for a cocktail shaker, and there are many good designs, in a wide range of prices. The best, which is made in glass of all qualities, is well balanced, very slightly bulbous at the bottom, with a wide mouth. The top is usually double—a pierced strainer and a solid stopper—and it fits so tightly that

there is never any danger of its leaking. Some of the more expensive shakers have single tops, carefully grooved so that with one turn they are safe for shaking and, with another, they are ready for pouring. The best designs have no handles to be broken and no ornamentation. They are solidly and successfully functional, and they look it.

For those who like to stir cocktails, rather than to shake them, there are oversize balloon brandy glasses, made with a lip for pouring. Another excellent design is like this, but with a handle added.

Cream Pitchers and Sugar Bowls

Glass cream pitchers, and sugar bowls to match are very useful substitutes for silver. Like silver, they look well with almost any china, and their lack of durability is compensated for by the fact that they need not be polished. There are many very good modern designs in fairly heavy glass. And although all the glass is not of a very fine quality, this is not so important as it is with other, bigger glass pieces. In any case the sugar and cream do as much as most ornamentation to conceal any flaws and imperfections.

A matching cream pitcher and sugar bowl make an excellent wedding present; but one should be careful, if the glass is not of a very good quality, to avoid any design with a pedestal foot. The best design for inexpensive glass is one in which there is no superfluous glass, because any pedestal foot of inexpensive glass, with no cream to line it, will show all its imperfections. Fine glass, both old and new, is often designed with a pedestal foot and very fine cutting.

Decanters

There are two basic types of decanters, one with handles and the other without. Decanters with handles are designed for red wine which is to be served at the dining-room table. White wine is not usually decanted. Decanters without handles divide again into two categories: One kind, without stoppers, is used for water or wine on the dining-room table; and the other kind, with stoppers, is used for sherry, whiskey, etc. which is often left on the sideboard or on a drink-tray.

Before we go any further, it must be said again that any glass which pretends to brilliance, as all cut glass does, must be of very fine quality. It is unfortunately true that there are more bad designs, both old and new, for decanters than for almost any other kind of glassware. For some reason, perhaps because glass is such an ideal container for alcoholic drinks, glass workers of every period seem to have made inept copies of brilliantly cut glass decanters. Among modern designs, there are not only these copies to be avoided but also a whole family of most unattractive, rather clinical shapes, which suggest a laboratory much more strongly than they do a pleasant evening of good cheer. Apart from these unfortunate specimens, there are, however, many lovely decanters: simple ones in plain glass, old or new; magnificent old ones, of brilliantly cut crystal; simpler old ones of white pressed glass or of colored glass; modern ones of fine crystal, either plain or beautifully etched.

It might be helpful to say a word about the labels that often hang about the necks of decanters. The best old ones are made of silver, china, or enamel and the best modern ones are made either of silver or of enamel. All of them should have a good stout chain in proportion to the size of the label. And, if possible, the character of the label should be adapted to that of the decanter. A beautiful old silver label goes well with almost any of them, but a chromium label will not look well with cut glass, and an elaborate label of old plate is not always very becoming to a simple decanter.

Finger Bowls

Finger bowls may be bought as part of a matched set of glass for the table, or they may be assembled one by one, or six by six. One might, for example, collect finger bowls of old clear cut glass, all of more or less the same period but each slightly different in design; or one might make a collection of which half would be clear glass and the other half colored: old red Bohemian or Bristol glass, for example, alternating around the table with old clear glass. If one has decided to make a collection of finger bowls rather than to buy a matched set, one must be sure that each of the finger bowls is old and interesting, and looks it. A collection of old, unusual pieces is attractive; a collection of odd, modern finger bowls, each one of

which might easily be bought by the dozen, is entirely senseless. As usual, pretentious, imitative cutting and etching should be avoided.

Jam Pots, Mustard Pots, etc.

As in the case of cream pitchers and sugar bowls, inexpensive glass is often used most successfully for jam pots, honey jars, and mustard pots. The rule here, also, is to choose the simplest and most functional design in inexpensive glass, and more elaborate designs only in glass of a better quality. The most functional design is one in which the glass is used only as a shell or container; the top is wide and the shape is as simple as possible. If any of these jars or pots has a cover, the cover should be pierced to allow for the spoon. Many of the modern jars are sold with a matching plate of glass, which is convenient but not necessary. As always, the most elaborate designs for fine glass can be extremely beautiful, and correspondingly expensive.

Plates

Although many designs have been tried, very few designs for glass plates to be used at the dining-room table are dependably successful. Glass and hot foods are not usually an attractive combination. There are only three glass plates that have been generally accepted, and even these are not very widely used. The first is a small glass plate which matches the finger bowl. Dessert is sometimes eaten on these plates, which then are used as a protection for a very fragile and valuable dessert plate underneath; usually, however, they are taken off the dessert plate with the finger bowl and are, therefore, only a completely useless sort of extra doily. The second glass plate is a butter plate (the finger-bowl plate can usually double for this) which is used when the entrée or main-course plates cannot be matched with another china. The third is a crescent-shaped salad plate, designed to fit against the big plate on which the meat course is eaten. These are not so popular as they used to be, because it has become fashionable to eat salad and meat on the same plate. But if one does not like this new fashion, the glass plates are very practical. They do not take up much room on the table and, like the glass butter plate, they look well with almost any kind of china.

Obviously, crescent-shaped plates must be bought in matched sets. It is a modern design, and there is no way of making up a collection of interesting old pieces. Finger-bowl plates should match the finger bowls unless they are old ones, in which case they can be used with any very simple modern finger bowl.

Saltcellars and Pepper Bowls

There are some very well designed old glass salt and pepper shakers with silver tops, but, as a rule, glass shaker designs are not entirely successful. The best design is a small round bowl, or a straight-sided oblong container shaped rather like a window box. Modern containers are sometimes made in the shape of a square block with a depression for the salt or pepper; old ones are often octagonal or hexagonal, with a pedestal foot. But since the salt and pepper do not entirely fill the glass in either of these designs, the glass must be of a fine quality.

With any of these, a silver spoon is used, or a little glass shovel. The glass shovel is, of course, the more practical of the two because it never needs polishing, but it is strangely difficult to find good, simple designs. All too often, the handles are ornamented with would-be-cute little cat's heads, or rough, badly executed designs of fruit in colored glass.

As in the case of silver saltcellars and pepper pots, four of each is the most useful number; two of each, a minimum. But since there is no difference between the functional design of a glass pepper container and that of a glass salt container, they must be bought and used in pairs.

Sea-food Glasses

The best design for glasses in which to serve sea-food cocktails avoids any suggestion of the old-fashioned long-stemmed sherbet glass. Sherbet glasses are now out of fashion, and are not used in private houses. One of the best designs is a small round bowl, a little like a narrow finger bowl with slightly flaring sides. Other designs are made with a very short pedestal foot; but a long stem is not advisable.

Water Pitchers

Surely it is unnecessary to say one word further about cheap cut glass and pretentious ornamentation, and so we shall proceed at once to list some of the best designs for water pitchers: light, inexpensive, modern glass, in a functional shape with rounded sides, a broad, curved lip and a strong handle; fine, modern crystal in this same functional shape, or in a hexagonal or octagonal shape, with or without a pedestal foot; old, pressed glass, usually made with a pedestal foot, and decorated with a design of wheat, crossed swords, or patriotic figures; old glass in the classic, rounded shape, with a design of vine leaves or grapes (these are often not made in a very fine glass but they are usually unpretentious, inexpensive, and extremely good-looking); very fine old pitchers, some octagonal or hexagonal, with a pedestal foot and decorative bands of cut glass, others rounded, with fine ornamentation. One must avoid, however, the extremely tall, narrow shape so popular in the Nineties. This was often made in cut glass; but no matter how fine the glass or how fine the cutting, it is basically a bad, unfunctional design. There are also water pitchers of colored glass, but, unless they are very old and very beautiful, they should be avoided. Clear glass is the best.

There is another excellent modern design for water pitchers, so useful that it must be described in a paragraph by itself. It is tall and straight-sided, round as a column and perfectly plain, with a short lip for pouring and a stout handle. Although it may be made of glass of any quality, it is usually most satisfactorily inexpensive. And although this design is not used as much as the others for serving water at the dining-room table, it easily might be. It is ideal, of course, for serving such drinks as fruit juices and iced tea. Other pitcher designs for long drinks are made with a separate well for the ice, so that the melting ice will not dilute the drink. These are practical, but the best are often quite expensive. The design is complicated, and the pitcher is apt to look rather clumsy unless it is really very well made.

51

China

THE MODERN approach to buying china has wisely departed from the classic conception of a matched set which included plates, serving dishes, and all the table decorations except perhaps the candelabra. This might have been a sound approach in the days when huge sums were spent for magnificent and complete sets of china. (And huge sums were spent. As recently as forty years ago, one American paid $88,000 for a made-to-order set of table china.) When each piece is beautiful, the design can well withstand the emphasis of repetition, course after course, and beauty and uniformity can easily be achieved together. When it comes to buying inexpensive sets of china, two difficulties are at once apparent: If the design is bold and not well executed, it is a bad choice, because the eye grows very quickly tired of things which clamor for attention and are not worth it; if it is unpretentious and unobtrusive, it is a bad choice, because it is monotonous and without decorative value. These are two of the reasons why the classic conception of uniformity has been abandoned, or, to be precise, almost abandoned. A rigidly formal dinner still adheres somewhat to the classic standards. But such dinners are scarcely examples of the modern approach to entertaining and, in any case, they are now extremely rare.

A third and more important reason is that, from the point of view of common sense, the first aesthetic consideration in buying china should always be its decorative value rather than its uniformity. Since beauty and uniformity can be bought together only at such an impossibly high price, uniformity is the one that must be sacrificed. Today, a complete set of china is very often the mark of a lack of interest in table decoration. Varied sets of plates, of different designs and patterns, which cost very much less than an equally beautiful and decorative set, have been accepted as the standard.

From a common-sense point of view, however, it is obvious that other aspects of the classic conception are still valid. A soup plate of one pattern, followed by a meat plate of another, gives pleasing variety because the two patterns are not seen together. But a batch of completely unrelated china decorations, herded together in the middle of the table, suggests past breakage and present confusion. These are the points at which the classic conception of a set still has some validity and where indiscriminate mixing is almost sure to be unsuccessful:

1. The table decorations, consisting of centerpiece, candy dishes, etc., are still considered as a set, particularly in their relation to each other and, also, to a lesser degree, in their relation to the other plates (such as place plates and butter plates) which are on the table when the guests first come into the dining room. The plates for subsequent courses are less important.

2. Tea sets are still considered as a set.

3. Coffee sets are also regarded as a set.

4. All the plates for any one course must be a matched set.

At the end of this chapter, this china is discussed in detail, but first we must consider the general principles of mixing china successfully.

HOW TO USE DIFFERENT CHINAS TOGETHER

Most fortunately, mixing chinas is a matter of knowledge, which can be acquired, as well as taste, which is a more elusive commodity. The basic principle is that whenever one is departing from the still valid rules as to which china should be a "set," one must use great discrimination and care in deciding which chinas can be used together. These are the points to watch for:

Scale. This is an obvious point. A very big cream pitcher is not becoming to a small teapot; mammoth fruit dishes should not dwarf the centerpiece.

Pattern. This is a more complicated subject. The first question is color. If the colors clash, the chinas cannot be used together. If they match or are in harmony, one proceeds to the second question: the character of the design. At the risk of making a grossly imprecise generalization, one can reduce all the patterns for china to four basic types: a scenic or landscape pattern, usually confined to a definite space in the middle of the plate and often combined with a banded border; an all-over pattern; a banded or geometric pattern around the rim of the plate; and a loose, scattered pattern—for example, flowers, butterflies, fish, etc. There are, of course, hundreds of variations and combinations of these four patterns, but the over-all impression determines to which category each china belongs. For example, if there is a design of flowers confined within definite limitations, whether marked or not, around the edge of the plate, the pattern is basically a banded one. The safest rule of thumb is that banded chinas can be combined successfully with any of the other patterns, but that the others should not be used together. In the interpretation of this rule, there are infinite subtleties; for example, a banded design of stylized flowers is not apt to look well with a loose, scattered design of naturalistic flowers. But, on the whole, banded patterns, or perfectly plain china without any pattern, are the best mixers.

404

Texture. The texture of a piece of china is a very important factor in deciding whether or not it can be used with another china. A heavy, coarse-grained piece of earthenware rarely looks well next to a fine, close-grained piece of porcelain. Earthenware, also called pottery or faïence, is opaque and usually quite thick; porcelain, called also fine china (and technically the only true china), is translucent and often very thin—light in weight and appearance. These are the two basically different textures. In addition, there are two other minor categories: soft paste which is an artificial porcelain and very rare, and stoneware which is a cross between porcelain and earthenware. Subject to all the other considerations as to scale and pattern, the rule of thumb is that stoneware can often be used with both porcelain and pottery, that soft paste looks best with porcelain, and that earthenware and porcelain can rarely be mixed successfully. As in the case of almost every other rule, there are exceptions. There are a few very fine earthenwares that can be used with porcelain; there are a few heavy porcelains that look well with earthenware. Experts, who would probably laugh at such simple definitions, can find an infinite number of such exceptions, but for the amateur the rule of thumb is a safe one to follow.

FAMOUS CHINA FACTORIES

The following lists are not by any means a complete roster of all the different kinds of china. They are only a partial listing of some of the best-known factories and the most widely available chinas, and they are included here only in the hope that they may be useful to those who are planning to buy.

Stoneware

Mason: Mostly old; most commonly found in blue, orange, and brown on an oyster-white body.

Spode: One of the biggest manufacturers of stoneware. Most famous old pattern is very much like that of Mason stoneware; today making very fine reproductions of armorial Lowestoft.

Soft Paste

Sèvres: The best-known factory; most of it extremely rare and equally expensive.

Fine China

Old Fine China:

Meissen: Sometimes called Dresden. Best-known patterns were landscapes or flowers: small, spread, or scattered flowers; large bouquets with insects and butterflies. Also famous for figurines, and candelabra.

Vienna: Styles and patterns very like Meissen.

Derby: One of the best-known patterns is the famous Imari pattern: cobalt blue, mandarin red and gold, on a white background.

Worcester: Best-known for monotone and gold patterns on a white ground; and for variations of the Imari patterns.

Spode: Famous for fine enameled floral designs, and variations of the Imari pattern.

Rockingham: Best-known for pale-green, pink, red, and blue solid-bordered patterns, with flowers or landscapes in the middle.

Sèvres: Famous for flowered designs and more recently for white-and-gold banded porcelain.

Chantilly: Best-known for very fine white porcelain with scattered, delicate patterns.

Copenhagen: Well-known for underglaze blue designs on a gray-white body, and for scattered flower patterns in a lovely soft red monotone.

Capo di monte: Best-known for scenic patterns with raised, embossed figures; also for figurines and candelabra.

Lowestoft: Famous for its unique "orange-peel" texture, and for its armorial, floral, and oriental designs.

Chelsea: Best-known for its rustic figures and candelabra.

Contemporary Fine China:

Minton: Best-known for its very fine banded patterns, usually cobalt-blue, or red, and gold. Also encrusted gold.

Lenox: Best-known for its very fine pure cream-colored porcelain.

Derby: This factory still makes modern variations of its famous cobalt-blue, mandarin red, and gold Imari pattern. Also beautiful printed patterns of flowers and birds.

Worcester: Well-known for its solid and banded patterns with floral centers and enameled floral patterns and fruits.

Castleton: Best-known for its decorations by modern artists, and for its white, unpatterned, semi-oriental design.

Copenhagen: Best-known for its fine gold-and-white china, and its blue-and-white or multi-colored figurines.

Booth: Famous for monotone floral patterns in red, blue, or green; also multicolors. Booth "silicon china" is often made in very good reproductions of the Imari pattern.

Spode: Best-known for its rose patterns —"moss," "maritime," "Billingsley" and others—often with solid-color banded borders.

Herend: Best-known for its scattered patterns: flowers, butterflies, etc., with many shades of green, on a fine white background.

Earthenware

Old Earthenware:

Creil: Famous for its black-and-ivory colored patterns, often scenic.

Leeds: Famous for its unpatterned, cream-colored ware.

Spode: Best-known for over-all, monotone patterns of pink, pale mauve, and royal—or purple—blue.

Wedgwood: Best-known pattern is its cream-colored "Queensware," sometimes unpatterned, sometimes with a border pattern.

Enoch Wood: Best-known for over-all, purple-blue, monotone patterns; often historic scenes.

Turner: Usually an ivory body with a simple border pattern, very like Wedgwood.

Adams: Over-all prints, very like Enoch Wood.

Contemporary Earthenware:

There are so many makers of modern earthenware that it is impossible to list more than a few of the best generic types:

Simple, functional shapes in pale colors, unpatterned. Pedestal feet, sharp angles, and other formal or classic designs are never found in the best ware of this kind.

Printed designs like those of old earthenware. This china is made in light, pretty colors. The best designs are very simple: a sprig of flowers, or a border pattern of ivy.

Peasant china, decorated with crude but colorful patterns. This comes in many colors; light and bright colors are better than the dark ones. The best of this kind is decorated by hand.

A WORD ON REPRODUCTIONS

Among the many modern "reproductions" of household objects, there are few that can be so classified with complete accuracy and truthfulness. Most of them, it must be admitted, are imitations. In silver and wood, for example, it is impossible to reproduce the patina of the antique, and so, quite apart from other considerations, such as workmanship, there can be no true reproductions in these two fields. On the other hand, most old chinas can be reproduced exactly. The clay can be mixed according to the same formula; it can be fired at the same temperature, in the same kiln; it can be decorated and glazed in the same way. Such modern reproductions are not, of course, as valuable as the originals, and there are some old patterns which are impossible to copy under modern economic conditions. But if a piece of china is a true reproduction—strictly accurate as to pattern design and, above all, texture—it should not really be called an imitation.

Imitations, in china and everything else, should be avoided as a rule. And this is one of the safest of all rules for those who are finding their way in any new field. A piece of imitation china is one which copies an old and valuable original, in a different mixture of clay, produced under different conditions and often in a less expensive adaptation of the pattern. Anyone who has seen an imitation Meissen figurine, with heavy lumps replacing the sharp, delicate laces, and coarse colors instead of subtle and brilliantly executed designs, will know what imitation china can be.

WHETHER TO BUY FINE CHINA OR EARTHENWARE

When one adds up all the pros and cons of earthenware and porcelain, it becomes quite clear that in most cases, porcelain is an infinitely better buy. The great practical advantage of porcelain over earthenware is that porcelain is so much more durable. When it comes to breakage, one might almost compare porcelain to oakwood and earthenware to cork: porcelain will withstand a blow which would crumble most earthenware. (There are some outstanding exceptions to this: Spode, for example, makes a most durable earthenware.) When it comes to chipping, one might compare porcelain to metal and earthenware to wood. The tight resilient body of porcelain resists chipping, but the looser, softer body of earthenware gives way; and being porous, when it does give way, it often darkens irremediably. The quality of resilience is one of the particular advantages of bone china but, subject always to a few exceptions, it can safely be said that all fine chinas are tougher than earthenware.

Apart from these practical considerations, there are some aesthetic ones. When earthenware is gilded, the gilding is often overbright at the start and nonexistent at the finish. The reason for this is that fine china is decorated with "best gold," and an inferior alloy (called "liquid gold") is often used for earthenware. And then there is the fact that earthenware, being a heavier and coarser material, is always somewhat limited as an artistic medium. The great drawback of porcelain is that it is usually much more expensive than earthenware and, although it might be argued that it is never wise to consider the initial expense only, it must be admitted that the initial expense is often the one that hurts. Buying china on a budget, therefore, is our next consideration.

BUYING CHINA ON A BUDGET

When it comes to buying china on a budget, the wisest and least expensive course is to use a simple, unobtrusive, open-stock pattern as one's basic or standard set and to buy interesting and perhaps slightly more expensive pieces to give it flavor. Whether one buys a basic set of earthenware or fine china is entirely a matter for the budget to determine. If it can possibly be managed, in the long run fine china is an economy, as we have said. (See immediately above.) And if one can afford a few pieces of fine china, certainly the first to buy are cups, both teacups and demitasses. An earthenware cup is even more likely to chip than an earthenware plate; and when it is chipped, it is even more unattractive. Fine china for one's tea set and demitasses, and earthenware for the rest of one's table china is a practical division followed by generations of housewives. If one follows this division, the minimum list on page 230, in "China for the Bride," will have to be enlarged to include six extra tea plates of fine china. From now on, in the rest of this section, we shall take it for granted that these practical considerations have been understood.

From the purely aesthetic point of view, interesting table decoration is just as easy to achieve with earthenware as it is with porcelain. Just as easy, and usually a good deal less expensive. In either case, the "interesting" pieces will be more important and more expensive than those in the basic set. They should be bought with the greatest care, with these three points in mind:

1. Which are usually the most expensive? An interesting teapot, for example, is apt to be less expensive than a set of interesting teacups, saucers, and tea plates. One should plan, therefore, to make the teapot the dominant piece on the tea tray.
2. Which pieces of china are apt to be used the most? It would be unwise to choose interesting pieces of china for the ones which must be used and washed unremittingly after every meal.
3. Granted a very limited budget, which pieces will be the most decorative in relation to their cost?

All these questions are answered in the list which follows; but first we must discuss the key to all table china: the centerpiece. If there is any budget problem, china is by far the best material for a centerpiece. Silver is expensive and needs polishing. Inexpensive glass demands flowers or fruit. But a china bowl, a china tureen, or a group of china figures are not only colorful and attractive but need no maintenance of any kind. Bowls and tureens can, of course, be used with flowers, too. (Centerpieces are discussed in detail on pages 418 and 419.)

If the budget is so small that it cannot cover more than the basic and practical necessities, the plates will have to come first, but the centerpiece should be the mental starting point. The standard set will probably be made of earthenware but, as a rule, it is just as easy to buy such a set in a color which will look well with attractive and interesting pieces of old earthenware, as it is to buy it in a color which, from this point of view, is utterly impossible. For example, a great deal of old earthenware is made in deep-blue and purple-blue monotones. If one likes these colors, one might buy a standard earthenware set in a very pale, unpatterned hyacinth blue, planning to add more interesting pieces in the future. Or, one might buy a set of plain, cream-colored earthenware, with all the many lovely old cream-colored earthenwares in view. The essential point is that the smaller the budget, the greater the thought that must be given to all buying.

Whether the "interesting" pieces of china are an immediate or an eventual possibility, the minimum china list on page 230 can be divided as follows:

Interesting
Centerpiece
Teapot
Coffeepot
Vegetable dishes; these should be a pair
All other serving dishes: these need not match each other or anything else
Dessert plates: if these are carefully chosen to go well with the centerpiece, they can be used as place plates also

Standard
Big plates for the main course
Entrée plates
Soup cups, and soup plates, or bowls
Cereal bowls
Teacups and saucers
Tea plates, also used as butter plates
Hot-milk or hot-water jug
Sugar bowl and cream pitcher
Demitasses

This division of china is the most practical and the least expensive. Everything is carefully planned so that there should never be a conflict of pattern and so that there should always be at least one interesting piece to relieve the monotony of the standard set. And yet most of the china which must stand the hardest wear belongs to the basic set and can easily be replaced.

If one wanted to save further, the platters could be bought in the standard pattern. The vegetable dishes, too, might have to be added to the standard list because a pair of interesting ones is often expensive. But a deep bowl for dessert is always easy to find and need not be expensive at all. So is a sauceboat, or a pretty little bowl which can be used for sauces.

If the budget were a little less limiting, the soup plates could be removed from the standard list. They should be chosen to harmonize with the dessert plates which, as we have suggested, can also double as place plates. (In small households where the most formal service is never necessary, the soup plate can be set down on the place plate.) But even more important are the sugar bowl and the cream pitcher, which would then be bought with the teapot as part of a three-piece set. The coffeepot could then be eliminated entirely, if necessary, and one would plan to serve filled cups of coffee on a tray with the pretty sugar bowl and cream pitcher. This very sound arrangement was not suggested in the list because a matched set of teapot, cream jug, and sugar bowl is usually more expensive than a single teapot and a single coffeepot would be. If one can afford silver, it would be even more practical to buy a silver sugar bowl and a cream pitcher, and perhaps a silver hot-milk or hot-water jug, in a very simple pattern which would look well with all one's china, and with any other silver one might buy in the future. Further suggestions for budget buyers are given in the detailed lists below.

CHINA FOR THE TABLE

Whether one is buying a complete set of table china or not, very few sets include all the pieces that are usually needed on modern tables. The following list makes no attempt to cover all the different pieces of china that may be used on the dining-room table. It is designed only to give specific and helpful suggestions concerning the pieces which are usually needed, and the characteristics which are usually considered desirable in each piece, whether decorative or functional.

Ashtrays

All ashtrays for the dining-room table, and particularly, perhaps, china ashtrays, should be very small, and always less noticeable than the rest of the table decorations. It is basically unattractive to make much of a point of smoking at the dining-room table. The only exception to this rule are ashtrays made in the shape of lettuce leaves or vine leaves. These seem more appropriate than others and can be bigger. Some of them are old and expensive. There are beautiful ones made by Derby, Worcester, and Spode, for example; and there are many lovely modern earthenware leaves made by Wedg-wood, and Lenox, and by French and Portuguese factories. The most usual ashtrays of old china are saucers which have lost their cups, although these are sometimes a little too big for the dining-room table. Ideal for this purpose are the old, traveling-salesmen's samples of china: miniature plates which were made by almost every firm in England during the nineteenth century. In modern china, there are some good designs, but the better ones are apt to be expensive. If there is a budget problem, it is wiser to buy glass.

Unless the cigarette containers are made of china, ashtrays need not match any of the other china on the table, but it is wise to avoid violent contrasts in pattern and quality. Heavily gilded ashtrays of fine white china, for example, would not be becoming to earthenware plates, or vice versa. They should all be of the same size and quality and, unless they are old—in which case variations would be permissible—they should be of the same pattern.

Breadbaskets

China breadbaskets, designed as such, are rare. But one could well use a shallow china bowl for this purpose, as suggested below in the paragraph "Bowls," under "Serving Dishes."

Breakfast Sets

Breakfast sets are made for three different kinds of breakfasts: breakfast at the dining-room table, a big breakfast in bed, and coffee and toast in bed. The only points that apply to all three are these: Simple patterns and light colors are the best—no matter how beautiful it may be, china with an elaborate pattern, heavy with gold, is never appealing at breakfast-time; and, as always, since cups are brought into the picture, the better the china, the greater the economy in the long run.

Breakfast sets for the dining-room table come in various sizes for various numbers of people. They usually consist of the following: a teapot and coffeepot, a hot-milk or hot-water pitcher (sometimes both); a sugar bowl and cream pitcher; dessert-sized plates and butter plates; teacups and saucers, which are used also, of course, for coffee; cups for boiled eggs; and a serving platter, or sometimes two platters. In some sets, there are also cereal bowls and extra-big cups for coffee. Whether one buys a special breakfast set or, as is more usual, uses the regular household china, these are the pieces that will be needed for breakfast. The most practical arrangement is to use one's standard set and supplement it with any pieces that are specially needed at breakfast. (See also page 412, "Coffee Cups.")

Tray sets for breakfast in bed consist of the following pieces: a coffeepot, a hot-milk pitcher, a sugar bowl and cream pitcher, a cup and saucer, a cereal bowl, a butter plate, an egg cup, and a plate about eight or nine inches in diameter,

with a cover, for bacon and eggs. Very complete sets have a teapot as well, but these are often lacking in American sets. If a teapot is needed, one can use either a small thermos jug with a handle (which obviously need not match the set) or a brown earthenware teapot which many tea fanciers insist is the best.

Sets for coffee in bed are an innovation, borrowed from the English tradition of early-morning tea. They usually consist of a china tray with special ridged places for the cup, the coffeepot (or teapot), the cream pitcher and sugar bowl. All these are sold as a set, usually in pale, pretty colors or flowered, sprigged patterns. And although they are made of earthenware which is not, of course, as practical as china, they have the practical advantage of being comparatively inexpensive.

Cigarette Containers

China cigarette containers and ashtrays, used together on the dining-room table, should be a set. There are many very small boxes of old china with little trays to match; and there are modern china urns or cups in white or cream color with matching ashtrays. Both of these can be very useful, but they should always be very much subordinated to the rest of the china. Failing a perfect match, it is wiser to use glass or silver; or, as suggested on page 262, in the chapter "Setting the Table," to use no cigarette containers at all.

If the ashtrays are not china, it is not difficult to find good china cigarette containers which look well with the table decorations. In fact, once they are separated from the ashtrays by being made of another material, they may even be part of the decoration. There are small cups in almost every china of almost every period; the best have two handles or none. There are many beautiful small china urns and vases, often made with a pedestal foot, but sometimes difficult to find in the right size, as they should be no deeper than the cigarette is long. There are small china boxes, some of them metal-hinged, others plain; Wedgwood made many of these. Best of all perhaps are very small eggcups, designed for eggs eaten in the shell. Many of these belonged to magnificent sets of old porcelain, but even in the finest china, they are usually most satisfactorily inexpensive. The best inexpensive modern design is a small earthenware urn in a monotone white or cream color. Good modern designs with colors are apt to be quite expensive.

Coffee Sets

A perfect set for after-dinner coffee consists of the following: a coffeepot, tall and narrow with a long spout; a sugar bowl, with or without a lid; a cream pitcher; and demitasses with saucers, the cups quite big and straight-sided (they hold about half the amount a teacup does). Most of the old, beautiful coffee sets are made in these classic shapes, and a few have a matching china tray as well. Other sets have smaller rounded cups, like a teacup one-third the usual size. This is a later design and some of these sets are extremely attractive. Many, however, were made in the "dainty" period of the early 1900's and are too heavily gilded for modern taste.

If one is making up a china coffee set, the best division of the china falls into two groups: cups and saucers of one pattern; coffeepot, sugar bowl, and cream pitcher of another. Or, china coffeepot of one pattern; sugar bowl and cream pitcher of silver; china cups of another pattern. As explained on page 404, this mixing of china cannot be done indiscriminately. It is obvious that Derby demitasses in the bold cobalt-blue, mandarin-red, and gold pattern, however magnificent they might be, would never look well with a delicately flowered Meissen coffeepot; plain modern coffee cups, in a brilliant white porcelain, would be much better. With such elaborate Derby cups, one could use a pot in one of the many variations of the same pattern, perhaps made in another china or even in earthenware.

The least expensive way of making up an attractive coffee set is to buy an interesting or beautiful coffeepot and to use with it another china of a very simple standard set. It is usually not difficult to find coffeepots such as these in old china and, besides, there are also old chocolate pots which are most attractive and often less expensive. Chocolate pots are more rounded than the classic coffeepot and they have a short lip rather than a long spout. But, whichever one buys, it is a sound rule to avoid a pedestal foot design unless the china is of a fine quality, or unless the piece is unusually interesting. A pedestal foot is essentially a formal design and, in inexpensive china or earthenware, it often seems pretentious.

A matching sugar bowl and cream pitcher are often sold as a set with the coffeepot. But a matched set is proportionately very much more expensive as a rule than a single coffeepot, and so we have suggested for a very limited budget a sugar bowl and cream pitcher that match the cups. If the budget is less limiting, a silver cream pitcher and sugar bowl are perhaps the ideal solution, because the cups, which are apt to be expensive if they are "interesting," can still be a simple pattern and the coffeepot can supply the decoration and color. Less expensive than silver are a cream jug and sugar bowl of glass but, if one is using glass, one should use only one china with it. Glass does not look well combined on a tray with two different patterns of china.

Mixing chinas in a coffee set cannot be carried beyond this point. All the demitasses and saucers used together on the same coffee tray should be a set. If everything else on the coffee tray were silver, one might be able to use together exceptionally rare and beautiful demitasses of an almost similar pattern. But otherwise, one should stick to the rule of thumb and buy a perfectly matching set. In old and beautiful chinas a set of demitasses can be quite expensive, and fine modern chinas are not inexpensive either, particularly if they are elaborately and beautifully decorated. This is why we have so often suggested simple cups, with a more elaborate old coffeepot as the decorative note. Modern cups in a simple pattern are the least expensive, and fine china is the best buy. (This is fully discussed on page 407.) With an old coffeepot of fine china with a white background, white porcelain cups are best, and if the pot has gilding, porcelain with a narrow gold band. With most of the old earthenware coffeepots, cream-colored cups in fine china, but not too thin a china, would be an excellent choice. Or, with all-over red, or purple-blue, earthenware, the thinnest cups of shell-pink or pale hyacinth-blue.

Coffee Urns

China coffee urns are harder to find than china coffeepots, but they are most decorative. Almost all of them are made of old china; big ones which would be ideal for buffet meals and as a decoration on the sideboard, and smaller ones, which could be used on the after-dinner coffee tray. They can be used also, of course, as centerpieces.

Cups

Coffee cups: Coffee cups come in three sizes: small ones—demitasses—used for coffee after luncheon or dinner (these are discussed under the heading "Coffee Sets" above); medium-sized cups for morning coffee, which are exactly like teacups and are covered under the heading "Tea Sets"; and jumbo-sized coffee cups, or huge "magnum" cups, which are used only for morning coffee and usually by those who like coffee mixed with hot milk instead of cream. These very big coffee cups are shaped exactly like teacups but they hold about two or three times as much. They are not usually made in the less expensive standard sets, but odd ones are not difficult to find and, as a matter of fact, odd ones are very practical. They are made in durable fine china, in many pretty or amusing designs, which were obviously never part of any set or ever meant to be. If one has a standard or basic set for breakfast, it is quite easy to find jumbo cups that will look well with it. And if the budget has not allowed for teacups of fine china, the more tender earthenware ones will be spared as a matched, and un-chipped, set for teatime. Some of these coffee cups are made with "French drip" tops, a most practical arrangement for breakfast for one, or perhaps even two, people.

Soup cups: There are three kinds of cups that can be used for serving soup at luncheon: the standard soup cup which is exactly like a two-handled teacup and always has a matching saucer, sometimes called "bouillon cups"; the wide bowl called "cream-soup" cups or bowls, a modern design halfway between a soup cup and a rimmed soup plate, which is sometimes sold with a matching saucer (this bowl can be used also at dinner); and pottery ovenware bowls, usually made with a cover, with a capacity almost twice that of the usual soup cup.

Very few soup cups are old ones. They can be found in china of almost every quality, but most of them are modern.

Many modern china manufacturers have made reproductions of old patterns which can be used very satisfactorily with old china of the same pattern or period. (See "A Word on Reproductions," page 406.) For those who do not like copies of any kind, there are dozens of good simple modern designs from which to choose: thin white cups with a narrow gold band, which would go very well with any of the very fine gilded chinas; plain ones in white and pale colors, in fine china and earthenware.

The great practical virtue of the modern wide soup bowl is that it can be used not only at luncheon but also at every dinner except the most formal. Its great drawback is that, like so many dual-purpose gadgets, it is not really perfect for either. It holds a little too much soup to be perfect for luncheon and it is never quite as attractive as a soup plate at dinnertime. Some of these bowls are made in very fine china with gilding of the highest quality, but for some reason—perhaps because they are not a classic shape—the best are made either in fine china with less formal decoration, or in earthenware which is very often beautifully painted. If the dining-room table and all its decorations are classic and formal, the design of the modern soup bowl is a discordant note. If the table is colorful and informal and makes no effort to be anything else, soup bowls can be very practical and compatible.

Pottery ovenware bowls are often used at informal meals for soups such as onion soup au gratin, which are put briefly under the broiler before being brought to the table. They can be used also as a practical convenience whenever soup must be served quite a while before it is to be eaten. But they should really be used only for hearty soups (onion soup, clam chowder, etc.); for thin soups, such as consommé or bouillon, they are much less appropriate. Some of these bowls are made in colored ovenware with an all-over glaze and a matching plate, but the best are completely functional and make no effort to be decorative. They are made of brown earthenware, glazed on the inside, plain on the outside. These are sometimes made in the shape of a tiny casserole, with two very small curved handles and a cover—a design which is ideal for buffet meals, or for any meal when the soup is set on the table before the guests come into the dining room. Another design, perfect for any soup au gratin, is shaped like a deep, open frying pan with one short thick handle.

Teacups: See "Tea Sets" below.

Pitchers

China pitchers, whether fine china or porcelain, are often used for serving water or milk. For some reason, china is not a good container for fruit juice, iced tea, or iced coffee: Glass is much better. Pitchers are not usually made in cheap modern chinas; so many of the available pitchers are old and most of them are extremely attractive. As always, it is wise to avoid a formal design, such as the pedestal foot, in earthenware. Some old china pitchers are made with a cover, or with a hinged lid of pewter or silver, ideal for serving milk whenever it is to be left on a tray.

Plates

The first point in buying plates is the rule given on page 404: All the plates used together for the same food at the same time should match each other exactly. This is certainly the rule of thumb, but exceptions can be made when the plates are interesting or beautiful enough to warrant them. Consider black-and-white Creil, for example. A great deal of this china was made in variations of the same basic pattern: a border of leaves, flowers, or patriotic emblems, with a big central design, often a landscape or a historic scene. A set of place plates of this china, all black and white, all the same size, would be most attractive whether or not the central design or even the borders were exactly the same. And this is true not only of place plates and not only of Creil china but of many other chinas, of which Worcester is another outstanding example, and of every kind of plate except small butter plates or tea plates.

In all the welter of plates of different sizes and different patterns, there are only four desirable types which have any basic differences: a small flat plate for butter; a deep plate for soup; a big, flat plate for the main course; and a smaller flat plate for dessert, salad, etc. All the others—fruit plates, place plates, fish plates, and oyster plates—are different only because

special decoration has made them so. There are, however, certain characteristics that are particularly desirable in plates that will be used for different foods; so that, although there are only four basic types, the nine different kinds of plates will be taken up one by one.

Butter plates: The classic butter plate is a smaller replica of the place plate, usually four to six inches in diameter. By tradition and convention, butter plates should appear on the dining-room table only at lunchtime; although many who happen to like them use them at every meal except the most rigidly formal dinner. If one is buying varied sets of plates rather than a complete matched set, butter plates are often a rather difficult problem. Like the place plates, they must be carefully chosen to look well with the table decorations and, besides, they must look well with the place plates and with the china used for any subsequent courses. If one is having difficulty in finding a butter plate of the proper kind, one can sometimes use a saucer instead, but it must be a very flat one. In extremely difficult cases, glass or even silver can be used. There are no customs concerning the patterns of butter plates; they can be elaborate or simple, but each one should match the other.

Dessert plates: The classic dessert plate is a flat plate about eight or nine inches in diameter. Elaborate patterns, and even patterns with dark colors, which would be unattractive in fish or meat plates, can be used for dessert. In some old chinas, the dessert plates were not quite flat but rather like a shallow soup plate, sometimes with a flat rim and sometimes without any rim. These are not a wise choice if one is planning to use the dessert plate as a place plate, because the place plate must be flat. Otherwise, they are charming. And it is better also, if one is planning to interchange dessert plates and place plates, to buy dessert plates a little bigger than the eight-inch minimum.

Fish plates: A classic fish plate is almost exactly like a dessert plate: flat, and about eight or nine inches across. A great many china factories made plates especially for the fish course, with designs of fishes, very often beautifully painted. Such specialization is not necessary; in fact, it should be avoided unless the decoration is very fine. And if there is a budget problem, it would be most unwise to buy plates which could be used only for one course. The best pattern for a fish plate is a fairly simple one. If there is an over-all design, the colors must be light; dark colors, and bold over-all designs, are not the best for fish plates.

Fruit plates: The classic fruit plate is flat, about seven or eight inches in diameter, and decorated with fruit designs. But, as in the case of dessert plates, almost any pattern can be used: dark colors as well as light ones; simple banded patterns, or more elaborate over-all designs.

Meat plates: From a common-sense point of view, the meat plate is the most important one in any meal. It should be big, about ten inches in diameter, and it should be solid. A super-thin china (Beleek, for example) should never be used for the meat course. Like fish plates—but even more so—meat plates should have a very simple pattern. The border of the plate can be elaborate but, if there is an over-all design, the middle of the plate at least must be in a monotone. Bold designs in vivid colors, dark colors and, particularly, embossed gilding should be avoided.

Oyster plates: Oysters or clams on the half shell are served on a bed of cracked ice which covers the plate from rim to rim. The pattern, therefore, is unimportant. The size is entirely a matter of convenience. The right size is one in which all the shells fit comfortably, without crowding and without wide separation. The important point is that the plate should have a rising edge, rather than a flat rim. Some plates are designed especially for oysters with scooped depressions for each shell and place in the middle for a glass of cocktail sauce. But since the plate is completely hidden, these have always seemed a little pointless—in fact, many are so badly designed that they seem to spill the ice rather than to contain it.

Place plates: From the point of view of aesthetics, if the centerpiece is made of china, place plates are more important than any others. Traditionally, they should match the centerpiece exactly but, as we have said so often in this chapter, interesting chinas, chosen carefully to look well together, are infinitely better than a matched set of which homogeneity is the only virtue.

Place plates are flat, about nine or ten inches in diameter, and as much decorated or as simple as the centerpiece would suggest. Those that have an elaborate design can be used also for dessert but, if one is planning to use place plates for another course, such as salad or fish, one would have to choose a simpler design.

Salad plates: The classic salad plate is flat and about seven to nine inches in diameter. A border pattern, or an over-all pattern in light clear colors is the best, although this point is not so important as it would be in the case of a plate which is to be used for meat or fish.

In addition to the usual round plate, there are also crescent-shaped salad plates, designed to be used when meat and salad are served in the same course. A small round salad plate can also be used for this. Technically, if a crescent-shaped china plate is used, it should match the meat plate exactly, but an almost-match can sometimes look very well. An absolutely plain white crescent-shaped plate of fine china could very well be used, for example, with a meat plate of fine white china with a brilliant red or blue border. The only mistake would be a pattern that fought with, or dominated, the pattern of the meat plate. (See also "Glass," page 401.)

Soup plates: The classic soup plate is about nine or ten inches across with a broad bowl about an inch deep, and a broad flat rim. This design is made in china of every quality, both old and new. In some old chinas this design is made in a smaller size, about eight or nine inches across, and there are some old plates which are even bigger, with an even deeper bowl. The rimless soup plate, really a broad, shallow bowl, is a variation which is often found in old porcelain and in modern earthenware. On the whole, however, it is wise to avoid such variations unless the plate is unusually interesting or fine. Unusual designs are more noticeable than standard ones, and anything which calls for attention must be worth it.

The question of how much or how little decoration there should be on a soup plate has a very practical answer: for clear soups, a border pattern only; for thick soups, whatever pattern one likes. This is the traditional rule, and at the most elaborate and formal dinners, where clear soups are also the rule, it is usually quite strictly followed. For any dinner short of this standard, the rule is interpreted a little leniently: any pattern for thick soups; for clear soups, a bold pattern only if it is beautiful or particularly interesting.

The usual proportion of a soup plate to its underplate is about ¾ of an inch less than the underplate, allowing a scant half inch of the underplate's rim to show beneath the soup plate. In matched sets of soup plate and underplate, these are the standard proportions. In using unmatched plates together, one must be careful not to choose an underplate too small for the soup plate. The underplate can be exactly the same size as a soup plate, or even an inch and a half greater in diameter, but if it is smaller, the soup plate looks topheavy.

By the most conventional standards, the soup plate and its underplate should match exactly, but modern usage and modern taste approve almost any combination short of an obvious conflict of color, pattern, or quality. For example, one could use together any of the multitude of fine white chinas with cobalt-blue-and-gold borders, whether or not the design were exactly the same. One could use a red-and-gold bordered soup plate with a plain gold bordered underplate. One could use old earthenware soup plates of a monotone pattern, with a fine china underplate heavily patterned in the same color. The border of the underplate is the only part that matters, since the rest of it is completely hidden by the soup plate; but one should be careful not to choose a brilliantly bordered underplate to use with a plain soup plate. A heavily decorated soup plate can look very well on a comparatively plain underplate, but a plain soup plate looks poor and pallid with a more brilliant companion. Soup plates are used only at dinner. See page 412 for a description of the cups and bowls used at luncheon.

Saltcellars

China saltcellars are comparatively hard to find. There are some made of fine modern china in a simple bowl shape, usually not very decorative or interesting but inconspicuous and practical. Other modern ones are made in earthenware, in the "trencher" design often found in silver and in old china, especially Lowestoft. The classic trencher shape is oblong or oval with solid sides and a depression in the middle for the salt. These modern saltcellars are made in bright colors and some of them, particularly the handmade Italian ones, are very pretty. Their main drawback is that they are difficult to use with china of any other kind.

Like china ashtrays and cigarette containers, china saltcellars should be bought carefully with the rest of the china in mind. Like the cigarette containers, and unlike the ashtrays, they can be a small but conspicuous part of the table decorations. China pepper pots are rare, and so china saltcellars are usually used with a silver pepper pot. If one wants to avoid silver, one can use a pair of china cellars for salt and pepper; but they must be a pair. A set of four saltcellars is the best number. Four pairs of china saltcellars—which would be almost impossible to find in old china—would be needed if one were planning to use china for the pepper as well as the salt.

Serving Dishes

China serving dishes which will be used at the dining-room table are exempt from all the rules outlined on page 407. They need not match each other or any of the other china because they are never used as a set with anything else. But if one is planning to use china serving dishes on a buffet table, all the rules must be applied in full. As much as any dining-room table, and in the same way, a buffet table must present a harmonious picture when the guests first come into the dining room.

Bowls: From many points of view, china is the best material for bowls which can be used not only for serving but also as centerpieces. Although they are not so durable as silver, they need no polishing. They are more decorative than most glass, and, unlike glass, they may be used for hot foods as well as for cold ones. (Covered bowls which are bought primarily as centerpieces are discussed on page 418, with other centerpieces.) Here we shall consider only bowls used primarily for serving, which can be used as centerpieces, without flowers or fruit, only if they are exceptionally interesting or beautiful.

Except for bowls used as sauceboats, which are discussed below, china bowls used for serving need not match any of the other china. The interrelation of pattern, quality, texture, and scale is irrelevant. One might quite well, for example, use a heavy earthenware serving bowl with fine china plates, and table decorations. Or a Nymphenburg bowl might be the only piece of fine china in the midst of earthenware. For this very reason, just because there is so much latitude of choice, one should avoid using the bowls which are often sold as part of an inexpensive standard set. As we have said on page 231, in some inexpensive sets of china, the plates may be most attractive, whereas the other, would-be-more-decorative pieces of the set are completely lacking in charm. This is particularly true of bowls and vegetable dishes (and tureens, too, of course, but these are rare in inexpensive modern sets). Platters are covered with food, and a simple rim, even a coarse one, is rarely conspicuously ugly. But a coarse bowl, without any authentic decorative value, can be almost offensively ugly. Simple earthenware casseroles, which are used for serving as well as cooking, are never offensively ugly because they are strictly functional and do not pretend to have anything to do with decoration. But a china bowl or vegetable dish is not entirely functional. The food has been transferred to it from the pot for aesthetic reasons. And any object which is thus brought into the field of decoration should be decorative.

Among all the hundreds of bowls of different shapes and sizes, the three most useful serving bowls are these:

A shallow bowl not more than two or three inches deep and about eleven inches in diameter with a broad, flat bottom and fairly straight sides. The trade name for this is a"nappy" and it comes in all sizes. This is used for serving any of the carefully arranged fruit desserts, or a molded dessert with a great deal of sauce or filling. This bowl can be used also, with a lace or paper doily, as a breadbasket. As a centerpiece, it would be a little flat by itself, but it could hold waterlilies or any other flowers which need a shallow bowl. Or it could be filled with sand and water and used to hold snowdrops or narcissus.

A bowl about five or six inches deep. This can be used for serving any dessert which is neither molded nor carefully arranged. If it has a broad flat bottom and straight sides, it can be used for serving spaghetti or hot foods, such as crab gumbo or lobster Newburg, which need a specially deep platter. If it is interesting enough, this bowl is big enough to use as a centerpiece without flowers.

A bowl about eight inches deep. This is used for serving desserts at buffet meals and, if one does not like wooden salad bowls, for serving mixed salads. And it is big enough—usually about 12 to 14 inches in diameter—to be used as a centerpiece.

Platters: China platters come in all sizes in almost every conceivable kind of china. Some of these platters are especially decorated for different foods—a design of fish for the fish course, game for the meat course, etc.—but it is wise to avoid such specialization unless one plans to have a great many platters. A good minimum list of platters is very like that suggested on page 389 for silver.

A small oval platter about fifteen inches long. This is used for meat or fish for four people and for a molded dessert for any number up to eight.

A big oval platter about eighteen inches long. This can be used for big roasts, for cold meat for buffet meals, etc. Platters in this size are sometimes designed especially for roasts, with a gravy well at one end and often a "tree" design leading into the well.

A round platter, about twelve inches in diameter. This is used for serving pies, cakes, canapés, or cookies, and for serving any food in a round mold or ring, as salads, desserts, entrées, etc.

The above is a minimum list, but china platters are not necessarily expensive, and if one has room for them, graduated sets of three or four oval platters and two or three round ones are very practical. The most usual sizes for the oval platters are fourteen, sixteen, eighteen, and twenty inches long; for the round platters, twelve, fourteen, and sixteen inches in diameter.

Sauceboats and sauce tureens: The classic china sauceboat or gravy boat is almost exactly a copy of the silver one. It has the same general shape, the same lip and handle; but instead of feet, it usually has a very low pedestal foot or rim base. These are quite easy to find in fine modern china and earthenware, and there are many old ones. As in the case of silver sauceboats, it is not necessary to stick to the classic shape. One can use a round bowl or an oval one, provided only that it is deep enough to hold the gravy ladle safely. If two sauces are served together on the same tray, they must be served in matching sauceboats, so a pair of sauceboats is the best present, and the best buy.

Sauce tureens are usually found only in old porcelain or earthenware. They are sometimes round, sometimes oval, but they almost always have a cover and a matching underplate. In modern households, they are used mostly as table decorations: as a centerpiece on a small table, or as secondary decoration on bigger ones. But there is no reason for their not being used also for serving, a purpose for which they were designed and for which they are perfectly suited.

Vegetable dishes: Vegetable dishes can be round, oval, oblong, or square, with or without a low pedestal foot. The only essentials are that they should have a broad, flat bottom and that the sides should be deep enough to keep the vegetables hot. In modern china, vegetable dishes are usually either oblong or oval. These are the most useful shapes, because two vegetable dishes are often served in matching dishes on the same tray, and round or square dishes are not convenient.

The ideal number of vegetable dishes would be two pairs: a smaller pair for every day and a bigger pair to be used when there are many guests. A more usual arrangement is to have a pair of medium-sized vegetable dishes which will do for either. Vegetable dishes which are to be used only for serving need not have covers. Even for a buffet table, covered vegetable dishes, although very good-looking, would be unnecessary.

The only caution about vegetable dishes is that those which belong to very inexpensive sets of otherwise satisfactory china are often most unattractive. This is true also of bowls used for serving and is fully discussed under the heading on page 416. To be avoided, also, as a rule, are vegetable dishes divided into compartments, so that two vegetables may be served in the same dish. If one wants to save service, it is much better to put the vegetables on the platter with the meat.

Table Decorations

"Table decorations" is a very elastic phrase. It can mean a single centerpiece in the middle of a small luncheon table, and it can mean a complete set for a big dinner table: a centerpiece, and a pair of small replicas of the centerpiece, which will be used halfway down each side of the table; two candelabra, or four candlesticks (on a very long table, perhaps six candlesticks); small dishes for candies and bigger dishes for fruit. On a small table and at informal meals, one can use almost any piece of decorative china as a centerpiece. On a big table, for a very elaborate and formal dinner, china designed to be a centerpiece is usually the best; a tureen, for example, which is usually an ideal centerpiece could never be considered quite as classically "formal" as a bowl of flowers, an urn, or an epergne.

The traditional ideal was a set of table decorations designed primarily to be decorative, not functional. A china set included everything that was set in the middle of the table, except for the pepper pots and saltcellars and the candelabra, which were often made of silver or glass. Only a few of the most elaborate sets included candelabra, so silver and glass were accepted as standard. For an elaborate and rigidly formal dinner, this classic pattern might still be followed, but such elaborate dinners are extremely rare, and in this section, we shall not further concern ourselves with the question as to whether or not one table decoration is more "formal" than another.

When one is planning china for the table decorations, the first and very sensible point is that the centerpiece is the most important; and, if one must make a choice, it should be the most noticeable and the best. On a luncheon table, there is no way in which this rule can be broken without absurdity. But on a dinner table there are one or two exceptions. For example, if one had a magnificent pair of ornate china candelabra, the centerpiece might be only a low platter of fruit, or a flat bowl of floating flowers, entirely subordinated to the candelabra. However, "a magnificent pair of candelabra" will always be a pretty big "if," and the rule that the centerpiece should be the focal point of the table is generally a pretty sound one.

The second rule for table decorations is that each half of the table must be an exact duplicate of the other half. If there are two candelabra, they must be a pair. If there are four candlesticks, they must be a set. If there are six candlesticks, the four at the middle of the table must be a set and the two at each end of the table must be a pair, although not necessarily the same as the set of four. If there are sauce tureens flanking the centerpiece, they must be a pair. If there are fruit dishes, whether there are two or four on the table, they must be a set. (Rules and a chart for table setting are on page 242.)

For a small table, a centerpiece and a pair of candelabra, or four candlesticks, are usually all the table decorations there is room for. For a slightly longer table, one might add a pair of sauce tureens, or fruit dishes, or low bowls. On a very long table, there is room for three sizes and types of decorations besides the candlesticks: a centerpiece for the middle of the table; two smaller or "secondary" centerpieces halfway down each side of the table; and low plates or dishes for candy and fruit. All these can, of course, be bought in sets. Most sets consist of three pieces: a big tureen and a pair of smaller sauce tureens; or a big fruit basket with a pedestal foot, with a pair of smaller ones of the same design. Some of the more complete sets include also flat dishes for fruit and candy. But all such sets are apt to be expensive. If one is making up a group of decorations, it is wise to avoid the usual "set" groups. It is wiser, for example, to buy a tureen and a pair of baskets than to buy a tureen and a pair of smaller sauce tureens or vegetable dishes. The change of design makes the difference of pattern more understandable and more sensible.

Under their separate headings, below, we have listed a few table decorations which are among the most interesting and the easiest to use.

Candelabra: Compared to other china, china candelabra are hard to find and quite expensive. And (to put all the difficulties first) a great number of the discoverable ones are made of flowery and ornate china, notable exceptions being old French candelabra: Paris and Sèvres. Granted, however, that one can find them and afford them, and that one can find and afford other china to go with them, they are among the most decorative of any pieces of china. Some of the best old ones were made by Spode, Minton, Bow, Chelsea, Chantilly, Nymphenburg, and Meissen. These are some crude but colorful "peasant" earthenwares (often Italian), but most of the others are fine china.

Candlesticks: China candlesticks were made in almost every kind of china during the nineteenth century, and they are still being made by many factories today. Since candlesticks are rarely a stumbling block in making up a set of table decorations, all questions of texture, pattern, and scale are easy to solve and the design of the candlesticks is usually just as satisfactory. The only designs that are apt to be really bad are modern ones which strain to avoid the very sensible and entirely functional lines of the classic form.

Four candlesticks are the usual number for the dining-room table, and they must be a set. On a very long table, if six candlesticks are used, the general practice is to have a set of four bigger ones for the middle of the table and a smaller pair for each end. This smaller pair need not match the others.

Centerpieces: The first point is that the centerpiece is the focal point of the table. In a set of table decorations, the centerpiece has no difficulty in dominating the rest of the china because it is obviously the biggest and most important piece in sight. But if one is mixing chinas, the matter is not so simple. In many shops there are tureens of china with very little decoration, sole survivors of the many big matched sets that were made in the nineteenth century. If the design or even the texture is interesting or beautiful, these make ideal centerpieces, but if they are anything less, it is unwise to choose one of these as a centerpiece. One will always be caught in the difficulty of making the table interesting and decorative without making the centerpiece lose its proper position as the dominant decorative note. It can be done, of course, but it is a question of great subtlety and skill.

On the whole, it is easier and, in the long run, wise to choose a centerpiece which is interesting in itself and can make the table attractive almost on its own. There are dozens of these among the suggestions which are given below. The seven best and most usual designs for china centerpieces are these: covered bowls and vegetable dishes; tureens; bowls with a pedestal foot, with or without a cover; high-sided baskets or bowls, openwork or with openwork decoration on the sides, with or without a pedestal foot; epergnes; china figures, or group of figures; and covered wine or fruit coolers.

Covered bowls and vegetable dishes: Covered bowls and vegetable dishes make ideal centerpieces for a small table, provided only that they are high enough in relation to their size. On bigger tables, they are used as "secondary" centerpieces for the long sides of the table. One can find them at any price in china of almost every period and quality. The exceptions are modern bowls and vegetable dishes of inexpensive china, which are usually made without covers. Very good modern designs, both in earthenware and in fine china, are usually expensive, and old ones are apt to be a much better buy. Exceptions are modern pottery in the shape of vegetables, most attractive and not expensive.

Tureens: Everything that has been said concerning covered bowls and vegetable dishes used as centerpieces is true also of tureens, except that tureens are usually perfectly proportioned. The difficulty one sometimes finds in vegetable dishes, which is that they are often too low to be the focal point of the table, is rarely found in tureens. All the suggestions concerning those which are apt to be more or less expensive apply also here.

Bowls with a pedestal foot: Bowls with a pedestal foot are scarcely ever found in modern china. But there are a great many lovely ones that were made in the eighteenth and nineteenth centuries. Some are octagonal or hexagonal (these usually have no cover), and were designed to hold fruit. Some of the round ones (which often have a cover and a matching underplate) were used for serving, but many of these, too, were designed to be decorative rather than useful. The only drawback to these bowls is that they are comparatively difficult to find.

Openwork baskets: Openwork baskets are often extremely beautiful and almost always, by virtue of their design, inter-

esting. Some of these have high sides and make very good centerpieces, but in those which have no pedestal foot, one is apt to find the same difficulty as in vegetable dishes: They are often a little too low in proportion to their size. For a small table, of course, this is not a relevant point, but for bigger tables, those which have a pedestal foot are usually much better. Like the covered bowls, these baskets can often be found with a matching plate. One of the best designs is almost round, with a cover and a great deal of openwork. Old baskets in this design are called "chestnut baskets" or "twig baskets" and some of the best of these (although, unfortunately, quite expensive) are Leeds, Lowestoft, and Worcester. They can be found, however, in a very wide range of prices in many kinds of china: German and French, as well as English. When they have low sides and no covers, they are very like epergnes which are discussed immediately below.

Epergnes: Epergnes were originally designed to hold fruit. Some are almost flat, others have fairly high basket sides, usually openwork, but all have a pedestal foot. They are usually not made in inexpensive modern china and they are easier to find in French or German china than in English. Their great drawback as a centerpiece is that they were designed to hold fruit and many of them look empty without it. The high-sided basket design with openwork sides is usually the best.

Figures: Figures, or groups of figures, big enough to use as centerpieces, are ideal decorations, and there are many very fine designs. Best known among the old ones of fine china are those made by Chelsea, Bow, Spode, Meissen, Derby, Rockingham, or Sèvres; most famous of the modern ones are Doulton, Minton, Worcester, Spode, and Copenhagen; among the fine old earthenware figures are Staffordshire and Wood. Most of these were not designed as centerpieces, but they have always been so desirable as decoration that they have inspired a host of most unfortunate imitations, both old and modern. It is difficult to describe here which are the good ones and which are the bad ones, but a safe rule is to avoid all imitations. Another good rule is to avoid inexpensive, colored, modern designs; monotones in white or cream color are usually better.

Apart from these two warnings, there is another point, an obvious one, concerning china figurines used as centerpieces. Unless the dining-room table is against the wall, the centerpiece must be designed so that it can be seen from all sides. Many of the old Chelsea figures were designed for mantelpieces and are flat in back. One might use a pair of these, back-to-back in the middle of the table, but a design that is meant to be seen in the round is usually more attractive.

In addition to these big single figurines, one can also use a set of small china figures as decoration for the middle of the table. A set of four or six Meissen figures, combined with old mirror plaques or "plateaux," are often used as a centerpiece for a small table. Bigger figures in cream-white biscuit-ware are used with bowls of flowers, or china balustrades, which are made in sections so that they can be fitted to a table of any size.

Wine and fruit coolers: Wine and fruit coolers are ideal centerpieces: not too tall, broad and heavy enough to hold the center of the table and, usually, made in lovely old china. The typical cooler has two short handles and a cover, and often a removable collar. Worcester made a great many of them, with monotone decorations in brown or deep blue, combined with gold on a white background. Others were made by Sèvres, Meissen, and Rockingham.

Fruit dishes: We have discussed under other headings épergnes and other china dishes designed to hold fruit. We are concerned here only with fruit dishes that lie flat on the table, which can be used as secondary decoration on small tables or as a third, subsidiary decoration on big tables. Such dishes are usually part of old sets of china. Some are round like a very low bowl, others are shell-shaped, triangular, or square. Almost all of them have a rising lip instead of a flat rim. They come in many sizes and can be used, of course, for candy as well as fruit. If they are very beautiful, which they often are, they can be left empty and used purely as decoration. The minimum and most usual number is a pair. A set of four, which

would be necessary only for quite a big table, is apt to be very expensive.

In addition to the dishes which are designed to hold fruit and candy, one could also use flat plates of the standard, rimmed design. If an ordinary plate, such as one of these, is used as part of the table decorations, it must be more than usually interesting or else it must be particularly well suited to the more important table decorations. For example, with a flowered tureen as a centerpiece, one could very well use a pair of plates with beautiful flowered borders that suggest the pattern of the tureen. With a centerpiece of silver or glass, one might use a pair of plates with elaborate openwork borders. (Lowestoft and Wedgwood are conspicuous examples of these.) Unless they are extremely rare or unusually beautiful, however, plates in the standard rimmed pattern should not be used purely as decoration, but only to hold candy or fruit.

Tea Sets

There are two quite different but equally correct ways of arranging a tea tray according to the traditional pattern. The first is to have a silver tea set, complete except for cups, saucers and tea plates of china. The second is to have a china tea set, complete except for a silver kettle. Judged by even the strictest standards, one is just as desirable as the other. On page 390, silver tea sets are discussed in detail. Here we shall consider, first, complete tea sets and, further on, their component parts.

From a practical point of view, as we have said on page 407, a complete china tea set should be made of fine china and not earthenware. And if it is complete, and classically perfect, it will consist of the following: a teapot, short and fat, round or oval, with a long spout; a sugar bowl, with or without a lid; a cream pitcher; a bowl into which the dregs of the teacups can be emptied; cups and saucers; and tea plates, flat as a butter plate and no smaller than the saucers. (They are usually bigger than the saucers, but they must not be smaller; they are usually hard to find in old sets.) In many tea sets, there are also bigger plates for cakes and sandwiches, which are all to the good if the set is interesting or beautiful but which need not, technically, be a part of the set. On the other hand even in the most magnificent old sets, a tea caddy, which really is necessary, is extremely rare. Tea cost about $120 a pound in those days and was locked up. Later, tea caddies were often made of china; but, at this level of perfection, if the tea caddy were not part of the set, it would probably be made of silver.

This is the perfect china tea set: magnificent old porcelain on a tray with an old silver kettle and tea caddy. But it is perfection at a very high price and at an impractical level. To begin with, if one must have a kettle, a copper kettle is much less expensive than a silver one, and looks very well with all-gold luster china and with most of the less expensive "peasant" designs. With a yellow peasant earthenware, for example, a copper kettle would be ideal. To be even more practical, one can ignore the traditional way of setting a tea tray and leave out the kettle, which is no longer the necessity it used to be. Modern living rooms are nearer the kitchen, and a continuous supply of very hot water is needed only if there are many guests. In our times, the tea is often made in the pot, in the kitchen. A kettle and a tea caddy are superfluous and, instead, a pitcher for hot water becomes a necessity. With a beautiful and otherwise complete china tea set, a silver hot-water pitcher would be the best. But beautiful and complete tea sets are always expensive, and now we come to the point of making up a tea set, a much less expensive way of making a tea tray attractive and decorative.

Making up a tea set: In making up a tea set, the division of the china falls into two groups: cups, saucers, and tea plates of one pattern, and the rest of the tea set in another; or, tea plates of one pattern—a plain one—with the rest of the china in another. The first is certainly the best arrangement. All the china which is given to each guest is of one kind; all the china that stays on the tea tray is of another. And, obviously, if the china is divided in this way, the most interesting and decorative pieces should be those which are left on the tray. The cups and saucers and tea plates might belong to a standard open-stock set of fine china; the rest of the tea set could be either fine china or earthenware. The general principles which should be followed whenever one is using different chinas together

are explained on page 404, and they should be followed very carefully when one is making up a tea set. However, if the china is divided in this way (which, after all, is only an extension of the old division of silver and china), the rules can be interpreted with a certain liberality. Almost any two patterns which do not obviously conflict in character or color can be used together. When one starts mixing chinas beyond this division, one must be a little more careful.

In the first place, it is no longer wise to plan to use two different patterns together unless they are ideally suited to each other. The best plan is usually to buy a completely plain china which is obviously subordinated to the more interesting pieces. And the more interesting pieces must include the teapot. Under pressure from the budget, the bowl or the hot water pitcher is usually the first to join the standard set, leaving the teapot, the sugar bowl and the cream pitcher to supply the pattern and decoration. Or the sugar bowl and the cream pitcher might be the first, leaving the bowl and the water pitcher in the same pattern as the teapot. (Whichever group they belong to, the sugar bowl and the cream pitcher should always be treated as a pair.) If the teapot is the only decorative and vivid note—and this is, of course, the least expensive system—it should be very fine and a little oversized.

Whether the teapot or any of the "stationary" pieces of the tea set are earthenware or fine china is entirely unimportant, except insofar as the pattern or character of the earthenware imposes restrictions on the choice of fine china for the teacups. As we suggested on page 407, no matter what the teapot is made of—silver, earthenware, or fine china—porcelain is in many ways the most practical material for teacups. The aesthetic, and perhaps less practical, rules about teacups and tea plates are that, no matter what the division of the china, all teacups and saucers should be a set and all the tea plates should match them. Those are the rules and these are the permissible ways of breaking them:

1. Under certain conditions, the teacups need not be a set. For example, if the rest of the tea set were silver, one might have a set of fine white china tea plates

with a narrow dark-gray-and-gold band, and odd cups and saucers of porcelain, all black and white, all gold-edged, but with different designs.

2. If the tea set is complete except for tea plates, as so many old sets are, one can use a set of any small plates that are entirely subordinated to the rest of the china. Silver butterplates have also been used; but glass, which is sometimes a good substitute at the dining-room table, is never as pretty on a tea-table.

3. With an otherwise complete set, of which many cups have been broken, one can use simple standard cups and saucers even though they do not match the tea plates. The only rule that can never be broken is that each teacup must match its saucer.

Cups and tea plates for buffet teas: The rules about cups and saucers and tea plates are predicated on the assumption that the tea tray will be brought into the living room and that tea will be served there. Whenever there are so many guests that they must be served at the dining-room table, the rules do not apply. No hostess is expected to have such a big set

of cups and saucers and tea plates, all matching. All the cups and tea plates of one pattern are put at one side of the tea tray, all those of another pattern at the other side. But all the china in each group should be a set.

Plates for cakes and sandwiches: Plates for serving cakes and sandwiches at tea-time are often not part of a tea set. Such dishes are set on the tea table, not on the tea tray, and although it is obvious that their pattern should not conflict with that of the rest of the china, it is not at all necessary that it should clearly have been chosen for it. With a complete china tea set, one's choice of china for the serving dishes would be extremely wide. And one can always use silver dishes, too. With a set made up of two different patterns, it is better if the pattern of the serving dishes at least suggest one of the others. If the teapot is the only vivid and decorative piece on the tea tray, it is best that the pattern of the serving dishes have a marked affinity with that of the teapot; but this is only a matter of taste and not a rule. China serving dishes need not match one another, although two dishes the same size are always more decorative if they are a pair.

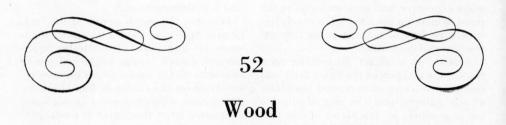

52

Wood

THERE ARE many very attractive and practical household objects, used for serving and on the dining-room table, which are made of wood. In buying these, the first point to consider is the rule, "Avoid pretentious decoration or carving." Some wooden bowls and trays, both old and new, have simple, peasant carving, which may be crude but is unpretentious and charming. Elaborate designs are attractive only if they are beautifully executed. The second rule, a practical one, is, "Avoid wood with a shellacked surface which may peel or blister." Old wood often has a beautiful patina, which modern shellacs try to copy. But since most of the modern pieces have an interesting grain, it is better to let a patina accumulate in its own solid time.

WOOD FOR THE TABLE

Bowls

There are a few good-looking, old bowls with a beautiful patina and sometimes fine carving, which can be used as a centerpiece for the dining-room table. But the most useful wooden bowl, of course, is a big one which can be used for serving salad. These come in all sizes, from twelve to twenty inches in diameter. There are very expensive old ones, with a dark, rich patina; fairly expensive modern ones in beautifully grained wood; and very inexpensive modern ones, plain as a chopping bowl and most satisfactory.

Salt and Pepper Grinders

From a gourmet's point of view, wooden salt and pepper grinders have always been desirable and now they have become fashionable as well. They are ideal for every kind of informal meal because they are simple, functional, and practical. Unlike silver, they need no polishing; unlike glass or china, they cannot break. And unlike so many other household objects, wooden mills are almost never badly designed.

These mills are usually bought in pairs, one for pepper and the other for salt. However, freshly ground pepper is more important to the gourmet than freshly ground salt, so one often sees a wooden pepper mill with a glass or china saltcellar. Needless to say, since wooden mills are inexpensive and easy to find, all of them should match, unless they are old and interesting in themselves.

Serving Spoons and Forks

Big wooden serving spoons and forks are ideal for a salad served in a bowl, whether the bowl is made of wood or of glass. With most china bowls, too, one could use a wooden serving fork and spoon, although silver would look better with elaborate, gilded china. The design of wooden forks and spoons should be as simple and functional as though they were intended for the kitchen. Some very expensive ones are made with silver handles, but this is a little pointless and these are often not as attractive as all-wooden ones with a fine, close grain.

Trays

From a practical point of view, the great drawback to wooden trays is that they may warp, or that the finish may be damaged. There are many ways, however, of treating the finish of trays so that they are proof against almost any kind of damage and, if the wood is well-seasoned, there is not too much danger of warping. The more expensive trays are more carefully treated and are made of better wood than the inexpensive ones, and therefore it is never wise to buy the least expensive wooden trays.

The best modern wooden trays are either pickled or left in their natural color. Trays which belong to the modern school of decoration are often oblong and pickled; those which belong to the more classic school are usually round, with a Chippendale border. Both are good-looking and whichever one chooses is purely a matter of taste, depending on which looks best with one's china and glass.

As we have said on page 391, where the various uses of trays are fully described, the most practical sizes for round trays are eight, thirteen, and eighteen inches in diameter. In addition to these, and perhaps more useful than any of them, there are big oblong or oval trays, about twenty inches long, not counting the border. In a small household, one might have only two trays: this big one, and the middle-sized round one, thirteen inches in diameter. These big trays, which are used for tea or as a drink tray, usually have handles. On some trays, the handles are cut out of the wooden border. On others, particularly those of the modern school, the handles are made of chromium. Wooden trays rarely have feet, but there are some very big sizes which have long folding legs. These can be used as a tea table and tea tray combined, or as a drink-tray and table.

Another very good-looking tray which is particularly useful for drinks is made of glass with a wooden border. Some of the best of these have borders made of bamboo, with bamboo or chromium handles and strips of bamboo under the border to keep the surface of the tray away from the table.

53

Ovenware for Cooking and Serving

OVENWARE which can be used for serving is an extremely practical idea, completely in accord with modern taste and usage. It is particularly practical, of course, in small households and in small houses, where there is little space for storage and little time for transferring the food carefully from the pot to a heated serving dish or platter. But it is used, also, in many households where such factors are not an urgent consideration. The best of this ovenware is completely functional and makes no effort whatever to be pretty or decorative. Some of it, however, has a very definite character which can add a great deal to a carefully thought-out decorative scheme.

COPPER

There are three kinds of cooking utensils which can be used for serving as well as cooking: copper, earthenware, and glass. Of the three, copper is apt to be the most expensive and, since it has such a very definite character of its own, it is also apt to be a little more limited in its use. It is particularly well suited to French food and to short, informal, but hearty meals. It is not very becoming to elaborate table decorations; plates without gilding, plain silver, wooden pepper mills, and wicker breadbaskets are its natural companions. Most of these copper dishes are now made with a tin lining which makes them much easier to clean and in no way detracts from their functional good looks. Copper can be used for serving meat and vegetables, but it should not be used for serving desserts.

EARTHENWARE

Earthenware that can be used for cooking and serving is made in several basically different types. One is all-brown, glazed on the inside, unglazed on the outside. This is made in two shapes: a deep covered casserole, usually with a lid and two tiny handles; and a shallow, open casserole with one thick, stubby handle; and in miniature replicas of these two designs. Another kind of ovenware is glazed all over, usually white on the inside and red-brown or liver-brown on the outside. This is most often made in flat, deep platters of various sizes and in small individual cups such as would be used for custard or baked eggs; big, deep casseroles are not common in this ware. A third type is all white, thinner and more delicate than the first two. This is usually found only in soufflé dishes and in the small custard cup size. All these three types are standard ovenware which has been used, particularly in France, for many years. A newer kind, of which a great deal is now being made in America, is colored: pale gray on the outside with pale yellow, or pale pink, on the inside; all brown, or blue, etc. Much of this is made in every kind of dish: big deep casseroles, very shallow open dishes which can be used for serving, custard cups, and so on. This new American ovenware is apt to look best with other modern table appointments; the three standard types can be used with a greater variety.

Deep, semiglazed brown casseroles are particularly well suited for serving meat stews, hot fruit compotes, and vegetable dishes such as scalloped tomatoes or stewed eggplant. The open shallow casseroles in this same semiglazed brown earthenware can also be used for hot compote desserts and for serving all vegetables and fish dishes such as lobster or crab Newburg. The miniature replicas of these two dishes are used for soup (the deep covered one is best for this) and for baked egg dishes. Like copper serving dishes, but to a lesser extent, brown earthenware is most appropriate for informal entertaining. Its character is, however, a little less definite than that of copper, so it can be used with a greater variety of table decorations and other china. For example, even though the rest of the serving dishes and platters were of silver or the finest china and even though all the table appointments were quite elaborate, at any meal short of the most rigidly formal pattern an earthenware serving dish would be quite suitable, provided only that it were particularly appropriate to the food for which it is used.

The brown and white platters can be used for serving meat, fish, and any vegetables; although they are, perhaps, particularly well suited to dishes in which meat and vegetables are combined; breaded veal cutlets, for example, served with neat little clumps of baby beets, string beans, and noisette potatoes. The little cups, of course, are ideal for baked eggs or custard. In character, this ware is a little less informal than the brown earthenware. In elaborate households, it might be used in town only for informal entertaining. But in the country, it is used whenever the appropriate food is to be served.

All-white, glazed overware is usually made only in a deep open shape, in a big size for soufflés and in a small size for baked eggs and custard dishes. It can be used for any kind of entertaining, and since it has almost no character of its own —aesthetically speaking—it can be used with any kind of table appointments or china.

GLASS

Glass ovenware is like white glazed ovenware in character; in other words, it is so unobtrusive it can go anywhere. On the other hand, it is also true that it lacks both the decorative value of other glass, and the sturdy, obviously functional charm of other ovenware. It is made in a wide variety of shapes and sizes: shallow dishes, oblong or round, and deep ones. The flat glass dishes are used as they come from the oven for serving pies, eggs au gratin, and hash en bordure. The deep dishes are wrapped in a folded napkin and used for food such as soufflés or baked macaroni. And they should always be wrapped if they are at all darkened or discolored by the oven heat. As a rule, careful housekeepers use white oven-ware, rather than glass, for any baked individual dishes.

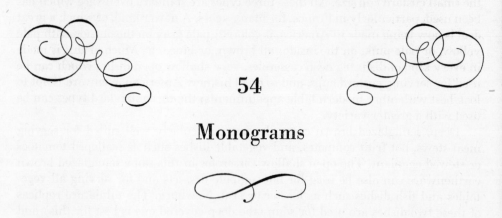

54

Monograms

IN HAVING anything monogrammed or marked with one's initials, there are three main considerations. The first is a just proportion. Too small a monogram will be lost, too big a one will look overwhelming. Good linen stores have a regular formula for the sizes of monograms on sheets and towels; good jewelers have the same formulas for silver, but there is no rule that holds for everything. A good eye is needed!

The second factor is the number of letters. It is impossible to make a monogram with one initial, a monogram being by definition two or more letters intertwined. And in marking anything except nursery linen, beach linen, or things of that kind, the use of one letter should be avoided. Unless a crest is being used, a monogram—or initials—is the best marking, and the best number of letters is three. (Two or four are perfectly correct but difficult to work into a pretty design.) It is better, if the marking seems too expensive, to save up and have it properly done later than it is to use one initial.

The third consideration, and the most complicated, is the form of the letters, or what printers would call the "type." Old-English letters are not very good taste; to mark a beautiful piece of plain, heavy silver with a single Old-English initial is neither good usage nor good taste. Block letters are better, or the rounded letters derived from script lettering. For a wom-an's personal things—linen, cigarette cases, underwear—the letters may be as full of curlicues as she likes. For silver, or other things that will be used by all the family, simple letters are better. And for a man's things, block-letter initials, rather than a monogram, are by far the best.

Finally, it is better to under-monogram than to over-monogram one's possessions. Handkerchiefs, linen and silver are often marked, but when playing cards, glass, cigarette boxes, automobiles, and everything else are monogrammed, the over-all effect is unpleasant. Examples of modern marking for linen, silver, and glass are given below on page 429; the marking of writing paper is discussed separately on page 532.

MONOGRAMS FOR A MARRIED WOMAN

After a woman is married her things are no longer marked with her maiden initials. Any new acquisitions are marked or embroidered with the initials of her new name. There are two ways of doing this, one correct but archaic, the other less correct but accepted. Consider, for example, Mary Livingston Beecher, married to a man named Allen. Her things may be marked with the initials of the names given her in baptism plus the initial of her husband's surname, as *Mary Livingston Allen;* or with the initial of her first name followed by the initials of her maiden surname and her husband's surname, as *Mary Beecher Allen.* The first version, using the baptismal names and discarding the maiden surname, is the more old-fashioned and, technically, the more correct of the two: The names given in baptism never change and even the old song admits that a woman changes her name when she marries. The second way is based on a fallacy: that a woman adds a name when she marries, discarding her second baptismal name for convenience' sake. Once thought impossibly wrong, this is now accepted modern usage—so accepted that to use the first version would be surprising and a little anachronistic. (See also page 228, "Marking the Trousseau.")

WOMEN'S BELONGINGS

A woman's personal belongings, such as handkerchiefs, underwear, or cigarette cases, may be marked either with initials, a monogram, or a short first name. Any of these markings may be used, also, for the linen a woman will use in her own bedroom and bathroom. For other linen and other belongings, a monogram or initials is more appropriate than a name.

A SHORT NAME USED AS A MARKING

These are suggested for a woman's personal belongings, and for the linen which will be used in her own bedroom and bathroom.

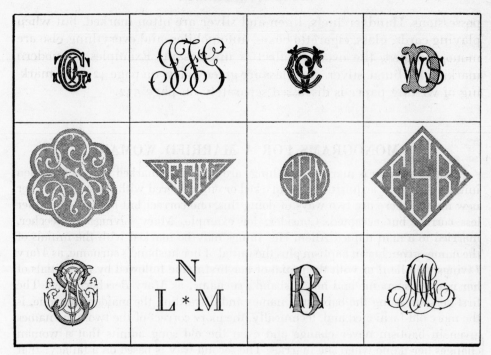

WOMEN'S MONOGRAMS FOR LINEN AND OTHER BELONGINGS

These monograms may be used for all the bedroom and bathroom linen in a woman's house. In fact, anything a woman might want to mark, except writing paper (see page 532) and silver, glass, or table linen (see below), may be marked with one of these monograms, which are less personal than the names shown on the preceding page.

INITIALS FOR NURSERY OR BEACH LINEN

Any of these simple initials may be embroidered (perhaps by machine) on the linen which will be used by children, or in a bath house.

SILVER, GLASS AND TABLE LINEN

Silver and glass and, to a lesser extent, table linen are less personal belongings than other linen and other belongings. They may be inherited generation after generation, and suggest a family, rather than an individual, ownership. They are best marked in one of the standard ways shown below.

Some of these markings—the triangular one shown at the upper left, for example—are very old designs; all may be used both by men and by women. As a matter of custom, when silver or glass or table linen is to be marked with a monogram or initials, the wife's initials are used; but when it is marked with a crest or coat of arms, it is always that of the husband's family. The triangular marking already referred to may incorporate the initials of both husband and wife: the initial of his first name at the lower left, her first name at the lower right, and their last name at the top; or it may be used by a single man or woman in the same way: the first initial at the lower left, the second at the right, and the initial of the family name at the apex. A final word about marking—if one has inherited marked silver, glass or table linen, it is wise to mark subsequent additions to a set in the same general style.

MARKINGS FOR SILVER, GLASS, AND TABLE LINEN

Left to right, across the top: old-fashioned triangular marking; crest with motto; crest; good marking for two initials—often hard to find. All these may be used for marking small pieces. Second row, for marking big pieces: circle around a triangular monogram; reversed cypher; coat of arms; wreath to use around initials or a monogram. Bottom row, for large or small pieces: entwined script letters; old-fashioned decorated lettering; simple reversed cypher; simple monogram.

MEN'S BELONGINGS

A man's personal belongings are usually marked with initials or (but this is rare in America) with a crest or coat of arms. And this applies also to the linen which will be used in the bedrooms and bathrooms of a bachelor establishment.

FOR A MAN'S LINEN AND PERSONAL BELONGINGS

All these, although suggested specifically for marking a man's belongings, may be used also to mark a woman's things. In other words, a man is limited to simple designs and letterings such as these; a woman's choice is much wider.

55

Introduction

ENTERTAINING should be a simple matter and, in prehistoric times, perhaps it was. One liked someone, one asked him to come and share whatever game had been caught, and that was the end of it. But this happily logical state of affairs can't have lasted long, if it ever really existed at all. Even in Biblical times, a philosophy and a ritual for entertaining had already crept into the picture, and they have stayed ever since.

In our present philosophy of entertaining, three elements are obvious: a human feeling of friendliness, which we like to think of as natural to man; a conception, perhaps nomadic in origin, of the obligation of hospitality; and the Old Testament tradition of honoring the guest. The fairly complicated ritual used to express these is the accumulation of centuries; and the process of accumulation is still going on.

Friendliness cannot be legislated, but the obligation of hospitality has its rules. The accepted custom is that one must entertain those by whom one has been entertained. This does not mean that a rigid quid pro quo must be maintained, or that one can only invite to tea those who have invited one to tea, or to dinner those in whose houses one has dined. But it does mean that one should not accept hospitality unless one is prepared to make a more or less equal effort to return it. Obviously, there is often some element of inequality in the exchange of hospitality, springing from the inequalities inherent in many situations. He who has a house in the country and a tiny flat in town may accept many dinners in town and return the hospitality by inviting his hosts to come and stay in the country. He who has a tiny flat in town, and nothing more, may return the most elaborate hospitality by giving a small, simple dinner or a cocktail party. The essential point is not the absolute, but the relative, return. A further point is that one should not accept hospitality from those whom one would not want to entertain in return. The modern tendency to accept, with no intention of returning, an invitation which sounds amusing, is a form of opportunism which, though practiced, is still very much criticized. To accept an invitation, and later to criticize or make fun of one's hosts, is an extreme example of the abuse of hospitality.

Another flagrant and very common example is to invite a new acquaintance without including also those in whose house the acquaintance was made. For example, the first time one invites Mr. and Mrs. Cartwright to dinner, one should also invite Mr. and Mrs. Ruston, in whose house one first met the Cartwrights. This rule is not always binding on unmarried men (see page 29) or on those of a younger generation who have met in the house of one of an older generation. But it must apply to women, whether married or unmarried, who are planning to entertain new acquaintances.

A further custom based on the obligation of hospitality is that of entertaining newcomers to the community. In the early part of this century, when community life was closely organized, this obligation was taken very seriously and the established members of the community were always expected to call on the newcomers shortly after their arrival. Although this is no longer a rule of American life, remnants of it can be found in the matter of who invites whom first. As a rule, among new acquaintances, the older or more established of the people involved should make the first gestures of friendliness and issue the first invitation.

The conception of honoring the guest, which is certainly a most attractive idea, is probably the most ill-used of any of the three major elements of entertaining. One cannot go too far in true friendliness and, if one considered the obligations of hospitality too strictly, one would only be thought a little stuffy. But the abuses in the matter of honoring the guest are many.

Ideally, honoring the guest should be expressed in this attitude: One is pleased to see one's guest; one has made efforts to arrange the rooms and the table with flowers and lights, in order to give him pleasure; one has made efforts to give him good food and agreeable companions. All this, because it is without pretense or selfish motive, is the very essence of hospitality. But the moment that one tries to impress the guest, or to profit by the guest's presence, the abuse creeps in. Quite apart from its connotations of bad taste, an ulterior motive is the basis of most unsuccessful entertaining.

THE PROCEDURE OF ENTERTAINING

The procedure of entertaining is detailed and explicit. Like all good systems, it saves time and thought. It conveys all the elements of entertaining—friendliness, the obligation of hospitality and the honoring of guests—in a way which is immediately understandable to all concerned. The form is, in fact, so accepted that hosts and guests are like actors in a semi-extemporaneous play, with certain stage directions to follow, certain lines to say. It may be objected that such rigid casting and stage directing will inevitably kill all spontaneity, that it will be impossible to enjoy oneself if one must continually be conscious of lines and stage directions. But there are two points against this objection. The first is that one cannot ignore the great usefulness of all manners, by which at least a pretense of agreeable emotions is maintained, glossing over the unfortunate moments which spontaneity cannot always cover. The second point is that rules are not necessarily the mortal enemy of spontaneity. One might as well argue that one cannot enjoy a game of tennis if one must keep one's eye on the ball, the head of the racket up, the opposite foot forward, calculate accurately what one's opponent will do, and at the same time remember to be perfectly relaxed. The conclusion is, obviously, that all the detailed rules about stance and form, and all the code of manners that cover the giving and receiving of hospitality, must be so well learned that they become second nature. The only person who suffers from a consciousness of the rules, whether on the tennis court or in the drawing room, is the one who has not learned them well.

As always, the process of learning is not an unmitigated delight, and if one could entertain successfully without bothering to learn or follow the code, one might be justified in feeling that the effort was not worthwhile. Certainly, it is easier to sit and greet guests with a careless "Hi," than it is to get up and go to the door and make them feel really welcome. But in the long run, even if one is entertaining fairly intimate friends, such carelessness is neither successful nor practical. Friends may not get angry or annoyed but they will notice the lack of manners and wish it were otherwise. Too often they will find themselves left to cope too long with a bore whom a more disciplined hostess would have shifted along to another. Too often they will notice guests, brought to the house by others, made uncomfortable by the hostess' cheerful carelessness.

The only dependable successful bases for entertaining are a spirit of true hospitality, or a thorough knowledge of the accepted code of manners; preferably both. The ideal hostess is not only frankly delighted to see her guests, and interested in seeing that each one will have a good time, but she is also well-trained in the disciplined unselfishness which makes entertaining run smoothly in the accepted form. The hostess who may not know or follow the accepted form will entertain a little less smoothly than this ideal hostess. Her parties may have a few awkward moments, but if she is full of the spirit of hospitality, they will be just as successful as those of the ideal hostess, and her guests will enjoy themselves just as much.

Although the procedure of entertaining is almost uniform throughout, certain modifications must be made for its two major categories, entertaining at home, and entertaining away from home. It is more of a compliment to a guest to entertain him at home than in a club or restaurant. For this reason, and because entertaining at home is probably the more usual of the two, we shall discuss this half of the subject first.

56

Entertaining at Home

THE OUTLINE given here describes the generally accepted pattern of the actions and attitudes of guests and hosts at a luncheon or dinner in a private house. To continue the metaphor of the theater, it is a description of the play itself, and does not enter into any of the inevitable stage-setting preliminaries which are the concern of the hostess only. (These will be found in the chapters "Setting the Table," "Serving," "Fashions in Food," "Fashions in Table Decorations," and "The Household Staff.")

The basic pattern is that observed in almost all American entertaining. But because there are certain technical differences and degrees of formality (as shown on page 237) we have used the word "informal" to describe dinners and luncheons at which the guests and hosts may co-operate in the service, and the makeshift word "semiformal" for meals at which the service is complete. Formal entertaining, which is in many cases different in kind as well as degree, is discussed separately on page 477.

IN THE HALL

In semiformal entertaining there is a maid or butler in the front hall, to open the door and take the guests' coats. If only a few guests are expected, the coats may be left in the front hall, folded neatly on a chair or sofa, or hung in a convenient cupboard. If there are as many as twelve or fourteen guests, it is usually more convenient to have the women's coats left in another room. Women guests may be directed to this room by the one who opens the front door. The men take their coats off in the hall and wait there for the women to come back, so that couples can go together to greet their host and hostess. At very large dinners, the men are directed to one room and the women to another; and there may even be racks for the coats set up in each of these rooms. No guest at a dinner should, however, be given a ticket for his coat, as he might quite properly if it were a reception, or a dance, or an official dinner in some hotel. At informal dinners in small country houses, or small apartments in town, the door is often left unlocked when guests are expected, especially if the guests are friends who know the house and expect such informality. If the guests are acquaintances, rather than friends, the host usually opens the door, helps them with their coats and escorts them to the living room.

IN THE LIVING ROOM

The host and hostess should be ready to receive their guests in the living room at least five minutes before the hour for which guests have been invited. Whether they stand or sit during the intervals of the guests' arrivals depends on the size of the luncheon or dinner. The only requisite is that they should be in a position from which they can conveniently go forward to greet each guest as he comes in. If only three or four couples are expected, they will very probably sit and talk to the other guests until the last one has arrived. If sixteen or twenty guests are expected, it may be more convenient for them to stand, talking to some of the guests, than to get up every time another guest arrives. Whenever the hostess is standing, men guests must also stand, unless they are in a separate group with women who are all seated.

The Guests Arrive

The guests should always speak to the hostess first, the host next, and then the other guests. Since a man follows his wife into the room, it is probably unnecessary to add that the woman guest speaks first to the hostess and then to the host, followed by her husband. (The only exceptions to this are important officials who may precede their wives. See page 491, "Entertaining Officials.")

The hostess should be the first to speak, and the classic phrases are: "Good evening, Mrs. ————, I'm so glad to see you. Good evening, Mr. ————." Or at luncheon, "How do you do, Mrs. ————," etc. The guests need only say, "Good evening" or "How do you do?" The host or the hostess, depending on which can more conveniently do so, makes any introductions that may be necessary. (See page 58 for the formal introduction and the acknowledgments.) If there is a guest of honor, or an important guest whom arrivals should be sure to greet, the hostess will probably be talking to him, and new arrivals will automatically be introduced as soon as they have greeted their hosts. If the important guest is sitting in another part of the room, the host will bring the new arrivals to him, in order to make the introductions. If the new arrival is a stranger to the other guests, and particularly if he seems shy or inexperienced, the host might end the introductions with one of the easier and more affable guests, so that the stranger will have a comfortable berth while the host is welcoming other guests. If there are a great many people, it is not feasible or necessary—since "the roof is an introduction"—to introduce each new arrival to all the guests. (See page 59.) But a stranger should be introduced to all the members of a group, at least.

A Guest Brings Friends

When a guest brings friends, they are introduced at once to the hosts, as soon as the greeting is over. The host or the hostess should then introduce these friends to some of the other guests; or, at a small party, to all of them. It should never be left to the guest to make the introductions.

Late Guests

If guests are late, apologies and explanations are made when they greet their hosts. The hosts minimize the lateness with some such remark as, "But you're not at all late; the others were just more than prompt." Or, if the lateness is so exaggerated that such a remark would be absurd, the hostess stresses the excuse as an inconvenience to the guests rather than to herself. For example, if the excuse is, "It took twenty minutes to get a taxi," or, "The tire blew out just by the bridge," the hostess should answer, "It doesn't matter at all, but how awful for you!"

Cocktails

At small or informal dinners or luncheons, when the host is mixing and serving the cocktails himself, he asks each arrival if he would like a cocktail as soon as the introductions are over. He must, of course, interrupt his mixing and serving of cocktails to greet each new arrival. If the cocktails are being served by a waitress or butler, they are brought when about a quarter of the guests have arrived, and to each later guest soon after his arrival. (See page 291, "Serving Cocktails Before Meals.")

Announcing Dinner

When all the guests have come, dinner is announced by the waitress or butler, who has been keeping count of the arrivals. (The more informal version of this procedure is described on page 447, "Entertaining Without a Maid.") If one guest, or a couple, seems hopelessly late, the hostess must decide whether or not to keep the other guests waiting. For example, she may ring and say to the butler or waitress, "Would you please telephone Mr. and Mrs. Bradley's house and see if they have left yet." Or, she may say, "We won't wait for Mr. and Mrs. Bradley: you can announce dinner (or luncheon) whenever it is ready." Delaying dinner until the last guest has come is more polite to the late arrivals, but less considerate of the guests who have already arrived. If the late arrivals are very much younger than those who have already come, after a wait of twenty minutes or so, the hostess often takes her guests in to dinner. The forms of announcement used by a waitress or butler are on page 361.

Going in to Dinner

The length of time between the announcement of dinner or luncheon and the moment when the hostess says, "Shall we go in?" is entirely at the discretion of the hostess. If many of the guests seem to be just starting their cocktails, she may want to delay a minute or two. If she knows there is a soufflé, she will probably want to start her guests toward the dining room immediately. At a semiformal dinner or luncheon, the hostess goes to the guest who will sit at her right and says, "Shall we go in?" Led by the host, who has taken his cue from his wife, the other guests go into the dining room with whomever they happen to have been speaking to when the movement toward the dining room started. Two women who have been talking together may go into the dining room together, preceded and followed by men and women. Two men who may have been talking together should wait until all the women except the hostess have gone through the door. The hostess waits with the guest of honor until the last. This system stems directly from the order of formal entertaining by which the host, with the woman who will sit at his right, goes in first, and the hostess, with her right-hand dinner companion, goes in last. At small or informal dinners or luncheons, however—in other words, nine-tenths of the time in America—the hostess says to the guests in general, "Shall we go in?" and she shepherds the women in front of her, followed by all the men, with the host last. In any case, it is unusual, except among very much older people or at the most formal dinners, for everyone to go into the dining room arm in arm.

IN THE DINING ROOM

If there are no place cards, the hostess directs each guest to his place at the table. (See page 273 for suggestions concerning place cards.) There is no special order or system covering the question of who sits down when, except that the host should not sit until everyone else has been seated. The hostess may sit down when-ever she chooses, either before or after the other women guests have found their places. Men do not, as a rule, sit down until all the women have been seated, but it is better for them to sit than to stand too obviously, like children, with eager eyes on the hostess, waiting for her to sit down. When there are many guests, the waitress or butler sometimes helps the guests to find their place cards: "Madam's card is here—Your place is over there, Sir."

Conversation

The hostess starts the conversation first with the man at her left, the host with the woman at his right. If there is an uneven number of guests, the hostess may talk to two guests (the two at her left, or the ones at each side of her), but if she has not done this, guests should be careful not to leave one of their number stranded. (See, however, "General Conversation" in "Memos to Hosts.")

Turning the Table

"Turning the table" is the responsibility of the hostess, who, at a point about halfway through the meal, should make a smooth transition from her conversa-tion with the guest at her left to a new conversation with her guest at her right. A practiced hostess does this by drawing the guest at the right into her conversa-tion or by joining in his. (The woman beyond him then turns to the man at her right, and so on around the table.) When the guest at her left is an older man who should not be left stranded, even temporarily, the hostess can draw the woman beyond him into the conversation and, having settled him comfortably in a new conversation, then turn to the man at her right. Guests should be on the watch for these moments, because it is their co-operation which will make the whole process easy and graceful and smooth.

Leaving the Table

When the service of dinner is over, and everyone has finished eating, the hostess pushes back her chair and stands up, moving slowly away from the table in order to give the other women time to break off their conversations. If, as is usually the case in America, the men are not going into the living room with the women, the hostess stands by the dining-room door until all her women guests have left the room, and follows them back to the living room. The men stand until the women have left the room.

The host stays at his end of the table unless special respect or attention is due one of the guests. For example, when the man seated at the hostess's right is an older man, a foreigner, or an official, the host often moves down to the hostess's place to arrange a conversation which will be interesting to him. This is particularly true when there are so many guests that general conversation is difficult. At small dinners, the men in the dining room usually gather at the host's end of the table; at large dinners, when no guest needs special attention, two or even three groups may be formed. Coffee, cigars, and liqueurs are then served. (See pages 293 to 295.) After about half an hour, or at the most forty minutes, the host pushes back his chair and says, "Well, I think we'd better be getting along," and the men go to join the women in the living room.

In some houses, the men go into the library after dinner, instead of staying in the dining room, and coffee, liqueurs, and cigars are brought to them there. (If so, the service follows the pattern suggested for serving in the living room; see page 295.) Either course is correct; whether one stays in the dining room or goes into the library is entirely a matter of convenience.

IN THE LIVING ROOM AFTER DINNER

During this interval of half an hour or so, the hostess and the women guests will have been having their coffee and liqueurs in the living room. At informal dinners the hostess during this interval usually asks the women guests, "Would anyone like to go upstairs to my room?" or, "Would anyone like to go upstairs for a moment?" and the host does the same for the men. If the hostess plans to have bridge or other games after dinner, this is also the moment for her to arrange the tables. If some of the guests are strangers whose tastes may not be known, the hostess may ask the wives, "Do you and your husband like to play bridge, or would you like backgammon or conversation better?" In answering, the guest should avoid the extreme of a flat, "My husband and I dislike all games," and the opposite fault of, "We'd love to do anything; whatever is convenient for you." The ideal answer gives the hostess some inkling as to the guest's true preference, with an escape clause in case it is not convenient; as, "I like bridge and my husband backgammon, but we both love conversation." Unless they are intimate friends of the hostess, no guests should presume to arrange their own games.

After very informal dinners, and after almost all luncheons, the men do not stay in the dining room but instead have their coffee with the women in the living room. A short time after luncheon, perhaps half or three-quarters of an hour, everyone usually goes home, so no plans need be made. The after-dinner period, however, usually lasts at least an hour; and some plan, however vague, must be made. The evening is usually one of these three different kinds: There may be bridge or other card games; there may be pencil and paper games, or some energetic acting game, such as "The Game"; there may be general conversation or, and this is most usual after formal dinners, conversation in scattered tête-à-têtes and small groups.

The first two, once organized, are very easy on the hostess. General conversation is a little more difficult to do well. At the very beginning of the evening, the hostess will have to make the guests understand that she wants a general conversation. In a small room, her tactics are usually to corral any separatist elements by asking a question which will involve them in the general topic. In a big room, she may say to those who seem about to wander off, "Won't you both come and sit here with us?" But once the pattern has been set, general conversation requires nothing more from the hostess than an occasional prodding and the usual surveillance. (See the heading "General Conversation" in the chapter, "Memos to Hosts," on page 461.)

Conversation

Conversation in tête-à-têtes and small groups often needs some attention and arranging on the part of the hostess. Some of the tête-à-têtes will break up by themselves, if the guests have sense and experience enough to move around and handle themselves. But very often the intervention of the hostess will be needed. In fact, unless a tête-à-tête seems to be particularly animated and gay and the hostess is sure that both guests are enjoying themselves thoroughly, she should change the combinations from time to time.

To outline these maneuvers from the very beginning: As soon as the men come in from the dining room, the hostess should go up to the guest who needs the most attention, whether by reason of age, position, shyness, or what not. In this way, if the guest is a woman, she is assured of a partner, because at least one man guest is sure to join his hostess. If the guest is a man, she can take him to whichever woman guest she thinks will entertain him most. In either case, after seeing the conversation well launched, the hostess is free to leave and see how the other guests are getting along. If the numbers of men and women are equal, and the hostess is moving around from group to group, there will be one extra man who will also be free to wander. The hostess can detach him and move him to another group in the following way: She joins the group to which the extra man is talking, enters into the conversation and, at an appropriate moment, with some phrases such as, "Won't you come with me? I want you to talk to Miss Barclay," moves him on to another part of the room. Whatever man Miss Barclay had been talking to can then be moved on to the next group. By using this relay system indefinitely, each group or conversation can be changed at least once during the evening. No one, not even the host, will be left to suffer all during the evening with a difficult conversationalist. There is danger, of course, in overdoing this system. If a group seem particularly interested in their conversation, and if it is plain that they are well suited, it would be wiser not to interrupt them. All this requires constant vigilance, surveillance, and activity on the part of the hostess, and guests should co-operate by being, at least apparently, quite willing to follow her suggestions. (See "Co-operation," on page 466, in "Memos to Guests.")

During the evening, food is often served after a semiformal dinner. See pages 296, 265 and 332 for suggestions concerning the service, the setting of the table, and the food. The service of drinks is also described on page 296.

SAYING GOOD-BYE

When the moment has come to leave, the guest of honor, or if there is no guest of honor, the first person who wishes to leave, should go to the hostess and say, "I really think I must be going home. It has been such a pleasant evening; thank you so much," or, "I'm afraid we must go; thank you so much." The hostess, who must rise to say good-bye to her guests, answers, "It was a great pleasure to see you; good-night," or less formally, "Good-night; I'm so glad you could come." If the host sees that someone is leaving, he should immediately excuse himself and get up to say good-bye to his guest. At informal and semiformal dinners and luncheons, both host and hostess often accompany the guest to the door of the living room, but in any case, a host with good manners always does. If the guest is a woman, or an older man to whom special respect is due, the host follows into the hall, and stays with the guest until he has gone out the front door.

SEEING THE GUEST OFF

"Seeing the guest off" is an essential point of hospitality. A member of the household should be on hand to take care of every guest until he has left the limits of the house, and the limits of the house extend beyond the front door. If a member of the staff is waiting to see guests off, the hosts can leave this responsibility to him; if not, the host must see to it himself. In a country house, the butler or waitress will wait at the open door until the guest has gotten into his car, or has walked away from the front door limits; if the host is seeing the guest off, he usually goes with the guest, particularly a woman guest, as far as the automobile. In a city apartment house, this responsibility ends when the guest has got into the elevator; the host, or the butler or waitress, rings, and waits at the door of the apartment, holding it open until the elevator door has closed. Very polite hosts often ask the elevator man to "make sure that Mrs. ———— will get a taxi."

The guest should say, "Thank you," and "Good-night," to the butler or waitress who has been waiting to see him off.

VARIATIONS FOR OTHER FORMS OF ENTERTAINING
Tea

The door is opened by the butler or maid, or, more informally, by one of the hosts, and the guests' coats are taken according to the standard procedure described on page 436, "In the Hall." In the living room, the hostess comes forward a few steps to receive her guests. Tea may be served as soon as the first guests arrive, unless the hostess wants to pay one of the guests the compliment of waiting. As later guests arrive, the hostess gets up from behind the table to greet them. (See also pages 251, 289, and 318, for the setting of the table, the service and the food.) Guests and hosts say good-bye according to the standard formula: "I really must be going; thank you so much"; and "Good-bye, I'm so pleased you were able to come." The hostess accompanies the guest to the door of the living room, or, in the case of a very much older woman, to the front door.

If there are men and women at the tea, and a host as well as a hostess, the host and the other men will wait on the women guests. This does not mean that the women guests must cling like limpets to their chairs, avid for service and incapable of fetching a second cup of tea for themselves, but if the host or any other man happens to notice that a woman's teacup is empty, that there is no food on her plate, he should ask her if she wouldn't like something and fetch it for her. The host accompanies the guest to the front door, as suggested above.

Receptions and Cocktail Parties

Cocktail parties and informal receptions are among the most informal ways of entertaining. There is no set hour at which guests must arrive, as there is for a luncheon or a dinner; nor are all guests expected to do any one thing, such as go into the dining room, simultaneously. Some of the guests will be arriving as others leave, and the atmosphere is one of informality.

The front door may be left open or on the latch; it is not at all necessary at small parties to have a maid at the door, because the guests can quite easily let themselves in and leave their coats in the hall. If it is a very large party, however, there should be someone in the hall to direct the guests to the rooms where they will leave their coats.

Guests should, of course, greet their hostess and host as soon as they arrive. If the guests are strangers, the hostess introduces them to some of the guests: to all the guests at a cocktail party of ten or twelve people; to all of the guests in a group, if there are more guests than this. When they say good-bye the standard procedure is followed both by the guests and by the hosts.

Buffet Luncheons, Dinners, and Suppers

At a buffet dinner, supper, or luncheon there is no change in the first part of the standard procedure, unless the hostess has planned a seated meal without place cards. In this case, she tells each woman guest in the living room before-hand who the other guests at her table will be, and the women guests are responsible for arranging each table.

In the dining room, the men wait on the women unless the women want to choose their own food from the buffet table. Wise women often do choose their own; too many men come cheerfully back with two plates loaded with meat and potatoes, having overlooked a wonderful aspic, or a delicious cheese.

When the coffee is set out on the buffet table or on a side table in the dining room, as it usually is, there is no separation of men and women, even after a buffet dinner. The only exception is a buffet dinner where all the tables have been set in the dining room. In this case, the men often stay behind and smoke their cigars in the dining room, and the women come into the living room by themselves for their coffee.

The rest of the pattern of a buffet supper or luncheon follows the standard procedure.

Dances

At informal dances, the names of the guests are not announced. The host and hostess stand within striking distance of the door, very much as they do at a dinner party. After about half an hour, they start dancing and only keep an eye on the door, to greet the new arrivals as they come in. Supper is not announced, and there are usually no seated supper tables. The hosts suggest to a few guests that they might go in to supper, and this starts a movement in that direction which operates by its own momentum. The tables are arranged as described on page 266: big buffet tables for the food and drink, smaller tables for the guests. The men guests wait on the women, unless it is a very big dance, in which case there will probably be waiters from the caterer's.

At other dances the procedure is patterned fairly closely on that of a formal reception. At both semiformal and formal dances, the guests are announced and the hostess stands by the door to receive them, with her husband near by. At a very big dance in the traditional pattern, both the host and hostess with any guest of honor are expected to stay in the receiving line for an hour or more; at less formal ones, only the hostess and the guests of honor stand in line, while the host circulates among the guests. (See also "Debutante Dances," page 42.)

Dancing usually starts before the receiving line breaks up, unless the dance is almost officially formal. At a semiformal dance, a table may be set up for drinks at one side of the ballroom or, as is more usual at formal dances, in a room near by. There may be a fairly elaborate seated supper or an informal buffet supper.

Musicales

At a musicale for which the guests have been invited after dinner, they must be prompt. The procedure can follow either that of a semiformal dinner or luncheon, or that of a formal dinner with a butler to announce the names to the host and hostess. (See page 479.) Late arrivals should be careful not to go into the music room while the performer is singing or playing. They should wait until the piece is finished, slip in as unobtrusively as possible, and make their apologies to their hostess after the music is over. The arrangements for supper may follow either the procedure given on page 481, "Formal Dances and Receptions," or the simple system described above for informal dances.

The hostess should decide beforehand whether or not the performer would enjoy staying to supper and meeting the guests after the music is over. Usually the invitation to stay to supper is given to the performer or to his agent when the hostess makes arrangements for the evening.

CHILDREN AT MEALS

The increasing informality of living, to say nothing of the increasing shortages of domestic help, has made the combination of children and guests at the same table a much more usual part of entertaining than it used to be. And, as always when a practice becomes very widely accepted, a very practical and attractive pattern has developed for it.

These are the essential points:

To begin with, whenever there are more than three or four grown-up guests who are not relatives or intimate friends, children do not appear at dinner. No matter what the strain on the household, no children—and, for that matter, no boys and girls of school age—come down to their parents' dinner parties.

Luncheon, however, is quite another matter. Unless there is some special, almost official, reason for keeping them away, children and guests almost always lunch together, and it usually works out very well. Ideally, of course, the children should be old enough and expert enough to feed and help themselves neatly; but very often children too young to serve themselves can eat very nicely. In such cases, the food may be portioned and cut by the maid in the pantry, or by the mother at the table. Any child this age should sit beside his mother.

Children of the house sit in a row at the hostess' left, the youngest child nearest her; children of guests sit between their mother and the hostess. The idea behind these seating arrangements, which should prevail at every meal except a purely family one, is that children are not scattered among the guests as though expected to take part in the conversation. The perfect picture is a row of cheerful, clean, fresh faces, alert and responsive, but aware that this is a grown-up party and not a field day arranged for them.

The before- and after-luncheon routine is equally simple: Children come in and say how-do-you-do just before the meal; afterwards, having followed the guests through the dining-room door, they go directly to their room, or outdoors, without necessarily saying good-bye.

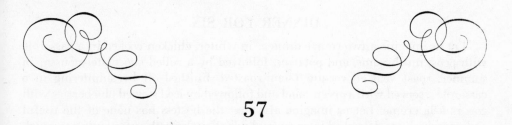

57

Entertaining Without a Maid

THE BIG difference between entertaining with a staff and entertaining without one is that, in entertaining without a maid, the mechanics become a major problem. When there is a staff, the guest is never made aware of these mechanics; when the hostess is doing everything herself, the guest may often, with acute discomfort, count every trip that she must make to the kitchen. The essential point in arranging the mechanics, therefore, is to shelter guests as far as possible from being made aware of the hostess's work.

From this point of view, the cooking is less of a problem than the service. The sauce for a curry may take days of preparation and the chocolate roll may take hours of beating, but since the guest sees none of this, he will be able to accept either quite calmly. On the other hand, repeated trips to the kitchen, even if nothing more complicated than a plateful of fresh toast is involved, will make him uncomfortably aware that he is sitting while the hostess works. A big point in such entertaining is a wise choice of the menu. The first rule, therefore, is this: few courses, and as much food on the table or in the dining room as can be arranged. The second rule is that whatever service is necessary must never be done as a maid would do it. In other words, the hostess must make no effort to approximate the kind of service that is usually given by a household staff. The purpose of this, like that of the first rule, is to save the guests embarrassment and a feeling of giving their hostess a great deal of trouble.

The easiest way to entertain without a maid is to invite people to tea or to a cocktail party. Next in order are buffet luncheons and suppers. The most difficult of all are seated dinners, and therefore it might be useful to discuss first the preparation and the procedure of a seated dinner for six people, without outside help of any kind.

DINNER FOR SIX

Let us imagine a two-course dinner: in winter, chicken cooked in a casserole with peas, mushrooms, and potatoes, followed by a rolled chocolate mousse; in summer, roast veal en cocotte (semi-roasted, finished off by simmering in a casserole), served with a green salad and followed by iced stewed blueberries with coeurs à la crème. Let us imagine also that the hostess has none of the useful gadgets which are described later on, and which make such entertaining so much easier.

Preparations

These are the first steps on the morning of the party: to set the table; to put the dessert plates on the sideboard; to make the dessert; to prepare the chickens and vegetables, or the veal and the salad; to decant the red wine or, if white wine is to be served, to put it on ice; to arrange the coffee tray with the cups, spoons, and sugar.

The next step is to arrange the drink trays, which are put on an inconspicuous table in a corner of the living room. On a big tray, decanters of whiskey and brandy are set, together with the appropriate glasses, bottles of soda, an opener, etc., leaving room for the ice thermos bucket and for a pitcher of water. This tray will stay in the room all evening. Next to it, a smaller tray is arranged, with the cocktail ingredients, shaker and glasses, a sherry decanter and glasses, and room for a dish of nuts or crackers. This tray can be taken into the pantry on the way in to dinner. As an extra time and space saver, one can also mix the cocktails in the shaker, so that there is nothing to do but put in the ice when the guests come. All this can easily be done in the morning. The table is set as it would be for any dinner, with two minor exceptions. The first is that the dessert forks and spoons are put on the table, above each place, as suggested on page 258, "Setting the Table." This is very helpful, because it means that the clean dessert plates can be stacked and passed easily from one guest to the other with no danger of silver falling to the floor. The other exception is that the table is set without place plates, with the folded napkin in the middle of the doily or mat at each place.

About two hours before the guests arrive, depending on the size of the chickens, the cooking should begin. The ice thermos is then filled and put on the drink tray. The nuts, olives, or anything else that is to be served with the cocktails, are got ready. Then there is time for a bath, for dressing, for another look at the food that is cooking. One should finish one's make-up as late as possible; the best is about fifteen minutes before the guests are expected. In the last fifteen minutes before the guests arrive, nuts or crackers that will be needed for cocktails should be heated in the oven; the bread, which might be French bread cut in fairly thick slices, or French croissants, or rolls, is put conveniently near the stove so that it can be heated before being served; and the plates for the main course are put to warm in the oven. The water is put on to boil for the coffee, and a pitcher of iced water is put on the sideboard. After checking on the cooking, the hostess can bring the cocktail food into the living room and wait to receive her guests.

When the Guests Arrive

Since there is no maid, the hostess will open the door and serve the cocktails (for the purposes of this example, we are not counting on help of any kind, not even a husband's). When all the guests have arrived, and all have almost finished their cocktails, the hostess should go into the kitchen, put the bread into the oven, start the coffee, take the casserole and the stack of heated dinner plates into the dining room and put them at her place at the table. Then, she brings the heated bread and the dessert, which she puts on the sideboard. In summertime, even iced berries can be left on the sideboard throughout the meal, in big double glass bowls, with ice between.

All this being done, the hostess goes back to the living room and says, "Shall we go in to dinner?" She gathers up the cocktail glasses, puts them all on the small cocktail tray with the shaker, and shepherding the guests ahead of her into the dining room, leaves the tray in the pantry.

At the Table

At the dining-room table, she serves each plate from the casserole in front of her. The guests pass the plates along until all of them have been served. In the same way, the bread and wine circle the table. At the end of this course, the hostess will have to be firm about guests wanting to clear the table. All that she need say is, "No, really. Please stay where you are; I'd rather—and it's so easy." If it is said with sincerity and firmness, guests will usually obey. Carrying them two at a time, the hostess takes the plates to the kitchen; or, better still, to a table behind a screen near the pantry door. The casserole and the breadbasket are taken last. The hostess should not take the pepper and salt, or the crumbs off the table (but the guests should put any big crumbs and any uneaten pieces of bread on their plates). The hostess then brings the dessert and the stack of dessert plates from the sideboard and serves this course as she did the last one. At the end of this course, she fetches the coffee, which may be served either at the table or in the living room.

HELPFUL GADGETS

This brief outline presupposes a living room and a dining room and no gadgets except the indispensable ice thermos. If there is a living room-dining room, the same system can be followed, but in either case one or two gadgets will be found helpful:

A rolling cart with many shallow shelves. The uses of this cart are many. Used plates can be put on the shallow shelves which, since they are close together, hide the plates very well. The top shelf can be used for the dessert plates and the dessert platter, making it unnecessary for the hostess to get up at all, until it is time to fetch the coffee. When the hostess goes in to get the coffee, the used dessert plates can be on the cart too, and the whole thing can be taken into the kitchen and left there.

A spirit lamp which acts as a stand for the coffeepot, or a coffee urn with a burner underneath it. Either of these will spare the hostess the trip to the kitchen to fetch the coffee.

Silent butlers. Perhaps it is unnecessary to add this to the list, but nothing is more useful than one of these covered dishes into which ash trays can be emptied.

TEA, COCKTAIL PARTIES, AND BUFFET MEALS

Since so little service is required for any of these ways of entertaining, the descriptions given in the chapters, "Setting the Table" and "Serving," cover the subject quite fully, but a few suggestions may be helpful. At a tea party, the table and tray are prepared before the guests arrive, either in the living room or in the dining room. All the food is in place, except the hot food which, with the hot water, is brought at the last moment. At a cocktail party, the cocktails are mixed in the shaker, the ice is in the thermos, and all the food is in place before the guests arrive. Hot cocktail food is not at all necessary.

At a buffet dinner, the best plan is to have all the guests seated at the dining-room table, which is set as suggested above on page 446. The only differences between this and the other dinner, described there, is that the guests wait on themselves and get up between courses to put their used plates on a side table; and the food is set on the sideboard, rather than in front of the hostess. If there are too many guests for the dining-room table, small tables can be arranged. All these details, and more describing the setting of tea trays and buffet tables, are discussed on pages 251 to 265, and there is nothing more that need be added here except to suggest one or two things that might be useful.

Gadgets

The rolling cart and the spirit lamp to keep the coffee hot suggested immediately above, on page 447, would be as useful for a buffet dinner or luncheon as for the seated dinner suggested there. In addition, there are very good, wide-mouthed, crockery thermos containers which will keep food hot or cold; copper or silver burners heated by spirit lamps; electric hot plates; and big Sheffield plate hot-water stands, fitted with heavy covered dishes.

Perhaps, before we leave the subject of entertaining without a maid, it might be wise to say a word about the many other gadgets which are suggested to make such entertaining easy. As a rule, it is wiser to avoid them all. Many of them belong only in a kitchen, where their streamlined chromium surfaces and brightly colored plastic handles look extremely attractive. On a very large table, at a most informal buffet luncheon or supper, a toaster might not be too conspicuous, and certainly if one were having lobster or crabmeat Newburg, absolutely fresh toast would be good. But, on the whole, if one is in any doubt, it is better not to plan to use a toaster, a waffle iron, cafeteria trays, or anything else of that kind, except at breakfast.

58

Seating and Precedence

THE QUESTION of where to seat the guests at table falls into two parts: the first one which must be decided is which guest should take precedence over another; the second is where the guests, having been thus ranked, are seated at the table. In other words, there is the question of the order of precedence, and the question of a plan of seating. The order of precedence is again divided into two parts: official and unofficial. Since most entertaining in America is unofficial, we shall start with that. The plan of seating will be found on the next page; the order of precedence of officials on page 492.

UNOFFICIAL ORDER OF PRECEDENCE

Seating guests at table is too often, in America, a haphazard un-thought-out business. Too often, it must be admitted, one guest is given precedence over another according to the generally accepted estimate of his business standing or financial position—obviously not a sound approach, or one that is apt to add to the amenities of entertaining. Although it is very often true that a man's prestige and position in the community have some relation to his financial situation, it is not *always* true, and too often the latter is used as the only criterion. The outline which follows, listing guests in the order of precedence, is the only one which is widely accepted in this country.

Everything else, particularly the ages, being equal, guests are ranked as follows:

1. A foreigner.
2. A stranger; for example, a guest brought by a friend.
3. One who has held an official position in the past.
4. A guest invited for the first time.
5. Guests who have been in the house only a few times.
6. Constant guests.
7. House guests and relatives.
8. Children of the house.

Official position automatically ranks a guest above any in this unofficial list, and age can alter it greatly. In fact, age is such an important factor that it should be used as a coefficient all the way down the scale. Great age, for example, would give a guest precedence over a younger foreigner; even ten years' seniority might give No. 4 precedence over No. 3. Scholarly or professional achievement, too, should be considered a factor—in fact, as usual, common sense is a good guide.

As in official entertaining, women take their husbands' rank unless they have higher rank of their own. Women whose husbands are not present lose their rank if there is anyone of superior rank among the guests. For example, an ex-senator and his wife would take precedence over a guest who had never before been invited to the house; but if the ex-senator were not present, his wife would sit on the left of the host, and a guest invited for the first time, providing she were not conspicuously younger, would sit at the host's right. Particular care should be taken whenever there is a question of seating foreigners, or those who have held official positions. This is not only because such people may care where they are placed at the table, but also because they are fully aware of the rules of seating and will, therefore, be equally aware of any errors. (See page 492 for order of precedence used in seating officials.)

Another rule of thumb is that, in seating women, married women take precedence over widows, widows over divorced women, and divorced women over unmarried women, unless, of course, there is a marked difference in their ages. But this is a fine point observed only when there is nothing else to go by.

BASIC PLAN OF SEATING

In America, the host and hostess sit facing each other at each end of the table with the ranking guests at their right. In some foreign countries, and at very big dinners in some American houses, the hosts sit facing each other across the middle of the table. The following plan of seating is the basic one. "First man" means, first in order of precedence, whether according to the unofficial order of precedence given just above, or the official one on page 492. The "first woman,"who sits at the host's right, is either the wife of the most important man guest, or a woman who outranks the wife of the first man by virtue of her position; a very much older widow, for example, would be ranked above the young wife of a guest who had never before been invited to the house. If the "first man" is unmarried, the wife of the second man takes precedence over the other women. It is probably unnecessary to add that husbands and wives are never seated side by side.

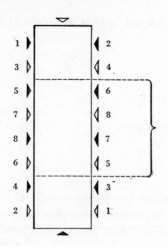

THE STANDARD PLAN OF SEATING

In this diagram, the men are represented by black triangles; the women by white ones. The host, at the lower end of the table, has no number, and neither has the hostess at the far end. The numbers for the guests show how they are seated—the first man at her right, the second at her left; and, at this end of the table, the first woman at the host's right, and so on.

This is a dinner table drawn out to exaggeration, for the sake of example. At a more normal dinner of ten, the bracketed center section would not have to be considered.

SEATING GUESTS IN MULTIPLES OF FOUR

An alteration of this basic plan is always necessary when there are eight people at the table, or when there is any multiple of four. The hostess cannot sit opposite the host and the table is arranged as follows.

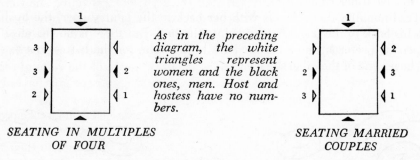

As in the preceding diagram, the white triangles represent women and the black ones, men. Host and hostess have no numbers.

SEATING IN MULTIPLES
OF FOUR

SEATING MARRIED
COUPLES

This arrangement presupposes the fact that "third man" and "third woman" are not married. If, instead, "second man" and "second woman" are not married, second and third men can change places. At a dinner of eight or twelve it is always better to invite one unmarried pair, especially if "first man" has an important or official position. When all the guests are married couples, and when protocol need not be so strictly observed, the plan right, above, can be used.

When there are four people only, the hostess keeps her place, with the man guest at her right and the woman guest at her left. Another way of seating multiples of four, feasible only at a fairly wide table, is to put two places at each end of the table.

When There Is No Hostess or No Host

When there is no hostess, the place of honor for a man is at the right of the woman who sits at the host's right. When "first man" and "first woman" are not man and wife, the plan below, right, is followed.

When the first man is married, the plan below, left, must be used.

When there is no host, exactly the same plans are followed in reverse. In other words, the first woman, if not the wife of the first man, sits just beyond the hostess' right. When she is married to the first man, she sits just beyond the hostess' left.

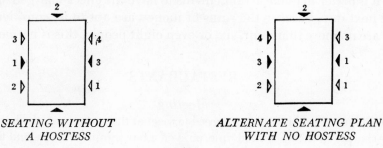

SEATING WITHOUT
A HOSTESS

ALTERNATE SEATING PLAN
WITH NO HOSTESS

THE PLACE OF THE HOST AND HOSTESS AT TABLE

When the host and hostess cannot sit opposite each other at the table, it is she who must move from her place. This rule is too often broken in America, although it is unheard-of in other countries for a man to move from his place at the head of the table. As we have indicated above, in the diagram of the seating for a table for eight, the hostess usually moves to the place at the left of her end of the table so that the most important man guest will be seated opposite the husband and will still be at her right.

Traditionally, the wife sits with her back to the pantry door, the husband, with his back to the door that leads into the hall. But there is no reason, if she happens to prefer sitting with her back to the light, for the hostess not to sit at whichever end of the table she pleases.

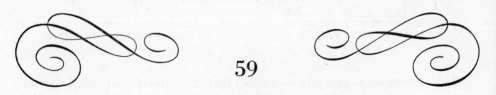

59

Entertaining in Clubs, Restaurants, Night Clubs, etc.

THE PURPOSE of entertaining is always the same, but the procedure in a club or restaurant is necessarily a little different from the procedure at home. The only point that is common to all entertaining which is not done at home is that guests must be protected as far as possible from the cost element involved. In private clubs, this problem is almost automatically solved because one never pays on the spot. If one is giving a very big dinner in a restaurant, or if one is entertaining a great many people in a night club, it is better to make arrangements to have the check charged, or to pay it the next day, because the sums of money are apt to be considerable. If there are no more than four, six, or even eight people, this is not necessary.

RESTAURANTS

Meeting

When guests and hosts have agreed to meet at the restaurant, the hosts should arrive sharply at the appointed time, or even a few minutes before, and the guests should never be more than ten minutes late. As soon as the hosts arrive, they should speak to the headwaiter to make sure that everything is in order. It is always better to reserve a table beforehand when entertaining in a restaurant. In many restaurants there is no comfortable place to sit and wait but, even so, the hosts should not go alone to the table, before the guests arrive; they should wait near the front door, so that they can see their guests as they come in and go forward to meet them. As in a house, the guests should look for their hosts as soon as they have taken off their coats and hats. Men check their coats and hats; women keep both on until they are seated at table, when they slip their coats off and back over the chair. The only things women usually check are raincoats and umbrellas.

If the first guest to arrive is an older woman or anyone to whom special attention is due, the hosts should not keep this guest waiting near the door for the other guests. Instead, they should all go to the table, leaving word with the headwaiter for the other guests to join them. If the early arrival is a man, or a younger woman, this guest should wait with the hosts near the door for the older and more important guests.

Cocktails

If one is entertaining in the restaurant of a hotel, or in a restaurant which has a comfortable waiting room, the problem of late guests is less difficult. When the guests accept the invitation, the hostess can suggest a meeting place, usually a sitting room or a comfortable lobby near the dining room. As a rule, it is better not to suggest meeting in the bar if one is entertaining older people, strangers or foreigners, unless the bar is particularly well known as a meeting place. In any case, one should arrange to meet where there are small tables and comfortable chairs. Cocktails and cocktail food can be served as soon as the first guest arrives, and it is quite proper, in such circumstances, for the host and all his guests to wait here until the last guest has come and has had his cocktail.

Going in to Dinner

As in all entertaining, it is the hostess who suggests going in to dinner. At the table, unless the guests have just had cocktails, the host asks each guest what kind of cocktail he likes and gives the waiter the orders. Cocktails can be ordered before all the guests have arrived, but the host should wait for late arrivals before ordering dinner. He should wait, that is, for anyone who is not unforgivably late, and twenty-five minutes' or half an hour's lateness is unforgivable in a restaurant.

Seating

When one is entertaining at a large table or at a table in the middle of the room, the seating at a restaurant table is exactly like that at one's own dining-room table. (See diagrams on pages 450 to 451.) Differences arise only when one has a table along the restaurant wall, or in a corner. At such a table, the "best" places are along the wall, facing the room, and at a dinner of four people the women sit there, with the men facing them. The only exception to this rule would be a very much older couple dining with a younger couple when the young ones might well sit in the outside seats. At a corner table, the host—unless he is very much the oldest of the men—should sit in the outside seat, with the others along the wall.

453

The only other considerations are practical ones. The more exposed seats—exposed to draughts, bumping, or whatever—go to young men, or, in a party of women, to younger women; the sheltered seats, with the best view of the room, go to women and older people.

Finally, there is the question, "When a man and a woman are dining together in a restaurant, should she sit at his right?" The answer is that, in America, few pay any attention to this point. The woman goes first to the table and sits down first, as a rule in whichever seat is the most convenient. This is the accepted practice, although many quite justly feel that it is not so attractive as the custom of seating a woman always at a man's right. "After all," they argue, "if a man were dining at home, the woman would sit at his right; so why not when she is his guest in a restaurant?" There is no answer to this except that a few agree, but most people ignore the question completely.

Ordering Food

There are two ways of ordering the food. The host can either plan and order the meal in advance; or else he can wait to order it until he and all the guests are together at the table. The first system is a timesaver, particularly useful when there are more than six people, or when the time element is important. It is also used by gourmet hosts, or hosts who are entertaining gourmets and want to be sure of a specially good meal. The second system is, of course, much less trouble and is more or less standard practice in America.

The procedure of this system is as follows: The waiter gives the hosts and each guest a menu. After a moment, the host turns to the woman on his right with a phrase such as, "What would you like?"; and then more generally to the table, "Do you see anything that sounds good?" If any guest seems timid about speaking his mind, the host can make suggestions, but, as a rule, each guest makes his own choice. (See Memos to Guests, "Being Entertained in Restaurants," on page 471.) If there is a table d'hôte meal, guests should, as a rule, stick to the dishes listed there. But whether there is or not, each guest should decide first on the main course, choosing neither the most expensive of the dishes listed nor, unless he happens to like it, the least expensive. There are two very good reasons for choosing the main course first. One is that it is a sound plan of eating: just as a hostess who, in making a menu, decides first what the main course will be, and builds up to and away from that course, so anyone ordering food should follow that plan. The second reason, which is most pertinent in a restaurant which has no table d'hôte meals, is that by ordering the main course first, guests do not automatically commit the host to a meal of more than two courses. The host is then free to say, "Wouldn't you like something first?" or not, as he chooses. No guest need hesitate to order two courses —a main course, dessert and coffee—but he should leave it to the host to suggest a first course, extra vegetables to be served with the main course, salad, or anything else of the kind. As a rule, at luncheon the host need only suggest one dish besides those his guests have asked for. This might be either a first course, or a vegetable to go with the main course. At dinner, hosts usually suggest both. The host does not, of course, order three courses for himself without suggesting that his guests do likewise. But if he should, a guest is at liberty to say, "Oh, I think clams sound delicious. Could I change my mind and have some too?"

Ordering Wine

Unless one has ordered both the food and the wine in advance, the wine should be ordered after all the guests have decided what they would like to eat. As soon as the host has finished giving his order to the waiter, he asks for the wine card; or, if there is a wine steward, he asks the waiter to send him to the table. Unless one is a great gourmet or is entertaining a guest who is particularly fond of wine, in America one does not usually order more than one wine when entertaining in a restaurant. If one of the guests has chosen a fish for his main course, the host should order a white wine. The reason for this is that white wine can be served either with fish or with meat, whereas red wine is best with meat. (See "The Choice and Handling of Wines and Liqueurs," in the section, "Household Customs," page 334.)

The Check

When it is time to leave, the host signals to the waiter and asks him for the check, which will be brought face down on a small plate. The host glances at the total, and, rapidly calculating, puts enough money on the plate, under the check, to pay the bill and tip the waiter. (See "Tipping," page 65, in the chapter on "Manners in General.") Unless there has been a blatantly outrageous overcharge, the host should not scrutinize the check or argue with the waiter about it. There is no reason, however, to carry this too far. If there *has* been an outrageous overcharge, then the host should ask, very quietly, and without any trace of embarrassment or anger, to speak to the headwaiter. He gives the headwaiter the check, not in the spirit of carping crossly at the overcharge but rather with the attitude of one who is quite happy to put the entire matter in the hands of the headwaiter, whom he expects to set the matter right.

When the check has been paid and the hostess decides that it is time to leave, she gets up and goes toward the door, the women guests following, the men guests next and the host last. As he passes the headwaiter, the host can thank him and tip him. He tips the wine steward, who is usually hovering around the table, in the same way.

NIGHT CLUBS

If one is dining in a night club, the procedure is exactly the same as though one were dining in a restaurant, and the suggestions given immediately above all apply. The most usual time, however, for entertaining in a night club is later in the evening, after dinner or after the theater, and for this reason some of the procedure is a little different. In the first place, since there is no question of dinner, guests need not be quite so punctual and hosts need never wait by the door. The only exception to this is a man who is expecting only one woman guest; he should wait by the door, no matter how late she might be. As soon as the hosts arrive, whether the guests are with them or not, they go directly to their table, telling the headwaiter the number of guests they expect and asking him to show them to the table. At the table, the question of seating is, of course, much less formally arranged than at dinner. If one of the women guests is older or more important than the others, the host asks her to sit at his right hand, and when the time comes to dance, it is she whom he first invites to dance. The host should then, in turn, ask each of the other women to dance and, finally, his wife. In the same way the older or more important man should sit at the right of the hostess and ask her, then the other women, to dance. The other men guests are also under obligation, if they dance at all, to ask each woman at the table to dance at least once. The only further point is that no woman should be left alone at the table; there should always be at least one man or another couple with her. (The matters of ordering and of paying the check follow the suggestions given above under "Restaurants" on page 454; tipping is discussed on page 70, and the behavior of guests on page 471.)

WHEN THERE IS NO ONE HOST

If a party at a night club, or a restaurant, is a matter of joint suggestion, rather than specific invitation, the men often share in paying the check. The best way to do this is for one man to pay at the table, and for the others to pay him back later when they are getting their coats, or even the next day. The one who has given most of the orders is usually given the check and he immediately starts to pay; the others say, "Let me take care of this," or "Let me come in on this." He answers, "We'll fix it up later," and tells them what their share is at some convenient moment later on. Ideally, the others should ask, but if they don't, he can tell them; it is always best to avoid, if possible, a complicated interchange of money at the table.

WHEN A GUEST BECOMES THE HOST

When an evening lasts beyond its normal span, one of the men guests often takes over the responsibility from the host. For example, if one has dined and gone to the theater with one's host and it is suggested that "we might all go on to a night club," one of the guests can quite properly become the host at the night club and pay the check. He shows his intention by asking the others what they would like to eat or drink and by giving the orders to the waiter. When the check comes, if his dinner-host is determined to pay, he must allow him to do so; if the dinner-host offers only mild resistance, he can insist on paying. This is an accepted custom among contemporaries. If the dinner-host is very much older than any of his guests, the process will have to be handled with more diffidence and less determination. One of the guests can still offer to pay when the check comes by saying, "Won't you let me take care of this?" But even mild resistance on the host's part will have to be respected.

WOMEN ENTERTAINING WITHOUT A HOST

When a woman entertains both men and women in a restaurant or night club, the moment when the check is paid can be a very awkward one. Basically, it is not very becoming, either to the woman herself or to the men who are her guests, if she must open her pocketbook and pay the check in cash. The best solution is to order and pay for everything in advance: cocktails, food, wine, and tips. A check can be sent later to cover any unexpected orders and, if the service has been particularly good, to increase the tips. Another system is to entertain in a restaurant where one is so well known that the check need never even be signed. The bill can be sent the day after the dinner, and paid, together with the tips, by check. Still another system, not quite so attractive but perhaps wiser in restaurants or night clubs where such a trustful plan might not be feasible, is to arrange to sign the check just before leaving. The tip can be slipped unobtrusively under the check when it is signed or better, a note can be added to the check: "tip $5.00" with the signature beneath. There are moments, of course, when none of these systems is possible and in such cases the best thing to do is to give an adequate amount of money to one of the men guests who is an old friend or a relative. If one has made no arrangements to pay beforehand or to sign, if none of the guests is a friend or relative, the only alternative is to pay on the spot and to do it as gracefully as possible.

If a man entertains without a hostess, the question of payment is no problem. The only difference in procedure is that if there is no hostess, the host must suggest going into dinner and decide when it is time to leave the table.

ENTERTAINING AT THE THEATER AND MOVIES

Theaters

The procedure of entertaining one's guests by taking them to the theater is obviously a simple one. The host can, but need not, pay for the taxi. In fact, if it happens to be convenient, one of the men guests should make an effort to pay. The host carries the tickets, which nowadays are usually bought well in advance, and shepherds all his guests through the door before he goes in himself. If the seats are divided, the question of who sits with whom can be discussed in the taxi or at the dinner beforehand. The host and hostess should separate, each sitting with one group of guests.

In theory, as soon as the host has shown his ticket stubs to the usher, he should follow his guests down the aisle. Actually, if for any reason this is awkward, he can quite properly precede them down the aisle, although he should never sit down until all of them are seated. The host usually sits on the aisle, so this is a very practical arrangement. The hostess is usually the one who arranges the order of seating: "George, will you go first, and then will you go next, Mrs. Taylor? . . . ," etc. If the host and hostess are separated, each one will arrange the seating of each group. As a rule, no woman, and certainly not one of the women guests, should be the first or last to be seated. If the numbers are even, this will mean that two women will sit together, but the group should always begin and end with a man. As a matter of politeness, if two women must sit next to each other, the hostess must be one of them, and husbands and wives should never, of course, be seated side by side. If the seats are separated, and one pair or one group of seats is very much better than the other, the seating arrangements are difficult. When there are four people, the host should always sit in the seats which are the least good, but in a party of four this automatically condemns the woman guest to the less desirable place. The best solution is to alternate places between acts, the host and the woman guest sitting in the less desirable seats for the first act, the hostess and the man guest during the next act, etc. If there are six people, of course, the matter is fairly easy to resolve: The host and the younger of the women guests sit in the less desirable seats throughout the play. If by any chance the seats should be divided three and three, the hostess should always sit with a woman and a man; the women guests can alternate in sitting with the two men.

457

Movies

At the movies, the host usually buys the tickets at the box office, while the others wait near by, but otherwise the procedure is exactly like entertaining at the theater. The accepted politenesses of standing in line are referred to on page 13, in the chapter, "Manners in General."

Operas and Concerts

Entertaining at the opera or at a concert is exactly like entertaining in the theater unless one is sitting in a box. In a box at the opera, the hostess always sits in the first row, in the seat farthest from the stage. In the boxes facing the stage, the hostess sits at the right. And this is true at all musical performances, whether opera, concert, or ballet. The older and more important women guests sit in the first row with the hostess, the younger women in the next row with the older and more important men guests, the host in the last row in the least desirable seat.

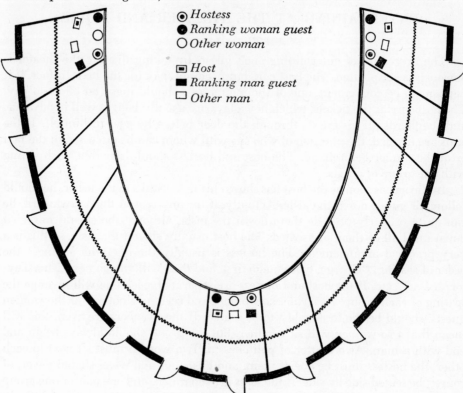

PLAN OF SEATING IN A BOX AT THE OPERA

The hostess, represented by the circle with the solid black center, is sitting at the right, with the ranking man guest behind her. The older of the two women guests is sitting at the left, also in the front row, with the younger woman guest between her and the hostess. If there are only six people in the box, all the men will sit in the second row —with the host behind the ranking woman guest—except in a box very near the stage, where the back seats away from the stage will afford a better view. Under any such circumstances, the host always takes the worst seat, unless there is a young male relative, or a very much younger man, among the guests.

The hostess shows each guest where to sit when they have reached the opera box. Turning first to the ranking woman guest and then to the others she indicates the seats the guests are to take. For example: "Will you sit here, Mrs. Barclay? And, Jane next to me? Mr. Barclay, will you sit here?" Having thus settled the women and the most important man, the other guests will find their own places. If the opera has already begun, the hostess whispers directions to her guests, or shows by gestures where they are to sit.

During intermissions, the mass migration to the lobby "for a cigarette," which is standard practice in the theater, is not the rule at the opera. The old-fashioned and conservative procedure was that the hostess, the older women guests, and at least one of the men guests stayed in the opera box from the moment they arrived until the opera was over. And this procedure is still followed by many of the more conservative modern hostesses. In some opera houses, however, a sitting room or a bar has become the usual meeting place in the intermission, and if such is a local custom, there is no reason not to follow it. Failing such a local custom, the hostess should not leave her box to speak to friends unless, as is most unlikely, all of her guests have already done so. The host can accompany one of his guests; but he should not, without apology, go off by himself to speak to other friends.

If one of the younger women guests wants to go to speak to a friend during the intermission, one of the men should offer to accompany her; or she may even, if necessary, ask one of the younger men guests to go with her. Men guests go off by themselves after a suitable word to the hostess: "I want to speak to Mrs. Borroughs for a minute; I'll be right back." But at least one of the men guests must stay in the opera box if the hostess, or any woman, is there.

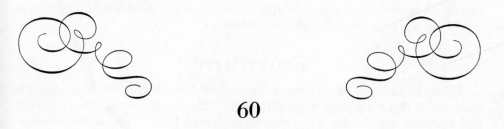

60

Memos to Hosts

THE WHOLE approach to the subject of entertaining has been discussed on pages 433 to 435 in the introduction of this section, but the following specific examples will illustrate some of the principles of the behavior of a host and hostess.

PROTECTION

As a host or hostess, one has a responsibility to protect one's guests from all the hazards of any gathering of people: from the bad manners, the faults and the overenthusiasms of others; from boredom and embarrassment; and most of all from paying a penalty for their own good manners. Classic examples of guests in need of protection are these: the guest who has gallantly taken on a bore and been allowed to suffer, unrelieved; the guest who is a lonely minority in a heated political discussion; the guest who, all unwilling, is being pressed into a conversation about business.

This sense of protection must extend, if necessary, to a point where the hosts even protect a guest from his own shortcomings. For example, if Mr. A becomes hotly involved in an argument with the rest of the guests, having taken not only an unpopular but perhaps a slightly foolish stand, the host or hostess should rally to his support. This need not be carried to the extent of denying any of one's own principles or beliefs, but should be done in such a way as to develop whatever there is of sense on the side of Mr. A's argument. Very adroit hosts can sometimes manage to change the subject before it has reached a point where such intervention becomes necessary, but if guests have got out of hand, there is often nothing else one can do. And needless to say no host should himself ever harass a guest with argument or too pointed discussion.

Guests must also be protected from knowing how grave a mistake they may have made. If anything is spilled or broken, the damage must quickly be minimized; a faux pas must be smoothed over and covered. As far as possible, no guest should be allowed to feel that his behavior has been awkward or upsetting to others. (A more serious aspect of this protection is involved whenever there is gambling; see page 88 in the section, "Manners.")

IMPARTIALITY

Hosts, like princes, must seem to be impartial. Each guest must be equally welcome. If there is a very important or very much older guest, special respect and attention may be due him, but the hosts will have to be careful to avoid monopolizing him. A long tête-à-tête between the hostess and the most interesting guest, excluding the other guests, is an egregious rudeness. The best solution is a more general conversation, in which at least several of the other guests can be included. And it is axiomatic that a good hostess never allows a guest to sit or wander about alone, left out of any group or conversation. (See "Surveillance" immediately below and "Conversation," on page 15, in the chapter on "Manners in General.")

SURVEILLANCE

The code of behavior for guests strictly limits them as to what they can do and what they can ask for; and knowing this, the hosts should always be watchful for the guests' comfort. They must offer drink, knowing the guests can ask for nothing but water. They must offer cigars. They must remember to offer guests a second cocktail or a second cup of tea or a candy from the jar on the table, sparing the guests the necessity of asking. At the dining-room table, the hosts should watch to see which guests refuse wine; if they are near by, the host or hostess should ask them if they would perhaps not like to have whiskey and soda or something else, and see that they are given what they want. If the guests are too far down the table for this, the hosts should tell the maid or butler to offer them something else. The question of what "something else" may be should be decided upon beforehand between the hostess and the maid. It may cover the whole field from a cola drink, ginger ale, and milk to two or three different kinds of whiskey; but whatever it is, the maid will know it. And this is why guests must never ask for anything, but always wait for suggestions either from the hosts or the maid. In the same way, if a guest's water glass is standing empty and the maid seems not to notice, the host or hostess should order it to be filled.

As long as guests are in the house, this same surveillance must continue, not only in matters of food and drink, but in every way that might contribute to the guest's enjoyment.

LOOKING AFTER WOMEN GUESTS

It is extremely considerate and polite to make sure that women guests will not have to come to dinner, or leave, alone. For example, at the time of the invitation, the hostess can say on the telephone, "We're asking George Wheeler that night. Suppose I telephone him and ask him to stop for you?"

It is even more important, of course, to see that a woman guest need not go home from dinner alone. During the evening the host suggests to one of the extra men, or to a couple who live near the guest, that she might like to be taken home. For example, "I don't know if she has made any other plans," says the host to one of the men guests, "but if not, could you take Jane Barclay home?" "I'd be delighted to," answers the guest. "Oh, that's splendid. Then will you speak to her about it?"

OVERANXIOUS HOSTS

Hosts should be careful not to confuse hospitality with overanxiety. There are two ways in which this confusion is made evident. The first is that many hosts too anxiously and too often urge their guests to eat, or drink, to sit down, to come out on the porch where it is cool, or to come nearer the fire where it is warm. Guests like to be offered food or a drink once, and perhaps even a second and third time if there is a suitable interval between, but no one, except perhaps the pathologically timid, likes to be urged repeatedly.

The second form of overanxiety in a host or hostess is to deprecate one's hospitality, putting the guests under the embarrassing necessity of continually reassuring their hosts that they are comfortable and are having a good time.

GENERAL CONVERSATION

General conversation is probably the most rewarding and agreeable of all forms of dining-table and after-dinner entertainment, particularly when there are two or three interesting and authoritative dinner guests. It always requires, however, a certain amount of management and organizing on the part of the hostess. In the first place, the dinner cannot be too large; ten or twelve people are usually the maximum number in the living room, and eight at the dining-room table. (A dinner party of ten or twelve can be broken into two groups of five or six each at the dining-room table.) The second requisite for general conversation is that there must be at least one or two people whose opinions will be interesting to the rest of the guests. And, if this one or these two are authorities and know it, the rest of the guests must be willing to be audience most of the time. In order to prevent the conversation from turning into a series of monologues, the host or hostess will have to intervene from time to time, questioning other guests whose opinions are known to be apropos and valuable. Ideally, the guests should have been so chosen that each one will have something to contribute and each one will be interested in what the "authorities" have to say. Adroit hosts will draw the best out of each guest, and present him in the best and most interesting light to the others. Questions can be phrased to include the reasons for the importance and validity of the guest's opinion. For example, if government control or censorship is being discussed, "You worked on the Manhattan Project. How binding were government regulations there?" Or, "There must have been thousands of farmers who did business with your bank. What did they feel about the A.A.A.?" It is probably unnecessary to add that the host and hostess should never hold the floor themselves, or show off at their own parties. They should act as chairmen, prompters, moderators, never as shining lights.

All these suggestions concerning general conversation are directed to the host and hostess. See also "Conversation," on page 15, in the section on "Manners," and on page 441, in the chapter, "Entertaining at Home."

GUESTS OF HONOR

In other chapters of this section we have discussed the procedure of entertaining and inviting a guest of honor, but it might be useful here to outline the accepted ways in which one goes about making the arrangement. In speaking to the prospective guest of honor, the classic phrase, whether by writing, telephone, or face to face, is, "I would like so much to give a dinner for you," or, "for you and your husband." The cardinal point is that, although either may be the true guest of honor, if the guest is married, the invitation must be framed to include both. When the day has been agreed upon, the hostess asks, "Would you like me to call again and remind you?"; or, if it is a formal dinner for which engraved invitations or reminder cards will be sent, "Would you like me to send you a reminder card?" In case the guest of honor may have friends or business associates whom the hostess does not know, it is always polite for the hostess to ask, when the date has been agreed upon, "Is there anyone you would like me to invite?" If the prospective guest of honor is an official or a high-ranking member of the government or of the church, the official channels of his staff or secretariat should be used in making the arrangements, unless he is an intimate friend. And it should be noted that when entertaining officials formally, one must consider the old rule, "Never invite those of higher rank to meet those of lower rank." (See "Invitations" on page 490, and "Order of Precedence of Officials," page 492.)

Informally, one may often give a dinner for a friend of lower rank than many of the other guests. And this is sensible because the guest of honor would otherwise be able to meet none but his juniors. At such a dinner, the guest of honor might sit far down the table, with higher ranking guests at his hostess's right and left hands. When there are no official guests, the guest of honor always sits at the hostess's right and his wife at the host's.

WEEK ENDS

There are certain rules and requisites that are necessary to make week-end guests happy and comfortable. The requisites are simpler, so we shall begin with them. Apart from good food and drink and pleasant company—which are most important, but sometimes a little difficult to command—there are four quite simple things that are absolutely vital to a guest's comfort. The first is a good bed; the second is plenty of hot water; the third is a good reading light; and the last is plenty of covers. Many guests would add a bedside pitcher of water to this list. And for others, one must add also a fifth requisite: a bed so placed that the first light of the sun will not inevitably fall on the pillow. Without these, in the biggest and most beautiful house, guests will be uncomfortable; with them, the basis of comfort is assured.

The entertainment of week-end guests is, of course, a more complicated subject than their comfort. Guests are more apt to agree on questions of comfort than they are on questions of entertainment. There are only two rules that can apply to all week ends, whether in winter or summer, town or country.

The first is that guests should not be overorganized. Nothing is more depressing than a hostess who has ticketed every minute of the guest's time. The ideal hostesses are those who, if they do not know the tastes of their guests, make diffident suggestions: "Would anybody feel like playing a little tennis this afternoon, or would you rather just sit around?" Or, "I thought we might play a little golf tomorrow. Does that appeal to anybody?" There is a new school of behavior for week-end hostesses which allows them to go off alone to play golf and tennis if none of the guests wants to play. This is condoned by some hostesses on the basis that it "allows the guests more freedom," but by any name it is not a politeness to the guests, and hostesses should never do it if any of the week-end guests is a stranger or a foreigner. If some of the guests want to play tennis and others prefer to stay quietly at home, the hostess can quite properly go off to tennis if she wants to. If the guests play tennis and the hostess doesn't, she should organize the games for them; she will either go and watch, which is most polite of her, or stay at home and rest, which is less polite but still perfectly permissible.

The second rule is that week-end guests should not be taken out to lunch or dine in other houses for every meal. In fact, as far as guests are concerned, the less they go out, the more they usually like it. This is particularly true of the first evening. Nothing is more tiring and confusing than to arrive at teatime, to be told that one must soon rush upstairs to dress, and to be taken off to a strange house full of people one has never met.

61

Memos to Guests

GUESTS VARY: some sit like pitchers waiting to be filled, others spill over, as though no evening were long enough to hold all the ideas crowding the mind's lip. But all good guests, whether passive or active, identify themselves with the others. The passive ones are alertly and appreciatively listening. The talkers are aware of the others' interest; and they are willing to take a hint, ready to change the subject, or even to be still. Bad guests sit in inert and unresponsive passivity, or gallop into runaway monologues. And such guests are bad guests because they are not accepting the responsibilities of the role.

A great deal has been written about the responsibilities of hosts—and they are many—but too seldom is it said that the guests have their own obligations, parallel and similar to those of the hosts. The ideal guest's manners express delight in his hosts and their other guests; they convey the fact that he thinks the food delicious, and that the conversation or games his hostess has suggested are the very ones he would have chosen. Narrowed down to one sentence, a guest's manners should express, "I know you have tried to please me, and I am touched and made happy by that; but most of all, I want you to know that all the ways in which you have planned to please me have been most successful." It may sound a little elaborate, but it is nevertheless true that every good guest, whether consciously or subconsciously, manages to convey this attitude towards his hosts.

Towards other guests his attitude is very much the same. The ideal guest laughs at jokes, is interested in anecdotes and seems to find everyone most attractive. The wit and charm that give warmth and life and personality to a guest's code of manners cannot be prescribed. But the principles of behavior which are the basis of this code are listed here.

THE UNPRESUMING GUEST

The ideal guest shows his virtues in many subtle ways, but one of his salient qualities is that he is unpresuming. It is a pity that this wonderful attribute of a guest is so often destroyed by the abuse of the cozy, old-fashioned phrase, "Make yourself at home." There is almost nothing that a guest can do that is worse than making himself too obviously at home in a house that belongs to someone else. The most blatant examples of being too much at home are these: fetching playing cards, water, food, drinks or anything else, except at the hostess's suggestion; offering drinks, or anything else, to other guests; telling other guests where things may be found; telephoning without asking permission first and making long distance calls without paying for them; parading one's frequent visits or one's familiarity with the house, before other guests; and above all, giving orders to the staff.

A guest with perfect manners never asks for special service at the dining-room table, even for water, because it may interfere with the serving routine. After luncheon or dinner, if the host or hostess is not in the room, he may ask the maid or butler for cigarettes or water, or for anything else which has already been served. For example, if orangeade or whiskey and soda has been served after dinner, a guest may quite properly say, "I'd like a little more orangeade, please," or "Will you bring me another whiskey and soda, please." But he should not take it upon himself to ask for milk, or brandy and soda, or anything else which has not already been offered. The maid, however, can quite properly suggest alternatives to a guest who has refused what has been offered. (See page 460.)

A more important point of manners is that a guest should never interfere with the discipline of children or dogs. If children are supposed to go to bed at a certain hour, no guest should plead, and certainly not before the children, that they be allowed to stay up longer; if dogs are supposed to stay on the floor, no guest should take it upon himself to cuddle them on the sofa.

The unpresuming guest is careful, too, not to interfere with the duties of the staff and with the household routine. Friends who know the household ways can be extremely helpful without lacking in proper diffidence, but acquaintances should be careful not to confuse the two. A typical victim of this confusion is the week-end guest who, without asking the hostess or knowing what the customs are, makes his own bed. He not only disrupts the household customs but he also suggests to the hostess that, in his opinion, her household arrangements are not adequate to cover the service that is usually given to guests. There is no situation in which a guest can take it for granted without any hint from his hostess that he may make his own bed. Even in a household where there is no maid, it is just possible that the hostess might prefer to make the guests' beds herself, while her husband takes the guests for a walk or to play tennis.

If the hostess does want the guests to make their beds, or to help with the dishes, she may suggest it herself: "I hope you won't mind, but we all make our own beds." In such cases, the hostess often gives a hint of the situation in the invitation: "We live a very picnic life, but we are looking forward to . . ." If the household seems strained, the guest can ask the hostess, "May I make my bed in the morning? We always do at home when we have guests," to which the hostess will answer either, "How awfully kind of you! That would be wonderful," or, "How kind! but you mustn't—Nora would feel dreadfully." A guest should always, however, keep his room and his bathroom neat. In small houses, when the guest shares a bathroom with others, he should wash the tub and tidy the bathroom before he leaves it.

When the unpresuming guest has come to call, whether by appointment or not, he will be found sitting in a small straight-backed armchair when his hostess comes in, not sprawling on the sofa or in a very deep chair, smoking, and reading a magazine. Neither will he be discovered making an inspection tour of the rooms, picking up bibelots and looking at the markings on the china, as though he were making an appraisal for insurance purposes. The hostess may be quite pleased to find a guest looking at one of the pictures on the wall, the suggestion being that he has been struck by its beauty. But she will not be pleased to find that he has made free with all the comforts and objects of interest in the room.

Like other virtues, this diffidence can be overdone. If there are no cigarettes on the dining-room table, a guest will be quite justified in feeling a little hesitant about taking out one of his own cigarettes and lighting it whenever he wants to. But if there are cigarettes on the table, there is no reason why the guest should not take one, although he should not do so until after the meat course. If one has refused champagne, and the hostess or the butler offers a still wine instead, it would be overdiffident not to accept. A proper diffidence suggests that one should not leap to one's food the minute one has served oneself; but after two or three other guests have been served, it is overdiffident to feel that any more delay is necessary.

CO-OPERATION

One of the first duties of a guest is co-operation. The spirit in which this obligation should be met is almost that of a fellow conspirator of the hostess. She is making every effort to see that all the guests will enjoy themselves and that no one's feelings will be hurt. And every guest should help her. In other words, no matter what one thinks of one's dinner companions, one must talk to them with the appearance, at least, of as much interest and pleasure as possible. If a guest seems stranded, one should help out by taking him into the conversation or going across the room to join him. The hostess, too, will naturally be on the alert for this sort of situation, but a problem guest becomes more obviously a problem when the hostess must repeatedly come to the rescue. It is extremely bad manners for a guest to show reluctance to any of the hostess's suggestions whether direct or indirect; to be conspicuously slow in turning when the table turns; to play cards with bad grace if one is at a table with very much inferior players; to demur, if games are suggested; or make suggestions counter to those of the hostess, unless the hostess asks for them. Guests should be quick to take any hint, however slight, from the hostess.

DISCIPLINE

There are two things that make guests difficult. One is lack of knowledge, the other, and much more important of the two, is lack of discipline. Most guests know how late they can be, how long they can stay, how much diffidence they should show in the houses of others. But too many are unwilling to discipline themselves enough to obey the rules.

In some guests there seems to be a curious spirit of exploitation towards those who are civilized enough, and disciplined enough, to feel bound by the rules of good manners; others cannot protest when one takes a cigarette after the soup course, so the undisciplined guest takes advantage of this. A hostess cannot protest when one smears lipstick all over her napkin, so the undisciplined guest makes no effort to eat tidily. No one can protest if one reads in the middle of a group of conversationalists. "So why not do it?" the undisciplined guest seems to say. "Deep chairs are more comfortable than hard ones, lateness is easier than punctuality, and let the hostess take the rap." It is an attitude without charm for others.

DISCRETION

One of the primary rules for guests is that they must never repeat anything they have learned about their hosts when they were guests of the house. This rule is almost as binding for a guest as it is for a doctor, who should never repeat anything he knows about his patients. To be scrupulously polite to one's hosts, no guest should ever repeat anything about another guest, either, since the hosts are responsible for the protection of all their guests while they are in their house.

APOLOGIES

Guests must apologize for any lateness beyond that which is considered acceptable. (See "Punctuality," page 468.) The reasons for their lateness should be given and their apologies should be made, as they greet their hostess. Apologies are also due if a guest should damage or break anything, or spill a drink. He should bring it immediately to the attention of the hostess, apologize and, if possible, replace within a day or so anything broken or seriously damaged. If whatever he has done was inconvenient, or if the object was irreplaceable, he should send flowers the next day to the hostess, again apologizing.

In the same way, if a guest has been rude or has behaved badly, he should apologize the very next day not only to the hostess but also to any fellow guest whom he may have offended. The hostess should receive flowers and a note of apology and so also should a woman guest to whom he has been rude. If the rudeness involved another man, the hostess should still receive flowers and a note, and the man should receive a letter of apology. The reason for this is that an offense to any of the guests in the house is a double offense, first to the one who has received it and second to the hostess who is responsible for the protection of guests while they are in her house.

EMERGENCIES

When a guest has arrived at his hostess's house, no matter how boring the party may be, there is no way of getting out of it before the usual time (see "When to Go Home," page 469), unless there is a real emergency. If one has left a child ill at home, it is better to mention it early in the evening or even on arrival, so that an early departure will not seem to be prompted by one's opinion of the party. If one feels suddenly ill, the best thing to do is to go to the hostess and explain, and leave without ostentatious farewells to the other guests. The point is that one should try to make his departure as inconspicuous as possible. And this is why it is easier to leave a roomful of people after dinner than it is to leave the dining-room table.

467

If one suddenly feels ill at the dining-room table and is sitting next to the hostess, an excuse need be made only to her: "I'm so sorry to be such a nuisance, but suddenly I feel rather ill; I wonder if I might lie down for just a moment." An older man—or any man guest at a small dinner—is taken by the host to his room; at a very big dinner, the butler would accompany the guest. The hostess should always accompany a woman guest. If one is not sitting next to the hostess, an excuse must be made to one's dinner companion as well as to the hostess. All this is, obviously, a nuisance for the hosts, no matter how politely they protest, and a guest should avoid such situations if possible. One should use all one's good sense and self-discipline to avoid leaving the dining-room table. An empty chair during a meal is conspicuous, inconvenient, and awkward.

PUNCTUALITY

Lateness is a curious thing. Chronic lateness, we are told, can be a manifestation of neurasthenia, a subconscious effort to escape the rigidity of time, or a desire to bolster one's ego. But as a rule, it has no such serious connotations, and can be traced to nothing more interesting than carelessness mixed with a little selfishness, in more or less equal parts. Lateness is frowned on in Europe, where anything less than perfect punctuality for a social engagement is considered a rudeness. But in America, supposedly the very nest of efficiency, lateness is strangely tolerated. In fact, with three exceptions, overpunctuality is not admired.

The first exception are hosts and hostesses who, in theory at least, must be punctual. Their tendency to come down late for their own dinners is still considered rude, although it may explain why super-promptness in a guest is regarded as somewhat unattractive. And more than any hostess, a man must be prompt when he has an appointment with a woman. The third inevitable promptness applies to occasions when royalty or chiefs of state are involved: Everyone *must* be present when they arrive. Apart from these three exceptions, there is a pat little scale of accepted lateness of which guests can—and do—take full advantage.

1. Luncheon or Dinner

> With another person of the same sex: five to ten minutes.
> With a man, if one is a woman: anything up to fifteen minutes.
> With a married couple at a restaurant: never more than ten minutes.
> At dinner, if one knows there are to be fewer than ten guests: fifteen minutes.
> Up to twenty guests: twenty minutes.
> At a very big dinner, of perhaps fifty or sixty people: lateness up to half an
> hour is tolerated. At buffet dinners, especially, such lateness is expected.

2. Tea

> A small tea party (five or six guests): fifteen or twenty minutes.
> A large tea party, cocktail party, or any large afternoon reception to which
> one is invited for a given length of time: lateness from fifteen minutes
> after the first hour mentioned in the invitation, up to half an hour before
> the reception is to be over.

3. Dances

> An hour's lateness is entirely permissible at dances and all large evening parties except musicales.

4. Musicales

> No more than five or ten minutes' lateness, unless one is sure what time the program will begin. In this case, one should arrive at least ten minutes beforehand.

WHEN TO GO HOME

It is impossible to give an exact schedule for the amount of time one should spend as a guest in someone else's house. At a reception, one might want to copy the American ambassador who allowed three to five minutes for a quick hand-shake and a surreptitious departure. Or, one might want to spend two hours with the kindly intention of making an inexperienced hostess feel that her tea party had been a great success. The one rule is that one must not leave before a guest of honor. (The matter of the guest of honor's departure is discussed below.) Apart from this one certainty, the schedule cannot be fixed exactly and the following suggestions can only be taken as a rough guide, to be changed to fit any local customs.

At tea or an afternoon reception: twenty minutes minimum, if there are ten or twelve guests or more; forty-five minutes minimum for smaller parties. The maximum depends entirely on when one's hosts may be expected to be dining; one should always leave at least an hour before the dinner hour customary in the community.

At an evening reception: forty-five minutes minimum at very large receptions; an hour and a half at smaller ones. The maximum depends on the number of people still remaining. If there are only ten or twelve left out of a hundred, it it probably time for anyone but an intimate friend to leave.

At luncheon: the margin here is very small; anyone asked to come at a quarter past one, and planning to leave before half-past two, might feel the necessity of explaining his departure to the hostess. The usual duration of a luncheon is one and a half to two hours.

At dinner: about three hours minimum, or three hours and a half. The maximum, as in the case of an evening reception, depends on the other guests. One can always leave after one or two couples have already gone, and, as an acquaintance rather than a friend of the hostess, it is always wise to leave while there are still one or two couples left.

As the guest of honor, one has a special responsibility in the matter of going home, because none of the other guests, no matter how tired he may be, can leave earlier. If the dinner is very formal, the usual minimum of three, or three and a half hours, should be observed. At a less formal dinner, when sandwiches are served at about half-past eleven, the guest of honor should leave at about twelve or half-past. In a very protocol-conscious gathering, a guest of honor's responsibility may be given to those who have been seated at the right of the host and hostess at dinner. Therefore, if there seems to be a lull, and if three and a half hours have gone by and the hostess is not apparently planning to have sandwiches or supper served, it would probably be wise to leave.

FORMALITY WITH THE STAFF

Conversation with the household of one's host should always be extremely polite, formal, and brief. One should always greet the one who opens the door with "Good evening," "Good morning," or "Good afternoon"; at the door, in leaving one says, "Good night" or "Good day" and "Thank you." Suggestions as to where the guest should wait, or leave his coat will come from the members of the staff, and it is they who will ask for the keys of the luggage, if unpacking is to be done for week-end guests. After many visits, when the guest has become a friend of the house, a little less formality is proper. The guest can say, "Good evening, Carter," or, "Good evening, Mary," and inquire about the servant's health or that of the family, comment on the weather, etc. Members of the staff should not be greeted by, "Hello." The essential point in all this, as in all politeness, is to make others feel at ease. A very highly trained butler, for example, or a maid trained in the English tradition, will be made uncomfortable by an overcasual, overhearty behavior, however well-meant, because he will not know how to respond. On the other hand, a cheerful general houseworker, accustomed to entering freely into the family's conversation, will be quite at home in a less formal atmosphere. To a maid such as this, guests should say, "Thank you," or, "Thank you, Mary," as she waits on table. This need not be done each time a guest has finished serving himself, but it should be done at least once or twice during a meal. With more formal maids, and at all formal luncheons or dinners, no comment is necessary.

WHEN A GUEST BRINGS A GUEST

When one has accepted an invitation for luncheon or dinner, and a friend arrives to spend the week end, there are two ways of handling the situation. Suppose, for example, one was dining on Saturday night in a big house, with plenty of room for extra guests. It would be quite in order, to call up the hostess and ask to bring guests, because the chances are that she will not be at all inconvenienced. For example: "George and Mary Paine have telegraphed that they are coming for the week end; may I bring them to dinner on Saturday?" On the other hand, if the house were small, it would be wiser to suggest staying home; as, "I'm so sorry, Mrs. Bigelow, but George and Mary Paine have just let us know that they are arriving for the week end; that will make so many of us that perhaps it would be more convenient for you if we didn't come on Saturday."

In either case, the hostess is free to answer, "Oh, I'm so sorry, but I'm afraid there just isn't room for any more. That's most disappointing, but I hope you'll come sometime soon again." Or she may say, "Oh, how nice; do bring them. I'll look forward to seeing you all on Saturday at eight."

Any guest who comes for a week end or even to spend the day is a legitimate candidate for such an invitation. But there are three other points to bear in mind. The first is that one can more easily ask for an invitation to a reception, dance, or cocktail party than to a dinner or bridge party, and asking for an invitation for a man is almost a favor to the hostess who is giving a dance. The second is that one should never ask to bring a friend who lives in the same community as the hostess, unless one knows the hostess intimately. For example, if Mr. Blank is well known to the hostess, and is not invited to her dance, it may be that there are reasons for omitting him which she would find embarrassing to discuss with an acquaintance. If the hostess is an intimate friend, she will not mind being frank.

Finally, one should never ask to bring anyone whom the hostess would not have asked herself had she known him.

ON BEING ENTERTAINED IN RESTAURANTS
AND NIGHT CLUBS

We have stressed the fact that guests should not give orders to the staff, in their hosts' house, and it is equally true that as a guest in a restaurant or night club, one should not give an order directly to a waiter. Well-trained waiters will never question a guest directly, and well-trained guests always make their requests to their hosts. But it is a curious fact that guests who would never dream of ordering anything in their hosts' houses are very often guilty of this particular form of bad manners in restaurants. When a guest has been given a menu by the waiter, he should wait to declare his choice until the host asks him what he would like. After a few minutes delay, if the host has not done this, the guest can quite properly tell his host what he has decided. If the waiter makes suggestions directly to the guest, the guest should accept these as information and ignore the invitation to give the order directly to him. When the food is brought to the table, it is, of course, perfectly proper for the guest to answer such questions of the waiter's as, "Who ordered the curry?" But, except when there are so many guests that the host may have suggested that each order for himself, the orders should be given through the host. Questions as to how much and what kind of food to order are discussed on page 454 of "Entertaining in Restaurants."

VISITING

In addition to the other suggestions given above, there are a few further points which apply particularly to visiting. The first is that guests must arrive when they have promised to arrive and leave when they have indicated they will leave. The second is that they must, to all appearances, at least, enter gladly into whatever entertainment the hostess suggests. Further, as always, they must be prompt. (See page 522, "Invitations for Week Ends.") The other points are covered in question and answer form here. (Suggestions for clothes for the country for men and for women are on pages 620 and 629.)

Must I take a present? And if so, what?

No, you need not take a present, although it is polite to do so. If you do, it should be a present for the hostess or the children. Candy and books are the standard presents for the hostess; toys, of course, for the children. If the woman knows the hostess fairly well, some special bath salts or bath oil, soap, or sachets would be a good present. Husbands need not bring presents; that is the wife's job. Except in times of known shortages, wine, cake, or any utilitarian food presents are not a good idea, because they suggest that the guest may feel that the hostess's larder is not adequately stocked. This applies to acquaintances, not intimate friends.

Should I telephone from the station to let my hostess know that I have arrived?

No, the best thing to do is to take a taxi without telephoning beforehand. Presumably, the hostess will have known what train you are taking and a telephone call from the station may sound like a hint on your part that you would like to be fetched.

Must I take my hostess to a restaurant for one meal during a week-end visit?

Certainly not. While you are visiting, you are a guest. The moment for reciprocity comes later, when you invite your hostess for a return visit, or show your gratitude and sense of obligation in another way. For example, a single man who has no way of returning a week-end invitation could invite his hosts to dinner once or twice; or, he could send game, or a salmon, books, or phonograph records, as a present after his visit.

If I have friends in the neighborhood, may I telephone them and suggest that they come over?

Certainly not. If you have friends in the neighborhood whom you want to see, all you can do is to say something like this, "The Barclays, who are great friends of mine, live near here. Do you know them?" Unless the hostess leaps to this hint, you must leave it at that. The only exceptions are visits which are a matter of obligation rather than pleasure. If you have a relative, a business associate, an old employee, or an invalid friend in the neighborhood, you can quite properly explain the circumstances to the hostess, arrange to go whenever it will be convenient for her, and order a taxi at the agreed-upon time. You can even ask to borrow a car to make a visit such as this.

Can I accept invitations from friends in the neighborhood?

Certainly not. You should never use your hostess's house as a springboard for other activities.

If I am invited by friends to come and bring my hosts, what should I do?

You should never relay invitations to your hostess. If friend and hostess know each other, the best thing to do is to ask the friend to speak to the hostess. If they are strangers to each other, it is better to refuse. "I'm awfully sorry; I think Mary has invited some people here for the evening." If the friend presses, which she shouldn't, you can only say, "May I call you back? I'd like to talk to Mary and see what her plans are." You can then call back later, making further excuses.

If there is a disagreement between my host and hostess as to my entertainment, what should I do?

The answer to this depends on the reasons behind the disagreement. For example, if the hostess is obviously trying to protect the guest from her husband's overenthusiasm for his hobby, the most tactful guest will try to convince both his host and hostess that he is sincerely interested in farming, or birdcalls, or whatever the hobby happens to be. If the disagreement is a matter of conflicting conveniences—the hostess wanting the guest to make a fourth at bridge, the host wanting the guest to make up a foursome at golf—it is more tactful to agree with the dominant one of the two.

If I feel tired, is it all right if I go up to bed before my hostess and the other guests?

Certainly. If you are not involved in a bridge game or anything else, you can quite easily go up to the hostess, explain that you are tired, say good-night and leave as inconspicuously as possible.

Can I sit up with some of the other guests when the host and hostess have gone to bed?

No. You should follow the hosts' lead unless they go to bed unusually early.

For example, if your hosts say good-night an hour or so after dinner is over, they will probably quite sincerely urge their guests to stay up as late as they like, and it is quite all right to do so. But, as a rule, guests should not stay downstairs unless either the host, the hostess, or a member of the family is with them.

Should I ring for the maid?

Unless there is an emergency, you should not ring for any employee except when the hostess has indicated that she expects you to do so. Obviously, you may ring if she has said, "Ring for breakfast whenever you wake up." But even in a very large household, the guests are not expected to ring for help in dressing unless the guests are very old or infirm, in which case the hostess will probably have suggested it herself. The rule is that week-end guests may ring from their bedrooms for the upstairs maids in these circumstances, or to tip them before leaving (see below). No guest, not even a week-end guest, should ring from any other room in the house, if the host or hostess is in. If the hostess and host are out, and a guest has arrived or returned unexpectedly, he can ring to announce his arrival, to leave a message for the hostess, or to find out where she has gone, or whether there are any messages for him. Like all guests, whether for a week end or for an evening, one should not ring to order tea or drinks or anything else.

When I leave, do I shake hands with the staff?

No, unless there is some special reason for doing so. Women never, except in the most unusual circumstances, shake hands with menservants, or men with womenservants, and women shake hands less often than men. If, for example, a guest had known the butler or footman a long time, or if he were an ex-army comrade, he would shake hands on arrival and departure. But if there is any question as to whether one should or not, the safest answer is no.

When my husband and I are invited to come for the week end, what should we pack?

In theory, a woman's week-end luggage should contain the following: two evening dresses—a simple one for a small dinner party and a more elaborate one; two dresses or suits for daytime. A man should have with him a dinner jacket, and a daytime suit. If you have any reason to believe that your hosts may not dress for dinner on one of the evenings, you will have to add an afternoon or "don't dress" dinner dress and your husband should add a blue suit. And if they never dress for dinner, of course, you leave out the evening clothes and add another afternoon dress. These are the basic elements of week-end packing and other things are added for special reasons: bathing suits, tennis or golf clothes, riding or shooting clothes, etc. (Specific suggestions for these will be found in the chapters "Men's Clothes" and "Women's Clothes," pages 615 to 628, and 629 to 638.)

For the sake of example we shall list all the things a woman might and should take with her for a week-end visit to the country in cold weather. (Specific suggestions concerning suits, blouses, sweaters, shoes, etc. for country wear are on page 630.)

As suggested above, two evening dresses—one simple and the other more elaborate. Or this might be changed to one dress which may be worn with or without its jacket. If one is visiting friends one might take a tea gown or evening pajamas, but if one is visiting acquaintances it is better to stick to dresses.

As suggested above, two suits or dresses for daytime. Or this might be changed to one suit, and an odd skirt which can be worn with a cardigan sweater on Saturday. Or one suit to be worn with a cardigan sweater on Saturday and its own jacket on Sunday.

Two blouses, unless one is taking dresses.

A pair of country shoes with moderate heels, and perhaps also a pair of heavy walking shoes.

A warm coat; this can be worn, of course, or carried, and need not be packed.

At least one sweater; and if only one, then a cardigan.

A pair of gloves for the country.

A country handbag.

An evening handbag.

Evening slippers.

Bedroom slippers.

A dressing gown; this is really a necessity in many houses where the bathroom may not be next to the bedroom, and bedroom slippers are necessary too. It is extremely unattractive to pad around in bare feet before getting into bed or to wear an overcoat over the nightgown for a trip to the bathroom.

Others might extend this list even further: a bed jacket for reading and breakfast in bed, a hot-water bottle, scarves—all these are "indispensable" to some. But apart from the usual extras such as toothbrushes, powder, and underclothes, this list is all one could really call necessary.

Is there a "correct" way to pack?

The word "correct" has several interpretations. From a practical point of view there is a "correct" way to pack in order to save space and prevent creases. From an aesthetic point of view there is also a "correct" way to pack which is entirely a matter of what is attractive and what is not. Quite apart from the chaos which must result from the reckless packing one so often sees in movies, there is a basic lack of proper fastidiousness in it. Underclothes should be carefully covered so that other clothes do not touch them; a clean white layer of tissue paper will do, or a silk case. Shoes should go in special shoe bags, or in a good wrapping of tissue paper. Hair brushes and combs should also be wrapped, or put in a bag; toothbrushes should have special containers. In fact everything in one's bag should be wrapped except the clothes themselves and these, particularly bed jackets and dressing gowns, should be separated from each other by a piece of tissue paper. Some women use pieces of silk instead of tissue paper, specially cut to fit the bag and always in pale washable materials, but that is a matter of personal taste and we are discussing here only matters of form.

TIPPING AFTER A VISIT

There are only two points that apply to all tipping, by all guests—men and women, married and single. The first point is that, in the United States, domestic employees are not tipped unless the guest has spent a night or more in the house. The second is that one does not tip those whom one has not seen. The only exception to this last would be a special situation: for example, if one were on a rigid diet, it would be quite in order to give the cook three to five dollars after a weekend visit, depending on the amount of trouble the diet had caused her. But otherwise, neither she nor the kitchenmaid would be tipped. Beyond these two points, the question of tipping must be divided into separate scales for men and women guests. The paragraph, "When and How to Tip," which is given at the end of this chapter, applies, however, to all guests.

Women Guests

In America a woman rarely tips a manservant unless he has done some special service for her. In a very large household, where the duties are very much departmentalized, the only manservant the woman guest would be apt to tip after a week-end visit would be the chauffeur, who might have had to make a special trip to the station to fetch her or her bags. For this, the most usual tip, and the minimum, would be a dollar; it would be more if it were a very long trip or a very complicated errand; and if he had washed her car, it would be two dollars. In a smaller household, where the butler might combine all the duties of chauffeur and butler, a woman guest would give him two dollars if he has given special service in either one of those capacities. If a woman guest has had riding boots or heavy walking shoes that have had to be cleaned, she should ask who has performed this service and give him a dollar also. A woman who visits repeatedly might give the butler five dollars every third or fourth visit but, in theory, the only one a woman guest must *always* tip is the maid who takes care of her clothes.

The question of how much to tip the maid can be approached in either of two different ways: In a very big household, tips should be bigger than they are in a small one, because there is less danger of making the wages or the next guest's tip seem inadequate. Or: In a small household, the tip is the same as in a big one; although there is less service in a small house, a guest is more of a strain, and a tip is even more in order. After a visit in a big household, women who belong to the first school of thought usually give the head housemaid or lady's maid five dollars for a week end, and two or three for a night. In a smaller household they give one or two dollars for a night, and three—or four, perhaps—for a week end, whether there is a chambermaid, or a chambermaid-waitress, or one general houseworker. Women who belong to the second school, usually give one or two dollars for a night, and three or four for a week end no matter what the size of the household.

Men Guests

As a matter of rule, a man is expected to tip not only the one who looks after his clothes and packing, but also the one who is in charge of the pantry department; and he is expected to tip at the highest scale. In very large households, when there is a butler as well as a valet, or a first footman who does the valeting, the usual tip is five dollars to each for a week end of three nights, two or three dollars each for one night. The chauffeur is tipped a dollar minimum if he has given any special service, and three dollars if he has washed the guest's car. In households where the butler is also the valet, he is not tipped doubly but is given the usual two or three dollars for one night, five dollars for a three-night week end. In a household with three women servants—a cook, waitress, and chambermaid—a man would be expected to tip both the waitress and the chambermaid, if the latter had taken care of his clothes. If the waitress had acted as valet, he would tip her five dollars, as he would a butler-valet. If there are two maids—a cook and a chambermaid-waitress—he tips only the latter. In a household with one maid, he gives her the tip. And all these at the same scale.

475

Married Couples

When husband and wife are visiting together, in a very large household they tip as though each were a single man and a single woman. In other words, the husband tips the butler and valet, or butler-valet, and the wife the lady's maid or chambermaid-maid, according to the scales given above. In smaller households, the scale changes. If there are three women servants—a cook, waitress, and chambermaid—the husband gives the waitress five dollars at the end of a week end and the wife gives the upstairs maid five dollars. In households of two women servants—cook and chambermaid-waitress—only the husband tips, and he gives the chambermaid-waitress five dollars. If there is one maid, he gives her the five dollars.

When and How to Tip

All tipping is done just before the guests leave the house. In very large households, the guests ring for the upstairs servants who have done the maiding and valeting and tip them before going downstairs. In a household where there is a butler-valet, the butler is usually standing in the front hall when the guests are due to leave and he can be tipped then. If the chauffeur is taking the guests to the station, he can be tipped when he is taking the luggage out of the car. In smaller households, one can also ring for the maid, or if it seems more convenient, watch for the one who must be tipped. Guests should not search out the maid in the back of the house; nor, if possible, should they give a tip in front of their hosts or other guests, except in the most unobtrusive way. If the one who should be tipped does not seem to be available, the guest should go downstairs and ask the host or hostess if he may ring: "I'd like to speak to Nora before I go. May I ring for her?" All tips should be accompanied by "Thank you and good-bye."

Presents Instead of Tips

There are times when, from every point of view, a present is better than a tip. For example, a friend, a relative, or a young couple, who visits regularly in a large household where all the servants are established fixtures of the family, might well give presents instead of tips. A box of candy or a scarf for the maid, pipe tobacco for the butler, or a defroster for the windshield of his car—any present such as this shows more interest and appreciation than a tip, and will give a great deal more pleasure. In the circumstances, one might also bring a present for the cook and the chambermaid whom, as a less steady visitor, one would not tip at all.

In smaller households, where the staff is often more transitory, or where there is a part-time maid, tips are perhaps better than presents. This is particularly true if one has made only two or three visits. But, even in a small household, if one visits repeatedly it is an attractive custom to alternate tips and presents or, perhaps, to give a box of candy every now and then, as well as a tip.

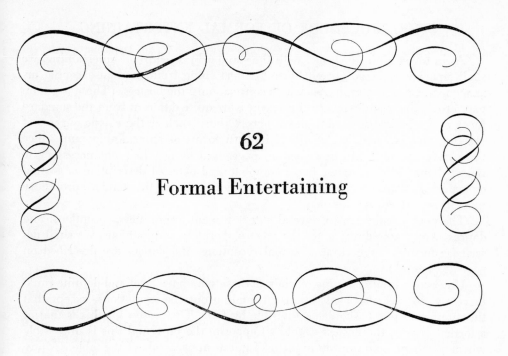

62

Formal Entertaining

In practice and in theory, formal entertaining is quite unlike any of the other ways of entertaining which are described in other parts of this book. The most important difference is that it is based on adherence to tradition and form for their own sake. Considerations which are basic in other American entertaining, such as practicality, convenience, or comfort, are secondary in formal entertaining. At most dinners in America, for example, guests are not announced, because it's not a practical necessity that they should be; at most big dances and receptions when they are announced, it is only because it is convenient for the hostess, who is probably receiving a great many acquaintances, as well as friends. But in formal entertaining, *all* guests are announced, whether the hostess is receiving the entire staff of a Government Bureau, or only twenty-four people whom she could quite easily recognize.

All this being so, one might perhaps wonder why a description of formal entertaining is included in a book about modern American customs and manners. There are two answers. First, it may be useful to those who are beginning an official or diplomatic life where such entertaining is still part of one's job. And, second, it may be interesting to others as a minor sociological study, a record of a curious, already somewhat archaic, form.

THE PROCEDURE OF FORMAL ENTERTAINING

As in the section concerned with the standard procedure of entertaining, we shall separate the procedure of formal entertaining from the housekeeping arrangements, and preliminaries which concern only the hostess. (These begin on page 481.) Many of the points of procedure are quite different from the standard form, and will be discussed in detail here. Others, such as the classic phrases of greeting and farewell, are identical in both forms of entertaining; and, since these have already been described on pages 436 to 442, it is not necessary to repeat them in this chapter. For a complete and detailed description of formal entertaining, therefore, both this and the section outlining the standard procedure must be read together.

The most usual forms of formal entertainment are dinners, receptions, and dances. And, since dinners are the most elaborately ceremonious, we shall describe a formal dinner first. (Formal receptions and dances are described on page 481 below.)

Unless one is entertaining officials or those who have a set and definite rank, there are no special considerations in sending out the invitations, except that the number of guests should be divisible by four. The reason for this is that at a formal dinner, the hostess should sit opposite the host, and this is impossible whenever there is an uneven number of guests at each side of the table. (Many hostesses who insist that there be exactly eight people to each service invite two extra men to get around this difficulty. See "Entertaining Officials," below.) The invitations follow one of the forms suggested on pages 507 to 514, and the plan of seating is arranged according to the examples given on pages 450 to 451. The first change in procedure comes in the matter of arranging the dinner partners— something which is common to all formal entertaining whether or not officials are involved.

Dinner Partners

At a formal dinner, each man is assigned a dinner partner, with whom he will go arm in arm from the drawing room to the dining-room table. The host takes in the woman who will sit at his right hand, and in those foreign countries where the hostess sits at the right of the ranking man guest, each man conveniently takes in the woman who sits at his right. In America, however, the ranking man guest sits at the hostess's right and takes her in to dinner, so the pairs can no longer be worked out this way. The dinner partners are therefore arranged in pairs so that each man will take in a woman who sits next to him, with the exception of one pair, usually the youngest or those with the lowest rank, who will separate and sit at opposite sides of the table.

When these matters have been decided, envelopes and cards are prepared as follows: The name of each man at the dinner (with the exception, of course, of the host) is written on a small envelope, which contains a small card with the name of his dinner partner written on it. The envelopes are then neatly arranged on a tray and put on a table in the front hall, so that each man guest, as he takes off his overcoat, can take his envelope.

The Table Diagram

At very big formal dinners, a diagram showing the places of seating at the dining-room table is often put in the front hall, so that each man guest will know where he and his dinner partner are to sit. The diagram most commonly used is one made of stiff leather, in the shape of a table, about four or five inches wide and ten inches long. Cards inscribed with each guest's name are stuck between two layers of the leather and the completed diagram is put on a tray next to the dinner-partner envelopes, on the front hall table.

These are the only preparations for a formal dinner which the guests must know about as well as the hosts. We come now to the evening of the dinner party.

In the Hall

At a formal dinner, a footman waits in the front hall to open the door, to take the men's coats and to direct the women to the coatroom where the maid is waiting. No guest should have to wait to have the door opened, and, ideally, he should not even have to ring. At very big dinners, there is usually a chauffeur or a footman outside the door, to open the door of the automobiles, and inside the hall there are often several footmen (or the butler's "adjutant" and one or two footmen) so that one footman will always be ready at the door, another ready to help with the men's coats, and a third, if necessary, ready to direct the women to their coatroom. In houses where there is no room conveniently near the hall for the women's coats, a table in the corner of the hall is arranged with a mirror, and the lady's maid waits there.

As soon as each man has taken off his overcoat, he chooses from the tray the envelope bearing his name, which contains the card with his dinner partner's name. He glances at the card (and he must be sure, if she is a stranger, to be properly introduced before dinnertime) and while he is putting it in his pocket, he studies the diagram of the dinner table.

Announcing the Guests

At the head of the stairs, or just outside the drawing-room door, within easy earshot of the hosts, stands the butler. He asks each guest his name, and announces it to the hostess in a loud clear voice. When married couples arrive, the wife, who is walking ahead of her husband, is the one to whom the butler directs the question, "Name, please?" The wife answers in exactly the form the butler will use: "Mr. and Mrs. Scott," for example. A woman arriving with an extra man answers for herself only, "Mrs. ———," and the butler, after announcing her, then questions the man.

In announcing foreigners, unless they hold one of the official positions listed on page 491, the form used for introductions is also followed: "Lord and Lady Winchester," for example, "Count and Countess de Noailles." (The British, French, and Spanish forms of introduction are on pages 582 to 597.) The only exceptions to this are foreigners without any title other than "Mr." and "Mrs." These are usually announced as "Mr. and Mrs. ———," although one introduces them as "Monsieur de ———" or "Señora de ———."

In the Drawing Room

At all formal dinners and receptions, the hostess stands by the door of the drawing room to greet each guest as he comes in, and the host stands a short distance away. (See also page 437, where the typical phrases and procedures are described.) Any guest, or guests, of honor stands near the hostess, so that new arrivals can be introduced as they come in. As soon as all the guests have arrived, the host and hostess can move about among the guests making any further introductions that may be necessary. After dinner has been announced, when the hostess decides it is time to go into the dining room, she goes to the man who will sit at her right and says, "I think we might go in to dinner." The host goes also to the woman who will sit at his right, and leads the way to the dining room with her. According to the traditional form, each man offers his right arm to his dinner companion and leaves the room arm in arm with her. There is no special order of precedence except that the host and his partner go first, the hostess and her partner last.

In the Dining Room

At a formal luncheon or dinner there must be place cards written with the full name of each guest (see page 490, "Place Cards"). There is, as a rule, no general conversation and the table will turn (there is a description of this on page 439) halfway through the meal. After the most elaborate dinners, when the women have gone into the drawing room, the men do not stay in the dining room. Instead, they go into the library where they are served the usual coffee, liqueurs, and cigars. This is true only in houses which observe the Anglo-American custom of separating men and women after dinner; according to the Continental custom, men and women have coffee and liqueurs together in the drawing room.

After Dinner

The procedure in the drawing room after a formal dinner is exactly like that of the standard procedure described on page 440 until the point at which the men come into the drawing room. Although there may be bridge or other card games, by far the most frequent form of entertainment after a formal dinner is conversation. And, since the dinner is apt to be too large for general conversation, there is inevitably conversation in small groups and tête-à-têtes. (This is described on page 441.) Guests are apt to leave earlier after a formal dinner than after a semiformal dinner and an evening of bridge. Nothing more will be needed, therefore, than the minimum after-dinner service. (See page 296.)

Saying Good-bye

Even if there is no guest of honor, the most formal tradition holds that those who sat at the right of the host and hostess during dinner should be the first to go home. The hostess rises to say good-bye but does not move from her place in the drawing room. The classic good-bye phrases are described on page 441. The host accompanies all guests to the door of the drawing room, and older women who are leaving by themselves to the front door. At a formal dinner, the host does not go to the door of the elevator or outdoors to the automobile, since he has other guests whom he must entertain. In any case, there will be a lady's maid and a butler or footman to help with the coats and to see the guests safely away.

Formal Dances and Receptions

At a big formal reception or dance, the arrangements in the hall are very like those for a formal dinner. The only differences are that each guest is given a ticket for his coat and there are no dinner-partner cards or table diagrams. As at a formal dinner, the butler announces the guests, and the host and hostess stand by the door of the drawing room to receive them. Half an hour, or at most three-quarters of an hour, after the hour set in the invitation, the host and hostess leave their position near the door and move about among the guests. Any late arrivals are not announced, and they must seek out the hosts and make apologies for their lateness. If there is a guest of honor, the hostess may take late arrivals up to be introduced to him, but she need not do so unless there is a reason good enough to warrant interrupting his conversation. At an evening reception, when supper has been announced, the hostess goes to two or three of the older and more important guests and suggests that they go into the dining room. The host goes first with the ranking woman guest and the hostess goes last, as usual, with the ranking man guest.

At very big receptions, however—particularly when there are officials— there is often a seated supper table, in a room separate from the main buffet tables for the other guests. The guests who are to be seated are specially invited by the hosts, during the interval between dinner and supper. There are no dinner-partner cards and there is no table diagram. Instead, when the time comes the guests are shepherded in the usual way between the host who goes first and the hostess who goes last. The supper table is arranged as though for a formal dinner (see immediately below) and all the rules of seating and precedence are observed. (See page 490.) The service follows the formal pattern described on page 483, and there are suggestions for the food on page 484.

Saying good-bye follows the procedure suggested after a formal dinner.

HOUSEKEEPING ARRANGEMENTS FOR FORMAL ENTERTAINING

The essential preliminaries to any formal entertaining are the arrangements concerning the table, the service, and the food. They are discussed here in that order.

Setting the Table

Reduced to its strict technicalities, these are the earmarks of the formal dinner table: It is covered with a cloth, and the cloth is white or the palest cream color, with napkins to match; there are no butter plates, ashtrays, cigarettes or matches; the candles are thin and tall, as all candle flames should be above eye level, plain white or ivory color—no curlicues, no colors, no twisted candles. There are place cards at each place and menu cards. (See page 487.) The place settings remain, in theory, the same; there will be more glasses and more knives and forks than at informal dinners, but the basic pattern of table setting is still followed. The diagrams on the next page show how it is adapted to a formal dinner.

Anything beyond this is a question of taste or aesthetics (the choice of china, glass, linen and silver is discussed on page 339, under "Fashions in Table Decoration"); here, we are concerned only with the theory and technicalities of setting a formal dinner table, and this short little list of three or four items is all that could be considered rules.

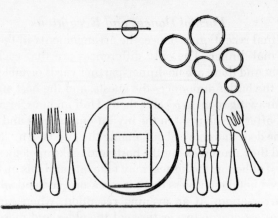

A PLACE SET FOR A FORMAL DINNER

Starting at the table edge, left to right, are: fish fork; meat fork; salad fork; the plate with its napkin and place card; salad knife; meat knife; fish knife; soup spoon; and oyster fork. Above the plate is the menu card, standing upright in a holder. Nearest the menu, in the lower row of glasses is the water glass; just above the meat knife, the red wine glass; and near the soup spoon, the sherry glass. The big glass at the top is a saucer champagne glass, and the smaller one below and to the right of it is for white wine.

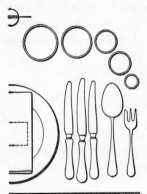

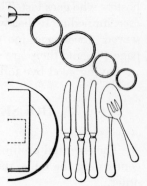

ALTERNATE PLACE SETTINGS FOR A FORMAL DINNER

These places are set for the same menu as that in the above diagram: oysters, soup, fish, meat, salad and dessert. (And probably fruit, too—but, as is true also of dessert, plans to serve fruit at the end of the meal are never apparent in the place setting.) The differences are these: In the diagram at the left, the four wine glasses are arranged in another way: champagne at the left, with water, red wine, white wine and sherry trailing off to the right in that order; and the oyster fork is set parallel with the other implements, instead of resting on an angle on the spoon. In the diagram at the right, three wines are provided for, instead of four: water at the left, and champagne, red wine, and white wine (or sherry) following. All these arrangements of glasses may be changed to fit the circumstances. If there is plenty of room, the best arrangement to follow is the last, with the four glasses in a straight line. When there are many guests, however, and many wines are to be served, one of the other arrangements will probably be the most practical.

Like all rules, of course, they have exceptions—the question of color, for example. White is traditional for formal dinners, but no one could deny that a table set with beige lace over beige satin with candelabra and centerpiece of silver gilt would also be extremely formal. The essential point is that any departures from the traditional are not formal unless they are more elaborate than usual, rather than less: A shell-pink damask tablecloth is considered less formal than a white one. (The mechanics of setting a table with a cloth are given on page 259, and diagrams of the placing of candelabra, flowers, etc., are on page 242.)

The structure of a formal dinner of seven courses—the most elaborate given today—is as follows:

Oysters, clams, or caviar.

Clear soup, hot (in plates) or cold.

Fish, hot or cold.

Meat, always hot—with vegetables.

Salad or asparagus.

Dessert.

Fruit.

Suggestions for food for each of these courses are on pages 484 to 487. Setting the coffee tray is discussed on page 260; serving the coffee, page 293. The serving of cigarettes and cigars is given on page 295; the serving of liqueurs on page 303.

The Service

The service of a formal dinner provides the most striking example of the differences between formal and other entertaining. The traditions on which it is based are all French in origin, and the philosophy which inspired them is concerned mainly with respect for food and decorum, and only secondarily with such usual considerations as practicality and convenience.

To begin with, the formal tradition demands menservants: a butler, and footmen in livery. Two footmen are considered necessary for each service, and the butler, sometimes assisted by an "adjutant," often does nothing but pour the wine. The classic formal dinner is one of thirty-four people, but for the purposes of example and to be a little more realistic, we will imagine a dinner of twenty-two people with three services, a butler and six footmen.

A word of explanation is perhaps necessary here concerning the relation of the number of services to the number of guests. (As explained on page 277, a "service" is a complete set of the serving dishes of each course.) According to the most traditional and formal French custom, a meal should not be served too quickly. The dishes and sauces of each course must be served together, one immediately after the other, since it would spoil the mixture of flavor were there any delay, but a little delay between courses is not objectionable. Therefore, formal custom demands two footmen to each service, but the strictest and most formal opinion does not approve fewer than eight, or at least seven, guests to each service; and nine, for example, is preferred to seven. American custom has sometimes leaned toward six guests to a service, but this is not approved because it suggests that speed, and not the food, is all-important.

When the guests come into the dining room, the butler is standing behind the hostess's chair, the first footman behind the host's chair, and the other footmen (if the topography of the dining room allows it) at equal distances between these two, at a point about eight or ten feet back of the chairs. Naturally, all the guests will not seat themselves at precisely the same moment; and it is, therefore, quite easy for the butler to push in the chair of the hostess and of the two women nearest her, and for the first footman to push in the chair of the woman to the right of the host and of two other women guests, and so on. If neither the butler nor footman seems available at the proper moment, a man can push in the chair of the woman whom he has taken in to dinner, but in most cases it is unnecessary.

As soon as each guest has been served the oysters, the butler pours the wine for that course; and when the first course has been eaten, soup is served. (See page 300.) As soon as all the guests have received their soup, the butler pours the sherry, followed by a footman who offers Melba toast in a breadbasket to each guest. When the soup is done, the soup plates are removed and the fish plates set down. The three services of fish are brought in and the butler then brings the wine. The footmen follow after with the breadbasket. The services of meat, the sauces, vegetables, wine, and rolls follow in that order. The meat plates are removed, the salad plates are brought and the table is finally cleared for the dessert course. (See pages 276-279.) Dessert plates are then brought with only a spoon and fork on them, since this is a most formal dinner. Dessert is served, followed by any cake or cookies; the wineglasses are filled. As soon as dessert is over the plates are removed and replaced immediately by the fruit plates with finger bowl, fruit knife and fork. Fruit is served and, without having the fruit plates removed, candy.

If this is a formal dinner in the French tradition, the men and women will leave the room together and have their coffee and liqueurs together in the drawing room. If it follows the more usual American and English tradition, the women will go into the drawing room and the men will go to the library for their coffee, cigars, and liqueurs. In England, the men would remain for their port. At less stiffly formal dinners, or whenever it is more convenient, the men stay in the dining room and they are served their coffee, cigars, and liqueurs at the dining-room table. The details of this service are given on page 293, "Coffee"; page 295, "Cigarettes and Cigars"; and page 303, "Liqueurs."

The Food and Wine

The choice of food for a most elaborate formal dinner is still governed by the traditional rules of the great school of French cooking. The old rules have been given a slightly different interpretation to fit them better into modern life, but there is still a very definite and somewhat inflexible form which is accepted both here and abroad. Dinners such as these, of course, are extremely rare today, in any country in the world. But in official and diplomatic life, they must still be given, and so we have listed here a few dishes as samples of those which are considered correct according to the very highest and most critical standards, together with the customary wines. The correct French title for each dish is given in parentheses to show how it is written on the menu. (See page 487.)

As we have said, the maximum number of courses is seven. Suggestions are listed course by course:

1. Oysters on the half shell ("Huîtres en coquilles"); or clams on the half shell ("Clams"); or caviar ("Caviar"). See pages 305 and 306 for customary ways of serving. The classic wine is a white Burgundy.

2. Soup almost always hot and, if so, always served in plates. Because formal dinners have more courses than informal dinners, a clear soup is naturally chosen more often than a heavy one and, therefore, clear soups have come to be regarded as more "formal" than thick ones. The most usual soups for formal dinners are beef consommé with finely cut-up vegetables ("Consommé Brunoise"); essence of tomato, very clear and strengthened with beef stock ("Consommé Madrilène"); turtle soup, with small pieces of turtle meat in it, flavored with sherry ("Tortue verte"); oxtail soup ("Oxtail soup"; this soup did not originate in France and, therefore, the English form is correct on the menu); and chicken consommé ("Consommé de volaille"). The classic wine is sherry.

For a formal dinner in hot weather, jellied soup can be served in cups. Jellied soup is, of course, impossible in plates, but even cold soup in plates is entirely against the formal French tradition. The soup should be chilled until it begins to thicken and is only very lightly jellied; stiff jellies should be avoided. The most usual cold soups are beef or chicken consommé ("Consommé en gelée") or tomato consommé ("Consommé Madrilène en gelée").

Another soup for formal dinners is borscht, a clear beet soup with a beef and duck stock base, served with a few shreds of beets and a dollop of sour cream in the middle. It can be served either hot ("Borscht à la Russe") or cold ("Borscht à la Russe en gelée"). The wine served is sherry.

3. Fish, hot or cold: filets of sole in a sauce of cream, mushrooms, and shallots ("Filets de sole Bonne Femme"); halibut cooked in fish stock and white wine, with hollandaise sauce served separately ("Chicken halibut au court-bouillon—Sauce Hollandaise." "Sauce Hollandaise" is listed on a separate line in the menu—see the rules for writing the menu on page 270. "Chicken halibut" is written in English on the menu because it is a fish that is unknown on the Continent, where the nearest equivalent is "turbot." In France it is written, "Turbot au court-bouillon . . . etc."); pompano cooked with white wine and shallots ("Pompano Bercy"); filets of sea bass, cooked in the same way ("Suprême de sea bass Bercy").

The more usual cold fish dishes are salmon with mayonnaise sauce ("Saumon froid—Sauce mayonnaise"), or salmon with "sauce verte," a sauce made with a mayonnaise base which is mixed with a paste of finely chopped tarragon, chives, chervil, watercress leaf, and cooked spinach ("Saumon froid—Sauce verte"); brook trout with tarragon in aspic, served either with mayonnaise sauce or sauce verte ("Aspic de truites à l'estragon—Sauce verte" or, "Sauce mayonnaise"). Note that potatoes are not served with fish at a formal dinner, except when they are included in the garniture on the platter. The suitable wine is a white Rhine wine.

4. Meat dishes for a very elaborate dinner are rich and heavy: filet of beef, served with a "garniture" of stuffed mushrooms and tomatoes filling out the platter and with Madeira sauce ("Filet de boeuf Richelieu—Sauce Madère"); saddle or leg of lamb served with a garniture of artichoke hearts, string beans, peas and carrots ("Selle d' agneau jardinière" or, "Gigot d'agneau jardinière"); saddle of lamb, served with a garniture of artichoke hearts ("Selle d'agneau Chivry"); or veal cooked in the same way ("Selle de veau Chivry"); rump of beef served with a garniture of small carrots, small potato balls, and peas ("Culotte de boeuf bourgeoise"); smoked beef tongue cooked in the same way as the rump of beef ("Langue de boeuf fumée bourgeoise"); guinea hen with bread sauce ("Pintades rôties"); and in our modern rules almost any kind of game: wild duck, pheasant, grouse, quail, or woodcock. Details concerning the serving of game will be found on pages 306 to 307.

In the old-fashioned and most strictly formal dinners, vegetables were not always served separately, except for asparagus which was a course by itself. Most of the garnitures included vegetables, and since there were so many courses, extra vegetables were not considered necessary. Now that there are fewer courses, however, it has become the fashion to serve vegetables and to list them on the menu. Since potatoes are listed first on the menu and are served before other vegetables, we shall discuss them first.

The classic ways of serving potatoes are: potato cakes made of mashed potato mixed with egg ("Pommes Duchesse"); potato balls, made with mashed potato and puff paste, mixed half-and-half, and cooked in deep fat ("Pommes Dauphine"); potato balls, cut out of the whole potato to a size about as big as an olive, browned in fat ("Pommes noisettes"); a ballooned potato, cooked in a most complicated way, in fats of different temperatures ("Pommes soufflées").

The second vegetable is often one of these: braised celery ("Céleris braisés"); spinach—plain ("Epinards en branche") or creamed ("Epinards à la crème"); string beans ("Haricots verts au beurre"); and peas ("Petits pois"). A rule of formal dinners is that onions cannot be served, even in a garniture. There are some elaborately concealed exceptions to this, but it is a rule. The standard wine is claret (red Bordeaux) or, with game, Burgundy.

5. At a most formal dinner such as this, the course that comes immediately before the dessert can only be one of the following: a hot roast meat, often game, served with salad (this is extremely rare nowadays, when two heavy meats are almost never seen on the same menu); a cold dish served with salad; or asparagus, either hot or cold, served with hollandaise, mousseline, or vinaigrette sauce.

The most usual fifth course is one of the following: cold Virginia ham, served with a vegetable salad with French dressing ("Jambon de Virginie froid—Salade de legumes frais"); a platter of breast of chicken covered with white "chaud-froid" sauce stuffed with pâté de foie gras and resting on aspic ("Suprême de volaille Jeannette"), served with a romaine salad ("Salade de romaines"), or a vegetable salad with Russian dressing ("Salade Russe"); a mold of pâté de foie gras covered with aspic ("Aspic de foie gras de Strasbourg"), served with endive salad ("Salade d'endives"). Note that pâté de foie gras should never, according to the highest standards, be served on a platter with lettuce because the oil and vinegar of the dressing destroys the flavor of the pâté. In its most rigid interpretation, this means that lettuce even without dressing should not even be used as the garniture on a platter containing pâté de foie gras. Broken aspic can be used as a garniture instead. Another cold dish which could be used for the fifth course is a ring of Roquefort cheese in aspic, with mayonnaise sauce in the middle of the ring ("Aspic de Roquefort à la mayonnaise"), served with escarole salad ("Salade d'escaroles").

If asparagus is served as the fifth course, it is presented by itself on a platter resting on a folded napkin, followed by a hollandaise sauce ("Asperges—Sauce Hollandaise"), or a more delicate sauce of hollandaise mixed with whipped cream ("Asperges—Sauce mousseline"). If asparagus is served cold, it is presented in the same way and followed by a vinaigrette sauce ("Sauce vinaigrette"). Note that cold asparagus is one of the few dishes that should never be served very cold, as icing destroys the flavor completely. No new wine is served with the salad course.

6. The classic desserts for a formal dinner are: ice cream, water ice, a stiff variation of water ice which is called "granité"; or mousse, which is frozen, flavored whipped cream. Among the ice cream desserts are: a mold of vanilla ice cream covered with fine shavings of bitter chocolate ("Glace vanille"); a hollow mold of vanilla ice cream filled and sprinkled with powdered chocolate ("Glace vanille"); a mold of plain vanilla ice cream edged with crystallized ginger ("Glace Manchu"); a mold of vanilla ice cream bordered with whole marrons glacés ("Glace vanille Nesselrode"), or a hollow mold of vanilla ice cream filled and decorated with riced puree of marrons glacés ("Glace Nesselrode"); a hollow mold of vanilla ice cream filled and decorated with a mixture of powdered coffee and chocolate ("Parfait au café"); a mold

of vanilla ice cream mixed and decorated with finely chopped, toasted hazelnuts ("Glace pralinée"). Among the water ices there are: a mold of pineapple water ice flavored with rum ("Sorbet d'ananas"); a mold of strawberry ice flavored with kirsch ("Sorbet de fraises"); or a mold of orange water ice flavored with Cointreau ("Sorbet à l'orange"). Any of these three water ices can be served with a border of strawberries, and wild strawberries are the best. The two most usual granités are flavored either with orange or lemon ("Granité à l'orange," or "Granité au citron"). The best mousses are: a mold of strawberry mousse with a border of fresh crushed strawberries ("Mousse aux fraises"); a mold of vanilla mousse with a border of fresh crushed raspberries ("Mousse aux framboises"), or a raspberry mousse with a border of raspberries ("Mousse aux framboises"). And there is also, of course, that somewhat overworked standby, "Bombe Alaska," which is ice cream in a baked meringue shell.

With the dessert, and listed on the menu, an assortment of flat brittle little cookies and macaroons is usually served ("Friandises"). The classic wine is champagne.

7. The only possible course after the dessert is fruit. One or two of the following could be served: pears, peaches, nectarines, grapes, cherries, apricots, plums. Such fruit is usually served on a flat dish or in a shallow bowl sometimes edged with grape or laurel leaves. There is another way of serving grapes, however, which is particularly good after a long heavy meal. The bunches of grapes are cut into small clusters and served on ice in a deep bowl which is filled with ice about three-quarters of the way up. Cherries can also be served in this way. Fruit is never listed on the menu (see page 271).

After the fruit, one kind of chocolate candy and one kind of mint or candied fruit may be served, but these do not, of course, constitute a course.

MENU CARDS AND PLACE CARDS

In a Private House

Menus for formal, or official, meals in a private house must be written or engraved in French, with the very few exceptions of those dishes which are English or American in origin; as, for example, clams, oxtail soup, and halibut. If the menus are engraved, which is done only on extremely rare occasions, script is used. But it should be noted that, although the coat of arms is embossed in silver or gold, the script should always be engraved in black. (A description of the card itself, which is the same as that used for a semiformal dinner, is on page 270.) When a menu is written, black ink should be used, and the handwriting should resemble script as much as possible; an irregular handwriting, or any handwriting which departs too widely from the script form, is out of place on formal tables. The names of the dishes may be preceded by "Le," "La," or "Les"—"La salade Russe," for example, or "Les épinards en branche"—but this is entirely a matter of taste.

The menu card should be held upright in a small stand. As a rule, these stands are made of silver or silver gilt, although there are some modern ones of clear glass or colorless plastic. There should be one menu in front of the host, about six or eight inches above the upper rim of the place plate, one in front of the hostess, and one for each three guests down each side of the table. In writing the menu, all the rules given on page 271 must be observed, and it is also customary to write the date in French in the lower corner of the menu card, usually the left corner, as follows: "le 17 Janvier 1947" or "12 Mai 1948."

Menu

Les huîtres en coquilles

Le consommé Brunoise

Le pompano Bercy

Le filet de boeuf Richelieu
  La sauce Madère
  Les pommes soufflées
Les haricots verts au beurre

Le suprême de volaille Jeannette
  La salade Russe

La mousse aux fraises
  Les friandises

Le 15 Décembre, 1948

MENU OF A FORMAL DINNER

*PLACE CARD FOR A
FORMAL DINNER*

Mrs. Walcott

*Like the menu card
shown above, this place
card is decorated with a
full coat of arms em-
bossed in gold. The
beveled edges of both
cards are gilded, also.*

At Public Banquets

For the most elaborate public banquets, special menu cards are usually planned far in advance. The classic menu card for formal dinners can be used, but a folded menu card on which the wines can be listed is more generally chosen. These are made of a single fold of heavy glazed paper about 5½ by 8½, or 6 by 9 inches. The outside is often engraved in color with an emblem or device (flags, of course, are inevitable at international banquets), and below this is the name of the organization or society which is giving the dinner. The date also can be engraved here. For example:

Annual Dinner of the Society of . . . .
January 17th, 1948

or if the dinner is given in honor of someone:

Dinner of the Society of the . . . .
in honor of
The Honorable . . . .
January 17th, 1948

On the back of this page is the wine list, with the menu facing on the third page. Each wine is listed separately on a single line directly across from the course which it accompanies, and the name, not the generic type of the wine, should be given. For example:

Chablis 1940 (This would be opposite oysters or caviar; the wine suggested is a dry white Burgundy.)

Solera 1847 (Opposite the soup; the wine suggested is a sherry.)

Traminet 1924 (Fish; the wine suggested is a Rhine wine.)

Haut Brion 1933 (Meat; the wine suggested is a red Bordeaux, or claret, but it might be a Burgundy—Chambertin, 1941, for example—instead. Two red wines are rarely served at the same meal, now that the custom of serving two heavy meats has been abandoned.)

Bollinger 1928 (Dessert; the wine suggested is champagne.)

On the third page, the menu is written or, more often, engraved in French, exactly as it would be for a most formal dinner, as shown on the opposite page. The date is written or engraved in the lower corner of the menu as suggested on page 488 unless it appears on the first page as shown above. For a public dinner of a business nature, the first two pages are engraved in the same way, but the menu is often written in English instead of French.

Another menu for public banquets consists of eight pages instead of four. The first page is engraved with an emblem or device only; and the second page is blank. The third page carries the heading "Annual Dinner . . . ." or "Dinner of the Society . . . ." The fourth lists the wines; the fifth, the menu; and the following pages are blank. This menu is usually held together by a tasseled silk cord in some color that goes well with the decorations.

The food served at a formal public banquet is exactly like that served at a formal dinner in a private house. (See pages 484 to 487 for suggestions.)

Place Cards

At formal meals, the names must be written on the place cards in full. The form to be followed is that used in introducing one guest to another. For example, "Mr. Carpenter," "Mrs. Walcott," "The Chief Justice," "The Speaker," "The Secretary of Agriculture," "The American Ambassador," or in countries where the title "Excellency" is given to ambassadors, "H. E. the French Ambassador." (Note that "His Excellency" is abbreviated on a place card; "His Highness" and "His Royal Highness" are abbreviated in the same way, "H. H." or "H. R. H.") The correct forms to be used in introductions are fully covered in the chapter, "Forms of Address," except for a few personages of such importance that no form of introduction is ever used. A list of these exceptions follows to show how their place cards are written:

For the President of the United States: "The President" or, in a foreign country, "The President of . . . ."
For an apostolic delegate: "H. E., the Apostolic Delegate"
For a patriarch: "H. H., the Patriarch of . . . ."
For a cardinal: "His Eminence, Cardinal . . . ."

For formal dinners, script handwriting should be used for place cards, as it is for menu cards. (On pages 273 and 274, in the chapter, "Setting the Table," the cards and their placement on the table are fully discussed.)

ENTERTAINING OFFICIALS

It should be made clear at the very beginning of this section that we are not here discussing the protocol and procedure of state dinners or official entertaining. We are discussing only the procedure that is followed when important officials or those who have a set and definite rank are entertained formally by private individuals.

At an informal or semiformal dinner, no matter how important or official the guests, there would be no change in the usual procedure described on pages 436 to 442. If several important guests are expected, the hostess will, of course, make sure that they are properly seated in the order of their rank at the table, but apart from this minor detail there is no change. Friends who happen to be officials need not make the dinner "official" or even formal. But the formal entertainment of officials is another matter.

The Invitations

When one is entertaining officials, or guests who have a set rank, points which need never be considered in the usual procedure of formal entertaining become immediately evident. The first point comes when one is making up the list of guests. If one is giving a dinner, or a reception where there will be a seated supper, one must be careful not to invite together so many high-ranking guests that some will be offended by being seated—as they quite properly would have to be—far from the head of the table. Although the order of precedence is fairly explicit (see page 492) there are often borderline decisions of great delicacy, and it is wiser to avoid them if possible.

The second point concerning the invitations arises only if one is entertaining in honor of a guest of rank or official position. This point is the old rule that one should not send an engraved, formal invitation to one whose rank or position is higher than that of the guest of honor—one should not, for example, invite an ambassador formally "to meet" a minister, or a general "to meet" a colonel. This does not apply, of course, to informal verbal invitations; nor to partially engraved invitations which bear no mention of ". . . in honor of ————." But it does apply to all fully engraved invitations and to partially engraved invitations by which guests are specifically invited to meet a guest of honor.

Seating Officials

An important point to remember in seating officials is that husband and wife are treated as equal in rank. A woman takes her husband's rank; and a man also, if he is married to a woman official, is seated in a place equal to hers. In other words, the husband of a woman-Senator is seated above a Representative. This is never a desirable situation and hostesses who entertain a great many such officials are careful to avoid it as far as possible.

Other Preliminaries

The other preliminaries of the dinner are exactly like those for any formal dinner. The arrangements concerning the table, the food, the menus and place cards and the service are unchanged. The procedure in the front hall, with footmen, trays of dinner-partner envelopes and table diagram are all as described on pages 478 to 481, but there is a change in the way certain guests are announced, and in the order in which the hosts and their guests go in to the dining room.

Announcing the Guests

Most of those who hold official positions are announced according to the usual form, which is exactly like that used in introductions. (See page 479, "Announcing the Guests.") But certain very important officials are announced by title, rather than by name, and not always as they are introduced. Further, if one of these officials is accompanied by his wife, his name is announced before hers, and technically he precedes her into the room. (Most officials ignore this.) This is the list of those to whom these rules apply:

> Chiefs of State
>
> Vice Presidents
>
> The Chief Justice of the Supreme Court
>
> Members of the Cabinet
>
> Governors
>
> Archbishops
>
> Bishops
>
> Mayors of very large cities
>
> Ambassadors of foreign countries
>
> Ministers of foreign countries

The forms used by the butler in announcing these officials are:

> "The President" or, for a president outside
> his country, "The President of ...."
> "The Vice President"
> "The Chief Justice"
> "The Secretary of the Interior"
> "The Governor" or, outside his state,
> "The Governor of New Mexico"
> "The Archbishop of New York"
> "The Bishop of Baltimore"
> "The Mayor" or, outside his city,
> "The Mayor of ...."
> "The Ambassador of ...." *
> "The .... Minister" *

The wives of all these gentlemen are announced according to the form used in introductions. For example, after the butler has announced the title of the official, there is a slight pause and the wife's name is announced: "The Secretary of the Interior"—a pause—"Mrs. Gibson." Only at official or state functions are official or titled guests announced with the full ceremony of all their complimentary titles: "His Excellency, the Chinese Ambassador." (See "Forms of Address"; pages 557 to 581.)

Going in to Dinner

When entertaining a chief of state, a member of a royal family, an archbishop or a cardinal, there is a change in the usual order for going in to the dining room. At most formal dinners, the host goes first with the ranking woman guest and the hostess last, with the ranking man guest, as described on page 480. When one of these important officials is present, however, the hostess goes in first with the ranking man guest, the host following next with the ranking woman guest.

Order of Precedence of Officials

Official, ecclesiastical, and diplomatic seating is a matter of rigid protocol. In the hierarchy of church and state, and, in foreign countries, in the ranking of nobility, each position carries a specific rating. Because such rankings may differ in different countries, it is impossible to list all the variations here, and we shall confine ourselves to the American order of precedence. Americans who plan to do a great deal of entertaining in a foreign country should consult the official in charge of protocol in the Foreign Office of that government. American embassies and legations can also be very helpful in these matters.

It has often been objected that protocol is a boring and tiresome preliminary to any official entertaining. And, of course, if one is entertaining a great many official people, the seating of a dinner can mean a great deal of work. It has, however, an immensely practical basis. Before the Congress of Vienna in 1815, there was no such thing as an internationally accepted protocol. Ambassadors were

---

* Note that ambassadors are sometimes, "The .... Ambassador" and sometimes, "The Ambassador of ....," and that some ministers are "The .... Minister," and others, "The Minister of ...." A list of the exact titles will be found on page 565 in the chapter, "Forms of Address."

ranked according to the relative importance of the countries which they represented, and entertaining had become a matter of great political significance and a source of much ill feeling. The value of protocol, or of any such system, is that it removes the element of personal judgment and appraisal.

Whenever the protocol is exact and explicit, age has no bearing on the order of precedence. A very young ambassador must outrank the most venerable senator in an American house, because he is the representative of a foreign chief of state in America. A foreign ambassador who is only visiting America en route to his post in another country has, however, no official position in this country and would not be ranked above any important American official, even in an American house. The question of whether a house is "American," or not, is not only a matter of whether or not the house is literally standing on land within the borders of the United States. All foreign embassies and legations in Washington are technically "on foreign soil" and the customs followed there are not like those of American houses. This is also true of the houses of members of the diplomatic missions, and even of the houses of foreigners in America. In a "foreign house" Americans are given courtesy precedence whenever possible, and the same is true of foreigners in American houses.

Foreign hostesses, however, have a much easier time arranging the seating of important officials than American hostesses have. Foreign protocol is quite definite and the position of each official is clearly listed in relation to other officials. For example, there is no question in England as to where a bishop ranks in relation to a member of Parliament because there is an official and explicit rating for each in books and official lists which are open to the public. In the United States, however, there are no such lists. The order of precedence is locked in a State Department safe and there is no way of knowing—certainly and officially—whether or not a bishop should be ranked above a Senator. With the subject thus left open to guess work, a few lists have been drawn up unofficially, based on common sense and practical experience of past decisions. Such a list cannot be accepted as final, and the one given here is offered only as a guide.

The following is the order of precedence for American houses:

Foreign Chief of State

The President of the United States

The Vice President

The Chief Justice

The Apostolic Delegate or a Cardinal. (Ecclesiastics are often, by courtesy, accorded a very high ranking, but this is open to question. In a Catholic house, or on a special occasion, a Cardinal might be given this place, otherwise he might be placed just above the Cabinet.)

Foreign Ambassadors ranked according to date of presentation of credentials

Speaker of the House

Ministers Plenipotentiary representing foreign countries, ranked as are Ambassadors

Associate Justices of the Supreme Court

Special Ambassadors—not accredited to the United States Government (e.g., representatives at the United Nations); but note that the United States representative to the United Nations, although ranked with other Ambassadors, is never put before the Secretary of State.

The Secretary of State

The Secretary of the Treasury

The Secretary of Defense

The Attorney General

The Postmaster General

The Secretary of the Interior

The Secretary of Agriculture

The Secretary of Commerce

The Secretary of Labor

Governor of a State—in his own State outranks all but Presidents. Among Governors, a Governor is ranked according to the length of office or, if two Governors were elected in the same year, according to the date of the entry of their respective States into the Union.

Archbishop

Senators ranked according to the date of their election, or, if elected in the same year, according to the date of the entry of their respective States into the Union.

Representatives—ranked as Senators are

Secretary of the Department of the Army

Secretary of the Department of the Navy

Secretary of the Department of the Air Force

Chief of Staff of the Army

Chief of Naval Operations

Chief of Staff of the Air Force

General, 5 stars

Admiral, 5 stars

Under Secretary of State

Chargés d'Affaires of foreign States

Other Under Secretaries and the Solicitor General, in Cabinet order

General, 4 stars

Admiral, 4 stars

Commandant of the Marine Corps—by Act of Congress, passed in 1947, the Commandant is a "4-star" General.

Assistant Secretaries of Cabinet

Bishop

Lieutenant General

Vice Admiral

Counselors of foreign Embassies and Legations

Major General

Rear Admiral (upper half)

Brigadier General

Rear Admiral (lower half) and Commodore

Military and Naval Attachés of foreign Embassies and Legations according to rank—but given precedence over American officers of equal rank

First Secretaries of Foreign Embassies and Legations

Lieutenant-Governor of a State, President of a State Senate, Speaker of a State Assembly

State Senator, State Justice, Mayor

Monsignor

State Assemblyman

Directors of the Federal Reserve

Commissioners of Interstate Commerce

Secretary of the Smithsonian Institution

Director of the Pan-American Union

Second and Third Secretaries of foreign Embassies and Legations

Generally speaking, the rule of thumb for the precedence of officials follows the order suggested by this list: elected executives (the President), the legislative branch (the Vice President, as representative of the Senate) and the judiciary (the Chief Justice). For example, if one had invited the Lieutenant Governor, a State Senator, a State Assemblyman, and a judge of the local court, the seating would follow that order. A Monsignor invited to the same dinner would be placed below the State Senator and above the Assemblyman. By courtesy, clergymen may be placed very high in the order of precedence; and foreigners who represent a foreign state, or belong to a foreign mission, must be given an important place.

The order of precedence for members of the armed forces follows the order of precedence of the services: Army, Navy, Air Force, Marine Corps. Officers of equal rank in separate services are placed accordingly. For example, a full Lieutenant in the Navy, although of equal rank with a Captain in the Army, is seated below him at table. Officers of equal rank in the same service are placed according to the date of their commission.

Again, it must be emphasized that all the suggestions given here are offered only as a guide—not as a definitive listing. They explain some of the general principles on which American precedence is based, but courtesy is the basis of them all. Whenever it is hard to decide which guest should precede another, a decision based on obvious considerations of courtesy and kindness is always the wise one.

Order of Precedence in the United Nations

The order of precedence of officials of the United Nations has not yet been finally or definitely established, and it is always wise to consult the office of the Chief of Protocol when officials of almost equal rank are to be invited together. The broad outlines of precedence may, however, be set down and, when the decisions are not too difficult, they may be used as a guide.

Generally speaking, the representatives of foreign governments accredited to the United States government outrank the representatives of foreign governments at the United Nations except at gatherings given by the United Nations or in honor of the United Nations and of its representatives. Within the hierarchy of the United Nations itself, the General Assembly during the time it is in session outranks the Security Council and all other councils. The order of precedence at such times is:

> The President of the General Assembly
> The Secretary General of the United Nations
> The President of the Security Council

When the Assembly is not in session, the President of the Security Council outranks the Secretary General of the United Nations.

Within the Assembly itself, the order of precedence is alphabetical, but one must take two other rulings into consideration. The first is that heads of missions with the rank of Ambassador are usually placed above heads of missions with the rank of Minister Plenipotentiary; and the second is that the function of an official may sometimes cause both alphabetical order and diplomatic rank to be ignored. For example, let us consider an official dinner given for the General Committee of the General Assembly. (The General Committee is made up of the President of the General Assembly, the seven Vice Presidents of the General Assembly, and the Chairmen of the main Committees of the Assembly.) At such a dinner, a Minister Plenipotentiary, Vice President of the General Assembly, would be placed before an Ambassador, Chairman of a Committee. This would apply also to other Councils and Committees.

Among the organizations of the United Nations, the Security Council outranks all others (e.g., the Economic and Social Council, the Trusteeship Council) because it is listed first under the Charter, it is in permanent session, and it is the political expression of the United Nations. The order of precedence of Councils and Committees below the Security Council is determined by the order of listing. Within the Security Council this is the order of precedence:

> The President of the Council
> The outgoing President of the Council
> The incoming President of the Council
> The representative who, in Council meetings,
>   sits at the right of the outgoing President
> The representative who sits at the left of
>   the incoming President
> The representative who sits at the right of the one
>   at the right of the outgoing President, etc.

The order of seating at the Council meetings determines the precedence of each member and follows the monthly rotation of the Council Presidency; so when two representatives—both of Ambassadorial rank—are invited together, the seating must be planned as of the date of the dinner.

Junior members of missions who have equal rank in each mission are ranked according to the precedence of their chiefs. If the Chinese representative, for example, is President of the Security Council, the member of his delegation who is immediately below him would outrank the second member of any other delegation.

Beyond these very rudimentary points, there is no safe guide except the Protocol Office of the United Nations itself.

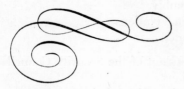 

63

On Being Entertained at the White House

LIKE AN invitation to a royal palace, an invitation to the White House cannot be refused. No previous engagement, no trip out of town, no family wedding or christening can be used as an excuse.

FORMAL INVITATIONS TO THE WHITE HOUSE

A formal invitation to the White House is sent according to the usual engraved form, but the answer is worded a little differently:

Mr. and Mrs. Herbert Charles
have the honour of accepting
the kind invitation of
The President and Mrs. Adams
to dine
on Thursday, the fourteenth of December,
at eight o'clock

Like other acceptances, this is written by hand on formal house writing paper, either engraved or plain. See page 519 for a facsimile of an acceptance.

If one has already accepted an invitation to dine informally somewhere else on that night, one need only telephone or write a letter excusing oneself (. . . "I'm so sorry but we have been asked to the White House on that evening . . .") If one has already accepted a formal invitation for that evening, one must send a formal written excuse to the original hostess in this form:

Mr. and Mrs. Herbert Charles
regret exceedingly that an invitation to
the White House
prevents their keeping
their engagement to dine
on Thursday, the fourteenth of December

There are, however, three valid grounds for regretting an invitation to the White House, and although a reason is not always given in regretting an engraved invitation, a reason must be given in regretting an invitation to the White House (or a royal invitation). The grounds are severe illness, absence in some distant place (Europe or South America, for example) from which return is obviously impossible, and the very recent death of a very close relative. The form is:

Mr. and Mrs. Herbert Charles
regret that owing to the illness *
of Mrs. Charles
they will be unable to accept
the very kind invitation of
The President and Mrs. Adams
to dine
on Thursday, the fourteenth of December

or,

owing to the absence in Scotland
of Mr. Charles

or,

owing to the recent death
of the mother of Mrs. Charles

INFORMAL INVITATIONS TO THE WHITE HOUSE

Informal invitations to dinner or luncheon often come in letters, telegrams, or telephone messages from the President's secretary or his wife's secretary. In any of these cases, the answer should be sent, in the same form, to the secretary who sent the invitation. For example, to an invitation worded like this:

Dear Mrs. Charles,

Mrs. Adams hopes that you will be able to lunch with her at the White House on Saturday, February fourteenth. Luncheon will be at one o'clock.

Yours truly,
Margaret Hanson
Secretary to Mrs. Adams

one would reply in this form:

Dear Miss Hanson,

Would you be kind enough to tell Mrs. Adams that I shall be

* Or, very grave illness.

delighted to lunch at the White House next Saturday, the fourteenth of February, at one o'clock. With many thanks,

Sincerely,
Mary Charles

Or, to this invitation:

Dear Mrs. Charles,

The President and Mrs. Adams have asked me to invite you and Mr. Charles to dine at the White House on Tuesday, the twenty-second of February, at eight o'clock, black tie.

Yours truly,
Elizabeth Hawkes
Secretary to the President

the acceptance would be:

Dear Miss Hawkes,

My husband and I shall be delighted to accept the very kind invitation of the President and Mrs. Adams to dine at the White House on Tuesday, February twenty-second, at eight o'clock. With many thanks,

Sincerely,
Mary Charles

These acceptances should be written on formal "house" paper, either engraved or plain. The placing of the date and the addressing of the envelope are shown on pages 540 and 539 in the chapter "Letters."

AT THE GATE

The names of the guests expected at the White House are always given to those who guard the gate. Guests need only stop, wait a moment while their names are checked against the list, and proceed as soon as they have been given permission. At the door, the butler will indicate where coats and hats are to be left, and in which room the guests are to wait. It cannot be emphasized too strongly that all guests at the White House must be prompt. They should arrive at the gate at least ten minutes before the appointed hour.

SAYING "HOW DO YOU DO"

When all the guests are assembled, the President and his wife "make the circle," greeting each guest in turn. Whether at the most formal dinner or the most informal luncheon, guests are expected to stand when the President and his wife come in. Men bow as they shake hands, and women incline their heads, but there is no other ceremony. (See also "Official Introductions," page 6.)

ADDRESSING THE PRESIDENT AND HIS WIFE

In speaking to the President, the correct form of address is "Mr. President." This is used at least once or twice during any conversation, but not, necessarily, in every sentence. Men can vary "Mr. President" with "Sir," but "Sir" is not used by women except in speaking to royalty. There is no special form of address for the President's wife. She is always spoken to and referred to as "Mrs. ———" —"Mrs. Adams," for example.

GUESTS SHOULD STAND

Guests should remain standing as long as the President or his wife is standing. But, of course, should the President (or his wife) start a conversation and sit down, those to whom he is talking should sit down also.

GOING IN TO THE DINING ROOM

At formal dinners, the President and his wife will go first in to the dining room, he with the ranking woman guest, she following immediately after with the ranking man guest. At informal meals, this system may be followed in a less rigid way; or it may be abandoned entirely and the procedure will follow the usual informal American pattern. In any case, the guest who goes in to the dining room with either the President or his wife should always step back to allow the other to go first through the doorways. As a rule, at informal dinners or luncheons, the President will always ask a woman guest to precede him, but the gesture of stepping back must be made by a woman guest.

AFTER DINNER

After dinner, the President and his wife will say good-bye to their guests when they decide the time has come. Again, all guests should rise, the President and his wife will make the circle, and leave the room. When they have gone, the guests say good-bye to each other, find their coats and hats and leave. It is a rule that no one can leave—or make any suggestion of leaving—until the President and his wife have left the room.

RECEPTIONS AT THE WHITE HOUSE

Official receptions at the White House are, as a rule, so crowded that there is nothing that a guest need do but arrive on time, leave his hat and coat as directed, stand in line, shake hands briefly (and, if he is considerate, gently) with the President and his wife, stand around with other guests until the last one has greeted the President, and finally go home. One is not expected, on being presented to the President and his wife, to say anything more than "How do you do." Before and after one has been received, one may talk to any stranger who seems agreeable and friendly, since, as everywhere, the roof constitutes an introduction.

At smaller receptions, one follows exactly the same procedure as at a dinner. The two cardinal points of White House etiquette are that no guest is late and that no guest leaves before the President and his wife have gone upstairs.

LEAVING VISITING CARDS

When one has been entertained at the White House, one must leave cards the next day; or, at least, not longer than three days afterwards. The customs described in detail on page 598 should be followed, a single man leaving two cards; a single woman, one; a married couple a "Mr. and Mrs." card and one of the husband's cards. The other points are taken up one by one on page 598, but it should be mentioned that in leaving cards at the White House, or at the house of any important personage, it is always more polite to leave them oneself.

DRESSING TO GO TO THE WHITE HOUSE

As in the case of other engraved invitations, an engraved invitation to the White House now means "Black tie," unless "White tie" is written on the card. At the White House, "Black tie" means that the men wear stiff shirts and collars with the usual dinner jacket. Women need not wear gloves.

When the invitation bears the notation "White tie," or "Decorations," full evening dress is worn. (Men's evening clothes are fully described on page 619, decorations on page 627.) Women wear evening dresses and long gloves. (See page 35, "Gloves.")

For any luncheon, no matter how informal, women should always wear a hat, stockings, and gloves. Gloves worn at luncheon should be taken off in the living room before one goes into the dining room. Or one can take them off when one takes off one's coat and carry them with the purse. Men should dress with equal formality. If the luncheon is official, or formal, they should wear cutaways or a black sack coat with striped trousers. (See page 617 in the chapter, "Men's Clothes.") At informal luncheons, the first choice would be a dark blue serge suit with a white shirt, or a gray suit with a white or a blue shirt. But no man should wear a seersucker suit, or a fancy shirt, or unmatched coat and trousers to the White House.

These rules of dress should also be followed if one is invited to a White House reception. If engraved invitations have been sent for an afternoon reception, the men should wear formal afternoon dress (cutaways) and women should wear afternoon clothes, as for an afternoon wedding. If one has received a formal and engraved invitation to an evening reception, full evening dress must be worn. For informal afternoon receptions and garden parties, one dresses as one would for an informal luncheon.

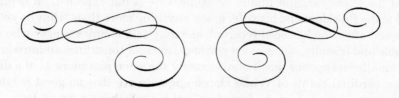

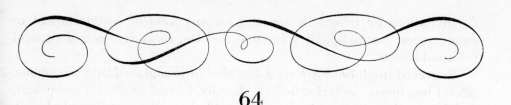

64

Invitations, Acceptances, and Regrets

THE FIRST point in connection with invitations is that, with certain exceptions such as engraved invitations, they are sent by a woman, or in her name only, even if she is married. They are sent in a man's name only when he is unmarried. The wife is the mistress of the house, and only the most casual, on-the-spot invitation should be given by the husband. This is particularly true when women guests are concerned.

The second point is that, although even the most informal invitation could conceivably be used for formal entertaining, informal invitations *must* be used for asking guests to any entertainment which is, by its very nature, informal. For example, one might invite eight people to dinner—white tie—before going to the opening of the opera or to a formal reception, without any invitation other than a verbal one. But it would be ridiculous to use an engraved invitation for an essentially informal party, such as a buffet supper, a picnic, or a luncheon out of doors. Before describing in detail the usual forms for invitations, it may be useful to show which forms are used for the various ways of entertaining. (Invitations for week ends are at the end of this chapter, on page 522, together with acceptances.)

Verbal invitations, whether face to face or by telephone, are given for: luncheon, tea, cocktails, dinner (informal or semiformal), suppers, children's parties, christenings, anniversary parties, restaurant or night club entertaining, dances (very small, informal), and picnics.

Note: Verbal invitations should never be given within earshot of the uninvited (see page 14, in the chapter, "Manners in General"). An invitation to any of the above may also be sent in a letter. Many hostesses send reminder cards if the invitations were made verbally, especially in the confusion of a party or meeting.

Invitations by card (folding card or visiting card) are sent for: tea, cocktails, receptions (both afternoon and evening), buffet suppers, children's parties, and dances (informal).

Invitations by telegraph are sent for any kind of entertainment in emergencies. Normally, they are sent for: tea, cocktails, receptions, and informal dances.

Engraved invitations are used for: weddings and wedding receptions, official luncheons, formal or official dinners, formal or official receptions, and dances. An engraved invitation should always be sent for very big or official entertainments, when lists may have to be checked at the door.

It is not necessary here, of course, to discuss the different ways in which one invites friends and family. The following suggestions are all based on the assumption of a rather distant, if not formal, acquaintanceship. And, incidentally, they are all suggestions for invitations issued by the hostess herself. (The form to be used by butlers and waitresses in sending invitations by telephone will be found on page 360, in the chapter, "The Household Staff.")

VERBAL INVITATIONS

Invitations given in conversation are, of course, as informal as the conversation itself. The only thing to avoid is an invitation so casually or tentatively given that it leaves the guest wondering whether or not it is definite. As always, the hostess and her guest should be in clear agreement about the time, the place and the degree of formality.

The exact forms of face-to-face invitations cannot be cut and dried, because so much depends on the circumstances. In substance, however, with the obviously necessary changes, they are very like the following telephone conversations.

Hostess and Guest

"May I speak to Mrs. Ewing?" says the hostess.

"This is Mrs. Ewing," answers the prospective guest.

"Oh, hello, Mrs. Ewing, this is Caroline Beecher. I wonder if you and your husband (or, if the Ewings are an older couple, "If you and Mr. Ewing") could dine with us next Wednesday."

"Yes, indeed; thank you, we'd like to very much." (Or, more informally, "Why yes, we'd love to.")

"Oh, that's splendid, eight o'clock then."

In communities where there is an established custom about dressing for dinner, no further comment is necessary. But if there is any doubt, the hostess may add "—and it will be black tie." Or the guest may ask, "We're not dressing, are we?"

There is no necessity, of course, to ask to speak to Mrs. Ewing, as the message can quite properly be left with whoever answers the telephone. (See the following page.)

Hostess and New Acquaintance

If the guest is a new acquaintance whom one has just met for the first time, the invitation cannot be as simple as the above example. Unless there has been some suggestion about a second meeting, an invitation after one meeting must be explained, or be immediately understandable to the person to whom the invitation is given. (See also page 29, in the chapter, "Men's Manners.") Otherwise, there is an unfortunate suggestion of overeagerness on the part of the hostess; as though, perhaps, she needed new friends, or thought the strangers socially useful. The reason for this is that, traditionally, an invitation to one's house is a compliment not lightly given to those whom one has met only once, unless some other basis for the invitation exists. (After two or three meetings, none of this applies.) If the meeting has been immediately and particularly congenial, that, in itself, constitutes a basis that can be referred to in the invitation. Or, the basis might be friends in common, or a mutual interest. For example:

"Hello, may I speak to Mrs. Ewing?"

"This is Mrs. Ewing."

"Oh hello, Mrs. Ewing. This is Caroline Beecher. I so enjoyed our conversation last night." (Here some chat arising from the conversation would probably follow, as "Did you get home safely last night?" or "I found the name of the flower we were trying to remember." And then the invitation.) "My husband and I wondered if you might be free and could lunch with us next Wednesday?"

Or, "It was such a joy to hear about Winthrop and Eleanor after so many years; I wondered if you and your husband could stop in for tea next Sunday. It would give us both so much pleasure if you could come."

Or, "You told me you're interested in modern French painting, and I wondered if you would like to come to tea next Wednesday to meet the director of our museum, who has just returned from France."

Since the hostess must give some indication as to the basis for this invitation, it is better not to leave a message. If Mrs. Ewing is not at home, the hostess can ask when she is expected, and call back again; or ask that Mrs. Ewing telephone upon her return. See page 360, "The Household Staff," for the form.

Hostess Leaving a Message with a Maid or Butler

"Mrs. Ewing's residence," or "Miss Ewing's apartment," says the butler answering the telephone.

"I'd like to leave a message for Mr. and Mrs. Ewing, please," says the hostess, "to ask if they could dine with Mrs. Beecher" (or, "with Mrs. Robert Beecher," if the circumstances are such that "Mrs. Beecher" would be too indefinite) "on Monday night, the seventh of September, at eight o'clock."

"To dine with Mrs. Beecher on Monday, the seventh of September," the butler repeats ending, "Very good, Madam, thank you."

"Thank you," says the hostess. ("Good-bye" is not used in this case.)

Hostess Leaving a Message with a Member of the Family

"Hello," says the one answering the telephone.

"Hello, is this Mrs. Ewing's house?" asks the hostess.

"Yes, it is," answers the voice.

"I'd like to leave a message for Mr. and Mrs. Ewing . . ." Then follows the same message as above.

"Yes, indeed, I'll give them the message," says the voice.

"Thank you very much; good-bye." says the hostess.

"Good-bye."

Butler Leaving a Message of Invitation

See page 361.

INVITATION BY CARD

Invitations written on a card are, in a way, more informal than invitations sent by telephone. Cards are not often used, for example, for a luncheon or a dinner invitation, whereas the telephone is standard for either of these. Nor are they often used for invitations to very small tea or cocktail parties. The moment when these cards are really useful is when one is giving a big informal party, whether tea, cocktails, a hunt breakfast, or anything else of the kind. (See the list on page 501.) The implication is that there will probably be at least twenty or more guests, and that the hostess wants to avoid so many telephone calls. The examples given here all have "R. s. v. p." written on them but if one does not want or need an answer, this will, of course, be omitted.

Cocktails Sunday
May 5th, 5-7

M̶r̶ Edward Benton

R. s. v. p.   50 Ladue Road

AN INVITATION WRITTEN ON A VISITING CARD

This card shows the wording which is most often used in invitations of this kind, but five other forms which are also commonly used are shown below. In each of these, the handwritten message is shown in italics; and when the name is written in, as shown in Nos. 2 and 4, the engraved name is struck out in ink.

---

1.   *Tea, Sunday, May 5th* *
            Five o'clock *

            Miss Ethel Beecher

            R.s.v.p.*   60 Franklin Road

---

2.   *Won't you both come to tea,* *
            Sunday, May 5th *

                Mr. and Mrs. Robert Beecher

                            Love, *
                            Caroline *

            R.s.v.p.*   60 Franklin Road

* Written by hand.

3.

Tea, Wednesday, May 8th,*
five o'clock*

Mrs. Robert Beecher

To discuss plans for the benefit.*

R.s.v.p.*   60 Franklin Road

4.

Do come to tea on Wednesday,*
May 8th at five o'clock *
to discuss plans for the benefit.*

Mrs. Robert Beecher

Caroline Beecher *

R.s.v.p.*   60 Franklin Road

5.

I hope you will come to Bobby's birthday *
party on Saturday, May 11th at four o'clock.*

Mrs. Robert Beecher

R.s.v.p.*   60 Franklin Road

* Written by hand.

No. 3 and No. 4 are invitations to a tea—in this case a committee meeting —when the husbands of the women guests will not be expected. All these examples are written on visiting cards, which are discussed in detail on pages 597 to 610, but there are other cards, as well.

For children's parties one may very well use the little cards which are printed in gay childish designs and sold at any stationer's. As a rule, one need only fill in the date, time, and address. (If a visiting card is used, it should be the mother's, as shown in example No. 5, not the father's and mother's.) The envelope is addressed to "Master" or "Miss ———," in care of the mother.

Another card which may be used for invitations is the folding card. This is about four by three inches, in a heavy paper (not card or pasteboard) with a smooth finish, either white or cream-colored. There is a small envelope to match. The name is engraved on the outside in any of the letterings used for engraving visiting cards; and the message is written either above and below the name on the outside, or on the lower half of the inside. For example, on the outside:

6.

To meet *

Dr. and Mme. van Kleburg *

Mr. and Mrs. Robert Beecher

Monday, May 20th *
5:30 — 7 o'clock *

R.s.v.p.*   60 Franklin Road

or on the inside:

To meet *

Dr. and Mme. van Kleburg *
Monday, May 20th *
5:30 — 7 o'clock *

R.s.v.p.*

* Written by hand.

A new card very like a visiting card is replacing the folded card. It is used for the same purposes: informal invitations, and also to send with flowers when more writing space is needed than the usual visiting card affords. This card is flat, not folded; it is about 4½ by 3½ inches, made of heavy white or cream-colored paper, not card or pasteboard. The name is engraved in the center top, with the address above and to the right and, sometimes, with the telephone number above and to the left. The following example shows the use of two different kinds of lettering, one used for the name and the other for the address. But it could be engraved in one lettering in any of those suggested for visiting cards. Since these cards are sent in the mail, they must have envelopes to match, and, like folded cards, they are never, of course, used as visiting cards.

60 Franklin Road

MRS. ROBERT BEECHER

Cocktails 5:30 — 7:30
Sunday, May 5th

R.s.v.p.

THE NEW FLAT INVITATION CARD

INVITATION BY TELEGRAPH

Invitations sent in a telegram suggest a fairly large, impromptu, informal party and are particularly useful if two or three, or even six or eight, people are entertaining jointly.

The form is simple and logical: "Won't you come to a cocktail party (or "dance" or whatever) at the River Club, 90 Euclid Avenue, at 5:30 Wednesday, January 28. R.s.v.p. Mrs. Henry Thayer, 121 Olcott Street." The signatures are written as follows:

Grace and Henry Thayer
Caroline and George Sears
Edward Benton
Arnold Stover

ENGRAVED INVITATIONS

Apart from wedding invitations which are discussed separately on pages 199 to 212, there are two basic types of engraved invitations. One is engraved especially for the occasion, with everything except the name of the guest, which must be written in in ink. The other is only partially engraved, with space left open for writing in the names of the guests, the nature of the entertainment, and the date and hour. The latter kind is, of course, more practical than the other and is more often used for entertaining in a private house. (See page 514 below.)

The Paper

The best paper for a fully engraved invitation is a heavy paper with a kid finish and it should always be white, or at most cream-colored, with black engraving. No decoration should be used other than a coat of arms, a crest, or a lozenge (no monograms, no addresses), and if a crest or coat of arms is used, it should be embossed in the paper without color. The most conservative and traditional size for a formal invitation is about 5½ by 7 inches; it is folded in half before being put into the envelope. But modern taste leans toward a smaller size, about 4 by 5½ inches; this is slipped sideways into the envelope without folding. The same paper may be used also for partially engraved invitations, but these are more usually engraved on a stiff white or ivory card (3 or 4 sheet board) about 3½ inches by 5 inches.

The Lettering

The lettering most commonly used is Shaded Antique Roman, although Shaded Modified Roman, Script and London Script are also used.

Examples of these are shown on page 202. Only the wording of engraved invitations will be given in this chapter.

Names

Those who are sending engraved invitations identify themselves fully, on the modest assumption that there are perhaps others named "Mr. and Mrs. Parrish," and that "Mr. and Mrs. Anderson Parrish" (or ". . . Anderson Parrish, junior") may be necessary for full identification. Those to whom the communication is sent are addressed as "Mr. and Mrs. Beecher" on the flattering assumption that further identification is unnecessary. This does not, of course, apply to the envelope, which is addressed "Mr. and Mrs. Robert Beecher," unless—and this is a pure technicality—Mr. Beecher is the head of the family by primogeniture. In this case, although the procedure is unusual and rather stiff, the envelope may be addressed "Mr. and Mrs. Beecher."

The form, "the company of Mr. and Mrs. Beecher," is preferred to "Mr. and Mrs. Beecher's company," because it is not polite to hook " 's" onto their name for convenience's sake. Further, it should be noted that there are no abbreviations on an engraved invitation other than "Mr.," "Mrs.," "Dr.," and "R.s.v.p." The word "junior" is fully written without capitalization. The date and the hour are also written out but only the day and month are capitalized.

Addresses

Addresses may be written out, or they may be engraved in numbers; for example, either "Ten North Third Street" or "364 Duane Road," a more modern practice which is particularly useful when an address is awkwardly long. As a matter of form, "One Fifteen East" is not a desirable pattern. When a number cannot be written in one or two words—as, "Eleven" or "Eighty-four"—numerals should be used. On such a formal document as a wedding announcement, "One thousand, nine hundred and forty-seven" or, "Nineteen hundred and forty-seven" is justifiable. On an invitation, "One hundred and fifteen East One hundred and sixth Street" would be absurd. The halfway measures such as "One fifteen East 106th Street" are scarcely better. Note that the letters "th," "rd," or "nd" after a numeral should always have ditto marks or a line underneath them; as, "82nd". When an address is written out, the first letter of the number of the house and the first letter of the number of the street should always be capitalized. Such words as "East," "Street," "Avenue," and "Boulevard" should also begin with a capital letter.

The Hour

The word "ten-thirty" should not be used in an engraved invitation; "half past ten o'clock" or the more old-fashioned form, "half after ten o'clock" should be used. Engraved invitations are not often sent for the quarter-hour, but the form is "at quarter past ten o'clock," or "at quarter before . . ." And finally, "R.s.v.p." and "R.S.V.P." are both correct, although the first is more usual today.

When There Is a Guest of Honor

The words "in honour of ———" should be used only on engraved invitations. By telephone, the classic phrase is "for ———." For example, "We are giving a dinner next Friday, the 29th, for Mr. and Mrs. Clayton, and George and I hope so much that you and your husband will be able to come"; or, if leaving the message, "I'd like to leave a message for Mr. and Mrs. Ewing. Mrs. Beecher would like to know if Mr. and Mrs. Ewing could come to a dinner for Mr. and Mrs. Clayton on Friday, ———." On a card: "To meet ———" (see page 506 above). On a partly engraved invitation, the fifth line may read "At a dinner in honour of Dr. and Mme. van Kleburg"; but if, as is often the case, this supplementary phrase is too long to fit comfortably in the body of the invitation, "To meet ———" may be written across the top, above the hosts' names.

An example of the official, fully engraved invitation "in honour of ———" is shown on this page; invitations to a debutante party are shown on page 510; to wedding anniversaries, on page 512.

Official Invitations

On invitations to very big official entertainments, the very polite custom of writing in the guest's name is often omitted as follows:

The President and Trustees
of
The American Museum of Natural History
request the pleasure of your company
at a reception
in honour of
The Security Council of the United Nations
and
The Secretary General
on Wednesday evening, the twenty-second of May
at nine o'clock
in the Theodore Roosevelt Memorial of
The American Museum of Natural History
Central Park West at Seventy-ninth Street
R.s.v.p.
The President's Office

If the reception is of a more or less public nature, the notation "Dress Optional" is sometimes engraved at the lower right-hand corner, balancing the "R.s.v.p."

For Dances and Special Occasions

The best form for invitations to dances, official luncheons, dinners, and receptions (and the form, incidentally, which is used by our Department of State) is as follows:

Mr. and Mrs. Anderson Parrish, junior
request the pleasure of
the company of
Mr. and Mrs. Beecher *
at a small dance
on Saturday, the tenth of January
at half-past ten o'clock
R.s.v.p.   Three East Third Street
* Written by hand.

509

Another form, a little less polite and less desirable is:

Mr. and Mrs. Anderson Parrish, junior
request the pleasure of
Mr. and Mrs. Beecher's *
company at a small dance
on Saturday, the tenth of January
at half-past ten o'clock

R.s.v.p.　　　　　Three East Third Street

A third variation, used for dances and receptions but not for dinner or luncheon in a private house, requests "the pleasure of your company at . . ." omitting the written name. (See the opposite page.)

Note that when one is giving a dance, whether large or small, it is the fashion today to send invitations to "a small dance" or to "a dance," never to "a ball." Balls are public or official entertainments.

For a Debutante Dance

For a dance in honor of a debutante there are two forms, both fully engraved except for the name of the guest, and both very formal. The first is:

Mr. and Mrs. Robert Vallon
request the pleasure of
the company of
Miss Barnes *
at a dance in honour of their daughter
Miss Marguerite Vallon
on Friday, the tenth of December
at eleven o'clock

R.s.v.p.　　　　　Ten Audubon Place

If the dance is being given by someone other than the debutante's parents, the fifth line reads "at a dance in honour of."

The second form is:

Mr. and Mrs. Robert Vallon
Miss Marguerite Vallon
request the pleasure of
the company of
Miss Barnes *
on Friday, the tenth of December
at eleven o'clock

R.s.v.p.　　　　Ten Audubon Place　　　　Dancing

* Written by hand.

If the dance is not so formal, the guest's name is usually omitted. The following example is an invitation to a dance given in the country.

Mr. and Mrs. August Davis
Miss Elizabeth Davis
request the pleasure of your company
at a small dance
on Thursday, the fifteenth of November
at ten o'clock
The Bayou Club
River Oaks

R.s.v.p.
123 Inwood Drive
River Oaks
Houston

For a Debutante Reception

Mr. and Mrs. August Davis
Miss Elizabeth Davis
At Home
Saturday, March seventeenth
at five o'clock
123 Inwood Drive

R.s.v.p.

"At Home" Invitation

The most formal invitation to a dance or a reception in a private house is still, technically, "At Home." But, except for rather pompous occasions, "At Home" has become a much less fashionable phrase than it used to be. Engraved "At Home" invitations for the afternoon are now unheard of except for a debutante reception. This is the form for a very formal evening reception:

Mr. and Mrs. Robert Vallon
At Home
Friday, the tenth of January
at ten o'clock
Ten Audubon Place

The favour of a reply is requested

If it is to be a dance, and not a reception, the word "Dancing" is engraved at the lower right, balancing "The favour of a reply . . ." (For "At Home" cards for the newly married, see page 216 in the chapter, "Weddings.")

For a Joint Party

When two or three people of the same generation are giving a party together, the names are engraved in alphabetical order:

Mr. and Mrs. William Gwathmey Crosby
Mr. and Mrs. Grenville Humphries
Mr. and Mrs. George Gordon Talbot, junior
request the pleasure of
the company of
Mr. and Mrs. Beecher *
at a small dance
on Saturday, the fourth of May
at ten o'clock
The Crystal Room
The Plaza

R.s.v.p.
Mrs. George G. Talbot, junior
12 St. Johns Drive

* Written by hand.

If there is a marked difference in age between those who are giving a joint party, the names of the older generation should come first. This is particularly true in the case of parents and children. Further, if the children are entertaining in their parents' house, even if they are well over age, the parents' names should appear on an engraved invitation. The only exception to this rule might be in the case of a parent who is a confirmed invalid, with children who are middle-aged.

For a Wedding Anniversary

Invitations to a wedding anniversary should always be as simple as possible; or, if one wants to give a formal dinner or reception, the customary form should be used. Funny or clever invitations are not in good taste.

Invitations may be sent by telephone, letter, or telegram, as the following example will show. By telephone, after the usual preliminaries suggested on page 502, the message would be ". . . if Mr. and Mrs. Beecher could dine on Tuesday, the fourth of September, to celebrate Mr. and Mrs. Parrish's wedding anniversary." By telegram: "Could you both dine on Tuesday, September fourth, to celebrate our wedding anniversary." By letter, ". . . hope so much that you and your husband will dine on Tuesday, the fourth of September, to celebrate our fifteenth wedding anniversary." Presents need not be brought to a wedding anniversary party, but, if one wants to be sure that none of the guests will feel that he should bring a present, one need only omit mention of the anniversary in the invitation and bring up the point after the guests have arrived. (See page 64 for a list of wedding anniversary presents.)

In an engraved invitation the words "to celebrate" are used if the anniversary dinner is being given by the couple themselves. If others are giving the dinner in their honor, the words "in honour of" are used. The dates—as "1922-1947," for example—often used to be engraved at the top of the invitation, although the fashion now tends toward omitting them.

Mr. and Mrs. Russel Yates
request the pleasure of
the company of
Mr. and Mrs. Sargent *
at a dinner to celebrate
the twenty-fifth anniversary of their marriage
on Tuesday, the fourth of September
at eight o'clock

R.s.v.p.   12 Orlando Road

If a reception is being given by their children:

Mr. and Mrs. Russel Yates, junior
Mr. and Mrs. Edward Adams Sears
request the pleasure of
the company of
Mr. and Mrs. Sargent *
in honour of
the fiftieth wedding anniversary of
Mr. and Mrs. Yates
on Tuesday, the fourth of September
at ten o'clock
Three St. Pierre Road

R.s.v.p.
Mrs. Russel Yates, junior
Three St. Pierre Road

If the reception is being given in a hotel, the last line reads, "The Westbury Hotel" or "The Baroque Room, Hotel Plaza." If a dinner is being given, the line under the guests' names is engraved "at a dinner in honour of."

If many sons and daughters are giving a party for their parents, their names can be omitted in the invitation. But this form is not as desirable as the other and should never be used if there are fewer than four separate names. The form is:

In honour of
the fortieth wedding anniversary of
Mr. and Mrs. Russel Yates
their sons and daughters
request the pleasure of
the company of
Mr. and Mrs. Sargent *
on Tuesday, the fourth of September
at ten o'clock
Three St. Pierre Road

R.s.v.p.
Mrs. Russel Yates, junior
Three St. Pierre Road

* Written by hand.

For Big Dinners and Small Dances

The partly engraved invitation is sent for big dinners of about twenty or more, for formal dinners whether large or not, and for dances which are not big enough to warrant the more fully engraved invitations shown on page 510. In the form, which follows, the words "a small dance" may be substituted for "dinner":

Mr. and Mrs. Robert James Beecher
request the pleasure of
the company of
Mr. and Mrs. Ewing *
at *dinner* *
on *Saturday, the eleventh of May* *
at *eight o'clock* *
60 Franklin Road

* Written by hand.

Traditionally, an engraved invitation meant full evening dress, and "Black tie"—or "Decorations"—written in the lower corner, indicated an exception to the rule. Now the "Black tie" is the rule, "White tie" shows the exception. "Decorations," as always, means full evening dress.

FORMAL WRITTEN INVITATIONS

Formal invitations need not, of course, always be engraved. They may be written on any personal writing paper. This is the form:

Mr. and Mrs. Anderson Parrish, junior
request the pleasure of
the company of

Mr. and Mrs. Beecher

at dinner

on Wednesday, the fifteenth of May

at eight o'clock

HANDWRITTEN INVITATION IN THE THIRD PERSON

If the address is engraved at the top of the sheet of paper, nothing more is needed. If a monogrammed paper is used, the address is written below the hour, as in an engraved invitation.

LAST-MINUTE INVITATIONS

A last-minute invitation is rarely a compliment, but it is often the only resort of a hostess suddenly faced with the prospect of an empty place at her dinner table. Guests who have accepted invitations must, sometimes, excuse themselves at the last moment (see page 17) and there is nothing for a hostess to do but ask a friend to fill a place.

The classic phrase is, "Would you be kind enough"—or, more colloquially, "Would you be an angel"—"and dine with us tonight to fill a place?"

It is never wise to invite someone who is an infrequent guest at the house; such an invitation smacks of "I ask you only because I must have someone." An intimate friend is a much better prospect for the role of last-minute guest, although even a friend's good nature can be strained by repeated last-minute invitations. In any case, one should always make a point of inviting a last-minute guest soon again, in the normal way.

REMINDER CARDS

Engraved reminder cards are sometimes sent to those who have accepted an invitation, when the invitation was given verbally or sent by telephone. They are not sent when a written answer has been received by the hostess. Reminder cards are usually engraved in black in script, shaded Roman, or shaded modified Roman lettering, on a stiff white or cream-colored (two-sheet) card of about four by three inches, and are sent in a matching envelope of heavy paper. They are partially engraved, with space left for writing in the necessary details. There are three forms, of which the first is the most old-fashioned and conservative:

To remind
Mr. and Mrs. Beecher *
of *dinner* *
with
Mr. and Mrs. Anderson Parrish, junior
on *Wednesday, the fifteenth of May* *
at *eight* * o'clock
Three East Third Street

---

or

To remind you of dinner with
Mr. and Mrs. Henry Elliott
on *Wednesday, March 26th* *
at *eight* * o'clock
12 Commonwealth Avenue

* Written by hand.

---

or

To remind you that
Mr. and Mrs. Henry Elliott
expect you for *dinner* *
on *Thursday, March 4th* *
at *eight* * o'clock
12 Commonwealth Avenue
* Written by hand.

Simple Reminder Cards

A visiting card is often used as a reminder card; in fact, now that formal entertaining is becoming so rare, visiting cards are fast being accepted as the usual form of reminder. Across the face of the card, "To remind" is written at the upper left center; just below this, above the engraved name, is written, "Dinner, Saturday, May twelfth" (or "12th"); and below the name, the hour: "at eight o'clock." If there is no address on the card, it may be written in the lower right-hand corner. This card is sent in the mail, in an envelope that fits the card exactly. (See page 599.) It is used for any kind of informal or semiformal entertaining for which no written invitation has been sent; it is particularly practical when an invitation has been given verbally to a guest who obviously had no engagement book at hand.

CANCELING OR CHANGING INVITATIONS

The simplest way of canceling or changing an invitation is either by telephone or by telegram. By telephone for example, if the message is sent by the maid or butler, or by a member of the family: "Mrs. Beecher is very sorry, but she is obliged to cancel her invitations for dinner on Saturday, the eleventh of May, owing to the very grave illness of Mr. Beecher's mother." A telegram from the hostess might read: "Hope so much that you will be able to dine on Saturday, the eighteenth of May, at eight o'clock instead of Saturday, the eleventh of May. Very much regret necessity for postponement but must be away on the eleventh. Caroline Beecher." If engraved invitations were sent originally, reminder cards are then mailed to all those who have accepted the invitation for the second date.

Those who entertain very formally and have issued engraved invitations may want to send a printed notice (there is usually no time for engraving), and this is a correct, although somewhat old-fashioned, procedure. The lettering most often used is antique Roman, as shown on page 202. The form is:

Mr. and Mrs. Anderson Parrish, junior
regret exceedingly
that owing to the illness of Mrs. Parrish
they are obliged to recall their invitations
for Saturday, the eleventh of May

Official dinners or receptions, for which invitations have been sent long in advance, may be canceled, advanced, or postponed by sending an engraved notice using the form shown opposite, in the same lettering as the original invitation.

Owing to the
unavoidable departure of
The Secretary General
the reception in honour of
The Security Council of the United Nations
and
The Secretary General
will be advanced from
Wednesday evening, the twenty-second of May
to
Friday evening, the seventeenth of May
at nine o'clock
in the Theodore Roosevelt Memorial
The American Museum of Natural History
Central Park West and Seventy-ninth Street
R.s.v.p.
President's Office

Ways of recalling or changing wedding invitations are discussed on page 219; see also page 20, in the chapter, "Manners."

ANSWERING INVITATIONS

The first rule in answering invitations is that they must be answered promptly, and in the form in which they were sent. This is an old rule, evolved in the days when invitations were either given face to face, or sent in a note or in the engraved form. The modern interpretation of this rule is that invitations must be answered with the same degree of formality as that which has been used in sending them. For example, an invitation sent in an informal letter can be answered either by telephone or in the same kind of letter. An engraved invitation is answered in the third person, and is written in a form exactly like that of the invitation. The only exception to this rule of strict reciprocity is in answering invitations sent on a visiting card, and even here one does not go beyond the corresponding degree of formality. (See below, page 518, "Accepting Invitations Sent by Card.")

The first and very useful rule in accepting invitations is that one must specify the hour as well as the day, although this is not necessary in regretting. The point is that by a repetition of the hour, a mistake or misapprehension can be corrected. This is always a good rule, particularly in accepting an invitation for a week end (page 522).

Accepting Verbal Invitations

There is no definite form for accepting face-to-face invitations beyond the normal "Why, yes, thank you so much, ..." Telephoned acceptances, although they have no rigid forms, follow a more recognizable and definite pattern.

The conversation between guest and hostess is discussed on page 502. When the guest leaves an answer with the maid or butler, the conversation is usually somewhat as follows:

"Mrs. Beecher's residence," says the butler answering the telephone.

"This is Mrs. Ewing," says the guest. "Would you please tell Mrs. Beecher that Mr. and Mrs. Ewing will be delighted to dine on Saturday, the seventh of May, at eight o'clock."

"Very good, Madam."

"Thank you."

"Thank you, Madam."

When a guest leaves a message with a member of the family, after the usual preliminaries, he might say:

"I'd like to leave a message for Mrs. Beecher, please. Would you tell Mrs. Beecher that Mr. and Mrs. Ewing will be delighted to dine on Saturday, the seventh of May, at eight o'clock."

"Yes, indeed, I'll give her the message," is the answer.

"Thank you very much, good-bye."

"Good-bye."

When a Butler Leaves a Message of Acceptance

See page 360 for the form when a butler leaves a message of acceptance.

Accepting Invitations Sent by Card

Invitations written on a visiting card, or on a flat or folded invitation card, need be answered only if they read, "R.s.v.p." They may be answered on a visiting card, but a telephone call or a letter is better and more the custom. A folded card, or its newer flat counterpart, should not be used. Accepting invitations by telephone has been fully discussed above. The degree of formality in the letter would entirely depend on the intimacy of the correspondents and would have nothing to do with the way the message had been written on the card. For example, if form no. 4 on page 505 had been sent, the answering letter might read: "Dear Mrs. Beecher, I would be delighted to come to tea on Wednesday, the eighth. It will be a great pleasure to see you again, and I am looking forward to it very much. With many thanks, Sincerely,"; or, "Dear Caroline, I'd love to come to tea on Wednesday. See you then. Affectionately." If a printed invitation has been sent from one child to another, the guest can answer in writing: "Dear Bobby, I would love to come to your party on Saturday, the eighteenth." Usually, however, it is simpler to have the invitation answered by telephone, and a message may be left for the mother of the child who is giving the party.

If one does accept an invitation on a visiting card, one need only write: "Delighted to come" with the date and the time. To a friend, one might write: "So looking forward to Sunday at five!" If one has crossed off the engraved name, one adds, "Love, Kitty" or, "Affectionately, Jane."

Accepting Telegraphed Invitations

These can be accepted by telegram, telephone, or letter. If by telegram: "Delighted to come on Wednesday at five-thirty. Anderson and Louise Parrish"; or, if by telephone or letter, any of the forms suggested on the preceding page, or immediately above.

Accepting All Invitations in the Third Person

An answer to an engraved invitation, or any invitation sent in the third person, should always be written by hand on one's own writing paper. The only exception is in the case of invitations to formal business luncheons, dinners, or receptions, which have been sent to one's office. These may be written on paper with a business heading. As in issuing invitations, in accepting it is always more polite to use the form, "the kind invitation of ———," than the form, "Mr. and Mrs. ———'s kind invitation."

Mr. and Mrs. Albert Ewing

accept with pleasure

the kind invitation of

Mr. and Mrs. Beecher

to dine

on Saturday, the eleventh of May

at eight o'clock

WRITTEN ACCEPTANCE IN THE THIRD PERSON

The acceptance which follows immediately below is given as an example of another rule, which is that the names of all those who have issued an invitation must be listed in the acceptance. This, too, is written by hand, and spaced as shown here:

Mr. and Mrs. Robert Beecher
accept with pleasure
the kind invitation of
Mr. and Mrs. Crosby
Mr. and Mrs. Humphries
Mr. and Mrs. Talbot
to a dance
on Saturday, the fourth of May
at ten o'clock
The Crystal Room
The Plaza

Note: although the invitation reads, "to a small dance," the acceptance omits the adjective. An alternate form omits this line entirely and reads, "for Saturday, the fourth of May," etc.

Reminder Cards

Reminder cards need no acknowledgment of any kind.

REGRETTING INVITATIONS

The first rule in regretting invitations, as in accepting them, is that it must be done in the same form and spirit as that of the invitation. But there is another rule which applies only to regretting: A simple, "No, I'm sorry," cannot be substituted for, "Yes, I'll be delighted." And, depending on the degree of intimacy of the hostess and guest, reasons must be given, except in regretting an engraved invitation. The important point is that the invitation was a polite compliment on the part of the hostess and one must show equal politeness in refusing.

The second rule is that any joint invitation to a married couple must be refused if one or the other cannot accept. This does not apply to brothers and sisters who may accept or regret separately even though they have been invited in a joint invitation.

Regretting Verbal Invitations

The form for regretting is very like that used in accepting and described on pages 517 to 518. But it might be useful, nevertheless, to give a few sample telephone conversations.

To an acquaintance, after the invitation has been given, the one who has been invited says:

"How kind of you! We would have been delighted to come and I'm so sorry we have another engagement for that evening."

"Oh, I'm so disappointed," says the hostess.

"So am I, but thank you very much for asking us."

If the hostess is the older and more experienced she might add, "We'll try again very soon." If the guest is the older and more experienced of the two, she might say, "But I hope we shall see you soon."

A less formal example of regretting an invitation would be:

"I am terribly sorry. We're dining with the Clarks that night; I couldn't be more disappointed."

"I couldn't either," answers the hostess.

"Anyway, thanks a lot for asking us."

There is a fine point of manners connected with the mention of "the Clarks," but since it is not strictly part of the technique of regretting invitations, it will be found on page 15, in the chapter, "Manners in General." The forms used when a message of regret is given to, or by, a butler are described on page 360.

Regretting an Invitation Sent by Card

Again, as in accepting, the degree of formality used in regretting an invitation by card, whether visiting card or folded card, depends on the intimacy of the correspondents, and has nothing to do with the way the message was written. For example, if one were regretting by letter an invitation such as card No. 4, on page 505, one might write either, "Dear Mrs. Beecher, I would so love to come to tea on Wednesday, but there is a Parents' Day tea at my child's school that afternoon, and I'm afraid I must go. I am so sorry to miss the discussion of our benefit, and if there is anything I can do to help with it, please let me know. Sincerely, Jane Ewing" or, "Dear Caroline, I'd love to come to tea on Wednesday, but that is Parents' Day at Mary's school, and I just can't get out of it. We must lunch some day soon. Affectionately, Jane." If a child must regret a party, it is better for his mother to do it for him by telephone, explaining the reason, whether illness, another engagement, or whatever.

If one uses one's visiting card one may write to an acquaintance, "So sorry— will be away on the eighth of May; or, to a friend, "So sorry—will be at Mother's on the week end of May eighth. Love, Kitty," with the engraved name, of course, struck off. As in accepting, the flat or folded invitation card should not be used.

Regretting Invitations Sent by Telegram

As in accepting invitations of this kind, one may regret by telegraph, telephone, or letter: "Very sorry unable to come on Wednesday. Thank you for asking us. Anderson and Louise Parrish." Or, less formally, "So sorry, can't come on Wednesday. Most disappointed, but thanks for asking us." The forms for regretting by telephone and letter have already been discussed above.

Regretting All Invitations in the Third Person

The only difference between an acceptance and a regret are these: instead of "accept with pleasure," one writes "regret that they will be unable to accept"; instead of "kind invitation," one writes "very kind invitation"; and the time and place are omitted. Otherwise, the form is the same—the names of all the hosts and the usual information must be written out. On page 519, there is a facsimile of a written acceptance; the form and spacing given below are used in regretting. The excuse or reason for being unable to accept may or may not be given, although it must if the invitation comes from the White House or a crowned head (see page 599). When an excuse is given, the standard phrases are always used—"regrets that owing to a previous engagement, she will be unable—" or "regrets that owing to her absence from New York, she will be unable . . ." Some use the more polite and old-fashioned "regrets that a previous engagement prevents her accepting" or "regret that their absence from New York will prevent their accepting . . ." Modern usage, however, tends towards omitting all excuses. For ing . . ." Modern usage, however, tends to omit all excuses. For example:

Mrs. Robert Clark
regrets that she will be unable
to accept the very kind invitation of
the President and Trustees of
The American Museum of Natural History
to a reception in honour of
The Security Council of the United Nations
and
The Secretary General
on Wednesday evening, the twenty-second of May

A shorter form, less punctilious but now considered permissible, is:

Mrs. Robert Clark
regrets that she will be unable
to accept the very kind invitation of
the President and Trustees of
The American Museum of Natural History
for
Wednesday evening, the twenty-second of May

EXCUSING ONESELF FROM AN ENGAGEMENT ALREADY ACCEPTED

This is fully discussed on pages 16 to 20, in the section, "Manners."

INVITATIONS FOR WEEK ENDS

Giving and accepting invitations for the week end is a fairly complicated matter. A mutual exchange of information between hostess and guest, which is unnecessary in connection with other invitations, is inevitable when week ends are concerned. We are not, of course, discussing invitations to old friends or habitual week-end guests but, rather, invitations to new friends or to those who will be visiting for the first time.

Invitations for the week end may be sent by letter or telegram, or they may be given verbally, either by telephone or face to face. Whichever means she chooses, the hostess will indicate in the invitation the date she expects the guests to arrive; and, unless there is some specific countersuggestion, guests should arrive about five or six in the afternoon of that day. Usually, "Come for the week end" means, "Come from teatime Friday until Monday morning." Guests who will have to leave Sunday evening, or late Sunday afternoon, should tell their hostess this in accepting the invitation. If the hostess does not expect to have her guests arrive before Saturday, she should ask them to come for lunch on Saturday; for example, "Could you and your husband come for the week end of the eleventh" (the eleventh being a Saturday) "and I hope you will be able to arrive in time for lunch." No suggestions as to trains or hours of arrival need be made in the invitation, unless the place is very remote, or unless the hostess has a plan for the guests' transportation; as, "George is driving out from town on Friday at five and would love to bring you."

In accepting an invitation, it is a great convenience to the hostess if the exact hour and method of arrival can be given. In a letter for example, "I'd be delighted to come for the week end of August tenth. If it is convenient for you, I plan to take the 4:16 train on Friday, arriving at Stockton at half past five, and I'll take a taxi up from the station." By telephone, the guest could convey the same information a little less stiffly.

Regretting an invitation for the week end follows the principles suggested on pages 520 to 521 of this section. There should always be polite words of thanks for the invitation, an explanation if possible of the reasons for refusing, and expressions of regret that a refusal is necessary.

SECTION SEVEN

CORRESPONDENCE

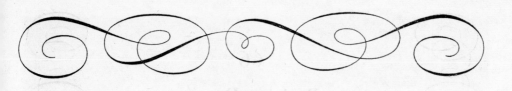

65

Introduction

THIS SECTION is concerned entirely with writing and cards, and everything that goes with them—writing paper, forms of address, and forms of engraving. Most of it is plain, serviceable material, fairly conservative in approach and like many of the earlier sections of this book, designed for relations with acquaintances, rather than with family or friends. Some of it is useful every day; great parts of it may be used only once or twice in a lifetime, if ever. And because writing is such a personal expression, all the suggested letters must be used as a guide, rather than a complete and limiting pattern.

So much having been said, a word of warning must be added. Letters and visiting cards have a great deal in common, because both serve as representatives of an absent person. They are inheritors of a long line of usages and forms and there are certain among these forms which should never be ignored. ("Never," it is understood, means "now"; customs, like Congresses, will not be bound by their predecessors, although they may choose to continue earlier regulations.) In each section, these forms are carefully outlined and only the really significant ones are stressed. All, of course, are broken every day; but no one should be confused by the gap between what is and what should be. Most of the more important rules, such as the rules against sympathy cards and thank you cards, are soundly based on the fundamentals of courtesy towards others; others have less obvious roots; and still others—the forms of address, for example—are almost entirely practical. But all are part of the accepted good usage of our time.

There are two old rules, however, which still hold and which must be mentioned. It is *always* polite to write a letter as an expression of thanks or sympathy; and it is *always* a severe rebuke—whether justified or not is another matter—to return a letter to the one who has written it.

66

Writing Paper

For many reasons, writing paper should be chosen with the greatest care. In the first place, it is a personal belonging, and like all personal belongings, it should express one's taste and even the quality of one's personality. But, unlike other personal belongings, it must stand alone, without the supporting evidence of one's presence, one's glance or smile or manner. The only thing to which it can be compared is a voice on the telephone; but the sound of a voice is transitory and ephemeral, and a letter can last for years. In many cases, a letter is all that one person will know of another on earth—and all he needs to know.

The second cardinal point about writing paper is that there is a very definite and limiting set of rules as to what is appropriate and what is not. There is an accepted standard for the paper itself: the colors, sizes, and shapes, and the ways in which papers are marked. And there is an accepted standard for the kind of writing paper which is used for certain kinds of letters. But within these limitations, there is an almost infinite number of subtleties and nuances which can express the personality of the writer. The weight, color, size, and finish of the paper, the different kinds of monograms and engravings, the different kinds of lettering that can be used, are all factors that make it possible to have almost as many kinds of writing paper as there are kinds of letters.

THE PAPER

The question of quality and expense is simple. All-rag paper is more expensive than wood pulp paper, and is generally conceded to be of a finer quality. Wood paper is often used for business correspondence, and rag paper for personal correspondence. Beyond this point, there is a multitude of baffling details concerning the weight, the finish, and so on which are of no use at all to someone who just wants to buy some nice writing paper. The best advice is to buy the best quality and to stick to conventional colors and finishes. Heavy, medium, and light are the only words a layman needs to describe the weight he wants. Glazed and dull are the two most conventional finishes; "kid finish" means a plain paper with a dull, velvety finish, sometimes called vellum. And these are the few necessary details concerning the texture: "Laid" means a paper with striations in the body of the paper; "lawn" means that almost invisible lines, like the lightest pencil lines, are

526

drawn horizontally across the surface of the paper; "granite" means a paper with shredded threads in the body of the paper, almost like dollar-bill paper; "plain" is what it sounds like, a paper without pattern; "bond" is stiffer and more transparent. The uses to which these papers are best adapted are described below, together with the colors and weights which are best for each one.

PRACTICAL SUGGESTIONS FOR BUYING AND MARKING

A very full list of writing paper is suggested below but it is not, of course, a list of necessary papers. From a practical point of view, only two kinds are needed: one for business letters or any impersonal correspondence; and another, which might be of a better, more expensive quality, for more personal and more formal correspondence, such as thank-you letters or letters of condolence. Air-mail correspondence would raise this minimum to three. Equally, although engraving—and, in some cases, printing—is suggested, writing paper need not be marked at all. It cannot be overemphasized that a simple paper of the best quality, without any marking whatsoever, is much better, and, incidentally, usually much less expensive, than a paper of inferior quality with elaborate printing and unusual colors. If one wants to avoid the expense of engraving, a plain paper of good quality is correct for all correspondence. According to the conventional rule, printing should be used on business writing paper only. Those who like a marked paper, and want to avoid the expense of engraving, often use a simple single sheet, printed with the house address. (See "Printed Names and Addresses," page 536.) But this is not a completely useful paper, as an unmarked paper of good quality would be, because it should not be used for any formal correspondence.

If one has decided to have engraving, the most practical plan is to have one die made with the house address. This can be used to mark papers of different weights and sizes for all the members of the family. On the other hand, someone living alone might prefer to have one die made with initials or a monogram. There are two drawbacks to an initialed or monogrammed paper: One is that it cannot be used by anyone except the person to whom it belongs; and the other is that, because it is more personal, it is not so desirable as the others for formal correspondence, business letters, and letters to acquaintances. In many cases, however, particularly if one travels a great deal and has no settled address, a monogrammed or initialed paper is the only practical one. The engraving may be made on a light-weight paper, in large single sheets, for air-mail letters, and on a very fine heavy paper, in a dull or kid finish, for formal correspondence.

WRITING PAPER FOR A WOMAN

This is a list of the writing papers most widely used today. The weights, colors, sizes, and finishes suggested in this list are those particularly well suited to women's paper. The qualities considered desirable in men's writing paper and in business writing paper will be discussed next.

Personal Writing Paper

For personal correspondence, such as letters to friends and acquaintances: medium-weight paper in a kid, glazed, or dull finish, in a plain, laid, or lawn paper. In white, cream color, gray, gray-blue, light-blue, medium-blue or oxford blue, but not in aquamarine-blue or turquoise-blue. Engraved with a monogram, initials, or entwined cipher (see page 532 below). The most useful size is about 5 by 7 or 6 by 8 inches, and, in this size, paper engraved with a monogram or cipher may be used for answering formal invitations, although "house paper" (see below) is the accepted standard. Some women like a bigger size, about 8 by 10 or 8½ by 11 inches, for very long letters, to be folded in four; and a smaller size, about 4 by 5 inches, for short notes which fit into the same envelope without folding. A double sheet is the standard form for the smaller sizes; but single sheets, which must be used for the larger sizes, and are often used in the 5 by 7 or 6 by 8 sizes, are becoming increasingly fashionable. When single sheets are used, very often the first page of the letter is the only one that is engraved; subsequent pages are all exactly like the first, of course, but they are not marked. For very informal correspondence with friends, a single sheet, often white and printed with initials, is sometimes used by those who like to typewrite.

House Writing Paper

For formal and more impersonal correspondence, answers to engraved invitations, letters to acquaintances, congressmen, shops, etc.

The formal paper of a town house: Used for answers to engraved invitations and for formal letters. Heavy-weight plain paper in a kid or dull finish. In white, cream color, or perhaps pale gray. Engraved with the house address only. (See page 534 below, "The paper of a formal town house. . . .") The standard size is about 5½ by 7½ and a double sheet should always be used.

The paper of a country house: Used as suggested above. A medium-weight paper, plain or laid, in a dull or glazed finish. In white, cream color, light blue, medium blue, oxford blue, or gray. Engraved with the name of the house and the address. (See page 535 below.) This paper is usually the same size as the formal town-house paper: about 5½ by 7½ inches. The double sheet is the standard form, but single sheets are also used for informal correspondence.

A more informal country-house paper: For letters to acquaintances, congressmen, and shops. A lightweight or medium-weight plain paper in a dull or glazed finish, or a lawn, or granite paper; glazed or dull. In white, cream color, light blue, gray blue, medium blue, oxford blue, or gray. Engraved—or, if single sheets, printed—with the telephone number and address, or just the address (see page 535 below). The most practical size, if one is buying one size only, is the standard one—about 5½ by 7½ inches; if one is buying two sizes, a small paper about 4 by 6 inches will fit without folding into the envelope of a bigger paper about 6 by 8 inches. Double sheets are used in the smaller sizes, but single sheets are more practical and more appropriate for the bigger size. A very big single sheet, 8 by 10 or 8½ by 11 inches, is often used, particularly by those who like to typewrite very informal personal letters. Some of these, like air-mail paper, are made in pad form.

Cards

For informal personal correspondence. In card or pasteboard of a fine quality, in any of the colors suggested above for writing papers; engraved with a monogram, initials, or the house address. These cards are sent in envelopes and they are usually made in a size to fit the envelopes of the standard writing papers—about 3½ by 5½ or 4 by 6 inches.

Business Writing Paper

For business letters: letters to shops, public utilities, etc. Medium- or light-weight paper; plain or bond, lawn or laid, glazed or dull. In white, gray, or gray blue. Printed with the address or the full name and address. (See page 536 below.) The most usual size is about 5 by 7 inches. Single sheets are the standard form, but double sheets are also used.

Post Cards

For business correspondence and very informal correspondence, short notes to shops, etc., to be sent through the mails without envelope. In card and paste-board (technically, two-sheet or three-sheet board). In white, cream color or gray blue. Printed with the address, or the full name and address, usually in a straight line across the top of the card. (See also page 537 below.) The best size is the standard postcard size: about 3½ by 5½ inches.

Air-Mail Paper

The lightest-weight paper, in a glazed or dull finish, in a plain, lawn or laid paper. In white, cream color, light blue, medium blue, oxford blue, gray blue, or gray. A considerable amount of pigment is often practical in such lightweight paper, because the writing from the other side does not show through so easily. Engraved with a monogram, or with a house address. Single or double sheets about 5½ by 7½ inches are sometimes used, but large single sheets about 8 by 10 or 8½ by 11 inches are becoming standard. These are often made in a very prac-tical pad form. Here, too, an engraved first sheet is often used with other sheets that are not engraved.

Air-mail paper may be interchanged with personal writing paper. In other words, one may use air-mail paper even if the letter is not going by air mail. One should not, however, according to the most conventional standards, use air-mail paper for formal correspondence.

Folded and Engraved Cards

For informal invitations: Folded cards, and the newer, flat invitation cards, are discussed on page 506 in the chapter, "Invitations, Acceptances, and Regrets."

Partly Engraved Invitations and Reminder Cards

See page 514 and page 515.

WRITING PAPER FOR MEN AND WOMEN IN BUSINESS

Men and women in business use the company's writing paper for all business correspondence and, unless their positions are very important, the paper is not marked specially for them. Important executives or officials, however, often have specially marked paper and usually it is engraved. Under the company's letterhead, at the left hand margin, the full name is engraved, without prefix and with the title of office directly underneath. For example,

Alice Taylor
Vice President

John Harding Fuller
Editor in chief

This form is not advised unless the position is an important one. (See the last paragraphs on page 609, under example 2, in "Business Cards," for a list of those which are so considered.) Nor should it be used with a printed letterhead, which automatically suggests a more informal, less weighty letter. It is best used on white or pale-gray paper of a fine quality, which is fully engraved in black, gray, or dark blue. Other colors should be avoided. The lettering may match that of the letterhead; or else a different lettering, carefully chosen to complement the letterhead, may be used instead.

Men and women in business on their own, and others such as artists or doctors, use their full name and address as a letterhead; women with the prefix "Mrs." or "Miss" as shown on page 537 of this section, men without prefix. Doctors' names are followed by the abbreviations of degrees. The only exceptions to this rule would be women known to the public by their Christian names: "Mary Compton Duncan," for example, instead of "Mrs. James Howard Duncan." In such cases, the prefix is left off. This paper may be engraved or printed, and again gray or dark-blue marking is best, and white or gray paper of a good quality.

WRITING PAPER FOR A MAN

Like his clothes, a man's writing paper is usually much less varied than a woman's. Men who are in business may use business writing paper (see directly above) for any correspondence, except an answer to a formal invitation or a letter of condolence, or an answer to a letter of condolence, to a personal friend. For such personal correspondence, the best paper is heavy or medium-weight, of fine quality, and engraved with the house address or with initials; initials are better than a monogram for a man's writing paper. The suggestions given above for women may be used by a man with the following limitations:

Weight: Heavy or medium-weight paper for all correspondence except air mail.

Size: About 6 by 7 inches for all correspondence other than air-mail correspondence. This fits into an envelope about 6 by 3½ inches, more oblong, and more masculine, than the more nearly square envelopes suggested for a woman. For air-mail correspondence, the standard sheet is about 6 by 8 inches.

Color: White, cream color, gray blue, oxford blue, or gray—but gray only in a dull finish. Light blue is a feminine color.

Finish: A plain paper in a glazed or kid finish for formal personal correspondence, but white or cream color only. A plain bond or granite paper, glazed or dull, for other correspondence; lawn paper in gray with a dull finish.

Engraving: Plain block letters, or French Roman letters—all in capitals. As we have said, initials are better than a monogram, but an address is better than either. The best color for engraving on a man's paper is dark blue. Black can be used for a house address.

ENVELOPES

The best shape for envelopes, no matter what their size, is a near-square or a moderate oblong. Near-square is best for a woman; an oblong, as suggested above, for a man. On the back of the envelope, there should be either a deep, pointed, gummed flap, coming evenly down from each upper corner, or a straight gummed flap, reaching halfway down the envelope. It is wise to avoid very unusual shapes —a tall, narrow envelope, or an exaggeratedly long oblong, for example—or an unusual closing, such as a flap that closes on an oblique angle. Unless the engraving is in a very dark color, the lining of the envelope often matches it. Otherwise it may be the same color as the paper, or slightly darker, or, for a woman's envelope, white. These are three good shapes:

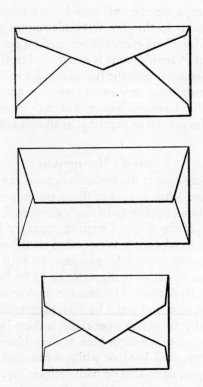

THREE STANDARD SHAPES FOR ENVELOPES

An envelope like the one at the top of this drawing is often used for the paper of an informal country house, or for a man's writing paper. The envelope in the middle, with its heavy flap, is best for a man's paper. The smallest one is standard for almost all women's writing paper, and for formal "house" paper.

FOLDING THE PAPER

As a rule, writing paper for personal correspondence is folded only once before it is put into the envelope. For the most formal correspondence—answering engraved invitations, for example—a double sheet is used, folded once across its length before being put into the envelope. But whether one uses a double sheet or an informal single sheet, this is the standard procedure. For informal notes, one might use a very small double sheet which is put sideways into the envelope without folding, or one might use a very big sheet which is folded twice, in a near-square. As far as possible, for personal correspondence one should avoid using writing paper which, like most business paper, is folded twice across—in three—before being put into the envelope.

MARKING THE PAPER

The conventional rule, as we have said, is that any paper used for private correspondence should be engraved if it is marked at all. And the second rule is that only an address, a cipher, a monogram, initials, or a device should be engraved on such papers. Exceptions to this are women's names which are very short: "Jean," "Ailsa," and "Mary" are names often used on personal writing paper in the form of a monogram. A man's name is never used in this way. A form which should never be used in engraving is the full name; for example, "Ailsa Scott" or "John Kerr." A professional man or woman (see page 530) may use this form in special circumstances, for business letters, but not otherwise. The full postal address is the standard form used in printing, as shown below on page 537.

Women's Monograms

For a woman's writing paper, the best monograms are those of fairly simple and conventional shapes: square, round, diamond-shaped, oval, or oblong; or elaborate but stylized shapes such as entwined or reversed ciphers. These are engraved at the center top of the sheet of writing paper, or in the upper left-hand corner. The upper right-hand corner is not often used because the date may be put there. On a sheet of paper about 5 by 7 inches or 6 by 8 inches, the monogram should not be bigger than $\frac{3}{4}$ inches in diameter or $\frac{3}{4}$ by $\frac{1}{2}$ inch. On a very large sheet of air-mail paper about 8 by 10 inches, the monogram is usually about the size of a twenty-five cent piece but could be even bigger: about one inch in diameter. As a rule, the most satisfactory engraving is done in the following colors: on a white or light-blue paper, medium-blue or dark-blue engraving; on a pale-gray paper, a darker gray, dark-blue, or white engraving; on an oxford-blue, or any fairly deep blue paper, dark-blue or white engraving. Very beautiful monograms are also engraved in a combination of white with medium blue, dark blue or gray. Dark red or dark green are sometimes also used for engraving, but they are not as traditional as blue, gray, or white; and, in the long run, one is apt to grow tired of them. Black engraving is used on white or gray paper for mourning. (See also page 153.) The following are examples of some of the best ways of marking a woman's paper:

MONOGRAMS FOR A WOMAN'S WRITING PAPER

Initials

As with monograms, initials are engraved either at the center top of a sheet of writing paper, or in the upper left-hand corner. Plain block initials—three initials are the most usual, but there may be two or four—are usually engraved in a straight line with a period after each one. This is by all odds the best way of engraving initials on a man's writing paper. The best size for a paper about 5 by 7 inches is an initial about 3/16 of an inch high, spaced so as to take up about ¾ inches over all. On big single sheets of paper, the initials are about ¼ of an inch high, covering an over-all space of about ¾ inches. These are examples of initials and monograms which are used both by men and by women:

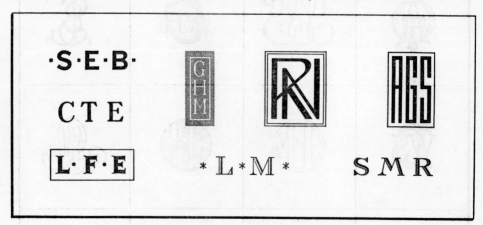

FOR A MAN'S OR A WOMAN'S WRITING PAPER

Engraved Addresses

The classic paper for a formal town house is engraved at the center top in dark gray or dark blue. Black may be used, also, but many feel that it suggests mourning. As a rule, only the street and the number are engraved and usually as follows:

4000 MASSACHUSETTS AVENUE

This is an example of block lettering

When it would not be inconveniently long, the address is sometimes given without numerals:

One Courtlandt Square

This is an example of shaded modified Roman lettering

or

Ten Blackland Street

This is an example of solid antique Roman lettering

If the line is not long enough, the number of the street may be written out: "22 East Seventy-second Street." But, to make a fine point, it is better, if possible, not to write in full an address which consists of two numbers: "Eleven South Sixty-fourth Street" seems a little pretentious, whereas "Ten Blackland Street" seems quite natural. As a rule, the number of the house is given in numerals, and the number of the street or avenue is engraved in letters: "11 South Sixty-fourth Street" or "1012 Fifth Avenue." But when the number of the street is not written out, "th" or "rd" or "nd" is written after the number with a line or ditto marks underneath; for example, "66th Street," "23rd Street" or "72nd Street." "Street" and "Avenue" should never be abbreviated, but in a city such as Washington, D. C., where the zone follows immediately after the street address, the abbreviation of the zone may be engraved: "5340 Massachusetts Avenue, N. W." When the house is in a big city, the name of the city and state are not engraved, according to the most conventional and formal practice, and the city zone number is therefore omitted. When the address is that of a small town, it is both practical and correct to engrave the full postal address, usually in two lines:

500 West Jefferson Place

Delafield, Massachusetts

This is an example of shaded antique Roman lettering

The best letterings for a formal town-house paper are block letters or French Roman lettering—all in capital letters. Antique Roman, shaded or solid, and shaded modified Roman, in capital and small letters, are also used.

The most formal country-house paper is engraved in the same colors as town-house paper, but not in black, with the name of the house given on one line, and the name of the town directly underneath it:

MALVERN
SAN RAPHAEL, CALIFORNIA

This is an example of French Roman lettering

If the house has no name, the address only is engraved, usually in two lines.

Less formally, there are many variations for engraving the address of a country house. In the first place, in addition to the usual colors, green or brown is often used for engraving on white or cream-colored papers; red on blue. Second, when the post office, telephone exchange, and railroad station are all in different towns, each may be engraved with its symbol usually in the upper left corner.

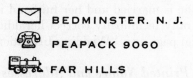

BEDMINSTER. N. J.

PEAPACK 9060

FAR HILLS

This is an example of block lettering

or, better and more modern,

TEL. ST. JAMES 3940   RIPPLEBROOK,

ST. JAMES, L. I.,

NEW YORK.

This is an example of block letters with large and small capitals

or,

PLEASANT VALLEY FARM

ENDHAM, NEW JERSEY

This is an example of block lettering in two sizes

Engraved Devices

Some women, instead of having their initials or a monogram engraved on their writing paper, choose a device or symbol which they use whenever their personal belongings are to be marked, embroidered, or engraved. A cornflower, a garland of laurel, a stylized rose—all these have been used as an engraving for a personal writing paper. Most of these devices are extremely attractive and the only difficulty lies in choosing something which will be neither too personal nor too irrelevant.

Country-house writing paper, also, is often engraved with devices instead of, and sometimes in addition to, the usual address. A working farm, for example, which raises Angus cattle, might have the head or the figure of an Angus steer engraved on its writing paper; a country place called "Apple Tree Farm," an apple tree, or a stylized engraving of an apple orchard. These are engraved in the middle of the sheet, above the centered address. The only engravings to be avoided are those which are pretentious, or self-consciously cute, or totally irrelevant.

Coats of Arms and Crests

In the United States, coats of arms and crests are not often used on writing paper but only on wedding invitations and announcements, menu cards, and place cards. Heraldic devices are discussed in detail on page 201 in the chapter, "Wedding Invitations," and there are only two points that need be made here. The first is that if a coat of arms or crest is used on writing paper, it must be engraved. This point has been made before, in connection with monograms, initials, and addresses, but it is even more mandatory as far as heraldic devices are concerned. The second point is that, to be technically "correct" according to heraldic custom, a woman should never use writing paper engraved with a crest or coat of arms unless she is married and her husband is alive. For widows, or unmarried women, the only technically correct heraldic device is a "lozenge." This is fully explained on page 201, "Wedding Invitations."

Printed Names and Addresses

When the full name and address are given on writing paper or on post cards, printing is often used. A paper so marked should be used only for business correspondence. The best printing is dark blue, in plain block letters. If the city is not very big or if there might be confusion, the name of the state is included; for example:

MRS. HUSTON WHITLOCK
CURTIS WOODS LANE
SPRINGFIELD, ILLINOIS

The form "Mary Duncan" should not be used. The printing should read like a postal address; if the woman is unmarried: "Miss Mary Compton Duncan, 40 Rolling Road . . .," etc. The name and address are usually printed in three lines at the center top of the page. Or they may be printed in a straight line across the top, a form used on post cards; for example:

| MRS. JAMES DUNCAN • 40 ROLLING ROAD • BALTIMORE • MARYLAND |

A printed address, with no name, is used on single sheets for informal personal correspondence as well as for business correspondence. It is an infringement of the conventional rule, but it is done every day. The standard 5½ by 7 inch size is best for business, but the large typewriter size is used for informal personal correspondence. Variations other than the form shown below should be avoided.

300 LAKE WASHINGTON BOULEVARD
SEATTLE, WASHINGTON

TO BE AVOIDED

1. Avoid crinkly, bumpy paper; it is hard to write on and can look very "arty."
2. Avoid rough-edged paper, called "deckle edge." Unless the paper is handmade, of the finest quality, a simple straight edge is in better taste.
3. Avoid any double-sheet paper with a first page narrower than the second.
4. Avoid unusual colors. Pale lilac and pink are too fragile for the mails; fuchsia and chartreuse show too clearly an effort to be original.
5. Avoid gilding or any metallic touches of any kind, either on the paper itself or in the lining of the envelope.
6. Avoid inappropriate lettering of any kind. The name and address on business paper are printed in block letters in a straight line; women's writing paper may be engraved in rounded and flowing letters, but "house" writing paper, which would be used by many members of the family, should be engraved in a simpler form.
7. Avoid curious lettering, such as pseudo-Oriental or imitation Chinese.
8. Avoid envelopes in strange or unusual "novelty" shapes. A square or an oblong is best.

67

Letters

As we said in the beginning of this section, the letters in this chapter are written as a tentative guide, not as examples which must be followed exactly. At its best, letter writing is an art, with infinite nuances and subtleties; and like all arts, it is intimately personal. Within the accepted limits of the form, personal inventions are an asset and empty phrases, polite though they may be, are from this point of view a failure. Any honest emotion, provided it is bound by a sense of proportion and fitness, makes a letter become alive. But these small truths have been said before and the catch is always the same: What are the "accepted limits"? How can one be sure of a "sense of fitness and proportion"?

The accepted limits of the form begin, from the reader's point of view, with the envelope, the way the address is written and placed. Handwriting is important. And although handwriting is not properly subject to etiquette it is irresistible to seize this moment to urge a departure from the lifeless, stereotyped handwriting taught in most of our schools. Legibility is immensely valuable, but once children have learned to write clearly, they should be encouraged to develop a form which will express their own personality. And apart from the handwriting—and the paper, which we have already discussed—there are many small but revealing details in the way the address is written.

Most important, of course, is the substance of the letter: the thought and the way it is expressed. For certain letters, there are certain forms, sometimes beautifully concealed in an original and ingenious pattern, often quite nakedly obvious. A sense of proportion fits the emotion of the letter to the purpose for which the letter was sent. And the great practical value of usage is that for almost every letter which is sent as a matter of form (and these are the only ones we are concerned with), there is an accepted form which those who are not geniuses in the art of letter writing may safely follow. This is the great difference between letter writing and other arts. There are times when a letter is expected and must be forthcoming. The comfort is that at such moments the important element is not the originality of the thought, or the facility of expression, but only the willingness to comply with the accepted rules; in other words, the desire to be polite.

The forms for envelopes, salutations, closings, and signatures are all in this chapter, but other letters, as the index will show, will be found in the chapters "Christenings," "Weddings," "Funerals and Mourning," and "Clubs."

ADDRESSING THE ENVELOPE

In writing any letter which is not a business letter, the envelope is correctly addressed as follows:

Mrs. Robert Maitland Wilson

62 York Avenue.

Cedar Rapids

Iowa

This is the classic form for writing an address. It is not always followed in writing to intimate friends or members of the family, but it illustrates several basic points:

1. Middle initials, which are an accepted part of a business letter, are not approved for other correspondence by those who are sticklers for form. The middle name is written or omitted. The only exception to this rule is in the case of those who use a second name as a general practice. A man who is known to his friends as "Maitland Wilson" and whose visiting cards read, "Mr. R. Maitland Wilson," should be addressed on an envelope as "Mr. R. Maitland Wilson" or "R. Maitland Wilson, Esq." (See page 556 for a discussion of the use of "Esquire.") An envelope is addressed to his wife: "Mrs. R. Maitland Wilson."

2. The second line, which carries the street address, should be abbreviated as little as possible. "Avenue" and "Street" should always be written in full. The most formal old-fashioned usage required that numbers, also, be written out, but this is not now observed unless the numbers are conveniently short. For example:

One Courtlandt Place
Ten East Jefferson Street
976 Fifth Avenue

539

Very often, one part of the address appears in numerals, and the other part is written out, as shown in the last example. The rule follows that of engraving: When there are two numbers, the number which "names" the street or avenue is written out, and the number of the house is left in numerals. When numerals are used, as in ". . . East 53$\underline{rd}$ Street," or ". . . East 79$\underline{th}$ Street," "th" and "rd" must be written after the numeral. The best usage demands also that these letters be underlined.

3. Cities and states should not be abbreviated ("Va.," for example, should be "Virginia"), and neither should they both be written on the same line. These are correct:

Chicago
Illinois
Richmond
Virginia

There should not be a comma after the name of the city.

4. Ideally, each line in the address should extend a little further to the right than the line above, or should make a straight margin at the right, as shown.

5. An envelope addressed to a shop or a company may be written according to any of the forms we have given here. But very often a variation of the business form is used. For example:

Good and Company
51$\underline{st}$ St. and Ninth Ave.
Pittsburgh
Pa.

DATING THE LETTER

In any letter which is not a business letter, the date is often written on the last page, at the left-hand margin, a little below the signature. In a very formal or very short letter, nothing more is written than the day:

. . . are looking forward so much
to seeing you.

Sincerely,

Jane Cowperthwaite

Wednesday

A long letter is usually dated in the upper right-hand corner:

Monday
December 9$\underline{th}$

In very informal letters to friends, the month may be abbreviated: "Dec. 9$\underline{th}$." But the rule of thumb is that the more formal the letter, the further one departs from the abbreviations which are usual in business correspondence.

Business letters, even those on the most trifling subjects, should be fully dated in the upper right-hand corner:

Dec. 9$\underline{th}$ 1948.

SALUTATIONS AND CLOSINGS

As indicated in the chapter "Forms of Address," for the most formal correspondence, the salutation is, "My dear ————." Otherwise, "Dear ————" is the classic salutation, and "Sincerely yours" the classic closing for all forms of correspondence other than business correspondence or correspondence between friends. In addition to the forms listed below there are two rules:

1. Any letter addressed to a firm and beginning "Dear Sirs," is signed "Yours truly."
2. Any letter written to an unknown reader, as, for example, a letter of reference, has neither salutation nor closing. Such a letter becomes a simple statement of fact, attested to by the signature.

The Most Formal Letter:
　My dear Mrs. Crowley,
　　Sincerely yours,
　　Thomas Rush Eliott

This salutation is considered most formal and distant in American usage. In British usage, it implies a fairly intimate friendship. (See page 582.)

The More Usual Formal Letter:
　Dear Senator Smith,
　　Sincerely yours,
　　Lucy Delafield Crowley

Letter to an acquaintance, whether a man or a woman:
　Dear Mr. (or Mrs.) Andrews,
　　Sincerely,
　　Lucy Crowley

Woman to a Man:
　Dear George,
　　Sincerely, (or "Until very soon, I hope" or "As ever")
　　Lucy Crowley

Man to a Woman:
　Dear Lucy,
　　As ever, (or "Yours ever")
　　George Andrews

Woman to a Woman:
　Dear Helen,
　　Affectionately,
　　Lucy Crowley

Man to a Man:
　Dear George,
　　Sincerely, (or "As ever")
　　Clarence Hoyt

In any but the two formal examples, the last name may be left off if the first name is enough identification. There is no need to discuss correspondence between intimate friends and relatives so close that formalities would be absurd, but it might be useful to give a few suggestions for closings used in such correspondence. For example, in any letter to a relative, even one whom one sees rarely and with whom one is not on intimate terms, the closing should still never be as stiff as "Sincerely." These are better: "Affectionately," "With love, Affectionately," or even "Devotedly." Older relatives-in-law should always be the first to set the general atmosphere of the correspondence and a closing of equal warmth should be used in answering their letters.

PHRASES TO AVOID

"Dear Friend," and "To Whom It May Concern."

"Cordially," "Kindly . . . ," "Faithfully," all of which may be used in business, but not in private correspondence.

"Yours of the 14th inst.," "Thanking you in advance," and other such clichés, should never be used, even in business letters.

THE CLOSING MESSAGE

At the end of many letters, just before the closing, there is often a phrase such as, "With love to George," or, "Henry sends his love." The most formal and polite phrase for this, which would be used in any letter signed "Sincerely," is "Please remember me to your Mother" or "your husband" or, if one is writing to an older woman, "Please remember me to Mr. Barnes." In a letter from an older woman to a younger woman, "My husband has asked to be remembered to you." In a letter that ends "Affectionately," "George has asked to be remembered to you all." A slightly less stiff version is "George has particularly asked to be remembered to you." In a letter that ends "Devotedly," the phrase is "With love to Aunt Harriet," or, "With best love to you all."

"Please remember me to . . ." is a better form for private correspondence than "With regards to . . ." or "With best regards to . . ." or, the classic business phrase, "With kindest regards." "Give my regards to . . ." is never a desirable form.

SIGNATURES

The unbreakable rule concerning signatures is that "Mr.," "Mrs.," "Miss," "Dr.," "Prof." or any other title is incorrect in a signature to a letter and must not be used. A letter is signed with a first or full name only. Men are less apt to break this rule than women, particularly married women. Mistakes one often sees are letters signed "Mrs. John Smith" or "Mrs. Mary Smith," or parentheses giving the woman's married name after or under her signature. No matter what the circumstances, all these must be avoided in a letter. In business letters, when the postal address is really more important than one's signature, one can use paper printed or engraved with the full name and charge address or postal address. (See page 536.) Lacking such paper, the name and address are written at the left-hand margin on the last page, a little below the signature, as follows:

". . . and send it to me as soon as possible. With
many thanks for all your trouble,

Yours truly,
Lucy D. Crowley

Mrs. Robert Crowley
221 Walnut Grove Road
Memphis
Tennessee

Or, if one is writing on "house" paper which is engraved with the address only, "Mrs. Robert Crowley" is written as shown here and the address is omitted.

In writing to domestic employees, and to small shops, women sign letters with their initials and last name—"L. D. Crowley," for example—as they do notes and telegrams. But "Mrs." is indefensible in a letter.

The last question concerning the signature of letters is whether to sign with the first and last name only or to include the middle name or its initial. As a rule, the signature of social correspondence is either the first name or the first and last names only, for example, "Lucy" or "Lucy Crowley." In business-like correspondence the signature is "Lucy D. Crowley" and the full three names ("Lucy

Delafield Crowley") are used only in formal or legal matters, or in letters where one wants to avoid the curtness of the abbreviation and the friendly implication of the social form.

Signatures to Notes, Telegrams, etc.

Women's signatures to certain telegrams and notes are not subject to the rules for signatures to letters. The exceptions, which may be signed "L. D. Crowley" or "Mrs. Robert Crowley," are telegrams to members of the household staff (signed "L. D. Crowley"), and telegrams to shops, hotels, travel agencies or any transportation service such as steamship lines, or public utilities such as telephone companies. These are signed "Mrs. Robert Crowley." Men should never sign anything, "Mr. ———" but these exceptions are sometimes necessary for women for obvious reasons. A man's name is full identification for charge accounts and reservations, whereas a woman who signs herself "Lucy Crowley" could be either "Miss Lucy Crowley," or "Mrs. Delafield Crowley" (divorced), or, "Mrs. Robert Crowley" (married). The forms for these telegrams are on page 554.

Short notes without the usual salutation "Dear ———" and without any closing such as "Yours truly" or "Sincerely" are also exempt from the general rule concerning signatures. For example, if one were leaving a note for the milkman, and there were any danger of confusion, a woman would sign "Mrs. Crowley," or a man "Mr. Andrews." If identification were unnecessary, as it would be if one were returning a dress with the sales slip enclosed, a note to the salesgirl might read, "Miss Angele—Would you try to get this for me in size 16, please?", and the signature might be "L.D.C." or "L. D. Crowley." Or, if one is leaving a note for the maid:

Bessie:

There'll be four people to tea.
Will you get some English muffins, please.

LDC (or "L. D. Crowley")

OBLIGATORY LETTERS

Entirely apart from any business or legal considerations, there are certain letters which must be written, and from which there is no escape other than severe illness. All of them are written on personal or "house" writing paper, and they must be written by hand unless there is some valid excuse, such as a broken wrist. They are:

1. Bread-and-butter letters.
2. Thank-you letters for wedding presents. Thanks for other presents are often given verbally, although the punctilious always write.
3. Thank-you letters for letters of condolence.
4. Letters to prospective and distant sons- or daughters-in-law upon their engagement.

One might include in the list letters of condolence, which certainly should be sent to friends and members of the family and which must also, incidentally, be written by hand. But the obligation is not quite the same as it is in the case of the four we have listed. All are a matter of feeling, but the four listed here are also a matter of form. One who fails to write a letter such as this, when there is an obligation to do so, is guilty not only of a lack of feeling but also of rudeness. The implication, in other words, is not only, "My feelings do not prompt me to write you," but also, "You are not important enough to warrant observance of the rules."

Bread-and-Butter Letters

These must be written when one has spent a night or more in someone's house. They are addressed to the mistress of the house, even if the guest is a very young friend of one of the children. It would not be useful to outline here the form used by children or by intimate friends. The first might confine itself to "Dear Mrs. Whitney, Thank you for inviting me to stay. I had a good time. I liked the pony. Love, David"; the second might read, "Darling, We had a wonderful visit, and it was sweet of you to ask us. Thank you a thousand times. Am rushing to meet Jim at the station, but could you both dine with us in town next Thursday? Love, Lib." But neither of these could be called a form, and in neither case is a form necessary.

Although it may be varied in infinite ways to cover an infinite number of circumstances, the form of a bread-and-butter letter is supposed to be as follows: in the first paragraph, thanks and expressions of one's enjoyment of the visit; in the second, a short anecdote or a phrase or two about one's trip home, or something else indirectly connected with the visit; in the third, renewed thanks. The general tone of the letter should reflect the atmosphere of the visit. If the hosts were older and rather formal, the letter should be somewhat formal; if they were contemporaries, it might be as witty and gay as possible. It should be written within a day or so; or at most, five days, after the visit; a greater lapse of time will mean that apologies must be made for the delay in writing.

To a Contemporary:

This illustrates the form and the general tone; the wit must be personal:

Dear Evie,

Thank you so much for the wonderful week end. We so loved seeing you and Harry again, and we couldn't have enjoyed ourselves more.

Our arrival home was clouded by the news that every chicken had escaped from the coop and, although it was by then eleven o'clock, Louis felt it necessary to make efforts to retrieve them from the trees where they were roosting. I missed the peace of our week end very much indeed!

I hope we shall see you both very soon. Louis sends you his love, with many thanks again from us both,

Affectionately,
Muriel

To an Older Woman:

Dear Mrs. Barnes,

Thank you so much for the lovely visit. It was so kind of you to ask us, and we had a wonderful time.

I am writing to Sutton's today, as you suggested, to ask them to send me some of the pansy seed. But I'm afraid it will take years—and a very green thumb—to get the same effect!

Our new apartment is almost ready, and Mother will be visiting us in September, so I hope you and Mr. Barnes will come and lunch with us when you come back to town. Thank you so much again for the week end. With love from us both,

Affectionately,
Ann

From a Man:

Dear Mrs. Barnes,

Thank you very much indeed for a very agreeable week end. It was a great pleasure to see you both again, and I am most grateful to you for inviting me.

The luggage and I arrived safely at the station, but I was sorry to have had to leave at such an inconveniently early hour—and sorrier still not to have been able to see you to say good-bye.

I shall look forward to seeing you both in Plymouth next month. Please remember me to your husband, and many thanks again.

Sincerely,
George Cosby

Thank-You Letters for Wedding Presents

These are discussed on page 225.

Thank-You Letters for Letters of Condolence

These are discussed on page 152.

Letters to Prospective Sons- and Daughters-in-Law

As a rule, of course, engagements take place under a mother's eye, or at least near enough so that a letter to the prospective in-law is unnecessary. But if for any reason the mother is away from the scene, she should write to her future son- or daughter-in-law, to give the engagement her blessing and make it official. (Granted, of course, that it has her approval!)

The form is very simple because the only point is that one is pleased and happy. The first paragraph contains this information; the second usually outlines some plan for a future meeting, and the letter ends with an affectionate closing.

My dear Edith,

Howard has told me of your decision to be married, and I wanted to write you at once to tell you how delighted my husband and I are, and how happy it has made us.

We plan to come to Philadelphia within the next few weeks, and I shall telephone your mother this evening to arrange when and where we shall meet. In any case, it will be very soon, and we shall both be so pleased to see you all again.

This letter brings you much love and many, many hopes for your happiness.

Affectionately,
Mary Osborne

Dear Winslow,

Genevieve has told me that you and she have decided to be married and, although I shall see you so soon, I felt I must write you to tell you how happy we are.

We are expecting you next Friday, and we plan to have a little dinner on Saturday, the day the engagement is to be announced. I have already telephoned your mother and I hope your parents will be staying with us, too. It will be a very happy time for us all.

Until very soon then, dear Winslow, with all my best wishes,

Affectionately,
Mary Osborne

LETTERS OF INTRODUCTION

All letters of introduction involve a certain number of customs which have nothing to do with the content of the letter and which can best be illustrated by an example: Mrs. Abbott gives Miss Barclay a letter of introduction to Mrs. Crowley. This letter is neither stamped nor sealed. Miss Barclay takes it with her on her trip, or receives it, enclosed in another letter from Mrs. Abbott, when she has already arrived. (Letters of introduction obviously imply a journey, because if all three lived in the same town, Mrs. Abbott could easily arrange a meeting without all the fuss of letters.)

Miss Barclay leaves the letter at the Crowleys' house—or sends it there with a visiting card of her own, since letters of introduction should not be handed directly to the one to whom they are addressed. If the Crowleys were very much older than Miss Barclay, or very formal, or if this were a business matter rather than a purely friendly one, Miss Barclay would write only her new address on her card; since they are more or less contemporaries, she writes also, "So looking forward to seeing you." If Miss Barclay had no visiting cards, she would write a short note on her hotel writing paper:

Dear Mrs. Crowley,

Eleanor Abbott gave me this letter of introduction to you. I am staying here until a week from Thursday, and I am looking forward so much to meeting you.

Until very soon,

Sincerely,
Helen Barclay

Mrs. Crowley writes or telephones Miss Barclay immediately, inviting her to tea or to luncheon. Had Mrs. Crowley been away when the letter was delivered, or had there been any delay in answering, a letter or a telephone call of profuse apology would have been necessary.

Having been thus kindly received and entertained by Mrs. Crowley, Miss Barclay writes to Mrs. Abbott, thanking her for the letter of introduction, and expatiating on the charm and the kindness of Mrs. Crowley. Mrs. Abbott then writes Mrs. Crowley thanking her in turn for her kindness to Miss Barclay, hinting that Miss Barclay found the Crowleys charming and enjoyed very much meeting them. If Mrs. Crowley is exquisitely polite, she writes to Mrs. Abbott, minimizing the trouble she has taken and dwelling on the pleasure she has had in meeting Miss Barclay. This completes the circle of letters and the round robin of customs that are set in motion by a letter of introduction.

But all this has been standard practice for many years. The big change in letters of introduction in recent years has been in their content. The embarrassingly fulsome description of Miss Barclay's charm and of Mrs. Abbott's feelings for her, which were considered an integral part of every letter of introduction of the past generation, have been very much toned down. The following are a few examples which may be helpful.

Introducing One Intimate Friend to Another

Dearest Lucy,

This letter will be brought you by Helen Barclay, who is planning to spend a few weeks in Memphis. She is a great friend of mine (an older woman might say, "a very old and very dear friend")—but you have heard as much about her as she has about you, so I need not expatiate here!

I was delighted to receive your lovely long letter about the Christmas parties. It all sounded so gay. Now that the children have gone back to school, I'll have time to answer it properly.

Do remember me to George. With love,

Affectionately,

Eleanor

Such a letter should always be written by hand, and it should never be written on paper with a business letterhead, even if it is being sent by one man to another. It should be addressed to "Lucy's" house, never to a business address.

Introducing an Acquaintance to an Intimate Friend

Dearest Jane,

I am sending you this letter to introduce a charming friend, Mrs. Henry Willetts, whom you will enjoy meeting. She is to be in San Francisco for only a few weeks, and I hope you will do everything you can to make her stay agreeable. Perhaps George could also arrange to have her meet some of the Museum trustees—her great interest is sculpture and she has been a trustee of the museum here for some time.

I was so pleased to receive your last letter and to know that you and George are well. Please give him my love.

Affectionately,

Eleanor

This letter should be written in the same way and on the same paper as the previous example.

Introducing a Friend to a Friend

When neither is an intimate friend, but both are more than acquaintances, the letter might be as follows:

Dear Jane,

I am sending you this letter to introduce Bill Field, a friend who will

547

be spending a few days in San Francisco on his way to Honolulu. I know you will both enjoy meeting—he is great fun and most attractive—and I shall be most grateful for anything you can do to give him a good time in the short while he will be there.

Do write soon and give me all your news—in any case, Bill will be coming home in about six weeks via Panama, so I shall have a first-hand report!

With love to you all,

Affectionately,
Eleanor Abbott

As in the case of the first two letters, this should be written by hand, on one's own writing paper.

Introducing a Friend to an Acquaintance

Letters of introduction are rarely sent to an acquaintance and the example below is included only to illustrate the essential points. The letter does not emphasize the friendship between Mrs. Abbott and Miss Barclay, since Mrs. Cowperthwaite is not a great friend of Mrs. Abbott's, and will not be interested. Instead, it stresses the reasons for Miss Barclay's visit, and the reasons why Mrs. Cowperthwaite might be interested in meeting her. A letter of introduction should not be sent unless these reasons exist, or unless Mrs. Cowperthwaite is under an obligation to Mrs. Abbott which she will be pleased to be able to repay. If Mrs. Cowperthwaite is a business acquaintance, this letter would be written on business paper; if not, one's own writing paper should be used and it should be written by hand.

Dear Mrs. Cowperthwaite,

This letter will be brought you by Helen Barclay, a friend of mine who is coming to San Francisco for a few weeks to look into the Physical Therapy work the Red Cross is doing in the hospitals there. Since your interests are so similar, I felt sure that you would enjoy meeting, and I hoped that perhaps you would be able to help her to get any information she might need.

Should you be coming to Cincinnati soon again, do be sure to let me know. It was such a pleasure to see you on your last visit.

Until very soon, I hope,

Sincerely,
Eleanor Abbott

Business Letter of Introduction

Mr. Arnold Remsen
First Chemical Bank
33 O'Farrell Street
San Francisco
California

Dear Mr. Remsen (or "Dear Arnold"),

My friend, David Fielding, is leaving shortly for San Francisco on business in connection with his work in the Lincoln Engineering Company.

(Or, if he has an important position such as president, vice president or general manager, his title can be given—". . . his work as general manager of the Lincoln Engineering Company.") He expects to be there for some time, and I want very much to have him meet you. I know you will enjoy knowing him, and I shall be most grateful for anything you can do for him.

With kindest regards,

Sincerely yours,
Alexander Williams

Such a letter must include some reference to the business of the one who is presented. It should be typed on business writing paper and be sent to a business address. A closing phrase such as "With kindest regards" is correct and customary in business letters but should not be used in private correspondence.

LETTERS OF REFERENCES

An employee who is leaving one's household is entitled to a reference to show that his services have been satisfactory, unless the contrary is very much the case. The first point in writing a reference is that one must be truthful and fair, both to future employers and to the employee. The second point is that one must be kind, because these letters are extremely important to one whose life is spent in domestic employment. They are unquestionable testimony as to his record and character, and they should be withheld only for the most serious reasons, when it would be impossible in all truthfulness to write a letter which would be useful to him in finding a new position. Further, one should never write or suggest anything in a reference which one might contradict later, when a prospective employer telephones to ask for details. Although one must be honest in answering a prospective employer when he asks for information, justice to the employee demands that one should never give him a favorable and enthusiastic reference and speak slightingly of him when questioned. If one has reservations about any important factor, there are ways of indicating it in the reference. (See page 550 below.)

The classic letter of reference covers the following points in the following order:

The name of the employee.
The length of his employment.
The nature of his work.
His honesty.
His sobriety.
His competence, and any other qualities, whether pertinent to his work, or of a general nature, such as his ability to work well with others, etc.
The reasons for his leaving, regret at losing him (if such is the case) and willingness to answer any further questions concerning him, are included in a closing paragraph.

References need neither salutation nor closing. "To Whom It May Concern" should never be used. Although they can be typewritten, it is better if they are written by hand, on the "house" writing paper. In any case, they must be signed by the mistress of the house or, if there is none, by the employer or the house-keeper.

For a Satisfactory Employee

The following is a sample reference for a satisfactory maid.

May 12<u>th</u>
1948

Hilda Matthews has been in my employ for the last three years as chamber-maid-waitress. I have found her most satisfactory in every way—scrupulously honest, sober, and a willing worker. She is an excellent waitress and a competent housemaid, and has always worked well with other members of the household.

She is leaving for family reasons of her own, and I am extremely sorry to see her go. I shall be glad to answer any questions concerning her at any time.

Eleanor Chase Abbott

Mrs. Henry Abbott
12 Forest Avenue
Cincinnati
Ohio

This enthusiastic reference indicates a most satisfactory employee and a mutually happy relationship. If conditions were not quite so ideal, the adjectives would be less glowing and the general tone of the letter would be more guarded. Hilda would be described as a "capable waitress and chambermaid," "honest and sober." If she had given notice, the last paragraph would read, "She is leaving of her own accord." If her character were satisfactory and she were being dismissed for incompetence, all references to her capability as waitress-chambermaid would be omitted from the body of the letter, and the last paragraph would read, "She is leaving because my household arrangements demand a more fully trained worker. I cannot, however, recommend her character too highly and I shall be very glad to answer any questions concerning her."

Other reasons which may be given in this last paragraph are: "She is leaving because I am moving to town and plan to rearrange the duties of the household." Or, ". . . expect to make other household arrangements."

For an Unsatisfactory Employee

When an employee has been unsatisfactory, omissions in the reference are the only way of indicating it. And such omissions should be made if one plans to mention any of his faults later, when a prospective employer telephones for fur-ther information. For example, if he has a bad disposition, no mention of his temper, good or bad, need be made in the reference, and one is free to say any-thing one likes about it when questioned.

But these are minor points. The two vital factors in any reference, as in any-one's character, are honesty and sobriety. To impugn either of these is to make it extremely difficult for him to find new employment, and, therefore, every generous interpretation should be strained to avoid implicating him on these counts. If one has good reason to believe that he was inclined to drink too much, one can leave out any mention of sobriety in the reference. In this case, of course, the first question a prospective employer will ask will be on this point. In answering, one must be both honest and generous. Any possible excuse, such as illness, war service, or an earlier accident, must be suggested.

The same is true of honesty. Although an employee will rarely present a reference in which no mention is made of his honesty, if he does, one must explain the circumstances, in all truthfulness and with as much generosity and kindness as possible. For example, "Well, I didn't say anything about his honesty in the reference because a very disagreeable episode took place while he was here. Some silver was discovered missing. On the other hand, he had been with us for two years at that time, and there had never been any other trouble of that kind before. Besides, it happened in the country, where a great many people have access to the house. I was never sure about it one way or the other, but that explains why I didn't mention honesty in the reference."

WOMEN'S BUSINESS LETTERS

This section describes two or three of the most useful forms for writing to business firms. Business letters written from one firm to another are not included, because they are strictly a matter of business usage. The examples given here are all written to large companies; in writing to a small tradesman, whom one knows by name, the letter should begin, "Dear Mr. ————," and end "Yours truly," or "Sincerely yours." In writing to a specific salesman in a big shop, if one does not know his initials or first name, the envelope is addressed:

Marshall Field and Co.
Chicago
Illinois

Attention of Mr. Bolton
Shoe Department

It is not correct to address the envelope:

Mr. Bolton, Shoe Department
Marshall Field & Co.
etc.

The letter may begin either "Dear Mr. Bolton," or "Dear Sirs." All such letters should be dated.

Placing an Order

June 15th
1947

Woodward and Lothrop
Washington
D. C.

Dear Sirs,

　　　I should like to order the tennis dress advertised in the *Sun* last Tuesday.

I enclose my cheque for $15.00 and the advertisement that appeared in the paper. Please send the dress, in white, size 14, to:

> Mrs. James Howard Duncan
> Rolling Road
> Baltimore
> Maryland

> With many thanks,
> Yours truly,
> Mary C. Duncan

Returning Unsatisfactory Merchandise

> December 10th
> 1947

Douglas and Co.
Fifth Avenue at 57th Street
New York
New York

Dear Sirs,

      I have returned to you today, by parcel post, three of the dozen whiskey-and-soda glasses which you sent me last week. Although the others arrived safely, these three were found broken when they were being unpacked. I hope you will be able to replace them with three others but, if this is not possible, please credit them to my account. I enclose the sales slip which came with the order.

> With many thanks,
> Yours truly,
> Lucy D. Crowley

Reporting a Mistake or Unsatisfactory Service

> September 8th
> 1947

New Vernon Power and Light Co.
Highland Park
Oklahoma

Dear Sirs,

      I am afraid there has been some mistake in the enclosed bill. The house at New Vernon has been shut for the past months, and I cannot understand how this amount can be owing you in the circumstances. Is there, perhaps, a service charge, whether or not electricity is used?

      Please let me know about this as soon as possible. With many thanks,

> Yours truly,
> Alice H. Cartwright

LETTERS TO CONGRESSMEN

The example given here is a letter to a United States senator. The forms of address for representatives and state senators and assemblymen will be found on page 562 in the chapter on "Forms of Address." The envelope is addressed:

The Honorable William Addison Smith
United States Senate
Washington
D. C.

and the letter might be worded as follows:

Dear Senator Smith,

I hope so much that you will use your valuable influence in support of (or "against") the proposed legislation for continuing the Office of Temporary Controls. As a registered voter (or, if the writer is a member of the same political party as the Congressman, "As a registered Republican") in the state of Wisconsin, I feel that the passage (or "defeat") of this bill is in the best interests of the country.

Sincerely yours,
Alice Harwood Cartwright

LETTERS OF RECOMMENDATION FOR THE YOUNG

A letter such as this is sometimes needed in connection with organized activities for young people. It is usually written at the request of a parent whose child is being proposed for admission, and it is sent to a friend, or at least to an acquaintance, who is a member of the admission committee. Some organizations accept letters from other members, or parents of members, whether or not the writer is known to any member of the admission committee. But, usually, one should not write such a letter except to a friend or acquaintance.

Dear Mrs. Barnes (or "Dear Ethel," if one is on more intimate terms),

I understand that Diana Crowley's name is coming up at the next meeting for admission to the School Holiday dance. She is fourteen years old and in the ninth class at the Brearton School. I have known her parents, Robert and Lucy Crowley, for many years, and I have known Diana since she was a little girl. She is a most attractive and charming child—I am sure that she would enjoy the dances and that you would enjoy having her.

With many thanks for anything that you can do,

Sincerely (or "Affectionately"—
see "Salutations and Closings")
Jane Fowler

LETTERS OF RECOMMENDATION

Letters of recommendation are sometimes required by women's residences or by families with which young men, or young women, are planning to board. The following example, written to the secretary of a residential club, is the standard form:

Dear Miss Adams,

Margaret Ellsworth has told me that you have asked for a letter of recommendation, which I am delighted to send you. I have known Margaret and her parents, Mr. and Mrs. Robert Ellsworth, for many years. Her father is District Manager of the Lincoln Engineering Company here, and they have lived in Berwick for a long time.

Margaret is a forthright, able, and serious girl, and has always been a good student. I have every confidence in her, and I am sure that she will be a most valuable resident member of the club.

Sincerely yours,
Eleanor Chase Abbott

The envelope would be addressed:

Miss Martha Adams
Secretary, Student Artists' Club
Chicago
Illinois

TELEGRAPHIC FORMS

We are listing here two or three different forms for telegrams which may be useful, not only as examples of the text, but also to show how the signature of a telegram may differ from that of a letter.

Reserving Rooms in a Hotel

PLEASE RESERVE DOUBLE ROOM AND BATH FOR ONE WEEK STARTING FRIDAY, SEPTEMBER 24. WIRE CONFIRMATION COLLECT.

MRS. WILLIAM ANDREWS
2100 PACIFIC AVENUE
SAN FRANCISCO
CALIFORNIA

If the telegram were sent by a man the signature would, of course, read "William Andrews." "For self and wife" is not a desirable phrase.

Telegram to a Shop

PLEASE CHARGE TO MY ACCOUNT AT 342 WALNUT GROVE ROAD, MEMPHIS, TENNESSEE, THREE STURDY QUART-SIZE THERMOS BOTTLES AND SEND TO ME AT FAIRLEE, VERMONT.

MRS. ROBERT CROWLEY

To a Public Utility

PLEASE RESUME SERVICE STARTING SEPTEMBER 15TH.

MRS. ROBERT CROWLEY
342 WALNUT GROVE ROAD
MEMPHIS
TENNESSEE

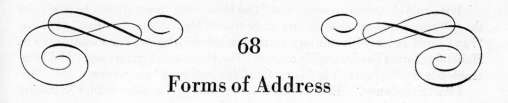

68

Forms of Address

In this chapter will be found the forms of address used in the United States. We have included also some of the British forms, and French forms which are correct in any country when writing or speaking French. Spanish forms, which are used in Spanish-American countries as well as in Spain, are listed also. But it should be noted that in speaking in English to foreigners of any nationality, women are usually addressed as "Madame" or "Mademoiselle —"; men as "Mr. —." For example, "Madame Pavlov," and "Mr. Pavlov."

TITLES USED IN THE UNITED STATES

"Excellency"

According to the standard official practice of the United States government, the courtesy title "Excellency" is not used in addressing American officials. It is used in addressing a foreign president, a foreign cabinet minister, a foreign ambassador or high foreign officials in general.

Ecclesiastical usage differs from this in that "Excellency" is used in addressing all Roman Catholic archbishops and bishops. And social usage, also, makes certain exceptions. In many States, for example, the governor is always called "Excellency," and in social correspondence, American Ambassadors also.

Like all courtesy titles, "Excellency" is used by others as a form of address— never by the holder. For example, "The Chinese Ambassador requests the pleasure of . . ." not "His Excellency, the Chinese Ambassador, requests . . ." Or, on a visiting card "Vigo Jenssen, Ambassador of Denmark"; not "His Excellency." Or, in answering invitations, "The American Ambassador and Mrs. Choate."

In writing the envelope, the formal practice is to write out "His Excellency," usually on the line above the name and a little to the left. Informally, it may be abbreviated—"H. E."—and written just before the name.

"Honorable"

High American officials are often given the courtesy title "Honorable," both while they are in office and when they have left office. (The old rule is, "Once an Honorable, always an Honorable.") A former Senator, for example, is not officially addressed in writing as "Senator," but he is always "The Honorable . . ." (In practice, a former Senator, particularly one who has held the office a long time, is often spoken to as "Senator" and is often, informally, addressed in writing as "My dear Senator . . .")

It is a rule of American usage that "The Honorable" must always be used with the full name, and never with any other title ("Mr.," "Mrs.," "Miss," "Dr." or "Esq.") and never with military rank or scholastic degree. For example, "The Honorable James Fox Strong" is correct. "The Honorable Strong" and "The Honorable Mr. Strong" and "The Honorable Captain Strong" are wrong.

Like "Excellency," "Honorable" is never used by the office-holder in issuing or answering invitations, on visiting cards or in any other way.

Formally, "The Honorable" is written out in full, and, if the line would be too long, it may be written above and to the left of the name. Less formally, it may be abbreviated: "The Hon." or "Hon."

This is a list of the offices which carry the right to the courtesy title "Honorable":

American Ambassador
American Minister
Cabinet Officer
Clerk of the United States House of Representatives
Commissioner, District of Columbia
Commissioner or member of a board of equal rank
Counselor of the Department of State
Foreign Minister not of Cabinet rank
Governor of a State, Territory or Island Possession of the United States. (In certain states, the Governor is given the courtesy title, Excellency, as a matter of rule. In most states it is a custom, but is not followed by the Federal government.)
Head of an independent Federal agency
High Commissioner
High officer of a State government
Judge (judge of the Supreme Court excepted)
Legal Advisor, or an office of comparable rank

Mayor of a city
Minister resident
Public Printer
Representative
Secretary to the President
Secretary of the United States Senate
Senator
Sergeant-at-Arms of the United States Senate
Speaker of the House of Representatives
State senator or representative
Under- or assistant secretary of an Executive department

In addition, a former President or Vice President, and any former member of the Supreme Court is an "Honorable." While they are in office none of these is addressed in writing as "The Honorable" but a member of the Supreme Court, when it seems fitting or appropriate, might be presented at a banquet or on the radio with the use of his full name and the title "Honorable" as shown on page 558.

"Esquire"

"Esquire" is a complimentary title not used in commercial correspondence. It is used only in addressing a man in writing; not on an envelope addressed to a man and his wife and never on a visiting card. In official American correspondence, "Esquire" is written in full, but in social correspondence the abbreviation is used. It should never be used together with a title such as "Mr." or "Honorable," or with military rank or scholastic degree, but only as follows:

James Howard Duncan, Esq.
44 Rolling Road
Baltimore
Maryland

or,   James Howard Duncan, Jr., Esq.
or,   James Howard Duncan, II, Esq.

"Junior," "Senior," "II"

"Junior" is used in addressing a man whose name is exactly the same as his father's, and whose father is living. Although this is not a rule, "junior" is often used without the prefix "Mr." and it may be followed, but never preceded, by "Esq." (see above). If he is married, an envelope sent jointly to a man and his wife is addressed: Mr. and Mrs. George Henry Adams, Jr. "Junior" should never be used by an unmarried woman, but only by a married woman whose husband is "junior." A capital "J" is used only when "junior" is abbreviated—"Jr."

Senior cannot be used with a man's name. No matter how famous the son, he is junior to his father as long as his father is alive. The only possible use of senior is after the name of a widow, and this is not really desirable (see "A Widow," page 568). Like "junior," "senior" is either written in full without a capital letter, or abbreviated: "Sr."

II is used to identify a younger man, other than a son, who has the same name as an older living relative. For example, a man named after his living grandfather, uncle or great-uncle, Mr. Alan Flagg, is Alan Flagg, II. Any younger namesake of Mr. Flagg, other than his son, would be Alan Flagg, III, and so on. (IV, and even V, can conceivably be used.)

If father, son and grandson are all called Alan Flagg, the father is Alan Flagg, the son is Alan Flagg, Jr., and the grandson Alan Flagg, III, because he is the third of that name. As soon as the grandfather dies, the son becomes Alan Flagg, the grandson, Alan Flagg, Jr. Like "junior," "II" or "III" may be followed, but never preceded, by "Esq." No numerals are ever used by a woman in her own right.

AMERICAN FORMS

Officials

The forms given here are based on the official forms used by our State Department, with a few exceptions made to accord with social rather than official usage. The official form for inviting an official and his wife, for example, is based on the assumption that one invites the official and includes his wife. An official invitation, therefore, sent to a United States Senator and his wife is addressed: "The Honorable John Blank and Mrs. Blank." This is quite proper in official life, but socially the official and his wife are invited together and the envelope is therefore addressed either "Senator and Mrs. Blank" or "The Honorable and Mrs. John Blank."

In the same way, and for the same reasons, in official communications the name or title of a woman official is written first, and her husband's name follows. Socially, this form is followed only in the case of very important women officials, such as Cabinet officers, ministers and ambassadors. In other words, if the post is of such importance that a man who holds it is entitled officially to precede his wife into the room at an official dinner, the title must go first on the envelope whether or not the office-holder is a woman. (A list of these officials will be found on page 491.) When envelopes are addressed jointly to other women officials and their husbands, the husband's name must come first on the envelope, or in any invitation, according to the accepted social form shown in this chapter.

Written Address	Spoken Address	Introduction * and (Form of Reference)	Presentation at a Banquet or on the Radio

* The form of reference is usually the same as the form of introduction: "The Vice President announced . . ." When there is a difference, the form of reference will be put in brackets under the form of introduction. No form of introduction is given for those who are so important that everyone is introduced to them.

The President

The President
The White House
Washington
D. C.
My dear Mr. President,
Very respectfully,
Business: "Respectfully yours,"
 	
(in writing to all other American
  officials the business closing is
  "Very truly yours,")
 	
The President and Mrs. Adams †
The White House
Washington
D. C.
	Mr. President	(The President)	The President of
			the United
			States

The Vice President

The Vice President United States Senate Washington D. C. My dear Mr. Vice President, Sincerely yours, The Vice President and Mrs. Quincy address at home	Mr. Vice Presi- dent, or Mr. Quincy	The Vice Presi- dent	The Vice Presi- dent of the United States

The Chief Justice of the Supreme Court

The Chief Justice
The Supreme Court
Washington
D. C.
My dear Mr. Chief Justice,
Sincerely yours,
 	
The Chief Justice and Mrs. Mar-
  shall
address at home
 	
  Mrs. John Quincy Adams
  The White House
  Washington
  D. C.
  My dear Mrs. Adams:
  Sincerely yours,
	Mr. Chief Justice,
	or Mr. Mar-
	shall
		The Chief Justice	The Honorable
			John Marshall,
			Chief Justice of
			the Supreme
			Court of the
			United States
			(abroad add "of
			America")

The spoken address and introduction are: "Mrs. Adams"; the presentation is: "Mrs. John Quincy Adams."

† The wives of all American officials are addressed in the usual way, without any special form or courtesy title:

Written Address	Spoken Address	Introduction and (Form of Reference)	Presentation at a Banquet or on the Radio

Associate Justices

Mr. Justice Johnson The Supreme Court Washington D. C. My dear Mr. Justice, Sincerely yours, Mr. Justice and Mrs. Johnson address at home	Mr. Justice, or Mr. Justice Johnson	Mr. Justice John- son	The Honorable Henry Johnson, Associate Jus- tice of the Su- preme Court of the United States (abroad add "of Amer- ica")

The Speaker of the House of Representatives

The Honorable Francis Clay,
    Speaker of the House of Repre-
    sentatives
The Capitol
 	
or, according to social usage,
 	
The Speaker
The Capitol
 	
My dear Mr. Speaker,
Sincerely yours,
 	
The Speaker and Mrs. Clay
address at home
	Mr. Speaker, or
	Mr. Clay
		The Speaker, Mr.
		Clay (The
		Speaker, or
		Mr. Clay)
			The Honorable
			Francis Clay,
			Speaker of the
			House of
			Representatives

American Ambassador

NOTE that in Central and South American countries the phrases "Embassy of the United States of America" and "Ambassador of the United States" are used in preference to "American Embassy" or "American Ambassador."

NOTE also that when an American Army officer is appointed Ambassador or Minister, a courtesy title is never given him. The correct address is: General John Blank, American Ambassador (or Minister). The salutation of the letter may be either "My dear Mr. Ambassador" or "My dear General Blank"; and in speaking to him, either "Mr. Ambassador" or "General Blank" may be used.

The Honorable Joseph Choate
American Ambassador
London
England
My dear Mr. Ambassador,
Sincerely yours,
The American Ambassador and
    Mrs. Choate
American Embassy
London
England
The Honorable and Mrs. Joseph
    Choate (in other countries)
 	
or the accepted social form:
	Mr. Ambassador,
	or Mr. Choate
		The American
		Ambassador
		(The Ambas-
		sador, or Mr.
		Choate)
			The Honorable
			Joseph Choate,
			the American
			Ambassador
			(When an am-
			bassador is not
			at his post, the
			name of the
			country to
			which he is ac-
			credited must
			be added:
			"American
			Ambassador
			to ———")

His Excellency The American Ambassador London England H. E. The American Ambassador and Mrs. Choate	Your Excellency, or Mr. Ambas- sador		His Excellency the American Ambassador

Written Address	Spoken Address	Introduction and (Form of Reference)	Presentation at a Banquet or on the Radio

American Ministers

The Honorable Henry Armour American Minister Dublin Ireland	Mr. Minister, or Mr. Armour	The American Minister, Mr. Armour (The Minister, or Mr. Armour)	The Honorable Henry Armour, the American Minister (not at his post: —— American Minister to ——)
My dear Mr. Minister, Sincerely yours,			
The American Minister and Mrs. Armour American Legation Dublin Ireland The Honorable and Mrs. Henry Armour (in other countries)			

American Minister—woman

The Honorable Margaret Lloyd Owen American Minister Damascus Lebanon	Madam Minister, or Mrs. Owen	The American Minister, Mrs. Owen (The Minister, or Mrs. Owen)	The Honorable Margaret Lloyd Owen, the American Minister (not at her post: —— American Minister to ——)
My dear Madam Minister, or My dear Mrs. Owen, Sincerely yours,			
The American Minister and Mr. Owen American Legation Damascus Lebanon			

American Chargé d'Affaires, Consul-General, Consul, or Vice-Consul

George Edward Benson, Esquire American Chargé d'Affaires (or American Consul-General, Consul, or Vice-Consul) Paris France	Mr. Benson	Mr. Benson	Mr. George Edward Benson, the American Chargé d'Affaires
My dear Mr. Benson, Sincerely yours,			
Mr. and Mrs. George Edward Benson address at home			

Cabinet Officer—man

The Honorable John Hay Secretary of State Washington D. C.	Mr. Secretary, or Mr. Hay	The Secretary of State, Mr. Hay (The Secretary, or Mr. Hay)	The Honorable John Hay, Secretary of State

Written Address	Spoken Address	Introduction and (Form of Reference)	Presentation at a Banquet or on the Radio

If written from abroad,

The Honorable John Hay
Secretary of State of the United
   States of America
Washington
D. C.

or, the accepted social form:

The Secretary of State
Washington
D. C.

(or address at home)

My dear Mr. Secretary,
Sincerely yours,

The Secretary of State and Mrs.
   Hay
address at home

NOTE: Other members of the Cabinet follow the same form: "Secretary of Labor," "Secretary of the Interior," etc. In writing to the Attorney General, the envelope is addressed either: "The Honorable Richard Walbeck, Attorney General," or "The Attorney General"; the salutation is "My Dear Mr. Attorney General."

Cabinet Officer—woman

Written Address	Spoken Address	Introduction and (Form of Reference)	Presentation at a Banquet or on the Radio
The Honorable Frances Williams Secretary of Labor Washington D. C.	Madam Secretary, or Miss (or Mrs.) Williams	The Secretary of Labor, Miss Williams (The Secretary, or Miss Williams)	The Honorable Frances Williams, Secretary of Labor
My dear Madam Secretary, Sincerely yours,			
The Secretary of Labor and Mr. Williams address at home			

Under Secretary

Written Address	Spoken Address	Introduction and (Form of Reference)	Presentation at a Banquet or on the Radio
The Honorable William Anderson Under Secretary of State Washington D. C. or, in social correspondence The Under Secretary of State	Mr. Anderson	Mr. Anderson	The Honorable William Anderson, Under Secretary of State
My dear Mr. Anderson, Sincerely yours,			
The Under Secretary of State and Mrs. Anderson address at home			

Written Address	Spoken Address	Introduction and (Form of Reference)	Presentation at a Banquet or on the Radio

Assistant Secretary

Same as above except that envelope is addressed only:
The Honorable William Anderson
Assistant Secretary of State

or,

The Honorable and Mrs. William Anderson

| | | | The Honorable William Anderson, Assistant Secretary of State |

Head of a Division or Bureau of a Department

Winslow Fowler, Esquire
Chief, Division of Latin-American Affairs
Department of State
Washington
D. C.

My dear Mr. Fowler,
Sincerely yours,

Mr. and Mrs. Winslow Fowler
address at home

| | Mr. Fowler | Mr. Fowler | Mr. Winslow Fowler, Chief of the Division of Latin-American Affairs |

Head of a Federal Agency

The Honorable John Canfield
Administrator, Federal Works Agency
Washington
D. C.

My dear Mr. Canfield,
Sincerely yours,

The Honorable and Mrs. John Canfield
address at home

| | Mr. Canfield | Mr. Canfield | The Honorable John Canfield, Administrator of the Federal Works Agency |

Senator—man (The form is the same for a State Senator, with the appropriate change of address)

The Honorable Emmet Johnson
United States Senate
Washington
D. C.
or, the accepted social form,
Senator Johnson
address at home

My dear Senator Johnson,
Sincerely yours,

| | Senator Johnson, or Senator | Senator Johnson | The Honorable Emmet Johnson, Senator from New Jersey |

Written Address	Spoken Address	Introduction and (Form of Reference)	Presentation at a Banquet or on the Radio

The Honorable and Mrs. Emmet
   Johnson
address at home

or, in social correspondence

Senator and Mrs. Johnson
address at home

NOTE: No Senator uses the title "Senator" in issuing or accepting invitations; "Mr. Emmet Johnson requests the pleasure . . . ," for example, or "Mr. and Mrs. Emmet Johnson accept with pleasure . . ." Neither is it used on visiting cards—according to the best practice, the only difference between the visiting card of a Senator and that of any other American is that the name of the State he represents is engraved in the lower right-hand corner.

Senator—woman

The Honorable Mary S. Carraway United States Senate Washington D. C.	Senator Carraway, **or** Mrs. Carraway	Senator Carraway	The Honorable Mary S. Carraway, Senator from Washington

or, according to social usage:

Senator Carraway
address at home

My dear Senator Carraway, or,
My dear Mrs. Carraway,
Sincerely yours,

There are no clearly established
   forms for addressing a Senator
   and her husband. The best
   usage is to ignore her office and
   address the envelope in the
   usual way:

Mr. and Mrs. George Carraway
address at home

Representative—man (The form is the same for an Assemblyman, with the appropriate change of address)

The Honorable Charles Weston House of Representatives Washington D. C.	Mr. Weston	Mr. Weston or Representative Weston	The Honorable Charles Weston, Representative from New Jersey

My dear Mr. Weston,
Sincerely yours,

The Honorable and Mrs. Charles
   Weston
address at home

Written Address	Spoken Address	Introduction and (Form of Reference)	Presentation at a Banquet or on the Radio

Representative—woman

| The Honorable Helen Rogers House of Representatives Washington D. C. | Mrs. Rogers | Mrs. Rogers | The Honorable Helen Rogers, Representative from New Mexico |

My dear Mrs. Rogers,
Sincerely yours,

This is the best way to address an envelope to a woman Representative and her husband (see note concerning women Senators above):

Mr. and Mrs. Gordon Rogers
address at home

Governors (According to the customs of many states, the governor is given the title "Excellency," but the first form is the one used by our Department of State)

| The Honorable Thomas Lennox Governor of New York Albany New York | Governor Lennox, or Governor | Governor Lennox, or The Governor | The Honorable Thomas Lennox, Governor of New York (or: ——— of the State of New York) |

My dear Governor,
Sincerely yours,

The Governor and Mrs. Lennox
(outside the State, "The Governor of New York and Mrs. Lennox")
address at home

| His Excellency the Governor or His Excellency the Governor and Mrs. Lennox or, outside the State His Excellency the Governor of New York and Mrs. Lennox | | | His Excellency the Governor or His Excellency the Governor of New York |

Mayors

| The Honorable William Walker Mayor of New York New York | Mayor Walker, or Mr. Mayor | Mayor Walker | The Honorable William Walker, Mayor of New York (or: ——— Mayor of the city of New York) |

My dear Mayor Walker,
Sincerely yours,

The Honorable and Mrs. William
Walker
Gracie Mansion
New York
New York

Written Address	Spoken Address	Introduction and (Form of Reference)	Presentation at a Banquet or on the Radio

Judges

The Honorable August B. Gibb Judge of Whatever Court New York New York	Judge Gibb	Judge Gibb	The Honorable August Gibb, Judge of Whatever Court

My dear Judge Gibb,
Sincerely yours,

NOTE: The exception to this is the Presiding Justice of an Appellate Division. A letter to him begins, "My dear Mr. Justice"; and on the envelope, "Presiding Justice, Appellate Division, Supreme Court," is written in place of "Judge of _____" as shown here. He also is given the courtesy title, "Honorable."

The Honorable and Mrs. August
   Gibb
address at home

Foreign Representatives

The correct titles of Ambassadors and Ministers of all principal countries are "Ambassador (or Minister) of _____" (the name of the country); for example, "Minister of Ireland," "Ambassador of Brazil," with exceptions as listed below:

Ambassador of the Argentine Republic	Embassy of the Argentine Republic
American Ambassador	American Embassy
Ambassador of the United States (in Latin America)	Embassy of the United States (or:— United States of America)
British Ambassador	British Embassy (see also British forms)
Chinese Ambassador	Chinese Embassy
Ambassador of the Dominican Republic	Embassy of the Dominican Republic
Ambassador of the French Republic	Embassy of the French Republic
French Ambassador (unofficial use)	French Embassy
Italian Ambassador	Italian Embassy
Japanese Ambassador	Japanese Embassy
Ambassador of the Netherlands	Embassy of the Netherlands
Ambassador of Siam	Embassy of Siam
Minister of the Union of South Africa	Legation of the Union of South Africa
Ambassador of the Union of Soviet Socialist Republics	Embassy of the Union of Soviet Socialist Republics
Minister of the People's Republic of Bulgaria	Legation of the People's Republic of Bulgaria
Ambassador of the Federal People's Republic of Yugoslavia	Embassy of the Federal People's Republic of Yugoslavia
Minister of the People's Republic of Rumania	Legation of the People's Republic of Rumania

In the same way, the official residence of an Ambassador or Minister is usually the Embassy (or Legation) of _____; as, for example, Legation of Ireland, Embassy of Brazil. The exceptions are shown above.

The following officially approved American forms for addressing foreign ambassadors and ministers may be used for unofficial correspondence by any

American, whether or not in the government service: "Excellency" is always used for foreign Ambassadors, Cabinet Ministers, and Presidents, unless they have a royal title such as "His Highness," or "His Serene Highness."

Written Address	Spoken Address	Introduction and (Form of Reference)	Presentation at a Banquet or on the Radio
Foreign Ambassador			
His Excellency 　The Ambassador of the 　Netherlands Washington D. C.	Mr. Ambassador, or Mr. van Wort	The Ambassador of the Nether- lands, Mr. van Wort (The Ambassador, or Mr. van Wort)	His Excellency the Ambas- sador of the Netherlands Mr. Jan van Wort)
My dear Mr. Ambassador, Sincerely yours,			
His Excellency 　The Ambassador of the 　Netherlands 　and Madame van Wort Washington D. C.			
Foreign Minister Plenipotentiary			
The Honorable George Walker Minister of New Zealand Washington D. C.	Mr. Minister, or Mr. Walker	The Minister of New Zealand, Mr. Walker (The Minister, or Mr. Walker)	The Honorable George Walker, Minis- ter of New Zealand
or, according to social usage,			
The Minister of New Zealand Washington D. C.			
My dear Mr. Minister, Sincerely yours,			
The Honorable 　The Minister of New Zealand 　and Mrs. Walker Legation of New Zealand Washington D. C.			
or the accepted social form,			
The Minister of New Zealand 　and Mrs. Walker			

Private Individuals

With two exceptions, the formal presentation (see below) is exactly the same as the superscription on the envelope. The first exception is in the case of "Esquire," which is correct only in writing (see page 556 above); and the second is in the case of married women who are famous in their own names. If, for example, one were presenting Mrs. Duncan at a banquet or over the radio, instead of using her married name—Mrs. James Howard Duncan—one might present her as Mary Compton Duncan. This would be entirely correct, and obviously more sensible if she were known to the public under that name. But one must never present her as Mrs. Mary Compton Duncan. Men and women are always spoken to, referred to, and introduced as "Mr.," "Mrs.," or "Miss," followed by the last name.

Written Address	*Spoken Address*	*Introduction and (Form of Reference)*	*Presentation at a Banquet or on the Radio*
A Man			
Mr. James Howard Duncan (or, but socially only, James Howard Duncan, Esq.) 44 Rolling Road Baltimore Maryland	Mr. Duncan	Mr. Duncan	Mr. James Howard Duncan
Dear Mr. Duncan, Sincerely yours,			
A Married Woman			
Mrs. James Howard Duncan 44 Rolling Road Baltimore Maryland	Mrs. Duncan	Mrs. Duncan	Mrs. James Howard Duncan
Dear Mrs. Duncan, Sincerely yours,			
Mr. and Mrs. James Howard Duncan 44 Rolling Road Baltimore Maryland			

A Divorced Woman

A divorced woman usually takes her maiden surname followed by that of her former husband. Mrs. Alexander Auchincloss, who was born Mary Elkins, is addressed as follows after her divorce:

Mrs. Elkins Auchincloss Bryn Mawr Pennsylvania	Mrs. Auchincloss	Mrs. Auchincloss	Mrs. Elkins Auchincloss
Dear Mrs. Auchincloss, Sincerely yours,			

If, by an unfortunate coincidence, her maiden name was Mary Alexander, she may use this form:

Mrs. M. Alexander Auchincloss

There are further details on page 602, in the chapter concerned with visiting cards.

Written Address	Spoken Address	Introduction and (Form of Reference)	Presentation at a Banquet or on the Radio

A Widow

NOTE: The form used in addressing a widow is the same as that used in addressing a married woman. Changes are made only for practical reasons, when the widow has a married son whose name is the same as his father's. Suppose, for example, that Mrs. Duncan had a daughter-in-law, Mrs. James Howard Duncan, Jr. After Mr. Duncan's death, the daughter-in-law becomes Mrs. James Howard Duncan and, if there is any danger of confusion, the widow is addressed either as Mrs. Duncan—which is the preferred and most correct form—or, if necessary, as Mrs. James Howard Duncan, Sr. "Senior" is not, however, a desirable form; it should never be engraved on a card or invitation and should never be used as an address in formal social correspondence.

The best practice, which is always followed when the widow and her daughter-in-law live in different cities or at different addresses, is to make no change at all in the form of address. In no case should a widow be addressed as "Mrs. Mary Duncan."

An Unmarried Woman

Miss Ethel Grafton 23 Lightfoot Road Louisville Kentucky	Miss Grafton	Miss Grafton	Miss Ethel Graf- ton

Dear Miss Grafton,
Sincerely yours,

Correspondence to the eldest daughter may be addressed simply "Miss Grafton," without a first name. In writing to younger daughters or cousins, the first name must be used.

Multiple Addresses

Envelopes should never be addressed to "Mr. and Mrs. —— —— and family." "And family" is not a correct form for any kind of correspondence. With the single exception of "Mr. and Mrs.," it is always best to address envelopes separately, to each person, rather than to lump people together in the less flattering, blanket form of a multiple address. Under certain circumstances, however, multiple addresses are extremely practical and certainly not incorrect. Wedding invitations or announcements, and invitations to big dances, are often sent in this way. These are the correct forms:

1. Mr. and Mrs. George Mason
2. The Misses Mason
3. The Messrs. Mason

These standard forms may be combined as follows:

4. Mr. and Mrs. George Mason
   The Misses Mason
5. Mr. and Mrs. George Mason
   The Messrs. Mason
6. The Misses Mason
   The Messrs. Mason

More than two of these standard multiple addresses should never be used together on the same envelope, and it should be noted that No. 6 is not used when the parents and children are all invited. In this case, daughters are always included with parents, rather than brothers. For example, if one wants to address the entire Mason family (which consists of Mr. and Mrs. Mason, two sons and two daughters), two envelopes will be necessary. The first should be addressed:

Mr. and Mrs. George Mason
The Misses Mason

The second:

The Messrs. Mason

Two single forms may also be combined on the same envelope, as (for a brother and sister):

Miss Mason (or, if she is not the elder or only daughter, Miss Mary Mason)
Mr. James Edward Mason (or, James Edward Mason, Esq.)

and one of the standard multiple forms may also be combined with a single form, as:

Mr. and Mrs. George Mason
Miss Mason

The Armed Forces

The Armed Forces of the United States have recently re-named many of their ranks. These are complete lists for each branch of the services, incorporating any of the changes which have definitely been established.

Army:

1. General of the Armies of the United States *
2. General of the Army
3. Chief of Staff
4. General
5. Lieutenant General
6. Major General
7. Brigadier General
8. Colonel
9. Lieutenant Colonel
10. Major
11. Captain
12. First Lieutenant
13. Second Lieutenant
14. Chief Warrant Officer (A Cadet ranks below a Chief Warrant Officer and above a Warrant Officer.)
15. Warrant Officer
16. Master Sergeant (First Sergeant is now an occupational title only.)
17. Sergeant, second grade
18. Sergeant, third grade
19. Corporal
20. Private, first class
21. Private
22. Recruit

Navy:

1. No rank comparable to "General of the Armies"
2. Fleet Admiral
3. Chief of Naval Operations
4. Admiral
5. Vice Admiral
6. Rear Admiral (upper half)
7. Rear Admiral (lower half—"Commodore" is an almost equal rank, but it is not a permanent rank on the active list of the United States Navy. A Commodore is ranked below a Rear Admiral and above a Captain.)
8. Captain
9. Commander
10. Lieutenant Commander
11. Lieutenant
12. Lieutenant, junior grade
13. Ensign
14. Commissioned Warrant Officer (A Midshipman is ranked below a Commissioned Warrant Officer and above a Warrant Officer.)
15. Warrant Officer
16. Chief Petty Officer
17. Petty Officer, first class
18. Petty Officer, second class
19. Petty Officer, third class
20. Seaman (There are other titles in this rank—among them, Stewardsman, Fireman and Airman.)
21. Seaman Apprentice (or Fireman Apprentice, etc.)
22. Seaman Recruit (or Airman Recruit, etc.)

Air Force:

The ranks of the United States Air Force above the rank of Warrant Officer follow those of the United States Army, except that there is no rank higher than "Chief of Staff" (No. 3 on the Army list). The titles of Warrant Officers and of the personnel below this rank are being changed and are not yet definite.

As in the Army, the phrase "United States Air Force" is changed to "Air Force of the United States" to show the reserve. For example, a Captain in the Air Force is "Captain John Blank, United States Air Force" (or "USAF"). A Reserve Captain is "Captain John Blank, Air Force of the United States" (or "AFUS").

* This rank has been given only to the late General John J. Pershing.

Marine Corps:

The ranks of the Marine Corps follow those of the Army with these exceptions:

There are no ranks comparable to the first two in the Army.

The first rank in the Marine Corp is "Commandant of the Marine Corps" —a rank comparable to Chief of Staff in the Army, since 1947 held by a full General.

Rank No. 14 in the Marine Corps, comparable to Chief Warrant Officer in the Army, is Commissioned Warrant Officer.

Below the next rank, which is Warrant Officer, the ranks are:

16. Master Sergeant
17. Technical Sergeant
18. Staff Sergeant
19. Sergeant
20. Corporal
21. Private, first class
22. Private

As in the Navy, "United States Marine Corps" (or "USMC") indicates regular service: "United States Marine Corps Reserve" (or "USMCR") indicates the Reserve.

Coast Guard:

The Coast Guard follows the titles of rank of the Navy with these exceptions:

There are no comparable ranks for the first three grades. The top rank in the Coast Guard is "Admiral" which is comparable to No. 4 in the Navy.

Rank No. 14 in the Coast Guard is Chief Warrant Officer.

The Coast Guard equivalent of a Midshipman in the Navy is Cadet.

The forms of spoken and written address are exactly like the Navy's. And, as in the Navy, "Reserve" is added to indicate a member of the reserve on active duty. For example, "United States Coast Guard" or "United States Coast Guard Reserve."

Army Forms:

The only abbreviations which are always correct in correspondence addressed to members of the Army are "USA" which is written after the name of a regular Army officer, and "AUS" which is written after the name of a Reserve officer on active duty. When the name and rank are long, however, the following abbreviations may be used in writing informally and unofficially:

Lieut. Colonel

Brig. General

Lieut. General

In conversation, the title by itself is not correct as a spoken address: "Colonel" or "Major" is wrong—"Colonel Wheeler" or "Major Wheeler" is correct. There is a very useful rule of thumb for this: in conversation all Generals are "General _____"; all Colonels are "Colonel _____": all Lieutenants are "Lieutenant _____": all Warrant Officers are "Mr. _____": all Sergeants are "Sergeant _____": and all Privates are "Private _____."

Written Address	Spoken Address	Introduction and (Form of Reference)	Presentation at a Banquet or on the Radio

General, and Lieutenant, Major, or Brigadier General

NOTE: Socially, it is not necessary to mention the various ranks of general—"General" is enough. At official banquets, however, or on the radio, the explicit title is used once.

Written Address	Spoken Address	Introduction and (Form of Reference)	Presentation at a Banquet or on the Radio
General of the Army Ward D. Curtis, U.S.A. Department of the Army Washington D. C.	General Curtis	General Curtis	General of the Army, Ward Dwight Curtis

My dear General Curtis,
Sincerely yours,

General of the Army
  and Mrs. Ward Dwight Curtis
address at home

Written Address	Spoken Address	Introduction and (Form of Reference)	Presentation at a Banquet or on the Radio
General (or Lieutenant General, etc.) Mark Crosby, U.S.A. Fort Leavenworth Kansas	General Crosby	General Crosby	General Mark Crosby (or Lieutenant, or Major, or Brigadier General Mark Crosby)

My dear General Crosby,
Sincerely yours,

NOTE: In unofficial, social correspondence, it is not always necessary to give the precise rank of a General on an envelope addressed to him and his wife. This form is often used:

General and Mrs. Mark Crosby
address at home

Colonel, and Lieutenant Colonel, Major, and Captain

(As in the case of Lieutenant General, Lieutenant Colonel is used only on an envelope or in a presentation; otherwise "Colonel" is always used socially.)

Written Address	Spoken Address	Introduction and (Form of Reference)	Presentation at a Banquet or on the Radio
Colonel (or Lieutenant Colonel, etc.) Allen Wheeler, U.S.A. Fort Sam Houston Texas	Colonel Wheeler	Colonel Wheeler	Colonel Allen Wheeler (or Lieutenant Colonel, Major, or Captain Allen Wheeler)

My dear Colonel Wheeler, (or
  My dear Major Wheeler, etc.)
Sincerely yours,

Colonel (or Major or Captain)
  and Mrs. Allen Wheeler
address at home or on the post

Written Address	Spoken Address	Introduction and (Form of Reference)	Presentation at a Banquet or on the Radio

First and Second Lieutenant

NOTE: The old Army usage was that officers below the rank of Captain should be addressed, even in writing, as "Mr." Modern usage, however, sanctions the following forms and omits "First" or "Second" in unofficial correspondence.

Written Address	Spoken Address	Introduction and (Form of Reference)	Presentation at a Banquet or on the Radio
Lieutenant George Ellis, A.U.S. Fort Sill Oklahoma	Lieutenant Ellis	Lieutenant Ellis	Lieutenant George Ellis

My dear Lieutenant Ellis,
Sincerely yours,

Lieutenant and Mrs. George Ellis
address at home or on the post

See page 575 below for the address of an Army chaplain.

Warrant Officers

Written Address	Spoken Address	Introduction and (Form of Reference)	Presentation at a Banquet or on the Radio
Mr. Peter Grey Fort Lewis Washington	Mr. Grey	Mr. Grey	Chief Warrant Officer Peter Grey (or Warrant Officer Peter Grey)

My dear Mr. Grey,
Yours sincerely,

Mr. and Mrs. Peter Grey
address at home or on the post

Cadet

Written Address	Spoken Address	Introduction and (Form of Reference)	Presentation at a Banquet or on the Radio
Cadet Peter Grey	Cadet Grey	Cadet Grey	Cadet Peter Grey

My dear Cadet Grey,
Yours sincerely,

Non-Commissioned Officers

Written Address	Spoken Address	Introduction and (Form of Reference)	Presentation at a Banquet or on the Radio
Master Sergeant Peter Grey Fort Lewis Washington	Sergeant Grey	Sergeant Grey	Master Sergeant Peter Grey

My dear Sergeant Grey,
Yours sincerely,

Master Sergeant and Mrs. Peter Grey
address at home or on the post

NOTE: The same form is used for Corporals and other Sergeants (the grades—"Sergeant, first grade" or "Sergeant, second grade"—are omitted in social correspondence): A letter is addressed "Sergeant Peter Grey" or "Corporal and Mrs. Peter Grey." On the radio the full title would be given.

Privates

Written Address	Spoken Address	Introduction and (Form of Reference)	Presentation at a Banquet or on the Radio
Pfc. Peter Grey Fort Lewis Washington	Private Grey	Private Grey	Private, first class, Peter Grey

Written Address	Spoken Address	Introduction and (Form of Reference)	Presentation at a Banquet or on the Radio

My dear Private Grey,
Yours sincerely,

Pfc. and Mrs. Peter Grey
address at home or on the post
The same form is used for Privates, with the appropriate changes. The abbreviation of "Private" is "Priv."

Recruit (This is a new Army grade and these are the proposed Army forms)

Recruit Peter Grey Fort Lewis Washington	Recruit Grey	Recruit Grey	Recruit Peter Grey

My dear Recruit Grey,
Yours sincerely,

Recruit and Mrs. Peter Grey
address at home or on the post

Naval Forms:

As in the case of army officers, "Captain" or "Commander" is an incorrect spoken address: "Captain Beadleston" or "Commander Ellis" is correct. The only abbreviations that may always be used in formal social correspondence are these: "U.S.N.," which follows a regular Naval officer's name; "U.S.N.R.," which follows the name of an officer in the Naval Reserve; and "(jg)" which may be written on an envelope addressed to a Lieutenant, junior grade. However, if abbreviations are absolutely necessary, the following are approved by the Navy:

Ens.	Capt.
Lt. (jg) or Lieut. (jg)	Commo.
Lt. or Lieut.	Rear Adm.
Lieut. Comdr. or Lt. Cdr.	Vice Adm.
Comdr. or Cdr.	Adm.

Those approved by the best social usage are:

Lieutenant (jg) or Lieut. (jg)
Lieut. Comdr. or Lieut. Commander

Fleet Admiral

Fleet Admiral Chester W. Haven, U.S.N. Chief of Naval Operations Department of the Navy Washington D. C.	Admiral Haven	Admiral Haven	Fleet Admiral Chester Wyllis Haven, Chief of Naval Operations

My dear Admiral Haven,
Sincerely yours,

Fleet Admiral
   and Mrs. Chester Wyllis Haven
address at home

Written Address	Spoken Address	Introduction and (Form of Reference)	Presentation at a Banquet or on the Radio

Admiral, Vice Admiral, or Rear Admiral

(Vice and Rear Admirals are spoken to as "Admiral . . ." On the envelope and in official presentations the explicit title is used.)

Admiral (or Vice Admiral or Rear Admiral) Thomas C. Royal, U.S.N. Commander, Eastern and Gulf Sea Frontiers 90 Church Street New York 7 New York	Admiral Royal	Admiral Royal	Admiral (or Vice Admiral, etc.) Thomas Craven Royal, Commander of the Eastern and Gulf Sea Frontiers

My dear Admiral Royal,
Sincerely yours,

As in the case of envelopes addressed jointly to a General and his wife, the differentiation between Rear Admiral, Vice Admiral, and Admiral is not always made. In unofficial social correspondence, this form may be used:

Admiral and Mrs. Thomas Craven Royal
address at home

Commodores, Captains, and Commanders

Commodore (or Captain or Commander) Henry Beadleston, U.S.N. U.S.S. Wyoming Norfolk Virginia	Commodore Beadleston	Commodore Beadleston	Commodore (or etc.) Henry Beadleston

My dear Commodore Beadleston,
Sincerely yours,

Commodore (or Captain, or Commander) and Mrs. Henry Beadleston
address at home

Lieutenant Commander; Lieutenant; Lieutenant, junior grade; and Ensign (these are "junior officers")

Lieutenant Commander (or Lieutenant, Lieutenant, junior grade, etc.) George Ellis, U.S.N. Operations Crossroads Fleet Post Office San Francisco California	Mr. Ellis	Lieutenant Commander Ellis, etc. See below	Lieutenant Commander (or Lieutenant, Lieutenant, junior grade, or Ensign) George Ellis

Written Address	Spoken Address	Introduction and (Form of Reference)	Presentation at a Banquet or on the Radio
My dear Mr. Ellis, Sincerely yours,			
Lieutenant Commander and **Mrs.** George Ellis Lieutenant and Mrs. George Ellis Lieutenant (jg) and Mrs. George Ellis Ensign and Mrs. George Ellis			

NOTE: Introductions of junior officers should include mention of their **rank**. Thereafter, junior officers of the medical or dental corps are addressed and referred to as "Doctor _____," others as "Mr. _____." For example, "This is Lieutenant Commander Ellis. Mr. Ellis has just returned from the Pacific." A Protestant or Jewish chaplain is introduced and presented as "Captain (or "Commander") ——" according to his rank, but afterwards is spoken or referred to as "Chaplain ——." Roman Catholic chaplains and certain Anglican priests are also introduced or presented according to rank, but are referred to and addressed as "Father _____." Envelopes are addressed with the chaplain's name on the first line and the rank below. For example:

Chaplain John Doe
Captain, U.S.N.
Department of the Navy
Washington
D. C.

Chaplain John Doe
Major General, U.S.A.
Fort Myer
Virginia

Warrant Officers

Chief Photographer John Jones, U.S.N. Photographer John Jones, U.S.N. U.S.S. _____	Mr. Jones	Mr. Jones	Chief Photographer John Jones Photographer John Jones
Dear Mr. Jones, Yours sincerely,			
Mr. and Mrs. John Jones address at home			

Midshipmen

Midshipman John Jones United States Naval Academy Annapolis Maryland	Mr. Jones	Mr. Jones	Midshipman John Jones
Dear Mr. Jones, Yours sincerely,			

Written Address	Spoken Address	Introduction and (Form of Reference)	Presentation at a Banquet or on the Radio
Petty Officers			
John Jones, Chief Yeoman, U.S.N. or (John Jones, YNC, U.S.N.) John Jones, Yeoman, first class, U.S.N. or (John Jones, YN₁, U.S.N.)	Mr. Jones	Mr. Jones	Chief Yeoman John Jones Yeoman, first class, John Jones
Dear Mr. Jones, Yours sincerely,			
Mr. and Mrs. John Jones address at home			
John Jones, BMC, U.S.N. John Jones, BM₁, U.S.N.	Mr. Jones	Mr. Jones	Chief Boat- swain's (pro- nounced "Bo'sn's") Mate John Jones
Dear Mr. Jones, Yours sincerely,			
Mr. and Mrs. John Jones address at home			
Pay Grades 5, 6, 7			
John Jones, Seaman, U.S.N. or (John Jones, SN, U.S.N.) John Jones, Seaman Apprentice, U.S.N. or (John Jones, SA, U.S.N.) U.S.S. ————	Mr. Jones	Mr. Jones	Seaman John Jones Seaman Appren- tice John Jones
Dear Mr. Jones, Yours sincerely,			
Mr. and Mrs. John Jones address at home			

Church Dignitaries and Clergymen

The Papacy			
His Holiness, The Pope (or His Holiness, Pius XII) Vatican City Italy	Your Holiness	(His Holiness, or The Pope)	His Holiness, the Pope
Your Holiness: Respectfully yours,			
Apostolic Delegate			
His Excellency, The Most Reverend Amleto Giovanni Cicognani	Excellency	(The Apostolic Delegate)	His Excellency, the Archbishop of Laodicea di

Written Address	*Spoken Address*	*Introduction and (Form of Reference)*	*Presentation at a Banquet or on the Radio*
Archbishop of Laodicea di Frigia The Apostolic Delegate Washington D. C. Your Excellency: Respectfully yours,			Frigia, the Apostolic Dele- gate

Patriarch

His All Holiness Photios Patriarch of Constantinople Turkey Your All Holiness: Respectfully yours,	Your All Holi- ness	(His All Holi- ness, or The Patriarch)	His All Holiness, the Patriarch of Constan- tinople

Cardinals

His Eminence, George Cardinal Wilmot Archbishop of New York New York New York Your Eminence: Respectfully yours,	Your Eminence	(His Eminence, or Cardinal Wilmot)	His Eminence, Cardinal Wilmot

Anglican Archbishop

To His Grace, The Lord Archbishop of Canterbury Canterbury England Your Grace: (or, "My Lord Archbishop:") Respectfully yours, Less formally, My dear Lord Archbishop, or My dear Archbishop, Sincerely yours,	Your Grace	(His Grace or The Archbishop)	His Grace the Archbishop of Canterbury

Roman Catholic Archbishop in United States

His Excellency, The Most Reverend Michael Emmet, S.T.D. Archbishop of Baltimore Baltimore Maryland Your Excellency: Respectfully yours, Less formally, My dear Archbishop, Sincerely yours,	Archbishop Emmet	Archbishop Emmet	His Excellency, The Most Rev- erend Michael Emmet, Arch- bishop of Baltimore (or, His Excellency, The Archbishop of Baltimore)

Written Address	Spoken Address	Introduction and (Form of Reference)	Presentation at a Banquet or on the Radio

Greek Orthodox Archbishops of Cyprus, Athens, Georgia and Poland

His Beatitude
  The Archbishop of Cyprus
  Macarios
local address
	Your Beatitude	(His Beatitude,
		  or the
		  Archbishop)
			His Beatitude,
			  the Archbishop
			  of Cyprus

Your Beatitude: Respectfully yours,			

Greek Orthodox Archbishops of Mount Sinai and Albania

His Eminence
  The Archbishop of Mount Sinai
  Porphyrios
local address
	Your Eminence	(His Eminence,
		  or the
		  Archbishop)
			His Eminence,
			  the Archbishop
			  of Mount Sinai

Your Eminence: Respectfully yours,			

The Presiding Bishop of the Protestant Episcopal Church in America

The Most Reverend
  Henry Harper Knox, D.D.,LL.D.
Presiding Bishop of the Protestant
  Episcopal Church in America
local address
	Bishop Knox	Bishop Knox	The Most Reverend Henry Harper Knox, Presiding Bishop of the Protestant Episcopal Church in America

Most Reverend Sir: Respectfully yours,			
Less formally,			
My dear Bishop Knox, Sincerely yours,			

Protestant Episcopal Bishops

The Right Reverend James E. Alston, D.D., LL.D. Bishop of —— local address	Bishop Alston	Bishop Alston	The Right Reverend James E. Alston, Bishop of ____
My dear Bishop Alston, (or more formally "Right Reverend Sir:") Sincerely yours, (or " Respectfully yours.")			
The Right Reverend and Mrs. James E. Alston address at home			

Anglican Bishop

The Right Reverend James Blair The Lord Bishop of _____	Bishop Blair	Bishop Blair	The Right Reverend James Blair, the Lord Bishop of ____
My Lord Bishop: Respectfully yours, or My dear Bishop, Sincerely yours,			

Written Address	Spoken Address	Introduction and (Form of Reference)	Presentation at a Banquet or on the Radio

Roman Catholic Bishop in United States

His Excellency
   the Most Reverend
   Andrew Turner, S.T.D.
Bishop of Trenton
Trenton
New Jersey
 	
Your Excellency:
Respectfully yours,
	Bishop Turner	Bishop Turner	His Excellency,
			   the Most Rever-
			   end Andrew
			   Turner, Bishop
			   of Trenton (or
			   His Excellency,
			   the Bishop of
			   Trenton)

Methodist Bishop

The Very Reverend
   Edwin Austin Sage, D.D., LL.D.
Bishop of _____
Kansas City
Missouri
 	
My dear Bishop, (or "Reverend
   Sir,")
Sincerely yours, (or Respectfully
   yours,)
 	
The Very Reverend
   and Mrs. Edwin Austin Sage
address at home
	Bishop Sage	Bishop Sage	The Very Rever-
			   end Edwin
			   Austin Sage,
			   Methodist
			   Bishop of ____

Mormon Bishop

A Mormon Bishop is addressed without any title other than "Mr. _____," as a private individual would be.

Monsignor

NOTE: An Archimandrite of the Greek Orthodox Church is addressed in writing in the same way: "The Very Reverend Archimandrite _____." In spoken address he is called "Your Reverence."

The Right Reverend
   Monsignor Francis Barrett, S.J.
local address
(or "The Very Reverend Mon-
   signor _____" depending on
   his rank—see Catholic direc-
   tory)
 	
My dear Monsignor Barrett,
Sincerely yours, (or "Respectfully
   yours,")
	Monsignor Bar-
	   rett
		Monsignor Bar-
		   rett
			The Very Rever-
			   end (or Right
			   Reverend)
			   Monsignor
			   Francis Barrett

Protestant Episcopal Archdeacon

The Venerable
   Francis J. Ford, D.D.
Archdeacon of Mountain Work
Diocese of Virginia
	Archdeacon Ford,
	   or Doctor Ford
		Archdeacon Ford,
		   or Doctor Ford
			The Venerable
			   Francis J. Ford,
			   Archdeacon of
			   Mountain
			   Work in the
			   Diocese of
			   Virginia

Written Address	Spoken Address	Introduction and (Form of Reference)	Presentation at a Banquet or on the Radio

Protestant Episcopal Archdeacon, continued

My dear Archdeacon,
Sincerely yours,

Deans

The Very Reverend George Benson Tucker, D.D. Dean of Washington Cathedral Washington D. C.	Dean Tucker, or Doctor Tucker	Dean Tucker, or Doctor Tucker	The Very Reverend George Benson Tucker, Dean of Washington Cathedral

My dear Dean Tucker,
Sincerely yours,

The Very Reverend
and Mrs. George Benson Tucker
address at home

Canons

The Reverend Richard Amory Phelps, D.D., LL.D. Canon of Washington Cathedral Washington D. C.	Canon Phelps, or Doctor Phelps	Canon Phelps, or Doctor Phelps	The Reverend Richard Amory Phelps, Canon of Washington Cathedral

My dear Canon Phelps,
Sincerely yours,

The Reverend
and Mrs. Richard Amory Phelps
address at home

Protestant Minister with a scholastic degree

The Reverend Joseph R. Sutton, D.D., Litt.D. local address	Dr. Sutton	Dr. Sutton	The Reverend Joseph R. Sutton

My dear Dr. Sutton,
Sincerely yours,

The Reverend
and Mrs. Joseph R. Sutton
address at home

Protestant Minister without a scholastic degree

The Reverend William B. Hale local address	Mr. Hale	Mr. Hale	The Reverend William B. Hale

My dear Mr. Hale,
Sincerely yours,
The Reverend
and Mrs. William Hale

Written Address	Spoken Address	Introduction and (Form of Reference)	Presentation at a Banquet or on the Radio

Roman Catholic and Greek Orthodox Priests and Anglican Priests who are addressed as "Father _____"

The Reverend Edward P. McAdams, S.J. St. Joseph's Church Washington D. C.	Father McAdams	Father McAdams	The Reverend Edward P. McAdams

My dear Father McAdams,
Sincerely yours,

Rabbi

Rabbi Aaron Simon address	Rabbi Simon or Rabbi	Rabbi Simon	Rabbi Aaron Simon (or Doctor Aaron Simon)

My dear Rabbi Simon,
Sincerely yours,

Rabbi and Mrs. Aaron Simon
home address

NOTE: If a Rabbi has a scholastic degree he may be addressed either as "Rabbi" or "Doctor." In writing, if the title "Rabbi" is used, the abbreviation of his degree is added after his name.

Professors and Doctors

John W. Matthews, Ph.D. (or M.D.) (or, Dr. John W. Matthews) Columbia University New York New York	Dr. Matthews, or Mr. Matthews; (Doctors of Medicine: Dr. Smith)	Same	Dr. John Wadsworth Matthews

(If writing to the President of a University, "President," is written directly before the name of the University: "President, Columbia University")

My dear Dr. Matthews,
Sincerely yours,

Dr. and Mrs. John Wadsworth
Matthews
address at home

NOTE: When the wife is a doctor, or when man and wife are both doctors, the wife is not usually given her title on an envelope addressed jointly to the couple. This is based on the assumption that correspondence addressed jointly is social or personal—not a matter of business. If, for example, Dr. John W. Matthews were married to a woman doctor, a Christmas card or an invitation would be addressed "Dr. and Mrs. John Matthews"; professional correspondence is addressed, "Dr. John W. Matthews" on the first line and, under this, "Dr. Hilda Matthews"; or even, if Mrs. Matthews uses her maiden name professionally, "Dr. Hilda Wilson."

BRITISH FORMS

The State Department has an official form for official correspondence. For unofficial correspondence, Americans may use a salutation and closing which accords with the best American usage, as suggested below.

The Use of Titles

The forms for addressing the king and queen may be followed in addressing the crowned heads of any other country when writing in English.

It should be noted, however, that only in very exceptional cases should private individuals address the King or Queen or any other member of a royal family. In no case should correspondence be addressed to them except through the usual diplomatic channels, or through members of the royal household.

Further, in speaking in England of the British royalty or nobility to tradespeople, domestics or employees, the formal address is correct. For example, "Has His Grace come in yet?" not "Has the Duke (or "the Duke of ———") come in yet?" Similarly, the phrases "His Lordship" or "Her Ladyship" are used for all other peers. Baronets and knights are referred to by name ("Sir Charles" or "Sir Sidney"), although their wives are referred to as "Her Ladyship." The complimentary titles of peers—"His Grace," "The Most Honorable," and "The Right Honorable"—are not shown here because they are used only in official correspondence or in an official presentation, never in social correspondence, introductions, or spoken references.

It will be noticed that British and American customs are exactly opposed on the question of the salutation "Dear" and "My dear." In America, "My dear" is the formal salutation; in England, "My dear" is used only between fairly intimate friends.

Another difference between British customs and our own is that the practice of addressing an envelope jointly to a man and his wife is somewhat contrary to the British form. Examples are shown here only because it is very much the custom in America. In England the envelope of an invitation is addressed to the wife only; the names of both husband and wife are written in the body of the invitation, or across the top of the page or card.

And—one last note—"Honorable" is always abbreviated in British usage, as shown here.

The Royal Family

Written Address	Spoken Address	Introduction and (Form of Reference)	Presentation at a Banquet or on the Radio
The King			
His Majesty the King Buckingham Palace London S. W. 1 England	Your Majesty, or Sir	(His Majesty, or The King)	His Majesty, the King
Sir: (or "Your Majesty"; write in third person) Very respectfully, (The British closing is: "I have the honor to be Your Majesty's most obedient servant")			

Written Address	*Spoken Address*	*Introduction and (Form of Reference)*	*Presentation at a Banquet or on the Radio*
The Queen			
Her Majesty the Queen Buckingham Palace London S. W. 1 England Madam: (or "Your Majesty") Very respectfully, (for the British closing, see above)	Your Majesty, or Ma'am	(Her Majesty, or The Queen)	Her Majesty, the Queen
The Queen Mother			
Her Majesty Queen Mary Marlborough House London S. W. 1 England Madam: (or "Your Majesty") Very respectfully, (See British closing above)	Your Majesty, or Ma'am	(Her Majesty, or Queen Mary)	Her Majesty, Queen Mary
Royal Princes and Dukes			
H.R.H. The Prince of Wales H.R.H. The Duke of Edinburgh H.R.H. The Duke of Gloucester H.R.H. Prince Arthur of Connaught local address Sir: (or "Your Royal Highness") Respectfully yours, (the British closing is: "I have the honor to be Your Highness' most obedient servant")	Your Royal Highness, or Sir	(His Royal Highness, or the Duke or Prince Arthur)	His Royal Highness, and name, as in the written address
Prince Consort			
H.R.H. the Prince Consort local address Sir: (or "Your Royal Highness") Respectfully yours, (see closing for Royal Dukes)	Your Royal Highness, or Sir	(His Royal Highness, or the Prince Consort)	His Royal Highness, the Prince Consort
Royal Princess or Royal Duchess			
H.R.H. the Princess Elizabeth, Duchess of Edinburgh H.R.H. the Princess Margaret Rose H.R.H. the Princess Royal H.R.H. the Duchess of Kent Madam: (or "Your Royal Highness") Respectfully yours, (See British closing for Royal Dukes)	Your Royal Highness, or Ma'am	(Her Royal Highness, or the Princess ———; or, the Duchess of ———, or the Duchess)	Her Royal Highness and name, as in the written address

583

Written Address	Spoken Address	Introduction and (Form of Reference)	Presentation at a Banquet or on the Radio

The Peerage

Duke and Duchess

The Duke of Hampshire local address Dear Duke: Yours sincerely,	Duke	The Duke of Hampshire (The Duke, or the Duke of Hampshire)	The Duke of Hampshire
The Duchess of Hampshire local address Dear Duchess, Yours sincerely,	Duchess	The Duchess of Hampshire (The Duchess, or the Duchess of Hampshire)	The Duchess of Hampshire

The Duke and Duchess of Hampshire

The younger sons of a Duke are given the prefix "Lord" followed by their Christian and family names. (The eldest son of a Duke, Marquess, or Earl uses his father's second title until he succeeds to the first.)

The Lord Charles Jarvis local address Dear Lord Charles, Yours sincerely,	Lord Charles	Lord Charles Jarvis (Lord Charles)	Lord Charles Jarvis

The wives of younger sons of Dukes are addressed as "Lady _____" followed by their husbands' names.

The Lady Charles Jarvis local address Dear Lady Charles, Yours sincerely,	Lady Charles	Lady Charles Jarvis (Lady Charles)	Lady Charles Jarvis

Lord and Lady Charles Jarvis

The daughter of a Duke is given the prefix "Lady" followed by her Christian name and family name.

The Lady Angela Jarvis local address Dear Lady Angela, Yours sincerely,	Lady Angela	Lady Angela Jarvis (Lady Angela)	Lady Angela Jarvis

When she marries (unless her husband is a peer) she is: The Lady Angela Morrell local address Dear Lady Angela, Yours sincerely,	Lady Angela	Lady Angela Morrell	Lady Angela Morrell

Mr. Eric and Lady Angela Morrell
(or, Sir Eric and Lady Angela Morrell)

If her husband is a peer, she is addressed according to his title.

Written Address	Spoken Address	Introduction and (Form of Reference)	Presentation at a Banquet or on the Radio

Marquess and Marchioness

The Marquess of Clanricorn local address	Lord Clanricorn	Lord Clanricorn	The Marquess of Clanricorn
Dear Lord Clanricorn, Yours sincerely,			
The Marchioness of Clanricorn local address	Lady Clanricorn	Lady Clanricorn	The Marchioness of Clanricorn
Dear Lady Clanricorn Yours sincerely,			
The Marquess and Marchioness of Clanricorn			

The younger sons and the daughters of a Marquess are given the titles Lord or Lady as are the sons and daughters of Dukes. Wives of younger sons follow the same ruling.

Earl and Countess

The Earl of Ashburnham local address	Lord Ashburnham	Lord Ashburnham	The Earl of Ashburnham
Dear Lord Ashburnham, Yours sincerely,			
The Countess of Ashburnham local address	Lady Ashburnham	Lady Ashburnham	The Countess of Ashburnham
Dear Lady Ashburnham, Yours sincerely,			
The Earl and Countess of Ashburnham			

The younger sons of an Earl, and their wives:

The Hon. James Jameson local address	Mr. Jameson	Mr. Jameson	The Honorable James Jameson
Dear Mr. Jameson, Yours sincerely,			
The Hon. Mrs. James Jameson Dear Mrs. Jameson, Yours sincerely,			
The Hon. James and Mrs. Jameson			

Should the younger son of an Earl—or any other "Honorable"—be knighted, he is addressed in writing as "The Hon. Sir ___ ___" and his wife as "The Hon. Lady ___."

The daughters of an Earl follow the ruling for daughters of Dukes.

Written Address	Spoken Address	Introduction and (Form of Reference)	Presentation at a Banquet or on the Radio

Viscount and Viscountess

The Viscount Alverstone local address	Lord Alverstone	Lord Alverstone	The Viscount Alverstone
Dear Lord Alverstone, Yours sincerely,			
The Viscountess Alverstone local address	Lady Alverstone	Lady Alverstone	The Viscountess Alverstone
Dear Lady Alverstone, Yours sincerely,			
The Viscount and Viscountess Alverstone			

The sons of a Viscount and their wives are given the prefix "Honorable" in exactly the same form as the younger sons of an Earl and their wives.

The Daughters of a Viscount

The Hon. Gladys Devereux local address	Miss Devereux	Miss Devereux	The Honorable Gladys Devereux
Dear Miss Devereux, Yours sincerely,			

NOTE: When she marries (unless her husband is a peer) she is: The Hon. Lady Spencer or the Hon. Mrs. Hamilton (the husband's first name is omitted when the wife, but not the husband, is an "Honorable").

Dear Lady Spencer, (or, Dear Mrs. Hamilton,) Yours sincerely,	Lady Spencer or Mrs. Hamilton	Lady Spencer or Mrs. Hamilton	The Honorable Lady Spencer, or The Honorable Mrs. Hamilton
Sir Anthony and the Hon. Lady Spencer or, Mr. and the Hon. Mrs. Victor Hamilton			

Baron and Baroness

The Lord Anslow local address	Lord Anslow	Lord Anslow	The Lord Anslow
Dear Lord Anslow, Yours sincerely,			
The Lady Anslow local address	Lady Anslow	Lady Anslow	The Lady Anslow
Dear Lady Anslow, Yours sincerely,			
The Lord and Lady Anslow			

A Baroness in her own right

The Baroness (or The Lady) Harries local address	Baroness (or Lady) Harries	Baroness (or Lady) Harries	The Baroness Harries

Written Address	Spoken Address	Introduction and (Form of Reference)	Presentation at a Banquet or on the Radio

Dear Lady Harries,
Yours sincerely,

George Talbot, Esq. and the
 Baroness Harries, or,
George Talbot, Esq. and the Lady
 Harries

The children of a baron or baroness are given titles according to the rules for the children of Viscounts.

Widows of Peers

If the widow's son is unmarried, or if the title has passed to an unmarried nephew or relative, the widow is addressed as before her husband's death. If the son has married, or if the title has passed to a married relative, the widow obviously cannot retain her husband's title. The term "Dowager," as used with a title to indicate widowhood, is now confined almost entirely to official British communications, such as Court Summons; in any case, only a woman who is the mother, stepmother or grandmother of the incumbent has the right to it. Modern custom has sanctioned the use of the first name of the widow, followed by the title, a form correct for the widow of any titled Britisher; as follows:

The widow of a Duke is Helen,
 Duchess of Hampshire
The widow of a Marquess is
 Rachel, Marchioness of Clanri-
 corn
The widow of an Earl is Felicity,
 Countess of Cowperis
The widow of a Viscount is An-
 gela, Viscountess of Avonmore
The widow of a Baron is Eleanor,
 Baroness Moulton

Upon remarriage, widows lose all rights to precedence or title. However, modern social usage, contrary to official usage, permits a divorcée once married to a peer to be addressed as though she were his widow until she remarries.

Baronets and Knights

Baronet (The letters Bart. or Bt.—abbreviations of the title "Baronet"—are written after the name)

Written Address	Spoken Address	Introduction and (Form of Reference)	Presentation at a Banquet or on the Radio
Sir Anthony Spencer, Bart. local address	Sir Anthony	Sir Anthony Spencer (Sir Anthony)	Sir Anthony Spencer
Dear Sir Anthony, Yours sincerely,			
Dear Lady Spencer, Yours sincerely,	Lady Spencer	Lady Spencer	Lady Spencer
Sir Anthony and Lady Spencer			

Knight

A Knight and the wife of a Knight are addressed exactly as are a Baronet and his wife.

Written Address	Spoken Address	Introduction and (Form of Reference)	Presentation at a Banquet or on the Radio

Widows of Baronets and Knights

Widow of a Baronet

Penelope, Lady Spencer local address	Lady Spencer	Lady Spencer	
Dear Lady Spencer, Yours sincerely,			

Widow of a Knight

Lavinia, Lady Clayton local address	Lady Clayton	Lady Clayton	
Dear Lady Clayton, Yours sincerely,			

NOTE: The correct terms to describe the assumption of a title are these: one *succeeds* to a Dukedom, Marquisate, Earldom, Viscountcy, Barony, *or* Baronetcy; one is *awarded* a Knighthood.

Government Officials

The British Prime Minister

The Right Hon.
    Clement Winston, P.C., M.P.
    Prime Minister
No. 10 Downing Street
London
England
	Mr. Winston	Mr. Winston, or
		The Prime
		Minister
			The Prime Minister, The Right Honorable Clement Winston (abroad: The Prime Minister of Great Britain, The Right Honorable Clement Winston)

Dear Mr. Prime Minister, (or Dear Mr. Winston,) Yours sincerely,			
The Right Hon. and Mrs. Clement Winston local address			

NOTE: Prime Ministers of the Commonwealth Countries are addressed as above, except that the name of the country is added after "Prime Minister." For example:

The Right Hon. Rufus Baldwin, P.C., M.P. Prime Minister of Canada Ottawa Canada			In his own country—The Prime Minister, the Right Honorable Rufus Baldwin; abroad— The Prime Minister of Canada, the Right Honorable Rufus Baldwin

Members of the British Cabinet, as members of the Privy Council, are given the title The Right Honorable, followed by the name and the title of the post. For example:

Written Address	Spoken Address	Introduction and (Form of Reference)	Presentation at a Banquet or on the Radio
The Rt. Hon. Ernest Ford, Secretary of State for Foreign Affairs Foreign Office Dear Mr. Ford, Yours sincerely, The Rt. Hon. and Mrs. Ernest Ford	Mr. Ford	Mr. Ford	The Right Honorable Ernest Ford, Secretary of State for Foreign Affairs

A woman cabinet officer—member of the Privy Council

Written Address	Spoken Address	Introduction and (Form of Reference)	Presentation at a Banquet or on the Radio
The Rt. Hon. Edith Hager, Minister of Education Ministry of Education London England Dear Mrs. Hager, Yours sincerely, Invitations sent to her house are addressed as follows: if unmarried: The Rt. Hon. Edith Hager if married: John Hager, Esq. and the Rt. Hon. Edith Hager	Mrs. Hager	Mrs. Hager	The Right Honorable Edith Hager, Minister of Education

Members of the Privy Council, of any title lower than Duke or Marquess, are entitled to be addressed as "The Right Honorable." In social correspondence, however, it is used only in addressing those who have no title other than "Mr."

Written Address	Spoken Address	Introduction and (Form of Reference)	Presentation at a Banquet or on the Radio
The Rt. Hon. Cecil Gore local address Dear Mr. Gore, Yours sincerely, The Rt. Hon. and Mrs. Cecil Gore	Mr. Gore	Mr. Gore	The Right Honorable Cecil Gore

Members of Privy Councils of the Commonwealth Countries are given the title "The Honorable."

Written Address	Spoken Address	Introduction and (Form of Reference)	Presentation at a Banquet or on the Radio
The Hon. John Angus local address Dear Mr. Angus, Yours sincerely, The Hon. and Mrs. John Angus local address	Mr. Angus	Mr. Angus	The Honorable John Angus

Written Address	Spoken Address	Introduction and (Form of Reference)	Presentation at a Banquet or on the Radio

Members of the House of Commons are given the initials "M.P." after their names.

George Edward Adams, Esq., M.P. House of Commons London England	Mr. Adams	Mr. Adams	Mr. George Adams, Member of Parliament from Woking on Trent
Dear Mr. Adams, Yours sincerely,			
Mr. and Mrs. George Edward Adams			

Governor-General of a Dominion or Colony

His Excellency The Earl of Windmere Governor-General of the Union of South Africa Victoria Union of South Africa	Excellency, or Lord Windmere	His Excellency the Governor-General, or Lord Windmere (His Excellency, or The Governor General, or Lord Windmere	His Excellency The Right Honorable The Earl of Windmere The Governor-General (or, away from his post ———— of Windmere, Governor General of the Union of South Africa)
Dear Governor-General, or Dear Lord Windmere, Yours sincerely,			
His Excellency The Governor-General and the Countess of Windmere			

Ambassadors and Ministers

NOTE: As a matter of courtesy, American citizens, not in government service, may use the British forms in addressing British Ambassadors and Ministers. (For the officially approved American forms for addressing foreign representatives, see page 566.)

His Excellency, H.B.M.'s Ambassador British Embassy Washington D. C.	Lord Marpole	The British Ambassador, Lord Marpole (The Ambassador, or The British Ambassador, or Lord Marpole)	His Britannic Majesty's Ambassador, the Earl of Marpole
Your Excellency: or, Dear Lord Marpole, Yours sincerely,			
H.B.M.'s Ambassador and the Countess of Marpole British Embassy Washington D. C.			
Spencer Dickson, Esq. H.B.M.'s Minister British Legation Bogotá Colombia	Mr. Minister or, Mr. Dickson	The British Minister, Mr. Dickson (The Minister, or The British Minister, or Mr. Dickson)	His Britannic Majesty's Minister, Mr. Spencer Dickson

Written Address	Spoken Address	Introduction and (Form of Reference)	Presentation at a Banquet or on the Radio

Dear Mr. Dickson,
Yours sincerely,

H.B.M.'s Minister and Mrs.
  Dickson
British Legation
Bogotá
 Colombia

Private Individuals

It should be noted that Esq. is used in preference to Mr. in all British correspondence except business correspondence: John Smith, Esq., not Mr. John Smith. The rules of usage are the same as in America, and so are the forms for addressing women. A small point of difference in the customs of spoken address is that surgeons in England are always spoken to as "Mr. ———" not "Dr. ———."

FRENCH FORMS

The French forms for diplomatic and unofficial correspondence are included here for many reasons. As the traditional diplomatic language, French is the second language of many foreigners and French forms are used in correspondence with many countries other than France. Most of these forms, however, can be used only in French and are quite incorrect in English. For example, "Madame l'Ambassadrice" is a courteous form of address unknown and utterly incorrect in English; "His Excellency, Mr. ———" is not approved in English.

When speaking to tradespeople, domestics, or employees, an ambassador is referred to as "Son Excellence" ("Son Excellence est rentrée"); ministers as "Monsieur le Ministre"; those who have the title of prince are spoken of as "Le Prince"; others with titles as "Madame la Comtesse," etc.; others as "Monsieur" or "Madame."

In speaking directly to an ambassador, the form of address is "Excellence"; to a Minister, "Monsieur le Ministre." But as a rule titles are not used in spoken address—the correct form is "Monsieur" or "Madame." Exceptions are princes and dukes and their wives, for whom the forms are "Prince," "Princesse," "Monsieur le Duc," and "Madame la Duchesse." Royal princes are "Monseigneur" or "Votre Altesse"; royal princesses, "Madame" or "Votre Altesse."

In letter writing, French salutations are extremely simple—with few exceptions, all letters to acquaintances begin "Monsieur," or "Madame," or more informally, "Chère Madame" or "Cher Monsieur," or to be more friendly, "Chère amie" or "Cher ami." Closings, however, are an extremely complicated and delicate matter. There is no French equivalent for "Sincerely yours," which is used by men and women, young and old, in writing in English to anyone except a president or a high church dignitary. The French forms have almost infinite variations and subtleties of shading which take into consideration not only the position or sex of the writer but also that of the one who is addressed. Therefore, to each of the closings listed below, a note is attached explaining the relative position of the writer.

Written Address	Spoken Address	Introduction and (Form of Reference)	Presentation at a Banquet or on the Radio

Officials

Ambassadors

Son Excellence
  Monsieur A. I. de Texeira
Ambassadeur du Brésil
Paris
France
	Excellence, or
	Monsieur
	l'Ambassadeur
		Son Excellence,
		  l'Ambassadeur
		du Brésil
		(L'Ambassadeur
		or
		Son Excel-
		lence)
			Son Excellence
			Monsieur de
			Texeira, Am-
			bassadeur du
			Brésil

Monsieur l'Ambassadeur:
Veuillez agréer, Monsieur l'Am-
  bassadeur, l'assurance de ma
  très haute considération. (From
  a man to a contemporary or col-
  league, very formal)			

Son Excellence
  Madame de Texeira
   or
Madame de Texeira
Ambassade du Brésil
Paris
France
	Madame, or
	Madame
	l'Ambassadrice
		Madame de
		Texeira (or
		Madame, or
		Madame l'Am-
		bassadrice)
			Madame de
			Texeira

Madame:
Veuillez agréer, Madame, l'ex-
  pression de mes sentiments
  respectueux. (From a young
  woman to an older woman)			

Son Excellence l'Ambassadeur du Brésil et Madame de Texeira			

Ministers

Monsieur Carlos Saavedra y San- chez Ministre de Cuba Paris France	Monsieur le Ministre or Monsieur	Le Ministre de Cuba, Monsieur Saavedra (Le Ministre, or Monsieur, or Monsieur Saavedra)	Le Ministre de Cuba, Mon- sieur Saavedra

Monsieur le Ministre:
Veuillez agréer, Monsieur le
  Ministre, l'assurance de ma
  haute considération. (From a
  man to a contemporary or col-
  league, very formal)			

Madame de Saavedra Légation de Cuba Paris France	Madame, or Madame de Saavedra	Madame de Saavedra (or Madame)	Madame de Saavedra

Madame:
Veuillez agréer, Madame, l'ex-
  pression de mes sentiments les
  meilleurs. (From a woman to a
  contemporary acquaintance)
Le Ministre de Cuba
  et Madame de Saavedra			

Written Address	Spoken Address	Introduction and (Form of Reference)	Presentation at a Banquet or on the Radio

Titled Persons

Prince and Princess—not royal

Royal Princes and Princesses are addressed in writing with the prefix "Son Altesse Royale (or "Impériale") Monseigneur le Prince de _____" or "_____ Madame la Princesse de _____." In the plural, "Leurs Altesses _____," etc. Other titles, often not French, may be accorded the prefix "Son Altesse Sérénissime le Prince de _____"; but the use of this title is impossible to fix by rule—the Almanach de Gotha must be consulted. The only fixed rule is that a Prince addressed in writing as "Son Altesse Sérénissime _____" is spoken to as "Prince," as suggested here, not as "Votre Altesse" or "Monseigneur," as a royal Prince would be.

Written Address	Spoken Address	Introduction and (Form of Reference)	Presentation at a Banquet or on the Radio
Le Prince de Soubise local address Prince: Veuillez agréer, Prince, l'expression de mes sentiments les plus distingués. (From a young man to an older man)	Prince	Le Prince de Soubise (Le Prince)	Le Prince de Soubise
La Princesse de Soubise local address Princesse: Veuillez agréer, Princesse, mes hommages les plus respectueux. (From a young man to an older woman, very formal) Le Prince et la Princesse de Soubise	Princesse	La Princesse de Soubise (La Princesse)	La Princesse de Soubise

Duke and Duchess

Written Address	Spoken Address	Introduction and (Form of Reference)	Presentation at a Banquet or on the Radio
Monsieur Le Duc de Guermantes local address Monsieur le Duc: Veuillez agréer, Monsieur le Duc, l'expression de mes sentiments trés distingués. (From a man to a contemporary man, formal)	Monsieur le Duc	Le Duc de Guermantes (Le Duc)	Le Duc de Guermantes

In writing to other men, the phrasing is identical but the title is changed. For example, in a letter to a bank director "Monsieur le Duc" would be changed to "Monsieur le Directeur."

Written Address	Spoken Address	Introduction and (Form of Reference)	Presentation at a Banquet or on the Radio
Madame La Duchesse de Guermantes local address Madame la Duchesse: Veuillez agréer, Madame la Duchesse, mes très respectueux hommages. (From a young man to an older woman, less formal) Monsieur le Duc et Madame la Duchesse de Guermantes	Madame la Duchesse	La Duchesse de Guermantes (La Duchesse)	La Duchesse de Guermantes

Written Address	*Spoken Address*	*Introduction and (Form of Reference)*	*Presentation at a Banquet or on the Radio*
Marquis, Count, Viscount, or Baron			
Monsieur le Marquis (or Comte, Vicomte, or Baron) de Lafayette local address	Monsieur	Le Marquis (or etc.) de Lafayette (Monsieur)	Le Marquis (or Comte, Vicomte, Baron) de Lafayette
Monsieur: Veuillez croire, Monsieur (or "Monsieur l'Ambassadeur," etc.) à mes sentiments déférents. (From a young woman to a much older man; if there were less difference in age, the closing might be "＿＿＿ mes sentiments très distingués"; a woman writing formally to a contemporary might end the letter, "Croyez, Monsieur, à mes sentiments très distingués.")			
Madame la Marquise (or Comtesse, Vicomtesse or Baronne) de Lafayette local address	Madame	La Marquise (or etc.) de Lafayette (Madame)	La Marquise (or Comtesse, Vicomtesse or Baronne) de Lafayette
Madame: Veuillez agréer, Madame, mes respectueux hommages. (From a man to a woman contemporary)			
Monsieur le Marquis et Madame la Marquise de Lafayette Monsieur le Comte et Madame la Comtesse de Lafayette Monsieur le Vicomte et Madame la Vicomtesse de Lafayette Monsieur le Baron et Madame la Baronne de Lafayette			
Private Individuals			
Monsieur Pierre Tassigny (or "de Tassigny" if he is entitled to the prefix "de") local address	Monsieur	Monsieur Tassigny (Monsieur)	Monsieur Tassigny
Monsieur: Croyez, Monsieur, à mes sentiments les meilleurs. (From a man to a younger man, less formal)			
Madame Tassigny (or "de Tassigny") local address	Madame	Madame Tassigny (Madame)	Madame Tassigny

Written Address	Spoken Address	Introduction and (Form of Reference)	Presentation at a Banquet or on the Radio

Madame:
Croyez, Madame, à mes sentiments distingués. (From an
older woman to a younger
woman)
Monsieur et Madame Tassigny

The closings suggested above may be used whether the salutation is "Monsieur" or "Cher Monsieur," "Madame" or "Chère Madame"; but when the salutation begins with "Cher(e)" the
closing should include it also ("Veuillez agréer, chère Madame . . ."). When the salutation is the
informal "Cher ami" or "Chère amie," which is often used between more friendly acquaintances,
these closings may be used:

"Croyez, chère amie, à mes meil-
leurs souvenirs"
"Croyez, cher ami, à mes sincères
amitiés"
"Bien à vous . . ."
"Affectueusement à vous"

The French form of the English closing, "Please remember me to . . .":

"Veuillez me rappeler au bon
souvenir de Madame Tassi-
gny . . ." (or ". . . de Monsieur
Tassigny," or ". . . de Madame
votre mère.")

Business letters begin, "Messieurs"; or, to a particular salesman, "Monsieur." The closing of a
woman's letter is "Je vous adresse mes salutations distingués . . ." A man would end, "Croyez,
Messieurs, à mes sentiments distingués . . ." A final flourish which may be used in any formal
correspondence when the superscription on the envelope begins "Monsieur" or "Madame" is to
write an extra "Monsieur" or "Madame" on a line above the name. Thus the address will read,
"Monsieur" (on the first line), then, "Monsieur de Tassigny"; or, on the first line, "Madame,"
then, on the next line, "Madame la Baronne de Lafayette."

SPANISH FORMS

In correspondence with any Spanish-speaking person, the complimentary
Spanish forms are used in addressing the envelope, even though the body of the
letter may be written in English. In Spain and in some South and Central American countries, in any correspondence except business correspondence, a man's
Christian and family names are followed by "y" ("and") and his mother's family
name. (In other South American countries "y" is omitted.) In the first example
below, the words "y Saavedra" are added to Señor Castillo's name because his
mother was born Saavedra. In the case of married women, the husband's name,
preceded by "de" ("of") is added to her own Christian and family names. In the
example given below, Señora de Caro's name shows that she was born Sofia Moro.
The abbreviated form is Señora de Caro or Señora Sofia de Caro; never, in writing,
Señora Caro.

The use of the words "Don" and "Doña" is a little more complicated and
subtle. "Don" (or the feminine "Doña") is a complimentary title, used to convey
respect for the position of the one so addressed. It is written on the envelopes of
all social correspondence, both to men and to women. It is not used in writing to
tradespeople, although tradesmen—perhaps on the theory that the customer is
always right—are very apt to use it in writing to their clients. In spoken address
it is used only for very much older or very distinguished people, and only with
the first name.

Written Address	Spoken Address	Introduction and (Form of Reference)	Presentation at a Banquet or on the Radio

Ambassador and Minister

| His Excellency, Señor Don Carlos Castillo y Saavedra
Ambassador of Peru
Washington
D. C. | Your Excellency, or Mr. Ambassador | The Ambassador of Peru (His Excellency, or The Ambassador) | His Excellency, Señor Don Carlos Castillo y Saavedra, Ambassador of Peru |

Dear Mr. Ambassador,
Sincerely yours,

His Excellency, the Ambassador of Peru and Señora de Castillo
Embassy of Peru
Washington
D. C.

NOTE: In addressing a Minister, "His Excellency" is not used. "Minister" replaces "Ambassador" and "Legation" replaces "Embassy."

Private Individuals—Men

| Señor Don Agustín José Caro y Balmaceda
Calle Almagro #9
Quito
Ecuador | Señor Caro, or Señor, or Don Agustín | Señor Caro | Señor Don Agustín Caro y Balmaceda |

Dear Señor Caro,
Sincerely yours,

Señor Don Agustín Caro and Señora de Caro (never "Señor and Señora _____" or, worse, "Señor Don Agustín Caro and Señora"; or "and Sra.")
Calle Almagro #9
Quito
Ecuador

Private Individuals—Married Woman (wife of above)

| Señora Doña Sofia Moro de Caro
Calle Almagro #9
Quito
Ecuador | Señora de Caro, or Señora, or Doña Sofia | Señora de Caro or Señora Caro | Señora Doña Sofia Moro de Caro |

Dear Señora de Caro,
Sincerely yours,

Private Individuals—Unmarried Woman (daughter of above couple)

| Señorita Doña Elena Caro y Moro
Calle Almagro #9
Quito
Ecuador | Señorita Caro, or Señorita | Señorita Caro | Señorita Doña Elena Caro y Moro |

Dear Señorita Caro,
Sincerely yours,

Written Address	Spoken Address	Introduction and (Form of Reference)	Presentation at a Banquet or on the Radio

For Business Correspondence—A Man

Señor Agustín **Caro**
Junin #27
Quito
Ecuador

Dear Señor **Caro,**
Yours truly,

For Business Correspondence—A Woman

Señora de Caro
Calle Almagro #9
Quito
Ecuador

Dear Señora de Caro,
Yours truly,

69

Cards

CARDS, and especially visiting cards, are very much a matter of form. In a way, the same may be said of visiting cards as of riding clothes: It is better to skip the whole idea than to make up little innovations of one's own. Formal visits are few, Christmas tags and florists' cards are acceptable, and letters will cover almost any other contingency which is apt to arise today.

VISITING CARDS

Visiting cards are very much less useful now than they were when it was the custom to leave cards in great numbers. They were once an essential part of the very strict routine of social life, and their comparative unimportance today is one of the marks of the change our customs have undergone.

Modern Customs

According to the modern custom, visiting cards are:

1. Sent with presents; except Christmas presents, when Christmas tags are usually used.
2. Sent with flowers.
3. Sent with letters of introduction (see page 546).

597

4. Sent with written inscriptions; as informal invitations (see page 504) or reminder cards (page 515).

5. Sometimes left when one makes visits of condolence or a visit to someone who is ill. Cards are not left if one has been received, but only in lieu of a visit.

Traditional Customs

The old-fashioned rule was "a woman never calls on a man," and when cards are used for calls, this rule still holds. For example, if a married couple should call on another married couple, one "Mr. and Mrs." card is left, with one of the husband's cards—or two of the husband's and one of the wife's—on the theory that the husband has called on both members of the family, whereas the wife has called only on the other woman. There is a slight change in this when officials are involved; see "The Cards of Diplomats," page 603.

The old-fashioned customs concerning visiting cards, although no longer observed in America except, perhaps, in official Washington, are less strictly observed abroad than they once were, and are included here only because it is advisable for those traveling abroad to observe the most rigid forms of courtesy.

1. Cards may be left at the house of anyone to whom one has been introduced. In the strictest Continental society, cards *must* be left, particularly by young couples or men, at the house of a woman to whom one has been introduced.

2. According to the old-fashioned American custom, cards may be left by established members of a community at the house of any newcomer. In Latin countries the reverse is true: newcomers must be the first to leave the cards.

3. Visiting cards must be returned; in other words, if Mr. and Mrs. A. have called, one must leave one's cards not longer than a week afterwards at Mr. and Mrs. A's house.

4. After one has been entertained, cards should be left at the hostess's house the following day, or at least within three days.

5. When one is leaving the city, cards are left at all friends' houses and at all the houses in which one has been entertained. In such cases, "P. p. c." ("pour prendre congé"—"to take leave") is written in by hand, either in pencil or in ink, in the lower left-hand corner. When one is making a visit of condolence, "p. c." ("pour condoler," "to condole") is written instead. "P. f. ("pour féliciter," "to felicitate") and "p. r." (pour remercier," "to thank") are the other conventional abbreviations.

6. The upper right-hand corner of the card is turned down with the point toward the name, to indicate that one has called in person—in most cases, a fiction of which nothing is left but this form. This custom is observed in Washington and in many foreign countries, but not in all. In Scandinavian capitals, for example, and in England, it only suggests that the cards have been mussed.

7. Although a husband almost never accompanies his wife in making calls, it is quite proper for her to leave his card as well as her own. Other members of the family, or even a friend, may substitute for the wife, but cards should never be left by a chauffeur. The chauffeur may take the cards to the door, but the wife, a relative, or a friend of the family should be in the car.

8. Cards should never be mailed, but should always be left at the door by hand.

9. Cards left as a matter of form, for the reasons given here, are left in the afternoon between luncheon and dinnertime. Between 4:00 and 6:00 P.M. are the ideal hours.

The Paper

The best material for visiting cards is a heavy white pasteboard or card (technically this is called two-sheet board) of the very best quality. Some use a very light cream color instead of white, but white is really the best. Single-sheet pasteboard is sometimes used, too, but this is less formal than the heavier card. The size may vary from about 3 by 1½ inches for the card of a single man to 3½ by 2⅜ for that of a married couple.

It is always wise to order envelopes to match the visiting cards, so that they may be sent with flowers or presents, or in the mail as an informal reminder card. Visiting cards left at someone's house are not, of course, left in envelopes.

The Lettering

Visiting cards should always be engraved in black—and the best lettering is one of those shown on pages 600 to 602: Roman, shaded Roman, script, London script, shaded antique Roman and shaded modified Roman. Unusual or heavy lettering, such as Old English, should be avoided.

Engraving the Name

As a matter of rule, no abbreviations other than "Mr." and "Mrs." and "Dr." should be used before the name. (See also page 604, "The Cards of Military and Naval Officers.") The initials of orders or degrees may be engraved after the name, as "Edward Everett Bates, M.D." but the better form is Dr. Edward Everett Bates"; for a doctor and his wife, "Dr. and Mrs. Edward Everett Bates."

"II" (or "III," etc.) is engraved in numerals after a man's name. According to the preferred form, "junior" is engraved in full although, if the name is very long, it is sometimes abbreviated and capitalized: "Jr." (The question of when to use "Jr.," "II," "III," etc. is discussed on page 557 in the chapter, "Forms of Address.") On a man's card, "Mr." is often left off if "junior" is to follow although, technically, "Mr." belongs on the card of every man over twenty-one; the cards of a married couple are engraved "Mr. and Mrs. Ogden Philip Hemingway, "junior," or "Mr. and Mrs. Ogden Philip Hemingway, II." Initials should be avoided as much as possible and, in any case, one name at least must be written out. A card might be engraved, "Mrs. Ogden P. Hemingway," for example, or "Mrs. O. Philip Hemingway"; but it should never read "Mrs. O. P. Hemingway." The best usage is always the full name: "Mrs. Ogden Philip Hemingway."

Engraving the Address

It is entirely a matter of choice whether or not the address is to be engraved on the card with the name. If so, it is engraved in one, or, if necessary, in two lines, in the lower right-hand corner. The only exception to this is a club address, which is engraved in the lower left corner. A business address should never, of course, be engraved on any visiting card except a business card; the only permissible address other than one's house is the name of one's club.

The customs governing the engraving of addresses on writing paper are followed also in engraving an address on a visiting card. In other words, a town address may be given almost entirely in numerals—"55 East 66th Street"—or it may be written out completely—"One Courtlandt Street." The suggestions given for formal town-house writing paper, on page 534, "Engraved Addresses," should be followed in engraving visiting cards marked with a town-house address. The cards of those who live in the country are engraved with the names of the town and the state, as shown on the woman's visiting card below.

Two letterings are often very successfully combined on the same card, one for the name and the other for the address. A name in shaded Roman, for example, looks very well with an address in script. But combined letterings must be very expertly done and, if there is any doubt, it is better to stick to the traditional form.

STANDARD FORMS

The following reproductions show the standard letterings and a few of the more usual forms for visiting cards.

A Man's Card

MR. EDWARD EVERETT BATES

THE LINKS CLUB

AN EXAMPLE OF ROMAN LETTERING

Club addresses are engraved in the lower left-hand corner, as shown here; all others, at the right.

A Married Woman's Card

Mrs Edward Everett Bates

Somerton, Maryland

AN EXAMPLE OF LONDON SCRIPT LETTERING

The address is that of a house in the country, or in a country village where no street address is necessary.

The Card of a Married Couple

Mr. and Mrs. Edward Everett Bates

20 Roble Road

AN EXAMPLE OF SCRIPT LETTERING
The address is that of a house in a city, or in a large town.

Mr. and Mrs. Gardner Meredith Shaw

10 West Genesee Street
Fayetteville, New York

AN EXAMPLE OF SHADED ANTIQUE ROMAN LETTERING

The address is that of a house in a small community—a practical form if one plans to use visiting cards away from home.

Dr. and Mrs. John Scott Ross, junior

AN EXAMPLE OF SHADED MODIFIED ROMAN LETTERING

An Unmarried Woman's Card

The most conservative tradition holds that no address should ever be engraved on the card of an unmarried woman. This custom is not always observed today, but it is still true that an address is not usually engraved on a young girl's visiting card.

MISS EDITH HAWKINS BATES

AN EXAMPLE OF SHADED ROMAN LETTERING IN TWO SIZES

This lettering is also used in capitals all of one size.

A Widow's Card

The visiting cards of a widow are engraved exactly as they were during her husband's lifetime. If, for example, while her husband was alive, a woman's cards were engraved, "Mrs. James Howard Duncan," her visiting card should still be engraved, "Mrs. James Howard Duncan." If there is any danger of confusion—as there might be if the widow's son were married and if the son bore his father's name—the widow's address may be engraved in the lower right corner. In no case should a widow's cards be engraved, "Mrs. Mary Compton Duncan," or, "Mrs. James Howard Duncan, Sr." As the widow or wife of the head of the family, a woman's card may be engraved simply, "Mrs. Duncan." But this is a technicality which, although correct, is not usually observed in the United States. Forms of address for the widow are discussed on page 568.

Children's Cards

Visiting cards for very small children are not advisable. There is something pretentious and extravagant about engraving a card for a very young child. Young children are not, as a rule, taken to call on acquaintances, and if one is calling on an intimate friend or a member of the family, one can always write on the card a message such as, "So sorry not to find you in; I brought Josephine with me to call on you." If children need a card to send with a present, they can always use a plain white card of a good quality, without engraving or decoration of any kind. A young girl might use her mother's card, with her mother's name struck out in ink and her name, with perhaps a short message, written in ink. When a boy has reached college age, cards may be engraved for him without the prefix "Mr." Technically, "Mr." should be engraved on a man's card only after he is twenty-one years old. Young girls may have visiting cards as soon as they are "presented to society"; in other words, when they are about seventeen or eighteen and have finished school.

The Cards of Divorcées

As indicated on page 567, in the section, "Forms of Address," there are three correct ways of addressing an envelope to a divorced woman and these forms are correct also on her visiting cards. The standard and preferred form is to use the maiden surname followed by the former husband's name. For example, the former Mrs. Alexander Auchincloss, born Mary Elkins, would engrave her visiting cards, "Mrs. Elkins Auchincloss." If, by an unfortunate coincidence, her maiden name had been Mary Alexander, this form could not be used. Instead, her visiting cards would be engraved, "Mrs. M. Alexander Auchincloss."

A third form, equally correct but less usual than these two, involves the use of a divorcée's second baptismal name. If her maiden name was Mary Foster Alexander, she could also engrave her visiting cards, "Mrs. Foster Auchincloss," or "Mrs. M. Foster Auchincloss." A woman's personal visiting cards should never be engraved, "Mrs. Mary Auchincloss" or, "Mrs. Mary Elkins Auchincloss." (See also "Business Cards for Women," pages 610 and 611.)

THE CARDS OF DIPLOMATS

Diplomats often have two sets of visiting cards, one engraved in the language of their own country, the other engraved either in French or in the language of the country to which they are accredited. Script used to be the standard lettering for American diplomats, but other kinds, such as shaded Roman, are now being used. Exact reproductions of these letterings are shown on pages 600-602; only the wording is given here. On all diplomats' cards, two sizes (and sometimes two kinds) of lettering are used, the larger for the name, and the smaller for the title. The title is centered on a line—or, if necessary, two lines—directly under the name. When the address is engraved, as it may be on the card of a diplomat's wife, it is placed in the lower right corner.

Further, as in the case of many officials, "Mr. and Mrs." cards are not often used; if, for example, an ambassador and his wife, or a Secretary and his wife, were calling on Mr. and Mrs. X, two of his cards would be left and one of hers. The title "Mr." is almost never used on the card of a diplomat. And in Latin American countries, "The United States of America" is always used in preference to "America" or "American."

An Ambassador's Card

This is the wording used on the visiting cards of an ambassador:

Henry Armour
Ambassador of the United States of America

The Cards of the Wife of an Ambassador

The visiting cards of the wife of an ambassador, or of any American diplomat of whatever rank, are engraved almost exactly as they would be if her husband were a private citizen. The only difference is that on the visiting cards of the wives of ambassadors or ministers, "The American Embassy" or "The American Legation" may be engraved in the lower right-hand corner, as shown also in the example, "A Married Woman's Card," page 600. For example:

Mrs. Henry Armour
The American Embassy
14 Prince's Gate

A Minister's Card

This is an example of the wording:

Norman Arnsworth
Minister of the United States of America

The Card of an American Minister—Woman

The wording of the card might be either

Margaret Bruce Scott
Minister of the United States of America

or

Mrs. Harrison Scott
Minister of the United States of America

Other Diplomats' Cards

On the cards of other members of the staff of an embassy or legation the line under the name reads as follows:

Counselor of Embassy (or Legation) of the United States of America
First Secretary of the Embassy (or Legation) of the United States of America
Second Secretary of the Embassy (or Legation) of the United States of America
Third Secretary of the Embassy (or Legation) of the United States of America
Attaché of the Embassy (or Legation) of the United States of America

To save space, on the cards of Secretaries and Attachés, the line is often broken in two after the word "Embassy" or "Legation." Or, after the title, a comma may replace the words "of the"; for example, "First Secretary, Embassy of the United States of America."

The Cards of Military or Naval Attachés

The card of a military attaché is engraved with his rank and name; as, "Major John Mills Locke." Under this is the line, "Military Attaché of the Embassy (or "Legation") of the United States of America." Naval attachés follow the same form; name and rank on the first line; as for example, "Lieutenant Henry Siedel Crawford," and on the second, "Naval Attaché of the Embassy (or "Legation") of the United States of America."

The Cards of a Consul General, Consul or Vice Consul

The title "Mr." is often omitted on the cards of consular officials as it is on the cards of all diplomats. For example, "Robert Louis Eliot" is engraved on the first line, and "Consul General (or "Consul," or "Vice Consul") of the United States of America" on the second.

THE CARDS OF MILITARY AND NAVAL OFFICERS

As a matter of form, abbreviations of military or naval rank should not be used on a visiting card. Navy rules make abbreviations unnecessary; but on an

Army officer's card, if the name is extremely long, abbreviation is sometimes unavoidable. For example, a name as long as "Lieutenant Colonel and Mrs. Harrington Howland-Russell" would present quite a problem. It is not customary to omit the first name, and one should never use an initial in place of it; therefore, there is nothing to do but abbreviate the rank, as "Lieut. Colonel and Mrs. . . ." These abbreviations are always, however, contrary to the best usage and should be used only if absolutely necessary and only on the card of an officer *and* his wife; never on his card only.

A second rule, and one which must never be broken, is that officers in the reserve Army or in the Naval Reserve should never use a military or naval title unless they are on active duty. Retired officers may, of course, use their titles. As a matter of military and naval practice, "Jr." is used after a man's name rather than "junior." This is practical because the full title or rank, followed by the name, often makes a very long line. It is not, however, a rule.

The paper and sizes of military and naval visiting cards are exactly like those described on page 599. Script lettering is standard, but shaded Roman and Roman are also used. Samples of these letterings are shown on pages 600–602; as in the case of the diplomats' cards discussed above, only the wording is given here.

Army Officers

The phrase, "United States Army" should be engraved only on the visiting card of an officer in the regular Army. To be extremely technical, it is correctly used only when an officer in the regular Army holds permanent rank in the regular Army; but usage does not always honor this technicality. Officers on active duty who are not members of the regular Army use "Army of the United States" on their visiting cards. An officer's regiment is now rarely engraved on his card, and whether or not his branch of service is mentioned is purely optional.

The Army approves two different wordings for visiting cards:

Lieutenant Richard Spooner Desmond
United States Army

or, with the rank in the "address" position:

Richard Spooner Desmond
Lieutenant
United States Army

An officer who wants to have his branch of service engraved on his visiting cards may use either of these forms as follows:

Major John Mills Leslie
Infantry, United States Army

or, with the rank in the lower right corner:

Thomas Carter Park
Lieutenant Colonel, Ordnance
United States Army

As a rule, officers of the regular Army are apt to use the first form; and Reserve officers on active duty the second one, with the name by itself in the middle

of the card, and the military rank in the lower right-hand corner. But this is entirely a matter of choice. In any case, of course, officers who are not in the regular Army cannot use the phrase "United States Army" on their visiting cards; they must substitute instead, "Army of the United States." Army rank is engraved as follows:

Lieutenant Richard Spooner Desmond
United States Army

Note that no difference is made between the card of a first lieutenant and that of a second lieutenant.

Captain Richard Spooner Desmond
United States Army
Major Richard Spooner Desmond
United States Army
Lieutenant Colonel Richard Spooner Desmond
United States Army
Colonel Richard Spooner Desmond
United States Army
Brigadier General Richard Spooner Desmond
United States Army
Major General Richard Spooner Desmond
United States Army
Lieutenant General Richard Spooner Desmond
United States Army
General Richard Spooner Desmond
United States Army
General of the Army Richard Spooner Desmond

The cards of military officers and their wives are engraved with the names and titles only:

Lieutenant and Mrs. Richard Spooner Desmond

When unavoidably necessary, the following abbreviations are sanctioned by usage for the cards of Army officers and their wives:

Lieut. Colonel and Mrs. Richard Spooner Desmond
Brig. General and Mrs. Richard Spooner Desmond
Lieut. General and Mrs. Richard Spooner Desmond
General and Mrs. Richard Spooner Desmond
(for a General of the Army and his wife)

"Major General" is written in full, since the abbreviation Maj. General is so little shorter than the full title. The cards of military and naval attachés are shown on page 603, "The Cards of Diplomats."

Naval Officers

The forms for the visiting cards of naval officers are extremely simple. The only difference between those of regular Navy officers and those of officers in the Naval Reserve is that the line under the name of a Reserve officer reads, "United States Naval Reserve" instead of "United States Navy." The form for the visiting cards of senior officers in the Navy is exactly like the first card shown for Army officers ("Lieutenant Richard Spooner Desmond"). These are the approved Naval wordings:

Commander George Albert Patterson
United States Navy
Captain George Albert Patterson
United States Navy
Commodore George Albert Patterson
United States Navy
Rear Admiral George Albert Patterson
United States Navy
Vice Admiral George Albert Patterson
United States Navy
Admiral George Albert Patterson
United States Navy

Senior officers and their wives may use joint visiting cards, but the second line must, of course, be omitted:

Captain and Mrs. George Albert Patterson

Junior officers (lieutenant commanders, lieutenants, lieutenants (j.g.), and ensigns use the following forms for visiting cards:

George Albert Patterson
Lieutenant, United States Navy

or, with the rank in the lower right-hand corner:

George Albert Patterson
Lieutenant, junior grade
United States Navy

Naval custom does not approve joint visiting cards for junior officers and their wives.

Officers of the Air Force

The forms suggested for the visiting cards of officers in the Army are used also for those of officers in the Air Force. The only difference is that "United States Army" is changed to "United States Air Force" for officers in the regular Air Force, and "Army of the United States" to "Air Force of the United States" for reserve officers on active duty.

Marine Corps Officers

The forms suggested above for the use of naval officers are correct also for officers of the Marine Corps except, of course, that the line under the name reads, "United States Marine Corps" instead of "United States Navy," or "United States Marine Corps Reserve," in place of "United States Naval Reserve."

BUSINESS CARDS

Perhaps it would be wise to make clear at the beginning of this section that we are not discussing visiting cards which are often used by business firms as a minor

607

form of advertising. Here we are concerned only with visiting cards which men and women in business use for their business life, in the same way and for the same purposes that they use personal visiting cards for their personal life. The difference between the wording of business visiting cards and personal visiting cards exactly parallels the difference between an introduction at a dinner party and an introduction at a business meeting. In society, a man's business affiliations are never mentioned in an introduction, although it is always perfectly correct and often very convenient to mention them at a business luncheon. In the same way, personal visiting cards are engraved only with one's name and address at home, whereas business visiting cards may be engraved with one's name, with the name and address of the company and even with the title of the position one holds in that company. To continue the parallel, business visiting cards, like business introductions, should never be used except in business. If one is sending flowers, or a Christmas present, to a business associate whom one has seen only during business hours and for business reasons, a business visiting card is sent with them. If, however, the business associate has become a friend, a personal visiting card should be used.

The Cards

All business cards except those used in advertising should be engraved in black or gray, on white pasteboard of a good quality; and the better the quality, the better impression the card will make. The best size is about 3½ by 2 inches, although the president of a company might use a slightly larger card, 3½ by 2¼ inches. Script, which is among the most usual forms of lettering for personal visiting cards, is not advisable for most business visiting cards. Except for specialty shops—particularly women's shops which might use script to give an impression of conservatism and femininity—the best lettering is Roman, shaded Roman, or plain block letters.

There are three basic forms for engraving visiting cards that are used in business: two for important officials and one for junior members of a company.

Important Executives

1. The first form, used by an important executive, is engraved without title, and with the name and address of the firm in a secondary position. An example of this is:

PERRY L. LINCOLN

LINCOLN COMPANY, INC.
BERWICK, OHIO

BUSINESS CARD ENGRAVED IN BLOCK LETTERS

One of the standard forms used by important officials in business, this card illustrates several principles common to all business cards:

a. Middle initials, which should be avoided on personal visiting cards, are quite proper on business visiting cards.

b. "Company" is always written out unless "Co." is part of the firm's registered name. "Inc." is usually abbreviated.

c. The name of the company is engraved in the lower left-hand corner.

d. If the company offices are not in a very big city, the name of the state is included with that of the town, as in the example shown above. If the offices are in a big city, the street address and the name of the city are engraved on two lines and the name of the state is omitted:

12 West Street
Detroit

The address of the company may be engraved either in the lower left-hand corner, as shown in the example above, or in the lower right-hand corner, as in the following example. The decision as to where it should be put rests on the question of where it looks best.

e. A telephone number does not belong on a visiting card, although it may quite properly be engraved on cards which the company uses as advertisements.

2. The second form for the card of an important official is engraved not only with his name and the firm's name and address, but also with his title:

JOSEPH P. MANTON

PRESIDENT
REEVE ENGINEERING COMPANY, INC.   SCOTT, IOWA

BUSINESS CARD ENGRAVED IN ROMAN LETTERING

The question of whether or not one uses one's title on a visiting card is entirely a matter of choice and convenience. A very important and well-known official would probably not include his title on his business visiting card. An official who has been newly elected or appointed to his position might feel that it was necessary for the sake of clarity. In any case, the only positions that should be engraved on a visiting card are: president, vice president, secretary, treasurer, and general manager, or equally important positions in other fields; as, editor, editor in chief, managing editor, etc.

The question of whether the title should be engraved above or below the name of the company is also a matter of choice and depends greatly upon where it will look best. In the example shown above the address is engraved on one line in the right-hand corner balanced against the name of the company in the left-hand corner. In this case, the title may look better when it is centered above the name of the company. If, however, the address of the company is engraved in two lines at the right, with the lower line very much the shorter, the title might be engraved underneath the name of the company.

Junior Executives

3. The visiting card of a junior executive is often engraved with the company's name in the dominant position and the official's name in the lower left-hand corner. The most important information the card conveys is the name of the business, and the name of the man is relegated to the secondary position in the lower left-hand corner.

CLAY AND WROTHERS, INC.

Mr. Gray L. Mason
Public Relations
60 West Street, Detroit

BUSINESS CARD ENGRAVED IN SHADED ROMAN AND SCRIPT

Note that "Mr." precedes the man's name. As in the case of card number 2, the man's name may be put over or under that of the department in which he works, depending on the balanced engraving of the card. Or the department may be omitted entirely.

Business Cards for Women

All the customs described above for men's visiting cards should be followed also by women in business. The only difference is that for convenience's sake, quite apart from any other consideration, a woman's name should be preceded by "Mrs." or "Miss." If one is using either card number 1 or number 2, a woman's first name should be written out, "Miss Frances Wilson," or "Miss Frances L. Wilson." If one is using card number 3, one may follow the same form, or use initials only, "Miss F. L. Wilson, Public Relations."

The question of whether or not to use "Mrs." on one's business cards is often a difficult one to decide. Many women in business keep their maiden names after they have married, either because they have made a position for themselves in business under that name, or because they would rather keep their business lives quite separate from their personal lives. This is entirely, however, a matter of choice. A woman's name may be engraved on her business cards exactly as it is on her personal cards, except, perhaps, that a middle initial is preferable to the formality of writing out the middle name, "Mrs. Robert W. Wilson."

If one is married and if one has become known to the public under one's married name—"Mary Compton Wilson," for example—one may engrave one's business cards, either "Mary Compton Wilson" or "Mrs. Mary Compton Wilson." The "Mrs. Mary . . ." form is, of course, entirely incorrect for a personal card and it is better to avoid it even in business. As a rule, the best solution is to keep one's maiden name, and to continue to engrave one's business visiting cards, "Miss Mary Compton," even after marriage.

CARDS FOR CHRISTMAS AND OTHER OCCASIONS

Engraved or printed cards are sent at Christmas, at Easter, for St. Valentine's Day, or for birthdays. And, except among the young or for special reasons, Christmas cards are the only ones sent as a matter of course. Incidentally, none should be called a "greeting card." It is unnecessary but not, of course, incorrect to write a message on a Christmas card. It need only be signed, as a letter would be. As in letter writing no title should be used in the signature. "Mrs." or "Mr." is wrong. Correct are signatures such as "Mary" or "Mary Andrews." Christmas cards sent by a husband and wife are usually addressed and signed by the wife and, therefore, her name comes after his: "Robert and Mary Andrews," rather than, "Mary and Robert." Another signature that should not be used is, "Mr. and Mrs. Robert Andrews and family." "And family" is not a desirable form. Much better are ". . . and love from us all, Robert and Mary"; or, more formally, ". . . from all of us" or ". . . and best wishes from us all."

When the names are engraved, the order is reversed and the message ends, "Mary and Robert Andrews." If one were sending such a Christmas card to a relative or intimate friend, "Andrews" would be struck out in ink, and "Love" or, "Affectionately" would be written in above the names.

Another way of engraving Christmas cards is to start the message "Mr. and Mrs. . . ." For example, "Mr. and Mrs. Robert Andrews wish you a Merry Christmas . . ." This is, of course, more formal than the first form suggested, but either is correct. A form which should be avoided in engraving, as in writing, is the one which ends, "Mr. and Mrs. . . ." because it suggests the impolite and improper use of "Mr. and Mrs." as a signature. And the abbreviation "Xmas" should never be used.

SYMPATHY CARDS

When a friend is ill, it is much better to send a letter than a "sympathy" card. Sympathy cards always suggest that the sender was too busy to write a personal message of sympathy, and decided to send a ready-made card instead. Flowers or a book, or a nice long letter are much more convincing evidences of sympathy and friendship. And a card of condolence should never be sent instead of a letter. See page 150.

THANK-YOU CARDS

A thank-you card is never a flattering way to send thanks in return for a present or a kindness, and every kind of thank-you card should be avoided, no matter how informal the relationship or how trivial the favor. They should *never* be sent as thanks for a wedding present or for a letter of condolence from a personal friend. The only ones who may use a thank-you card are public officials, or officers of a big business, who may need to send as many as a thousand "thank-you's" to official or business acquaintances. But even in such cases, the best usage is to write a letter of thanks, and the punctilious always stick to this practice. (There are sample letters on page 225, in the chapter on weddings, and on page 152, in the chapter on funerals.)

BIRTH-ANNOUNCEMENT CARDS

Engraved or printed cards should never be sent to announce the birth or adoption of a child. Adoptions are not announced, but a notice may be sent to the newspapers to announce a birth. (See page 97.) The only ways in which friends and relatives should be informed is verbally, by letter, or by telegram. All would-be funny cards, and tiny visiting cards attached to the parents' visiting cards, are bad form.

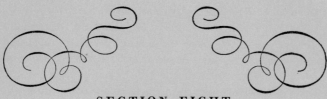

70

Introduction

This section is entirely devoted to clothes; not special clothes, such as those worn for funerals and weddings, or those worn by a household staff, but clothes in general, and clothes from a general point of view. We have come a long way from the time when certain clothes were an unmistakable badge of rank or occupation, restricted by law, but we have nevertheless evolved certain accepted ways of dressing for certain occasions. There are business men's clothes and country men's clothes, clothes suitable for women who live in the big cities in the North, and clothes for women in big Southern cities. Without bothering to study the subject, most normal American adults agree roughly on the wardrobe which is best suited to their own communities.

Differences of opinion arise, as a rule, only concerning the fine points of dress, the details which, for this very reason, reveal most about the taste and discrimination of the wearer. This section covers both the outlines and the details: the outlines for anyone who is moving to a new community, and the details for those who are interested in knowing exactly what the best usage approves and what it does not.

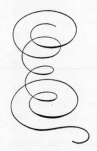

71

Men's Clothes

Men's clothes have often, and perhaps justly, been attacked as impractical and unaesthetic. However, despite all their rigidity and uniformity, they can be a remarkably subtle and accurate expression of a man's outlook, experience, and personality. The basic outlines of his wardrobe are dictated and the range of his choice is small; but just because the range is so limited, his choices are remarkably significant. In every city of the world, for example, men wear dark blue suits and gray suits and brown suits, and yet one can usually tell in half a glance to which country—or at least to which culture—the men belong. There is a true story about a young man in an Ohio town who was told to go to the station to meet a business friend of the company. The only identification given him was, "He'll be dressed like a New York business man," and it was quite enough.

Each culture has a slightly different conception of what makes a well-dressed man. In America, it is somewhat as follows: clothes not too tightly fitted, not too carefully matched, not too obviously thought out as a color scheme. Generally speaking, the American ideal is to be neat but never natty and—first, last and always—underdressed rather than overdressed. To be more specific, we shall list clothes for different occasions, different seasons, and different occupations. This list is not, of course, a final one. It would be impossible in one chapter to mention all the good and useful materials which may be used, and all the combinations of color which men who dress well can invent for themselves. But for each occasion we have made one or two definite and concrete suggestions which may be helpful, and which are safe and sure guides to follow. Details such as jewelry, handkerchiefs, mufflers, and umbrellas, are discussed separately at the end of this chapter.

TOWN DAY CLOTHES—WINTER

For Business

1. Suits. Either double-breasted or single-breasted, with waistcoats or without, pin-striped, chalk-striped, or plain; in gray flannel, dark blue worsted, basket-weave, or serge; brown worsted; gray worsted; or a smooth tweed, preferably herringbone, in gray, brown, or black-and-white. Black suits are now worn for business only by older men.

NOTE: All waistcoats, except evening waistcoats, should be worn with the lowest button unbuttoned. This is merely fashionable in America (where, however, waistcoats are becoming increasingly rare) but it is a must in England, where waistcoats are cut to be so worn. (An English joke tells of an Eton boy who ran away from school. Asked how he had done it, he answered, "I disguised myself. I buttoned the bottom button of my waistcoat.") When a single-breasted coat is worn without a waistcoat, the middle coat button is buttoned; the other two are left open. When a single-breasted coat is worn with a waistcoat, all buttons are unbuttoned. The top button of a double-breasted coat is the only one buttoned on the outside.

2. Shirts of plain solid colors (white or blue are the easiest to wear) or striped shirts. Broadcloth, oxford, and white-on-white Madras are the standard materials. Shirts for town often have detachable collars, and cuffs that are made for cuff links, rather than those that are buttoned. Shirts buttoned at the wrist are technically informal.

3. Ties of foulard, or rep silk, or wool in almost any classic pattern or color. Small patterns are usually safer than big ones.

4. Shoes of dark brown calf worn with brown or gray suits; black calf oxfords worn with dark blue or gray suits. Toe caps are standard for daytime.

5. Socks of lisle, wool, or wool-and-cotton mixtures; with black shoes, dark blue or black socks; with brown shoes, brown, dark red, dark blue or dark green socks. Never white socks in town.

6. Overcoats of brown smooth herringbone tweed to wear with gray or brown suits; or gray tweed (single-breasted is best)

to wear with blue or gray suits; dark blue overcoats to wear with dark blue or gray suits; very dark Oxford gray or midnight blue Chesterfields with velvet collar to wear with dark blue and dark gray suits, and at night. Overcoats worn in town should be fitted, but not too tightly, and never longer than just below the knee. The two most useful overcoats would be these: a gray herringbone tweed; and a heavy dark blue lamb's wool or cashmere made with a plain, not a velvet, collar, which could be worn in the daytime over a dark blue or gray suit, or a cutaway, and in the evening over either a dinner jacket or tails. In the spring or early autumn, overcoats of gray or tan covert cloth; useful also in the country.

7. Raincoats. Trench coats, belted or not, or anything that looks like a trench coat; or anything that looks like a covert cloth overcoat.

8. Hats. Gray or brown felt fedora, with or without bound brim; a derby hat; or a black Homburg.

9. Gloves. Brown leather, pigskin, gray buckskin; buttoned or pull-on. Never woolen gloves or mittens.

What to Avoid

1. Belted coats.
2. Overpadding and overfitting.
3. Trousers that are very high-fitting around the waist, unless a waistcoat is worn.
4. Shirts made of green-tinted broadcloth; or, for that matter, anything green except neckties and socks. Green hats, suits, and overcoats can be particularly bad.
5. Shoes—any shoes—which are not all brown, or all black, calf oxfords. Never two-tone shoes, and suède only in the country.
6. Overcoats that flare out from under the arms. These are not the best for town wear although they are often worn.
7. Shaggy overcoats and novelty buttons.

For Sundays and "Don't Dress" Evenings

1. Suits of dark blue, double- or single-breasted, with or without a waistcoat.
2. Shirts of white Madras, broadcloth, or silk; or, more formally, and for older men, shirts with stiff white collars. In the evenings, white silk shirts or white shirts and stiff collars.
3. Ties of foulard silk in some combination of blue and white. Bow ties are worn as well as four-in-hand ties.
4. Shoes. Oxfords of black calf. Brown shoes, and this is a rule, must never be worn with a dark blue suit after dark. And they should not—although this is not as inflexibly observed—be worn with a blue suit in the daytime, either.
5. Socks of black or navy blue lisle, wool, or wool-and-cotton mixture. Wool is not so good as the others for the evening.
6. Overcoat of dark blue (no velvet collar), or a Chesterfield (with a velvet collar).
7. Hat. Black derby, or black Homburg, or gray snap-brim fedora with black band.
8. Gloves of gray buckskin or yellow chamois.

For Official Occasions, Weddings, Funerals

The classic dress for formal daytime occasions is the cutaway, which used to be worn not only for weddings and funerals and official occasions, but also for church and for Sunday luncheons in winter in the city. Nowadays, they are rarely worn unless they are absolutely mandatory; as when: 1) one is a pallbearer at a very large funeral in a city; 2) one is the groom, best man, an usher, or the father of the bride or groom, at a large church wedding; 3) one is an important official appearing publicly at a formal, daytime function. At funerals and official occasions, the cutaway is worn exactly as described below; for weddings, certain variations are customary, all of which are discussed on page 221. (See also page 150, "Clothes for the Funeral.")

1. Morning, or cutaway, coat of lamb's wool or light cashmere, in black or oxford-gray, without braid.
2. Waistcoat to match the coat, double- or single-breasted; or double-breasted waistcoat of pearl-gray or fawn-colored doeskin. (See also "Dressing for the Wedding," page 220.)
3. Trousers of gray-and-black, or white-and-black, striped worsted or cheviot, without cuffs.
4. Shirts, always white, with pleated or

plain bosoms and stiff cuffs; stiff white wing or fold collar.

5. Tie of gray, black, or silver-gray silk (the latter brocaded in the pattern traditional for cutaways); but always a four-in-hand or a bow tie except at weddings when an ascot tie is worn (see page 221). A bow tie is worn only with a wing collar; a four-in-hand either with a wing or fold collar. Fold collar and black four-in-hand tie are classic for funerals.

6. Shoes. Black calf oxfords; those without toe-caps are more formal.

7. Socks. Black or very dark gray silk, wool or wool mixture.

8. Spats. Gray felt or doeskin. Spats are rarely worn by younger men except at weddings.

9. Hats. Black silk top hats.

10. Overcoats. Dark blue, dark Oxford-gray or black.

11. Gloves. Gray buckskin or mocha.

12. To be very technical, a stick or umbrella should always be carried when wearing a cutaway. And the handkerchief must be white (see page 626).

What to Avoid

Avoid any deviation from this pattern other than those suggested particularly for weddings, and the "sack coat" variation suggested below. Nothing is more rigorously dictated than the accessories worn with a cutaway.

"Sack Coat" Variation

This informal version of afternoon dress is never mandatory. It is now worn, mostly by older men, on Sundays in very big cities, when men of an earlier generation would always have worn a cutaway. Or it is worn at formal luncheons or for an official daytime function when one is neither the host nor the guest of honor. It may be worn also when one is appearing publicly as an official on some occasion when a cutaway and silk hat might be comically inappropriate; as, for example, if one were to meet a distinguished official and had to climb a swaying ladder from the pilot boat.

1. Coat. Black or Oxford-gray unfinished worsted (plain or diagonal weave); single-breasted is best.

2. Trousers as for a cutaway (above), waistcoat to match sack coat.

3. Shirt. White, with stiff cuffs; stiff white fold collar.

4. Tie of black or black-gray silk; some wear a polka-dot bow tie but a four-in-hand is standard.

5. Shoes and socks as listed above. Spats are not usually worn.

6. Hats. A derby, which used to be standard with a black coat and striped trousers; or a black Homburg, which has become the present-day classic.

7. Overcoat and gloves as listed above.

TOWN DAY CLOTHES—SUMMER

For Business

1. Suits. Always lightweight, in any of the colors suggested for winter. Tropical worsted is the almost standard material. In addition, gray "sharkskin" wool; natural-tan gabardine (but avoid pinkish or creamy-tan). Seersucker suits are usually unattractive, because they are apt to look more like pajamas than suits.

2. Shirts, as suggested for winter wear.

3. Ties of foulard silk, in lighter color than those worn in winter (see page 616).

4. Shoes and socks as suggested for winter.

5. Hats of panama or coconut-straw; or chip-straw hats; none is necessary.

What to Avoid

1. Sport shirts, or any novelty numbers.

2. White, and brown-and-white, or black-and-white shoes in any city in the United States or in the British Isles. This is an unbreakable rule, unless local custom overrides it, as it does in some southern cities in America.

For Sundays and "Don't Dress" Evenings

1. Suits of thin, dark blue wool.

2. Shirts of white broadcloth; soft collars. For evening, white silk shirts also. Ties, shoes, and socks as for winter; hats, if any, as suggested above for summer daytime.

For Weddings and Funerals

All as suggested above for Sundays. See page 220, "Dressing for the Wedding," and page 150, "Clothes for the Funeral," for further discussion.

For Official Appearances

Such occasions are rare in summer, but if they arise, the winter routine must painfully be observed. (See page 617.)

TOWN EVENING CLOTHES

Informal and Semiformal

During the war, for various reasons, dinner jackets were rarely worn in public places. In restaurants, at the theater, even at first nights, they became the exception rather than the rule. And this custom has taken root in America, particularly among the younger generation. Although dinner jackets are never incorrect for the theater or dinner in a restaurant, they are usually worn in public only on special occasions. At dinner in a private house, they are still the rule, unless one is planning to go afterwards to some place such as the movies, or a bowling alley, where dinner jackets would be inappropriate.

1. Coat of black or very dark ("midnight") blue wool, double-breasted, with satin or grosgrain faille revers, a plain collar and peaked lapels; or a single-breasted coat with a shawl collar, usually satin.
2. Trousers of same wool, without cuffs and with narrow strip of satin, or faille, or braid down the outside of the trouser leg. When braid is used, the old standard was "one stripe" braid for full evening dress; "two-stripe" braid for dinner-jacket trousers. Note: A belt must never be worn in the evening: suspenders always.
3. Waistcoat—necessary, of course, with single-breasted coat only—of black wool or silk, figured or plain, worn with wing or fold collar; or white waistcoat, worn only with stiff-bosomed shirt and wing collar, and worn mostly by older men only. Waistcoats can be either double- or single-breasted; a single-breasted one is more casual.
4. Shirts. Stiff-bosomed white shirt with stiff cuffs and wing collar is most formal; or semi-starched pleated white shirt, stiff cuffs, stiff fold collar; or white silk shirt, pleated or plain bosom, soft cuffs and soft fold collar; or white broadcloth shirts, soft collar (but *not* with buttoned-down collar points). The

last is the most informal and probably the most usual.
NOTE: See also "Jewelry," page 624.
5. Ties. Bow tie of plain dull black silk or black satin; never brocade.
6. Shoes. Black patent-leather oxfords without toe-caps, or pumps. Or extremely fine, thin, black leather shoes, or pumps, with a very high polish.
7. Socks of black silk, with or without black clocks.
8. Hat. An opera hat, a gray or black felt fedora, or a black Homburg, which is really the best.
9. Overcoat. Black, or dark blue, with or without a velvet collar.
10. Gloves. Gray buckskin, or chamois. If one is driving, brown leather is permissible.

Formal and Official; For Evening Weddings

Full evening dress used to be mandatory for the opera, for all the men sitting in boxes or the orchestra. Now, although one still sees many men, particularly older men, in full evening dress at the opera, it is no longer mandatory. On an opening night, the majority of the men in the boxes wear evening dress, and the rest dinner jackets. In the orchestra, the majority wear dinner jackets and the others, evening dress. In the balconies, dark blue suits are the rule, and dinner jackets the exception. On other nights, the men in evening dress are even fewer.

Evening dress is always mandatory, however, if one has received a formal engraved invitation to a dinner, ball, or official evening reception, with the notation "White tie," or "Decorations," written on it. A discussion of the customs concerning full evening dress for evening weddings is on page 223 in the chapter "Dressing for the Evening Wedding."

1. Coat of black or dark midnight blue worsted or Baretha with satin lapels. Tails of this coat should hang to a point just behind the knee.
2. Trousers to match the coat with a braid trimming down the outside of the trouser leg. "One-stripe braid" was always standard.
3. Waistcoat of white piqué; single- or double-breasted, with or without revers. See also "Jewelry," page 624.
4. Shirt of fine white linen with a stiffly

starched bosom made for one or two studs and with stiff cuffs. These shirts are sometimes made of piqué but plain white linen is better and more usual. The only collar is a wing collar, stiff and white.

5. Tie. The only tie is white, usually made of piqué.

6. Shoes. Black patent-leather oxfords without toe-caps.

7. Socks. Black silk, with or without black clocks.

8. Overcoat. Black or very dark "midnight blue" with or without a velvet collar.

9. Hats. An opera hat or a top hat.

10. Gloves. White buckskin; never white kid when gloves are worn out of doors. White kid always used to be worn for dancing.

COUNTRY CLOTHES—AUTUMN, WINTER, SPRING

For Daytime

1. Coats of tan gabardine, or of tweed in a mixture of gray, black and white, or of tan and brown. There are others, of course, but these are the easiest to wear. Always single-breasted.

2. Trousers of gray flannel. Older men sometimes wear tweed suits or flannel suits, but odd coats and trousers are more usual for younger men. In cold weather, older men often wear waistcoats, either of the same tweed as their coat or a bright waistcoat such as might be worn for hunting. Younger men are more apt to wear pull-over sweaters of cashmere or shetland yarn.

3. Shirts of broadcloth in white or blue are the most usual; or in pale "natural" colors. Or shirts of very thin flannel, plain white or in cold weather with Tattersall checks or a plain stripe.

4. Ties of cotton or wool in nice, loud colors. Or black crocheted ties, either silk or wool.

5. Shoes. Oxfords of dark brown calf, with leather or rubber soles. Or "officers" shoes of brown calf. Or "monks" shoes of reversed calf. Or brown calf moccasins.

6. Socks. Usually wool, brown or colored; anything but black or white. (See "Sports.") Woolen Argyle socks are particularly nice.

7. Polo coats, or overcoats of loose tweed. But never made of a huge bright plaid. Also overcoats of tan or gray covert cloth. For winter: sheepskin-lined gabardine, short or three-quarter length.

8. Raincoats. Any town raincoat, such as a trench coat; or a "slicker" of dark olive-green or yellow oilskin.

9. Hats. A gray or brown fedora, but never with a bound brim. Older men like, and wear, caps.

10. Gloves, if any, of brown leather, such as those sold for riding. Heavy sheepskin fur-lined, or wool-lined, for winter.

What to Avoid

1. Belted coats.
2. Coats made of two different materials: usually one for the sleeves, another for the body of the coat. These are impossibly ugly.
3. Waistcoats matching trousers.
4. Plus-four trousers, except for golf or older men. (See also "Sport Clothes.")
5. Black shoes.
6. Suède oxfords.
7. Alligator shoes of any kind.
8. Fitted overcoats.
9. Dark-blue overcoats.
10. Black Homburgs.
11. Felt fedoras with bound brims.
12. Derby hats, except for riding—and, of course, for detectives on the prowl!

For Evening

NOTE: Men should always change for dinner in a private house, but in the country, where restaurant dining is most unusual, "should" almost becomes "must."

1. Dinner jacket as in town (see page 619). Or, at home, smoking jackets of black or dark red, blue, or green velveteen with dull satin or grosgrain faille revers, worn with the usual black trousers.

2. Shirts of white silk, with or without a pleated bosom, worn with cuff links; or shirts of plain white broadcloth; but never those made with buttoned-down collar points. Starched, stiff shirt and collar for bigger dinner parties.

3. Black bow tie of plain silk or satin.

4. Shoes of black patent leather or black patent-leather pumps. At home, leather slippers, or slippers made of petit-point needlework.

5. Socks of black silk.
6. Overcoats of loose tweed, or polo coats.
7. Hats. Gray or brown fedora without a bound brim.

What to Avoid

Colored dinner jackets, correctly worn only by bandleaders.

COUNTRY CLOTHES—SUMMER

For Daytime

1. Coats of gabardine or lightweight gray flannel or lightweight tweed, single-breasted. Dark-blue coats to wear on Sundays, or for luncheon, with white flannel trousers.
2. Suits of gabardine or, in hot weather, suits of white linen or seersucker.
3. Trousers of white flannel or duck.
4. Shirts of white or blue broadcloth, or with a pin-stripe. Or the authentic polo shirt in dark blue or white, worn without a tie.
5. Ties of cotton in a light plaid; silk ties in light colors; wool ties.
6. Shoes. Oxfords of dark brown leather; moccasins; or for older men, brown-and-white or black-and-white oxfords. White doeskin shoes with rubber soles. Sneakers only for sports (see "Tennis Clothes").
7. Socks of wool, or wool-and-cotton mixtures, in pale colors.
8. Hats of panama straw, or coconut straw. Chip-straw hats are worn by older men. Younger men often go hatless.

What to Avoid

1. Brightly colored "slack" suits, or gabardine in any color but "natural-tan."
2. Shirts, except authentic polo shirts, designed to be worn without a tie; and, particularly, short-sleeved shirts. Regular shirts can be worn without a tie, and with the top button undone, but very few men look well in fancy shirts and bright trousers.
3. All-white shoes with hard leather soles.

For Evening

1. Dinner jackets for not-too-hot weather. (See page 619.)
2. Coats of white linen or light serge, also white, with the usual black evening trousers. Cummerbunds, if one must, but only black silk ones, with single-breasted coats. Or white linen suits.
3. Trousers of white flannel with the usual black dinner jacket.
4. Shirts of white silk, pleated or not, or of white Madras or broadcloth. Stiff shirts, with the regular black dinner coat and trousers, are worn in summer for formal evenings or by older men. For dances, many younger men wear white flannel trousers with stiff shirt and collar and a black dinner jacket.
5. Bow tie of plain black silk.
6. Shoes. Oxfords of black patent leather; or pumps.
7. Socks of black silk.
8. Hats of panama or coconut straw or chip-straw are "correct," but younger men usually wear no hat.

BEACH CLOTHES AND BATHING SUITS

There are two pitfalls in beach and bathing clothes that must be avoided: the overstiff, unaccustomed, "citified" look and the overpicturesque, overcolorful, overcasual look. So much of both kinds—and particularly, perhaps, the latter—is offered for sale that one needs the greatest care and tact in choosing. In a seaside village or resort, the more casual of the clothes suggested on this page for daytime would be entirely appropriate. But at a beach club or at a house on the beach, many of the younger men would be dressed a little more informally. The clothes listed below are worn only on the beach, at a beach club, or in a seaside village on the way to or from the beach. They could not be worn at a golf club or at any luncheon, except the most informal luncheon in a house on the sands.

1. Shorts of linen, canvas, sailcloth, spun rayon, or cotton herringbone tweed, in white, tan, or blue (light, medium, or dark blue). Natural tan gabardine shorts. These shorts are worn with a leather belt; the best are all "English length": i.e., an inch or two at most above the knee.
2. Trousers of white duck, linen, sailcloth, or cotton herringbone tweed. Natural tan gabardine trousers. These are all classic for beachwear and are preferred

to shorts by older men. There is also a new family of brightly colored trousers for men. (Men should never, incidentally, call any trousers "slacks." It may be necessary in a shop, where it has become an accepted commercialism, but it is not necessary in conversation.) Rust-color, blue, and dark maroon in any of the materials suggested above are often worn at a beach club, but unless one is consummately sure of oneself, bright colors should be avoided.

3. Shirts of white or blue cotton or linen, with sleeves rolled up and the top button left unbuttoned. Authentic polo shirts in white or dark blue; short-sleeved cotton knit sweaters with a high round neck in yellow, white, or light blue.

4. Sandals of plain, heavy, dark-brown leather, not too open in the toe; authentic Mexican "huaraches" in natural tan colors; canvas espadrilles. These are worn with shorts, rather than trousers, and always without socks. White sneakers, or white rubber-soled doeskin shoes, with white woolen socks, can be worn either with trousers or shorts.

5. Bathing suits. At most beaches nowadays, only older men wear tops as well as bathing shorts. When they are worn, tops are sleeveless, not very décolleté, and usually made of woolen jersey, in dark blue-and-white horizontal stripes. The best bathing shorts are made of gabardine or some heavy material, but with a straight squared-off leg and high enough to cover the navel. Young men's shorts are often made with "Hawaiian" patterns in different shades of blue, rust-color, brown, on a white or cream-colored ground; more conservative are plain dark blue or natural tan.

6. Bathing coats. Coats made of toweling, cut like a man's dressing gown, are perfect; or they may be short, like an odd coat; or one may wear a sweater of toweling cloth or even an ordinary knit sweater, with a bath towel tucked around the neck.

7. Beach hats. Any straw hat except a chip-straw; or a linen piqué hat, excellent protection against the sun.

What to Avoid

1. Suits in bright colors; colored trousers are often possible but bright trousers *and* coats are impossible.

2. All fancy bathing shoes.
3. Too abbreviated trunks such as those worn on the Riviera, which are only glorified loincloths.
4. Never a novelty beach coat or kimono.
5. Never a felt hat or any "novelty" number.

TENNIS CLOTHES

As with tennis clothes for women, the classic color is white.

1. Trousers or shorts. White duck or linen, white flannel; or long shorts (never short shorts) in any of the above materials. Or—a somewhat tentative new fashion for men—beige gabardine shorts (not trousers).

2. Shirts. White linen shirts, no necktie, with top button open, sleeves rolled up; or crew-shirts, sometimes called T-shirts, with short banded sleeves, banded round neck, with no collar and three buttons; or skivvies, the shirts worn in the Navy.

3. Socks. Short white socks, usually wool. Never long socks and never colored ones.

4. Shoes. White sneakers or tennis shoes.
5. Visor of white felt, lined with green, or white tennis cap of duck with a little visor, for those who want shade.

What to Avoid

Colored shirts, or colored shorts, loud socks. Or, worse, no shirt and short shorts.

GOLF CLOTHES

For Warm Weather

1. Trousers of gray flannel, beige gabardine or white flannel; or white linen, or duck. Rust-colored or blue linen trousers are sometimes worn in summer, but the ones listed first are really more suitable.

2. A plain shirt, but not with a stiff or detachable collar, white or unbleached linen color.

3. A necktie is optional, but it should not be of silk; crocheted string or cotton are standard.

4. Thin sweater, in a neutral color.
5. Heavy brown leather shoes, with rubber soles or metal cleats.
6. Wool socks in any color; canary-yellow is one of the best.

7. Hats. White duck, linen, or panama. Or a felt hat, as in cold weather, see below.
8. Gloves—if any, those made specially for golf.

For Cold Weather

1. Gray flannel trousers, or tweed ones. Older men still wear plus fours.
2. Heavy sweaters.
3. A shirt and tie as suggested above; woolen ties also.
4. Hats. Never a colored hat, never a bound brim; brown or gray felt is best, or, particularly for older men, tweed caps.
5. Gloves. Never any others except special golf gloves.

What to Avoid

1. Bright open-neck shirts.
2. Mesh shirts, novelty shirts.
3. Shorts.
4. Sneakers.
5. Hard straw hats.
6. Fancy silk neckties.

SKI CLOTHES

See the section "Ski Clothes" in the chapter "Women's Clothes"; the same clothes are worn by men.

Permissible Departures

For men, there is a fashion which is new in America but which has been the standard costume of Central European skiers for many years (the long straight ski-trousers were Scandinavian in origin): plus fours; heavy cable-stitch stockings (worn up under the knee band of the plus fours); ankle-length socks turned down over the boot tops; jacket or sweater.

What to Avoid

1. Shorts.
2. Bright colors for jackets and sweaters.

RIDING CLOTHES

See the section on riding clothes, on page 633, under "Women's Clothes." The same rules apply to men.

SHOOTING CLOTHES

See "Shooting Clothes," on page 635, where suggestions for men and for women are given together.

YACHTING AND SAILING CLOTHES

For men as well as women, the first point is to find out, tactfully, the size of the yacht. On small yachts, guests are expected to co-operate in the work of sailing. On bigger yachts, they are usually not. And, for men as well as women, it is a point of manners and of common sense to wear soft-soled shoes.

For Yachts under Fifty Feet

1. Shirts of almost any sturdy workman-like material in a simple cut; a white broadcloth shirt, for example, left open at the neck, with the sleeves rolled up; a polo shirt or a short-sleeved Navy T-shirt, or a sweater.
2. Shorts of khaki, tan gabardine, or almost any other material in a dull color; or dungarees; or trousers of gray flannel, khaki, or tan gabardine.
3. Socks of wool or cotton, in white or any light color.
4. Sneakers or rope-soled shoes.
5. Hat—if one wants one—that will not blow off. One of the best is like that worn by women for sailing: stitched white cotton or linen with a narrow brim and, sometimes, a green isinglass visor let into the brim. Or a swordfisherman's cap, with a long visor.

On any cruise of four days or more in hot weather, a long rubber coat. In cold weather, a fisherman's oilskin or rubber suit: rubber overalls and jacket, rubber sou'wester hat, and rubber boots.

For Yachts over Fifty Feet, or Going Ashore

1. Coat of gray flannel or dark blue serge, double breasted. Or a white linen suit.
2. Trousers of white flannel or linen. On board bigger yachts, men often wear shorts of a simple material such as gabardine or khaki; but a very conservative owner, particularly an older man, will probably wear long trousers all the time. An extra pair of gray flannel trousers is useful. For going ashore, for a visit to the local yacht club, or when guests are expected on board, the dark blue double-breasted coat and white trousers are standard.
3. Shirts of white or pale blue broadcloth or linen (white is better). With shorts,

these shirts can be worn open at the neck with the sleeves rolled up; or one can wear a polo shirt or a Navy T-shirt.

4. Neckties of cotton in light colors, or in light-colored plaids. With a dark blue coat and white flannel trousers, a plain dark blue four-in-hand necktie.

5. Shoes, always soft-soled (plain rubber or sponge rubber): white, brown-and-white, or black-and-white buckskin. To wear with shorts, a pair of sneakers or rope-soled canvas espadrilles.

6. Socks of cotton or, better, light wool, in white or light colors.

7. Hat of panama straw, or chip-straw, for going ashore. To wear on board with shorts or gray flannel trousers, a stitched white hat as described above.

On bigger yachts, in the evening, guests usually dress for dinner. Men usually wear a white linen coat, a soft white shirt and the usual black trousers and shoes (see page 619, "For Evening," under the heading "Country Clothes—Summer").

Yacht Club Members

On bigger yachts and on visits ashore yacht club members may wear the classic yachting coat and cap. The yachting coat is like a naval officer's coat, with black (instead of gold) stripes on the sleeves and with yacht club buttons instead of navy buttons. The yachting cap is like a naval officer's hat: a white or dark blue top with a black visor and yacht club insignia. These should be worn only by yacht club members. With these are usually worn white flannel trousers—or, sometimes and less formally, gray flannel trousers—and rubber-soled shoes. On very big yachts, according to the old-fashioned custom, members of a yacht club always wore stiff shirts and mess jackets with yacht club insignia, in the evening. This custom, together with the very big yachts that fathered it, has almost disappeared.

What to Avoid

Any imitations of the classic yachting coat and cap should be avoided. Only yacht club members are entitled to wear yacht club insignia, and any cap or coat that suggests an effort to imitate a yacht club member's costume is extremely bad taste.

JEWELRY

The first rule concerning men's jewelry is that nothing should be worn that is not functional, with the single exception of a ring. The second rule is that men should never wear diamonds, except very small rose diamonds as an edging on evening studs and cuff links. Light clear stones are not often worn by men; and they rarely wear rubies or emeralds. Sapphires, on the other hand, have been considered good taste for men for many years. A star-sapphire stickpin was often worn by men of the past generation with an ascot tie and a cutaway. And although stickpins in general and colored precious stones in particular are now somewhat out of fashion for men, still a man who would never dream of wearing a ruby, a diamond, or an emerald, might very well wear gold cuff links studded with a small sapphire. These are the only two rules that apply generally to all jewelry. Specific suggestions will be found in the list which follows.

Bracelets

Except for identification bracelets, which men often wear in wartime, there are no acceptable designs for men. And, except in wartime, men really should not wear a bracelet of any kind.

Collar Pins

A collar pin may be worn with a soft fold collar to keep the points of a collar tidy. The pin should be worn halfway between the points and the top of the collar under the necktie, and the only proper pin is a gold safety pin. Silver pins and all novelty clasps should be avoided. In America, these pins are worn with any soft collar in the daytime or for "Don't Dress" evenings. They should never be worn with a dinner jacket. In England, collar pins are not worn at all. A very good modern innovation is the "collar-stay," an invisible gadget which holds down the points of the collar.

Cuff Links

Daytime: Cuff links worn in the daytime should be made of gold, and the general effect should be plain, heavy, and functional, rather than decorative. These are a few of the most usual and attractive designs: plain gold bars, round or with squared edges, connected by a short chain of fairly heavy links; flat oval discs engraved with initials or a crest, also connected by a gold chain (the engraving is sometimes filled in with black or very dark blue); gold rings, on a stiff bar, that snap into position; single block initials, cut out of plain heavy gold, connected by a gold chain.

It would be impossible to list all the good designs that are made for cuff links, and these few are included only for the sake of example. The essential point is to avoid elaborately chased or sculptured gold or any design that looks as though it might be made for a woman.

Evening: Cuff links worn with a dinner jacket and a soft shirt can be made either of yellow gold or of platinum. Platinum or platinum-edged cuff links are more usual with stiff shirts for evening wear and are mandatory with full evening dress. The customs governing designs and materials are the same as those for waistcoat studs (see below).

Rings

In America and in England, men usually wear rings only on the little finger. The only exception to this rule is a wedding ring which, although not customarily worn by American men, is often worn on the fourth finger of the left hand (see page 174 for further discussion of men's wedding rings). Wedding rings and signet rings are the only ones that should be worn by men. Signet rings are made of plain yellow gold, or gold set with a semiprecious stone such as lapis lazuli. In either case, the gold should not be carved, or embossed, or chased, in a heavy design. The surface of the ring, whether it is stone or gold, may be cut or engraved with a monogram or, preferably, a coat of arms or crest. Class rings should never be worn by men.

Studs

Studs are worn only on stiff evening shirts and waistcoats. The most usual shirt stud is a single pearl, in any size big enough to function usefully. It should neither stand out like a large pea, nor slip uselessly through the buttonhole. There may be either one or two; but with a dinner jacket, one is slightly better. Other shirt studs are made to match the waistcoat studs; and, unless one is wearing pearl shirt studs, waistcoat and shirt studs should match. For these, and for cuff links worn with full evening dress, the most usual designs are crystal or white enamel, edged in platinum, or in tiny rose diamonds set in platinum. With a dinner jacket, studs of black onyx, or gold engraved with white enamel, are also worn.

Stickpins

Stickpins are hardly ever worn by the present generation, but this is a matter of fashion and individual taste rather than a matter of correctness or incorrectness. If one wanted to wear a stickpin in an ascot tie (they are hardly ever worn in four-in-hand ties today), it could be a black or white pearl, pearshaped or round, set in gold or platinum.

Tie Clips

Tie clips are a comparatively new addition to men's jewelry. They were encouraged by the fashion of wearing single-breasted suits without a waistcoat and are, therefore, essentially informal. From the aesthetic point of view, the best solution is to fasten a gold safety pin through the widest part of the tie; but, practically, this is very hard on the tie and men often, therefore, prefer a tie clip. The best tie clips are very small and purely functional. They may be made either of gold or of silver, engine-turned or plain, with or without engraved monograms or initials. One good design is about the size of a fingernail, and clips the edge of the tie in a strong spring. Other good designs are a tongue of stiff gold wire, without decoration of any kind; or a tongue of plain, solid gold. Tie clips in cheap materials and particularly in big sizes should never be worn, nor should ties be held down by silver or gold chains.

Pocket Watches

Any pocket watch that is made of plain metal with a plain white face and black or gold figures and a simple round or oval loop is in perfectly good taste. A man's evening watch can be very beautiful—very thin, made of platinum, and extremely expensive—but it is often argued that no watch is better than a plain gold one. The only thing to be avoided is an elaborate, embossed, or sculptured working of the metal case, or any novelty colors, such as red-gold, for the watch face.

Watch Chains

Watch chains are not often worn nowadays. They are made either of gold or silver, and the modern taste is for a simple, not too heavy chain design. In the daytime, there are two correct ways of wearing them: across the front of the waistcoat (one end in each of the lower waistcoat pockets); or from the trouser watch pocket to the side trouser pocket (on the same side, of course). An unbreakable rule is that a watch chain must *never* be threaded through a button hole. In the evening, the watch chain should never be worn across the waistcoat, but only from the trouser pocket to the side trouser pocket.

The question of what to put on a watch chain is very simply answered: Nothing should be hung on the watch chain. The watch goes at one end, and on a ring at the other end go the keys, emblems, lucky pieces, or anything else that a man may want to carry.

Wrist Watches

Wrist watches are a much more complicated subject than pocket watches because there are many different kinds. The two best are: the complicated chronological, shock-proof, water-proof, "airplane dashboard" kind, which is usually worn with a canvas or leather strap and a chromium or silver buckle; and the plain gold or silver wrist watch, square or oblong, with a white face, and a leather strap. As a rule, the best strap is plain pigskin with a simple buckle to match the watch. Novelty leathers and metal straps are not as reliably good taste. No wrist watch should be worn with full evening dress.

HANDKERCHIEFS

Handkerchiefs worn in the evening, or with a cutaway, should always be made of very fine plain white linen. If they are monogrammed, the monogram should be embroidered in white, gray, black, or any combination of white, gray, and black, but never in colors.

In the daytime, white handkerchiefs are, of course, perfectly correct, but there are also handkerchiefs with borders of a colored stripe and colored monograms; handkerchiefs in pale colors with darker borders and monograms; handkerchiefs of foulard silk. The only effect that must be avoided is one of studied matching; a foulard handkerchief to match the necktie is not as happy an idea as a foulard handkerchief with a necktie in a plain color. Or the overnatty effect that is produced whenever a handkerchief is too carefully folded, and six little prongs stand up along the breast pocket. It is probably unnecessary to add that handkerchiefs should never be tucked into the cuff; they belong either in the breast pocket or in one of the trouser pockets.

MUFFLERS

For the Country

Woolen, either knit or woven, in plain solid colors: dark brown, natural tan, yellow, or medium blue. Or, for summer after active sport, mufflers of white or yellow terrycloth.

For Town

In the daytime, large silk foulard squares folded into triangles and worn crossed but never tied under the overcoat. Or smooth woven wool mufflers in colors such as brown, gray, beige, or medium blue. In the evening, silk mufflers in the usual long narrow shape with fringed ends, with or without monograms but always white. If there is a monogram, it must be embroidered in black, gray, or white only. Long mufflers may be folded or tied in a single loop under the chin with the ends, of course, covered by the overcoat.

UMBRELLAS AND STICKS

The only umbrella a man should carry either in town or in the country is a black umbrella with a plain wooden handle. Very handsome and expensive men's umbrellas are made of black silk with gold-banded Malacca handles, but even a black cotton umbrella is better than a colored one.

A man's town cane (all canes should, technically, be referred to as "sticks") is made of Malacca wood with a curved handle, with or without a gold band. In the

626

country, men carry a stick of rough, knobby wood, usually with a right-angled handle. Shooting sticks of leather-covered metal, with a sharp point and handles that open out into a seat, are correct only if they will be useful. In other words, in the suburbs a shooting stick should not be carried. In the country, it is correct at any time.

TROUSERS AND TROUSER CUFFS

Trousers should cover the ankle, and, of course, the socks, but they should not hang in folds over the shoe.

Trouser cuffs belong only on trousers that are worn informally in the daytime. Striped trousers worn with a cutaway, and the black trousers worn with a dinner jacket or full evening dress, should never have cuffs.

WEARING DECORATIONS

This short section will not attempt to cover all the official military and naval rules for wearing decorations; and it would not be necessary because all branches of our Armed Forces have very detailed and explicit regulations. Here we are concerned only with civilians, and the question of wearing decorations with civilian dress. The suggestions given apply to women, as well as men.

Basic Considerations

Although these maxims spring from official regulations they must be honored also when decorations are worn with civilian dress:

1. Decorations are worn in this order:
   American decorations
   American service medals
   Foreign decorations
   Foreign service medals
   Hereditary decorations
2. American decorations are worn in the order of their importance.
3. Foreign decorations are worn in the order of their bestowal, but two decorations from the same country are not separated (e.g. a Croix de Guerre given in 1917 would be worn above a British decoration given in 1918, but if a Legion of Honor had been given in

1942 the two French decorations would be worn together, above the British).
4. All decorations worn at the same time must be properly ranked, but any decorations may be omitted with the single proviso that anyone who has received an American decoration, should wear an American decoration whenever he wears a foreign decoration (and the American, as we have said, above the foreign).
5. All decorations, other than the Medal of Honor, the Presidential Citation Ribbon, and certain foreign orders, are worn by men on the left lapel of civilian clothes, by women on the left breast. (The Presidential Citation is worn at the right; the Medal of Honor, with evening dress, around the neck.)
6. In wearing decorations with full evening dress the highest is at the upper left as seen by an observer facing the wearer; the lowest is at the right—or lower right, if there are two rows. With other clothes, more than one decoration is not usually worn; but if two are worn, the higher ranking is above the other.

These are the basic points. After listing American decorations in the order of their importance we shall take up the separate customs of day and evening wear.

Decorations Given to Members of the Armed Forces
1. Medal of Honor *
2. Distinguished Service Cross *
3. Distinguished Service Medal
4. Silver Star *
5. Legion of Merit
6. Distinguished Flying Cross †
7. Soldier's Medal (or Navy or Marine Corps Medal)*
8. Bronze Star Medal †
9. Air Medal †
10. Commendation Ribbon
11. Purple Heart

Decorations Given to Civilians
1. Medal for Merit, given on recommendation of the President's Medal for Merit Board. When worn with decorations earned as a member of the Armed Forces it is worn just below the Distinguished Service Medal.

* Given for valor.
† May be given for valor or for meritorious service.

2. Exceptional Service Award, given by the Army; or the Distinguished Service Award given by the Navy. With military decorations, either of these is worn just below the Silver Star.

3. Meritorious Service Award, given by the Army and by the Navy. Worn just below the Legion of Merit.

Given by the United States Maritime Commission:

1. Distinguished Service Medal, given for valor; worn below the Distinguished Service Medal, but above the Medal for Merit.

2. Meritorious Service Medal, given for valor; worn below the Silver Star but above the Exceptional Service Award or the Distinguished Service Award.

3. Mariner's Medal given automatically and posthumously to those killed by enemy action; may also be given for wounds received in action. Worn below the Purple Heart.

4. Victory Medal; a service award, worn below Service Medals given by the Armed Forces.

With Full Evening Dress

With full evening dress, the Medal of Honor is worn around the neck. A man wears the ribbon outside the shirt collar and inside the coat collar, with the medal hanging just under the middle of the white bow tie.

The Presidential Citation ribbon is worn in miniature at the right and, if that is the highest decoration, no other decorations are usually worn. Men wear it on the right lapel; a woman would wear it at the right, near the edge of her décolletage.

All other decorations, as we have said, are worn on the left. With evening dress, they are worn on the lapel, in miniature. There are three kinds of "miniatures":

There are miniature reproductions of the medals, which are worn on a chain; there are miniature reproductions of the ribbons, made in enamel, which are worn on a bar; and there are miniature ribbons, specially woven in a narrow width, which are also worn on a bar. Good jewelers have all of these. Although any of the three is allowed by the regulations, the miniature ribbons are usually worn. And although regulations permit the wearing of all awards and decorations, including service medals, the best practice is to wear only decorations given for individual action, unless there is a special reason to include another. Those who have the Medal of Honor, or the Medal for Merit, sometimes wear only that decoration, in rosette form.

As a courtesy to foreign officials, those who have several foreign decorations may give one or the other precedence on special occasions. For example, at official receptions in a foreign country, or at a dinner given in honor of an official of a foreign country, the decoration of that country would be worn above all other foreign decorations.

With Other Clothes

There are three kinds of miniature decorations that may be worn with civilian day clothes and informal evening clothes: miniature ribbons and miniature enamel reproductions of the ribbons, like those worn in the evening, but always worn in the buttonhole; and a long, very thin ribbon which runs from the buttonhole to the edge of the lapel and is fastened underneath. Among American decorations, only the Medal of Honor or the Medal for Merit may be worn in rosette form.

As a rule, only one ribbon, the highest, is worn at a time. When two are worn, the very thin long ribbons are best—one lying above the other, between the buttonhole and the edge of the lapel.

72

Women's Clothes

IT IS AXIOMATIC that a woman who dresses well always has an acute sense of fitness, as well as an understanding of the current fashion. And on the grounds of taste, the first is more important than the second. The best and biggest part of a sense of fitness is plain common sense. Few would wear a tennis dress to a wedding, or an evening dress to a high school basketball game. But there are more subtle points of fitness which often demand either a sure instinct or a rather wide knowledge and experience.

It is fairly easy, in looking into the closet, to say to oneself, "No, not that—it's too dressy; and not that—it's too bright; this is the best for traveling." But if one is suddenly asked to visit in a new community, it is not so easy to decide exactly what one needs. Every wise traveler, going to an unfamiliar country, asks an experienced traveler what to take with her. And that is exactly the role this chapter is designed to fill: that of an experienced guide.

Among all the specific suggestions given in this chapter, very few have anything to do with fashion. Fashion changes, and the clothes of each generation are interpreted according to its standards, but the basic standards of fitness and function change very little. The perfect skirt for walking in the country, for example, may not be exactly like those worn during the First World War; but it is still made of a sturdy material, it is still wide enough to walk in comfortably, and it is probably still made in one of the standard colors. The cut and the length may vary, but in relation to the rest of a woman's wardrobe, the character and purpose of the skirt are exactly the same. It is with these relatively unchanging elements of dressing that we are concerned.

COUNTRY DAY CLOTHES
AUTUMN, WINTER, SPRING

Clothes for daytime life in the country should always look practical and sturdy. For everything but evening clothes, this is the basic rule. Material that is conspicuously frail or that looks unequal to frequent washings or cleanings is almost never a good choice. It is often the fashion to use unexpected materials for city clothes, but in the country in the daytime, smooth, dark, perishable materials are never correct. And although a country suit, with a fashionable hat and a "dressmaker" blouse, often looks very well in town, the reverse is rarely true.

The most beautiful black town suit in the world is unfailingly out of place in a country house.

The suggestions we are giving here for country dressing do not, of course, apply without exception. In some sections of the American countryside, particularly in the South, there are local customs that contravene them and local customs should always be given preference. But as a rule of thumb, in wide areas throughout America these rules do hold. There is nothing local or ephemeral about them. They have been true for twenty years and they are still true in Burlingame, California, and in Lake Forest, Illinois, in Maryland's Green Spring Valley and in Newton Center, Massachusetts—and, for that matter, in any part of the British Isles.

The autumn, winter and spring months are the acid test of country clothes. It has been said that a good tweed suit will solve all one's country clothes problems. But this is just trying to dodge the issue by being falsely cheerful. A good tweed suit, marvelously practical though it may be, is not even vital. It is true that most women who dress fittingly for the country have one or two tweed suits, but there are many country women who wear odd skirts and sweaters and blouses and look very well indeed. The important questions are: what kinds of blouses? what colors? what shoes? what belts? what materials? The following lists are meant to answer these questions.

Dependable Standbys

1. Suits of mixed tweeds with brown, gray, beige or gray-green as the basic color.
2. Shirtwaists of plain white linen, cotton or silk, with long or short sleeves, round or V-neck, and turned-down collars; or simple blouses, with a round or high neck, with a plain bow.
3. Extra skirts of corduroy, whipcord, tweed or heavy gray flannel, cut with enough fullness for walking.
4. Sweaters, either pull-over or cardigan, of shetland or cashmere yarn.
5. Overcoats of tweed or rough woolens, fur-lined or not; camel's hair coats.
6. Pull-on hats of felt, tweed or leather in simple shapes with a simple ribbon band. The riding hat described on page 633 may be worn anywhere in the country.
7. Gloves of heavy supple leathers such as pigskin, doeskin, or chamois, riding gloves of knitted string or of brown leather; heavy woolen gloves in any bright color.
8. Belts of tan calfskin, with a plain harness buckle in brass or chromium.
9. Brown calf, alligator or lizard pumps, with medium-height, built-up leather heels, for luncheons, tea, Sundays, etc.
10. Brown reversed calf or calfskin "monk's" shoes for walking, with flat heels and sometimes a strap; flat-heeled calf "slip-on" shoes, brown or, for young women, red and green, too. Flat-heeled leather oxfords or "gillies" are country classics, but they must be well-made and are therefore apt to be more expensive than the others.
11. Scarves of challis, wool or silk foulard —in any of the colors listed below, or in one of the classic patterns of a man's foulard handkerchief.
12. Furs, such as nutria, beaver, muskrat, mouton or leopard-cat, which are flat yet sturdy; or rough country furs such as opossum.
13. Colors such as brown, gray, yellow, rust, light blue, green, beige, or rose-red.

To Be Avoided

1. Skirts and suits made of any thin, smooth, dark-blue or black woolen.
2. Fancy blouses; transparent silk blouses; satin blouses.
3. Sweaters of fancy yarns, such as bouclé.
4. Overcoats of any fine, smooth dark woolens.
5. Hats made of velvet or silk, or hats trimmed with satin or long feathers.
6. Tight gloves of thin leather, such as suède or kidskin, in any color; and any gloves, except woolen ones, with fancy work or decoration.
7. Belts of any fine, thin leather in dark blue or black; belts, in any color, which have rhinestone buckles.
8. Perishable leathers such as suède or thin kid.
9. Shoes with open toes or heels, in any color, if they have high heels.
10. Long-haired furs in any color, unless they are used as collars for tweed coats; flat black furs, such as sealskin or astrakhan.

11. Colors that look acidly synthetic; as magenta, fuchsia, chartreuse or hard aquamarine-blue; colors, such as dark blue and black, which are apt to look citified.

COUNTRY DAY CLOTHES
SUMMER

Country daytime clothes for the winter months are chosen for a way of life, but country clothes for the summer are chosen for the season. Different summer communities have different activities and different amusements and, therefore, although the principle of function still remains, there is more latitude in design and variety. When one is going into a new summer colony, it is always wise to dress in the most conservative way until one is able to sense accurately the community's special character or atmosphere. The clothes we are suggesting here would make a conservative backlog for a summer wardrobe. Personal variations can be added to fit the activities in any particular resort.

Dependable Standbys

1. Washable dresses in white or light pastel colors. The best one for the morning is a simple one; the shirtwaist dress is classic, but almost any very simple model without bows, or drapery, or openwork, or unnecessary elaborations is apt to be satisfactory. The best materials are linen, cotton, spun rayon, shantung, sharkskin and plain silk.
2. Afternoon dresses in silk or rayon, in prints with a light or white background and with predominantly light or bright colors. Since these dresses are worn in the afternoon and on Sundays, the cut is often a little more elaborate than that of the washable dresses suggested above. Elaborate drapery is not advisable in the country in the daytime, but many of the best of these dresses have a bow, or some simple ornamentation such as faggoting at the neck.
3. A cardigan to wear with the washable dresses, perhaps a short-sleeved, cotton knit cardigan, in a heavy cable stitch, in white, dark blue, a soft red or any pastel color; or a long-sleeved shetland cardigan in any of these colors. For the afternoon dresses, a cashmere cardigan

in any of these colors, or a short woolen jacket. Some of the most attractive of these are lined and bound in the print of the dress.
4. A straw hat in white or a light color; the best are usually the simplest version of the prevailing fashion.
5. Shoes. One pair of white buckskin with built-up brown leather heels. These may be all white, or the toe and heel may be capped in brown leather. A second pair for afternoon or "Don't-dress" evenings made of a thinner, lighter leather such as suède or kid—all white, with a higher covered heel. Some women wear red, beige, or green pumps, usually lizard or kid. Play shoes, worn without stockings, are a standby of girls and younger women, particularly at the seaside.
6. A woolen overcoat in a very simple cut and never tightly fitted. The best are these: a mixed tweed in light colors, or with at least one predominant light color; or a fairly rough woolen in a solid light color; or a monotone tweed in a practical color such as rose red, medium blue, bright green, or mustard yellow.
7. A tweed suit in a light color which is worn with summer shoes, for the first days of the autumn; particularly useful in any summer resort that is apt to have cool, rainy days. In almost every climate, there are some days in late September when one still wants to wear white or colored shoes, and a tweed suit in pale yellow, or light blue, or mustard yellow, or a soft pale green, or a mixture of almost any light color with white, is extremely useful.
8. Gloves. Heavy doeskin or cotton gloves, handstitched or machine-stitched but without decoration or fancy work, and always white or pale beige.

To Be Avoided

1. Clothes with a great deal of trimming or with a very elaborate or unusual cut.
2. Colored gloves and tight white glacé kid gloves.
3. Dark clothes and dark accessories. These are often worn, and most successfully, by women who dress extremely well, but anyone who is new to a summer community and is not very sure of herself would be wise to avoid them.

COUNTRY EVENING CLOTHES

On the theory, perhaps, that the dinner hour is the same all over the world, there are no special rules for country evening clothes. Satin evening suits, feathered evening hats and all the other "don't dress" evening clothes, which are so useful in city restaurants, are just so much extra baggage in the country. But long evening dresses, thin or thick, short-sleeved or long-sleeved, are even more useful in the country than they are in town. Evening dresses with jackets are ideal. Semi-evening dresses, such as pajamas and tea gowns (these are often sold as "housecoats") are almost a country evening specific for very small dinners or for dining at home.

TOWN CLOTHES

Town clothes do not really belong in this chapter because to a very great extent, they are more strictly a matter of fashion than of fitness and function. But, as always, there are some points of fitness and it might be helpful to the woman who plans to move to a big city from a small town to cover some of the broad general rules of town dressing.

In winter, in a very big city, dark clothes are the basis of every wardrobe. And these are the other most noticeable differences between town and country clothes: Shoes are lighter-weight and thinner than those worn in the country (whether they are high-heeled or not is a matter of choice, and, to some extent, of fashion); suits are less bulky—or, if the current fashion is bulkiness, they are dressmaker suits that lack the almost masculine bulkiness of country tweeds; dressmaker blouses, or thin, dressmaker sweaters replace the shirtwaists and shetlands; hats are designed according to the current fashion, unlike the simple round felt, that serves so well in the country, year after year. And there is a whole new category of clothes that have no country counterpart: short black silk, satin, or moiré dresses, or suits, if such is the fashion, for cocktail parties or "don't dress" evenings; thin elaborate blouses; and high-heeled black shoes. Beige gloves and dark gloves—thin suède ones for the afternoon and evening. Like country gloves, but usually dark, are the heavy, hand-stitched doeskin or cotton gloves worn in the daytime. But never glacé kid in any form.

In the summer in a Northern city, a country woman will notice that white shoes never look well; whether high-heeled or flat, whether pumps or sandals, the best city shoes are dark. She will begin to think about printed silk or rayon dresses, or "town ginghams," in colors that go well with dark accessories.

The biggest single difference between town and country dressing is that, in the country, daytime clothes are appropriate from nine in the morning until it is time to put on an evening dress for dinner. For shopping in the morning, in the country, a tweed suit and leather pumps and bag are just as appropriate as they are for tea. In very big cities, however, this is never true. If our country woman is invited to a tea party or a cocktail party, she will not wear the plain, tailored coat, the dark blue suit and low-heeled dark-blue shoes that looked so well when she went shopping early in the morning. Naturally, if she has been out shopping all day, and stops in to see a friend at teatime, she will not bother to go home and dress in a black satin suit. But at a cocktail party, black satin suits, or the equivalent, will be what all the other women are wearing.

TRAVELING CLOTHES

The ideal clothes for travel are those which would be worn for shopping in town in the morning. The old-fashioned rule for traveling clothes was: nothing so bright as to give the impression of wanting to attract attention; nothing too ostentatiously valuable; nothing too fragile or delicate-looking; nothing too richly formal, such as silk and satin; and nothing too informal (nothing such as a bare-backed dress covered with a scanty bolero). It still makes a very sensible picture. A tailored suit, a small neat hat, shoes that are halfway between the sturdiness of country walking shoes and the delicate lightness of town afternoon shoes, a loose overcoat that will slip on and off easily and if it is fur, of a fairly strong, practical fur—all these add up to the perfect clothes for travel. The summer version of this ideal picture is exactly like it in spirit: a practical, lightweight suit or dress which will wash or clean easily (unless it is really very hot, suits and blouses are even more attractive and more practical than dresses); the summer equivalent of winter's small, neat hat and, perhaps, the very same pair of practical dark brown, dark blue, or black shoes; an overcoat, if necessary, of mixed woolen tweed, brown and beige, black and gray, or dark blue and white. The essential point is that this conservative, practical attitude should be an automatic reflex to the word traveling. No white shoes, no floppy hats, no floating feathers or veils. This "morning shopping rule" holds for all train travel here or abroad and for debarking or going on board ship in any but the smallest port. Travel by motor, of course, does not come under this heading; neither does travel by plane from one country airport to another; nor travel on shipboard once a ship is underway; nor travel by train if it is a matter of a short train trip between two country stops. But all travel that begins or ends in a city of any size most definitely does.

Ocean Crossings and Cruises

Once a ship has put out to sea, the traveler should dress exactly as she would for the country, at whatever time of year it may be. (See pages 629 to 631.) In fact, the ship should be considered as though it were a country club, and one should dress accordingly. For active shipboard sports—sports clothes; for sitting around the swimming pool—beach clothes; for evening—evening clothes, or, on small ships, short dinner dresses.

Exactly the same rule holds for cruises. If one is traveling in a tropical climate, one will need a good supply of summer things; for North Cape cruises, or summer cruises to cool places, warm things in light colors. But every cruise traveler should consider the ports at which the ship will stop, and remember that, for most of them, one will need city morning, or shopping, clothes.

Long Airplane Trips

The only difference between dressing for a long airplane trip and dressing for a short trip is that for a long trip one should wear clothes that are more obviously sturdy and unmussable. A gray flannel suit, a small, close-fitting hat, shoes with heels of medium height, a good, warm overcoat of tweed or fur-lined wool—these would be perfect for a long airplane trip between two points in the temperate zone, in all but the hottest summer weather. In summer, a thin suit of shantung and a coat without fur would be most practical. The effect that is most attractive is one of neatness, of being stripped down and unencumbered with things that fly away or tangle or muss. Veils, flowers, fringes, blouses with lace and jabots—all these suddenly look impossibly fussy beside the clean lines of an airplane.

RIDING CLOTHES

Riding clothes offer one of the simplest and most definite examples of fitness in dressing. The rules given here are based on the English tradition, which has been generally accepted as sensible and smart. Their purpose is to make men and women look trim and workmanlike on a horse, and as trim after three hours in the saddle as they were at the start. These rules are ironbound, and vary almost not at all from one decade to another. Certain clothes are correct for hacking, whether it is in a city park or in the country, and certain others for hunting. There are some permissible variations, and there the matter ends. If these rules seem unattractive or too difficult, it is better to ignore them altogether and dress in blue jeans or corduroys than to vary the accepted form with little personal innovations. The following rules are for men as well as women.

For Hacking and Informal Riding

In a city park, or in the country when no jumping is involved, these are traditional:

1. For women, a soft, felt hat, dark brown, with a small brim, bound or unbound, a dull self-color ribbon hat-band and, for decoration, at most, a small flat feather in a neutral color; or in the country, no hat, and neat hair. (A net is always helpful.) For men, a soft brownish Fedora with an unbound brim, or a tweed cap with a visor; or no hat at all.
2. A tweed coat, single-breasted, in mixed beige and brown, or gray and gray-blue.
3. A shirt, like a man's, in white, beige or pale blue; wool, silk, cotton or linen.
4. A man's necktie, in wool or silk; or, in

summer, in cotton or linen; or a stock for slightly more formal riding. With a stock, which, for hacking, should be made of printed silk foulard, a collarless shirt is worn, and always a waistcoat. Stocks are tied in a traditional and indescribable way—a good men's shop can show you—but remember that one pin, the standard gold safety pin, is always needed.

5. A single-breasted waistcoat, for cold weather, as gay as you like.
6. A pair of breeches made of beige, cream-colored, or rusty-brown whipcord, or of Bedford cord, or cavalry twill, with a moderate flare between hip and knee; buttoned just below the knee, on the *inside* of the shinbone.
7. And, a pair of brown leather boots, as long and as narrow as the leg itself allows, either with or without a laced opening over the instep. Laced boots are called field boots.
8. Or, instead of the regular riding breeches and boots, a pair of fitted, ankle-length riding-trousers called jodhpurs—just as "correct" as breeches, and less expensive, but be sure they come well down to the ankle bone.
9. With jodhpurs, a pair of short boots, called jodhpur boots, which strap or lace around the ankle and slip up under the jodhpur.
10. Gloves, always, of plain chamois or brown leather, or of lined or unlined knitted string.
11. A bamboo or leather-covered stick, called a swagger stick, is smart and sometimes useful.

Permissible Departures

1. A turtle-neck sweater, worn with or without the tweed coat.
2. A chamois or leather shooting coat, for very cold weather and only for informal riding in the country.
3. A shirt of cotton, silk, or linen, cut like a man's shirt and worn without coat or necktie, with the neck open and the sleeves rolled up, but only for very hot weather and for very informal riding in the country.
4. A pair of heavy flat walking shoes, worn with jodhpurs, instead of the regular jodhpur boots.
5. Newmarket boots, made with canvas legs and leather feet, worn with the regular riding breeches.

6. Buttoned canvas leggings, worn with the standard breeches and ankle-high, laced shoes that fit under the leggings.

For Larking

For jumping informally across a countryside, wear a bowler (a stiff round black hat called a "hunting derby") with the traditional clothes for hacking. Children and young girls wear a special, reinforced velvet cap with a visor.

For Sidesaddle

Add a skirt of whipcord, Bedford cord, or cavalry twill, in tan or rusty brown. The only difference between sidesaddle and astride clothes, except for the skirt, is that sidesaddle breeches have almost no flare.

What to Avoid

1. Three-cornered hats. These can be correctly worn for riding only with the full French hunting dress, which differs in many respects from the English and is worn only in France. Foreigners riding with a French pack are not expected to conform to the French tradition.
2. Bandannas or turbans. Bandannas should only be worn in summer, in country places.
3. Waistcoats worn without a coat. These are all too often seen, especially in city parks. They are the very antithesis of the accepted standard.
4. Short, fat boots; loose boots.
5. Thin kid or suède gloves.
6. Dinky, fancy crops, miniature crops and crops without a lash.

Hunting

Hunting, during the formal season, is rigid with traditions, customs, and strict etiquette. (See also page 82, in the chapter "Games and Sports.") Before the formal season opens, there is an easier, less formal kind of hunting called cubbing, or cub-hunting, when the hounds are conditioned and young hounds trained to the sport. Cubbing usually starts at an almost impossibly early hour, at dawn or shortly after, and the clothes one wears are just about the same as those for larking, except that, for the longer, harder riding of cubbing, boots and breeches are better than jodhpurs.

Hunting during the regular season, however, demands a formal way of dressing. To begin with, there is the question of "hunt colors," which may be worn by members of the hunt at the special request of the Master. The hunt color—tan, blue, or other—is worn on the collar of the usual black hunting coat, which is worn by both men and women, or on the collar of the pink coat worn only by men. There are other elaborations of dress open to men—a "shadbelly" coat, for example —but this is the standard dress:

1. A stiff, neat-looking bowler hat, with a narrow brim. These are specially reinforced; ask for a "hunting-derby." Men wear top hats with pink coats.
2. For women, a thin hair net covering the hair, if it is short, plus a heavier net, if the hair is long, to hold the knot securely.
3. A white stock, secured with a plain gold safety pin.
4. A collarless white shirt, made of linen, cotton, silk, or wool; or knit-wool jersey.
5. A flannel waistcoat, usually canary yellow, beige, or Tattersall check.
6. A black single-breasted coat of Melton cloth, cut straight all around, like the coat of a business suit.
7. Beige or cream-colored or rusty-brown breeches of whipcord, Bedford cord, or twill, the same as those used for hacking.
8. Black boots, long and narrow, and without any lacing or decoration. With a pink coat, men wear black boots with brown leather tops (pinkish-brown or mahogany brown) and white breeches.
9. Small blunt spurs. These should be worn with the point down—never up— and are fastened with black leather straps; a chain goes under the foot.
10. Chamois gloves, or yellow string gloves, lined or unlined. String are better in case of rain.
11. A crop. The conventional hunting crop has a long leather lash. This is carried with the bone handle down and the lash held straight along the shaft. The lash should *never* be carried in a loop while riding and the crop should *never* be carried without its lash.

For sidesaddle, a dark blue habit is the best. Add a skirt to match the coat and a coarse veil (this is optional) to cover the face. For the most important hunting days, such as a great holiday, a woman riding sidesaddle will often wear a top hat, and with a top hat she must wear a veil.

Permissible departures do not exist. It is perfectly possible, of course, to hunt safely in larking clothes, but it's like wearing an afternoon dress to a ball.

Barbarisms too often seen in the hunting-field are top hats worn without a sidesaddle skirt; rings, bracelets, fancy stock pins, and other kinds of jewelry; heavy make-up, with eye-shadow and mascara, and hanging hair.

SHOOTING CLOTHES

Clothes for shooting are a complicated mixture of comfort, practicality, and in some cases physical safety. To some extent, like riding clothes, they are governed by rigid convention, particularly in the matter of game-bird shooting. Since this kind of shooting is the most popular in the United States, these are the only clothes we shall discuss here. The few who may be starting out on big-game expeditions may safely trust the advice of a really reliable sporting goods store.

There are three main types of game birds—upland birds, driven birds and waterfowl. Each type of shooting requires clothes of a somewhat different type, so we will list them separately; and it's a list that serves for men as well as women.

Upland Shooting

For upland shooting, when the birds are usually in front of the guns and will not be frightened by colors, clothes should be, above all, comfortable and practical. Boots may be either field-boots (laced with rawhide, with a moccasin foot) or tramping shoes, calf or knee length, depending upon the country. The Gokey boot pulls on like a riding boot and is fast becoming the most popular of all, as there is no bother with laces.

Breeches may be tightly fitted, like riding breeches, or cut with a little more fullness in the knees and seat. For quail shooting in the South, jungle cloth reinforced back and front with buckskin, because of the briars, is used a great deal. For northern shooting, breeches are often made in twill, or in a soft, beautifully woven material called safari.

From Charleston on south, white duck coats are worn for quail shooting. They are briar proof, and are worn for safety, because birds are found in thick country and the more visible one is the safer. For other upland shooting, gale-cloth, in a soft gray-tan, is very popular, as it is light and stands up well against the briars. In more northern climates, duck-shooting jackets may be worn for pheasant, woodcock, and grouse shooting also.

For Driven Birds

For driven birds—dove shoots and turkey drives—riding breeches and high boots are not necessary. Plain, heavy tweed trousers (or, for a woman, a sturdy tweed skirt), heavy shoes, and a comfortably warm jacket are all that is necessary.

Waterfowl Shooting

Waterfowl shooting, which properly means only ducks and geese, is almost always a cold proposition. Underwear is very important because, with warm wool next to the skin, fewer outer clothes are needed, and there is more freedom in shooting. Any clothes that will show must be in neutral colors to blend with the landscape.

The outer clothes begin with a sweater—a brown turtle-neck sweater, for example—or a heavy tan flannel shirt. The trousers may be specially made, long, with a knitted cuff at the ankle, slightly resembling ski-pants; these fit well under any boot; but field-shooting breeches, the ones worn for upland shooting, are just as satisfactory. The perfect boot is a hip-length, rubber overboot which fastens to the belt. In very cold weather it should be worn over shearling or sheepskin linings.

Coats for waterfowl shooting are short, a little less than fingertip length, and are usually made of Duxback, drab, or gabardine. Some of the coats made for northern shooting are hooded and lined with alpaca pile. Coats to wear in the South are lighter in weight, of course, but all coats worn for shooting except driven-bird shooting are made especially for the sport. They are plain and businesslike, with big pockets for shells and big game-pockets across the back. For one who does little shooting, special clothes like these would, of course, be a useless extravagance. A plain leather jacket, cut like a boy's, could be substituted for one of these shooting coats, but it would never look as well.

TENNIS CLOTHES

There are two ways of dressing for tennis, both equally acceptable. The first is to wear dresses, and the other is to wear shorts. The essential of both is that they must be white.

1. Dresses. One piece, sleeveless, with the skirts pleated all around; with round necks or little turned-down collars. The skirts come to just above the knee.

    Older women often wear long or short sleeves, and skirts just below the knee.

2. Shorts and shirts. Shorts should always be white; not tight; fingertip length, or "English-length," about two inches above the knee, is best. They are made of white flannel, linen, piqué, broadcloth, or sharkskin. All-in-one shorts (blouse and shorts in one), made in any of the last four materials, may be very practical.

    The shirts may be sleeveless sharkskin; or plain shirts with short sleeves; or "polo" shirts with a collar, a three-button neck, and short sleeves, made of very fine, tightly woven cotton mesh.

3. A visor of white felt, lined with green, or a white tennis cap of duck with a visor, if one likes shade for the eyes.

4. White wool socks, ankle length.

5. White sneakers, or Wimbledon tennis shoes.

What to Avoid

1. Sweaters worn without shirts.
2. Colors.
3. Halters.
4. Sun backs.
5. Bra tops.
6. Blouses.
7. Jewelry.
8. Ordinary shoes.

GOLF CLOTHES

For Warm Weather

1. Linen or cotton shirtwaist dress with short or long sleeves, or without sleeves; but never with a low décolletage.

2. Socks, wool or cotton; stockings are optional.
3. Heavy brown leather brogues or oxfords with flat heels; or brown-and-white leather golf shoes; but all golf shoes must have either rubber soles or, better, cleats.
4. A white stitched linen hat, or a visor —or no hat and neat hair.
5. Special golf gloves—white doeskin with brown leather palms are the most usual—or else no gloves at all.

For Cold Weather

1. Sweater and skirt, but no tight sweaters unless they are fairly heavy.
2. Plain skirts of flannel, wool, or tweed.
3. Shirt, of flannel, silk, cotton, anything, cut like a man's shirt, worn under the sweater.
4. Flannel or wool shirtwaist dress with a cardigan. The best are cut with special "action-pleats."
5. A brown felt hat, like a riding hat, with a narrow brim; or no hat.
6. Golf gloves as suggested above, or brown leather gloves.

What to Avoid

1. Shorts. These should never be worn on a golf course.
2. Slacks.
3. Barebacked dresses or halters.
4. Ruffles, or anything fussy and dressy.
5. Regular town gloves.
6. High heels, never on any golf course; fancy shoes or sandals; hats that are "fashionable"; or any hat but one of those suggested above.

SKI CLOTHES

The ideal look is inconspicuousness through conspicuous neatness: workmanlike, trim, every hatch battened down—like riding clothes. These are the details:

1. Black, navy-blue, gray or sometimes natural gabardine colors in gray tones.
2. Long and narrow ski trousers, drawn fairly tightly from the boot to the hip; usually of gabardine. It has become the fashion to wear the trouser over the sock, so that nothing shows but the boot and the trouser. This is trimmer and neater than the old-fashioned custom of wearing a heavy sock turned back

over the boot-top, but the latter is also permissible.
3. Windbreaker or parka, made of parka cloth, Byrd cloth, or any water-repellent material; usually matches the trousers.
4. Jersey hood-helmet or gabardine wool-lined helmet.
5. Under the jacket, a turtle-neck sweater, flannel shirt cut like a man's.
6. Wool gloves or mittens under parka-cloth mittens; dark or bright, preferably matching the suit.

Permissible Departures

Expert women skiers often wear a short neat skirt, a heavy cable-stitched sweater and matching stockings for spring skiing.

What to Avoid

1. Shorts: never wear shorts for skiing.
2. Fur (it mats).
3. Long-tasseled caps (untidy and amateurish).
4. Fuzzy, water-gathering woolly ski suits.
5. Brightly colored suits.

SAILING AND YACHTING

For a novice who has been invited to go sailing or yachting, the first point is to find out the size of the yacht. The size of the craft, even more than the length of the trip, determines the kind of clothes a guest will need. On any yacht under fifty feet long, guests must expect to take part in handling her and, on long trips, in the domestic routine. For an afternoon's sailing in a very small ten- or twelve-foot boat, most women wear a bathing suit with sunburn protection if necessary: a jacket or sweater and a short knee-length skirt or slacks. On boats a little bigger: shorts, slacks, or blue jeans, or a short divided skirt; a man's shirt, or a blouse cut in any simple pattern, or a sweater; sneakers or rope-soled shoes; a hat that will stay on in the wind—one of the best is made of stitched white cotton or linen, with a narrow brim and, sometimes, a green isinglass visor let into the brim. The essential point is that everything must be made of sturdy workmanlike materials that can stand sun and water. Although it might not seem suitable in theory, gray flannel is one of the best and most usual materials for skirts, shorts, or slacks. Plenty of warm sweaters are vital, and a waterproof of some kind.

As suggested in the chapter "Men's Clothes," if the trip is to last four days or more it is wise, even in warm weather, to bring a long rubber raincoat. On such a cruise in cold weather, a woman who will do any considerable part of the sailing should have a fisherman's oilskins or rubber suit like the men's. This consists of rubber overalls and a rubber jacket, and a rubber sou'wester hat and rubber boots. Oilskins are sticky and impossible for warm weather; rubber boots are heavy, but invaluable for cold climates or smaller yachts. If one plans to go ashore anytime during the cruise, one will need a summer day dress also, or, if it is late in the season, a light-colored tweed suit (see page 631, "Summer Clothes"). But

it is a point of good sense and good manners not to bring many clothes for a trip on a small yacht where there is little locker space for storage.

On the bigger yachts in the daytime, women wear clothes exactly like those worn in the country ashore, but one must always take a warm sweater and a good warm overcoat. Younger women who like slacks and shorts will probably wear them on board. In any case, on a long trip one will need simple evening dresses and afternoon dresses for trips ashore. Women should never wear yachting caps or any imitation of the traditional yacht club member's coat, and they must bring shoes which will not mark the deck (see page 83 in the chapter, "Games and Sports").

WEARING DECORATIONS
See pages 627 to 628.

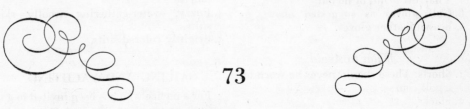

73

Children's Clothes

No ONE needs to be told how to dress a tiny baby. Any little white muslin dress, any afghan or shawl in pale pink, pale blue or white, any little bonnet will do. Or, for that matter, the prettiest pale satin coat, the finest embroidery, the richest laces and furs. But as soon as children can walk, the trouble begins.

Too many fat woolen tassels are loaded on them, too many hard, bright colors, too many flounces, and too much silk. Generally speaking, although an infant's clothes can be as elaborate as a dowager's, the plainer a child's clothes, the better. The most important element is to know what is fitting, and what is not—just as in all dressing. Simple materials and simple lines are best suited to the very young; sturdy materials for playing and everyday; darker colors for older boys. There is nothing very complicated about it. Any child that is big enough to play on the ground and get dirty should have a dark snow suit; babies in carriages should have pale ones.

The extraordinary fact is that, in a matter that is purely a question of common sense and a simple sense of fitness, so many mistakes are made. One major reason for mistakes is that common sense, through carelessness or lack of knowledge, is not applied. The other is that adult standards of beauty are sometimes, with disastrous results, confused with those of the very young. The very young should be clean, natural, and simple, and nothing more. A very faint permanent wave—so light as to resemble "ducks' tails" rather than curls—is the only permissible step towards the adult standards. Any little four-year-old girl in a dress of orange-pink shot-silk taffeta, with an unmistakable permanent wave and several bangle bracelets, is a very pitiable figure indeed.

As in the case of the other clothes lists, these lists of children's clothes are not supposed to be complete or final. The clothes listed as desirable are those which are easiest to find and most trustworthy. But they should be used as a guide, as examples of the best, not as the beginning and end of all good dressing. The other lists, which begin "And Not These," are equally incomplete. They include only the most salient examples of the clothes which are inappropriate for the children in each age group.

LITTLE GIRLS: EIGHTEEN MONTHS TO FIVE YEARS OLD

1. Very short dresses, of fine organdy or linen for parties; of linen, piqué, gingham, or cotton for everyday. In the country, seersucker or corduroy overalls, with plain or striped cotton knit shirts, as soon as they are active enough to walk and play on their own.
2. Pale colors, checked ginghams; simple flower prints in very small patterns. Darker and brighter colors—soft green, red, or medium blue—for snow suits and overcoats, when the children are no longer in a play pen or baby carriage.
3. Short ankle socks, always cotton; white for parties, white or brown for everyday.
4. Plain brown shoes or sandals for everyday; white, red, or emerald-green slippers for parties, or black patent leather. Modern medical opinion often does not approve high laced-up boots.
5. No jewelry, except possibly a seed-pearl or gold-chain necklace with a locket.

And Not These

1. Elaborate dresses of silk, taffeta or—worse—satin;
2. Hard, artificial colors, such as acid-green, fuchsia, and chartreuse;
3. Any rings or bracelets.

LITTLE BOYS: EIGHTEEN MONTHS TO FIVE YEARS OLD

1. Linen suits, with short trousers, and short-sleeved blouses to match; knitted cotton suits, with shorts in a solid color and striped blouses; corduroy overalls for the country with cotton knit shirts. For parties, velvet trousers in blue, red, black, emerald-green, or gray-green, with a shirt of white silk or fine white linen; but this only between eighteen months and four years. Linen trousers, with the same kind of shirts for summer parties. Gray flannel shorts for big five year olds.
2. Plain brown shoes and sandals for everyday; white or red sandals for parties, or "George Washington" slippers to wear with the velvet trousers.
3. Short, ankle-length cotton socks; white for parties and while they are babies; brown, when they walk around a lot.
4. Pale colors only in the baby stage. As soon as they start walking: gray, French blue, beige, or soft dark red; then, brown or dark blue combined with white or light blue; at four, gray flannel. One of the best and most practical models has suspenders attached to the trousers and is worn with a white silk overblouse with elastic around the bottom.

And Not These

1. Silk suits (except as noted above).
2. Heavy dark colors or materials on a very small boy; or pale fragile colors and materials on a child who is very large and robust for his age.

THE "HERD INSTINCT"

From the age of five years on—in fact, until the age of about twenty—a new factor enters into the matter of clothes: the herd instinct, the child's desire to look, act, and be an exact replica of his contemporaries. This urge, which is often most unfortunate in its manifestations, reaches a peak usually at about the age of fourteen. But it is often evident at eight or nine and, in precocious children, even at six. The one sure way to bring it on at an early age is to dress the child in clothes that are so different from those of his friends that he is forced to notice the fact.

All this is very easy for sensible parents to handle until the majority group in the school or kindergarten (boys are as subject to these fashion fads as girls) decides that snow suits are out—too sissy—and that The Thing is knickerbocker pants. So, the sensible parents are left holding a perfectly good snow suit, and are asked to buy a most unattractive pair of new trousers. As in all crises of deep conflict of opinion, a compromise can sometimes be a solution: the snow suit plus the new trousers, or a new overcoat and no knickerbockers. If the financial side of the matter really is a problem, an appeal on this basis will often solve the whole thing. But there is no use in making a false appeal on these grounds: Children are far too shrewd to be fooled and, if the parents buy new things for themselves, the child will notice and protest, or be deeply hurt, according to his temperament.

The only solution that is really wrong is to dismiss these childish fashions as childish, and to dismiss the child's longing to look like his friends as an unimportant, foolish whim. Affection for the child, and common sense—as well as the psychologists—suggest a moderate course of compromise, an intelligent surrender on certain points, sympathetic firmness on others. An uncompromising inflexibility, an insistence that the child dress only according to adult standards of taste, is a sure foundation for that unhappy cry of adolescence, "They don't understand me."

There is one more thing that should be said about clothes for children. Little girls look badly if they are dressed in a way that is too old for them; with boys, it is quite the other way: Clothes that are a little too old look better than those which are too babyish.

Here follows a list of desirable and undesirable clothes for girls between five and eleven, and, in two sections (five to nine, and nine to twelve) for boys—subject to the overriding herd instinct discussed above.

GIRLS FIVE TO TWELVE YEARS OLD

For Everyday and School

1. Suits of gray flannel for any large six-year-old and any older girl.
2. Skirts of gray flannel or plaid; light mixed tweeds or plain woolens in dark blue, gray or brown; or corduroy.
3. Blouses of white cotton, linen, rayon, piqué, or silk, in a simple model. The best often have short sleeves and round, turned-down collars.
4. Pull-over or cardigan sweaters in shetland, Jaeger, or cashmere yarns. Fancy yarns are unsuitable for children. In any pastel color, in soft reds or blues, in dark blue, beige or brown.
5. Shoes with flat heels, in plain brown leather, round-toed and sturdy-looking. Sharkskin toe-caps are very practical. Flat brown sandals for summer.
6. Short cotton socks in beige or brown; for cold weather, knee-length socks in mixed beige or gray wool.
7. Snow suits for younger girls in dark blue or dark brown, in wool or water-and-wind-resistant cloth lined with wool; girls over eight or nine rarely wear snow suits except for winter sports. Overcoats of tweed in neutral colors, mixed or plain, and in plain wools, gray, brown, soft red or blue, are standard. Any of these may also be used as a "party overcoat," although a rough tweed would not be as adaptable for this as a smoother wool.
8. Gloves of knitted string, plain or wool-lined; bright woolen mittens; leather mittens or gloves.

9. Summer dresses of cotton, piqué, spun rayon, gingham or linen, in light colors, white, checks, or flower prints (prints with a small pattern only). Sturdy cotton dresses, gingham or broadcloth, in practical colors for school in warm weather.

10. Cotton shorts and blouses to match, or knitted cotton shirts.

11. Overalls of light blue denim, or corduroy overalls in almost any color.

12. Hats of leghorn straw, or any other simple straw, for summer; for the rest of the year, a plain little round felt hat with a brim. A riding hat is most useful.

For Parties

1. Dresses of velveteen, for winter parties, in brown, blue, red, holly-green, or even black, with or without fine linen or lace collars; or simple, high-necked crepe de Chine dresses in any of these colors, but not dark blue or black. Very small six-year-olds can still wear thin organdy or muslin dresses, with satin ribbon sashes, but on bigger girls they look a little too babyish. For summer parties, linen dresses in light colors.

2. Short white cotton socks; ankle length is best.

3. Slippers of red or—very smart—bronze kid, with flat heels and a strap across the instep. Or patent leather.

4. Winter overcoats of monotone tweed or wool in brown, bright royal blue, red, gray, green, or even bright purple. Purple is not usually considered a child's color, but if it is becoming to the child, it looks very well. These overcoats may have a plain collar, a velvet collar of the same color, or a collar of some simple flat fur such as beaver. An old-fashioned tippet and muff are very smart, and would look very well with one of the overcoats suggested above for everyday, particularly the gray or soft red.

5. Hats made of felt to match or harmonize with the overcoat, or made of the same material as the overcoat; but always in a simple shape and with little trimming. Summer hats of straw, preferably with a brim of the same width all around, with a trimming of ribbon or simple field flowers, currants, cherries, or wheat, etc.

6. Summer or spring overcoats of thin wool or covert cloth; dark blue serge is smart for the city, but less attractive as a country coat; gray or a light mixed gray-beige would be the most practical.

7. Gloves of plain dark brown leather, like riding gloves; or, for spring and summer, of white cotton.

8. Jewelry of the simplest kind: gold chain and locket, seed-pearl necklace or bracelet, small gold chain bracelet, seed-pearl bar pin or a simple gold pin in the shape of a whip or riding-crop.

And Not These

1. Anything elaborate or too obviously expensive.

2. Colors such as shocking pink, cyclamen, chartreuse, and fuchsia, which are obviously designed for grown women.

3. Sweaters of silk yarn or bouclé.

4. Shoes or slippers that have any suggestion of a high heel.

5. White silk socks, or woolen socks with pseudo-Norwegian or Fair Isle designs. (Real Norwegian socks, or really good copies, can look very well, but they are expensive. The same is true of all knitted things, including sweaters and mufflers, and of all the Tyrolean things for children—cheap imitations should be avoided.)

6. Sophisticated prints.

7. Rings of any kind.

8. Silk or silk-knit underclothes; cotton or linen is standard for all children up to the age of twelve.

BOYS FIVE TO NINE YEARS OLD

For Everyday and School

1. Two-piece snow suits in dark blue or chocolate-brown. One-piece suits are not only impractical, but also too babyish.

2. Very short pants of gray flannel; or woolen shorts in dark blue, dark brown, or gray.

3. Pull-over sweaters in any dark color or in light yellow, medium blue, beige, gray, or kelly green.

4. Socks of brown or dark blue cotton for summer; knee-length gray or beige woolen socks, also, for winter.

5. Shirts of cotton, white or light blue. For five and six year olds, these shirts have narrow neckbands and rather wide turned-down "Peter Pan" collars, and

may be worn without a necktie if the pull-over is high enough to cover the button at the neck. Seven and eight year olds should wear neckties which come in a special short size. Mesh shirts with three buttons and a collar are very nice in light yellow and in white; they are left unbuttoned and are not worn with a tie.

6. For summer, gabardine shorts in dark blue or chocolate-brown, worn with striped, knitted cotton shirts to match; blue jeans; corduroy shorts or overalls.

7. Oxfords of brown leather, square and sturdy-looking; brown leather sandals for summer.

For Parties

1. Gray flannel suits, with very short trousers and with or without collars. With a collarless coat, a shirt with a round, "Eton" collar is worn, the shirt collar outside.

2. Overcoats and caps, with visors, of mixed beige-and-brown or gray tweed.

And Not These

1. Fur coats of any kind. Full-grown boys, at 18 or 20, can start wearing raccoon or bearskin coats in the country; younger boys look very foolish in furs.

2. Fancy socks, with elaborate designs and bright colors.

BOYS NINE TO TWELVE YEARS OLD

For Everyday and School

1. Short overcoat of tan, wind-and-water-resistant cloth, lined with alpaca plush or with sheepskin, with a sheepskin collar.

2. Gray or brown suits with long trousers. Long trousers, and when to let a child start wearing them, are almost entirely a question of the climate, the child's size, and of the prevailing school fashion. Very long legs, and legs that are at all fat as well as long, absolutely need long trousers.

3. White or blue or pin-striped shirts, cut like a man's and worn with a necktie.

4. For summer, tan, gray, dark-brown, or dark-blue shorts and cotton knit shirts with short socks and sneakers, moccasins, or low brown shoes.

For Parties

1. Dark blue suits with long trousers; for summer, long white duck trousers, or shorts, with the dark blue coat or a blazer.

2. Brown or black shoes; for summer, white shoes with rubber soles.

3. Simple foulard neckties.

4. Overcoats and caps to match; or his school cap, if there is one, as for the younger boys.

And Not These

1. Dinner jackets. No boy under fourteen or fifteen should ever wear a dinner jacket; sympathetic firmness should counter the herd instinct here.

2. Fedora hats.

3. Cuff links, or any other jewelry except a silver wrist watch, or a gold safety pin under the necktie, to keep the collar neat.

4. Silk socks.

THE TEENS

Dressing girls and boys over eleven and under sixteen is governed almost entirely by the customs and standards of the children's contemporaries, especially insofar as their school life is concerned. Provided that they keep clean, and as neat as the prevailing school fashion will permit, there is no sound reason why they should not look like all the other children. Extremes may have to be moderated a little; untidiness or overelaborate dressing should definitely be curbed; but, on the whole, the children should be allowed to fit into the accepted pattern. The parent who understands that a blue serge skirt can be terribly important—and right *now* —often receives a gratitude that is touching in its intensity. All the compromises suggested under the heading, "The 'Herd Instinct,'" will need to be remembered at this stage.

In the question of clothes for family parties and for Sundays, however, the children should not be given quite so much leeway. Thirteen- and fourteen-year-old girls often have a longing for black satin and sequins which must be ignored. Boys are averse to wearing a dark blue suit for church, but firm pressure should be applied to make them overcome the aversion. In out-of-school hours, and for parties of grown-ups and children, the parents' pattern should take precedence, just as the children's does during the school day or at children's parties. The following lists, therefore, are subject to infinite revision in the clothes for school, children's parties, and everyday, and to a less lenient interpretation concerning the clothes for family parties and Sundays.

GIRLS TWELVE TO FIFTEEN YEARS OLD

For Everyday and School

1. Simple suits of tweed or wool.
2. Sweaters and skirts.
3. Plain blouses that button up to the neck, with round collars; or shirtwaists, with V-necks.
4. Simple cotton dresses, in shirtwaist, "Princess," or "play clothes" models.
5. Flat sturdy shoes, but not necessarily oxfords; "monk's shoes" or low-heeled pumps are standard.
6. Winter overcoat of tweed; polo coats.

And Not These

1. Black clothes;
2. High-heeled shoes;
3. Fancy materials, such as satin or damasked silk;
4. Quantities of costume jewelry, or real jewelry that looks at all valuable;
5. Slacks, except for fishing (when they might be useful to protect the legs from the sun) or some other such sport;
6. Shorts, except for an active sport such as tennis or basketball; or for very hot summer days on a beach or in the country;
7. Any play clothes made in two pieces, leaving a bare midriff between.

For Children's Dances

Young girls of these ages may be allowed to dress a little beyond their years for children's parties; for grown-up dinners, they should underdress.

Girls of twelve and thirteen look best in the following:

1. Short (knee-length) dresses; in winter —dark red, dark green, or black velvet; in summer—plain or printed linen, or a simple silk print.

2. Black suède or patent-leather pumps with low heels and bows; or ballet slippers.
3. Girls twelve and thirteen, particularly if they are very big for their age, often wear long stockings instead of socks.
4. Simple jewelry.

At fourteen and fifteen girls usually wear long evening dresses, not décolleté, and usually made with short sleeves or a fichu. The best materials are muslin, organdy, faille, chiffon, and tulle; the best colors are white and pastel colors. Ballet slippers or low-heeled sandals of satin, silver or gold kid, are standard.

BOYS TWELVE TO FIFTEEN YEARS OLD

For Everyday and School

1. Brown or gray suits with long trousers; gray flannel or tan gabardine trousers with a tweed coat.
2. A jacket, or a long jacket of tan, wind-and-water-resistant cloth, lined with alpaca plush or sheepskin; or a polo coat; or a reversible, tweed and gabardine (or twill) single-breasted overcoat.
3. Fedora hat, brown or gray, with unbound brim. (But usually no hat.)
4. Argyle or brown cotton socks.

For Children's Parties

1. Dark blue suits with long trousers; for summer—long white duck or flannel trousers with a dark blue coat. At thirteen or fourteen, they start wearing waistcoats with dark blue suits.
2. Black shoes.
3. Socks of gray or blue cotton, or mixed wool-and-cotton, or lisle.
4. Overcoat of gray or brown mixed tweed.
5. Fedora hat.
6. Dinner jackets only for a boy of about fifteen, and only if he is very big for his age.

DRESSING THE YOUNG OVER SIXTEEN

Girls

Usually dress in a very modified version of the current fashion. In other words, no shoes with ankle straps or very,

very high heels. No dresses with very low décolletages. No black dresses in the day-time (girls under twenty do not, as a rule, look well in black in the daytime, but some black evening dresses can be very becoming—for example, black velveteen with a wide décolletage, little puff sleeves and a full skirt). No very valuable or conspicuous jewelry.

Boys

Boys begin to wear an informal version of the men's clothes described on pages 615 to 628, but no boy under eighteen should wear tails, a morning coat, or black-and-white striped trousers with a black sack coat. Derby hats may be worn at any age after eighteen or nineteen.

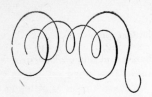
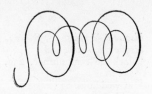